COGNITIVE DEVELOPMENT

Psychological and Biological Perspectives

ROSEMARY ROSSER

The University of Arizona

ALLYN AND BACON

Boston London Toronto Sydney Tokyo Singapore

To Dean Rosser Floerchinger

Editor-in-Chief, Social Sciences: Susan Badger
Senior Editor: Laura Pearson
Series Editorial Assistant: Marnie S. Greenhut
Production Administrator: Annette Joseph
Production Coordinator: Susan Freese
Editorial-Production Service: WordCrafters Editorial Services, Inc.
Manufacturing Buyer: Louise Richardson
Cover Administrator: Linda K. Dickinson
Cover Designer: Suzanne Harbison

Library of Congress Cataloging-in-Publication Data

Rosser, Rosemary A.
        Cognition development : psychological and biological perspectives
    /   Rosemary Rosser.
            p.   cm.
        Includes bibliographical references and index.
        ISBN 0-205-13965-5
        1. Cognition.   2. Nature and nurture.   I. Title
    BF311.R6543   1994   93-18889
    155.4'13—dc20   CIP

Printed in the United States of America

10 9 8 7 6 5 4 3 2 1   98 97 96 95 94 93

CONTENTS

PREFACE

Cognitive development concerns the processes of intellectual maturation that take an individual from infancy through childhood to adolescence. Cognitive development also concerns the evolution of knowledge and thought. This area of study has a place in a much larger enterprise: the scientific exploration of the mind. Contemporary cognitive scientists are engaged in building models of mind that are logically coherent, psychologically plausible, and biologically feasible. Findings from developmental studies contribute to the model-building effort and place restrictions on it as well, for developmental studies tell us about origins, the origins of mind. Our images of the adult are significantly proscribed by those of the baby and child who came first.

Questions about the nature of knowledge, thought, and mind have a long and rich intellectual history that greatly influences contemporary thinking. The philosophical treatises of the past formed the foundation of scientific psychology. Frequently, however, different philosophical perspectives were at odds. Today, those divergent philosophical contentions are encapsulated in psychological theories, including developmental theories about cognition. The richness and diversity of philosophical tradition reverberates in contemporary cognitive theory, and it is this theory that drives research. Just as philosophers during the Enlightenment found it quite impossible to be agnostic regarding their assumptions about the nature of reality, thought, and knowledge, today we find it impossible to evaluate cognition from a neutral point of view.

The first element of the viewpoint presented in this book is that empirical investigations make less sense when presented independently of the philosophical and theoretical premises that give birth to them. The intellectual tradition provides the impetus for research; hence, the implications of research data cannot be fully appreciated in a theoretical vacuum. Some books treat theory separately with a chapter or two at the beginning of the text. This book, which assumes that theory is integral to the research process, weaves theory throughout. *Every* chapter begins with an inspection of the theoretical premises and philosophical themes that influence research and shape interpretation.

The second element is that the meaning of data from research studies is very much dependent on the experimental methods used to collect them. Methodology is our tool for finding facts, but the facts we find are limited by the current adequacy of those tools. Methods are windows on the phenomena that frame the view we get. Like theory, methods should not be set off in an independent chapter. In this book, the techniques we use to look at cognition in babies and children are embedded in each chapter so that readers may see how methods and findings are coordinated in the research process.

And third, cognition is actualized in the brain; cognitive development goes hand in hand with brain development. Neurological and biological information form another window that clarifies the view of empirical findings; biology provides a backdrop for developmental facts. Reflecting this bias, and whenever possible, a biological thread is woven throughout, information from animal research is described, and relevant neurological processes are included in the depictions of cognitive events. In sum, the text stresses the contributions of theory, methodology, research, and biology to our full understanding of cognitive phenomena.

The book has a theoretical point of view, as well. The outcomes of human development are the consequences of complex interactions between an organism equipped for learning and a rich environment challenging the organism to adapt. Eons of evolutionary forces have provided individuals with survival equipment: mechanisms for figuring out how the world works, systems for representing information and observed facts, and intellectual tools for systematizing the facts encountered. Evolution and biology give people a leg up on survival by providing them with basic modes for dealing with reality as they make their way toward adulthood. But realities change, both with historic and developmental time; growing people must be flexible, ready to benefit from encounters with the novel, the idiosyncratic, the unexpected, and the varied. The growth of knowledge that comes with maturing reflects the interplay between innate stances and environment-provided press.

The Audience

This book is intended for those interested in cognition and cognitive development. Students in a variety of disciplines—psychology, cognitive science, neuroscience, educational psychology, and even linguistics, philosophy, and anthropology—should find information relevant to their respective fields. Although primarily envisioned as a text for a course in cognitive development for undergraduates, graduate students in cognitive disciplines and others, as well, may find the chapters useful in providing a theoretically grounded account of the various topics.

This book stresses theory, methods, and empirical research as they contribute to our general understanding of cognition. So, the compilation is neither especially applied nor practical except in one sense: A basic understanding of cognition is indispensable to any well-intentioned effort to foster intellectual growth in children.

Organization and Topics

Perhaps as a function of its acknowledged viewpoint, the text is organized in a somewhat unusual fashion. It begins with an introduction to the fundamental issues that drive investigation, reflection, and theory building in cognitive development. Chapter 1 introduces issue-driven questions such as: (1) How much of what we become is specified by innate biology and/or shaped by our experience? (2) How do mind and reality become coordinated such that our representations of the world turn out to be adequate? (3) How does developmental change take place? What changes? (4) How are infants, children, and adults alike? How are they different? (5) What is the best theory of development we can concoct right now anyway? These are the notions, themes, and questions introduced in Chapter 1. They resurface in various forms in the intervening chapters, and in Chapter 11, some formative, tentative responses are proposed.

Since theory, method, and the biological foundations for cognitive development are incorporated in all chapters, Chapters 2 through 10 deal with the actual content domains of cognition—separate areas held together by common threads of philosophical impetus, prototypic method, and the nature of the research questions underlying investigation. In Chapter 2, perceptual development is described, particularly development in infancy. It is here that the individual encounters the world—the sights, the sounds, and the feel of the environment—and brings the mind into alignment with reality. The description of the alignment process continues in Chapter 3, where the basic structure of the surrounding world must be located, sensed, discovered, or constructed. The world has a geometric, physical structure; it is also made up of things. The myriad of entities must be organized, too. And that is the topic explored in Chapters 4 and 5—the achievement of categories, classes, concepts, and dimensions for bringing order to what might otherwise be a random chaos of things, events, and entities. Percepts, concepts, classes, and scales make most sense as constructs for guiding intellectual behavior when we examine them as parts of organized knowledge systems. These organized belief systems—sometimes called naive theories—are the focus of Chapters 6 and 7. It seems intuitive for most of us to envision human intellectual achievement as marked by the capacity for language (Chapter 9), for problem solving (Chapter 8), and for storing and remembering information (Chapter 10). Then we come full circle to the initial inquiries, reconsidered in Chapter 11.

Acknowledgments

Many individuals made a variety of contributions to this book. They include the official reviewers, acknowledged below, and the editorial staff and production people, who turn visions into real product. Their role is undeniably vital. Others helped me greatly in unofficial roles, reading bits and pieces, providing me with feedback, correcting my stupidities, and informing me of missed observations. Many thanks to my colleagues at The University of Arizona—Karen Wynn, Lynn Nadel, Carol Sigelman, Charles Brainerd, and Laura McCloskey—who read versions of various chapters. And a special thanks to Paul Bloom, who graciously read several chapters in amazingly timely fashion and who guided me through the complex morass I found in the language-acquisition literature.

Thanks are also extended to the official reviewers of the text who patiently read the installments; provided much valued comment; and contributed their time, effort, and considerable expertise in shaping this final product. They are Pat Bauer, University of Minnesota; James Byrnes, University of Maryland; Franklin Manis, University of Southern California; Karl Rosengren, University of Michigan; Elizabeth Spelke, Cornell University; and Ken Springer, Southern Methodist University.

Throughout the chapters, you will find many of my "kid stories"—anecdotes, excerpts, examples, ideas, and comments that actually did come from various real children. I thank them, too—Noel and Ivy, Nathan and Joelle, and many an anonymous subject. But a special acknowledgment I reserve for my young son, Dean, who provided a wealth of comments, responses, insights, explanations, and especially patience when Mommy had to work. Dean is surely the one who has taught me the most about cognitive development in real children.

CHAPTER 1

FUNDAMENTAL ISSUES IN COGNITIVE DEVELOPMENT

INTRODUCTION

An 11-month-old infant is busy making her way about in a familiar playroom. It is a rich environment, filled with toys and textures, colors and forms. There are toy boxes, bookcases, small tables and chairs, and tubs filled with attractive objects to suck on, hold, throw, pile, and explore. There are cubby holes to crawl into, obstacles to hide behind, detours to maneuver around, mirrors to look into, and contraptions to climb on. There are other babies to watch, some adults to listen to. There are laps and teddy bears for cuddling, mats and blankets for napping. It is indeed an interesting, colorful, and thoroughly stimulating environment.

This infant will exhibit a lot of exploratory behavior—handling manipulatable objects, crawling about spaces, peering into corners and containers, and reaching for objects and experimenting with how they break, bounce, or bang when pounded on. Some behaviors will be very rare. For example, our crawler will *not* get lost, even if she moves behind a barrier and cannot see the rest of the room. She will

not get stuck as a consequence of crawling into too small a space. She is *not* likely to reach for objects clearly too far beyond her grasp, and when she wants her favorite stuffed animal at naptime, she will *not* have forgotten where it is. Although she is small, not too coordinated, pretty much nonverbal, and in need of protection and caretaking, this infant is *not* unknowledgeable about her environment.

But just how much does she know? Can she mentally represent the spaces she crawls through? Does she apprehend the physical characteristics of space, time, and motion? Can she anticipate events, sequences, and actions? Does she see the world as adults do? If she does, was she born with the insight? If not, how does experience in environments such as this change her?

These are the sorts of questions that intrigue psychologists who study cognitive development. What do infants and children know? How do they represent what they know? And how do they come to know it? How can we best describe their thinking and changes in thinking associated with growth? What is the initial state of a new baby's knowledge? How is thinking biologically actualized in the brain? How can we account for cognition and for changes in cognitive behavior and the biological substrate that supports it?

Research in cognitive development is exciting, intellectually rich, and challenging because it addresses questions like these. Figuring out how children think is no small feat; and as you will see in chapters to come, individuals who have made significant contributions to the field are remarkable for their innovation, ingenuity, and insight. Many of the research questions behind studies of developmental psychologists are broad; they are not restricted to concerns specific to infants and children. Rather, the questions are rooted in ancient philosophical argument about the nature of humankind.

Studies of infant perception, of number development in preschoolers, of language acquisition, of spatial cognition, and of conceptual growth are spurred by this heritage. Because of the intellectual context that influences investigation into child thought, the findings reverberate through the larger disciplines of psychology, philosophy, biology, linguistics, and related fields. Contemporary cognitive scientists are building models of mind that are logically actualizable, psychologically reasonable, and biologically feasible. Data about the intellectual and cognitive functioning of children play a part in, and sometimes even place a major limitation on, that larger enterprise (see Spelke, 1991).

Empirical research delves into the raw material of cognitive development; in chapters to come, much of that research will be reviewed. But developmental psychologists aspire to more than *describing* the facts of cognition in infants and children. An even more important goal is *explaining* cognitive growth, that is, constructing conceptual explanatory systems or theories. Child data are seldom, if ever, completely definitive. So, they must be interpreted; theory is rule-governed interpretation. Theory enriches data, explains data, and places data within a broader intellectual model. When data are ambiguous, subject to various interpretations, alterative theories are possible.

That is what we observe for cognitive development: multiple, competing, theoretical explanations of the phenomenon. Thus, in chapters to come, those theories will be evaluated, too. As you will come to see, theories differ in explanatory power, fit with the available evidence, and scientific rigor. They are alike, though, in that all of them must somehow deal with the same basic issues about cognition and development. The manner in which those issues are addressed forms the foundation for theoretical differences; so we explore that foundation in this initial chapter.

All theories face the following challenges:

1. How best to represent the organization of cognition, the way the mind must be structured.
2. How to incorporate experience and biology as causal contributors to the development of mind.
3. How to account for the connection between brain growth—development at the neurological level—and conceptual growth—development at the behavioral level.
4. How to best depict the nature, form, and pervasiveness of age-related change in cognitive ability and capacity.

THE STRUCTURED MIND

What is *cognition?* It is thinking and knowing. It is knowledge and knowledge acquisition. It is all the mental activity entailed in transforming stimulation from a physical source to a representation of reality that will guide behavior. Although it has not always been so, today virtually all psychologists agree that cognition, our mental representation of reality, is richly *structured*. Knowledge in the mind is organized, integrated, and unified and forms a complex system. Child cognition, just like the adult counterpart, is complexly structured, too. Developmentalists may disagree as to the nature of that structure—how abstract it should be, how general, and so forth (Flavell, 1982; Keil, 1986a)—but there is general consensus that some sort of structure forms the foundation for children's intellectual functioning.

Cognitive structures are hypothetical depictions of knowledge and thinking. We describe them in terms of abstract *models* of mind, kinds of formalized descriptions. The exact forms of those descriptions can vary and include the logico-algebraic system of Jean Piaget (1970a), the flow diagrams and production systems proposed by information-processing psychologists (Anderson, 1983; Klahr, 1984), and the semantic networks, schemas, scripts, and frames of others (Mandler, 1983). The common features across different hypothesized models of cognitive structure are (1) formal description of thought and (2) the belief that such description helps explain cognitive behavior.

Although the specifics of cognitive structure vary across theoretical perspectives, there are common themes. One theme is of a conceptualization of a structure as composed of cognitive *elements* held together in a network of *relationships* that direct and unify distinct-looking cognitive behaviors (Flavell, 1971). The cognitive element may be a mental symbol or sign for things, for example, a representation of a round object, a concept for the motion "roll." The relationship between elements constitutes a *rule* or *principle,* for instance, "round objects roll." The principle directs behavior toward objects, physical behaviors like throwing, perceptual behaviors like tracking an anticipated trajectory, and cognitive be-

haviors like computing the location of contact between the moving object and a stationary boundary. A network of like relationships/principles is a "naive mechanics" about how objects in the world behave in rule-governed ways. That network is an organized system of knowledge, a cognitive structure. We see theoretical differences as to what elements are identified as appropriate, what the organization among them is, and how best to describe the network, but there remains little controversy that it should be described.

All of us know that as children grow their behavior changes, but what else changes along with behavior? What develops? Perhaps it is that structure, the organization of mind, that also changes. Exactly how the change is envisioned depends on how the structure is initially described and on the class of transformations that are permitted on it. One view is of a fixed structure, constant from birth, that undergoes little if any substantive change with maturation. To propose a fixed structure is to equate the mind of the infant and the mind of the adult; it is to contend that while behavior indeed changes, the essential nature of thinking does not. An antithetical view is that mind is an evolving structure undergoing profound elaborations with development. Here the infant and adult are cognitively different species. Linking the two is an intellectual metamorphosis through which "infant caterpillar" becomes "adult butterfly."

Building a complete theory of cognitive development requires formulating a hypothetical structure, specifying the transformation processes the structure will undergo, and correlating the formalism with real behavior of real children. Logical requirements will limit the class of formalisms proposable as depictions of children's mental life since not all possible structures make sense. Behavioral data will impose limitations, too, since it is cognitive behavior we ultimately wish to explain. Cognitive development occurs in biological organisms comprised of cells and neurons, biological structures, and functional systems. So biology as well will restrict the class of possible explanatory models. Given those limitations, what formulations comprise the set of viable theoretical contenders?

One Structure or Many?

The influence of Swiss psychologist Jean Piaget on all theory in cognitive development has been profound. For many developmentalists, Piaget was their initiation to the concept of cognitive structure as a central, causal force behind observable behavior. Piaget, of course, was only one player in the "cognitive revolution" (Gardner, 1985), which, in the last 30 years, has transformed psychology; but for those interested in the realm of cognitive development, he was a major player. At one time, to describe one's theoretical predilections as "structuralist" was to identify with the Piagetian perspective (Flavell, 1982). That is no longer the case. Now, interest in deciphering the ontogeny of mental representation is shared by those adopting a multitude of theoretical perspectives. The influence of Piaget has even waned in recent years (Kessen, 1984), in part because of the scientific intractibility of some of his contentions (Brainerd, 1978a; 1979b), and in part because many Piagetian notions have simply been absorbed into other developmental models. While the theoretical distancing from Piaget among contemporary investigators is noteworthy, without his intellectual contributions, much of what currently goes on in developmental psychology would not occur.

Piaget envisioned a cognitive structure as a general, content-independent organization of mind, an organized set of abstract rules not specifically tied to particular things in the world. So, his network of rules was like an "algebra for thought." This single, global structure was at the center of all cognitive activity. During the course of development, that structure adapted through profound shifts in form, a mental metamorphosis. The structure was the root of cognitive competence; profound transformations in that structure were reflected in pervasive, global changes in intellectual competence. As a consequence, at different levels of development, levels roughly correlated with age, children were expected to behave in remarkably different fashion. A toddler might think of dreams as real events, might accuse the moon of following her about, and might treat her stuffed animals as living, breathing companions; a third-grader would not share her vision.

This approach to cognitive structure, with its accompanying sequential and radical reorganizations of knowledge, reflected Piaget's peculiar philosophical predilections (Gardner, 1973; Reese & Overton, 1970). These predilections were articulated in his philosophical position—**genetic epistemology**—a vision of knowledge formation as the product of each individual's active, constructive inventions (Piaget, 1980). From this philosophical foundation, Piaget built his familiar *stage theory*. A *stage* represented a level of organization in cognitive structure, and a *stage shift,* a global reorganization. The predicted consequences of stage and stage shift were radical changes in children's thinking and behavior.

Piaget's theory has attracted considerable criticism on multiple fronts (Brainerd, 1978a, 1978b; Flavell, 1985; Gelman & Baillargeon, 1983; Spelke, 1988a), but the notion of a single, general, cognitive structure underlying superficial particulars of intellectual behavior continues to be a popular notion (see, e.g., Marini & Case, 1989). In neo-Piagetian revisionist positions (Case, 1985b), in skill hierarchy theories (Fischer, 1980; Fischer & Pipp, 1984), and in some variations of information-processing models (Anderson, 1983) and their developmental extensions (Klahr, 1984; Klahr

& Wallace, 1976; Siegler, 1986a, 1989), general models of mental life are centrally important. Single-structure, revisionist proposals avoid the scientific ambiguity of the Piagetian original, but all, like Piaget's, depict cognition as a single entity, a *domain-general* system.

Another approach, still structuralist, replaces an emphasis on global structures with an emphasis on *local* ones (Ceci, 1989). Cognition is conceptualized as a set of more or less interrelated knowledge structures or multiple faculties specialized for specific cognitive functions (Fodor, 1983). This theoretical alternative presents cognition as *modular* (Chomsky, 1988), as composed of quasi-independent *modules,* local structures, or *domain-specific* knowledge systems (Carey & Gelman, 1991; Keil, 1984, 1986a, 1991). The perspective has very different developmental implications and leads to different empirical predictions than does a Piagetian-type, domain-general version of mind (Fodor, 1972; Rozin, 1976).

But what is a **domain**? It is a kind of information. In the process of acquiring information so as to adapt to the environment, all organisms (including humans) are faced with certain problems or challenges involving particular sorts of information. One of those problems, for example, is way-finding. Animals have to come up with a way of representing where they are located, where food supplies are, and how routes between locations are organized. The information is about space. The challenge is met with a cognitive representation of space to guide movements, and all animals must meet the challenge some way. There is also the problem of keeping track of how many entities there are, how many offspring in a litter, how many eggs in a nest, how many food caches have been stored, and so forth. Information about number must be dealt with, and the problem of enumeration must be solved with some system for representing numerosity.

There are many such problems. Those who would explain cognition must address whether different problems are ramifications of the same general information domain, representable in a generic mental structure. Or, alternatively, problems could be divided into different, nonreducible types; a number problem may not reduce to a spatial problem, for example. Appropriate mental representations would then need to be problem specific.

In the last 30 years, psychologists interested in cognitive development have become accustomed to structural constructs and ideas about mental representation. Many have accepted the perspective of structuralism; all have experienced the effect of such intellectual currents on the research literature. Now the issue has changed. It is no longer a question of whether structure is an important feature of cognitive development worthy of scientific inquiry or whether structural constructs are powerful explanatory tools. Current debate is about whether a global, domain-general or local, domain-specific structure system is the more fruitful representation, how that system should be described, and whether the two structural models are complementary or competitive explanatory systems (Ceci, 1989; Siegler, 1989; Sternberg, 1989).

The Concept of Constraints

Building hypothetical models of cognition that describe human performance is less difficult than initially surmised. In fact, multiple alternative models have been proposed. As philosophers and scientists have noted, it is possible to generate a large number of theoretical models for complex behavior, all of which fit the data equally well (Crick, 1979; Quine, 1961). A proliferation of models is particularly likely, when model building is data driven, or ex post facto, essentially designed after the fact from empirical observation. To arrive at the most adequate explanation of cognitive behavior, however, we must have solid means of distinguishing among what might at first appear to be equally viable models. We must limit the proliferation of models somehow by establishing boundaries, limits, or guidelines as to what constitutes an adequate model.

In short, **constraints** on the domain of possible models are necessary. Constraints limit the number of potential hypotheses that can be generated, and models are hypotheses. There are two ways in which constraints operate in the arena of cognitive development. The first is in terms of limiting the number of theoretical models that are plausible systems for explaining development. A model that does not adhere to a constraint is not a viable contender. The greater the number of constraints, the fewer models will remain in the running. Empirical data are one kind of constraint; a model must describe observed human performances.

Biology is a constraint, one with which developmental psychologists have always contended (Piaget, 1950; Werner, 1957). In fact, recourse to biological constraints, at least as they were understood in the nineteenth century, is a defining characteristic of the *organismic* model of development (Reese & Overton, 1970). Historically, however, developmentalists have tended to incorporate biological ideas metaphorically using a biological process as an analogy for a psychological process. An example would be equating embryonic development with postnatal psychological development (Werner, 1948). The biological process of evolution, and thus the ideas of Charles Darwin (1859, 1871), have always figured prominently in developmental thinking, although oftentimes Darwinian concepts have been perverted in the translation (Kessen, 1984). Whether in the recapitulation theory of G. Stanley Hall (White, 1968), the maturation theories of Gesell (1928), or the dialectic evolutionary proposals of Piaget (Boden, 1979; Piaget, 1971), developmentalists have

paid heed to biological limitations on their theorizing.

Most recently, developmentalists have appealed to emerging biological facts about how the brain works and grows. At something more than the level of metaphor, developmentalists want to figure out how behavioral development is biologically actualized. They may not always concern themselves directly with the activity of neurons, synapses, and the formation of connections in the cortex, but familiarity with how things work neurologically must be sufficient enough to preclude the proposal of implausible models. Brain mechanisms are the foundation of behavior and provide important limitations on any theoretical model designed to explain behavior (Grossberg, 1982).

So constraints operate at the level of theory to restrict the class of potential developmental stories. Constraints operate as well at the level of developmental mechanisms restricting the class of potential developmental outcomes. There are diverse sets of constraints— biological, environmental, formal—but most contemporary developmentalists recognize that complex mental structures cannot be generated without limits. Constraints are the limits.

At the level of the individual, biology constrains cognitive development. Human cognitive development must unfold within the boundaries permitted by the **genetic envelope,** (Changeaux, 1980), the genetic constraint on behavior, many features of which reflect our long evolutionary heritage (Black & Greenough, 1986). Variation is still possible within those biological constraints, a consequence of **plasticity.** Plasticity involves processes through which experience modifies neural circuitry, modifies the expression of genetic material, such that **phenotype,** the visible expression of biological endowment, and **genotype** do not exhibit a one-to-one correspondence. The genetic envelope sets the limits on the modifiability of the structure of the organism; plasticity explains modifiability within those limits. Together these concepts function as biologically derived constraints on cognitive development.

Still another kind of constraint is the structure of the physical environment in which the organism is developing. Human beings inhabit a universe that operates lawfully and has a describable structure; explaining the operation of that universe is the domain of physics. For example, the universe of the developing child is three dimensional, and distances within it can be metrically scaled. Physical laws specify that dropped things fall, pushed things roll, occluded things stop, and so forth. A developing organism that is sensitive to the existent physical structure and natural law is most likely to survive, as when species members are naturally inclined to avoid steep drop-offs and nonsupportive surfaces (e.g., water).

By some mechanism, the model of cognition built in the mind and actualized in the brain must share a basic correspondence with the physical universe, an **isomorphism** with natural laws. How that correspondence comes about has intrigued philosophers for centuries, and it is an issue to which we shall return in subsequent chapters. The structure of the physical universe, then, is another constraint on cognition, and it is reasonable to presume that through eons of evolutionary pressures, the essential features of the physical universe should be ingrained in our nervous system (Shepard, 1981).

Other domains of knowledge are also formally specifiable, and it is possible to describe the content of these knowledge domains independent of a particular knower. We can conceivably delineate the rules of Euclidean geometry, linguistics, algebra, calculus, and so forth. Our description of a knowledge domain includes the elements or concepts that make up the domain and the rules by which the elements are combined. The formal domain of

language, for example, consists of elements such as words and combinational rules like syntax for putting words together. If there is an isomorphism between the formal rules governing a domain and the ways in which we can think about content within a domain, then those formal rules may also act as a constraint on cognition. For example, if we assume that, by natural law, the universe divides into living things and nonliving things and that only living things engage in biological activity, then it is a violation of reality to form a relation between a nonliving object (e.g., a rock) and a living action (e.g., is hungry). If mental life is constrained to reflect natural law, then the literal combination "the rock is hungry" is nonsensical and cannot be represented in human thought.

Theories of cognitive development vary as to which constraints—biological, physical, or formal—are considered most important for explaining thinking and cognitive performance, and a few developmentalists will even choose to avoid the concepts of constraints altogether. Theories vary as to the sources of the constraints. Are they inherent in the nature of the developing mind? Are they imposed on the organism by the surrounding environment? These questions bring us to the next major issue in development.

THE NATURE-NURTURE CONTROVERSY

Constraints place limitations on mental modeling, but they also have implications for the origins of developmental phenomena. When one proposes that some constraint limits thinking, one must also acknowledge where the constraint comes from. It could be a characteristic of the environment to which we are all attuned, like three dimensionality; alternatively, a constraint could originate in the biological structure of the brain itself.

One of the oldest and most important conceptual issues in developmental psychology is the nature-nurture question: What controls the direction of development, heredity, or experience? Or put more tractably, What is given genetically? How much can the environment affect those givens? Which influence assumes the primary role? These questions have been debated for centuries by philosophers and biologists, as well as by psychologists. Resolutions are yet to be obtained. The questions do, however, spur research efforts; for while the nature-nurture debate has philosophical origins, the confrontation is now often conducted in the empirical arena.

Nurture

Developmental psychologists who avoid the notion of constraints or envision constraints as essentially a feature of the environment are **empiricist** in orientation. They acknowledge that the structure of the environment is a given, a limitation, on possible developmental pathways, as is the biological structure characteristic of a species. These factors are **constants** across individual species members and across developmental periods. Logically, constants cannot be the source of variability since the outcome of the action of a constant is also a constant. Development is supposedly about variability, particularly variability across age. Empiricists attribute developmental variability to experiential variability since only the action of a variable can explain variability. It follows that since experience can be highly idiosyncratic across individuals, developmental outcomes can likewise be quite variable. To extrapolate, it is the potential for movement within the genetic envelope that an empiricist would hope to explain, and experience is the driving force for that movement.

In developmental psychology, the radical empiricist position was represented in the **mechanistic model** and the theoretical perspective of behaviorism (Skinner, 1938; Bijou & Baer, 1961; 1978). The position is essen-

tially unconstrained (Kessen, 1984). Developmental change occurs as the individual experiences consequences for behavior by acting in the environment, and no a priori theoretical constraints need be placed on the selection process. That individuals share common features of functioning and that children show developmental regularities in behavior are explainable solely in terms of the actions of the environments and experiences. The explanation for each is parsimonious and positivist.

Although once the primary developmental model in American psychology, mechanism has fallen from favor in recent years. However, experientially driven processes still feature prominently in explanations of developmental phenomena, since they do constitute mechanisms of learning and could account for plasticity. Few contemporary developmentalists, however, embrace the extreme nurture perspective. The naive empiricism, which leads logically to an extreme nurture position, is just that—naive (Moshman, 1990).

Empiricists typically depict development as the result of an **unbiased learning mechanism** (Keil, 1991). *Unbiased* means there are no built-in, "hard-wired" mechanisms that lead the organism to construe environmental input in particular ways. Instead, the perceptually sensitive organism detects incoming information, picking up on regularities, associations, contiguities, and patterns inherent in the *information,* not in the detector.

Nature

Those who adopt a nature view of development, who place the primary impetus for cognitive development on innate, biological mechanisms, are **nativists**. Historically, developmentalists of an organismic world view were nativists, but in contemporary thinking, nativism is more sophisticated than its historic counterpart (which was as naive as its empiricist competitor).

The logic of modern nativism is as follows: First, human beings share many features of cognitive functioning. General principles of cognition cut across the specifics and the variability of idiosyncratic experience. It is illogical to attribute shared features of functioning to a source that is highly variable: experience in the environment. Therefore, universal aspects of cognition, where *universal* means expressed in all normal species members, must be attributed to some characteristic of organisms shared by all of them. Species-specific biology is a logical option.

Second, human beings often demonstrate cognitive abilities very early in life when it is unlikely, given limited time in the world, for much learning from experience to have occurred. The expression of early competence suggests a nonexperiential basis for cognition, an innate capability.

The observed rapidity with which children acquire knowledge in specific domains such as language (Chomsky, 1965; Keil, 1981) leads to a related argument. Were babies to enter the universe with no preconceived notions about how the world worked, they could entertain an infinite number of hypotheses about its nature. Knowledge acquisition would involve testing these hypotheses, rejecting those that are empirically disconfirmed (e.g., things fall up; cats bark), while retaining those consistent with observation (e.g., round things roll). Functioning like a scientist, the naive baby would hypothesize and test until the universe was discovered. The grown-up scientist, however, seldom operates from such an uninformed position. Instead, the scientist has preconceived notions derived from theory about how the world works. Those preconceived notions—constraints again—limit the class of possible hypotheses to be entertained. Testing a finite number of hypothesis to find "truth" is more efficient and takes less time than testing an infinite number. Extending the analogy, were the baby to possess intuitive, innate

"theories," or principled knowledge about how things work, there would be fewer reality hypotheses to test and knowledge acquisition could proceed more rapidly.

Many nativistically inclined developmentalists endow the individual with modes of construal built right into the system. These preconceived notions may take the form of innate information-processing capabilities, rudimentary concepts for organizing experiential input, or "first principles" (Gelman, 1990a). Specifically, naive organisms may have awareness, at some tacit level, of the constraints governing a cognitive domain (Chomsky, 1988). Knowledge of those constraints permits rapid intellectual development. This version of nativism is represented in prominent contemporary developmental positions (Keil, 1981) and serves as the impetus for a great deal of empirical activity.

Interactionism

Between the empty and the overstuffed infant, the one who knows nothing and the one who has mastered the principles of Euclid and Newton, is something else, an intermediate position. There are universals of cognitive functioning, certainly; there are individual differences, too. Biology, maturation, and genetic endowment exert a causal force on cognitive development; experience and learning do, too. Extreme positions on the nature-nurture controversy are probably unrealistic and hard to defend.

The child is a biological organism developing within a rich physical, perceptual, and social environment. From birth, complex interactions between biology, at all levels of analysis, and the environment take place, but the influence of biological and environmental forces are perfectly confounded. Teasing apart the relative contributions of each is difficult and perhaps next to impossible. Ignoring the contribution of one or the other is naive and overly simplistic. The nature-nurture question becomes not which propels development, biology or experience, but rather, Precisely what is specified biologically? What rudiments, kernels, or initial proclivities are given? How does experience modify and embellish those kernels? And perhaps most importantly, Through what mechanisms do the biological and environmental interact and give birth to a mature cognitive system?

A good part of the intuitive appeal of Piaget's theory is its interactionist flavor. The invariant function of **adaptation** and the developmental transition mechanism of **equilibration,** for example, are theoretical constructs that encompass complex exchange processes between the biologically derived cognitive structures and experience in the environment. Both equilibration and adaption represent a state of balance between **exogenous** environmental and **endogenous** biological influences.

In the balance of adaptation, the forces of the environment are paramount when **accommodation** occurs, and individuals must alter, change, or adapt their existing cognitive structures to meet the demands of new experiences. When a 3-year-old lost a pet to old age, he initially tried to equate death with a balloon losing its air. But he was forced to accommodate his thinking, to bring his internal notions into line with external reality, because the animal sadly could not be "blown back up." In **assimilation,** what the individual already knows is paramount and external reality is transformed into congruence with internal, existent ways of thinking. Old ideas (balloons losing air) are generalized without modification to new situations (animals no longer breathing). In development, both processes occur simultaneously—they counteract each other—and a balance, an interaction, is achieved.

On a larger scale, a state of **equilibrium** exists when the individual's intellectual tools can adequately meet the challenge of any experience encountered. **Disequilibrium** is created when the inadequacy or insufficiency of those tools is recognized. To regain a state of harmony and to achieve developmental progress, the individual must cognitively reorganize. Equilibration occurs when balance between the state of the organism and the press of the environment is restored through reorganization. Piagetian theory is rich and complex, so in chapters to come, there will be much elaboration on these and other specific theoretical concepts (see Chapters 3, 4, 7, and 8, particularly). The point for now is that Piagetian-derived concepts like adaptation and equilibration are definitely interactionist in essence and, thus, escape the naiveté of extremism.

Although some contend that Piaget favored the biological side and neglected the environmental (Fischer, 1980), Piaget was essentially both antiempiricist (Garcia, 1980) and antinativist. He perceived his *constructivist* theory of knowledge as a refutation of both empiricism and nativism (Piaget, 1980). To quote the Piagetian scholar, Jacques Voneche (1980):

> *The movement of knowledge is always incremental. It allows for a deeper understanding of both reality and the knower, if not of knowledge itself. It refuses to keep invariant both reality, as in empiricism, and the cognitive structures of the knower, as in nativism. It postulates an ever-changing system of checks and balances between the knower and reality.* Thence concepts such as equilibration, self-regulation, interaction, and feedback. For Piaget, knowing is interaction. *(pp. 1−2, emphasis added)*

Piaget's child invents knowledge through active exploration of the environment, first physically and later symbolically. The process takes time since there are no a priori, fixed, innate, knowledge structures to spur development. But knowledge acquisition is not simply experientially driven, because it is creative and constructive and because self-regulatory processes (e.g., equilibration) control the extent of change possible in a single experiential encounter. The developing child is a conservative creature, motivated to maintain an existing understanding of the world while only allowing experiences to slowly shift that understanding in controlled ways.

Because of the time it takes to build constructed knowledge, Piagetian predictions about cognitive performance in children are conservative. In his analysis, young children must be primarily unknowledgable and cognitively incapable. His view of the human infant, for instance, is particularly remarkable for the profound state of naiveté attributed to the neonate. Detection of early competence is damaging to Piaget's analysis since he constrained knowledge acquisition to specific time frames. Early competence violates that constraint.

Nativists, on the other hand, actually predict early competence, particularly for certain kinds of accomplishments predicated on forms of information to which the individual is uniquely attuned (see Carey & Gelman, 1991). Empiricists do not take a specific position on early competence. Learning from experience takes time, time to have *some* experience. However, since a priori constraints are not specified, there are no set limitations on *how much* time. For some kinds of learning, brief experience taking little time could suffice. Thus, the empiricist position is not automatically threatened by evidence of early competence. Nativists can account for early competence best, however.

In subsequent chapters, we will review the empirical evidence about the speed and nature of change in children's understanding of the world and in their cognitive abilities. And we shall see which of these perspectives—the empiricist, the nativist, or the interactionist—fits best with the majority of the available data.

Then, we shall recycle and reevaluate the status of the nature-nurture debate in Chapter 11.

THE ACTION OF EXPERIENCE

All behavioral development exhibited phenotypically arises from some sort of collaboration between the child and the environment (Gottlieb, 1983). About that, few would quibble. Determining the mechanism of collaboration is trickier business, however. The interactions between the child and the environment are convoluted, complex, and dynamic; it is an ongoing exchange process that takes place on multiple levels from a cellular one, to a representational one, to a contextual one. Teasing apart the direction of influence is more than a matter of dividing estimates of the amount of variance attributable to genetic and environmental factors (Plomin, DeFries, & Loehlin, 1977).

We can successfully partition the variance to explain observed individual differences in cognition at any one point in time. But cognitive development is a universal process that takes place over time. The analysis of individual differences can tell us little about that (Plomin, 1988). Since development occurs over time, the issue is not one of partitioning but one of figuring out how the two sources of influence combine.

Developmental Functions

Experience does not impose a single, uniform influence on behavior; the effects of experience can vary depending on the kind of competency or behavior examined. **Developmental functions** are hypothetical growth curves that capture the form of an association between age and developmental achievement. Experience can potentially affect development in at least four ways yielding four different developmental functions (Aslin, 1981b). Figure 1-1

FIGURE 1-1 *Schematic Depiction of Four Hypothetical Types of Developmental Functions for the Possible Relationships between Experience and Growth.*
The solid line anticipates development given a particular experience (marked by the vertical line); the dashed line reveals the course of development without the experience. The functions are ordered from least dependent *(maturation)* to most dependent *(induction)* on experience.

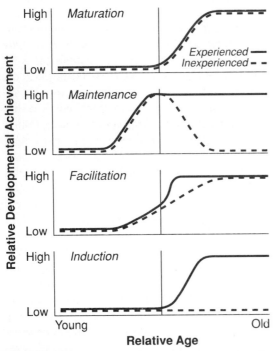

Relative Age

From "Experiential Influences and Sensitive Periods in Development: A Unified Model" by R. N. Aslin, in *Development of Perception* (Vol. 2), R. N. Aslin, J. R. Alberts, and M. R. Peterson (Eds.), 1981, New York: Academic Press. Adapted by permission.

shows these possible changes in cognitive proficiency in relation to age and the onset of experience. Adapted from conceptions of perceptual development and generalized to other cognitive phenomena, these hypothetical functions are ordered in terms of their increasing dependence on experience.

The first function, **maturation,** is least dependent on experience and thus includes developmental changes that occur without any particular experiential input. Organisms provided with an experience and those deprived of it would exhibit essentially the same growth function on the same schedule. Certain reflexive behaviors, such as sucking and swallowing (Black & Greenough, 1986), infants' preferences for patterned visual stimulation, which are correlated with gestational age (Fantz, Fagan, & Miranda, 1975), and many mammals' avoidance of steep drop-offs (Richards & Rader, 1981) show such a maturational pattern.

Experience can also serve a **maintenance** function. In this case, the behavior is manifested but it will disappear without environmental supports, without appropriate experience. For example, both normal infants and infants with hearing impairments begin to babble at about 3 to 6 months of age (de-Villiers & deVilliers, 1978), but babbling and subsequent oral language development fail to flourish in children not exposed to auditory input.

Facilitation is observed when a behavior that will typically develop in accord with a maturational schedule is hastened by appropriate experience. Babies, for example, may exhibit avoidance of steep drop-offs earlier if provided with the experience of self-produced locomotion afforded by infant walkers (Bertenthal & Campos, 1987). Most normal babies, however, exhibit avoidance on their own schedule after they have become proficient crawlers (see Gibson & Walk, 1960). Research in the 1960s and 1970s demonstrated that certain Piagetian cognitive concepts normally associated with older children (6–7 years of age) could be facilitated in young children (ages 3–4) through a variety of training methods (Brainerd, 1973b; Zimmermann & Rosenthal, 1974). Again, however, children typically display these competencies by about age 7 anyway without deliberate experiential intervention (Inhelder & Piaget, 1964).

Finally, **induction** describes developmental changes that are most dependent on experience, changes that will never fully transpire in the absence of appropriate experience. Children will not acquire the language of their social group without linguistic exposure to the lexicon; it is unlikely that they will learn to read left to their own devices. However, other cognitive preparations, perhaps less dependent on experience, do pave the way for an individual to profit from experience inductively.

It is not always clear which function best describes the development of a given behavior, and investigators will disagree depending on how they interpret developmental data. An experimental psychologist able to elicit positive training effects from young children on a conceptual task, for example, might be more inclined to interpret that result as a clear incidence of induction than would a Piagetian-inspired developmentalist (see, for e.g., Kuhn, 1974; Rosenthal & Zimmermann, 1978). An investigator who observes evidence of cognitive abilities in infants is apt to propose a maturational function that others might dispute. So, the interpretation of developmental functions is sometimes more ambiguous than we would like.

The kind of role the environment exerts on behavioral development is also affected by timing. For some behaviors, input must occur within a narrow time frame or it will not produce the normal effect. This is the concept of **critical period** (Bateson, 1979; Chomsky, 1988). The analogy is drawn between critical period and the brief opening of a window: experience can only have an effect when the window is open, not after it has been closed. The phenomenon of critical periods is documented in animal studies in which investigators can exert controlled manipulations of the environment, withhold crucial experience, and observe the subsequent effect on development (Greenough, Black, & Wallace, 1987). Gener-

alization of critical-period phenomena to normal human development is a reasonable extrapolation from animal research with indirect support from research with humans (see Newport, 1991).

Dimensions of Experience

Experience is not a unitary dimension, a fact that further complicates its role in development. For instance, some experiences are unique to an individual; they are idiosyncratic. Any child is exposed to an individualized environment and has a personal history. Environments vary in the particulars of experiences and caretaking provided, in the richness of opportunities offered, and so forth. In this way, experience is a **variable** across individuals; its variability can be quantified and the quantity used to predict variability in behavior. This is the way we are most used to thinking about experience, and we have access to mathematical models in statistics that exploit variability in explaining individual differences.

However, experience can also be a **constant.** The environment provides **ubiquitous experiences,** ones to which every normal member of the species is exposed. All normal babies develop within a social environment we call "family," and although families may differ in many ways (e.g., size, social status, available resources, cohesiveness), they share common characteristics. Similarly, all babies will be exposed visually to a three-dimensional spatial environment and virtually all will crawl and toddle about in it. All normal babies will hear the sounds of their soon to be acquired language. All will have some kind of toys and all will be members of a peer group.

It is more difficult to assess the causal contribution of ubiquitous experience on development. First, the statistical models that might help us address the question are most often models that depend on variance; the action of a constant is by definition nonvariable.

Second, there are built-in experimental limitations on our abilities to assess causal relations. To isolate causal relations, we need a control group, a group that is denied the ubiquitous experience. With human beings, a control group is unconscionable. We cannot withhold normal experience, deprive individuals of an appropriate rearing context and compare them with nondeprived individuals. Sometimes we find children whom nature has deprived in some way, but generalization from nonnormal to normal development is problematic. To some extent, we may be able to control experimentally the timing of a ubiquitous experience as when providing children with an experience before it is generally available (e.g., self-produced locomotion with infant walkers in precrawlers). However, since the control group would eventually obtain the target experience (e.g., crawling) anyway, the best we can hope to test is whether experience functions *facilitatively*. We cannot test whether ubiquitous experience functions *inductively* with an experimental study of human subjects. Yet, we need to know about the nature of the contribution ubiquitous experience makes to development. So, we turn to the animal literature, where the manipulation of rearing is feasible, and extrapolate, albeit cautiously, from animal data.

Models for Environment-Genome Interaction

Comparing humans with infrahumans is tricky business. There are differences in rates of maturation, learning histories, physical independence of young, and types of behavior displayed. Even so, sometimes comparative analysis can help establish the theoretical groundwork for development (Gallistel, Brown, Carey, Gelman, & Keil, 1991). But we must be cautious, especially when attempting to generalize results from studies of animal species (e.g., rabbit, rat, cat) that are phylogenetically distant from humans (Black & Greenough,

1986). Most animal research is done with these species. Still, the **comparative approach** does provide general models for how neural and cognitive development are controlled and organized by the **genome,** the genetic "package," and by the environment (Bullock, 1984).

An advantage of animal research is the potential for deliberate environmental manipulations to a degree not imaginable with human subjects. Rearing condition becomes an independent variable under experimenter control, and subjects, be they rats, cats, or monkeys, are randomly assigned to levels of the independent variable. In this way, the influences of genome and environment are rendered independent, permitting the partitioning of variance among factors. A second advantage of animal research is access to a wide range of dependent variables. One can, for example, obtain direct access to neurological data by observing brain states and neuronal function. This experimental model opens the way to examining the influence of ubiquitous experience on brain and behavioral development, and it enables the study of brain-behavior relationships.

A basic approach in animal research is to manipulate the housing environment of young animals. Two possible manipulations are (1) **deprivation,** exposure to an impoverished environment, and (2) the antithesis, environmental **enrichment.** The manipulation can be either general or specific. An example of a **general deprivation** condition is dark-rearing in order to observe the effect on an animal's sensory functioning. **Selective deprivation,** on the other hand, could be achieved by blocking vision in only one eye through the use of special lenses or by suturing. Selective manipulations yield narrower effects and are appropriate methods for testing specific hypotheses about environmental function and neural plasticity. Behavioral effects and neurophysical outcomes are assessed subsequently by comparing individuals reared under different housing conditions.

Experimental research like this reveals associations, both correlational and causal, between the environment of the immature animal (the "child") and two kinds of outcomes, neurophysiological and behavioral, the phenotype. The pattern of associations that can come from research of this variety is shown in Figure 1-2. Arrows indicate the direction of influence, and where no bonds occur, no association is presumed. Within the experimental framework, genotype of the parent is independent of the rearing environment since the latter is determined solely by the researcher. The genotype of the child is also independent of the environment, because of random assignment. So the environment is a function of *exogenous* sources, sources outside of the model—in this case, the laboratory manipulation. The model that results, as depicted in Figure 1-2, specifies two independent *paths* of influence on the child's neurophysiology which in turn serve as the essential substrate

FIGURE 1-3 *Hypothetical Model of Behavioral Development for a Child in the Natural Environment.*
Unlike in the animal model (Figure 1-2) the network of causal paths is much more complex. The environment of the child (E_c) is *not* independent of parental genotype (G_p), child's genotype (G_c), or even the child's behavior (P_c).

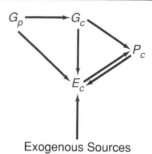

Exogenous Sources

From "How People Make Their Own Environments: A Theory of Genotype Environment Effects" by S. Scarr and K. McCartney, 1983, *Child Development, 54,* pp. 424—435. © The Society for Research in Child Development, Inc. Adapted by permission.

FIGURE 1-2 *Hypothetical Model of Behavioral Development for an Animal Subject in a Controlled Rearing Experiment.*
The outcome observed can be both behavioral, the phenotype of the "child" (P_c) and neurological (N_c). The causal influences on P_c include the genotype of the "child" (G_c) and the rearing environment (E_c), the latter of which is experimentally determined. While parental genotype (G_p) determines the "child's" genotype, G_p is independent of E_c. The summary picture is of two unidirectional and separable sources of influences on development.

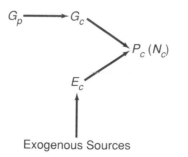

Exogenous Sources

for the child's behavior. Potentially the child's behavior may affect the physiology as well since both are concurrent products of two causal forces.

A human path model for cognitive development is different. The human model, adapted from Scarr and McCartney (1984), is presented in Figure 1-3. There are three important differences between this model and the one in Figure 1-2. First, in Figure 1-3, the dependent variable is typically limited to a measure of performance since direct assessment of the underlying neurology is rare. Second, transactions can occur between the child and the environment that change the environment; the consequence is a correlation between phenotype (P_c) and rearing environment (E_c). Third, and the greatest departure from the model in Figure 1-2, the rearing environment in the human case is *not* independent of the child's (G_c) or the parents' (G_p)

genotype. Rearing environment is not solely the result of exogenous sources determined by an experimenter who sets the parameters. Although there are extrafamiliar, exogenous sources, parental characteristics influence the sort of environment they create for their children. Parents provide both genes and environments for their offspring; thus, there is a rich pattern of correlations between the genotype of parent and child, the genotype of parent and environment, and the genotype of child and environment. As Scarr and McCartney (1984) exemplify it, parents who read well and enjoy it will probably provide their children with books they will read and enjoy, both for genetic and environmental reasons.

Children also help create their own environments, find their own ecological niches, by selecting compatible environments as a consequence of their personality ($G_c \rightarrow E_c$). The environment as experienced is, therefore, not identical to the one provided. A shy child, for example, might select solitary activities; a happy, active child elicits positive attention from caretakers; an intellectually inquisitive child demands challenging activities from teachers. A rat pup reared in isolation has few choices, nor will the rat pup's behavior change the environment the experimenter has selected for it ($P_c \rightarrow E_c$). The human child has choices and can affect the environment.

This causal model for how the genotype and environment affect human development is more complex than the one representing the experimental analogue. There are more paths and more dependencies. The rearing environment is richer. Ideally, the models could be instantiated with real data and parameters quantifying the relative strengths of sources of influence could be obtained. However, the parametric estimates from one model would not be directly generalizable to the other model. Depending on the actual state of nature, which is of course unknown, one or the other model could overestimate the contribu-

tion of the environment, or conversely biology, to human development. Therefore, we must always be cautious about the fit between experimental conclusions and natural developmental processes.

Neural Structure and Experience

Animal research permits a demonstration of the causal influence experience exerts on the phenotype. Such research also provides information about the neurological mechanisms through which the effect is actualized. Black and Greenough (1986) pointed out that mammals exhibit an extraordinary sensitivity to experience and depend on assimilating experience for survival. The fact that humans, in particular, have a lengthy developmental period may reflect the importance of this sensitivity and the necessity of extensive interaction between brain and environment. As Black and Greenough (1986) indicated, "The neural mechanisms supporting human cognitive development probably incorporate phylogenetically older and more recent plasticity mechanisms within an intricate and massive brain so that experience can be 'written' into the brain" (p. 5).

How the incorporation of experience into neural structures takes place is mechanically complex. The process involves regulation by intrinsic (i.e., organismic) factors, and it apparently depends on the quality and timing of information input from the environment as well. Even if the genetic envelope is relatively narrow, there is room to move about within it.

Were an organism's behavior entirely determined by the genome, then everything, every eventuality would somehow have to be coded in the DNA. The recipe for development would be a lengthy one requiring a lot of DNA. Such a conceptualization of the genetic blueprint is probably unreasonable, first because DNA is expensive stuff, and second because behavioral flexibility, as in mammals, could not be achieved through complete a priori specification. A more efficient system is one where the genetic blueprint serves to "prime" the organism rather than dictate behavioral outcome.

There are certain experiences, those we are calling ubiquitous experiences, that every normal species member can expect to encounter during the natural course of development. Every seeing animal will experience the contours and contrasts of the visual environment, for example. Conceivably, animals have evolved nervous systems that allow them to profit from the expected experience when it invariably comes. Then, what needs to be determined genetically is some mechanism for incorporating the experience and altering the phenotype accordingly. This economical approach is one way to account for induction processes in development. It does render the animal susceptible to deprivation, however, when the expected experience does not come or is withheld experimentally. **Experience-expectant** processes of neural development (Black & Greenough, 1986; Greenough, Black, & Wallace, 1987) have been extensively studied with regard to the development of sensory systems in animals. (We pick this up again in Chapter 2.) Moreover, it seems reasonable that similar mechanisms operate in human development.

Underlying cognitive activity at the performance level is a complex pattern of neural connections at the physiological level. The basic unit within this pattern is the **neuron,** the cell of the central nervous system, on which intercell connections, or **synapses,** form. Neurons interact with subsets of other neurons through regular synaptic associations. A given neural pattern should have a one-to-one correspondence with some aspect of behavior. Individual neurons, however, can form multiple synapses with other neurons. So, within a specific subset of neurons, the pattern, complexity, and sheer quantity of connections are

tremendous. Certain patterns of connections may be more cognitively or biologically efficient than other patterns; but how might a target network, an efficient "wiring diagram," get selected from among potential networks or available wiring diagrams? Studies with animals reveal that patterns of connections as well as the number of connections are influenced by experience in early development.

In early development in mammalian brains, synapse proliferation, overproduction, or "blooming" takes place. This is a process called **synaptogenesis** (Goldman-Rakic, 1987), which is cell growth where the animal generates many, many more synaptic connections and potential connections than it will eventually use. These multiple synapses compete with one another creating an opportunity for some variant of a "selection of the fittest" process to operate. In fact, periods of *synapse overproduction* are followed by periods of *synapse deletion* or "pruning" when excess synapses cease to function and, essentially, a winning wiring diagram remains. Experience may play a role in this "blooming-pruning" phenomenon; peak values of synaptic blooming occur about the time that sensitivity to gross manipulations of experience, particularly deprivation, is also maximal. Experience, then, may serve to stabilize or confirm a pattern of transient synaptic contacts. Perhaps by the use that the environment triggers, a stable pattern survives. Unconfirmed synapses, those not triggered and used, are eliminated (Black & Greenough, 1986).

To insure survival of the species, experience-expectant neural mechanisms, which can be studied with a deprivation paradigm, could not account for the operation of less universal experiences as well. If a cognitive function is essential to successful adaptation, for example, depth perception, then the experience that sets the function cannot be an idiosyncratic one available to only a subset of species members. Too many individuals would be debilitated if that were the case. Other sorts of mechanisms may account for neural plasticity resulting from experiences other than expected, ubiquitous ones. These **experience-dependent** processes (Black & Greenough, 1986; Greenough, Black, & Wallace, 1987) serve a different developmental function, one of synapse additions, the formation of new connections or the reactivation of old ones, in response to an experiential trigger. Perhaps idiosyncratic experience—special, individualized experience—elicits a local blooming-pruning phenomenon with an end result that overall mass and neural connections are increased. This analysis is consistent with data obtained with enrichment studies; enrichment constitutes the experimental provision of special experience. Figure 1-4 depicts the two experien-

tial functions proposed as mechanisms of neural plasticity operating in development.

Answers to questions about environment-genome interactions cannot always be sought at the neural level. Certainly neurophysiological research bears on the issue, and we have learned a lot from animal studies whose purpose it was to extract such data. Not all human cognitive phenomena, however, have correlates in animal behavior. Thus, while animal research findings provide useful generalizations to the development of sensory systems (Chapter 2) and perhaps some cognitive functions like spatial cognition (taken up in Chapter 3), information about other accomplishments (e.g., semantic and conceptual knowledge and language, examined in Chapters 5, 6, and 9) must be obtained elsewhere for now.

FIGURE 1-4 *Diagrams for Two Potential Effects of Experience on* Synaptogenesis. The experience-expectant figure depicts synapse overproduction ("blooming") and elimination ("pruning"). The experience-dependent figure shows synapse formation and selective retention. The arrowheads mark salient experiences that generate local synaptic overproduction and deletion (small curves). The cumulative effect of both types of process is more synapses per neuron for the experienced animal.

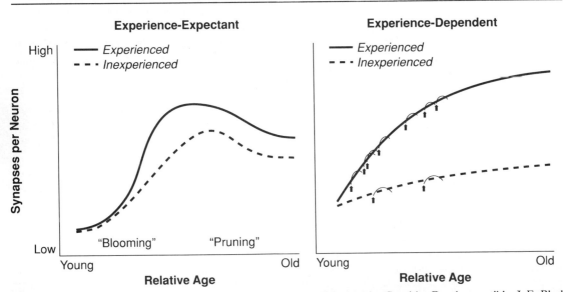

From "Induction of Pattern in Neural Structure by Experience: Implications for Cognitive Development" by J. E. Black and W. T. Greenough, in *Advances in Developmental Psychology* (Vol. 4), M. E. Lamb, A. L. Brown, and B. Rogoff (Eds.), 1986, Hillsdale, NJ: Erlbaum. Adapted with permission.

THE NATURE OF DEVELOPMENTAL CHANGE

Obviously, children change as they grow older. The increase in physical stature during the course of normal development is remarkable. The change in cognitive competence, skill level, expertise, and conceptual sophistication also covaries with chronological age. Some of these accomplishments, such as language development, are strongly correlated with physical development and with age. In fact, age-related change can be so salient that it tends to overshadow the similarities across age that also exist, albeit more subtly.

Psychologists have long noted the prevalence of age-related developmental change, but they have differed as to how best to conceptualize that change. Is change *quantitative,* depictable, and measurable in quantitative terms like more, less, and greater than? Or is it *qualitative,* a change in form or type? Qualitative changes involve increases in amount with age and alterations in form as well. The transition of a yearling filly to a mature mare is aptly represented by a quantitative function, since the filly's growth is a general increase in overall size and stature. In contrast, a butterfly is not quantitatively reducible to a caterpillar; a change in form has occurred. However, identifying the most appropriate growth function for human cognitive phenomena is a less tractable problem than it seems to be for fillies and caterpillars.

Questions about whether developmental change is quantitative or qualitative are questions about whether development is *continuous* or *discontinuous* (Berg & Sternberg, 1985; Fischer, 1983). There are three ways in which development can be continuous or discontinuous. In the first, continuity denotes a similarity in cognitive functioning between child and adult, when both are capable of the same accomplishment. For example, infants, children, and adults all exhibit some understanding of the natural number system (see Chapter 6). Discontinuity marks major discrepancy between what an adult and child can do; babies do not talk, children typically cannot reason abstractly (Chapter 8), and preschoolers do not comprehend the precise details of how biological systems operate (Chapter 7).

A second way references the pattern of growth. In a continuous pattern, growth is cumulative, gradual, and relatively smooth; increments in competence are added at a constant rate over time. This continuity shows up as a quantitative developmental function when measured values of cognitive competence are plotted against age (Appelbaum & McCall, 1983; McCall, 1979). Discontinuity is inferred when changes in the attribute over age are qualitative, indicated by abrupt, sharp bends in a developmental curve or by a change in slope (Fischer, 1983, 1987). Figure 1-5 shows a schematic contrast in the two types of developmental functions.

FIGURE 1-5 *Schematic Depiction of Two Contrasting Developmental Growth Functions.*
The dashed line represents continuous change where growth proceeds in relatively smooth fashion at an essentially constant rate over time. With discontinuous change (solid line) growth is marked by periods of stability and of rapid change.

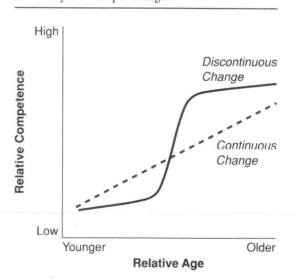

And third, developmental continuity is also associated with predictability over time; that is, knowledge of the individual's relative standing within a group of peers at one age permits better than chance prediction of that individual's relative position at a later age (Appelbaum & McCall, 1983; McCall, 1983). With discontinuous patterns, on the other hand, instability of individual differences is the rule (Berg & Sternberg, 1985). Discontinuity in cognitive growth, therefore, is associated with marked differences between the mature and the immature; for example, relatively stable periods of competence may be followed by periods of radical shift or rapid growth spurts. With respect to individual differences, competence at time 2 is not directly predictable from competence at time 1.

In general, traditional theories of cognitive development have favored explanations of change as discontinuous and qualitative in nature (Piaget, 1950, 1952b; Wohlwill, 1973, 1980; see Fischer, 1983). But the issue is not a simple one. It is particularly complicated and perhaps distorted by the means we use to observe developmental accomplishments and functions and even by the mathematics we employ to analyze them.

Empirical Detection of Continuity-Discontinuity

Ideally, we want to identify the nature and shape of the underlying growth function associated with a cognitive attribute. Typically, however, we only have access to behavioral data supposedly reflective of that attribute. We plot change in behavioral data as a function of time and extrapolate from the observed function revealed in *measured* values to the underlying function associated with the *true* values of the attribute. We are limited, however, by our ability to measure similar aspects of competence at different levels of maturity. We need both what Fischer (1987) calls a

"good clock" and a "good ruler" to plot cognitive ability over time.

To exemplify the potential difficulty, look at the quantitative function depicted in Figure 1-6. This growth curve typifies a **linear function** $(Y = a + bX)$ relating amount of detected competence to age. From data like those in the graph, we could compute initial competence, as represented at the **intercept** $(Y = a;$ $X = 0)$, rate of increase in competence indexed by the **slope** (b), and **strength** of the association between competence and age. We need a measurement device, a ruler that should work given any randomly selected age level. We then select a set of age levels, obtain the measures, graph the results, and extrapolate the function. Since age in our formulation is a **random variable,** we generalize to the association among points not actually measured from those that had been. For example, if we wanted to assess height in relation to age, measurement in inches would be an appropri-

FIGURE 1-6   The depiction of a linear function $(Y = a + bX)$ where change in the value of one variable (Y) is regularly associated with change in a second variable (X), and for all values of X the associated change in Y is constant.

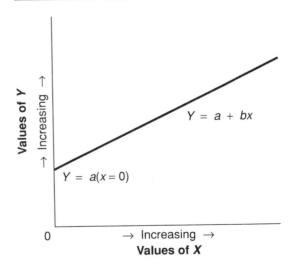

ate assessment at any randomly selected age. Then we could obtain our height values for a set of age values, plot the points, and compute the function (which would be smooth but not necessarily linear; see Lampl & Emde, 1983).

When determining functions associated with cognitive growth, instrumentation is often a problem. Seldom, if ever, do we have access to a single measurement device equally applicable at all age levels; the behavioral index of competence changes as we move from infancy to toddlerhood to the school-age period and so forth. We assess the competence of infants, for example, by observing what they attend to and inferring from attentiveness to cognitive state. With toddlers we use performance tasks that typically elicit a motor response. With older children, we evaluate symbolic behavior of some sort. There are enormous difficulties in equating conceptually diverse indices—looking, motor behavior, verbal responses—as different ramifications of the same underlying cognitive entity.

Our tasks and our theories have limited our attempts to arrive at definite solutions to problems about the shape of developmental functions. Beyond the ambiguity generated by the nonequivalence across age levels, tasks are usually designed to highlight competence at a particular level of development as predicted from theory. That makes it difficult to detect across-age similarities—continuities—in performance. Some Piagetian-derived tasks, such as those tapping knowledge of number, for example, serve well to differentiate the less numerically competent preschooler from the youngster in middle childhood. The same task, however, will prove insensitive to any cognitive difference between an infant and a toddler (both would fail) or between a school-age child and an adolescent (both would pass). Using the task across all age levels should yield a developmental function like that in Figure 1-7, a discontinuous pattern of growth. However, since the task itself is not designed

FIGURE 1-7   If a set of classic conservation problems was administered to children across age levels, the resultant data would probably yield a discontinuous growth curve as depicted here.

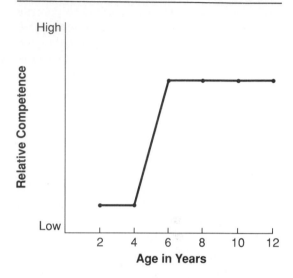

to elicit potential cognitive differences among 1-, 2-, 3-, and 4-year-old children or 8-, 9-, 10-, 11-, and 12-year-old children, the obtained function is artifactual. We cannot be certain whether the observed function reflects the true nature of developmental change in number knowledge or the apparent nature confounded by limitations of assessment, an **epiphenomenon** of measurement error. Indeed, when other sorts of number tasks are used with infants and young children, major and important continuities (not discontinuities) in performance surface.

There are additional cautions when drawing inferences from observed developmental-change data to underlying functions, cautions also originating in assessment. Since tasks are not age independent, we are unable to treat age as a random variable when selecting the age values from which to compute a developmental function. The ages are more apt to be *fixed* values with the scale gaps between them set a priori. With fixed variables as compared to random variables, we must be more conservative in extrapolating from the observed data points to the nonobserved data points (Kirk, 1982). Therefore, we really observe only a set of points, and we remain unsure as to the true shape of the curve on which those points fall. Depending on our analysis methodologies, available tasks, and measurement decisions, we may be predisposed to obtain certain kinds of data. Either we are "primed" to detect a qualitative developmental function, perhaps to miss the continuities in growth (Sophian, 1984), or, on the other hand, alternative techniques and tasks could blind us to true spurts, drops, and discontinuities in cognitive growth.

A related issue is how often we sample over time—the "good clock." Ideally, we should measure competence at multiple points in time (Fischer, 1987). If sampling is sparse, discontinuities might go undetected or growth might look discontinuous because intermediate changes are not represented. As we collect more and more data points, there are fewer and fewer potential lines that would connect all the points. Given only one point, for example, an infinite number of lines could pass through it. Adding a second point eliminates all but one straight line (one linear function); but since nonlinear functions are developmentally feasible, there remains an enormous set of plausible curves. Increasing the number of points will eliminate some contenders, but the function may still remain indeterminant. Thus, we continue to see alternative interpretations for observed developmental growth data (Fisher, 1983, 1987; Kenny, 1983; McCall, 1983; Siegel & Brainard, 1978); behavioral data alone are seldom self-evident.

Growth at the Neurological Level

Growth curves are ambiguous; they cannot clearly tell us whether or not development is continuous or discontinuous. There is a need for additional kinds of evidence, alternative indicators of growth, to disambiguate the de-

velopmental picture. Recently, developmental psychologists have begun looking at what neurobiologists have to say about brain growth. It is assumed, and reasonably so, that behavioral progress is marked (perhaps even preceded) by changes in the neural substrate. Logically, neurological development and behavioral development should go hand in hand, for without the necessary neural mechanisms, cognitive accomplishment could not occur. Our "hardware" has to constrain our capabilities (Crnic & Pennington, 1987). Perhaps observed correlations between brain growth and performance could provide additional evidence about the nature of developmental change.

Normal neural development is characterized by a primarily prenatal proliferation of neurons (Cowan, 1979) followed by a predominately postnatal period of proliferation of synapses until approximately 24 months of age when a maximum number of neurons and synapses have developed (Huttenlocher, 1979). The key feature of neurological growth relevant to developmental function is synaptogenesis, the synapse proliferation introduced earlier in the chapter. As Goldman-Rakic (1987) stated: "Synaptogenesis is the *sine qua non* of functional maturation, as it is the basis of cell-to-cell communication in the central nervous system" (p. 612). Perhaps we can discover something about the form taken by cognitive growth by looking at patterns of synapse proliferation.

Recall that discontinuity in development is defined as spurts in growth that surface behaviorally as abrupt jumps in competence. Synaptogenesis involves spurts in neural growth to peaks or plateaus where the density of neurons exceeds the adult level (Greenough, Black, & Wallace, 1987). These peaks are followed by periods of synapse elimination, selective synaptic degeneration that reduces the total number of synapses by 50 percent (Heumann & Leuba, 1983). The rate of reduction is slower than the proliferation rate, takes a longer period of time (Goldman-

Rakic, 1987), and continues into adulthood (Rakic, Bourgeois, Zecevic, Eckenhoff, & Goldman-Rakic, 1986).

Recent research with monkeys suggests that synapse proliferation occurs in many areas of the cortex at about the same time, though the timing of the peaks may differ. This **concurrent synaptogensis** means that there is a congruence in the timing and rate of synapse formation across different brain areas (Goldman-Rakic, 1987; Rakic et al., 1986). To again quote Goldman-Rakic's (1987) interpretation,

> *The finding that synapses develop rather synchronously in all areas of the cerebral cortex raises the possibility that functions mediated in these cortical areas might also emerge in relation to synaptogenesis, that is concurrently, or nearly so. . . . Perhaps the coincidental timing of a child's first utterance and first step are expressions of concurrent synaptogenesis in the language and motor areas of the cortex. (p. 615)*

Evidence of synaptogenesis and evidence that behavioral functions can be taken over by different structures in the brain as development progresses (Goldman-Rakic, 1974) provide a different kind of empirical support for discontinuities in development. In fact, if new synapses can be formed throughout life, as suggested in the earlier discussion of experience-dependent neuronal growth, then there might be important qualitative developmental changes in the circuitry underlying particular skills (Crnic & Pennington, 1987). A developmentally consistent interpretation of these biological data has been made (Fischer, 1987). It is important to bear in mind, however, that a second process, *synapse elimination,* is also involved in shaping the final form of a cognitive ability. The latter process is more gradual (continuous, perhaps) and may not show the same synchrony of pace across brain regions. Thus, at the neurological level, both continuity and discontinuity are possible.

Most developmental theories purporting discontinuity predict cognitive spurts in be-havioral competence across the period of childhood and adolescence. The number of proposed spurts may differ (see, for e.g., Case, 1985a; Fischer & Pipp, 1984), but qualitative change after infancy is expected. Excess synapse formation, however, is characteristic chiefly of the early postnatal period in mammals (La Mantia & Rakic, 1984); it occurs during infancy, with synapse elimination comprising the other essential determiner of the shape of the central nervous system (Rakic, 1986). The latter process takes place more gradually, throughout childhood and adolescence, and does not appear as likely to have the abrupt quality of the former process. Whether a growth curve looks discontinuous or continuous may be a function of the specific time frame represented.

Were we to ever determine the "truth" about the nature of development and the neurological foundation that supports it, we would probably discover that there are *both* continuities and discontinuities in growth, both qualitative and quantitative changes. Which variety best characterizes cognition is apt to depend on the particular facet of competence studied and the age span when change is most pronounced.

Theoretical Conceptualizations of the Nature of Change

The data, behavioral and neurological, are the raw material that developmental theory is challenged to explain. The theoretical conceptualizations, however, are framed at a different level of abstraction than are the empirical phenomena. The issue becomes how best to model or represent cognitive development, and while data constrain modeling attempts, there is no one-to-one correspondence between *the* data and *a* model. As in curve fitting, one tries to identify a theoretical "best fit" for empirical phenomena; but typically more than one contender surfaces. Discontinuities in development constitute competence spurts, abrupt bends, or plateaus of growth, all changes in the slope of a developmental function. Whether one accepts such discontinuities as true reflections of underlying developmental processes or as epiphenomena of psychological technology influences how one deals with them theoretically.

Piaget proposed that the discontinuities observed in the developing child's cognitive abilities are real, profound, and indicative of major shifts in the nature and organization of cognition. He identified sequences in behavior and contended that these sequences had a **stage** quality. The criteria for "stageness" from a Piagetian perspective are somewhat vague and not easy to operationalize, but most investigators agree that stageness presupposes discontinuity and a high degree of **synchrony** (correlations) among different behavioral indicators at a given point in development.

The stage hypothesis has not fared all that well empirically (Brainerd, 1978c; Fischer, 1980; Flavell, 1982). There are reliably observed discontinuities in development, but there is also reliable **dyssynchrony** in behavioral accomplishment. Children attain skills at different times, while theory predicts the skills should emerge at the same time; then, no correlation shows up where one was expected. Because of such discrepancies between theory and evidence, some developmentalists have opted for discontinuity-descriptive concepts like *level;* these concepts can account for growth spurts while avoiding some of the synchrony problems associated with stage concepts (Fischer & Pipp, 1984). Stage necessitates discontinuity; discontinuity need not be explained solely by stage.

Piagetian stage concepts are also criticized for the proposition that qualitatively different thought systems evolve in children at progressive stages of development (Fodor, 1972). It is the underlying shift in thinking that is presumably responsible for dramatic shifts in behavioral competence; and since the mental

shift is a global one, the behavioral shift should be a pervasive one. If it tends not to be, then stage will lose much of its explanatory power. Indeed, the stage concept becomes useless.

Those who reject the premise that development is qualitative change contend that the same representational and computational systems operate throughout life (see Fodor, 1972; Keil, 1986a; Rozin, 1976). Change in performance occurs because the child increases his or her ability to access and use those systems (Gelman, 1982; Gelman & Gallistel, 1978) or because, over time, the basic system becomes more elaborate and differentiated (Keil, 1986a). In either case, major metamorphoses in the fundamental nature of cognition are not anticipated, qualitative change is not a necessity, continuity as well as discontinuity is explainable, and stage is not a relevant construct. These contrasting styles of conceptualizing cognitive development, adapted from Keil (1981), are schematically depicted in Figure 1-8. Again, after reviewing the evidence, we will reevaluate these positions.

CONCLUSION

The focus of contemporary thinking in cognitive psychology has become the conceptualization of mental systems that capture the essence and typify the structure of knowledge and the processes of thought. We are engaged in filling up the "black box" with strategies and procedures, information-processing routines and skills, knowledge networks, intentionality, and even a central nervous system. Because the goal is to develop model systems that share a correspondence with human intelligence, rather than some nonhuman intellectual system, the model-building enterprise must be constrained by human factors. Many factors serve as constraints, but, quite importantly, information about development is one of them. Human intelligence is a dynamic,

FIGURE 1-8 Three views of the nature of change in cognitive structure with development: (A) represents structural reorganization as growth proceeds, consistent with a view of development as qualitative change. (B) depicts increasing access to an unchanging structure. In (C), growth proceeds as a structural elaboration in accord with specific constraints.

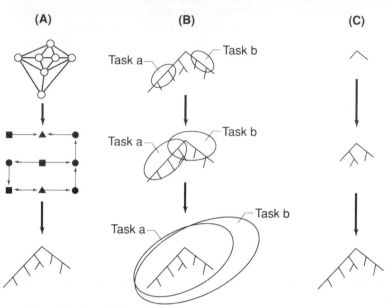

From "Constraints on Knowledge and Cognitive Development" by F. C. Keil, 1981, *Psychological Review, 88*(3), pp. 197–227. Copyright 1981 by the American Psychological Association. Reprinted by permission.

complex system(s) evolving within a biological being. Developmental psychologists have been observing the behavioral ramifications of that evolution for decades, and with the concurrent emergence of knowledge about neurological maturation, the scientific enterprise has become enriched. There now exists the promise that we might indeed achieve theoretical formulations of cognition that have a developmental reality and a biological feasibility.

In the past, developmental data have not been collected in a theoretical vacuum. Strong philosophical currents about the way we view knowledge and its origins have influenced developmental study and the formal explanation of children's thinking. This heritage is evident in the contrasting world views of empiricists and rationalists and in the genetic epistemology of Jean Piaget. Contrasting assumptions about the role of biology and experience and the interaction between them, the nature-nurture debate, have invariably played some role in empirical study and the interpretation of results. And too, predilections for whether cognition is best depicted as a single entity or a set of multiple components has affected the style, focus, and rationale of research efforts.

Empirical information about how cognition emerges from infancy to adulthood is the raw material of our science, and we have a lot of it. But that information must be evaluated from the perspective of the philosophical and intellectual currents that served as the impetus to collect it and melded with data from the neurosciences to forge a richer, more complete, and scientifically accurate picture of cognitive development.

In chapters to come, we will examine the conceptual themes, the methodological styles, the behavioral evidence, and the available neurological information as it bears on development in the cognitive domain. We shall see how the puzzle of intellectual development is being pieced together by scientists from a number of disciplines. And we shall see, so far, what makes the most sense as well as where full resolution continues to elude us.

CHAPTER 2

PERCEPTUAL DEVELOPMENT

INTRODUCTION
THE PHILOSOPHICAL AND METHODOLOGICAL FOUNDATIONS OF
RESEARCH IN PERCEPTUAL DEVELOPMENT
THE DEVELOPMENT OF VISUAL PERCEPTION
PERCEPTION OF SOUND AND SPEECH
CONCLUSION

INTRODUCTION

> *The baby, assailed by eye, ears, nose, skin and entrails at once, feels it all as one great blooming, buzzing confusion. (James, 1890)*

According to William James (1842–1910), the newborn finds the world a chaos of physical stimulation—a senseless, meaningless milieu. The baby must make order out of this amorphous bombardment of stimulation to achieve meaningful knowledge of the physical universe. Perceptual development is the psychological process through which the transformation would occur, but was James's perspective accurate? Do babies experience the environment this way? If so, how do they bring order to it? How does a human being come to know the world in an objective sense? These questions revolve around a fundamental epistemological query about the origins of human knowledge: How do mind and reality become coordinated? Rooted in psychology's philosophical underpinnings, this question provides an explicit impetus for the scientific investigation of perception and perceptual development.

It is perception that connects us with the surrounding environment, allows an interface with physical reality, and initially informs us about the world to which we must adapt in order to survive. So, perception has to play a fundamental role in virtually all other cognitive activity. At the same time, we engage in this basic process effortlessly, unconsciously, and reflexively. Indeed, perception seems automatic. We need not deliberately decide to see, hear, or feel physical sensation, although we may deliberately direct our attention toward specific stimuli. The fundamental role of perception in cognition and the obligatory nature of perceptual processing have attracted the attention of psychologists in the past and continue to intrigue them today.

The developing child must come to know and to represent the developmental environment. He must hear its sounds, feel its contours, and see its surfaces. He must organize its spaces, identify its features, learn to approach its comforts, and avoid its dangers. All of this begins with and hinges upon perceptual

27

ability, a capacity that, while basic, is far from simple or completely understood even in adults. However, given its importance to the interface between subjective mental life and objective external reality, we must rightly initiate our exploration of cognitive development with the development of this fundamental capacity.

The study of perception is one of the oldest areas in psychology and, given its relatively long history, perception research has evolved into a sophisticated enterprise. However, the experimental study of perception and perceptual development, and the creation of psychological theories to flush out and explain the resulting data, are difficult to understand fully without an appropriate framework. Research and theory in perception remain close to the philosophical issues that spawned the field, and philosophy provides such a framework. Before reviewing the research in visual perception—the process enabling the organization of light patterns into an ordered landscape of surfaces and objects—and auditory perception—the companion activity permitting the comprehension of language—we must look at the roots of perception theory and research.

THE PHILOSOPHICAL AND METHODOLOGICAL FOUNDATIONS OF RESEARCH IN PERCEPTUAL DEVELOPMENT

A most important issue, one central to an understanding of the intellectual heritage underlying inquiry into perception and its development, is the discrepancy between empiricist and rationalist world views. One of the big conceptual arguments behind research in perception is the philosophically derived, nature versus nurture debate (Gibson, 1987). The question of whether biology or experience drives development was introduced in Chapter 1 as a major focus of controversy in developmental psychology, and it will come up again in subsequent chapters. However, the influence this philosophical debate has on research

activity is more explicit in the area of perceptual development.

In its rudimentary form, the nature-nurture question is, What constrains development, biology or environment? Obviously, both do. Few contemporary developmentalists answer the question with an unequivocal preference for either influence, but the positions of most researchers looking at questions of perceptual development are still orderable on a nature-nurture, nativist-empiricist dimension (Dodwell, Humphrey, & Muir, 1987). That is important because an investigator's epistemological perspective affects the formulation of research questions, the means chosen to address those questions, and the interpretation of any data.

To the question, "What do we know before we have any experience in the world?" the empiricist responds, "Nothing." The infant's mind is a tabula rasa, according to the empiricist philosopher John Locke (1632−1704), a blank tablet waiting to be written upon; James's buzzing confusion is consistent with the empiricist position. Since empiricists reject infants' access to an innate conception of the world, what they come to know later must derive from the markings of experience. Therefore, to the empiricist the infant is a naive being who could not perceive or know the world as the adult does. The achievement of adultlike knowledge, an acquisition process in which perception plays a primary role, is experientially driven.

To the question, "How does experience produce knowledge?" the empiricist replies, "Through *sensation* and *association*." We perceive stimuli in the world through our senses, but for the baby these sensations are devoid of meaning or order. Meaning comes as separate sensations are associated in time and space, for example, the sight of a bottle, the taste of milk, and the feel of the rounded shape. These stimuli, which in turn elicit bodily reactions, occur together in a regular sequence, and with continual and repeated joint occurrence they become an aggregate, a global "idea." Order is brought to the world as a meaning is built up through the detection of repetitive associations among physical elements to which the biological mechanism is responsive. Implicit in this view is an assumption that continues to influence developmental study: that the world is comprised of elements lawfully associated in time and space. Those elements elicit corresponding sensations in the organism that are similarly related. Mind and reality are correlated because physical patterns and the mental patterns picked up by the senses are of the same nature. The infant, the receiver of this information, will eventually come to know the world, to perceive regularity, order, and lawfulness through this associative process. The process is conceptualized as gradual, cumulative, and developmental. And empiricists make no assumptions about inherent differences among types of stimuli as to their attention-eliciting potential.

While empiricists contend that experience fuels and constrains the acquisition of knowledge, nativists take an antithetical position: Much of what we know—shared meanings and perceived orderliness—is innate. It need not be gradually acquired because it is already there. The mind of the infant has an initial mental content that provides a structure into which forthcoming sense data fit.

Nativist views derive from rationalism, a position associated with philosophers René Descartes (1596–1650) and Immanuel Kant (1724–1804). For rationalists, knowledge is not a product of experience but an a priori condition of mind. There is something there even at the beginning of life; all subsequent mental contents are structured by this innate, mental apparatus that shapes knowledge acquisition. Mind creates reality and drives knowledge acquisition through its own active functioning rather than simply coming to align itself with the outside world through sensation and association. So, mind makes the ordered world rather than mirroring it.

To one of a rationalist bent, it is possible to disagree as to what content is initial and what is acquired, but the necessity of inborn knowledge to impose order and meaning on sensory experience is not disputed. Kant, whose influence on cognitive psychology is particularly important, postulated that initial, a priori knowledge includes the categories of size, form, position, motion, space, and time. In *The Critique of Pure Reason,* Kant ([1781]1924) argues how such dimensions could not be sensed. Thus, the infant, like her sophisticated adult counterpart, must perceive a meaningful, ordered reality.

To questions about what is known prior to experience, a nativist would likely respond, "The basic structure and dimensions of the physical world." To questions of how knowledge acquisition might proceed, the answer would be, "a structure-driven elaboration process." Rather than sensing order, the nativists' baby construes order by meshing and interpreting incoming sense information in accord with the existent organization of mind. The outcome of the knowledge-acquisition processes is highly constrained by the initial mental state. We as human beings share a universal conception of the world, not merely because we all sense the same elements and associations among them, but because we all begin with the same kind of mental equipment.

Implications for Perceptual Development

Predictions about perceptual development come from the basic philosophical tenets just discussed. Empiricists and nativists differ as to how they envision the newborn's perceptual abilities, for example, and what they propose as developmental pictures. Empiricists predict a naive organism who makes gradual progress to perceptual sophistication as a function of learning. Nativists' babies are perceptually capable and share important abilities with adults; development, if it were to occur at all, would be a maturational phenomenon following a preordained path. The psychological study of perceptual development is a clearly marked scientific battleground where nativist and empiricist premises can be put to the test (Bornstein, 1988), and, as you might expect, infants are the subjects of interest. In fact, the study of perceptual development has almost become synonymous with the study of infants. Perceptual processes are investigated in older children as well, but key theoretical arguments hinge on infant capabilities.

Less obvious, but equally important, is the implication that even the choice of research methods is influenced by philosophical perspective. A goal of research is to provide a description of a phenomenon (e.g., perceptual development), but the description can differ as a function of the specific procedures the scientist employs. Data alone are seldom self-evident, nor do they alone provide a complete picture for us. Particular investigative methodologies serve as windows that frame the view we get. If philosophical preferences affect methodological decisions, which in turn provide alternative pictures, the result may well be diversity of conclusions about the state of nature. For perceptual development, we must evaluate the data with methodology in mind.

Those of a nativist bent are inclined to document perceptual acuity very early in the baby's life, indeed, the earlier the better. Early competence, particularly if it is similar in nature to the mature version, is often taken as evidence of an innate, unlearned capacity. So, methods are designed to facilitate the demonstration of infant perceptual skill. Detection of an *age effect,* that is, a positive association between developmental time and increased efficacy, is less central to the nativist case. The opposite wisdom influences the empiricist's agenda. Age effects point to a gradualness in skill acquisition possibly as a consequence of experience and skill attainment. Depending on the investigators' initial philosophical pro-

clivities, research techniques are selected for their potential sensitivity to definitve outcomes.

Methods of Investigation

Scientific fields of study are characterized by their methods. The older sciences, like physics and biology, have long histories and have created sophisticated technologies, more so than newer sciences like psychology. Breakthroughs in knowledge across the sciences can and often do hinge on methodological innovation. New techniques permit fresh perspectives, an increase in obtainable information, or more sensitive measurement. The scientific study of perception is strong because of just such methodological advantages. Perception is an old area of psychological inquiry with a relatively long history of technical advances, strengthened by the contributions made by physicists and biologists. The result is a sophisticated and rich empirical literature.

Implementing an experiment to tap a perceptual process is tricky. In the general format, a subject is presented with some physically definable chunk of stimulation. Then, some aspect of the subject's performance is measured to determine if, in fact, that stimulation was perceived in accord with its defining physical characteristics. The objective is to identify a functional relationship between specific variation in physical stimulation and variation in the organism's response. However, the act of perceiving is a subjective experience so the observable performance correlates of the private mental event must be established and measured.

There are methodological choices to be made. Some choices are based on the requirements of objective procedure, but others are made on theoretical (and, thus, philosophical) grounds. Choice of subjects is an example of the latter and, because of philosophical currents, infants are likely candidates since their abilities bear directly on the nature-nurture issue. However, infant subjects pose special technical problems. How can we determine if a baby notices a stimulus, detects its differences from another stimulus, or prefers to perceive it rather than something else? Infants cannot tell us what they sense, and we cannot directly inspect sensory experience. Therefore, the developmentalist investigating perception must identify indirect behavioral or physiological measures from which to infer perceptual experience. Fortunately, in recent years, methodological breakthroughs for studying perception in infant subjects have enabled a blossoming of empirical inquiry into the perceptual development of the very young.

Preference paradigms.   Intuitively, judgments as to what infants perceive could be inferred from observing what they attend to. If an organism registers stimulation, then some sort of overt sign, such as an orienting response, might occur. Observing *orienting* behaviors is one viable method in perception research, and so many investigators, particularly those interested in the development of visual capabilities, examine what infants look at.

The now widely used technique of forced-choice preferential looking (Fantz & Yeh, 1979) introduced by Fantz (1958; Fantz, Ordy, & Udelf, 1962) was an important methodological breakthrough in perception research with infants. The logic of the procedure is straightforward: The infant is presented with two physically different stimuli. If she discriminates the difference, then she might prefer to look at one rather than the other. The result is differential looking times across the two stimuli. From looking times, capacities and sensitivities of the perceptual system are inferred. The subject need do very little.

The infant, lying face up in a comfortable position, is shown a display of two stimuli positioned to the right and left of midline. A peephole in the display permits the experimenter to observe gazing time in the direction of each stimulus. The technique proved useful

for Fantz, who demonstrated visual pattern discrimination and preference in infants 48 hours old. Preferential-looking methods have been refined as research in perceptual development has grown more sophisticated (Teller, 1979), but the general paradigm continues to be a useful one, particularly in the study of visual pattern discrimination and the detection of novelty.

The major limitation of the method is a built-in confounding in the dependent measure. Preference involves noting the difference between two stimuli and then preferring one over the other. If looking times are equivalent across stimulus choices, perhaps the infant *failed to discriminate* differences; or, discrimination might have occurred but *preference was not affected.* Therefore, we cannot determine unequivocally from null results what stimulus features babies cannot detect. Even when differential looking times are obtained, data remain ambiguous (Bertenthal, Proffit, Kramer, & Spetner, 1987). There is a difference between **encoding,** the process of extracting stimulus information, and the process of **discrimination,** which involves a detection of differences as well. Preferential looking could result from differential encoding alone in the absence of discrimination. So, what appears to be a "preferred" stimulus may simply have taken longer to encode.

Habituation.   An extension of the preferential-looking technique, one even more widely used in infant perception research, is the **habituation paradigm.** If infants are presented with stimulus information to which they are sensitive, we can expect them to attend to the stimulus, inspect it, encode its features, and gain familiarity with it. This behavior is another example of an **orienting response.** Continual presentation or the sustained presence of the stimulus is associated with a decline in orienting behavior as infants get used to or come to "know" the stimulus, and it subsequently loses its novelty. Decreased responding in conjunction with repeated presentation of a stimulus is referred to as **habituation.** Change the stimulus, reintroduce novelty, and an increase in orienting behavior, or *recovery from habituation,* occurs. When reliable changes in orienting behavior are associated with systematic variation in stimulus features, inferences are possible about what information the infants perceive.

The logic of habituation methods is similar to that of preferential looking. Investigators assume the subject is attending to and encoding presented information. When a change in stimulation takes place, it is the anomaly between the previously encoded and stored percept and the new encoded information that precipitates a behavior change. Some capacity for perceiving information and for forming and storing a percept is presumed. The objective is to infer something about the nature and characteristics of that percept from behavior changes correlated with anomalies. The methodology takes advantage of the observation that babies reliably react to novelty, to changes in stimulation, and to the violation of their expectations about how things should look.

A number of responses are potential indicators of orientation and attention. Inspection time is obviously one. However, there are measurable physiological indicators, too, such as heart rate (Berg & Berg, 1979). Heart-rate deceleration from a resting state (habituation) indicates interest (recovery) and can be reliably scaled. Respiration rate and sucking rate, as measured by a pacifier device, are other potential physiological indicators of attention.

Whether behavioral or physiological signs serve as the dependent measure, the objective is the same: to infer from response patterns which sources of physical stimulation are perceptually functional for subjects. Ambiguity is not altogether avoided, however. Habituation involves two processes: (1) encoding or perception and (2) retention of a stored percept. One shortcoming of the habituation proce-

dure is associated with a failure to find differential responding across stimulus variation. Such null results could be a consequence of a deficiency in either process (Bertenthal, Proffitt, Spetner, & Thomas, 1985). The strength of the technique is its wide applicability to the study of perception in virtually any modality (Bornstein, 1988).

Visual scanning. Another method useful for studying visual perception is recording the reflection of a stimulus on the cornea of the baby's eye, that is, filming what the baby sees. The technique, when backed up with appropriate technology, yields a record of the fixations infants make while scanning a visual pattern (Aslin, 1988). When babies fixate, they orient to segments of a stimulus array and, from those fixations, perceptual preferences can be inferred (Bornstein, 1988). The use of visual scanning technology reveals that infants, even from the first days of life, orient to their visual environments and show preferences for certain features such as areas of sharp contrasts, contours, edges, and bold patterns (Bornstein, 1988). Recording eye images and movements also permits examination of whether infants can locate visual targets (Aslin & Salapatek, 1975), track visual stimuli across movements in space (Aslin, 1981a), and visually anticipate the expected location of a stimulus (Haith, Hazan, & Goodman, 1988). Babies can do all of this within the first few months of life (Haith, 1966, 1980; Kessen, 1967).

Conditioning techniques. Still another technique exploits the finding that even the very young can be classically conditioned (Blass, Ganchrow, & Steiner, 1984). The sucking response, for example, is a virtually universal unconditioned response in normal babies to the presentation of milk or a sweet solution (unconditioned stimulus). Conditioning is achieved when a neutral perceptual stimulus (e.g., an auditory tone or visual pattern) is paircd with the nutrient solution often enough to elicit the response (e.g., sucking, head turning) with the perceptual input alone (conditioned stimulus). Infants can also be operantly conditioned. In the head-turn technique (HT), for example, a "background" stimulus consisting of a particular speech sound is repeated at a constant rate. Infants are trained to make a head-turn response whenever the background stimulus is changed to a "comparison" speech sound. Thus, the sound change elicits a head turn that is reinforced with an interesting visual stimulus (see Eilers, Wilson, & Moore, 1977). Once conditioning is achieved, characteristics of the conditioned stimulus are varied to assess generalizability. If the infant perceives a changed stimulus as equivalent to the conditioned stimulus, then the conditioned response will occur. If, on the other hand, the infant discriminates the stimulus difference, generalization is not expected. This technology tells us about the dimensions of stimulus variations to which an infant is sensitive and about the magnitude of change necessary to evoke discrimination.

Summary

Techniques for studying perceptual development in human infants are technically sophisticated, but they also are noninvasive, descriptive, indirect assessments of mental processing. They enable the identification of the kinds of stimulation babies detect and the determination of the age of onset of sensitivity. Data reveal age-related changes in capabilities and any continuity in perceptual functioning across younger and older organisms. In general, the methods yield information about systematic relationships between both behavioral and physiological variations in perceptual input and responding.

Indirect assessment with descriptive technologies has its limitations, however. Inferences drawn from data about mental processes often can be open to alternative interpretation. A particularly intractable ambiguity arises when infants do not demonstrate sensitivity to a given value or feature of perceptual stimulation. It is not possible to conclude straightforwardly that infants are incapable of detecting the feature, only that for some reason they fail to respond to it. The outcome could occur as a consequence of many factors besides perceptual insensitivity, such as failures of motivation, for instance, or some limitations in the method. Thus, while nativistically oriented investigators are challenged to elicit evidence of innate capabilities, their empiricist counterparts are at a disadvantage. Empiricists are hard pressed to demonstrate definitively that a neonate *lacks* a perceptual capability in the absence of experience given the ambiguity of null results. The nature-nurture controversy is not so easily settled simply by examining evidence of "initial" perceptual capacities.

Eventually, developmentalists aspire to explain the origins of perceptual abilities. That goal cannot be achieved solely through the description of infants' sensitivities because the data are often ambiguous and because potential causal variables cannot be manipulated. So, we must look elsewhere for evidence to disambiguate the experimental findings. Neurobiologists and developmental psychobiologists, for example, study perceptual processes, too, often with nonhuman subjects, but those data bear on human development. Moreover, animal studies have the advantage of permitting a degree of experimental control not possible with human subjects, up to and including direct examinations of the neurobiology implicated in perceptual functioning. Therefore, animal data are a rich source of information about perception that can assist us in our efforts to understand perceptual development in humans.

The general goal of research in perceptual development, whether subjects are immature humans, animals, or even adults, is to build models of functioning that are psychologically realistic and biologically feasible and have implications for the conceptual questions of a philosophical origin. The research varies in detail, but the studies are all variations on a similar theme.

THE DEVELOPMENT OF
VISUAL PERCEPTION

Perception includes a range of organismic activities, from sensitivity at the cellular and neural level to knowledge-driven, information processing at the representational level. Research and theory on perceptual development address the phenomenon on a variety of levels, yielding a vast and complex literature. Some of that literature focuses on the more psychophysical aspects of perception, what used to be called *sensation;* other research is more cognitive (see Salapatek & Cohen, 1987). The topic areas overlap, since the physiology of a sensory system limits which stimulus features can be responded to, that is, the perception of movement presupposes movement-sensitive neural mechanisms (Aslin, 1988). However, the cognitive end of the perception continuum has the most obvious bearing on the development of children's capacities to extract and manipulate meaningful information from physical stimulation.

Human infants are born with their eyes open and visual system operational, but their visual functioning is not identical to an adult's. For humans, as for most mammalian infants, the brain continues to grow, mature, and differentiate postnatally (Prechtl, 1984). These maturational processes contribute to changes in how sensory systems function following birth, a functioning fueled as well by experience in the postnatal environment (see Knudsen, 1983; Knudsen & Knudsen, 1990). How the initial biology of a perceptual system and early sensory experience interact to mold, shape, and elaborate the emerging informa-

tion-processing capacities is an important developmental question.

Newborn human infants do possess rich visual capacities (Hall & Oppenheim, 1987), but they may rely more on subcortical brain structures (Grusser, 1983) than they will a couple of months later when the cortex is more fully developed (Bronson, 1974; Johnson, 1990). The eyes also grow and change during the first months of life (Abramov, Gordon, Hendrickson, Hainline, Dobson, & LaBossiere, 1982), and neuron layers within the visual system mature at different rates following birth (Hickey, 1977; Hickey & Peduzzi, 1987). The cells in the **fovea,** for example, are changing in density through a process of cell migration at least during the first year and a half following birth (Yuodelis & Hendrickson, 1986). The fovea is a shallow depression in the retina containing many photo receptors; it is the area of the retina capable of greatest spatial resolution. Cellular changes in the fovea have implications for the development of visual acuity and pattern perception.

There must be a great deal of flux in perception for the developing infant. The visual system is changing structurally from endogenous influences, and the baby is experiencing visual events, an exogenous influence that also affects system function and structure (Black & Greenough, 1986; Greenough, Black, & Wallace, 1987). A basic task for the young perceiver is to achieve perceptual stability—to identify objects and calibrate their locations reliably in space even though they are viewed from different perspectives, in different places and contexts, and from different distances. The difficulty of this task is compounded because the visual apparatus itself is in a state of flux in early development (Banks, 1988).

In order to describe adequately this early perceptual development, investigators first need to identify the very early competencies—the preexisting or "hard-wired" capacities shaped by our evolutionary heritage, which are genetically specified and relatively crude in functional quality—that the neonate brings to subsequent visual encounters. Second, they need to describe how early competencies are readjusted with the growth of this rather unsophisticated, immature apparatus. Third, they need to determine the extent of **plasticity** in the system—how much the immature visual system responds to and modifies in the face of experience, particularly early experience. What does the literature tell us about the development of these essential information-extraction capabilities?

Research in Pattern Perception: The Neoempiricist Tradition

Do babies perceive complex patterns or elements of those patterns? Are they sensitive to changes in overall configuration or to alteration of elements within a pattern? Is pattern detection and preference age related? These questions have spurred research in **pattern perception**. A major stimulus for much of this work is the theory proposed by D. O. Hebb (1949). Hebb's interest was neurophysiology and the overlap of the problems in that field with those of psychology. He, like most cognitive psychologists today, assumed that behavior and neural function are perfectly correlated. So, the problem of understanding behavior is the same as that of understanding the action of the nervous system. Hebb proposed a theory at the neural level to account for some of the complex mental phenomena of interest to psychologists, one of which is visual perception.

Two key concepts in Hebb's theory are the **Hebb synapse** (Anderson & Rosenfeld, 1988) and the **cell assembly.** If an axon from one cell repeatedly or persistently excites a second cell and takes part in its firing, the two cells become associated or connected. Structural changes result that increase the efficiency with which the first cell facilitates the firing of the

second, and the synapse is strengthened. The growth process that accompanies synaptic activity makes the synapse more readily transversible; the changed facilitation constitutes learning. Sets of neurons associated this way come to form cell assemblies, diffuse structures comprising cells in the cortex. The action of an assembly could be aroused and activated by a sensory event, the preceding action of another assembly, or both. By building up systems of multiple and complex cell assemblies, the organism constructs neurological counterparts or models of features in the external world. Cell assemblies are presumed to operate in the perception of patterns, and since Hebb proposed that neural networks could act briefly as closed systems after stimulation ceased, their action constitutes the simplest instance of mental representation. A series of such neural events, a **phase sequence,** is the neurological counterpart of a thought process.

While Hebb did postulate certain primitive pattern elements of the perceptual world to which the organism intrinsically responded, the major operation associated with perceptual development is presumed to be learning, the gradual growth of assemblies. He projected that there would be significant differences in the properties of perception at different stages of perceptual integration as cell assemblies become connected, elaborated, and integrated. Moreover, he predicted marked differences between the perceptions of child and adult.

The implications of Hebb's thinking for research in perceptual development are straightforward. First, Hebb's view, like the empiricist philosophy with which it is consistent, is associationistic, reductionistic, and developmental. If the view is accurate, then there should be age-related changes in perceptual behavior that corresponds to neuronal changes and *not* much perceptual sophistication in the neonate. Second, growth should proceed from the perception of simple, primitive pattern elements to true pattern representation with the concurrent construction and integration of complex cell assemblies.

Hebb's theory has had a large impact on research in visual perception and space, particularly in research with animals. For example, with microelectrode recording techniques, investigators can observe the sensitivities of single neurons in the brain and associate neuronal sensitivity with specific "trigger" features in the environment (Bornstein, 1988). The contention that perceptions ought to have an identifiable neural substrate is a major impetus behind such work. In research with humans, we see similar attempts, although with different technologies, to relate changes in the visual behavior of the infant to anatomical and neurophysiological data. Research has revealed reliable differences in the perceptual sensitivities and visual preferences of infants under about 2 months of age, presumably when the visual system is quite immature, and those of infants a few months older (Dodwell, Humphrey, & Muir, 1987). And, in Hebbian style, there have been attempts to explain the developmental shifts on the basis of neurological models that could account for it (Bronson, 1974; Karmel & Maisel, 1975; Maurer & Lewis, 1979; Salapatek, 1975).

Hebbian influence is apparent in research on infants' pattern-perception capabilities. Working with stimuli composed of simple features, investigators examine the sensitivity of their immature subjects to primitive pattern elements. Stimuli tend to be geometric, abstract, static, and composed of molecular units arrangeable into more than one configuration, such as four small circles that can be arranged into a square or a diamond yielding two distinct patterns (see, e.g., Dineen & Meyer, 1980; Garner, 1974). Since these stimuli are fairly simple and the dimensions on which they vary are limited, when babies respond preferentially to the restricted stimulus varia-

tions or when they dishabituate to specific changes in patterns or elements, it should be possible to associate stimulus features and perceptual behavior. Investigators have looked at when infants are able to detect particular stimulus elements, when they first react to changes in those elements, and when they respond to patterns preferentially over elements.

From such studies, we conclude that newborns distinguish curved lines from straight ones (Fantz, Fagan, & Miranda, 1975), discriminate horizontal from vertical stripes (Slater & Sykes, 1977), and, by at least 1 month of age, differentiate right versus left oblique stripe patterns (Maurer & Martello, 1980). Young infants prefer to fixate on simple patterns with high contrast, such as bull's-eyes and large checker boards (Banks & Ginsburg, 1985). In the first few hours after birth, babies tend to look at the parts of stimuli having high contrast features like angles and along the contours of figures (Bornstein, 1988). At 1 month, they tend to scan external contours rather than internal details, which they note later (Salapatek, 1975). However, while research with animals has been consistent with Hebbian ideas—that is, simple elements are detected early—some of the evidence obtained with very young infants contradicts Hebb's predictions. Young babies, for example, detect simple form and dishabituate to changes in form but not to changes in orientation of the form (Schwartz & Day, 1979). Perhaps, even initially, infants are prepared to encode complex visual material and not just primitive elements.

An important aspect of pattern perception depends on the tendency to organize the visual field into the components of figure and ground. In a Gestalt psychology analysis of perception, this tendency is viewed as automatic, unlearned, and innate (Koffka, 1935). Even Hebb (1949) suggested that the capacity to separate figure from ground is innate. But how do infants do on tasks designed to test this capacity? Stephens and Banks's (1987) data with 6- and 12-week-old infants suggest that infants' ability to discriminate background differs markedly from that of adults. Apparently, contrast discrimination, essential to figure-ground organization as well as to other pattern-perception phenomena, is quite poor early in life.

Termine, Hrynick, Kestenbaum, Gleitman, and Spelke (1987) examined whether 4-month-old infants would perceive a background surface as continuous behind an occluder. Using a habituation paradigm, the investigators presented babies with visual stimuli like those depicted in Figure 2-1, which adults perceive as a continuous background partially blocked by a horizontal bar. If infants also perceive a continuous background, then they should not dishabituate to a test display with the occluder removed and the continuous surface revealed. They should, however, dishabituate to a test display depicting the surface with a horizontal gap. Data were consistent with this analysis, providing evidence of an early capacity to perceive backgrounds as continuous; the authors interpreted the findings as consistent with Hebb's predictions.

Pattern perception actually begins quite early, but preference for complex patterns increases with age (Fantz & Yeh, 1979). By 4 to 5 months of age, infants perceive gestalts, and by 6 to 7 months of age, they reliably dishabituate as readily to pattern changes as they do to feature changes (Dineen & Meyer, 1980). So, for example, they note when a square pattern made up of four small triangles is rotated to form a diamond as well as when the small triangles are replaced by small circles and no rotation is included. Infants under 6 months of age detect gestaltlike properties of vertical symmetry (Bornstein, Ferdinandsen, & Gross, 1981), good continuation (Van Giffen, & Haith, 1984), and good form (Bomba & Siqueland, 1983; Strauss & Curtis, 1981). In general, during the first year of life, measures of habituation, as well as those of preference, are systematically related to the complexity of the stimulus (Bornstein, 1985). Babies also demonstrate orientation preferences and, by 4 months of age, prefer simple patterns aligned on the vertical or horizontal (Bornstein,

FIGURE 2-1 *Occlusion Displays Used to Determine if Infants Perceive Figure-Ground Relationships.*
Both displays depict a background occluded by a horizontal bar.

From "Perceptual Completion of Surfaces in Infancy" by N. Termine, T. Hrynick, R. Kestenbaum, H. Gleitman, and E. S. Spelke, 1987, *Journal of Experimental Psychology: Human Perception and Performance, 13,* pp. 524–532. Copyright 1987 by the American Psychological Association. Reprinted by permission.

1978). During the first 6 months of life, they habituate most rapidly to vertically oriented stimuli and by 12 months prefer symmetrical vertical over matched horizontal and oblique patterns (Bornstein, Ferdinandsen, & Gross, 1981).

In short, during the first half-year of life, infants do develop sensitivity to configurations and patterns, to regularity and symmetry, and to "good form" in a gestalt sense. Clearly they can respond to more than molecular elements, such as lines, segments, or corners. In some subtle ways, infant perceptual behavior is not unlike that of adults (Bertenthal, Campos, & Haith, 1980).

There are, however, some cautions in order. Findings about infant pattern sensitivities and preferences, particularly data about the age of onset of sensitivities, are not robust. Conclusions vary across studies as stimuli change, as the dependent measures change, and as experimental procedures are altered. In fact, results tend to be study-specific. Sometimes it is difficult to draw unambiguous generalizations about what young infants perceive. Part of the problem resides in the investigator's choice of stimuli. They tend to be abstract and unlike any stimulus a baby is apt to encounter in the real postnatal environment. While stimuli of this sort afford maximum experimental control and physical definition, they lack **ecological validity,** a close relation to natural stimuli.

If babies are innately predisposed as a consequence of evolutionary pressures to respond to some particular environmental stimuli, then arbitrary, abstract patterns are not the most logical ones. Also, stimuli in pattern-detection research are usually presented in a static state. Babies, however, look more quickly and longer at moving static displays (Haith & Campos, 1977), and they are more sensitive to kinetic information (Banks & Salapatek, 1983; Gibson & Spelke, 1983). In fact, when the internal elements of a pattern are

presented in motion, such as when flashing, babies look at internal features and not the edge of the stimulus as commonly reported (Bushnell, 1979). Less Hebbian, less empiricist investigators, therefore, look elsewhere to study the development of visual perception.

Face Perception: Moving toward Nativism

A visual stimulus to which virtually all normal babies are exposed is the human face. Perhaps infants are differentially sensitive to faces as compared to other visual features of the postnatal environment. John Bowlby (1958, 1969), who adopted a theoretical perspective on development rooted in **ethology,** thought so. He argued that a baby's preference for human faces is innate and serves as the foundation of attachment. Logically, such stimulus selectivity, based on biological preparedness, would have adaptive value for human infants. Bowlby's position on the innateness of human face perception was not derived from experimental data, but recent evidence suggests some biological predisposition to perceive facial stimuli (Nelson, 1987).

Newborn infants will track certain types of facelike patterns (Karmiloff-Smith, 1991). According to most reports, by 2 to 4 months of age, infants show a preference for a normal version of a face as compared to one with scrambled features (Mauer, 1985; Maurer & Barrerra, 1981). By about 2 months, they fixate on internal features of faces in addition to the external border (Haith, Bergman, & Moore, 1977; Mauer & Salapatek, 1976), and by about 2 to 3 months, they are also able to discriminate a variety of facial expressions (Barrera & Maurer, 1981; Nelson & Horowitz, 1983; Young-Browne, Rosenfeld, & Horowitz, 1977), preferring happy ones (Kuchuk, Vibbert, & Bornstein, 1986). There is little evidence, however, that babies respond differentially to faces prior to about 6 weeks of age in the same way they will later. What does this imply for a biological preparedness hypothesis?

Null results in developmental research—in this case, the failure to observe differential responding to facial stimuli—do not disprove the hypothesis of innate capacity. The reliable observation, however, that a response is not observed before a certain age and is observed after that age begs an explanation. Recall from Chapter 1 that some developmental achievements emerge as a maturational function; proficiency might not appear until sometime after birth, but the process is a biological one, or a case of **predetermined epigenesis** (Gottlieb, 1983). Recall also that the age demarcation for the detectable emergence of face preference, 2 months, is also observed in a great deal of other developmental perception research as well. What might such convergent observations mean?

Banks and associates (Banks & Ginsburg, 1985; Banks & Salapatek, 1981, 1983; Banks, Stephens, & Hartmann, 1985; Stephens & Banks, 1985) proposed a model to explain differences between the visual perception of very young infants and that of older infants and adults. These investigators pointed out that the visual information available to an adult viewer is not the same as what is available to a very young infant. Because of the physiological immaturity of their visual system, young infant's may receive less information than their older counterparts. As a consequence, infants' preferences could reflect their attention to stimuli most visible for them. In short, young infants simply do not see as well as older ones do. The particular aspect of "visibleness" in this model is **contrast sensitivity,** and the index of the ability to detect contrast information is called a **contrast sensitivity function,** or CSF. This function permits a precise accounting of the actual visual information available to infants of different ages for a variety of stimuli. CSF is analogous to a filter; at younger ages greater amounts of visual information are filtered out, leaving what would be, by adult standards, a degraded stimulus. It was on the basis of contrast discrimination that Stephens and Banks (1987) observed differences in the pattern-discrimination ability of 6- and 12-week-old infants as compared to that of adults. Those data not only provided insight into the underlying neurophysiological mechanisms responsible for such visual deficits, they revealed how infants' contrast discrimination capabilities could place substantial restrictions on their ability to recognize, discriminate, and identify visual patterns. Figure 2-2 depicts a face filtered in accord with the CSF associated with various age levels.

Prior to 2 months of age, then, infants may fail to demonstrate a preference for facial stimuli due to limitations in contrast sensitivity. Using computer-generated, light and dark, schematic faces, Dannemiller and Stephens (1988) examined the stimulus preferences of 6- and 12-week-old infants. Stimulus variation was highly constrained by using schematic faces, preferable from the perspective of achieving experimental control; real faces are molar and complex, and their psychophysical characteristics are not obvious. The investigators created two stimulus patterns: a facelike one and an abstract one identical in contrast. Each stimulus could also be paired with a reverse-contrast version (i.e., one where the light and dark areas were reversed). The resulting four stimuli depicted in Figure 2-3 are identical in contrast, size, and optical characteristics, but one of them (a) is more facelike. If infants do possess differential sensitivity to faces, then they should prefer the facelike stimulus to the others in a forced-choice viewing task. Results revealed that 6-week-old infants do not demonstrate a preference for facelike stimuli, but 12-week-old infants do. Moreover, the older infants' viewing patterns are not predictable from the physical and optical characteristics of stimuli alone.

FIGURE 2-2   Beginning with the upper-left-hand picture and moving to the upper-right-hand, lower-left-hand, and lower-right-hand picture, faces filtered according to the CSF of the adult, 1-month-old, 2-month-old, and 3-month-old. Stimuli should be viewed from a distance of 15 cm.

From "The Recognition of Facial Expression in the First Two Years of Life: Mechanisms of Development" by C. A. Nelson, 1987, *Child Development, 58,* pp. 889–909.

This definitive preference test is consistent with a biological preparedness hypothesis and supports a plausible rationale for the absence of apparent preferences in young infants. (But there are others; see Johnson, 1988, 1990, and in press). Essentially, as soon as infants can see sufficiently well (2+ months), they demonstrate a preference for faces. There is also evidence from studies with monkeys, where actual cell activity has been measured (Perrett, Rolls, & Caan, 1982), and from studies with brain-damaged, adult humans (see Nelson, 1987) that the ability to recognize faces and facial expression is mediated by structures in the right hemisphere of the cortex (i.e., the occipital-temporal lobe junction). Nelson (1987), in his review of the data, contended that the nervous system of the human infant is indeed "prewired" to perceive facial stimuli, but experiential and maturational processes impact on this biological readiness.

The face-perception research points to a conclusion that potentially bears on underlying conceptual issues in the empiricist-rationalist debate. The findings lend support to the importance of contrast sensitivity and the contrast sensitivity function as a viable explanation for any absence of demonstratable per-

FIGURE 2-3 The four computer-generated stimuli used by Dannemiller and Stephens to assess infants' sensitivity to facial stimuli. The four stimuli are matched for CSF but A is more facelike.

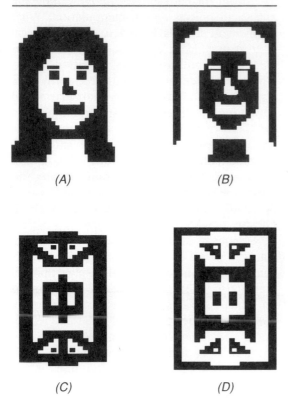

(A)   *(B)*

(C)   *(D)*

From "A Critical Test of Infant Pattern Preference Models" by J. L. Dannemiller and B. R. Stephens, 1988, *Child Development, 59,* pp. 210−216.

ceptual capacity in very young babies. It could be argued that babies might always be prepared a priori to perceive patterns, to organize the visual world into complex configurations. However, before 6 to 8 weeks of age, the information that specifies a pattern does not get through the sensory system. As soon as the babies can see it, though, the stimulus organization is perceived as a meaningful configuration, not as an accumulation of bits, elements, or features.

Therefore, an important theoretical question raised by the face-perception research is whether infants are predisposed to pick up other environmental features as a function of their biology. Many organisms, expecially in infancy, are attuned to certain key stimuli in their environment (Marler, 1991). But this is a nativist hypothesis, and to explore it we need further theoretical impetus for direction.

The Perception of Information in Motion

There are alternatives to an empiricist viewpoint. Babies may be innately predisposed to detect some perceptual features of the environment that are molar and complex if detection of those features has survival value. For example, the immature animal capable of detecting the approach of a predator has less likelihood of being eaten than one who cannot. Similarly, the baby mountain goat who can perceive and avoid steep drop-offs is more likely to survive than its oblivious counterpart. And the human infant who is able to discriminate the movement of a caretaker against a background of perceptual "noise" increases the probability of eliciting needed attention. In short, certain perceptual proclivities may have become ingrained in the nervous system through years of evolutionary selection pressures.

There are several important developmental ramifications of this perspective that contrast with the conceptual notions underlying much of the pattern-perception work. First, early visual competence in babies is anticipated. Second, the perceptual objects of this expected competence are most likely those with some ecological relevance. Third, ecologically valid stimuli are apt to be complex, dynamic, and informationally rich, much like objects in the natural environment. The investigator with philosophical sympathies of this bent will design and conduct research that looks considerably different from the empiricist variety. Particularly, the stimuli will be of an entirely different nature. A viable choice would be dynamic stimulus events organized in structure and lasting over time that simulate a more "natural" perceptual environment (Gibson, 1982).

If we are willing to ascribe considerable perceptual sensitivity to the infant, then the basis for that sensitivity must be identified. Is early perceptual competence a consequence of innate *cognitive* mechanisms, innate conceptions of the world? A positive response indicates strong nativism. The hypothesis is that infants display perceptual competence because they possess rudimentary, intuitive notions about the physical universe that direct behavior, including perceptual behavior (Spelke, 1991). Perhaps early competence is the result of conceptual, cognitive processes rather than perceptual ones; this would have to be the case if sufficient information with which to direct behavior is not adequately specified in the physical stimulus array. If infants act as if they have information about the physical layout and if the optical information is impoverished, then the information guiding action must have a cognitive source.

But is perceptual information absent? Is an optical array truly impoverished? If not, then it is only necessary to propose innate mechanisms for extracting important visual information from available stimulation. This weaker nativist position is consistent with James and Eleanor Gibson's *ecological* theory of perception (E. J. Gibson, 1969, 1982, 1984; J. J. Gibson, 1966, 1979).

The Gibsons see the information available in physical stimulation as rich in extent, lasting over time, and explorable by the organism. By exploring the ecological landscape, any perceptually equipped animal can **apprehend** properties of the world that are relevant to action. Apprehension connotes a direct process not cognitively mediated (E. J. Gibson, 1984). **Affordances** (E. J. Gibson, 1982; J. J. Gibson, 1979) are those action-relevant properties of the physical environment that afford, elicit, or suggest certain behavioral action. Chairs *afford* sitting on, hard surfaces *afford* walking on, and small objects *afford* manipulation. What an element affords is tied to the ecological context in which it appears and to the organism's needs, motivations, and intentions. Thus, a particular element does not necessarily have a stable set of affordances. A chair may afford sitting on for a tired organism or climbing on for the 3-year-old trying to reach the cookie jar. The organism will apprehend what the environment affords in ecologically valid, natural *terrains*. Features of this terrain offering important affordances for animals include paths, drop-offs, obstacles, steps, and slopes (E. J. Gibson, 1984).

Organisms also detect **invariants,** the constants in arrays of stimulation. An *invariant* is some aspect of a perceptual display that remains fixed despite changes in position or movement and temporally related variation in the stimulus array. Imagine, for example, being in a small boat on a slightly rough sea. Because of wave action, the perceptual view is continuously changing, but the line of the horizon is a constant, an invariant, detectable against the flux. In fact, looking at the horizon helps avoid the nausea accompanying too much flux. Invariants define the properties of space, objects, and the constraints of the physical universe. To Gibsonians, these are properties of the **distal** stimulus, the arrays themselves, not the **proximal** stimulus. It makes sense that the most pervasive and enduring constraints of the world in which we have evolved should be the ones most likely to be thoroughly internalized in the nervous system (Shepard, 1981, 1984, 1988). Perceivers, including infants, search for the invariant information specifying properties of the environment. For Gibsonians, such properties exist, and perceivers detect some of them without experience or learning (Spelke, 1987).

Essential to apprehending an invariant is a field of movement against which it is perceptible. Thus, motion is crucial to perception. In Eleanor Gibson's (1984) words, "The world to be perceived is not static, and this is fortunate for the perceiver, who uses change not only to perceive events (i.e., changes in the layout), but to get a handle on what persists" (p. 246). In the natural environment, the perceiver is not confronted by momentary views of static scenes but by a dynamic landscape with continuously changing scenes where information is specified over time. We determine what we are looking at from the succession of views and the transformations across them.

The information invariant across transformations specifies the structure of elements on the landscape. In fact, when confronted with a scene containing ambiguous information, we are very apt to move in order to obtain additional views that would disambiguate the input. As we travel through the environment, we not only experience motion, we perceive visual flow. Consequently, our perspective on objects within the landscape changes, although the layout itself does not. Conceivably, perceptual mechanisms sensitive to perspective change have developed over evolutionary time (Gibson, 1966, 1979; Kellman & Short, 1987) and have served as one basis for visual perception.

Motion is a very salient aspect of perceptual information for infants. Infants from 1 to 3 months of age can distinguish between stationary and moving stimulus displays (Volkman & Dobson, 1976). They show sensitivity and preference for dynamic displays, for kinetic information (Banks & Salapatek, 1983; Gibson & Spelke, 1983). After 2 months of age, babies demonstrate smooth ocular pursuit of moving contours (Aslin, 1981a). They are particularly sensitive to rapid velocities (Kaufman, Stucki, & Kaufman-Hayoz, 1985), although their sensitivity to slower velocities increases between 1 and 3 months of age. That

young infants are relatively insensitive to slow stimulus velocities (Kramer, 1986) is consistent with neurophysiological information about the immaturity of foveal vision (necessary to focus on stationary patterns and slow-moving stimuli) and the visual cortex.

Both the foveal region of the retina and the visual cortex undergo important postnatal developmental change (Atkinson, 1984). Sensitivity to rapid velocities, however, appears to be adultlike very early in life. Freedland and Dannemiller (1987) demonstrated that by 5 months of age infants' abilities for motion detection suggest a similarity to the motion-sensitive mechanisms of adults, specifically visual mechanisms of the periphery rather than the fovea. Motion-sensitive systems may develop very early in infancy, tuning infants into the dynamic features of their environment.

Perception of biological motion. A clever series of studies on the perception of biological motion reveals the importance of dynamic information for the apprehension of structure. In these studies, lights are attached to a person's major joints (hip, elbow, knee, etc.). When the person, dressed in black, is filmed against a black background in the dark, the only thing visible is the light points. The stimulus, called a *point-light display,* is obtainable with either a live performer, film, videotape, or a computer simulation. Adult subjects who view the static point-light display report perceiving a random array of lights, but as soon as the person begins to walk, they apprehend a human walking. Structure is quickly inferred from biomechanical motion (Cutting, Profitt, & Kozlowski, 1978; Johansson, 1973). Adults even discriminate familiar individuals on the basis of biomechanical motion (Cutting & Kozlowski, 1977).

In contrast, nothing is apprehended from nonbiomechanical light swarms even when the motion characteristics of the light movements are carefully controlled. Johansson (1978) argued that the apprehension of a three-dimensional structure from a point-light display is mediated by intrinsic perceptual processes; it is "prewired." This hypothesis suggests the study of infants' perception of biological motion. Do they also extract coherence and three-dimensionality from similar displays?

Infants do indeed differentiate biological from nonbiological motion in point-light displays. Fox and McDaniel (1982) reported that 4- to 6-month-old infants demonstrate visual preference for biological motion, running in place, over a random light swarm. Similarly, these infants differentiated the "runner" display from an inverted runner that served as a control. Younger infants (2 months old) did not make the same discrimination. However, infants under 2 months of age do not demonstrate sensitivity to a range of visual stimulation that only slightly older babies do.

Detection of a walker implies that three-dimensional structure is apprehended even though the point-light display in a video or computer version is two dimensional. What information present in the visual display would permit the infant to perceive three-dimensional structure? Suppose a person were to face sideways with respect to a viewer and walk. In the course of walking, parts of the elbow, knee, leg, hip, and so on of the side farthest away from the viewer would be momentarily occluded, or blocked from view. If only point lights are visible, then occlusion of these joints is signaled by a blinking light when the joint to which the light is attached temporarily disappears. Bertenthal, Profitt, Spetner, and Thomas (1985) manipulated this occlusion information in their point-light walker displays and found that, by the age of 36 weeks, infants detected the blinking-light occlusion information and preferred it as well.

Bertenthal and associates (Bertenthal, Profitt, & Cutting, 1984; Bertenthal, Profitt, Kramer, & Spetner, 1987) also varied the coherence of point-light walkers and investi-

gated whether degree of stimulus organization was relevant to the apprehension of structure. The investigators reasoned that coherent displays are apt to be encoded faster and remembered better than are less coherent displays, especially if viewers are inherently attuned to structure. Thus, they should observe a systematic relation between encoding time and stimulus coherence. The coherence of point-light displays can be metrically quantified (Cutting, 1981) and, therefore, computer simulation of walkers allows the variation of stimulus conditions in very precise ways. Bertenthal et al. (1987) presented 3-month-old infants with two point-light walker displays varying in coherence. The investigators interpreted the data as confirming their hypothesis: Infants revealed longer encoding times for the less coherent displays.[1]

This series of experiments suggests two important facts about visual perception in infants. First, there is a great deal of information available in kinetic stimulus events of which we are not always explicitly aware; that adults apprehend the information so uniformly and effortlessly and that babies do too suggests implicit awareness. Second, the findings from infant research tell us that these apprehension processes are present very early in life and could represent intrinsic processes of the visual system, even though they are not reliably detectable in infants less than 20 weeks old. But whether the ability to extract structure from movement is experientially based or hard-wired, the achievement is not the result of any lengthy developmental process, because considerable ability is detectable in early infancy.

Perception and optical flow.   When we move through the environment, the visual field changes. Surfaces in motion correlate with the moving pattern of light falling on the retina. The **optical flow field** provides information about the viewer's movement in space and about the three-dimensional layout of a scene (Gibson, 1950; 1966). So, in principle, optical flow delivers useful information about depth.

Imagine traveling across a landscape. Looking ahead you experience an expanding scene as surfaces spread out from a central point of focus. Behind, what you see is contraction. Thus, when moving through a static environment, optical flow is *centrifugal* ahead and *centripedal* behind. The location of objects in this scene is partially specified by relative differences in speed. Objects closer to the perceiver will seem to be moving more quickly than objects farther away.

According to Gibson (1950), expansion provides information about the direction in which the observer is moving while magnitude and position flow vectors indicate relative distance of points in a scene. There is additional optical information available in movement when surfaces on objects farther away pass behind surfaces on closer objects. This flow information is specified at the edges of surfaces. When an individual is stationary, optical-flow information is provided by objects moving toward the perceiver, and the effect is similar. Adults use optical-flow information quite effectively to determine the three-dimensionality of visual scenes (Rogers & Graham, 1982). And, apparently, sensitivity to optical flow develops quite early in life (Banks, 1988; Bertenthal, Dunn, & Bai, 1986).

T. G. R. Bower attracted attention when he demonstrated sensitivity to optical-flow information in infants under 1 month of age. Imagine yourself stationary with a cannon ball coming at you on a collision course. Optical-flow information specifies a rapidly expanding contour or **looming pattern** as the object approaches. Symmetrical expansion specifies collision, a hit; assymmetrical expansion specifies a miss. If the cannonball were moving away from you instead, a **zooming pattern** would emerge from flow information. You are more apt to take evasive action and duck in the case of a loom. Animals respond to the two visual patterns differentially too, backing away from the loom pattern (Schiff, 1965).

In similar fashion, Bower found that young infants become distressed and press their heads back when presented with looming patterns either created with real objects or simulated by a shadow caster. He interpreted the data as indicating evasive action taken to avoid a perceived impending collision (Bower, 1974; 1977b). The finding is somewhat controversial; the data are ambiguous and alternative inferences are possible. For example, if babies were tracking the expanding contour of the loom (and we already know young infants selectively attend to contours), the same behavior would result.

Yonas and associates (see Yonas & Owsley, 1987) were more conservative than Bower. Their conclusions as to infants' sensitivity to optical-flow information in looming patterns are qualified, and they date the age of onset in infancy later than Bower would. Still, Yonas and associates (Yonas, 1981; Yonas, Peterson, & Lockman, 1979) detected perception of looming patterns in infants by 3 months of age. Gibson (1982; Carrol & Gibson, 1981) reported that by 3 months of age infants can even differentiate approaching objects from approaching openings or apertures. With an approaching object, the optical-flow information reveals grain changes in texture; with an opening, of course, it does not. Thus, texture and grain changes constitute information about depth.

Another way in which changes in texture provide information about depth is when one surface slides behind another. At the edge of the front surface, there is a demarcation between the texture of the back surface and the texture of the one in front. J. J. Gibson (1966) contended that, from any vantage point, the world is divided into surfaces, some of which are visible and some of which are occluded.

When an observer moves through the environment or when a scene moves relative to an observer, some surfaces are revealed and others are occluded. The transforming pattern of light that reaches the eye is one of *accretion* and *deletion* of visible texture elements, which for adults provides unambiguous information about depth at an edge (Kaplan, 1969).

Does this kind of visual information specify depth for infants? Granrud et al. (1984) tested this hypothesis with 5- and 7-month-old infants. Previous studies had shown that infants will reliably reach for the nearer of two surfaces when they perceive a difference in depth (Granrud, Yonas, & Pettersen, 1984; Yonas, Sorknes, & Smith, 1983). Given that observation, Granrud et al. (1984) presented 5- and 7-month-old infants with computer-generated, random-dot displays that look to adults like one surface sliding in front of another. The stimuli were effectively discriminated by the babies; both age groups demonstrated a greater tendency to reach for the apparently nearer of the two surfaces (see also, Graton & Yonas, 1988).

This body of research, inspired by the Gibsons' ecological perspective, has delivered some powerful findings. Clearly, by the age of 3 months, babies demonstrate amazing perceptual capabilities. In virtually all cases, however, early competence is inferred from responses to *kinetic* visual information. In fact, kinetic sources of information seem to be the first type to which infants respond in perceiving spatial layout and depth (Granrud et al., 1984). Sensitivity to kinetic variables in stimulation is reliably detected by the age of 3 months; sensitivity to binocular discrepancy information, that is, the retinal position difference of the object's image between the two eyes that specifies depth, emerges next (3 to 5 months); and sensitivity to pictorial depth information emerges last (5 to 7 months) (Yonas, Arterberry, & Granrud, 1987b). Early sensitivity to motion is consistent with physi-

ological data about the immaturity of the very young baby's visual system, which constrains perceptual abilities.

Perception of Depth:
The Visual Cliff

Whether or not infants perceive depth at an edge intrigued Gibson and Walk (1960) over 30 years ago. In pioneering research, these investigators created a research apparatus referred to as the **visual cliff.** It consists of a transparent table-top apparatus divided into three regions: (1) a "shallow side" in which a checkerboard pattern is flush against the glass surface, (2) a "deep side" in which the checkerboard pattern is much closer to the floor, and (3) a centerboard separating the two regions. An animal or human infant placed on the centerboard could either stay put, move out across the shallow side, or transverse the deep side. If the infant is unable to differentiate the two sides on the basis of visual information (*note:* tactile information is identical), then the probability of transversing the shallow side and the deep side is equal.

If, on the other hand, young animals have a survival-motivated propensity to avoid drop-offs and if they can differentiate depth from visual information, then the probability of transversing the deep side is lower. In fact, early results showed that newborns of some species—notably, goats, monkeys, and chickens—did indeed avoid the deep side; other newborns (cats, rabbits) did so after a few weeks, although not at first (Walk, 1966). Goat and chicken babies, however, normally move about their environment right after birth, so there is survival value in an innate propensity to avoid drop-offs. Cat and rabbit newborns are not as mature and mobile, so they need not be so protected to increase species survivability. In any case, data suggest a maturational function for the avoidance of drop-offs (Walk & Gibson, 1961).

Once human babies start to crawl at around 7 months, they can be tested for avoidance of the "cliff." In the classic paradigm, the locomotor infant is placed on the centerboard and, with the mother's help, is coaxed to one or the other side of the apparatus. Whether the dependent measure is the response of traversing or of latency prior to initiating the traverse, human babies also demonstrate an avoidance of the deep side (Rader, Bausano, & Richards, 1980). However, the interpretation of these findings is controversial. The question is whether the data are best interpreted as a maturational function or as an inductive one. Richards and Rader (1981; 1983) provide a maturational interpretation since behavior on the cliff is correlated with age.

Deciding whether a developmental function is maturational or inductive is tricky business when experience is ubiquitous. Then age and experience are confounded, and their relative contributions must be separated somehow. Research by Campos and associates (Bertenthal & Campos, 1984; Campos, Hiatt, Ramsay, Henderson, & Svejda, 1978; Campos, Benson, & Rudy, 1986) challenged the maturational interpretation. Prior to crawling, infants can discriminate depth cues (Banks & Salapatek, 1983), and prelocomotor infants evidence heart-rate deceleration (an index of an orienting response) when lowered in the deep side of the cliff (Campos et al., 1978). They perceptually detect the difference between the sides in the optical flow associated with approach. But **avoidance** requires that the perceptual difference be given some interpretation. Avoidance depends on a fear response, and fear is signaled by heart-rate acceleration. Even if "detectibility competence" is innate and maturational, "interpretation competence" need not be.

Bertenthal, Campos, and Barrett (1984) were convinced that avoidance of the cliff is an induction function and the key experiential contributor is *self-produced locomotion.*

Adopting the animal paradigm of **enrichment,** the investigators provided prelocomotor infants with locomotor experience in the form of practice with infant walkers. These devices allow young infants to maneuver under their own power by pushing on the floor with their feet. As compared to control infants without walker experience, the experimental babies showed the more "mature" response indicative of avoidance of the visual cliff, and the difference persisted even after both groups of babies became naturally locomotor. Figure 2-4 depicts the findings.

These findings are buttressed by evidence from a case study of an orthopedically handicapped child whose cliff response was correlated with locomotor experience rather than age, and by a study with normal children in which the relative contributions of age and experience were statistically separated. For a depiction of the latter data, see Figure 2-5. The research evidence implicates self-produced locomotion as a ubiquitous experience essential to the development of avoidance of steep drop-offs (Bertenthal & Campos, 1987). It is experience that may function in an experience-expectant manner (see Chapter 1; also Bertenthal & Campos, 1987; Greenough, Black, & Wallace, 1987).

Human infants, unlike goats and chickens, need not have evolved to fear drop-offs at birth. They have little opportunity to fall off things until they are crawling about in the environment, so there is little survival advantage in the neonatal ability. Given the possible need of economy in genetic programming, it makes more sense to attune the organism for an upcoming experience (crawling) on which to base the acquisition of competence (cliff avoidance) and save "prewiring" for essential capabilities, the absence of which would threaten survival.

The research by Campos and associates leads to a qualification of maturational significance of the visual-cliff phenomenon. These

FIGURE 2-4 *Heart-Rate Reactions to Being Lowered toward the Deep Side of the Visual Cliff in Infants with at Least 40 Hours of Artificial ("walker") Locomotor Experience Compared to Age- and Sex-Matched Controls.*
Left panel shows data from infants tested when unable to move about without assistance. Right panel shows data from infants tested 5 days after beginning to crawl spontaneously.

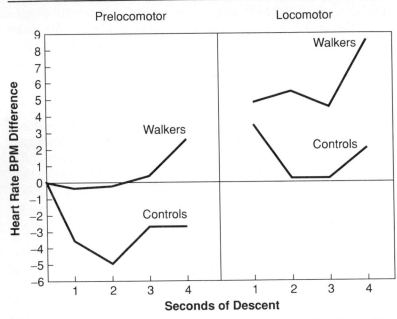

From "Self-Produced Locomotion: An Organizer of Emotional, Cognitive, and Social Development in Infancy" by B. Bertenthal, J. Campos, and K. Barrett, in *Continuities & Discontinuities in Development* (pp. 175–210), R. Emde and R. Harmon (Eds.), 1984, New York: Plenum.

data are consistent with the interpretation of developmental phenomena as *probabilistic* rather than *predetermined epigenesis* (Gottlieb, 1983). Also, the contention that activity of some sort, other than visual activity, is essential to perceptual competence is an empiricist contention (see Spelke, 1988a).[2]

Object Perception

Spelke (1988a) described the task humans face when perceiving objects from information in the visual field, and her comments reveal the potentially enormous difficulties involved:

Human adults experience the world as a layout of physical bodies that endure through time. Our ability to do this is both mysterious and fascinating, because the information we receive about physical objects is potentially so misleading. Consider the case of vision. Objects are bounded, but the visual scenes in which they appear are continuous arrays of surfaces. Somehow, we must determine which of the many surfaces that touch or overlap in a visual array are connected to one another. Objects are also integral units, but they are only partly visible at any given time and their visible surfaces are often separated from one another by nearer occluding objects. Somehow we must recover the integrity of each object from this mosaic of visible fragments. Finally, objects exist and

*move continuously through space and time, but
they are frequently occluded and disoccluded by
movements of surfaces or of the observer. Somehow, we must apprehend the continuous existence
of an object from our sporadic encounters with it.
(p. 197)*

It is not altogether clear how we can do this,
yet we adults perceive the world of objects effortlessly and automatically. Do babies perceive objects in the same way as we do? How
do they come to abstract objects as entities
from various patterns of light? The study of
development involves identifying not only developmental phenomena, those capabilities
and achievements that show change over time,
but also uncovering nondevelopmental phenomena—the characteristics of cognitive functioning infants and their older counterparts

FIGURE 2-5 *Proportion of Infants Failing to Cross
to the Mother Over the Deep Side of the Visual Cliff
in a 120 sec Period as a Function of Both Age and
Locomotor Experience.*

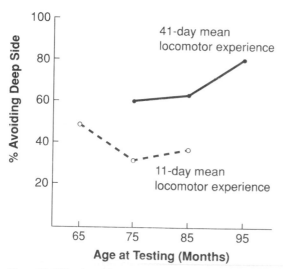

From "Self-Produced Locomotion: An Organizer of Emotional, Cognitive, and Social Development in Infancy" by
B. Bertenthal, J. Campos, and K. Barrett, in *Continuities &
Discontinuities in Development* (pp. 175—210), R. Emde
and R. Harmon (Eds.), 1984, New York: Plenum.

have in common.[3] These continuities in development are important to a full understanding of ontogenesis. When developmentalists look at object perception in infants,
they seek behavioral evidence for both types of
phenomena. Continuities in object perception
include any responsivity to object qualities
that is shared by infants, children, and adults.
Discontinuities are differences in responsivity.
From continuities and discontinuities in behavior toward objects, similarities and differences of physical reality are inferred.

When it comes to object knowledge, both
empiricists and Piagetians have emphasized
discontinuity between the infant and adult.
For empiricists, object perception begins with
the detection of the sensible properties of a
scene and the association of detected light reflections and tactile resistance. Children acquire knowledge about the world of objects by
associating the sights, sounds, and feel that accompany acting on elements in the physical
environment. By handling a block, a baby feels
the edges and corners and detects concurrently
changing patterns of light as the block moves
in her hand. As we know from earlier in the
chapter, the organization of the perceptual
world, in this case the world of objects, begins
to mirror these sensed properties, and the
child begins to perceive the three-dimensional
block. The developmental implications are
clear: (1) The infant should not exhibit object
knowledge prior to building the associations
of vision and touch over time, and (2) physical
action is central to the association mechanism.

For Piagetians, object knowledge is also
developmental and action is again implicated.
Babies construct conceptions of objects
through sensorimotor exploration. Perception
per se is less important in the Piagetian perspective than is cognition. Knowledge of objects as bounded, persisting elements with independent existence in time and space is a
cognitive act in this view. Moreover, the conceptual accomplishment is the child's construction that is extended in time and predi-

cated on interaction of organism and environment (Piaget, 1954). So, objects are not perceived; babies build an **object concept.** The task is not fully accomplished until the end of infancy at about 2 years of age. The object concept is examined in detail in Chapter 3.

The assumption made by empiricists and Piagetians alike is that perceptual information is inadequate and perhaps ambiguous and, thus, the organism must supplement external information with something else (Gibson, 1984). Piagetians propose mental schemata as the supplement; empiricists prefer learned associations. The conservative prediction is that behavior indicative of object knowledge is not expected early in infancy before association, learning, or construction processes could conceivably play a role. If handling of objects is central to the perception of objects as bounded entities that endure through time and space, then babies should not display evidence of such knowledge before they are motorically active. Babies start to engage in extensive manipulation and handling of objects (e.g., grasping and mouthing in particular) around 5 months of age. Important object properties like form, shape, substance, and so forth could require extensive motoric exploration to become known; behavior indicative of awareness of such properties is more likely to arise late in infancy.

An alternate analysis begins with an antithetical proposal: The optical display does constitute a rich source of information about objects for which supplementation is not necessary. Objects *afford* action and manipulation. Since babies and toddlers spend a great deal of developmental time manipulating objects, they may be attuned to the features of objects that afford handling. According to Eleanor Gibson (1984), the distinctive features and invariants, like form, for example, are the information for affordances. The baby must possess a set of perceptual processes permitting pickup of information.

Gibson (1984) proposed three basic activities involved in information pickup: "(1) *exploratory activity* of the perceptual systems, (2) *extraction of invariants* from information in the array, and (3) *observation of consequences* of exploratory action, resulting in detection of contingent relations" (pp. 254–255). Motoric exploratory activity is included here (number 3), but it is only one of the processes involved in information pickup. The first two processes are perceptual. Through these processes, infants increasingly *differentiate* information in optical displays, extracting more and more of it that is relevant to their activities. The infant does not perceive a display exactly as adults do since the differentiation process is incomplete, but infants are sensitive to some features very early.

Visual perception of objects in infancy. Spelke and associates (Kellman & Spelke, 1983; Spelke, 1985) have done a number of experiments testing young infants' object knowledge and identifying the object features to which they respond. Most of the experiments follow a prototypic format: First, the infant is habituated to a display that an adult would describe as an object partially obstructed by an occluder. The display is depicted in Figure 2-6. If the infant picks up "objectness" from the habituation display, he will "expect" the object to continue behind the occluder. Then this expectation is tested by presenting the infant with alternative test displays. The rationale for this is that a test display consistent with the expectation formed during the habituation phase will not lead to dishabituation because it does not constitute a novel stimulus. A test display inconsistent with the expectation, on the other hand, should result in recovery. For the object depicted in Figure 2-6, the test displays represent alternative views of the object with the occluder removed. One is a single object with its continuous form extending where the occluder had been. The second de-

FIGURE 2-6 *Prototypic Stimulus Display of a Partially Occluded Object.*
The upper portion of the figure depicts the display used during the habituation phase. The lower portion of the figure depicts the alternative test displays.

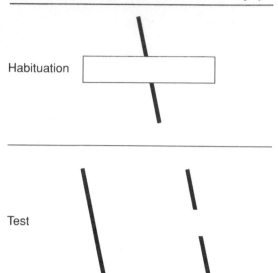

Habituation

Test

From "Object and Observer Motion in the Perception of Objects in Infants" by P. J. Kellman, H. Gleitman, and E. S. Spelke, 1987, *Journal of Experimental Psychology: Human Perception and Performance, 13,* pp. 586–593. Copyright 1987 by the American Psychological Association. Reprinted by permission.

picts two pieces, exactly as had been previously viewed, now separated by a gap.

Using looking time as the dependent measure, the investigators determined the characteristics of the habituation display that precipitated differential looking time to the test display. In all of the Spelke-inspired experiments, a similar control procedure was used: baseline-looking time to the test displays without prior exposure to the habituation display. Typically, infants do not inherently prefer one test display over the other. Therefore, subsequent differential looking to the test displays following exposure to the habituation display can only be attributed to the effect of the object-information manipulation.

Across a series of experiments (reviewed in Spelke, 1985, 1988a), the results were clear. The information feature that clearly resulted in differential looking times was *movement* in the habituation display. If the two extensions of the "object" moved together in relation to the occluder, then infants as young as 3 to 5 months of age looked at the display two to three times longer than if it were presented stationary, and they dishabituated to the test stimulus depicting the separated fragments. Spelke interpreted the data as evidence that infants perceive a center-occluded object as continuous behind an occluder if the visible ends undergo a *common motion.* Moreover, this aspect of object knowledge cannot be predicated on action-based constructive activity, because this early perceptual competence is elicited in infants too young to have had extensive motor experience.

Infants of this age do not reveal similar differentiation of test displays when the occluded object remains stationary during habituation (Kellman & Spelke, 1983), even when the occluded objects constitute "good forms" in the Gestalt sense (Schmidt & Spelke, 1984). They do dishabituate to the segmented test stimulus with a display whose pieces do not go together from a gestalt view but which have been associated through common motion (Kellman & Spelke, 1983). Figure 2-7 summarizes the outcome of the research program and identifies specifically which features lead to differential looking times and which do not. Clearly, movement is the key feature here, the perceptual characteristic infants pick up early in life. But not just any movement will do. Infants perceive an object's unity from lateral translations of the visible parts and from translations in depth (Kellman, Spelke, & Short, 1986), but they do not when the fragments and occluder together show a common motion, when the fragments undergo different

FIGURE 2-7 *The Types of "Occluded-Object" Stimulus Displays Used by Spelke and Others to Assess Infants' Perception of Objects.*
Infants dishabituate to test stimuli depicting a gap when the occluder is removed only for those stimulus varieties depicted on the right. Infants do not form an expectation of object completion behind the occluder for those stimuli on the left.

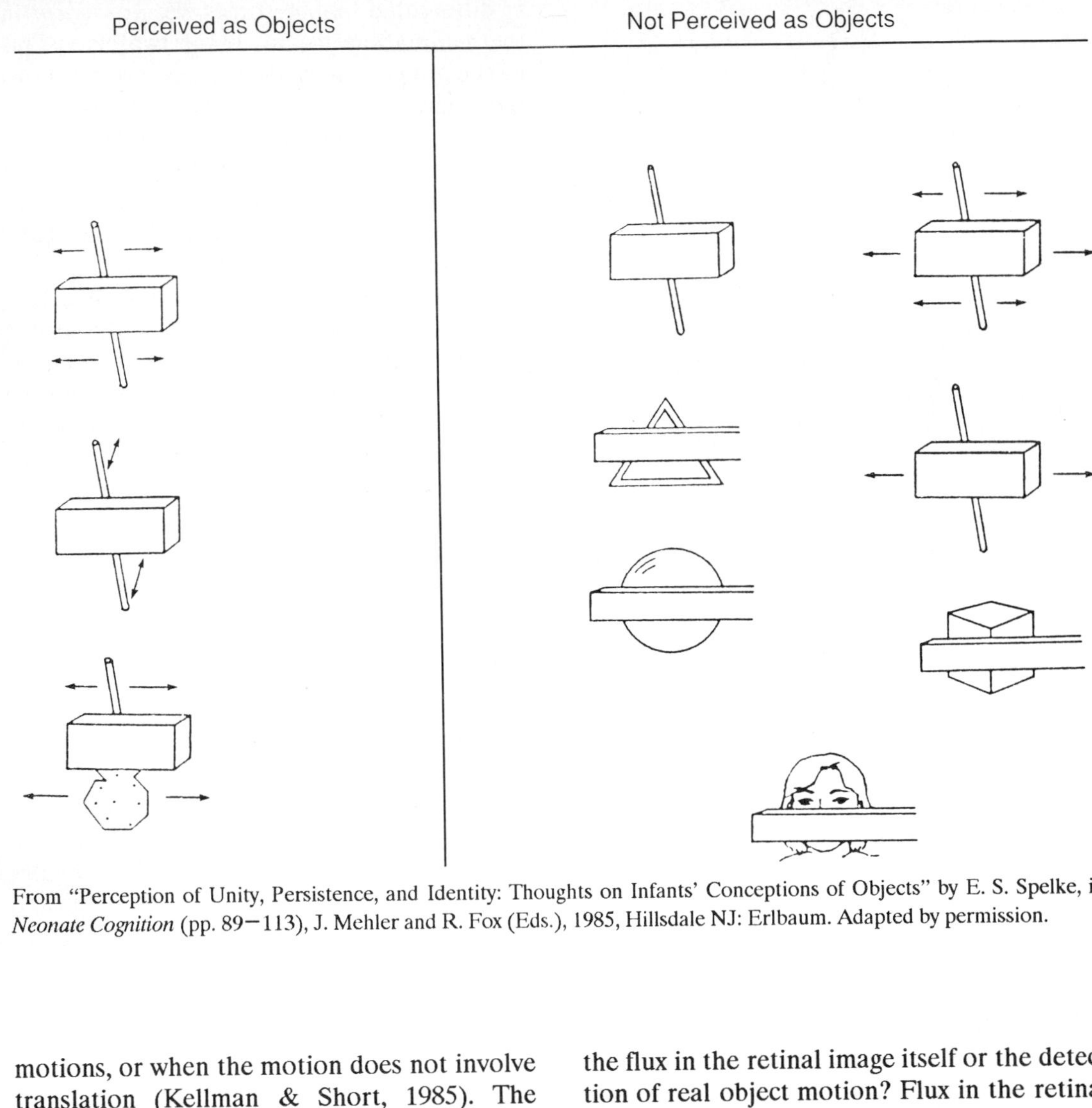

Perceived as Objects	Not Perceived as Objects

From "Perception of Unity, Persistence, and Identity: Thoughts on Infants' Conceptions of Objects" by E. S. Spelke, in *Neonate Cognition* (pp. 89−113), J. Mehler and R. Fox (Eds.), 1985, Hillsdale NJ: Erlbaum. Adapted by permission.

motions, or when the motion does not involve translation (Kellman & Short, 1985). The early capacity for object perception depends on the presence of changing stimulation of a particular type.

But what is the source of the information that yields the perception of object unity? Is it the flux in the retinal image itself or the detection of real object motion? Flux in the retinal image will occur both when an object moves relative to the observer and when an observer moves relative to an object. In the Gibsonian view, the two conditions should be perceptually different.

To examine this question, Kellman, Gleitman, and Spelke (1987) again used the occluded rod stimulus but varied the viewing conditions. Either the habituation display was static and the infant subject (3 to 4 months of age) was moved relative to it or the display and the infant were moved conjointly. In the first condition, the relative position of the rod and the observer would change; from an empiricist's perspective, the perceptual outcome should be identical if the observer is fixed and the object moves. In the second condition, the manipulation of both observer and object could have the effect of canceling out the movement. These manipulations are depicted in Figure 2-8.

The infants in the first condition did not dishabituate to the fragmented rod as did their counterparts in earlier studies who had viewed the object moving. Observer motion did not function the same way as object motion in the perception of object unity. Infants in the second condition, however, did dishabituate to the segmented test stimulus; apparently, they could indeed disentangle real object motion from self-motion and abstract object qualities

FIGURE 2-8 Apparatus used by Kellman et al. to examine subject motion (a) and conjoint motion (b) on infants' perception of object continuation behind an occluder. Top views of the object and observer positions at one extreme of movement are shown, with positions at the other extremes shown by dotted figures.

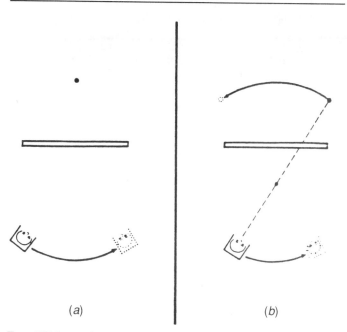

(a)   (b)

From "Object and Observer Motion in the Perception of Objects in Infants" by P. J. Kellman, H. Gleitman, and E. S. Spelke, 1987, *Journal of Experimental Psychology: Human Perception and Performance, 13,* pp. 586–593. Copyright 1987 by the American Psychological Association. Reprinted by permission.

FIGURE 2-9 *Looking Times during the Habituation and Test Periods.*
Panel (a): Stationary object and observer, data from Kellman & Spelke (1983). Panel (b): Stationary observer, moving object, data from Kellman & Spelke (1983). Panel (c): Observer movement condition (moving observer, stationary object). Panel (d): Conjoint movement condition (moving observer, moving object). (Backward habituation curves are displayed, showing looking times on the final six habituation trials. Test trials consisted of alternate presentations of broken and complete rod displays that had the same movement characteristics as the rod parts visible during the habituation period).

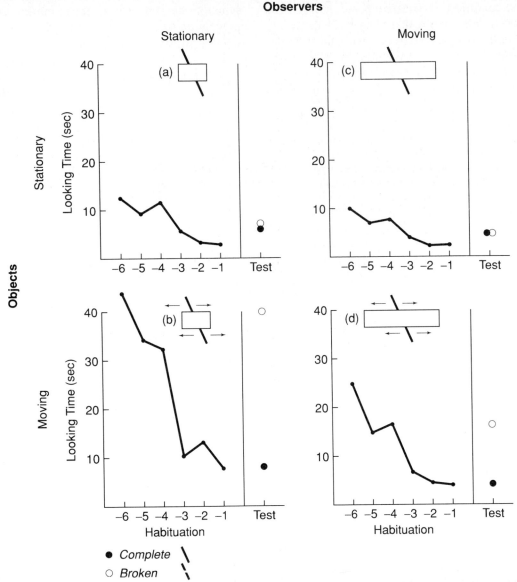

From "Object and Observer Motion in the Perception of Objects in Infants" by P. J. Kellman, H. Gleitman, and E. S. Spelke, 1987, *Journal of Experimental Psychology: Human Perception and Performance, 13*, pp. 586–593. Copyright 1987 by the American Psychological Association. Reprinted by permission.

from the display. The data, combined with findings from earlier studies, are presented in Figure 2-9.

Kellman and associates also did a series of experiments to show that infants abstract information about geometric *form* from kinetic information. Using the habituation paradigm with looking time as the dependent measure, infants were presented with a three-dimensional object undergoing a rotation transformation. The transformation of the object (either a wedge or *L*-shaped solid) could vary as to the axis of rotation and whether the transformation information was presented as continuous motion or as a series of successive status views. The stimuli and their appearance at different points in the rotation are depicted in Figure 2-10.

In one study (Kellman, 1984), 4-month-old infants were habituated to one of the two objects presented in rotation around two specific axes of rotation. The test stimulus was either the same object rotating around a third, different axis (movement change) or a different

object rotating around the same axis (object change). Only infants who observed the continuously moving stimulus showed differential recovery and reliably longer looking times to the new object. In a subsequent series of studies conducted in similar fashion (Kellman & Short, 1987), young infants perceived three-dimensional form even with stimuli whose form when presented statically is ambiguous. The same results are not produced when infants see multiple static views of the same three-dimensional objects. Apparently, infants must observe the continuous motion and the transformation across the motion to abstract the invariant feature of form.

Arterberry and Yonas (1988) examined whether infants could recover three-dimensional form solely from kinetic information. In a clever experiment, 4-month-old infants were shown computer-generated, random-dot displays. When presented statically, the stimuli look like dot swarms without any particular structure or shape. When presented in motion, adults report perceiving form in the opti-

FIGURE 2-10 Schematic views of objects and rotation axes used by Kellman and Short to assess infants' perception of geometric form. Successive views 60° apart are shown. All views in the same column are from the same three-dimensional object; views in the same row are from a single axis of rotation.

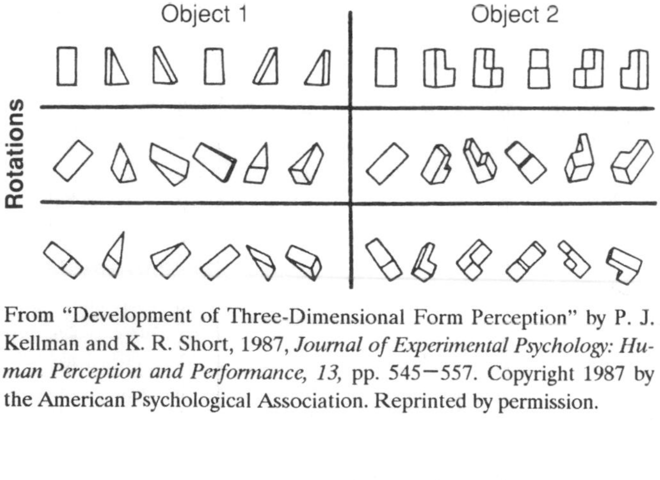

From "Development of Three-Dimensional Form Perception" by P. J. Kellman and K. R. Short, 1987, *Journal of Experimental Psychology: Human Perception and Performance, 13,* pp. 545–557. Copyright 1987 by the American Psychological Association. Reprinted by permission.

cal-flow information. There were two rectilinear, solid shapes specified by oscillating random-dot displays. Infants were habituated to one or the other undergoing two different rotations using procedures similar to Kellman's. Test displays consisted of the alternate form-dot display in a new rotation (object plus movement change) or the same form-dot display in a new rotation (movement change). As might be predicted from previous investigations, infants dishabituated to the former, looking significantly longer at the novel "object."

Other data (Gibson, Owsley, & Johnston, 1978; Gibson, Owsley, Walker, & Megaw-Nyce, 1979; Kellman & Short, 1985; Owsley, 1983; Yonas, Arterberry, & Granrud, 1987a) point again to the importance of motion for infants' detection of object characteristics prior to their ability to locomote through or to extensively manipulate objects in their environment. Typically, these investigators interpret their data as supportive of a nativist position and refer to the perceptual mechanisms as "unlearned." The impressive capability of infants and the adultlike quality of their perception of information from a wide variety of dynamic stimuli is a robust research finding. So, the perception of objects in motion would seem to represent a developmental continuity. This capability is reliably detected in infants of about 3 to 4 months of age, although even earlier sensitivity remains a possibility (Nelson & Horowitz, 1987). When it comes to the origins of the perception of objects, the bulk of empirical evidence gives nativists the edge. And the Gibsonian research tradition has provided us with a number of ingenious demonstrations of the functional significance of dynamic stimuli in the infant's environment.

Haptic and intermodal perception of objects. Information about the world of objects is not restricted to pickup through the visual mode. Objects can be touched, felt, mouthed, and sometimes heard as well as seen. And the particular sensations associated with different sensory-perceptual modes are quite different. An edge or corner has a feel to it, and it has a look to it; the sensation of touching an edge is distinct and separable from that of seeing one. Even the neural connections involved in the two avenues of apprehension are not the same. Yet, as adults, we recognize a single edge, not two, and we perceive its "edgeness" independent of the channel of perception. Acquisition of knowledge about the physical universe necessitates information pickup by a number of perceptual systems, but there is only *one* physical universe. How the senses cooperate, how perceptual systems coordinate in the extraction of this information, is a major epistemological issue (Rose & Ruff, 1987).

Cross-modal transfer is achieved when experience with information pickup is limited to one perceptual system, but the object of the experience is recognized with another. An infant, for example, might experience on object haptically by mouthing it and recognize it visually when it is presented in the visual field. Meltzoff and Borton (1979) claimed that infants are capable of such a discrimination by 1 month of age. **Cross-modal matching** occurs when an individual simultaneously experiences two objects with different perceptual systems and recognizes that the two objects are the same. The first kind of demonstration is more characteristic of research with infants (see, e.g., Gibson & Walker, 1984). In both cases, however, questions arise about the nature of the mediating process that bridges the gap between sensation in one modality and sensation in another.

Again, there are two alternative sets of premises for the origins of intermodal integration. Empiricists and Piagetians (for example, Piaget, 1954) posit an initial separation or independence of sensory systems at birth. Through either associative (the empiricists) or constructivist (the Piagetians) processes, the senses become coordinated. For Piaget, it is through sensorimotor activity, the coordination of grasping, looking, and manipulation schemas, that intermodal perception becomes possible. According to both experience-driven positions, the capacity is acquired, developmental, and not in the perceptual repertoire of the very young infant who has yet to coordinate prehension and vision. The Gibsonians do not assume an initial separation but, rather, an initial unity. What occurs in information pickup is the apprehension of **amodal** properties, like shape, size, and substance, which are invariant characteristics of the distal object. The modality detecting the invariant is irrelevant; it is the invariant to which the organism is attuned. The prediction is early competence.

Imagine yourself blindfolded and presented with a table top on which are placed multiple objects. Your task is to explore this "landscape" without benefit of vision and to discover its layout. Adults explore by touch, moving their hands across the surfaces, manipulating and feeling the objects encountered, and perhaps displacing the objects to mark relative position. The tactile encounters are fragmentary, brief, and transitory; but adults organize those encounters into a unitary "picture," a stable world (Gibson, 1962). The question is whether infants engage in a similar exploratory process and whether they extract sufficient information about stimuli through this means to recognize them. Whether nonvisual, tactile exploration is with the mouth (Gibson & Walker, 1984) or with the hand (Steri & Pecheux, 1986), infants do discriminate familiar from novel objects.

The main feature enabling the young infant to perceive visual stimuli as bounded and unitary objects is common motion. Steri and Spelke (1988) conducted a series of experiments to investigate whether similar principles could explain object perception haptically. Using the habituation paradigm, 4-month-old infants explored, through touch and handling, one of two stimuli. The stimuli differed in characteristic motion. The rigid object con-

sisted of two wooden rings connected by a fixed bar. If the infant were to hold the rings, one in each hand, and move them, the type of motion produced would be dependent; moving of one ring would move the other so the rings would move together. The alternative, a flexible-motion stimulus, also consisted of two rings but the connector was an elastic band, and the rings moved independently. On test trials, either the novel or familiar object was presented visually, whereas the habituation trials consisted solely of haptic exploration. The apparatus allowing babies to feel but not see the target stimulus and the stimuli themselves are depicted in Figure 2-11.

FIGURE 2-11 *Objects and Apparatus for Experiments on Haptic Exploration of Objects.*
The two stimuli at top vary in the type of connector: The solid stimulus results in dependent motion and the elastic stimulus permits independent motion.

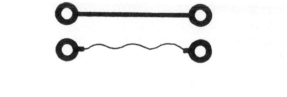

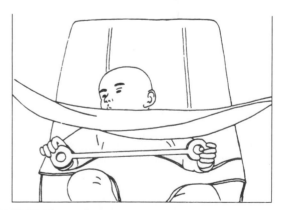

From "Where Perceiving Ends and Thinking Begins: The Apprehension of Objects in Infancy" by E. S. Spelke, in *Perceptual Development in Infancy: Minnesota Symposium on Child Psychology* (Vol. 20, pp. 197–234), A. Yonas (Ed.), 1988, Hillsdale, NJ: Erlbaum.

As it turned out, babies did explore the stimuli haptically even though the subjects were below the age when the coordination of prehension and vision is established. And when both habituation and test trials were in the haptic mode, holding times on test trials were longer (i.e., indicating dishabituation and thus object discrimination) for the novel object. The results were stronger when the infant had been habituated to the rigid-motion stimulus and tested with the independent-motion stimulus. Similar results were obtained when test trials were in the visual mode with looking time as the dependent measure.

The interpretation of the results of this experiment are as follows: Infants do perceive objects presented haptically and they perceive them according to the same principle of "objectness"—common motion—regardless of the modality of perception. Furthermore, the authors extend their interpretation to posit a common, central, cognitive mechanism responsible for organizing the surfaces seen and felt into objects (Spelke, 1988a). In short, what is proposed is not innate object perception but an innate object *concept*. Object perception in Steri and Spelke's (1988; Spelke, 1988a) view (see Kellman, 1988, for a counterargument) is cognitively driven—a product of thought rather than of direct apprehension. To propose that the process is innate as well as cognitive is to argue a strong nativist position.

The results of Spelke's (1987, 1988a, 1990, 1991) research program provide very convincing evidence of a fundamental human propensity to organize perceptual information into units corresponding to material bodies. Infants do so very early developmentally in accord with what their primitive sensory systems are capable of detecting (i.e., motion). It is not clear how the stimulation—the input itself, no matter how rich—could create such a uniform structuring so early in life. It has to be something the organizer brings to and imposes on the input data. The ramifications of this theoretical contention are profound and far reaching. We take this issue up again in Chapters 3 and 6.

Plasticity in Visual Perception

Behavioral research on visual perception in infancy points in a similar direction: to the amazing capacity of babies to respond to the characteristics of their visual world. With methodological and technological advancement, we have pushed back the time when visual competence can be documented. Perhaps, it is only technique that prevents us from finding more evidence of capacity in neonates. Twenty years ago, our current conclusions about the initial perceptual abilities of infants would have seemed counterintuitive; not any more.

Sometimes the role of experience in the development of visual perception is overshadowed by this emphasis on the organism's contribution. This results partly from the theoretical Zeitgeist, but it is partly a methodological artifact. When we study perception in human infants, we cannot use a true experimental paradigm in which experience is manipulated as an independent variable. For normal infants, there is little variability in visual experience. All are exposed to light and color, to a three-dimensional spatial environment, to objects, and to the movement of objects. In many respects, then, experience is a constant. This denies us the traditional means of identifying and examining the role of experience in shaping the normal visual system.

No such constraints face the scientist looking at neural development in young animals; visual experience can be manipulated in both extreme and subtle ways. Correspondingly, much animal research on visual development informs us about **plasticity**, neuronal responsivity to experience. Comparative psychologists and neuroscientists experimentally manipulate the rearing conditions and the visual experiences of young animals and examine the behavioral and neurological effects on those manipulations.

The hypothesis that experience will affect visual perception in young animals originates in *experience-expectant* mechanisms of neuronal development introduced in Chapter 1. The organism is "primed" for particular experiences ubiquitous under normal rearing conditions. Organisms then benefit, constructing a competence, when the experience comes. Priming entails *synaptogenesis,* the overproduction of neurons. Experience precipitates selective synapse elimination following synaptogenesis. Thus, activity serves to "prune" the wiring diagram and to "set" it by organizing the neural patterns (Greenough, Black, & Wallace, 1987).

Although the following illustration is an oversimplification, suppose the neural foundation for visual competence were a single, optimum circuit formed from a subset of neural connections. The organism by itself is unprepared to identify the optimum pattern from all potential patterns. There are possible alternative circuits, but these, built from other subsets of connections, would not yield the same level of visual competency or would not do so with equal efficiency. Without the activation supplied by input, the set of possible synapses generated in synaptogenesis might be prematurely shrunken by synapse death. There is also the possibility of "messy wiring," where a circuit is incompletely pruned and excess connections drain resources from ideal pathways. Experience becomes the "selector" of the circuit; however, selection can be hampered. For example, the outcome would be less than ideal if there is a dearth of existent neural connections from which to assemble the final set. Perhaps such an outcome would result if synaptogenesis were curtailed, inhibited, or incomplete, or if appropriate input failed to keep a sufficient set of synapses active. Also,

correct selection would not ensue if experience were so abnormal as to leave unpruned connections to create message "noise" or incorrect connections to interfere. Either way, the optimum pattern would not be achieved.

Neural associations take place through the formation of synapses, most of which are connections on the **dendrites** of neurons. **Spines,** structures on the dendrites of some cells, are a primary site where synapses relay messages from the **axon** of connecting cells. A schematization is depicted in Figure 2-12. Potential synaptic density will be limited by the adequacy of these structures. Density is as important to brain functioning as is the pattern of connectivity. Both density and pattern are influenced by visual experience during early development.

Experience-expectant neural plasticity is an efficient mechanism of behavioral adaptation, but it renders the organism susceptible to the effects of **deprivation.** Thus, the hypothesis: If a given experience does not occur when the organism is primed or sensitive, then the organism will be damaged. The normal pattern of experience will result in a normal pattern of neural organization, but abnormal experience will produce abnormal patterns. The relationship between experience and neuronal connectivity points to the appropriate paradigm in which to test the hypothesis: the deprivation study. In it, young animals are subjected to abnormal rearing conditions and the experimenter interferes with an experience otherwise common to the young of a species.

When the organizing function of experience on the visual system is studied, experimental animals are exposed to visually deprived environments. **Nonselective visual deprivation** is dark-rearing, and the behavioral deficits from the impairment of visual information processing wrought by such conditions are apparent in rats, cats, and monkeys (Riesen, 1975; Tees, 1979; Tees & Cartwright, 1972; Tees, Midgely, & Nesbit, 1982; Turner &

FIGURE 2-12 (A) A human brain, with much of the right hemisphere removed and many subcortical structures omitted to reveal a simplified view of the visual system. Visual information travels from the retina to the visual cortex via the lateral geniculate nucleus (LGN). As fibers from the retina pass back toward the LGN, some of them cross to the other side, reflecting the general principle that a sensory input originating on one side of the body is processed by brain structures in the hemisphere on the opposite side. Fibers from each retina that receive light from the right half of the visual field project to the visual cortex on the left hemisphere. Hence, the visual cortex in the left hemisphere "sees" only the right half of the world, through both eyes. (B) A section of visual cortex showing a neuron, as would be seen through a light microscope. The visual cortex, which is approximately 2 mm thick in a 2-year-old infant is actually much more densely packed with neurons and their interconnecting fibers than is depicted by this figure. At this level of magnification, spines appear as tiny dots along the dendrites. (C) Detail of a portion of a dendrite containing a synapse between an axon terminal (distinguished by the presence of spheres called *vesicles*) and a dendritic spine, a small projection from the dendrite trunk.

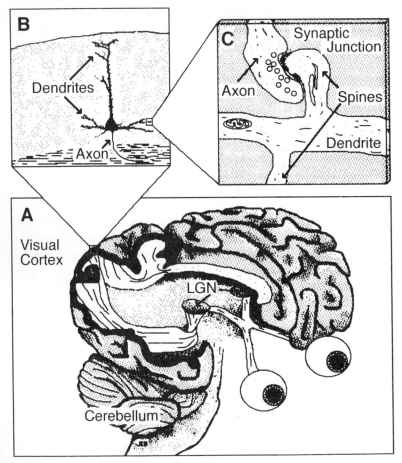

From "Experience and Brain Development" by W. T. Greenough, J. E. Black, and C. S. Wallace, 1987, *Child Development, 58,* pp. 539–559.

Greenough, 1985; Walk & Walters, 1973). Moreover, the deprivation effects become less reversible by later visual experience the longer the deprivation lasts (Crabtree & Riesen, 1979; Timney, Mitchel, & Cynader, 1980).

Patterns of neuronal connectivity are dependent on the structure of the neurons, especially the dendritic spines where synapses form. The more of these structures there are, the greater the possible number of connections. Neuronal circuitry depends on the complexity and number of connection between neurons that can be formed. Animals subjected to total pattern deprivation associated with dark-rearing show a reduction in the overall amount of dendrites (Coleman & Riesen, 1968) and they have neurons in the visual cortex with fewer spines on those dendrites (Fifkova, 1968; 1970; Rothblat & Schwartz, 1979). Thus, the nerve cells of visually deprived animals make fewer interconnections and the complexity of the visual cortex "wiring diagram" is subsequently reduced.

Black and Greenough (1986) concluded that visual experience is necessary for normal visual-motor development in mammalian species through the mechanism of experience expectancy. The kind and amount of experience need not be specific or extensive. In fact, relatively small amounts of normal visual experience may be sufficient to set developmental processes in motion and protect the animal against subsequent deprivation (Mower, Christen, & Caplan, 1983). However, the experience, even though general, must come at a particular time to stabilize the wiring diagram.

Dark-rearing is an extreme form of environmental manipulation yielding powerful results, but it is a crude technique. **Selective deprivation** is the more limited manipulation of experience, for example, denying the young animal binocular vision by suturing one eye shut or fitting the animal with special glasses. As an alternative, the animal could be reared in a limited abnormal environment in which

only some visual patterns are omitted, which allows visual information processing but of a nonnatural kind.

Limited interference studies address the deprivation hypothesis in specific ways. Additionally, a technological advance increases refinement of the dependent variable; microelectrode recording techniques enable measurement of the activity of single cells in the brain. Conceivably one can assess the neuronal activity occurring in conjunction with exposure to visual input and identify brain events underlying cognitive operation. To date, selective deprivation studies also provide a strong case for experientially driven induction of neural structure. Results suggest an orderly and direct connection between the patterning of visual input and the patterning of neural connectivity that in some cases corresponds to long-term alterations in visual-motor behavior (Black & Greenough, 1986).

For example, orientation is a measurable sensitivity in the visual cortex of cats. Neuroscientists identify differential subsets of neurons that fire when animals are exposed to lines of differing orientation. One type of selective deprivation manipulation entails rearing young animals in environments where visual experience is limited to lines of a single orientation (only vertical or only horizontal stripes). When reared in the absence of patterned visual stimulation, a sensitivity to stimulus orientation is lost, but kittens exposed only to horizontal or vertical stripes during development respond selectively to horizonal or vertical stimuli (Hirsch & Spinelli, 1970). Visual cortex neurons fire strongly only for lines in the orientation of the rearing environment.

Interestingly enough, subjects reared under these selective visual experience conditions show morphological differences as well as different sensitivities. Coleman, Flood, Whitehead, and Emerson (1981) observed that visual cortex neurons in cats reared with visual experience restricted to either horizontal or vertical lines had dendrites that were oriented differently, at approximately 90 degrees of divergence. Other evidence corroborates this observation (Tieman & Hirsch, 1982).

In another study, kittens were reared in a strobe-lit environment. When the strobe was fired, the subjects saw fully patterned flashes of their environment, but strobes were brief. Thus, the kittens were deprived of exposure to visual motion. They saw sequential "snapshots" of the world without the smooth transitions between snapshots. As a consequence, the kittens had impaired cortical sensitivity to motion (Cynader & Chernenko, 1976). Impaired motion sensitivity is associated with selective impairment of visual-motor behaviors that utilize motion (Held, Hein, & Gower, 1970).

The case for plasticity and the role of experience in the selection of the final wiring diagram is further buttressed with findings from studies in which selective deprivation consists of interruptions in binocular vision in mammals with binocularly overlapping visual systems (e.g., cats, monkeys). Temporary closure of one eye during sensitive periods of development is sufficiently disruptive to cause lasting visual impairment (Wiesel & Hubel, 1963). At the neurophysiological level, it seems the deprived eye loses its ability, at least temporarily, to control the activity of visual cortex neurons whereas the nondeprived eye gains control (LeVay, Wiesel, & Hubel, 1980). It is as if the eyes compete with each other for neuronal "space"; the advantaged eye, with visual experience input present to elicit active firing of synapses, ends up controlling more space. The resultant wiring diagram of one-eye subjects indeed differs from those of normal, two-eye subjects (see Greenough, Black, & Wallace, 1987, for a fuller discussion).

For the development of visual perception, empirical evidence of neural plasticity is strong. Experiential induction processes ap-

parently do occur and they can provide for greater precision in visual skills than genetic coding alone would allow. It is well to remember, however, that the final shaping process is still biologically constrained. It is not the case that *any* final wiring diagram is biologically possible; such an outcome might be conceivable if, prior to experience-driven synapse elimination, every neuron in the visual cortex were connected with every other. Such is not the case. Intrinsic, genotype-driven processes generate a pattern to form the foundation for final selection that is not completely crossed. The foundation is somewhat crude as compared to the final form the structure will take, but the initial sensitivities and visual proclivities are set. Experience fine tunes the original pattern, which in turn constrains the class of possible outcomes.

Summary

Visual perception permits the extraction of structure from light. Structure includes the relationships among surfaces, objects, forms, and patterns that define a terrain; sensitivity to structure enables adaptation to the environment. At the very least, detecting the structure of the terrain is prerequisite to successful movement through it and avoidance of hazardous features. Obviously, organisms whose biological equipment serves them well in this endeavor have a higher probability of survival than those not so endowed. "Well equipped," however, is interpretable as sufficiently "initially equipped" to insure the immature organism a good chance of avoiding calamity until mature status is achieved. Perception research with infants points to the rich visual capacities of newborns in detecting pattern, form, motion, and the rudimentary structural features of their environment, particularly objects.

Research shows us that babies respond to the perception of motion very early in development. Within the first few months, they use common motion as the essential attribute of objectness. They extract the form of objects, biological and geometric, from motion. They track moving objects, show preferences for movement, and pick up depth from optical flow. Abstraction of structure from motion is an early and fast developing, if not initial, capability of human infants; evidence of all these phenomena is found between 3- and 6-months of age.

However, infants' very early perceptual proclivities are not identical with those observed later in life. The baby, while well equipped, is in fact not fully equipped. With development, there is change in perceptual capacity. The neonate, who at first can see simple, bold patterns, comes to prefer and differentiate more complex ones as she moves through her first year; by 6 months of age, she can distinguish figure from ground, the symmetrical from the asymmetrical. While initially only movement defines depth, later static cues also augment depth information. Tracking ability, which is restricted to fast-moving objects in the neonate, generalizes to the tracking of objects moving at slow velocities. And, while especially sensitive to facial stimuli even in the first weeks of life, the baby's ability to detect faces is expanded to the differentiation of facial expressions. Thus, behavioral data point to developmental change. While there are continuities—perceptual competencies shared by neonate, toddler, child, and adult—initial competence becomes elaborated competence.

The change from initial kernels of competence to elaborated perceptual skill suggested by behavioral studies is supported by physiological and neurological evidence. Immaturity of the fovea, for example, is consistent with poor focus, poor contrast resolution, poor visual acuity for patterns, and limitations in the smooth tracking of slow-moving targets, all of which characterize vision in neonates. Marked changes in sensitivity at around 2 months of age are predictable from what we know about the maturing of visual structures and the increasing involvement of the visual cortex in seeing.

Synaptogenesis and selective synapse elimination provide a mechanism to explain a refinement in visual perception fueled by experience. In fact, the ontogenesis of visual perception well exemplifies how a multitude of developmental functions come into play sequentially in the formation of a complex human ability:

1. *Maturation* processes, basically endogenous in nature, serve to lay down the orderly connections as from the retina to the cortex.
2. *Maintenance* and *facilitation* processes respond to stimulation, preserve initial synaptic connections, and prepare the system for what is to come.
3. *Induction* processes use expected patterned stimulation to construct functional visual systems (Black & Greenough, 1987). A complex cognitive function has a complex developmental history.

PERCEPTION OF SOUND AND SPEECH

Visual perception is fundamental to the pickup of information from the environment. The capability is virtually indispensable to cognition. Through the visual channel, we come to know the physics of objects, the geometry of space, and the structure of the environment, topics we pick up again in Chapters 3 and 6. So, visual stimulation contains important information for successful adaptation, and the eyes are a major channel of information input. Additionally, however, people are sensitive to auditory stimulation embodied in sound and picked up with the ears. An enormous amount of information is conveyed in speech, for example, and a major accomplishment in infancy and early childhood is the acquisition of language, the ability to comprehend and produce speech (the subject of Chapter 9). The psychologist wishing to explain this representational landmark must evaluate the role of auditory input in the developmental process. Just how does auditory perception function for the infant in the extraction of information in sound?

Visual information has both spatial and temporal characteristics. Geometry constitutes a formal metric with which spatial displays and the transformations between displays over time are described. The metric is specifiable and provides a system of organization, of structure, for visual information. Developmental research in visual perception helps determine which particular aspects of that structure are functional for infants. Auditory information also has organizational characteristics or structure. As there is a physics of objects and optics, there is a physics of sound with metrics for quantifying the intensity, frequency, duration, and structure of sound stimuli. The metrics are sophisticated as are the technical means for obtaining precise measures of sound features. Having an advanced technology for describing auditory stimulation has important empirical implications; it makes it possible to define auditory input in precise ways, to alter features of the input in precise ways, and to observe the susubquent effect on behavior. Speech is the particular form of auditory input most relevant to the concerns of cognitive developmentalists. And a complex metric exists for characterizing, accurately measuring, and even reproducing the acoustics of speech.

Imagine what an infant lying in a crib might experience perceptually as caretakers move about the nursery, creating movement sounds, talking, and coming in and out of view. There are streams of speech sounds which, because they are projected from different speakers and locations, have different acoustical properties. There are pauses, changes in tone, and changes in intensity. There is great variability, just as there is in optical flow when an awake baby is carried through object-filled space.

Adult receivers readily determine the points of origin of the speech and differentiate individual speakers; competent listeners detect the spatial organization of auditory input. Can the infant? For the adult, the speech stream, temporally organized, is segmented into meaningful units, the most basic of which are **phonemes,** the elementary sounds of a language, and the units are interpreted for semantic content. How does the infant segment the sound stream, or does she? The adult discriminates acoustically subtle but semantically important differences in phonemes, like the *b* in *bat* and the *p* in *pat,* produced by the same speaker in the same tone with the same degree of loudness. The sounds may be acoustically similar but psychologically dissimilar. Would a baby make the same discrimination? The adult treats as equivalent the *p* in *pat* spoken loudly by a male speaker or whispered softly by a female speaker, despite acoustical dissimilarity. How about the baby? Does the baby experience an amorphous buzz or structured input? If the former, how is sensitivity to structure acquired? If the latter, is the structure similar to that perceived by the adult?

The auditory system is functional before birth (Hecox, 1975), although the uterine environment provides significant masking of most sounds (Walker, Grimwade, & Wood, 1971). Some sounds may be transmitted, however (Armitage, Baldwin, & Vince, 1980; Querleu & Renard, 1981). Newborns do discriminate and prefer their own mother's voice to that of a strange female (DeCasper & Fifer, 1980), and when exposure is experimentally manipulated during the last trimester of pregnancy, auditory preferences are affected (DeCasper & Spence, 1986). Newborns also show preferences for the *prosodic* characteristics—the intonation pattern and melodic features—of their native language over that of a nonnative language (Mehler, Jusczyk, Lambertz, Amiel-Tison, & Bertoncini, 1988). There is evidence that it is pitch contours, the characteristic "tune" of speech, that critically influence infants' responses to the mother's voice (Fernald, 1985; Mehler, Bertoncini, Barciere, & Jassik-Gerschenfeld, 1978).

Newborns also localize sound to some extent by orienting their heads toward lateral sounds (Muir & Field, 1979), including speech sounds (Brody, Zelazo, & Chaika, 1984). Sound produced off midline arrives at different times at the infant's two ears; it is perceived by the near ear first. The resultant time delay and relative difference in intensity of the sound between the two ears provides information for the calibration of location. Accuracy and precision of detecting shifts in the location of sound do change from infancy to adulthood (Ashmead, Clifton & Perris, 1987), and the infant is faced with the challenge of recalibration induced by growth (Clifton, Gwiazda, Bauer, Clarkson, & Held, 1988).

Head size increases during infancy when physical growth is rapid. As head size changes, so does interaural distance and so must the absolute difference in time cues for a sound in a given location. While the infant's map of auditory space undergoes refinement during infancy, clearly within the very first few months of life infants show sensitivity to binaural time differences. Precision in localization improves substantially during infancy, reaching near adult levels by 18 months of age (Morrongiello, 1988).

Auditory sensitivities are not exactly the same for infants and adults; sensitivities improve between birth and about 10 years of age

(Elliot & Katz, 1980; Yoneshinge & Elliot, 1981). But even the newborn perceives some, perhaps considerable, acoustic information. There is evidence that structure, although not necessarily the identical structure of the adult, is indeed perceived.

Auditory Perception of Speech Sounds

In the perceptual input achieved with optical flow there is motion, flux, and variability. Visual information processing entails apprehending the constancies, the invariants that do not change with the flux. Perception of structure, then, is at least partly dependent on distinguishing constants and variables. The same is true of perceiving structure in the speech stream; the infant must come to differentiate acoustic variability, sounds that are different, while aggregating into a single class sounds that are somehow the same. When speech is the input, the task involves discrimination at the phoneme level. The task is complicated, however, in some unobvious ways.

When a baby perceives a visual object such as a cup, the percept will remain constant across the contexts in which it appears; the cup does not look appreciably different whether it sits on the table next to a cereal box or next to a coffee pot. Not so for the phoneme. It may sound different depending on the other phonemes with which it is conjoined. Yet it is, from the perspective of perceiving speech, a constant. Another problem is the relationship between the **proximal stimulus,** the stimulus experienced by the ear, and the **distal stimulus.** For the mature receiver, the distal stimulus in speech is the meaning conveyed by phonemes, syllables, and words, but the infant is unlikely to be prepared to use meaning as the object of perception. Therefore, the distal and the proximal stimuli probably differ for the mature and immature perceiver. The auditory events must somehow emerge as units of perception before meanings are attached to those events (Aslin & Smith, 1988). This observation renders even more intriguing any finding of similarity in the phoemic perception of infants and adults. There is no parallel to this phenomenon in visual perception.

Much has been learned about the acoustics of speech. For each speech feature identified, there exists a detailed set of acoustic events sufficient to govern perception. At the level of the stimulus, description is precise with a metric for quantifying similarity and difference. However, for adults as well as infants, speech perception cannot be accounted for by acoustics. It is an accomplishment involving mechanisms beyond those of the auditory psychophysics (Liberman, Harris, Hoffman, & Griffith, 1957); the external stimulus features are simply insufficient to explain the perception of phonetic structure (Kuhl, 1987). The theoretical argument becomes whether adequate explanation of this accomplishment depends on proposing innate mechanisms specially evolved for the perception of speech, an innate phonetics or speech "module" (Fodor, 1983). Otherwise, the infant's initial responsiveness to speech must be attributed to general sensory and cognitive abilities. Then the infant can gradually develop a phonetic representation of speech as she learns the mapping between acoustic cues and word meaning.

The **sensory primitives**—that is, the elementary perceptual units such as intensity and frequency, which enable phoneme discrimination—are mature very early in life (Aslin & Smith, 1988). By 6 months of age, infants can discriminate virtually any acoustic difference that signals a phonologically relevant speech contrast used in natural languages (Aslin, Pisoni, Jusczyk, 1983; Jusczyk, 1981; Kuhl, 1987). Infants are able to discriminate speech contrasts used in their to be spoken native language and nonnative language speech contrasts as well (Eilers, Gavin, & Wilson, 1979; Trehub, 1976; Werker, Gilbert, Humphrey, & Tees, 1981). The initial presence of this ability suggests there are innately determined, universal acoustical categories.

So, the infant auditory system may be primed to detect the set of contrasts included in all languages. With lack of exposure to the nonnative sounds an alteration ensues, and discrimination becomes confined to a set of potentially meaningful contrasts within a cultural context (Werker & Tees, 1984). This priming-pruning phenomenon may reflect another example of experience—expectant neural plasticity (Greenough, Black, & Wallace, 1987). The comprehension and production of word meaning occurs just about at the end of this potentially sensitive period (Benedict, 1979; Oviatt, 1980; Thomas, Campos, Shucard, Ramsay, & Shucard, 1981).

Phoneme discrimination is nonlinear in both infants and adults. Basically, equal physical differences in acoustic dimensions do not correspond to equal psychological differences, a phenomenon referred to as **categorical perception.** Acoustically, the difference between two phonemes, for example *ba* and *pa,* can be represented on a continuous dimension (interval scale) rather than as two distinct categories of sound (nominal scale). With a clear *ba* marking one end of the continuum and a clear *pa* at the other, the acoustic changes in between are divisible into equal intervals. At some determinable point along the scale, adults detect auditory change and label a stimulus from one side of the point *ba* and from the other *pa.* They are less likely to differentiate two stimuli from the same side of that point even though the actual degree of acoustic change is identical. Thus, categorical perception is demonstrated when the listener's discrimination performance is near chance for phonetically equivalent stimuli (same label), but very good for phonetically different stimuli (different label).

Early data from adult subjects was of this nature (Liberman, Harris, Eimas, Lisker, & Bastian, 1961; Liberman, Harris, Hoffman, & Griffith, 1957; Liberman, Harris, Kinney, & Lane, 1961). Subsequent data revealed that while disciminability does indeed peak at the categorical boundary, significant increases in discriminability occur as one approaches the region of that boundary (Kuhl, 1987). The term **phoneme-boundary effect** more accurately reflects the empirical phenomenon (Wood, 1976).

The developmental question is, Does phoneme discriminability in infants take the same form as that found in adults? Eimas and associates (Eimas, 1974, 1975b; Eimas & Miller, 1980; Eimas, Siqueland, Jusczyk, & Vigorito, 1971) conducted a series of studies with infants under 4 months of age to address that question. Using a variation of the habituation procedure with sucking response as the dependent measure, the investigators presented infants with pairs of stimuli from a computer-generated continuum simulating the gradual change from one phoneme to another. Infants were presented with one member of the pair until habituation was observed; on test trials, the other member was presented. The second member, however, could be an acoustically different stimulus from the same phoneme category or one from the different phoneme category. If infants perceive change categorically as adults do, then the infants should dishabituate only to the second kind of change. Indeed, that is what was observed. Data typical of this effect are presented in Figure 2-13.

In summary, speech discrimination abilities are clearly present in babies, and those abilities are not unlike those displayed by adults. Neonates only hours old discriminate words (Brody, Zelazo, & Chaika, 1984), 1-month-olds distinguish phonemes (Eimas, 1975b); by 2 months of age, babies can discriminate contrasts embedded in bisyllabic strings, for example *bada* versus *gada* (Jusczyk & Thompson, 1978) and by 6 months, contrasts in multisyllabic strings (Goodsitt, Morse, Ver Hoeve, & Cowan, 1984). Infants also show sensitivity to holistic features of structure such as melody in sound. They discriminate changes in the order of sequentially presented tones (Demany, 1982) and in the rhythm of tone sequences (Chang & Trehub, 1977). Moreover, they recognize transpositions, treating as familiar tone sequences that preserve melodic contour across changes in key (Trehub, Bull, & Thorpe, 1984).

Melody and tone sequences bear resemblance to the prosodic features of speech, its characteristic tune. Before the onset of language, perhaps even before 6 months of age, infants have acquired sufficient information about the phonetic units and prosody of their native language to produce it in a manner characteristic of their culture (de Boysson-Bardies, Sagart, & Durand, 1984).

Intermodal Perception of Speech

The mapping between acoustic information and the perceptual units of speech, the phonemes, is enormously complex (Kuhl & Meltzoff, 1988). So, too, is the segmenting of the sound stream into an ordered sequence of those units. That infants demonstrate proficiency tackling these tasks, at detecting temporal and spatial structure in auditory input, is an impressive accomplishment. Yet recent evidence suggests that the accomplishment may be even more remarkable.

The perception of speech is not solely the domain of audition; vision is involved as well. Infant listeners look in the direction of sound, including speech sounds, and localize that sound in space; but speech has an additional visual component. The mouth movements accompanying the production of speech are perceived visually, and, as the success of lip read-

FIGURE 2-13 *Sucking-Recovery Data for Infants Tested for Categorical Perception Using a* ba—pa *Continuum.*
The first graph (20 D) depicts recovery for the between-category contrast while the others, (20 S and O) do not.

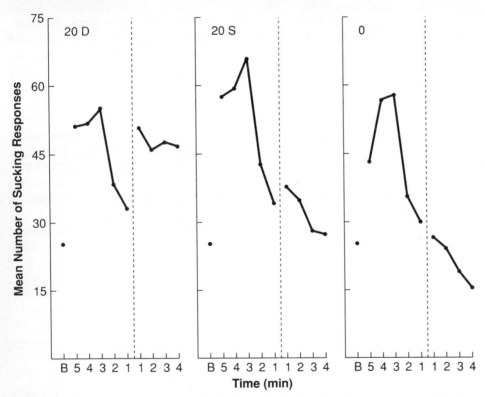

From "Speech Perception in Infants" by P. D. Eimas, E. R. Siqueland, P. Jusczyk, and J. Vigorito, 1971, *Science, 171,* pp. 303—306. Adapted by permission.

ing attests, convey information about the phonetic structure of speech. Although we can hear and perceive speech quite adequately with our eyes closed, visual information assists perception when the sound signals are ambiguous. Under impoverished listening conditions, for example, speech is perceived anyway if the face of the speaker is in full view (Grant, Ardell, Kuhl, & Sparks, 1985). Illusions are elicited when the auditory and visual informa-

tion, which are normally redundant, conflict. For example, when auditory information specifying *baba* is combined with the visual information of *gaga,* the illusion of *dada* is perceived (McGurk & MacDonald, 1976). Perhaps speech is an *intermodal* object of perception.

Young babies can detect and differentiate the kind of mouth movements associated with speech, and they can even imitate mouth movements from visual input (Meltzoff, 1985). Kuhl and Meltzoff (1982, 1984) undertook a series of experiments to find out whether infants could match sounds to those mouth movements. Subjects were familiarized with two identical female faces articulating two different vowel sounds; only one of the vowel sounds was audible, projected from midway between the faces.

The investigators reasoned that if the babies were sensitive to the visual speech information, then they would fixate on the mouth that matched the sound. And, indeed they did. Four-month-old infants looked significantly longer at the face that was consistent with the auditory input (see also Kuhl & Meltzoff, 1988). Remarkably, even in babies, speech is not solely an object of auditory perception. Perhaps speech, as an intermodal object of perception, is processed cognitively and centrally, much as Spelke (1988) argued for object perception. It is clear that infants are tuned into speech very early in life and that auditory, visual, motor, and perhaps even tactile systems participate in the perception of it.

CONCLUSION

The picture emerging of infants is one of perceptually capable individuals. Their sensory systems are fully functional at birth, and although changes are still to come, all systems work. But eyes, ears, and heads will grow; structures will change. So, too, will visual and auditory sensitivities. The nervous system is prepared and ready; and through the combination of endogenous maturational mechanisms and exogenous facilitative, maintenance, and inductive mechanisms, development proceeds. Much of the early development in the sensory systems likely follows a course of experience-expectant growth wherein synaptogenesis coupled with selective synapse elimination sculpts an efficient neural substrate. The developmental process is sufficiently biologically

constrained and experientially activated by ubiquitous encounters that species-typical perceptual competencies emerge very early in life.

The last 20 years of empirical inquiry have shown us that infants, even newborns, are extremely sensitive to their surroundings, selectively responding visually and auditorily only hours after birth. They coordinate motor, visual, and auditory systems, looking in the direction of sounds, tracking the path of moving objects, and anticipating how things will look, sound, move, and work. Although there is still much room for improvement—spatial maps for accurate sound localization are yet to be refined; smooth pursuit of moving targets has yet to be achieved—rudimentary abilities are in place. Most likely, early sensitivities are tuned to sources of stimulation with ecological validity that will be important for subsequent information processing and vital for successful adaptation. Thus speech sounds and moving visual stimuli function to elicit early fixation, recognition, and differentiation. And interestingly enough, babies not only respond to elementary units of stimulation but to the structure of the visual and acoustic environment.

With the early detection of structure, the world of the neonate is neither an amorphous buzz nor a blurry fuzz. If early competence is a reliable fact, and surely the bulk of the evidence is favorable, then we must account for it theoretically. We must equip the organism initially with something, some capability through which progress in perceptual and cognitive capacity can be made. For Piaget, the initial something consisted of basic reflexes and a motivation to adapt; for classic empiricists, a blank slate sensitive to and ready for impressions was sufficient. But the simple question remains, How do we get there from here?

A slate requires a means for making markings, and random actions need a mechanism for achieving organization. It is probably neither logically feasible nor empirically defensible to propose that order and structure can be abstracted from chaos without also proposing some sort of initial order detectors, however crude, for getting the process started. The initial package may be strictly perceptual; it may be cognitive. It may be modular; it may be central. One thing is very clear, though: William James underestimated babies.

The empirical literature in perception shows us that organisms are responsive to key stimuli early in development. This reliable observation suggests an innate *attuneness* to certain kinds of stimulation. Two of these, for human infants at least, are *phonemes* and *objects,* both of which constitute kinds of *individuals.* It is not inherent in either the sound stream or in visual input that information has to be analyzed or segmented at the level of individual units like these. After all, stimulation is continuous, not discrete. Perhaps human beings have a propensity to individuate stimuli, to organize the perceptual landscape into things—sound things, visual things, tactile things, and so forth. In upcoming chapters, we will explore how the cognitive system may possibly exploit this initial perceptual mode of construal in the creation of structures of knowledge to represent that perceived world.

ENDNOTES

1. There is some ambiguity in interpretation here, despite a positive statistical effect. It may be that the hypothesis was not disconfirmable. If infants had looked at the coherent display longer, then one could claim a preference for the ecologically valid, most realistic displays. Null results would have not been interpretable. But what would disconfirmatory data have to look like?

2. Actually, as you will come to see in Chapter 3, the importance of motor activity to cognitive development is a *constructivist's* contention. Piaget's position is that the organism must physically act on and in the environment to enable mental representation; Piaget also envisioned the philosophical basis for his theory as a synthesis of rationalism and empiricism.

3. The search for continuity is part of the nativist agenda.

THE DEVELOPMENT OF SPATIAL COGNITION

INTRODUCTION
FOUNDATIONS OF SPATIAL COGNITION
METHODS FOR STUDYING SPATIAL COGNITION
THE ORIGINS OF SEARCH
THE REPRESENTATION OF GEOMETRIC TRANSFORMATIONS
CONCLUSION

INTRODUCTION

An 11-month-old infant is crawling about the dining room floor under the table and chairs in pursuit of an elusive cat. The route laid down by the cat, who stays just out of reach, meanders about legs, through tight spaces, between obstacles, and up over laps. The baby is a persistent follower, continuing along the route traversed by the teasing cat, reaching out occasionally when the cat comes within range. But, the cat is nimbler and quicker than the child; so the animal is always ahead, sometimes disappearing behind a barrier to re-emerge in a new location. The more able cat can jump to high places, and the infant cannot follow. The cat is also smaller and thinner so is capable of squeezing through tight spaces. The plumper infant cannot exactly duplicate the cat's route. Chances are that the cat will escape, eluding the pursuer until one of them tires of the game. But in the process, the infant will reveal some formidable abilities.

For instance, the baby is more likely to reach for the cat when the cat is close, potentially within grasp, than when the cat is far away. Choosing when to reach and when not to suggests something about the computation of space. Second, the baby will not attempt to squeeze into the small spaces that permitted passage of the skinny cat but not the pudgy pursuer. How could the baby differentiate passable from impassable spaces without making some spatial computations? Third, perhaps the baby, when unable to follow the path precisely, will detour and intercept the cat by an alternate route. Or, similarly, when the cat disappears from view behind a barrier or up over the table top, the baby may head for where the cat's reappearance is anticipated. In sum, the baby's pursuit capabilities suggest a rudimentary mental representation of space in which cognitive symbols for landmarks, spaces, routes, and places function to guide behavior in space.

In Chapter 2 we saw that the year-old infant, like the pursuer in the anecdote, is a perceptually adept individual. Infants perceive the spatial layout, visually process information about spatial features, and adapt to the visual-spatial environment. But spatial representation is something more than the ability to apprehend features of the visual terrain. The perception of space and of objects in space presupposes sensory contact with that space; representation does not. In the latter, the contents of space are cognitive contents, symbols in a mental model subject to manipulation and transformation and from which inferences are drawn. Spatial "thinking" transpires in the absence of sensory contact. The cognitive status of spatial perception versus spatial representation may only be one of degree, since even object perception may be cognitively driven (Spelke, 1988a). However, spatial representation, or **spatial cognition,** is unambiguously a cognitive act.

Spatial cognition has long attracted the interest of psychologists. For instance, those concerned with the assessment of individual differences have factor analyzed spatial performance as one route to uncovering the nature of aptitude (see Lohman, 1979; McGee, 1979). Beginning with Thurstone (1938), standardized psychometric measures have included items for tapping spatial ability, for eliciting performances indicative of the capacity to encode, retrieve, and transform spatial representations. That line of investigation has yielded the fundamental distinction made between spatial and verbal ability in virtually all models of human cognition (Lohman, 1988). Empirical evidence from psychometric studies points to individual differences in spatial abilities associated both with gender (Harris, 1978, 1979; Hyde, 1981; Linn & Peterson, 1985; Maccoby & Jacklin, 1974) and with age (Liben, Patterson, & Newcombe, 1981). As for the latter, the acquisition of knowledge enabling the transformation of mentally coded spatial information is seen as a major developmental accomplishment (Lohman, 1988; Piaget & Inhelder, 1956, 1971).

Studies in spatial cognition comprise some of the cornerstones of cognitive psychology as well. For example, Tolman's (1948) studies of place finding, which gave rise to the term **cognitive map,** constituted a major challenge to the strictly behavioral view of psychological phenomena dominant in experimental circles at the time. About 20 years later, equally influential experimental studies of mental imagery for spatial information attracted attention (Paivio, 1971). And now, for more than two decades, some of the most reliable findings in cognitive psychology are associated with the phenomenon of mental rotation (Shepard & Metzler, 1971; Shepard & Cooper, 1986), hypothetically a fundamental cognitive process. In fact, in recent contemporary literature, it is around the phenomena of spatial representation in general and mental rotation in particular that notions about mind-brain relationships from neurological and psychological studies are converging (Georgopoulos, Lurito, Petrides, Schwartz, & Massey, 1989).

It is no accident that spatial cognition should emerge as a focal point of scientific interest. The analysis of space has served as a rich source of hypotheses about the nature of knowledge, of cognition, and of the correspondence between the human mind and the physics of the universe. The evolution of knowledge about the domain of space is the focus of this chapter. We will examine the philosophical traditions that have served as the impetus for psychological study, and we will evaluate the many varieties of research that function to clarify the nature of the individual's grasp of spatial concepts. This research springs from a rich intellectual past, exhibits a vigorous scientific present, and, most importantly, has far-reaching implications for contemporary models of cognition.

FOUNDATIONS OF SPATIAL COGNITION

The intellectual heritage behind theories of spatial knowledge is shared with theories of perception, and as expected, the familiar contrast between empiricist and rationalist views again emerges. The essential questions are, Docs the mental representation of space, that is, spatial and geometric knowledge, arise from sensory experience with the physical environment? A yes response affirms the empiricist position. Or is spatial knowledge a product of mind imposed on experience rather than derived from it? Now, affirmation is consistent with the rationalist stance. If mental space results from individual encounters with experienced physical space, then the mental content must be learned. It must be built from sensory inputs, and it must correspond to sensed space. If not, then it need not be learned. However, mental space must still sufficiently correlate with physical space to allow species survival.

The task for the empiricist is to describe the transformations that permit the construction of mature spatial knowledge from sensation—a task of building a geometry without initial postulates. Is such an endeavor logically, mathematically, and psychologically feasible? The rationalist, on the other hand, must explain how nonexperienced spatial knowledge is mentally actualized—how initial postulates are instantiated. If the environment, through experience, is not the source of the individual's spatial knowledge, then what accounts for the correspondence between the mental and the empirical?

How do children come to know space? What are the geometric characteristics of the space they do know? These are the narrower epistemological questions behind the developmental study of spatial cognition. Piaget's answers to these questions derived from his constructionist approach (Piaget & Inhelder, 1956). Some of his contentions have served as points of controversy for empirical inquiry (Diamond, 1991; Landau, 1988; Spelke, 1988a). Other investigators (Spelke, 1991) propose an alternative story. Theoretical differences emerge, not just from the data, but from our understanding of the nature of space, an essential content of mind.

Dimensions of Space

There are a number of ways in which properties of space can vary. O'Keefe and Nadel (1978) distinguished several potential points of divergence: (1) psychological versus physical space, (2) absolute versus relative space, and (3) Euclidean versus non-Euclidean space. To the developmentalist, there is an important fourth, the origins of spatial knowledge: (4) a priori or unlearned versus a posteriori, built on the basis of experientially driven processes.

Psychological space refers to the intuitive theory of space attributed to the mind of the individual. It is cognitive and representational and would not exist if minds did not exist. It is the equivalent of spatial cognition and is the focal interest of psychologists and neuroscientists. *Physical space,* in contrast, is the space of the external world; it is definable and describable with the principles of physics, and it is independent of mind. Psychological space need not demonstrate an isomorphism with physical space. However, if physical space serves as a constraint on an intuitive theory of space, or if psychological space is constructed through experience to mirror physical space, then some correspondence between the two systems is expected and must be explained. Then, the physics of external space has implications for the properties of psychological space; the same sort of mathematics could represent both systems.

Absolute space refers to space as a container of objects describable whether objects are in it or not. The container might be local, as with a box, regional, as in a neighborhood, or more extensive, as in the universe. It is continuous, immovable, connected and invariant and forms a coherent whole. To exemplify, think of a local space, a box. It has definable spatial features: it has size, dimension, volume, and a spatial reference system given by its walls. The spatial location of an object placed in the imaginary box is describable in terms of the reference system. The object could be located *against* the floor, slightly *to the right* of the west side, and *6 inches from* the south side. The location of another object placed in the box could similarly be identified. In this way, the spatial container is an objective framework. We can think about the framework whether or not it has objects in it. We can locate the position of objects within it, and via the framework, we can envision the relationships among objects that share the same container. Were we to walk around the box, view it from different sides, or move closer or farther away, the location of objects within the box would not change with those movements. The space is *independent* of the observer. If the box were emptied of items, the space would still exist; it is *independent* of the objects in it.

In *relative space,* the container provides no framework. Spatial dimensions and relations are those between objects and are nonexistent when objects are removed. Without an absolute framework, we need a point of reference that might very well be the observer's body. Objects are located vis-à-vis ourselves, the observers. So, one object can be described as being to our right, a second to our left and further away. But, when the observer's body changes position, as with a turn or movement, the location of objects relative to his or her body also changes and requires updating. The position of objects is relative, *dependent* on the position of an observer. Objects are described relative to each other. When not defined by the objects within it, the psychological space is not there. Can you envision an empty mental space even though physics permits its description?

Is the space of mental representation a Euclidean one? This question is about the *metric* of space, the *scaling operations* used to describe the relations among objects and among objects and observers. *Euclidean space* has a fixed metric in the form of a *ratio scale.* Appropriate mechanical analogies are the yardstick and the compass; the scale on either is fixed, specified by equal units of measurement. A reading on the scale indicates a specific value of spatial extent in those units. The reading has meaning, and it can be compared

with other readings in terms of greater than, less than, how much greater than, and so forth. Regardless of the point of origin, the location of the measurer, or the number of objects interspersed along the path to be measured, the distance between two objects in a Euclidean metric is fixed. The cognitive issue is whether the metric of psychological space is also fixed and in ratio form.

Euclidean space is three dimensional, and from a limited set of postulates about the nature and metric of that three-dimensional space (for example, notions about distance, lines, parallelness), the remaining properties of physical space can be derived. Geometries are characterized by the class of transformations that can be performed without changing an essential feature. In Euclidean geometry, form, for example, remains invariant across any *rigid transformation;* rigid transformations include *rotation,* movement of an object about a fixed axis; *translation,* movement of an object along a plane; and *reflection,* a flip movement on a fixed axis. Imagine a triangle made of wire. That triangle would retain its form if it were rotated, slid, or flipped. It would not remain invariant across a *deforming* or *nonrigid* transformation if it were stretched, flattened, or bent. As evidence presented in Chapter 2 attests, even infants perceive the invariance of an object's form across rigid transformations. Do spatial representations share this property with the results of direct perception?

In the mid-nineteenth century, mathematicians demonstrated how *non-Euclidean* geometries describing physical space were mathematically coherent. These were geometries where invariances across nonrigid transformations were possible, where metric need not necessarily be ratio, and where space of more than three dimensions could be defined. The demonstrations led to reconceptualizations about the nature of physical space which, in turn, had ramifications for conceptualizations of psychological space. If physical space is non-Euclidean, then why should psychological space be so structured? But as O'Keefe and Nadel (1978) pointed out:

> Any evidence which suggests that physical space does not have a Euclidean metric or that physical space can be described equally well by a Euclidean or non-Euclidean metric, far from counting against a Euclidean metric for psychological space, leaves the latter as one of the only possible sources of Euclidean notions and suggests that the mind (or a part of it) has a strong affinity for the laws of Euclid. (p. 10)

Whether intuitive theories of space are **a priori** or **a posteriori** is a question about the origins of human knowledge about space. Nativists propose that the structure of psychological space is given, is prespecified genetically, and is not acquired from experience. For development at the level of the individual, the nature of physical space is irrelevant to the nature of psychological space. Humans are predisposed to impose a structure on perceived, particular spatial information, and it is the innate structure that specifies the geometry. Nativists find philosophical justification in Immanuel Kant. Kant, whose ideas were introduced in Chapter 2, contended that space was an a priori condition of mind, a pure intuition, a mode of perceiving rather than a thing perceived. Knowledge of absolute space did not, and in fact could not, be derived through sense encounters with physical space. Physical space would function at the species (and thus the evolutionary) level to constrain the class of potential, a priori geometries; but at the individual (and thus the developmental) level, the constraint need not operate. From an evolutionary perspective, the individual could possess innately a geometry that provides a sufficiently good fit with the properties of physical space to insure survival. For Kant, space was a priori, absolute, and Euclidean.

A posteriori positions on the origins of spatial knowledge reject ideas of innate geometries. The individual must acquire geometry and develop a psychological spatial structure through one means or another. It could be acquired on the basis of experience with physical space, and then the mental entity would share a close correspondence with the external world. Since the universe we experience is essentially Euclidean, more recent mathematical reformulations notwithstanding, so is the resultant cognitive spatial structure. However, this need not necessarily be the case. If we inhabited a non-Euclidean world, the mental outcome could be non-Euclidean, too. Psychological space from this perspective is an empirical phenomenon derived from direct encounters with physical space.

Experience, however, is variable. There is the experience of sensation, of perceiving stimulation from the physical universe. Sensation might fuel the experience of space and function to constrain the representational geometry constructed. Experience also encompasses physical action in the environment: movement through terrains and interaction with elements in physical space. Conceivably, physical experience could function differently from perceptual activity to constrain the construction of spatial representations; psychological spaces derived from action could differ from those derived from vision. So, more than one a posteriori explanation of spatial knowledge is possible. The similarity among all experientially driven explanations, however, is the need to propose a mechanism for generating something—usually Euclidean geometry—from nothing, a spatially naive state.

Theories of Spatial Development

Theories of spatial development encapsulate perspectives on the nature of psychological space and the origins of spatial knowledge. Actually, there are few basic positions. A point of convergence is that, in virtually all contemporary positions, the mature spatial knowledge system is accepted to be Euclidean (but see Shepard, 1988). The point of divergence is whether the mature system develops, in which case spatial knowledge is a function of some acquisition process, or whether the mental representation of space is inherent and constant, its essential character shared by infant, child, and adult.

The Piagetian position.   A variation on the a posteriori theme is contained in Piaget's position on spatial cognition. Piaget rejected a priori notions of absolute space and insisted that each individual constructs spatial knowledge. Rather than serving as the starting point for the organization of spatial contents, for him Euclidean space was the culmination of ontogeny (Piaget & Inhelder, 1956), developmentally preceded by a non-Euclidean geometry of relative space. In Piaget's theory, spatial knowledge acquisition is wedded to and inseparable from nonspatial developmental acquisitions; both are derived from physical, exploratory action on environmental objects.

Active experience gives rise to a universally constructed Euclidean system of spatial representation. Such competence is not evidenced behaviorally until the achievement of concrete-operational structures (Piaget, & Inhelder, 1956; Piaget, Inhelder, & Szeminska, 1960). A prerequisite accomplishment to the mental representation of space is the mental representation of objects, a major accomplishment during infancy. Spatial knowledge emerges subsequently during the preschool years and middle childhood.

There are a number of interesting and unique aspects to Piaget's view of spatial cognition. First, since the means for knowledge construction is physical action on objects, the initial spatial system of the young child is object centered and object defined; psychological space for preoperational children is therefore *relative* rather than absolute. Second, the point of reference in this spatial system, the point of origin to which the child relates the placement of objects, is the self. A self-referenced psychological space is an *egocentric* one. Thus, the first spatial system the child constructs is characterized by an egocentric frame of reference. Third, the appropriate geometry for depicting this developmentally early form of psychological space is *topological* rather than Euclidean.

Topological space lacks the fixed metric of the Euclidean version and can be metaphorically conceptualized as elastic space. Objects, for example, do not violate their topological geometric properties across some deformation transformations, like stretching or squishing, as well as retaining them across nondeformational ones. The metric, as quantified in area or volume, need not remain invariant across a transformation for the geometric property to be the same.

Piaget has been criticized for distorting topological concepts (Kapadia, 1974; Mandler, 1983; Martin, 1976) and for not using geometric theory in a very precise manner (Beilin, 1984), which may be the case. Essential to his developmental thesis, nonetheless, is this contention: Young children possess a psychological space that is more general, more primitive, and generally cruder than the older child and adult (Newcombe, 1988).

Extrapolating from formal measurement terminology, the following examples might give some flavor of what this "cruder" space is like. It is as if the young child delineates space with an *ordinal* scale. Ordinal scaling describes a system based on ranks. Thus, relations of "greater than" and "less than" can be represented; but since the interval of measurement is not fixed, the difference between two ranks can vary along the scale. Imagine three objects at varying degrees of distance from a viewer along a single vector. Using a Euclidean metric, one could determine that object X is two feet from the viewer, object Y is three feet away, and object Z is nine feet away. At the crudest level, we can say the objects are *not connected* to the viewer since they are not touching; connectedness versus nonconnectedness is differentiated in topological space. Moving up a bit in precision, the objects are describable in terms of relative closeness to the viewer: X is closer than Y which is closer than Z. But we can go farther and note that Y is closer to X than Z is to Y (or Y-$X < Z$-Y) and, even more precisely, 1 foot (Y-X) is five units smaller than 6 feet (Z-Y).

Only the first and second levels of description are possible with an ordinal scale. More precise *interval* or *ratio* scales include the characteristics of the ordinal scale (greater than, less than) and additional characteristics (how much greater than?). With the metric of interval and ratio scales, only one configuration of objects would fit the spatial parameters of the description. With the less constrained ordinal scale, a much larger class of configurations would fit. So the ordinal scale, like a topological geometry, is more general and less constrained than an interval/ratio scale and a Euclidean geometry.

An ordinal scale is defined by the elements to be ranked, for no absolute reference system exists whether or not elements are measured with it. Thus, a set of 10 rankable elements would produce a "longer" scale than would a set of 3 elements. Applying this to distance judgments, imagine two configurations of objects. In one configuration, three objects are arranged on a line 10 feet long, while in the second, seven objects cover the same distance. From a Euclidean, fixed metric basis, the distance covered by each configuration is the same; there is an absolute scale that specifies the distance covered independent of the elements on it. From the cruder, ordinal-measurement basis, there is no absolute scale to use as an external standard of measurement for comparing the two configurations. We have no way of knowing that both configurations cover the same distance. So, the seven-item configuration is longer because there are

more elements to be ranked; ordinal scales are *relative to* the objects that make them up.

Spatial cognition is the **spatial representation** of spatial information. Knowledge of space need not be representational, and indeed Piaget distinguished the representational variety from *practical* and *perceptual* knowledge (Presson & Somerville, 1985). Practical spatial knowledge tops one's ability to get around in the spatial environment, to reach for and find objects, to direct and locate the body in space, and to use perceptual information to guide spatial behavior. This is spatial "doing" (Liben, 1988) which is not the equivalent of *knowing* as Piaget seems to have meant it. For Piaget, the development of practical spatial knowledge, the acquisition of a knowledge system to direct doing in space, is the infant's task during the sensorimotor period. Spatial knowing goes beyond doing to a conceptual representation of space that is symbolic and not action-dependent.

Essentially, then, there are three aspects of psychological space: (1) visual perception of space, (2) procedural knowledge of space, including sensorimotor schemes for how to move through and act in space (Mandler, 1983), and (3) conceptual representations of space. Piagetian theory explains the development of the third. It is representational space that is at first topological and then Euclidean, that is at first egocentric and then objective, that is at first ordinal and then ratio, and that is at first relative and then absolute.

However, Piaget and Inhelder assumed that the developmental sequence of conceptual, representational space recapitulates the development of the other two (Mandler, 1988). Thus, by implication, infants should *perceive* topological characteristics of space before perceiving Euclidean ones and *use* topological features to direct spatial doing before using Euclidean ones. The contemporary research reviewed in Chapter 2, which postdates the Piagetian thesis about space, suggests, however, that infants do perceive Euclidean characteristics of space (Franz & Miranda, 1975; Kellman, 1984). Empirical studies of spatial doing and spatial knowing presumably serve to test whether Piaget's premise holds for the other two aspects of psychological space.

For Piaget, the transition from practical to conceptual space, from relative to absolute space, and from non-Euclidean to Euclidean space is achieved through the individual's coordination of action in space. It is not perception that constrains spatial knowledge, but motor activity. The successive geometries built by the developing child derive from physical action on objects in space, an enterprise in which perception plays only a part. With action rather than visual perception as the driving force for spatial conceptualization, representations of space need not be isomorphic to the perception of space, and mental images need not share a correspondence with visual percepts. Rather, spatial representation shares a common nature with other cognitive phenomena, such as mathematical or logical knowledge, that also derive from the coordination of sensorimotor action.

Alternative positions. Piagetian ideas about spatial knowledge in children are quite controversial. Since the U.S. appearance of his books on space, geometry, and spatial imagery (Piaget & Inhelder, 1956, 1971; Piaget, Inhelder, & Szeminska, 1960), other developmentalists have sought to test his propositions, sometimes to corroborate the hypothesized developmental sequence (Beilin, 1984; Dodwell, 1963; Laurendeau & Pinard, 1970) and sometimes to challenge it (Mandler, 1983; Martin, 1976).

A number of issues raised by the theory are subject to empirical inquiry. There are, for instance, general questions about the reliability of the spatial behavior described in Piaget's books. Do young children respond to topological characteristics in the manner asserted (Rosser, Horan, Mattson, & Mazzeo, 1984)? Is spatial representation developmentally discontinuous with one geometry replaced by another? Spatial cognition could instead be continuous with gradual increases in geometric accuracy replacing shifts in the basic nature of geometric systems (Mandler, 1983).

There are also more specific questions. For example, Are infants and young children egocentric, using the self as the primary spatial referent (Acredolo & Evans, 1980; Borke, 1975; Cox, 1980; Rosser, 1983)? And finally, investigators question the mechanisms of development. Motor activity could be the means for generating shifts in geometric representation (Acredolo, 1988b; Kermoian & Campos, 1988), but it need not be. Vision is another possible mechanism (Bower, 1977a); and, in fact, developing knowledge systems might even be independent of specific experiential confrontations (Landau, 1988).

Although currently no one else has proposed as comprehensive an explanation of spatial cognition as have Piaget and Inhelder, research programs are yielding data that do challenge their basic contentions. Some data suggest that early spatial representation is indeed Euclidean (Landau & Spelke, 1985). Other data point to the essential role played by perception (Gibson, 1979; Pick, 1988), which Piagetians tend to overlook in favor of motoric processes. Many of the scientific challenges come from research studies whose designers make different choices than Piaget would have on the dimensions of space identified by O'Keefe and Nadel (1978). Models of spatial knowledge predicated on the Kantian position that psychological space is absolute, Euclidean, and a priori are indeed antithetical to the Piagetian thesis. And it is this nativist theoretical stance that is gaining considerable support from contemporary research investigations (Diamond, 1991; Gallistel, 1990).

Methods for Studying
Spatial Cognition

Eliciting some performance from which to draw inferences about the status of the subject's mental representations of space is a major task. The task is sufficiently difficult when subjects are adults; it is even more so when subjects are children and infants. To a large extent, the particulars of experimental procedure are shaped by two not entirely independent factors: (1) the age and species of the subjects under study and (2) the theoretical perspective of the investigator. Those who view spatial cognition as innate and a priori, for example, will be most apt to examine spatial knowledge in the very young with experimental tasks adapted to their available response systems. Minimal behavioral evidence becomes sufficient evidence from which to infer basic competence. The logic is much like that which directs the nativist research program in visual perception.

In contrast, the more conservative empiricist (and by extension, constructivist) position demands maximal behavioral evidence to infer conceptual knowledge, and that evidence is rarely within the response capabilities of the young subject. Contemporary psychologists choose to wage their theoretical arguments in the empirical arena, but their theory-derived hypotheses must be tested via alternative methodologies.

Research with Infants and Toddlers. Those of a nativist bent want to know how infants *think* about space. Spatial thinking presupposes some intuitive theory of how objects act in space when the particular space and those objects are not sensed. Thus, space research with infants involves determining whether they indeed have intuitive spatial theories and describing what those initial theories are like.

The first step is to hypothesize what a baby might know about space—that is, what a baby would accept as a basic geometric postulate or rule. If babies have some knowledge of basic rules related to space, then it follows that they have expectations about how things work spatially and about how objects move about in space. Then, the experimenter can expose infant subjects to a context in which objects should behave in an expected fashion, and one of two things can happen:

1. Some response indicative of anticipation is assessed, for example, looking or reaching in the direction of a spatial location where an event is expected to occur prior to the occurrence (Acredolo, 1978; Acredolo & Evans, 1980; Haith, Hazan, & Goodman, 1988).
2. The experimenter can violate the baby's anticipation with the illusory creation of an impossible event in space (Bower, Broughton, & Moore, 1971). A surprise reaction of some sort should accompany the violation of an expectation.

One variation of the **surprise paradigm** involves adapting the habituation technique used so extensively in studies of infant visual perception. An expectation is established during the habituation phase; for example, an infant might observe an object moving according to the principle that objects move on spatiotemporally continuous paths in space and time. This is the **continuity constraint** on object motion (Spelke, 1990). In the subsequent test phase, the object could either continue to move as anticipated, in accord with the expectation, or the object's movement could violate the expectation.

Dishabituation, as measured with looking times or with some physiological measure, should occur differentially to the violation. Spelke and Kestenbaum (1986, as reported in Spelke, 1988a) habituated infants to one of two sequences involving objects moving along a path and passing behind occluders during the process. In the **continuous-event condition,** subjects observed an object pass behind an occluder, reappear in an intervening space, pass behind a second occluder, and reappear again; the sequence is consistent with the movement of a single object on a single, continuous path. In the **discontinuous-event condition,** the sequence was the same except the object did not reappear in the intervening space; the second sequence would be expected if two objects were moving rather than one.

Infants were habituated to either the continuous or to the discontinuous event sequence and were then exposed to a test display depicting the movement of a single object or of two objects. Subjects who observed the continuous sequence, consistent with the movement of a single object, were expected to dishabituate to the two-object test display and vice versa. Indeed, that is what investigators found. The habituation and test displays and the data are in Figure 3-1.

Whether surprise reactions, startle responses, anticipatory behaviors, or dishabituation are measured, the logic is similar. Violation of an anticipation produces a behavioral signal, and violation is impossible unless a spatial event is mentally represented such that anomaly between the expected and the experienced is detected. To the extent babies react as if they are indeed sensitive to anomalies in the spatial behavior of objects, then some investigators are willing to infer possession of intuitive, perhaps innate, theories of space.

As babies get older, the response repertoire from which investigators infer spatial knowledge increases. Toddlers act in space; they do a number of things that seem to require spatial knowledge, like finding lost toys, negotiating routes around barriers, and intercepting elusive cats. With toddlers, methodologies typically involve observation of motor behaviors that might signal spatial representation.

By the time children engage in self-produced locomotion, their behavior within the spatial layout is not haphazard. In fact, it often appears goal-directed and suggests possession of at least a rudimentary system of spatial representation and location rules. Toddlers are quite able to engage in search behaviors for unseen goal objects, so search tasks are commonly employed in studies of spatial cognition with this age group (DeLoache, 1980; 1984; DeLoache & Brown, 1983, 1984).

Sometimes the goal object is sensible; typical behaviors then involve perceptually guided locomotion, reaching, or interception. Internal representations are not necessarily implicated. Other times, the goal object is not sensible, necessitating another level of spatial functioning. If access to a goal object were blocked, the situation might necessitate creation of a new route, a detour, through the layout, entailing locomotion of a different sort. In order to make a successful detour through a region, a youngster must represent the position of the goal and its relation to a starting point, and the youngster must infer what path or paths will lead from the starting point to the goal. When the mother leaves the immediate area and is no longer visible, and a crawler is able to maneuver a fairly direct route to intercept her, locomotion must be representationally guided.

Examples of this research methodology include the studies by Landau and associates (see Landau, 1988) of a young child's nonperceptually guided behavior in space. Data were interpreted as evidence of the ability to make spatial inferences (Landau & Spelke, 1985). Landau, Gleitman, and Spelke (1981) and Landau, Spelke, and Gleitman (1984) studied a young child, Kelli (2½ years of age in the first study), who had been blinded shortly after birth. One of the tasks Kelli performed was a navigation or triangulation task. First, she was exposed to a spatial layout containing four distinct objects or landmarks; the layout is diagramed in Figure 3-2. Kelli was trained along some of the paths (A to B, A to D, A to C in the figure), but then she was tested by having to navigate the other, nonexplored paths (C to B, C to D, B to D in the figure). Thus, the child had to find new routes among the landmarks. The investigators recorded Kelli's movement along the new routes and concluded that she did indeed know where she was going; she performed better than chance in locating the landmarks and moved quite di-

FIGURE 3-1 *Habituation Displays, Test Displays, and Looking Times in the Spelke and Kestenbaum Experiments to Assess Whether Infants See that Objects Move on Continuous Space-Time Paths.*
Habituation displays (left) show movement consistent with the continuous movement of a single rod behind two occluders or movement consistent with two rods. Test displays (right) present the movement of a single rod (as in the continuous event) or of two rods (consistent with discontinuous event). Looking times (center) show the patterns of dishabituation.

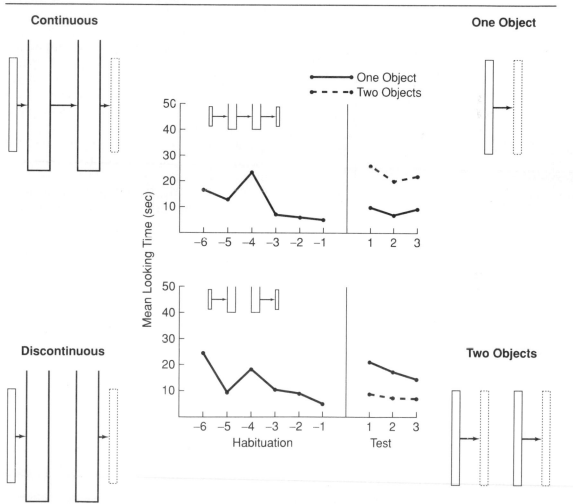

From "Where Perceiving Ends and Thinking Begins: The Apprehension of Objects in Infancy" by E. S. Spelke, in *Perceptual Development in Infancy: Minnesota Symposium on Child Development* (Vol. 20, pp. 197–234), A Yonas (Ed.), Hillsdale, NJ: Erlbaum. Reprinted by permission.

FIGURE 3-2 *Layout of the Room Where Kelli Was Trained and Tested for Route Knowledge.*

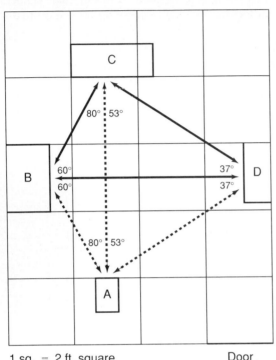

1 sq. = 2 ft. square   Door

←--→ Test Routes
←——→ Trained Routes
 A = Mother
 B = Pillows
 C = Table
 D = Basket

From "Spatial Knowledge in a Young Blind Child" by B. Landau, E. S. Spelke, and H. Gleitman, 1984, *Cognition, 16,* pp. 225–260. Reprinted by permission.

Neither perceptual cues nor simple spatial memory alone could account for these spatial inferences. The authors' conclusions from this series of studies were that Kelli's behavior was representationally guided and predicated on a Euclidean representation. Given that Kelli was both very young and blind further suggests an a priori, nonvisual origin for the representation as well. This decidedly nonempirical, nonconstructivist interpretation is not without contention (see Liben, 1988, for a counterargument) because Kelli did make errors in navigation. She performed better than chance; she did not perform flawlessly.

The research with Kelli exemplifies both a theoretical position on the origins of spatial knowledge in young children and a style of doing research with those young children. A motor performance is elicited and implications about spatial conceptualizations from spatial actions are drawn. But the tasks are "doing" tasks. Piagetians adamantly differentiate spatial doing from spatial knowing (Liben, 1988). The latter taps thinking about space in the abstract, **geometric knowledge,** as opposed to behaving within a particular concrete space, **place knowledge.** Although the two are related (Landau and associates would argue that accurate movement in a place demands a knowledge of geometric space), they need not be identical. Other types of tasks may better elicit the abstract, symbolic aspects of spatial thought. But what? How can one examine spatial thinking independent of spatial doing? Infants and toddlers have limited behavioral repertoires for expressing spatial knowledge.

rectly toward a goal (see Landau & Spelke, 1985). Kelli's actual routes are reproduced in Figure 3-3.

The interpretation is that Kelli possessed a spatial representation or *cognitive map* that guided her behavior and allowed her to infer new routes from knowledge of spatial relations computed from traversing old routes.

Research with preschoolers and school-age children. With increases in maturity, children become more capable of following directions and expressing their knowledge in a variety of contexts. As a consequence, a greater range of target tasks become available to the developmental investigator. Bear in mind, however,

FIGURE 3-3 *Kelli's Paths of Movement on navigation Test Trails after Training on Different Routes.*

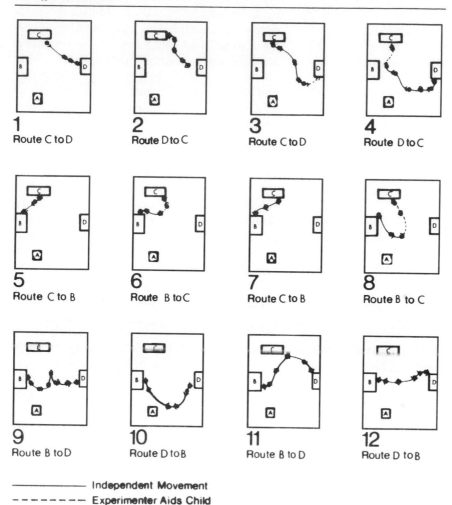

1
Route C to D

2
Route D to C

3
Route C to D

4
Route D to C

5
Route C to B

6
Route B to C

7
Route C to B

8
Route B to C

9
Route B to D

10
Route D to B

11
Route B to D

12
Route D to B

———————— Independent Movement

– – – – – – – – Experimenter Aids Child

From "Spatial Knowledge in a Young Blind Child" by B. Landau, E. S. Spelke, and H. Gleitman, 1984, *Cognition, 16,* pp. 225–260. Reprinted by permission.

that what is examined in any research study will only be a display of competence in a particular medium (Anooshian & Siegel, 1985). Knowledge per se is confounded by the task used to assess it. Conclusions about the extent of spatial knowledge in children are bound to differ across studies to the extent that tasks differ, to the extent that media diverge.

It seems intuitive that mental representations, mental symbols, become externalized in the symbolic productions or **artifacts** that people use to stand for some aspect of their knowledge about the world (Mandler, 1983). And, it may be equally intuitive to assume an isomorphism between what we know about space and what we depict in artifacts. Omissions of particular geometric features in spatial artifacts, or failure to identify distortions and misrepresentations of those features in symbolic products, could reflect limitations in spatial knowledge. One medium in which children's spatial knowledge is potentially actualized, is in their artifacts, in their drawings, models, constructions, scribbles, and descriptions. Obviously, artifact production is limited in infants and toddlers (but see Stiles-Davis, 1988); but with the increasing motor maturity emerging during the preschool years, children's spatial artifacts open another avenue of inference as to the status of their geometric sophistication.

Piagetian-inspired studies of spatial cognition include the analysis of children's artifacts as a prototypic dependent measure. Drawings, as an example, are examined for the purpose of detecting any discrepancy between a child's depiction and that expected of an adult. This approach is frequently a method of choice in clinical studies as well, particularly of patients who have sustained cerebral damage potentially affecting visual-spatial functioning (see, for example, Morrow & Ratcliff, 1988). The drawings of such individuals can differ in predictable ways from standard or normal drawings depending on the nature, extent, and location of impairment. Whether subjects are brain-damaged adults or young children, analysis of artifacts serves a *diagnostic* function; drawings are assignable to categories or prototypes. The method is well suited to a diagnostic system predicated on **typologies.**

The Piagetian perspective on spatial development is a kind of typology; the categories or types are determined by the underlying geometry that organizes the child's spatial knowledge. With preschool and school-age children, the theory predicts two categories or types: the topological type or, alternatively, the Euclidean type. The measurement operation involves something akin to diagnosis (the classification of artifacts), and the measurement

scale is *nominal*. The number of classes or categories can be expanded, perhaps to three or four, by adding mixed or transitional categories; but, nonetheless, the assignment operation must yield categories that are *mutually exclusive* and *exhaustive* (Hays, 1988). That means *any* artifact must be assignable to one and only one category and *all* artifacts must be assignable to some category. Stage theories, which predict qualitative shifts in mental structure as Piaget's does, are conceptually consistent with measurement systems designed to yield qualitatively distinct typologies.

For example, one might provide a child subject with geometric forms that he is instructed to recall and to copy. The child will produce a drawing preserving the geometric properties he thought were important. Several Euclidean features are potentially conservable, such as the metric of angles, lines, and area. Older children and adults will experience some success preserving these features although even they can encounter difficulties with accuracy; their angles, for example, might be a little off, plus or minus a few degrees, as compared to the model. So, adults and older children may encounter some problems with proficiency in replicating geometric stimuli.

The important developmental question is not whether young children are less accurate than older ones but whether youngsters preserve different features than their older counterparts. Piagetian theory predicts that young children's drawings of geometric forms will tend to show conservation of topological features, such as closure, with a disregard for Euclidean ones such as size; thus different, rather than less accurate, artifacts will be correlated with age.

In actuality, it is difficult to disentangle age-related differences in accuracy from age-related differences in type (Mandler, 1983) to determine when the inaccurate recreation of a 90 degree angle becomes failure to preserve angularity. Additionally, the measurement rule for nominal scaling should yield exclusive, nonoverlapping categories, but the geometries themselves do not constitute nonoverlapping mathematical systems. A topological geometry, at least in the Piagetian sense, is less constrained than a Euclidean one, so the latter is embedded within the former as opposed to distinct from it. Perhaps a nominal scaling system is really less than an ideal fit with a typology of the Piagetian variety after all. As a consequence, inferences made from children's artifacts to their underlying, cognitive representations of space are more ambiguous than it at first might appear.

The analysis of drawing surfaces appears in much Piagetian-inspired work on the development of spatial representation. In one example, Dean (1979) used drawings to determine whether children could represent the spatial transformations between two static end points, as when a vertical stick falls down to occupy a horizontal position. Piaget (Piaget & Inhelder, 1971) predicted that children younger than about age 6 should not be able to produce drawings depicting the intermediate states. Older children, who are solidly in the concrete-operational stage of development, should be able to. There should be a positive correlation between developmental level, indexed by age, and accurate depiction of the transformation. In the study, four categories were defined to reflect the degree to which accurate depiction of the transition was achieved; examples consistent with the prototypes are included in Figure 3-4. Dean's (1979) data confirm the theoretically predicted association between developmental level and nature of spatial depictions.

Others would contend that artifact production, particularly drawing, is an inherently confounded dependent measure even when such positive results are found (Brown, 1976; Goodnow, 1977; Kosslyn, Heldmeyer, & Locklear, 1977). The sophistication of children's cognitive representations of space may

be correlated with age; children's drawing ability most definitely is. Therefore, if the geometric accuracy of children's spatial artifacts turns out to be age related, we cannot determine whether the cause of the obtained relation is underlying cognitive competence or the superficial motor performance on which drawing depends.

Many would draw a distinction between observable *performance,* which is context bound and variable depending on the particular medium of assessment, and unobservable *competence* (Flavell & Wohlwill, 1969). The latter is supposed to be stable and context independent, the true state of the individual's knowledge. It is, however, impossible to evaluate competence without a context. But, the dichotomy between performance and competence is one we will encounter repeatedly in the interpretation of data from studies of cognitive development.

Spatial representations are internal, cognitive, and hypothetical entities. Researchers are hard-pressed to devise methods for extracting or externalizing representations in order to study their nature; no one method will be totally satisfactory. Evaluation of artifacts is one avenue, perilous perhaps, with its own set of acknowledged limitations, but one that still offers some insight into children's spatial thinking.

Traditionally, spatial ability has proved to be one of the basic "intelligences" (Thurstone, 1938). The analysis of individual differences in spatial aptitude suggests something about the structure of the ability by permitting identification of the major factors that seem to comprise it (Lohman, 1979; McGee, 1979). Basically, mathematical analyses permit identification of the sorts of spacelike tasks that correlate, and, from patterns of observed task intercorrelations, inferences are drawn about cognitive structure and about the hypothetical cognitive processes that must underlie task performance.

FIGURE 3-4 *Drawings Made by Children to Illustrate a Stick Rotation from a Vertical to a Horizontal Position.*
The sample drawings form the basis of a *typology,* a measurement system in which artifacts are assigned to category on the basis of specific criteria.

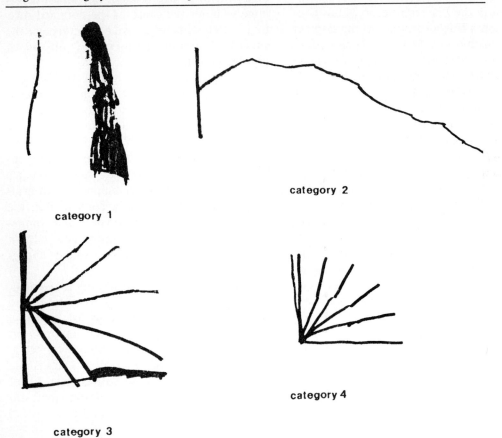

category 1

category 2

category 3

category 4

From "Patterns of Change in Relations between Children's Anticipatory Imagery and Operative Thought" by A. L. Dean, 1979, *Developmental Psychology, 15,* pp. 153–163. Copyright 1979 by the American Psychological Association. Reprinted with permission.

Cognitive psychologists, very often beginning with tasks identified through factor-analytic, psychometric work, attempt to decipher the nature of those underlying cognitive processes. Spatial tasks, taken from intelligence and aptitude tests, are analyzed as to the nature of the mental representations, operations, and strategies necessary to enable successful task performance (Pellegrino & Kail, 1982). The tasks identified by psychometricians and scrutinized by cognitive psychologists find their way into the developmental literature, too, but these tasks differ in important ways from the Piagetian-inspired variety.

First, these cognitive tasks look different. The look, reflecting the origins, is more test-like with the use of abstract figures as stimuli, two-dimensional representations of those stimuli, and perhaps even paper-and-pencil formatting of the test problems. Figure 3-5

FIGURE 3-5 *Sample Spatial Ability Problems Often Used on Tests of Spatial Aptitude.*
The top two sample problems are spatial-relation tasks; the bottom one is a spatial-visualization task. In all three, subjects must identify a form that is the outcome of a transformation perpetrated on a standard.

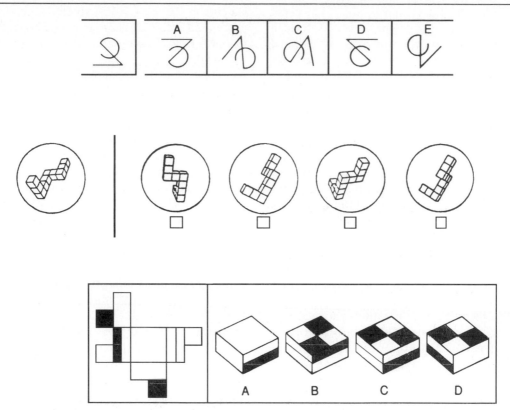

From "Process Analyses of Spatial Aptitude" by J. W. Pellegrino and R. Kail, in *Advances in the Psychology of Human Intelligence,* R. J. Sternberg (Ed.), 1982, Hillsdale, NJ: Erlbaum. Reprinted by permission.

depicts sample items used to assess some identified aspects of spatial problem solving. In all the samples, an abstract, two-dimensional stimulus functions as a standard. The respondent must select, from among a restricted class of choices, the option that correctly depicts the standard following an imagined, spatial transformation. The format is less open-ended than a drawing task, which permits a circumventing of the criticisms levied at the less constrained, artifact-production tasks favored by Piagetians. However, tasks like the samples are primarily appropriate only for older children.

Second, the theoretical foundations of this research style and the prototypic tasks associated with it, rooted as they are in contemporary cognitive psychology, differ substantially from the classic Piagetian style. Most cognitive psychologists build hypothetical models of one sort or another for how intellectual problems are solved by competent performers (Anderson, 1983; Pellegrino & Kail, 1982). The models precisely and explicitly convey how a cognitive system encodes, represents, transforms, and manipulates information (Sternberg, 1985). In short, modeling describes how a problem-solving process works. The level of specificity in information-processing models is very detailed, much more so than in the less explicit, holistic formulations favored by orthodox cognitive developmentalists. The detail is necessary. Models might be tested through computer simulation (Anderson, 1983) or, if not, the computer will provide an analogy for formatting a cognitive act. And computers cannot follow vague or implicit directions. Computer-based language is explicit expression. Hence, processing models, whether or not they are designed as simulatable programs, are typically carefully described, positing step-by-step analyses of the unobserved mental operations, presumed to transpire in real time, between information input and the production of a response. Very often the analysis is captured in a flowchart, again a technique borrowed from information theory. A simple flowchart, which was originally proposed to summarize the operation of mental rotation, is exemplified in Figure 3-6.

The theoretical formulations and analytical style associated with information processing yield dependent measures differing from the nominally scaled typologies produced with artifact diagnosis. Measurement scales for the former are quantitative (Cooper & Mumaw, 1985). With such scales, individual differences, including developmental differences, are reliably quantifiable (Pellegrino & Kail, 1982). Since investigators adopting an information-processing perspective assume that mental processes do take place in real time, it is conceptually feasible to measure the time it takes to perform them. Reaction time (or RT) measures the time elapsed between presentation of a stimulus and response to that stimulus. RT indexes efficiency of performance, or speed; accuracy, or proficiency of performance, is also quantifiable, such as in the number of problems of a particular type correctly solved.

One example of adapting the techniques of mainstream cognitive psychologists for developmental work is the research on mental rotation. The mental rotation paradigm originated with Roger Shepard and his associates who, starting in the early 1970s, studied mental imagery and related phenomena (Shepard & Cooper, 1986). Essentially, Shepard (Shepard & Metzler, 1971) proposed that the mental modeling of spatial phenomena shares fundamental common features with the physics of space; that is, there exists an *isomorphism* between psychological space and physical space.

In physical space, for example, if one were to take an object and rotate it around a fixed axis at a constant speed, the larger the distance of rotation, the longer the movement will take. A rotation of 80 degrees will take longer than one of 25 degrees which will take longer than one of 10 degrees. The object will also pass through all the intermediate positions between the starting point and the ending point. If the mental process is isomorphic, or *analog,* then the same should hold true for a mental representation of an object and its movement in space. It should take longer to mentally model a greater rotation, and the mental representation should mimic "passing through" intermediate states as well.

This hypothesis has been tested in a variety of ways (Cooper, 1975, 1976), but in a basic variation, subjects are asked to mentally rotate an abstract stimulus some *x* number of degrees, *x* varying between 0 degrees and 360 degrees. (Sample stimuli are shown in Figure 3-7). Then, subjects are shown a test stimulus rotated to *x* and asked to judge whether it is a simple rotation of the previous one or a rotation plus reflection of it. In order to make the decision, the subject must have rotated a mental "image" of the first stimulus into correspondence with the test stimulus and mentally compared the two. Adult subjects are invariably correct in their judgments, but that is not the theoretically important issue. Usually, the investigators want to observe RT, the time it takes to make the judgment. Is RT positively

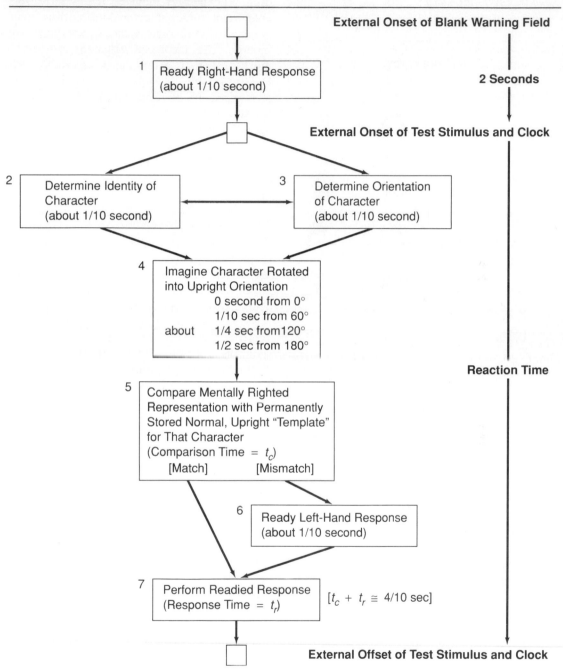

FIGURE 3-7 *Sample Stimuli Used in Mental Rotation Tasks with Adults.*
In this set, the standard shapes are to the left in each pair; the reflected shapes are to the right.

The Eight Forms

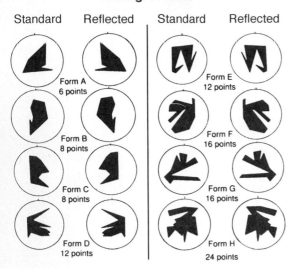

From "Mental Rotation of Random Two-Dimensional Stages" by L. A. Cooper, 1975, *Cognitive Psychology, 7,* pp. 20–43. Reprinted by permission.

related to the magnitude of *x*? Many studies conducted on this style and in variations of it yield the hypothesized, positive linear function between RT and *x* (Cooper & Shepard, 1973; Shepard & Cooper, 1986); a sample result can be found in Figure 3-8. The full interpretation of these data is still somewhat controversial (Just & Carpenter, 1985; Pylyshyn, 1979; 1981), but the style of investigation is theory-driven and yields a quantitative dependent measure.

Many researchers have adapted the paradigm for use with children (Childs & Polich, 1979; Kail, 1985, 1986; Kail, Pellegrino & Carter, 1980), the theoretical reasons for which will become apparent in upcoming sections. However, the usefulness of the technique is usually restricted to studies with older children. The measurement of RT is most reliable when subjects are making correct judgments; it is that cognitive act which the theory models. The incorrect judgment process is more obscure (Carter, Pazak, & Kail, 1983; Rosser, Ensing, & Mazzeo, 1985). Thus, subjects need to be performing *asymptotically,* producing high rates of accurate judgments, for RT data to prove useful. Young children simply are not sufficiently accurate. The more adultlike children behave or can be induced to behave (Kail, 1987), the more useful the research strategy.

It is instructive to compare the Piagetian-inspired study of the falling stick (Dean, 1979) described earlier with the prototypic, Shepard-inspired, cognitive paradigm described here. Both techniques were devised to test similar hypotheses about spatial cognition, yet the research style is very different. One targets subjects' artifacts, the other reaction time. In one, there is a reliance on categorical analysis of data; the other relys on quantitative methods. Differences in procedure reflect differences in the intellectual origins for the procedure and in theoretical tradition. Both styles surface in the developmental study of spatial cognition.

Research with animals. Spatial cognition is not a solely human capacity. Infrahuman animals, and certainly all mammals, move about in space, and their movements are systematic, not haphazard. The family cat knows where its food dish is located. The pet dog anticipates the appearance of family members at specific places. The trail horse negotiates its way home undirected by the rider, and the migratory grazing animal locates food sources along established routes. Clearly, many species maintain accurate spatial representations of their environment (Menzel, 1973; Olton, 1977; Peters, 1973). Thus, animals, like humans, must have the capacity to keep track of their position in space; effective navigation, way-

FIGURE 3-8 *Mean Reaction Time as a Function of Angular Disparity between Standard and Test Forms of the Stimuli Depicted in Figure 3-7.*

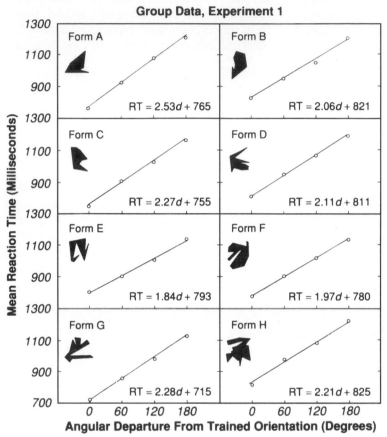

From "Mental Rotation of Random Two-Dimensional Stages" by L. A. Cooper, 1975, *Cognitive Psychology, 7,* pp. 20—43. Reprinted by permission.

finding, and foraging depend on some mechanism for recognizing and remembering places, registering routes, and using the knowledge to inform behavior. Because space is such an important aspect of animal cognition, crucial to the survival of many species, comparative psychologists and neuropsychologists have developed their own traditions for investigating these phenomena. Still, data from studies with animals tell us something about the cognitive development of children because those data:

1. Reveal information about the neural substrate underlying spatial functioning.
2. Uncover changes in the substrate associated with growth and experience.
3. Suggest parallels between the neurological and cognitive functioning and development of humans and other animals.

The tasks used in animal research and child-development research are not that similar. Animal research relies on "doing" tasks since infrahuman subjects do not produce diagnosable artifacts. Investigators must always adapt procedures to the species-typical response repertoires of subjects, and running, swimming, searching, and foraging are more characteristic of most mammals than are drawing and block building, the symbolic tasks preferred by many cognitive developmentalists. More recently, however, some tasks initially developed for use with animal subjects, such as search tasks in a radial-arm maze, show up in research with young children (Aadland, Beatty, & Maki, 1985; Foreman, Arber, & Savage, 1984). Use of equivalent tasks across species facilitates direct comparisons and generalizations (Diamond & Goldman-Rakic, 1983, 1985, 1986).

Animal research permits a degree of invasiveness impossible in child studies. With animals, it is feasible to selectively interfere with brain functioning as one means of deciphering brain-behavior relationships. For example, the brain of a subject might be lesioned (Zola-Morgan & Squire, 1986), influenced chemically (Sutherland, Whishaw, & Regehr, 1982), or mechanically altered (Parker & Walley, 1988) as a form of experimental manipulation. Then, spatial behavior elicited subsequent to the experimental manipulation is compared with that elicited in a nonaltered state or with that exhibited by normal individuals such that associations between actual brain states and behavioral functioning are clarified. Invasive recording techniques are also possible with animals (O'Keefe & Speakman, 1987). Neural activity is directly monitored and recorded as subjects engage in spatial activity.

Typical of developmentally important, recent research in spatial cognition is a set of empirical studies that utilize the Morris water maze and rats as subjects (Morris, 1984).

These studies exemplify how the driving role of theory, the implementation of task and method, and the interpretation of data are actualized in the contemporary animal literature. Researchers must capitalize on the characteristic behavioral repertoires of their animal subjects, and one thing rats, even young ones, reliably do is swim to escape immersion in water. Rats are good swimmers and take to water-escape tasks quite readily (Morris, 1984). The water-maze task takes advantage of this species propensity when subjects are placed in cool liquid from which they are naturally motivated to escape. Escape is a spatial task because investigators observe the rats' movement patterns and where they swim and evaluate how those patterns are affected by age (Rudy & Paylor, 1988; Rudy, Stadler-Morris, & Albert, 1987), cerebral damage (Morris, Garrud, Rawlins, & O'Keefe, 1982), drugs and neurotoxins (Hagan, Alpert, Morris, & Iverson, 1983; Sutherland, Whishaw, & Regehr, 1982), and electrical stimulation (Parker & Walley, 1988).

The water maze is a round tank filled with liquid, placed within a larger spatial environment without any natural escape routes for a swimming rat. The rat usually cannot climb over the edges of the maze or jump out of the tank itself. When a platform is added somewhere inside the tank, the rat is provided an exit. But placement of the platform is variable. Its base, for example, can extend above the water line, in which case the rat, using direct perceptual cues, will swim right to it.

However, the base placed just slightly below the water only permits effective escape if located. If the water is rendered opaque by adding milk, the platform becomes invisible. How, then, might the rat escape? Perhaps the animal will swim about randomly until it collides with the platform. If so, then across a series of trials, escape time should also vary randomly. That is not what happens, though. Normal adult rats learn to locate the platform rapidly, within four or five trials (Sutherland & Dyck, 1984). Their swim pattern is characterized by a fairly direct heading to the platform with decreasing escape time across additional acquisition trials. The swim pattern is similar regardless of where the rat enters the maze.

The surface of the water and the immediately surrounding tank do not provide direct, proximal cues to the location of the submerged platform. Platform location is unmarked; the rats are unable to simply swim toward a specific cue that marks the platform. How, then, do they find it so readily? One alternative is that the rats learn a specific **response strategy,** a pattern of turns and swim distances between entry point and escape. Acquisition of such a response chain is an unlikely explanation of effective escape, however, since a response sequence would not prove equally effective from different starting positions, which is how rats are usually tested.

The more accepted position is that the rats use distal cues in the larger environment to form a **cognitive map** (O'Keefe & Nadel, 1978; Tolman, 1948), a spatial representation, from which to compute platform location. This **spatial mapping strategy** (Sutherland & Dyck, 1984) is equally effective from any point of entry into the tank and can satisfactorily explain the empirical findings. As supportive anecdotal data, Sutherland and Dyck (1984) report that during early acquisition trials, the rats are apt to rear up on their hind limbs upon reaching the platform and turn to face in several directions while on the platform as if to look around.

In animal studies of spatial behavior, a distinction is made between **response learning** and **place learning.** The former involves the acquisition of the behavioral chain necessary to locomote between two points. Given a T maze, for example, there is a starting point at the base of the T, point A; one end of the T top holds a food well, point B. And the oppo-

site end is empty, point C. A rat learning the food's location in the maze could quickly learn a response strategy: Begin A → run straight → left turn → find B. The strategy is effective provided the rat always enters at A. However, the response sequence is specified in terms of the rat's own body. If the maze were flipped over 180 degrees, adhering to the response sequence would take the rat to C. In cognitive-development terms, the rat will produce an egocentric error. Had the rat learned a place strategy instead, locating B in relation to fixed, distal cues in the environment, it could still locate B in a flipped maze. Place learning, then, is like the spatial mapping strategy exhibited in the behavior of normal rats in the Morris water maze.

O'Keefe and Nadel (1978) implicated the **hippocampal formation,** a cortical structure in the limbic system, as the brain component mediating the rat's ability to use a spatial mapping strategy when locating itself in space and navigating in its environment. Indeed, there is considerable support for the critical role of the hippocampus in just this kind of place learning (O'Keefe, Nadel, Keightly, & Kill, 1975; Sutherland, Kolb, & Whishaw, 1982; Okaichi, 1987). Experimentally induced lesions to the hippocampus, for example, render animals incapable of learning to locate the submerged platform in the water maze (Morris, Garrud, Rawlins, & O'Keefe, 1982) even though their ability to find the visible platform is left intact (Morris, 1983). Similar results are induced when hippocampal function is disrupted with low-intensity electrical stimulation in trained rats (Parker & Walley, 1988).

Hippocampal development occurs relatively late in rat pups (Nadel, 1988), with substantial maturation occurring between the time the pups' visual system becomes functional at 15 days (Alberts, 1984) and 20 days when rats reliably escape the water maze by locating the submerged platform (Altman &

Das, 1965; Crain, Cotman, Taylor, & Lynch, 1973; Cotman, Taylor, & Lynch, 1973; Meiback, Ross, Cox, & Glick, 1981; Pokorny & Yamamoto, 1981). Between 15 and 20 days, young rat pups fail to locate the submerged platform even though they are excellent swimmers, can easily locate the visible platform, and can acquire response strategies (Rudy & Paylor, 1988). Apparently, response learning and place learning are disassociated in ontogenesis (Rudy, Stadler-Morris, Albert, 1987), implying that the brain mechanisms underlying the two behavioral systems are too.

Although it is an extrapolation, the development of these spatial abilities in rat pups is related to similar developments in humans. The shift from egocentric, or response strategies, to nonegocentric, or place strategies, is documented in infant studies on somewhat related tasks (Acredolo, 1977, 1985). Obviously, we cannot toss babies into water tanks, nor can we interfere with the hippocampus to see if animal findings are reiterated with humans. We can, however, draw tentative cross-species generalizations as to the possible role the hippocampus plays in aspects of spatial cognition.

Summary

One remarkable feature of the spatial cognition literature is its technical diversity. Developmentally related studies of spatial knowledge range from perception-looking ones, where infants are assessed within a habituation paradigm, to examinations of children's and adult's spatial problem-solving capacities with intelligence test items. In between are studies of normal and handicapped children, of normal and brain-damaged adults, of monkeys, rats, and even of honey bees (Gould, 1986) performing what we construe to be "spatial" tasks. Dependent measures include indices of latency and response time and accuracy and problem-solving power. There are

analyses of artifacts for their spatial characteristics and examinations of search strategies, way-finding, and navigation. We even see the direct recording of neuronal activity in the brain. There are spatial doing tasks, spatial representation tasks, and spatial registering tasks.

Interpreting the data from these myriad investigations in order to compose a reasonable developmental story is no easy feat. However, the plausible developmental accounts are not as diverse as the empirical literature that tests their feasibility—perhaps a reflection of the shared philosophical heritage that spawns psychological theory. Developmental accounts present spatial cognition as either experientially or maturationally driven. In the latter case, it is proposed that the individual comes equipped with at least some rudimentary concepts about how space is organized. Subsequently, those first concepts enable and direct the elaboration of spatial knowledge. But what are those first principles about? One possibility, central to many accounts of spatial cognition, is that they are about the nature of objects (see Spelke, 1991). So that is where we begin.

THE ORIGINS OF SEARCH

A 3-year-old toddler wants to play with all his toy cars, but he notices one of them is missing. Quick inspection of the immediate area does not turn it up, creating both frustration and some motivation to locate the lost object. The toddler faces a search task: Where is the car? How is it to be found? That the toddler notes a specific car is missing implies that he must have some mental representation of the object; no current, direct perceptual information about the car is available.

The toddler might begin the search by recalling what he can about the identifying features of the car—that it is little, red, and has a missing headlight. The features, like the existence of the object, must be "read" from some mental representation without access to perceptual data. Then, he might begin to look for the car in locations where it is normally found. He chooses to look in likely places—under the bed, in the toy box, in his closet, in his pockets, and so forth. Apparently, he can represent the lost object in context since he does not search all possible locations, only plausible ones. Still the car eludes discovery.

Next he extends the search to where the car was last seen. This places a bit more demand on memory; but, following some reflection, our subject searches the rest of the house after recalling having observed the dog carrying the little red car about in its mouth. The toddler has now consulted a representation of the object undergoing a spatial transformation as it was transported from one location to another. A search of the house, however, fails to produce the car. But, alas, our boy remembers placing the little car in the hollow seat of his tricycle and riding it out into the driveway where he left it. Thus, he infers that the car also must be out in the driveway with the tricycle. This bit of spatial knowledge encompasses an unseen transformation, an invisible displacement of the object through space. A search of the tricycle yields the wayward car.

Search presupposes knowledge of an object in its absence. Systematic search indicates knowledge of typical behaviors of the object and the spatial contexts it normally occupies. Successful search depends on creation of a retrieval plan. Positive identification of the object upon search completion implies a verification procedure in which the found object's features are checked against some mental list of those of the lost one. This act depends on cognition, even complex cognition, and virtually any normal 3-year-old can do it, provided the dog does not eat the little car or that the wheel of a big car does not crush it. Underlying search is the knowledge that the searched for object exists in time and space;

has boundaries, substance, and form; and has an existence independent of the perception and action of the searcher. Search behavior is based on inferences about the present location of an independent object from limited perceptual information, past memories, and predictions about an object's typical actions in space.

Piaget called this accomplishment the **object concept** (Piaget, 1954), an attainment he thought evolved gradually during the sensorimotor period. The concept originates in physical interactions between infant and object as the baby touches, feels, grasps, mouths, observes, and experiments with the physical world of things. Presence of the concept is the first clear indication of mental representation, of the **symbolic function.** And since object knowledge is constructed, it takes time. Extensive object interaction and manipulation, the action scheme on which Piagetian-inspired cognition is predicated, is maturationally restricted until around 4 or 5 months of age (Granrud, 1986; Spelke, 1988). So, too, should be any conceptual knowledge and spatial inference about objects.

Piagetian notions about knowledge acquisition through action-based construction place strict time constraints on the emergence of competence. That is not so of alternative theories. Other mechanisms would permit the acquisition of object knowledge from a more limited set of pertinent observations available earlier in development (Baillargeon, 1987a). Through such acts as rudimentary reaching and visual exploration, which are reliably observed in infant behavior prior to the age of 4 months, the baby may learn quite a bit about the displacement of objects and their action in space. Rudimentary experience takes some time, but not necessarily a great deal of time. Studies of infants' object perception strongly suggest innate knowledge of some object qualities, like boundedness and form (Kellman, 1984; Kellman & Spelke, 1983). Is this evidence of an innate object *concept* as well (Spelke, 1988)? What do babies and children know about the permanence of objects and how objects behave in space?

Piagetian Analysis of Search

Piaget assessed infants' inferences about the existence, location, and movement of objects by interpreting search behavior. Based on observations, primarily of his own three children, Piaget described scenarios in which he removed objects from view and hid them in various ways. He then watched children's attempts at recovery.

Search is quite a complex behavior. It involves both identification of the missing object's location (a mental representation of the object's position) and subsequent retrieval. Retrieval requires formulation of an action plan to guide behavior. Execution of the plan depends on the infant's ability to follow through motorically and reach for the hidden object. Failure to search and errors of search were the data from which Piaget inferred immature object knowledge. When elaborate manual search serves as the outcome measure, overt evidence of object knowledge cannot be expected during the first 6 months of life. Limitations in coordinated reaching and grasping could preclude success irrespective of the infant's knowledge of an object's permanence. It is important to bear in mind that failures in search might be attributable to a multitude of factors other than faulty object knowledge.

The object concept develops during the first 18 to 24 months of life. Piaget described six stages of object-knowledge attainment. The change in cognitive state across the stages is gradual and is generated by the coordination of sensorimotor schemes. There is a shift from the absence of any systematic search during the first months of life to the sort of sophisticated search exhibited by the toddler looking for his little red car. By the sixth and final stage, the infant can find an object even after it has undergone a complicated series of hidden movements.

In Stages I and II of the sensorimotor period (0–4 months), the infant does not exhibit active search. If the baby is looking at an object such as a toy and the object disappears, moves out of view, or is hidden by an occluder, the baby neither looks around for it nor requests its reappearance with any discernable signal. The Piagetian explanation is that, for young infants, an object's existence is tied to the immediate perception of it. When perception ceases, as it does with the object's occlusion, so does the object. The infant does not acknowledge that objects continue to exist when they are invisible.

The implication is that objects cannot have permanent stability, solidity, and substance if existence is tied to perceptual flux. By failing to search, the baby does not exhibit a conception of objects moving through time and space obeying the laws of physics. In the young infant's world, objects disappear and reappear; the infant must regard each reappearance as either the re-creation of the object or the creation of a similar one (Harris, 1987). Thus, objects are made and unmade with perceptual comings and goings. Objects are not yet independent of perception.

In Stage III of the sensorimotor period (4–8 months), the infant makes progress in search. If an object is partially occluded, for example, the baby will retrieve it using perceptual information as a cue for location; but the baby does not remove the occluder without the perceptual cue. When the baby observes full occlusion or disappearance, she may look briefly in the direction of removal or produce groping movements as if to signal a desire for the object's return. These motions cease rapidly, however, and true search is not exhibited. The Piagetian analysis is that even this late in development, when infants presumably have the motor skills to accomplish successful retrieval in a simple context, search does not occur. Objects still are not permanent entities existing continuously in time and space but are transient, ceasing to exist and beginning anew as they disappear and reappear in view.

The original observations are reliable (Gratch, 1975; Harris, 1987). However, controversy surrounds whether infants of this age really do have the physical ability to perform the coordinated search actions demanded by the search task (Bower, 1974); there is evidence suggesting limitations on complex motor schemes prior to 9 months of age (Uzgiris & Hunt, 1970).

By Stage IV (8–12 months), babies do exhibit true search. If they observe an object being hidden and they observe the hiding place into which it goes, they will retrieve it. The ability to coordinate action is now sufficient for successful removal of an occluder and retrieval of a hidden object. At this point, they must have some representation of the object in its absence, but that representation is not quite fully mature. Consider the following scenario: On Trial 1, the infant observes an object being hidden under an occluder at location A. The infant removes the occluder and retrieves the object. On Trial 2, the object is again hidden but at location B. Even though placement in the second hiding place is observed by the infant, chances are the infant will search the first location, A, and not the second, B. This curious, counterintuitive search error is referred to as *A not B, $A\bar{B}$,* or as a *perseveration* error.

For Piaget, the $A\bar{B}$ error revealed a lack of correspondence between the infant's object concept and the mature form. Obviously, the infant has endowed the object with permanence since search is conducted, but permanence is incomplete. The object is still conceived of as an extension of the infant's own action; the object's displacements are not governed by the objective laws of physics but by the subjective actions of self. Thus, the baby searches where the object was last found, where it was associated with a search action. This failure to separate object from self is an early form of **egocentrism,** which will be overcome by the end of the sensorimotor period, only to resurface again, as a conceptual cousin, during the preschool years. Because of its surprising nature, the $A\bar{B}$ error is the target of voluminous research efforts (Bremner, 1985; Harris, 1987; Sophian, 1984; Wellman, 1985; Wellman, Cross, & Bartsch, 1987) and reinterpretations. We shall return to this intriguing phenomenon.

In Stage V (12–18 months), the infant overcomes proneness to the $A\bar{B}$ error and successfully locates objects hidden at B. Now the limitations on search involve inferring the movements of the object when those movements are not seen. While an infant watches, an experimenter hides an object in a container and then moves the container to a variety of locations. The object is left somewhere along the path, the container comes up empty, and search behavior is observed (Sophian, Larkin, & Kadane, 1985). For Piaget, the mature response, once the infant observes the empty container, is signaled by systematic search along the traversed path. Until Stage VI (18–24 months), infants do not conduct systematic searches in accord with Piagetian criteria. The interpretation is that the object concept is still not fully symbolic because infants are unable to represent action and transposition of the object even though they can represent its entity.

Alternative Analyses

Piaget's search tasks, like many of the other original tasks he used, tap multiple representational, strategic, and motor skills. The assessment problems are designed to elicit maximal behavioral evidence from which to infer cognitive state. But the tasks are *noisy;* too much cognitive activity is required at one time.

When a child succeeds on a noisy task, we identify the set of competencies success signals. Failure, on the other hand, is inherently ambiguous. Which particular competency or subset of competencies precludes success? To answer that question adequately, "quieter" tasks are needed.

One way of avoiding the problems of ambiguity in search failures is to change the task so that the set of requisite competencies on which success depends is more limited or constrained. The purpose of task simplification is reduction in response demands. Then inferences from performance to cognitive state are less global, and it is easier to identify the particular competency blocking an appropriate response. Altered tasks may reveal memory as the limiter of search. Or perhaps it will turn out that the responder cannot motorically inhibit search at *A* once activated, even with the understanding that the object is now at *B*. Classic tasks are not suited to addressing the specific reasons for failure. Simplified tasks are better.

There is always the risk that a change in task changes the nature of what is assessed. Then, results obtained with one task are not directly comparable to those obtained with another. Be that as it may, investigators have revised, altered, and refined Piagetian procedures to test three of his most controversial formulations: (1) whether young infants lack a notion of object permanence, (2) whether the $A\overline{B}$ finding is a reliable, nonartifactual phenomenon, and (3) whether children truly fail to infer an object's movements in space.

Early evidence of search. Most studies designed to detect early signs of object permanence abandon manual search as the indicator of competence, because when search is examined, the Piagetian findings are generally replicated (Brainerd, 1978a; Gratch, 1975, 1976; Harris, 1975, 1987). Alternative behavioral indicators paint a more confusing picture, however. Bower and associates, for example (Bower, 1974; Bower & Patterson, 1973; Bower, Broughton, & Moore, 1971), assessed young babies' visual tracking of objects as those objects disappeared behind occluders. The presumption was that anticipatory tracking along an object's inferred trajectory indicates knowledge of the object's existence. The investigators claim to have obtained such evidence, but others dispute the robustness and meaning of those findings (Meicler & Gratch, 1980; Moore & Meltzoff, 1978; Muller & Aslin, 1978). Other studies—elaborate variations on visual tracking with attempts to violate expectations about typical object characteristics (Bower, 1967; Goldberg, 1976; Gratch, 1982; Meicler & Gratch, 1980; Moore, Borton, & Darby, 1978) or that manipulate the manner in which an object disappears (Bower, 1967)—yield similarly ambiguous, contradictory, or confusing data. Until very recently, reviewers of the literature concluded that subsequent research offered little serious challenge to Piaget's original analysis of the state of the object concept in early infancy (Bremmer, 1985; Harris, 1987).

There is one exception to that general conclusion. Bower and Wishart (1972) dangled an object in front of attending babies and then created occlusion by plunging the room into total darkness. Apparently, these babies, at only 5 months of age, retrieved the object even though it was invisible. However, this surprising outcome would occur if the babies were simply completing a retrieval action initiated when the object was still visible (Haith & Campos, 1977).

More recently, Renee Baillargeon and her associates developed an elegant, alternative means of assessing object permanence. Their procedure is a variation on the habituation paradigm and is well adapted to the response capabilities of young infants. One feature of permanent objects is that they are solid; and if an object is solid, another object cannot move through the space that the first object occupies. If babies know something about the solidity of objects, then they should have expectations based on that knowledge. It might violate those expectations, for example, if a visible object were to pass through the space occupied by a hidden object. Violation of expectations is an occasion to look at dishabituation.

In Baillargeon's studies, infants were habituated to one event: They observed a screen moving through a 180 degree arc from flat on the table, to upright, to flat on the table again. Once habituated, subjects were shown either a possible or impossible test event. For the possible event, a solid object, a box, was placed in the path of the rotating screen, but as the screen approached where the box, now rendered invisible, should have been, the screen stopped. For the impossible event, the screen continued its full rotation through the space that should have been occupied by the box. The task is depicted visually in Figure 3-9.

Baillargeon demonstrated that babies as young as 3½ months of age dishabituate, as evidenced by increased looking time, to the impossible event (Baillargeon, 1987a). Slightly older babies even behave as if they are making

quantitative inferences as to the extent of space the box occupies (Baillargeon, 1987b). The evidence from the series of studies is consistent and robust (Baillargeon, Spelke, & Wasserman, 1985; Baillargeon, 1987c; Baillargeon & Graber, 1987); the authors infer that babies indeed know something about the solidity of objects when those objects are not immediately visible. The Baillargeon findings are exciting and the best yet obtained indicating evidence of early object knowledge.

Stage IV search. Infants' performance on the $A\overline{B}$ object concept task variation continues to intrigue developmental researchers, and until very recently, the data were really quite baffling. Piaget's interpretation of the counterintuitive search error was that infants failed to view the hidden object as a separate entity independent of their own actions. He looked to egocentrism as the curtailer of appropriate retrieval, since babies search at the last location associated with their own successful search. However, since the original proposal, Piaget's formulations have been tested by many researchers (for reviews, see Bremner, 1985;

FIGURE 3-9 Illustration of the kind of stimulus displays used by Baillargeon to test infant's knowledge about solidity of objects.

Possible Event

Impossible Event

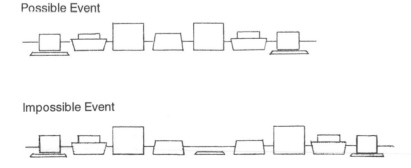

From "Object Permanence in Five-Month-Old Infants" by R. Baillargeon, E. S. Spelke, and S. Wasserman, 1985, *Cognition, 20,* pp. 191–208. Copyright 1984 Canadian Psychological Association. Reprinted with permission.

Harris, 1987; Sophian, 1984; Wellman, Cross, & Bartsch, 1987), and not all the data are consistent with the Piagetian analysis. The outcome—a multitude of alternative interpretations and partial explanations of the phenomenon—is truly confusing.

Immature or inadequate memory mechanisms are often proposed as an alternative explanation for the reliable observance of the $A\bar{B}$ error pattern in infants 8 to 12 months of age (Bjork & Cummings, 1984; Schacter & Moscovitch, 1983; Schacter, Moscovitch, Tulving, McLachlan, & Freedman, 1986). Error is rare when no delay, and thus no memory demand, is interjected between hiding and search, and error is reliable with delays up to 5 seconds (Diamond, 1985). With delays longer than 10 seconds, location choice is random rather than perseverative (Diamond, in press).

But generalized memory failure turns out to be an inadequate explanation also, since, in other contexts, infants can recall information across delay intervals considerably longer than those typically used in $A\bar{B}$ search experiments (Meltzoff, 1988; Rovee-Collier & Hayne, 1987). Moreover, infants do not fail when they are allowed to look at the B location during the delay (Cornell, 1979; Diamond, 1985) or when they can associate a landmark with the correct location (Butterworth, Jarrett, & Hicks, 1982). Task variations tapping similar object inferences with similar delays but with dissimilar response systems also do not yield the prototypic error pattern (Baillargeon & Graber, 1988). Memory failure explanations, like the classical explanation itself, simply cannot account for all the data.

Another explanation comes from work conducted by developmental psychobiologists (Diamond, 1985, 1988a, 1988b, 1990a, 1990b, 1990c, in press; Diamond & Goldman-Rakic, 1985, 1986). It turns out that the $A\bar{B}$ task is much like an object-search task used in animal research, the delay response (DR) task. In the latter version, nonhuman primates observe a food reward being hidden in one of two wells. Both wells are covered and a delay of 0 to 10 seconds is imposed; then the subject is allowed to reach. On DR, unlike $A\bar{B}$, hiding site from A to B is varied randomly; on $A\bar{B}$, the object (which for monkeys is food) is consistently hidden at A until the subject is correct, and then a shift to B is achieved. The important similarities between DR and $A\bar{B}$, however, include the brief memory requirement demanded by the delay between hiding and search. Across trials, the subject must deal with two potentially different pieces of information about hiding site: where the object was previously found on successful trials and where the object was last observed when hidden.

In the animal literature, DR is a reliable indicator of frontal-lobe function. Success is hampered by damage achieved with experimental lesioning, or mechanical and pharmacological intervention, to the *dorsolateral prefrontal cortex*. Moreover, the selective damage is specific only to DR performance, and similar behavioral interruption is not achieved with equivalent damage to other brain regions (i.e., the parietal lobe or the hippocampus; Diamond, in press). A reasonable hypothesis, given similarity of the tasks, is that $A\bar{B}$ performance also depends on the functioning of the prefrontal cortex. A test of that hypothesis could uncover the neurological basis for observed developmental deficiencies on $A\bar{B}$ tasks.

In a series of comparative studies, Adele Diamond and her associates have investigated and compared the performances of normal human and monkey infants and of lesioned adult and infant monkeys on several related search tasks including $A\bar{B}$ and DR (see Diamond, 1988a, 1991, in press for summaries of the research program). The results of the research program are striking. First, the developmental progression on the two tasks for human infants is very similar, with marked improvement occurring between 7½ and 12 months of age—Piaget's Stage IV. Second, infant monkeys make similar progress by 4 months of age—the developmental equivalent. Third, unsuccessful human and monkey infants make similar errors: First, they make the so-called perseverative error on $A\bar{B}$, and, second, they fail DR following a reversal shift (that is, when hiding place is switched following a successful prior trial). Third, while normal adult monkeys easily solve the tasks, those with lesions of the dorsolateral prefrontal cortex behave like unsuccessful infants, producing similar patterns of errors. Only lesions to that specific brain region produce the $A\bar{B}$ error under the same time delays (2–5 seconds) that elicit the error with babies. The prefrontal cortex is clearly implicated in the development of search. But how?

Investigators conjecture, from both behavioral and neurological data, that the prefrontal cortex is involved in the integration of information for purposes of action (Diamond, 1988a, 1991; Fuster, 1980). The DR and $A\bar{B}$ tasks in particular require integration of multiple pieces of information presented over time. The earlier piece is the object's location when last retrieved, while the second later piece is the object's location when last seen. The action is a reach to the present location. Neurological patients who have sustained damage to the frontal cortex have difficulty both with sequential information and with inhibiting a previously executed, reinforced motor response, a prepotent response or habit. On $A\bar{B}$ tasks and on reversal shift trials on DR, the prepotent, previously reinforced response is a reach to the wrong location. If the frontal cortex is not fully functional, as with damage or immaturity, subjects might be hard pressed to inhibit the retrieval habit and they might experience difficulty with the multiple bits of location information.

In support of this reasoning, Diamond (1991) reports that infants sometimes reach to A even *when the object is clearly visible at B.* Other times, they reach to A, *do not even*

search, and then reach to B! Or, they reach to *A while looking at B.* It is as if they "know" the toy is at *B,* as studies that use looking as the dependent measure suggest (Baillargeon & Graber, 1988), but the babies cannot inhibit the motor response of a reach to A. While a problem of inhibitory control of motor behavior is characteristic of damaged patients, it is not reflective of deficits in thinking. Diamond's well-reasoned interpretation (1988a, 1991, in press) is that infant's may well know much more about the location of hidden objects than they can express in their motor behavior.

The frontal cortex matures postnatally. The neurons are generated before birth, but they remain immature. Synaptogenesis continues through the first year (Huttenlocker, 1979), and neuronal density also decreases during that time period. These are two aspects of nervous-system maturation, the blooming-pruning phenomenon introduced in previous chapters. Changes after the first year, in both number of synapses per neuron and neuronal density, are more gradual (Huttenlocher, 1979). Diamond (1991, in press) observed striking age-related regularities across subjects as to the sequencing of object concept attainment, with very little individual variation in development. And the age-boundedness of conceptual attainment coincides very closely with the time frame for neurological maturation. She concluded that attainment exhibits a *facilitative* developmental function (see Chapter 1) primarily constrained by the maturation of the nervous system.

It is noteworthy that, yet again, self-produced locomotion is implicated in the attainment of object permanence (Kermoian & Campos, 1989) and related early indicators of spatial cognition (Acredolo, 1988a). This ubiquitous motor achievement, normally initiated in the second half of the first year of life, may function in an experience-expectant fashion in the acquisition of the object concept.

Stage VI search. The final accomplishment of object permanence is inferring the location of a hidden object following an unobserved transformation. Like the prototypic shell game, an object is covered by one of two or three cups, the cups are transposed, and the searcher must identify the original cover now in a new location. Since the movement of the object is invisible, its current location must be inferred from information about the movement of the cover. In another version of the task, an object is placed in a container, the container is moved to a potential hiding place (for example, behind a screen), and in an invisible transfer, the object is moved from the container to the new hiding place. When the container comes up empty, the new location of the object must again be inferred.

Infants less than 9 to 12 months of age do poorly in both of these tasks; at 9 months their search performance is at chance or below (Harris, 1987). The major source of error is search at the location that would have been correct had no transposition taken place (Sophian, 1984; Wishart & Bower, 1982).

Invisible displacement and transposition tasks are complex; the series of movements can vary as can the amount of perceptual information available about location. Because of this variability, these search tasks do not constitute a single test associated with one definable competence that differentiates the successful from the unsuccessful searcher. Actually, the tasks comprise a set, varying in difficulty, and, accordingly, the age associated with successful performance varies greatly as well, principally as a function of task demands.

When the task is a simple one, babies sometimes do make correct inferences about unseen movements (Sophian, Larkin, & Kadane, 1985). Infants of 9 months of age, for example, can identify the correct container covering an object following transposition if the container is distinctly marked (Bremner, 1978; Goldfield & Dickerson, 1981). The distinctiveness of an occluder functions as a loca-

tion cue that facilitates successful search. On the other hand, the tasks can be made sufficiently challenging (for example, with multiple alternative hiding sites, no perceptual location cues) that errors of inference persist well into the childhood years (Sophian, 1984; Sophian & Sage, 1983).

Memory for location and the ability to keep track of where one has searched is a cognitive competence with a lengthy development history. It may begin in late infancy, but improvement continues throughout childhood (Aadlard, Beatty, & Maki, 1985). In short, inferring movement and location is not an all-or-none accomplishment; the complexity of the unseen transposition as well as a number of other situational and informational factors (Acredolo, 1979; Somerville & Haake, 1983) affect the probability of conducting a successful search and the age of attainment. The Piagetian notion of invisible displacements is simply too global to explain variation in success rates, error types, and other age-related performance patterns (Harris, 1987).

In yet another variation of the task, the subject is moved relative to the hidden object. First, the infant is trained to find an object hidden at one of several locations. Then, on the test trial, the object is hidden at the trained location, and the subject is moved relative to the hiding place. For example, the baby is trained to make a left-right place discrimination, then he is rotated around the display 180 degrees such that the spatial relationship is reversed. Adoption of a **response-learning strategy,** one dependent on an egocentric frame of reference, would yield an incorrect location choice. A **place-learning strategy,** indicative of an **allocentric** frame of reference is the more mature choice (Cornell & Heth, 1979). This task is a lot like those used in animal spatial cognition literature.

Although the research with human infants is not entirely clear, it seems that babies do tend to respond with a response-learning strategy, and a cue-learning strategy as well, prior to approximately 9 months of age (Acredolo, 1978). But with very simple, single-movement transpositions, evidence of place-learning strategy could possibly be elicited earlier (see Landau & Spelke, 1988). However, if babies 9 months and older are provided with landmarks), for example, if the mother remains stationary throughout an assessment session, accuracy of performance improves considerably (Presson & Ihrig, 1982). Harris (1987) concluded that stable landmarks, even those at some distance from the hidden object, allow older infants to keep track of their own movements and correctly infer an object's hiding place. Before 9 months of age, landmarks do not affect behavior unless they are extremely salient and in very close proximity to the hidden object (Acredolo, 1988a).

From 9 to 13 months, less salient landmarks become increasingly functional in facilitating search. In fact, landmarks continue to assist accurate search behavior in toddlers and preschoolers as well (DeLoache, 1984; DeLoache & Brown, 1983; Foreman, Arber, & Savage, 1983). The pattern of development generally applicable to humans is similar to that found for the rat pups observed in the Morris water maze and similar contexts (Castro, Paylor, & Rudy, 1987; Foreman, Arber, & Savage, 1983; Morris, 1981, 1984; Rudy, Stadler-Morris, & Albert, 1987; Sutherland & Dyck, 1984). Recall that delayed maturation of the hippocampus is implicated in the late onset of place-learning in animals (Nadel, 1988). There is recent evidence implicating the hippocampus in place learning in children as well (Mangan, 1992).

Summary

The object concept, knowledge that objects exist and move in space in accord with physical laws independent of the knower, is a landmark accomplishment in spatial cognition. While concept attainment begins very early, indeed

earlier than Piaget originally conjectured, the display of knowledge does remain restricted until well into the second year of life. It does seem that an initial rudimentary object concept elaborates with development. But the Piagetian explanation, which attributes cognitive limitations to pervasive egocentrism, is not supported by the contemporary literature.

Sensorimotor spatial cognition is tapped by "doing" tasks; investigators observe tracking, looking, reaching, and searching. With this emphasis on action, there can be overlap between human development literature and animal research, which also addresses mammalian spatial behavior. While caution is necessary in cross-species, cross-paradigm generalizations, extrapolation from the experimental animal literature to similar processes in children enables insight into developmental mechanisms. The animal literature implicates the involvement of two late-developing brain structures in early spatial cognition. First, immaturity of the prefrontal cortex seems to be responsible for perseverative search during Stage IV; that limitation is overcome by the age of 12 months (Diamond, 1988a; 1991). Second, hippocampal development is implicated in place learning, the use of distal cues to locate invisible objects, achieved in Stages V and VI (Nadel, 1988). In both cases, it is the normal maturation of the structures that constrains spatial behavior.

Biological maturation processes are primarily the result of endogenously regulated mechanisms that are general across normal species members. To the extent experience fuels or enhances those mechanisms, it is probably ubiquitous experience that does so. This analysis predicts that development of a behavioral function so controlled should be fairly uniform in a species; that is, timing and sequence of accomplishment should not exhibit extensive cross-individual, idiosyncratic variation. Indeed cross-subject regularity is the rule for the object concept. The reliability of the original Piagetian observations attests to that, as do Diamond's findings. Individual differences are not a particularly noteworthy aspect of these accomplishments. The development of the object concept most probably exhibits a facilitative function; the experiential facilitator is perceptual activity and, perhaps later, self-produced locomotion.

THE REPRESENTATION OF GEOMETRIC TRANSFORMATIONS

The toddler is knowledgeable about the typical characteristics of objects and about their movements in space. The physical laws that constrain an object's possible movements and paths are sufficiently understood that most of the young child's inferences about the location, position, and trajectory of an object are accurate. And the developmental progression that yields such understanding is relatively uniform across individuals.

The empirical literature on spatial cognition after infancy, subsequent to the attainment of a mature object concept, shows a shift in focus to other geometric phenomena. In particular, developmentalists question how adequately children mentally represent complex geometric relations, for example, relations among sets of objects. There is speculation as to how the mental models of space possessed by children differ in complexity, richness, and function from those of adults. And there are questions about the sorts of mental processes children are able to perpetrate on those models.

The research is an interesting blend of Piagetian traditions and contemporary cognitive psychology. Piaget called attention to what he perceived as qualitative differences between the spatial cognitions of younger and older children and introduced intriguing tasks to highlight those differences (Piaget & Inhelder, 1956, 1971). Cognitive psychologists, in turn, have analyzed the information-processing demands of those tasks to reveal the cognitive mechanisms underlying the performance phenomenon. Following Piaget's lead, the qualitative shift attracting the most attention is the one between the preoperational and the concrete-operational period of development that occurs around age 6 or 7.

Piaget conjectured that the spatial cognitions of preoperational children were limited to static representations. Thus, young children should be unable to perform mental changes on those representations and to accurately estimate what the outcome of a change would produce. Imagine, for example, taking a length of string and winding it into a circle, or lowering a stick from upright to lying down, or viewing a place setting from the opposite side of the table. Such mental manipulations seem effortless to an adult, whatever the cognitive process is that permits us to engage in them, but that is not the case for young children. Piaget proposed that young children's mental "imagery," as he called it, is *static* and *reproductive*. Transformations on images are *kinetic* and *anticipatory*. So, the young child can imagine a scene from a single vantage point that is static, but not from another vantage point, the transformation to which is kinetic and requires anticipation. The child can represent a series of colored blocks in a line in front of him but cannot anticipate how the line would look reflected. Imagining an upright figure is possible; imagining it rotating 45 degrees is not.

Imagined spatial transformations are based on an understanding of **operations,** the class of **internalized actions** that can be applied to mental representations of objects, relations, sets, and collections. Mental action achieves a change of state between one mental representation and its successor. Without the action, the two states are not logically related. Thus, a child might correctly represent a full glass of milk, State 1, and an empty glass of milk, State 2.

The transition between State 1 and State 2 requires a representation of the action of pouring or emptying; that cannot be represented until the structures of concrete operations are achieved. It is as if the mind of the young child is a sequential series of snapshots fueled and simultaneously limited by immediate perceptual experience. The mental snapshots may be quite accurate; preoperational children are perceptually adept. But the mental links are missing. If the child cannot supply a mental link between a snapshot of State 1 and State 2, then she cannot anticipate the appearance of State 2 when she cannot look at it.

For Piaget, the emphasis was on operations. The differentiating cognitive characteristic between young children and their older counterparts is operational thinking, which is absent in the former. Explanations of young children's failure on spatial tasks is attributed primarily to the transformational inadequacy of mental life, although specifically how that manifests itself from task to task varies. There is less concern for the nature, richness, or type of the state representation. This is one place where Piagetians and many cognitive psychologists part company. There may, for example, be important, age-related developmental differences in how spatial features are coded, not just in how those spatial features are changed. The theory acknowledges potential differences in encoding, since young children are presumed to emphasize topological over Euclidean features in their perceptions and representations, and encoding is organized through an egocentric frame of reference. Nonetheless, transformational inadequacies remain paramount in Piagetian explanations for missing geometric competencies.

The Piagetian notion of a mental operation as an internalized action implicates an isomorphism between the cognitive process and the physical action from which the mental counterpart is derived. The actual, physical movement of objects in space is continuous, sequential, and connected. So if an object moves in a line from point A to point B, it must pass through all the points between A and B without the possibility of skipping any. Noncontinuous, disconnected movement would violate the laws of physics. Mental movement should follow the same rule system.

Suppose there is a red and blue ball, connected by a 3-inch bar, lying on a table in front of you. At the start of a hypothetical experiment, the blue ball is on the right. Then, you take hold of the blue ball and physically rotate it counterclockwise in a 180 degree arc around the red ball. The blue ball comes to rest to the left of the red ball. The action just described is physically constrained. The initial and final position of the two balls is constrained and the size of the arc of rotation is constrained by the size of the connecting rod. The blue ball would have continuously passed through all the intermediate points between its initial and final position. Even the speed of the transformation falls within physically defined limits. An isomorphic mental process would be constrained in the same way (recall Shepard and Metzler's mental rotation paradigm described in a previous section).

To assess whether or not an experimental subject actually engages in an analog mental process like this, one needs some external sign that the mental activity honors the constraints. Some options include (1) having the subject predict the final state, (2) having the subject predict the intermediate states, and (3) assessing any match between how the subject imagines a change and the characteristics of the physical change, as with the time it takes to accomplish each. Predictions are externalizable as artifacts. If the artifacts obey the rules of physics, then one infers that indeed the subject engaged in the analog process. Errors are violations of those rules and imply some inadequacy in the mental process. Developmentalists employ logic like this when examining aspects of age-related spatial thinking in children. While many tasks might be designed for this purpose, most studies are done with two of the most popular: visual perspective taking and mental rotation.

Visual Perspective Taking

After the appearance of Piaget and Inhelder's (1956) major work on spatial knowledge in children, numerous investigators sought to check the robustness of the original findings and to test the validity of the theoretical interpretations. A frequent target of empirical scrutiny is children's knowledge about visual perspective, their ability to anticipate the geometry of another's view. In the classic studies, subjects were shown a miniature model landscape with three distinctly marked mountains. The task entailed viewing the three mountains from a single vantage point and predicting how the arrangement would appear from other vantage points. Typically, a puppet, playing the role of "other," sits at some position around the scene and the subject must describe how the puppet sees the landscape.

One obvious difficulty is the anomaly between the spatial relations as directly perceived and the ones that must be computed. Correct solution demands, first, that the subject not be seduced by his own view, and second, that he engage in some sort of mental transformation, most likely one where he imagines himself transported to the position occupied by other (Huttenlocher & Presson, 1973). Since mental transformations are presumed to be difficult for young children, and since their ability to code geometric relations is also limited, theory predicts their failure on the three-mountain task.

Indeed, that is what happens. Children under 8 or 9 years of age invariably fail the classic version of the task. Not only do they fail, but, counterintuitively, they seem to treat their view and that of the other as equivalent. Thus,

if asked to build the view as the other sees it, describe the other's view, or select the other's view from a set of alternatives, they identify their own. Piaget described these errors as *egocentric.* The proportion of errors of this type decreases with age, as correctly selecting the other's actual view increases with age. In the Piagetian interpretation, response patterns reflect young children's dependence on a body-centered, relative representation of space rather than on an abstract, geocentric one (Presson & Somerville, 1985). The timing of the transition in mental representations of space coincides with the attainment of concrete operations.

Practical egocentrism, which affects doing in space, is overcome when the toddler emerges from infancy, but the child faces the challenge again in early childhood. **Conceptual egocentrism,** which affects thinking about space, is not reovercome until middle childhood. But do children really think everyone sees what they do? A toddler, looking at a book, will turn it appropriately to show another viewer a picture. The 3-year-old will actively direct her mother's line of sight to a target. The 4-year-old knows you can still see her even when she closes her eyes. Are these phenomena consistent with pervasive egocentrism?

Two decades of research have shown us that, in fact, the development picture is more complex. To some extent, Piaget's observations have been reiterated (Coie, Costanzo, & Farnill, 1973; Dodwell, 1963; Flavell, Botkin, Fry, Wright, & Jarvis, 1968; Fishbein, Lewis, & Keiffer, 1972; Laurendeau & Pinard, 1970), but other evidence does not fit the original formulations. Even very young children do not always fail perspective-taking tasks (Borke, 1975; Horan & Rosser, 1983; Liben, 1978; Masangkay et al., 1974). And sometimes tasks will precipitate failure even in children of formal-operational age (Cox, 1978; Laurendeau & Pinard, 1970). Taking all the results into account, the transition from an immature, egocentric orientation to a mature, decentered one extends down to 2½ years of age and up to 12 years of age (Rosser, 1983). Clearly, the research and conjecture about the nature of the transition spawned by it beg some alternative interpretation (Huttenlocher & Presson, 1973; Presson, 1980).

Findings in the empirical literature have raised widespread criticism about egocentrism as a satisfactory explanation for limitations in young children's spatial knowledge (Cox, 1980; Ford, 1979; Rosser, 1983). It seems that information and task variables constrain children's performance, not just developmental variables. When information demands are reduced or simplified, greater degrees of competence surface. Even 2- and 3-year-olds show implicit if fragile knowledge of another's view (Flavell, Everett, Croft, & Flavell, 1981; Lempers, Flavell, & Flavell, 1977). Sit across from a 3-year-old with a doll between you, and the child can infer that if she is looking at the front of the doll, you must be looking at the back. What complicates these tasks is not confusion about the line of sight of self and other but the computation of geometric relations for another's line of sight.

It turns out that children younger than 6 or 7 can only solve a limited kind of perspective-taking problems (Rosser, Chandler, & Lane, in press). They can, as exemplified, predict another's line of sight, but such tasks typically challenge children with geometrically simple stimuli, most often single objects. Going back to the red and blue ball connected by the rod, a child sitting opposite you cannot infer that if the red ball is on the right for her, it is on the left for you. She may know that you and she do not see the balls the same way, but it is very unlikely she can compute the exact nature of that difference. On line-of-sight problems, young children are not egocentric; on more complex computation problems, they might appear that way.

Young children also reliably exhibit knowledge of perspective within a surprise paradigm (Shantz & Watson, 1970). Here, the expectation that as subjects change position, they will observe different views is violated by experimental trickery, and indeed they are surprised at seeing the same view from multiple locations. Youngsters also succeed on rotation-response tasks (Borke, 1975; Horan & Rosser, 1983; Rosser, 1983; Rosser, Ensing, Mazzeo, & Horan, 1986). With this variation, children indicate what another sees by turning a Lazy-Susan-type apparatus holding a model of the stimulus display. They turn it and show an experimenter the other's view. Why do young children do well on these tasks while failing traditional ones?

To answer that question, we need to consider the nature of the child's mental representation of the original scene. Any scene that contains multiple objects can be described two ways (Bialystok & Vallance, 1989). The first description depicts the relation between viewers and the scene as a whole, probably in terms of the viewer and a single, salient constituent of the scene (Bialystok, 1989). The second description assigns the relations among the scene's components and structures the geometry of the scene itself. Children may differ developmentally as to how well they can represent both descriptions. Success on the classic Piagetian version of the task depends on both descriptions—the first to correctly reorient the scene and the second to compute the change in geometric structure that corresponds with the reorientation. Successful solution of a line-of-sight or of a rotation-response perspective problem does not require representation of the second description. On simple line-of-sight tasks, there is no geometry to structure; on rotation-response tasks, the response device holds the internal scene's geometry constant, so the child can ignore it (Rosser, Ensing, Mazzeo, & Horan, 1986).

In the first description, the salient constituent of the scene, which turns out to be the object physically closest to the other viewer (Bialystok & Vallance, 1989), is a sort of

landmark. Landmarks serve as points of reference for children, helping them organize representations of space (Lynch, 1960; Huttenlocher & Newcombe, 1984; Presson, 1987; Presson & Montello, 1988). Studies show that young children, even infants, successfully use landmarks to solve spatial problems, including some perspective problems (Acredolo, 1985; 1988; Acredolo & Evans, 1980; Rieser, 1979), just as rats do in a water maze.

One way to use a landmark on a three-mountain-type problem is through recourse to the first description: to look at the object closest to other and reposition it closest to self. If the child has been asked only to identify that object or to reposition it with a rotation-response device, then he will succeed and will look geometrically mature. Hence we observe early competence on tasks of that type (Rosser, 1983) regardless of the complexity of the internal geometry of the scene itself (Rosser, Ensing, Mazzeo, & Horan, 1986). But because of inadequate representation of the second description, success with repositioning the landmark piece is not followed by a correct restructuring of the remainder of the scene (Rosser, Chandler, & Lane, in press). Thus, in perspective-taking ability we observe **decalage,** differential success across tasks that were presumed to tap the same underlying cognitive mechanisms.

Landmark representations do not necessarily indicate a mature ability to mentally model geometric space in a Euclidean sense. Landmark codes could work within a general relative geometry for space (recall O'Keefe & Nadel, 1978). In a relative geometry, the coding of distance, proximity, and so forth need not be metric (Newcombe, 1988). In fact, young children could solve some perspective problems, those amenable to landmark coding, while still at a level of representing space ordinally. It remains to be seen whether the success of older children on more complex perspective-taking tasks is due to an overall shift in strategy and a shift in the underlying geometry—from landmark to computational, ordinal to an interval metric.

Mental Rotation

A task related to visual perspective taking but originating in cognitive rather than in developmental psychology, is the mental-rotation task (Shepard & Cooper, 1986). The mental-rotation paradigm and the prototypic findings associated with it were described earlier in the chapter. The cognitive process hypothesized to underlie performance is transformational and analog, and it is enough like the Piagetian construct of **anticipatory kinetic imagery** to have led developmental investigators to "borrow" the task. The developmental hypothesis is that if the mental rotation process is equated with related aspects of operational thought, and if the Piagetian analysis is correct, then young children should experience difficulty solving mental-rotation problems. In addition, the transition to competence should coincide with the emergence of concrete operational thinking. Piagetian-inspired observations of developmental progress on mental-rotation-type tasks lead to just that conclusion (Dean, 1976; Piaget & Inhelder, 1971).

Gloria Marmor (1975, 1977) was the first investigator to extend Shepard's paradigm to developmental study. She used a format much like the original and RT as the dependent measure. Her stimuli were pictures of teddy bears with one raised paw. Children were shown an upright teddy (the standard stimulus) and a second one (the test stimulus) rotated up to 180 degrees from the upright position. The task, adapted from Shepard's prototype, was to determine whether the standard and test stimulus bears had the same paw raised. Subjects were usually correct. The important finding was for RT: It increased linearly with the degree of angular disparity between the stimuli. Children as young as 5 produced adultlike data. Indeed, as Marmor computed it, the rate of mental rotation for children (60°/sec) was virtually identical to the adult rate. The implication is that if young children and adults produce data of a similar nature, then the psychological process responsible for the data must be the same. Marmor made the case that anticipatory kinetic imagery did not follow the developmental path suggested by Piaget; it is available to children of preoperational age, and it is not related to other, nonimaginal indices of operational thought.

Marmor's findings inspired controversy and attempts at replication; her procedures were extended for further child study (Childs & Polich, 1979; Dean & Harvey, 1979; Dean & Scherzer, 1982; Dean, Duhe, & Green, 1983; Kail, 1985, 1987; Kail, Pellegrino, & Carter, 1981). No one has achieved data as definitive as Marmor's with children as young. Most adultlike data are produced by children in third grade or older. Too frequently, young children are not sufficiently accurate in their judgments of whether the two stimuli match. They guess and RT for guessing is not interpretable. Analysis of solution time must be replaced by analysis of development trends in accuracy rates (Rosser, Ensing, & Mazzeo, 1985; Rosser, Ensing, Glider, & Lane, 1984).

In general, what we observe in the mental-rotation literature is decalage and a lengthy period of transition to competence. Under some circumstances, successful performance is achieved by very young children (Rosser, Ensing, Glider, & Lane, 1984), just as Marmor demonstrated. Other times, the task is difficult enough to delay success into late childhood (Rosser & Lane, 1987). And again, as with perspective taking, informational variables influence performance. While complexity of stimuli is not implicated as a source of variation in adult performance (Cooper & Podgorny, 1976), it is in child performance (Rosser, Stevens, Glider, Mazzeo, & Lane,

1989). As stimulus complexity increases, or as those stimuli become more abstract, accuracy in anticipating how rotated stimuli should look decreases. Rate of mental rotation is affected, too. Longer latencies are associated with complex, unfamiliar stimuli.

Children's ability to represent geometric relations is again implicated in relative task difficulty (Bialystok, 1989; Winestok & Bialystok, 1989). Apparently, children encounter problems coding the structure of a geometrically complex stimulus and maintaining coded relations across a rotation transformation. They may successfully encode and maintain a salient constituent of a stimulus, but not the whole thing. Stimuli that provide clear, salient features strongly cueing orientation elicit early competence; other kinds do not (Rosser et al., 1989). Marmor's teddy bears, with the strong cue of a raised paw, provided a salient constituent. Is such a cue a kind of landmark?

Summary

Traditional Piagetian explanations cannot fully account for the developmental findings associated with mental rotation and visual perspective-taking phenomena. Neither pervasive egocentrism nor a generalized incapacity to mentally model spatial transformations are necessarily characteristic of the young child. Display of these representational spatial skills seems to be a gradual accomplishment, not an abrupt one. Elaboration and generalization of initial competence spans the time period from late infancy to late childhood and probably beyond. Conceptualization of that elaboration as a qualitative developmental shift in ability is discordant with the evidence. The restrictions on the display of competence are not developmental in a strictly maturational sense. Rather, performance is constrained by informational variables. What we observe is change in the individual's ability to encode, represent, and mentally manipulate greater and greater amounts of geometric information. The capacity to represent landmark relations emerges early in childhood. Problems, which depend for their solution on landmark representation only, are solvable early as well.

If decalage and protracted developmental transitions are characteristic of perspective taking and mental-rotation ability, so, too, are individual differences. That is what makes tasks of this type interesting to psychometricians. Differences in aptitude are age related and gender related; some individuals are very good at these tasks and others are quite abysmal. This suggests that attainment of proficiency in the imaginal representation of transformations is not like the attainment of the object concept. Every normal individual achieves object knowledge; not everyone can efficiently engage in mental rotation equally. The developmental sequence for object concept knowledge is fairly uniform across individuals; the sequence for knowledge of transformational representations is less so. We may come to find that the developmental functions explaining this knowledge acquisition and the neurological mechanisms underlying knowledge acquisition are different too.

CONCLUSION

Spatial cognition is sometimes considered a semi-independent module of thought, as a vertical faculty with its own ontogenetic history and a unique neurological basis. The developmental evidence suggests, however, that spatial cognition itself is not a unitary cognitive entity. Some achievements, like object permanence, emerge early in life and show great uniformity across individuals as to level, timing, and the sequence of conceptual attainment. Others emerge late, and individual variation is the rule. Perhaps we are seeing the development of two different components of knowledge. One is a species-uniform achievement, constrained by biology and maturational in evolution. The second is a spatial aptitude whose attainment and developmental origins are variable across members of the species. While it is not always clear which of our tasks tap which component, it is clear that we are dealing with multiple components.

The intellectual history of spatial knowledge is long and rich. Multiple philosophical views on the subject have given rise to multiple theoretical perspectives to guide empirical inquiry. Multiple conceptual views generate multiple research traditions which in turn yield multiple developmental stories. The traditions most important for understanding spatial cognition, each making a unique contribution, are developmental neuroscience and developmental and cognitive psychology. The developmental evidence reveals age-related changes in spatial knowledge and possible shifts in the underlying geometry that organizes spatial representation. From neuroscience, we learn of the brain structures forming the neural substrate of spatial functioning. And cognitive psychologists provide us with hypothetical models describing the processing of spatial information.

This is the most likely developmental story: Babies, who begin life with impressive perceptual abilities that further elaborate very early in infancy, soon begin to display formidable knowledge about their spatial environments. Most recent evidence implicates early comprehension of the physical laws that govern the action and movement of objects in space (see Chapter 6 for more on this). Peculiarities and limitations in infants' spatial functioning are explainable by the neurological constraints imposed by late-maturing brain structures, specifically the frontal cortex and the hippocampus. By age 2, however, much of that is overcome; and as the toddler ventures forth into her spatial environment, she proficiently locates herself in space, locates her toys and caretakers, and does not get too lost in familiar environments.

In early childhood and probably beyond, mental models of space are most likely organized around ordinal representations. The underlying geometry is cruder and relative as compared to a Euclidean form, but coding scenes on the basis of relations among landmarks and the self still permits effective search, way-finding, navigation, route establishment, and even mental rotation and perspective taking in some contexts. Refinement of ordinal representations permits greater accuracy of geometric performance and increases in accuracy are age related. Thus, as children move into middle and late childhood, they become increasingly adept at spatial and geometric problem solving.

But the course of spatial cognitive development after toddlerhood is more variable than in infancy. Developmental sequences are protracted and much individual variation is observed. Variability even extends to the ultimate level of expertise achieved. If biology and maturation shape the form and establish the nature of early spatial development, and the role of experience is limited to a facilitative one, it is not clear how experience and biology interact in later spatial development. That mystery awaits further study.

CHAPTER 4

CLASSES, CATEGORIES, AND SCALES: TRADITIONAL VIEWS OF CONCEPTUAL DEVELOPMENT

INTRODUCTION

Human beings are organizers. They use their substantial cognitive powers to order and structure surrounding reality. That reality offers up a vast array of entities: artifacts, animals, plants, people, events, and so forth. Each entity appears in various locations and contexts and may come in multiple sizes, shapes, and colors. For example, the balls we play with come in numerous colors and sizes, from ping-pong balls—small, white, and light—to tennis balls—larger, fluorescent green, and fuzzy—to basketballs—larger still—to multicolored beachballs to footballs, which are not even spherical. Within this concrete, and unambiguous category, the individuals vary immensely; yet, virtually any adult will recognize the objects as members of a class sharing common properties.

Knowledge of class membership implies knowledge of common features (roundness), about shared physical properties (balls roll), and about appropriate actions toward category exemplars (balls are for throwing, bouncing, etc.). The adult need not have encountered a particular ball before to know something of its properties, its features, and generally what is done with it; those properties and features are specified by class membership.

Additionally, the category of balls has a place in a larger network of categories. The described group of balls belongs in two other categories: round things and recreational artifacts. The balls fit in a group, the group fits within a network of groups, and the order achieved with grouping specifies the place and function of any particular artifact in the reality of the orderer. No object assignable to a category within a network of categories is truly a novel object with unknown properties, because categorization allows us to make the unfamiliar familiar.

What if this were not so? What kind of world would confront the naive person unable to categorize and order experience? First, every entity would be unique and, if not specifically encountered before, novel as well. Given the sheer number of entities in the world, it would place a tremendous strain on the information-processing system to remember all those individuals. Second, the properties of each newly encountered object would have to be newly discovered. Prior knowledge about "objects of that sort" could not be called upon, which would put another strain on the information-processing system. Third, without prior knowledge about like objects, no particular set of actions toward the object is suggested. In short, this world would be immensely complicated, varied, diverse, unknown, and most likely overwhelming, unmanageable, and perhaps even unknowable. So, the ability to organize phenomena, to form categories and concepts, must be a very basic cognitive ability (Bruner, Goodnow, & Austin, 1956; Mandler, 1983; Markman, 1989). But what of children? Is the young child like a naive person?

The capacity to bring organization and order to the universe is truly fundamental because of the role this intellectual capacity plays in the formation of concepts. Conceptual knowledge forms the scaffolding around which meaningful models of reality are constructed. Concepts are the core of meaning, and the meaning of things is the heart of mental representation. Because of their central place in knowledge acquisition, what concepts are, how they are instantiated psychologically, and how they arise developmentally are basic issues that must be addressed in any comprehensive account of cognition. Indeed, conceptual development has figured prominently in all major developmental theories (Carey, 1985, 1988; Inhelder & Piaget, 1964; Keil, 1981, 1989, 1991; Markman, 1989; Vygotsky, 1986; Werner, 1948).

However, the developmental focus is only one part of an ongoing intellectual enterprise: the broader examination of what concepts are and how they figure in knowledge acquisition

(Lakoff, 1987; Murphy & Medin, 1985). Those concerned with epistemology and with the evolution of knowledge systems have grappled with the nature of concepts and their relation to the rest of cognition (Jackendoff, 1989; Langely, Simon, Bradshaw, & Zytkow, 1987; Nersessian, in press; Quine, 1960, 1977, 1981; Schwartz, 1977), and our understanding of conceptual phenomena has evolved as a result of the discourse. Developmental inquiry has been affected by this discourse, too. As our visions of concepts have changed, so have developmental conceptualizations.

Developmental explanations of conceptual development divide into two types: (1) traditional attempts that take their impetus from classical views of concepts and (2) contemporary reformulations (see Keil, 1991) that reflect a changing vision of the very nature of conceptual knowledge itself. In this chapter, the traditional view is presented and evaluated, along with accompanying empirical research. We will see which questions about conceptual development were addressed and answered by the inquiry spurred by this perspective, and we will discover which questions remained.

CATEGORIES AND COGNITION

All developmental theories must deal with the fact that adults are more knowledgeable than children. Children have had fewer encounters with the world and less time to have ordered those encounters and reflected upon them. In most ways, the adult is the expert and the child is the novice. Children are dubbed "universal novices" to capture the extent of their naiveté (Brown & DeLoache, 1978). Certainly, one important aspect of cognitive development is the accumulation of knowledge and facts, a process enabling the shift from novice to expert (Chi, Glaser, & Rees, 1982). But knowledge and facts are not simply accumulated in the same way papers are piled in a box. To be cognitively useful, knowledge and facts must be organized into systematically accessible files.

Every knowledge domain is complexly structured. The structure organizes the domain-relevant categories and specifies relations among those categories. One consequence of organizing knowledge on a categorical basis is the simplification of experience because, when objects or events are grouped in the same category, they can be treated equivalently. People's category judgments, however, tell us more than just how they sort things; category judgments implicate conceptual knowledge. Concepts are the *mental representations* that support cognitive activities such as categorizing, classifying, and scaling. Thus, when a child classifies a hippopotamus into the "mammal" category, we infer that the child has a concept of "mammal." The conceptual knowledge further enables the child to extend the characteristics associated with mammals to this particular instance. So the child who learns the hippopotamus is a mammal can surmise that the creature is warm-blooded, grows its babies in its tummy, and suckles its young. Children's ability to categorize reveals the nature and extent of their conceptual knowledge. The knowledge may be *intuitive,* because the child probably lacks the appropriate verbal label for the category and surely lacks a dictionary like definition of the concept, but the conceptual knowledge need not be unsophisticated.

In the desert Southwest, children must learn to discriminate pet dogs from wild coyotes. In physical features, a coyote resembles a small German Shepherd. So, in many ways, coyotes look like dogs, act like dogs, and are found roaming the neighborhood like dogs. Most desert-reared children learn to make the discrimination before the age of 3 on the basis of some not so obvious characteristics. Perhaps they know that the conceptual classification "dogs" divides into subclasses (pet dogs and wild dogs). Children behave differently toward exemplars of each class; they recognize

common features across subclasses (four legs and fur) and distinguish the differences (friendly or not friendly). Just to confuse the issue, however, dogs and coyotes do not always make the same distinction humans do. There are coyote-dog mixed breeds, or "Border Shepherds," ambiguous exemplars serving to remind us that the boundaries between categories are not always clear.

Less obvious, but implicated in the coyote instance, categories are organized into hierarchies, into **taxonomies** of nested class-inclusion relations (Markman, 1989). These hierarchies map relations among concepts (for example, coyote—canine—mammal—animal). The relations and connections enrich reality and provide more information than is available in a single encounter or context. Children who have organized their knowledge of the "coyote" concept into a "mammal" taxonomic system can deduce that a coyote, like a hippopotamus, breathes, eats, and can have babies, and that it does not have feathers or lay eggs. Knowledgeable children can make the claim without having personally observed a coyote doing any of those things. Hierarchical organization supports inference; inference results from knowledge beyond what is given in the immediate context. So, categorization simultaneously simplifies and enriches reality.

Categories and concepts are associated with words. Objects within the same category are labeled with the same name. Some categories are identifiable with single words, like *rabbit* or *rat*. Others, like "white furry objects," require multiword tags. The close correspondence between labels and categories highlights a correspondence between category acquisition and label learning. Learning to attach a label to some referent could facilitate subsequent learning about the referent's features. Children may only come to differentiate dogs from coyotes, for example, upon acquiring a verbal symbol for the second group. However, it could be the other way around. The child's basic categorical structure might enable acquiring a label. It is not clear how children could ever acquire category words without some conceptual framework to impose on empirical data (Markman, 1989; Quine, 1960).

Upon hearing the label *coyote* in the presence of an animal, how does the naive child determine that the word refers to the whole animal and not to some part of it, some aspect of its behavior and appearance, or some unique feature of the context at the time the label is applied? As research suggests, children's acquisition of new words is constrained by categorical taxonomies (Markman & Hutchinson, 1984). More about this in Chapter 9.

To summarize, the acquisition of categorical knowledge enables simplification of the many encounters with objects, things, and events; the knowledge also enriches a single encounter by supporting generalization of information from previous encounters. And, categorical knowledge is intertwined with learning the meaning of words. These facts about the cognitive functions of categories underscores the deeper connection between conceptual development and meaning. Categories come from concepts which in turn are bound up with a basic understanding of the objects and events making up the world. Systems of categorizing are associated with even more elaborate and molar aspects of knowledge, with **naive theories** about how things work (Keil, 1991; Markman, 1989; Wellman & Gelman, 1988). Naive theories (see Chapters 6 and 7) represent attempts to provide coherent cognitive structures for entire sets of concepts.

The complex interrelationship between categories, concepts, semantics (i.e., meaning), and facsimiles of theories raises provocative questions about the acquisition of knowledge in general and about cognitive development in particular. First, Where does such knowledge come from? Is concept formation data driven, built up from the facts of experience? Or, alternatively, is the generation of classes, categories, concepts, and scales theory driven?

Second, How does the organization of knowledge change with maturation? Does it elaborate? Differentiate? Accumulate? Or transform? Those are questions central to explanations of conceptual development. But, first, we must examine some aspects of the phenomenon to be explained: children's categorical and classification performances.

Age-Related Changes in Children's Categories

Given the sheer diversity in the environment confronting us, it is surprising how much uniformity there is in how people classify things. The world dishes up an infinite number of discriminately different stimuli, but the categories people create are a small subset of the possible ways those stimuli could be partitioned. Everyone's experience is unique, but the categories are not. We make very similar discriminations among objects and events, so much so that erroneous classifications are rare. No adult, for example, would misclassify a blue jay as an artifact, judge a tarantula to be a plant, fail to understand the difference between a living shrub and a plastic one, or infer that a child's stuffed raccoon has a heart. Variability among the stimuli to be classified does not correspond to variability in the classification systems humans generate.

Naturally occurring objects and fabricated artifacts present a huge array of features, perceptual and functional, obvious and nonobvious. Judgments about the category membership of objects must depend on reference to those features, but precisely how features affect grouping decisions is not clear. Since complex objects have multiple features and since features must somehow figure in classification decisions, then the number of different ways in which objects might be grouped is indeterminate. Animals, for example, could be variously classified by size, color, or whether or not they have legs, tails, or some other characteristic. On one basis, the presence of legs, snakes and fish are alike; on another basis, the presence of gills, they are different. On purely logical grounds, multifeatured stimuli are classifiable in multiple, alternative systems. Actually, people's classification schemes are more restricted than logic alone predicts.

The restriction of alternative classification systems is unlikely to be a posteriori, imposed solely by the characteristics of the stimuli themselves. Gills would be no more important than legs in grouping animals unless, by some other extra-stimulus criteria, gills take precedence. No one system of grouping can emerge as *the* appropriate system unless alternative systems are ruled out a priori. To achieve a restricted set of outcomes from an unrestricted set of possibilities, the categorization process must be constrained. The uniformity we observe among individuals performing classification tasks, even among children, suggests that constraints operate on classification judgments (Markman, 1989). For cognitive capacity to be constrained in both children and adults, consistency in performance across age is a necessary condition. The action of constraints produces developmental *continuity*. And evidence of such continuity is apparent for categorization and classification.

Adults, older children, very young children, and infants partition objects and events into groups. The capacity is detectable even in the behavior of very young infants (Bornstein, 1984). The established perceptual competence of infants (see Chapter 2) attests to their ability to organize and group stimuli on the basis of perceptual and even conceptual features. In studies of object perception, for example, dishabituation denotes the detection of differences among stimuli; failure to dishabituate implies detection of similarities. Differential responding, correlated with an object's features, is analogous to rudimentary categorization. Such evidence of early competence fuels arguments for the biological basis of these developmentally early forms of categorization.

However, experience also has a role to play. Children will not acquire a particular category (e.g., coyote) without exposure to exemplars of that category. Experience with category exemplars influences category acquisition, even if cumulative experience underdetermines the mature knowledge structure.

Continuity aside, conceptual knowledge is also developmental. The ways in which stimuli are grouped, ordered, and differentiated reveal systematic, age-related change (Bruner, Olver, & Greenfield, 1966; Inhelder & Piaget, 1964; Smith & Kemler, 1977; Vygotsky, 1962). There are numerous ways in which categorization can change. Many investigators have observed that the partitioning rules characteristic of young children are more apt to make reference to concrete perceptual features (Flavell, 1963, 1985). The differential *salience* of perceptual features, their "standout-ness," is age related, too (Odom, 1978). Shape and color, for example, are salient earlier in development than are height and width. Another example of a difference in classification between the mature and the immature is that, for younger children, judgments of "likeness," even with reference to perceptual characteristics, result from the global similarity of objects rather than from a feature-by-feature correspondence (Kemler, 1982, 1983; Smith, 1979, 1985).

Then, again, decision rules differ in stability. Young children switch partitioning criteria during classification more often than older children (Inhelder & Piaget, 1964); the former "change their minds" in the middle of a sorting task and shift their groupings idiosyncratically. Also apparently, younger children have a lesser tendency to organize stimuli around taxonomic categories (Mandler, 1983; Markman, 1989), preferring thematic ones instead (Inhelder & Piaget, 1964; Nelson, 1973, 1979). So, *saddle* and *horse,* which go together thematically, is a more likely combination for a young child than is *horse* and *rabbit,* which has a taxonomic association (Fenson, Vella, & Kennedy, 1989).

Children change developmentally in the subtlety of the distinctions they learn to make among stimuli. With increasing age, finer and finer discriminations become possible, yielding greater differentiation among objects and classes (Gibson, 1969). Essentially, children make finer and finer slices out of experience, as they gain maturity. The "child" category of *horse* might at first include horses, goats, cows, pigs, and other large farm animals. Then, over time, those additional distinctions are made and less inclusive categories result.

Developmental changes in the discriminability of stimuli yield changes in the sheer number of categories the child can represent. But in complementary fashion, children acquire the ability to see increasingly subtle similarities, which results in the collapse of previous distinctions. Dachshunds and Rottweilers are both dogs, whales and elephants are mammals, and motorcycles and dumptrucks are vehicles. Yet another kind of change in categorization occurs as the child extends a category to encompass additional, unusual exemplars; extending the category of *bird* to include penguins, roadrunners, and ostriches is an example. In sum, the number, exclusiveness, and inclusiveness of categories changes with age.

As categories expand and refine and the decision rules for classifying entities change, so does the organization among categories—the network in which the classes are embedded. When the child learns to partition cows and horses, not only does she create two basic classes where there was only one; she also changes the organization of knowledge. A higher level concept functions as a superordinate category. With increasing knowledge, the *horse* category can undergo further differentiation, into Arabians, quarterhorses, and thoroughbreds—subordinate categories. This elaborated system, depicted in Figure 4-1, is organized as multiple levels of related classes. Evidence suggests that the basic-level categories (horse, cow) are learned first (Horton &

FIGURE 4-1 Categories are organized into networks of subordinate and superordinate classes. Multiple levels of related classes are possible, although basic-level categories seem to be acquired first.

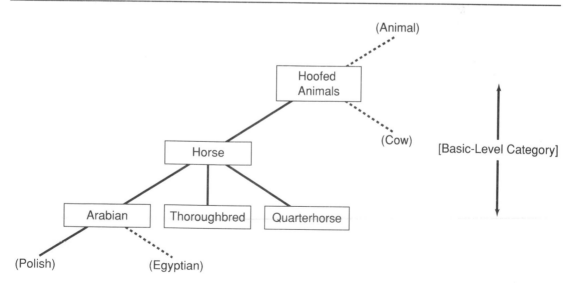

Markman, 1980; Rosch, Mervis, Gray, Johnson, & Boyes-Braem, 1976), refinements are made downward to subordinate classes (Arabians, thoroughbreds), and abstraction upward to superordinate classes (hoofed animals) comes later.

Explaining the Phenomenon

With most developmental achievements, there is evidence of both behavioral constancies, similarities in performance regardless of age, and of variability, age-associated differences in performance. This is true for the development of categorization and classification skills just as it is for many other cognitive phenomena. There is age-related variability in conceptual behavior, but the variability is constrained because people of all ages slice up the world in distinct ways. A comprehensive theory of conceptual development must account for age differences *and* for the similarities across age.

Adequate theory also must explain the fact that, with the accumulation of knowledge and the proliferation of categories, conceptual knowledge must undergo reorganization. The reorganization may reflect a quantitative change wherein the distinctions among classes are altered, different relations among those classes emerge, and additional inferences are supported. The structure grows like a tree, adding branches and boughs, into an increasingly complex pattern. However, the original tree trunk and the foundation branches, like core concepts, do not change as the foliage increases in density. Developmental change in categorical organization may also reflect qualitative reorganization: alteration at the level of core concepts as well as in the quantity and diversity of relations among concepts. In the tree analogy, the trunk itself would be transformed into a different kind of structure.

The nature of conceptual change is theoretically important. By implication, with qualitative change children and adults differ in the way they organize reality. Quantitative change, on the other hand, implies no such thing. It allows for developmental change, but the conceptual organization of children and adults need not be fundamentally different. We have encountered this discrepancy before; it is one of the issues basic to all development theories (Chapter 1).

Theories of conceptual development provide descriptions of what a child's categorical knowledge is like at various ages and how it is manifested in behavior. Behaviors such as the free classification of objects; the acquisition, application, and extension of object labels; inference about an object's properties; and the scaling of objects along quantitative dimensions reveal the status of conceptual knowledge. Theories of conceptual development also present hypotheses about how concepts are defined and how classification decision rules are formulated. From those hypotheses, behavior patterns and age-related changes in those patterns are predicted and tested.

Developmental theories provide explanations for how conceptual knowledge originates and evolves. Since the empirical facts are usually too incomplete and ambiguous to yield a solely data-generated picture of children's conceptual knowledge and change in that knowledge, theory fills in the gaps with an elaborated framework. The theoretical framework is also a knowledge system serving to direct empirical inquiry and the accumulation of more facts, facts that will in turn effect change in the framework itself. Perhaps, in some ways, the psychologist's task—building theories of conceptual development—parallels the child's task—building conceptual knowledge in the first place.

Theories, concepts, categories, and facts about phenomena are all cognitively interconnected. This principle holds for the scientist who operates from some theoretical base, collects data (facts), organizes the data and interprets them with the aid of theoretical constructs (concepts), and compiles a story to explain the interpreted facts (theory again). Adults who are not scientists function similarly, if less formally. Even children could be quasi-scientists. However, they will differ in functioning from the adult and the scientist to the extent that:

1. They lack an initial theory to direct fact-gathering.
2. They are deficient in fact-finding skills.
3. They lack constructs for organizing the facts they do acquire.

Developmental explanations diverge as to how young children are depicted in their role as potential intuitive scientists—discovering, organizing, categorizing, classifying, and integrating entities in the world.

TRADITIONAL VIEWS OF CONCEPTUAL DEVELOPMENT

In traditional approaches to conceptual development—perspectives associated with Piaget, Vygotsky, and Werner, for example—young children are presented as deficient in the capacity to impose categorical order on experience. One reason commonly proposed is that the young are primarily attuned to the perceptual characteristics of stimuli, and perception alone inadequately informs about the conceptual rules behind categories (Spelke, 1991). Things can look very different, for example, bicycles and rowboats, and still serve the same function and fit in the same category. Then again, things can look much alike, such as chicken eggs and ping-pong balls, and be conceptually far removed. The individual relying on the way things look must be oblivious to these sorts of distinctions and not so obvious similarities. If such an individual has access to classification rules, those rules must make reference to perceptual features and then the ability to categorize must be limited to percep-

tible dimensions. That is one point shared by traditional theoretical conceptions.

A second shared point is that the transition from an immature (perceptually based) to a mature (conceptually based) manner of categorizing entities in the world must involve a qualitative shift. At some point, the child has to adopt a very different system for organizing stimuli, a system that goes beyond appearances and the perceptually obvious. And the change has to be qualitative because it is not clear (perhaps it is even impossible) how a conceptual system could emerge from a perceptual one as a function of quantitative elaboration. Finer and finer perceptual discriminations, for instance, do not give rise to conceptual classification rules. One could perceptually compare a bicycle to a rowboat minute detail by minute detail and never arrive at a rule that puts them in the same class. Thus, it follows logically: If the young child is, first, a "perceptual classifier" and, second, a "conceptual classifier," a developmental transition of a qualitative nature must link the two states.

There are some less obvious consequences of this theoretical stance as well. First, we tend to think of perception as an *obligatory,* automatic process in cognition—one that we do not summon up deliberately nor one over which we exercise much cognitive control. It follows that a perceptually bound classifier will do so implicitly and not have explicit knowledge of the classification rule adopted.[1] Second, perception is *subjective*. How things look depends on the particular context one is in, the particular viewing circumstance, one's position, and so forth. And that is phenomenal. So, perception-based categories will change as phenomenal appearances change, and defining characteristics will not transcend the immediate circumstances. The category system of the perceptually bound classifier will, therefore, have little stability, and the classifier is going to look a lot less objective than his more mature counterpart. In sum, the traditional perspectives do not yield a picture of the young child as quasi-scientist. His fact-gathering skills are dependent on how things appear to be; he is subjective in his judgments about similarities and differences, and he cannot organize observations into a stable system that transcends appearances.

The Piagetian account typifies the traditional perspective. The acquisition of conceptual knowledge and the ability to think in terms of classes and scales is centrally important to Piaget's system. Moreover, his analysis of young children's abilities, his depiction of the transition to mature categorical thinking, and the techniques he used for eliciting knowledge about classes, categories, and scales, has stimulated much empirical inquiry.

Piaget's Approach

In Piagetian theory, it is qualitative, age-related change in cognitive capacity that is of central interest. The age-invariant aspects of cognition are less so. Continuity across age is restricted to the invariant functions (i.e., organization and adaptation), the universal strategies through which all human beings interact with their environment. Assimilation and accommodation occur at all developmental levels, but the cognitive structures that result are qualitatively different at each major stage of development. And those structures exert a pervasive effect on behavior, so much so that diagnosis of cognitive level is broadly predictive of cognitive performance. For instance, if a child is classified as concrete operational, then we should be able to predict how that child thinks about number, geometry, classes, relations, and so forth. Piaget's structures are *domain general*.

For Piaget, knowledge structures are symbolic representations of reality independent of the environmental contexts that gave rise to them. At a simple level, if we have a representation of "animal," then we can think about animals, draw inferences about animals' characteristics, and imagine types of animals. These animal cognitions can occur without accompanying perceptual input. A child in possession of the mental representation should be able to answer the question, Do cat's have fur and whiskers? without directly inspecting a real cat. Mental representations may result from the structuring of environmental encounters; but once constructed, the representation assumes its own cognitive status. It has existence in mental life and is consulted in the drawing of inferences about the world. Thus, for example, while children presumably construct the concept of "animal" from encounters with real exemplars, the conceptual representation is not bound to those specific encounters.

The degree to which thinking achieves independence from experience is the degree to which thinking becomes symbolic. The youngest children, sensorimotor-stage infants, are the least symbolic. The "thinking" of infants is practical and bound to their motor activity. The achievement of the object concept at the end of the sensorimotor period (see Chapter 3) was particularly important to Piaget because he viewed it as the first true instance of symbolic representation.

While achievement of the object concept marks the shift into the preoperational period, the thinking of preoperational-stage children is still symbolically restricted. Indeed, this group of children is sometimes referred to as *pre*conceptual. Their thinking is bound to the immediate perceptual context. Consequently, preoperational youngsters can be seduced into drawing illogical conclusions about reality if perception supports illogical conclusions. A preoperational child could conceivably think that a plane really becomes smaller as it takes off and travels into the sky; that is the phenomenal experience. A logical interpretation of the experience requires conceptual knowledge beyond the perceptual context, knowledge about the relationship between apparent size and distance.

Many of the tasks Piaget used to differentiate preoperational children from older children pitted appearances against logical necessity. The perceptually bound child would make characteristic, indeed defining, errors. In the classic conservation problems, the perceptual context is seductive in just this way. In mass conservation, for example, a round ball of clay is transformed and flattened into a pancake. The pancake looks bigger than the ball of clay and, predictably, the preoperational child will erroneously conclude that looking bigger implicates more mass.

The thinking of concrete-operational children is more symbolic and more conceptual than that of their younger counterparts. The prototypic conservation error—judging the bigger clay pancake to have more mass—no longer occurs. Logical solutions, rather than perceptual ones, become the norm. So, children's thinking achieves independence from sensorimotor action and from immediate perception. But, it is only in the culminating stage of cognitive development, in formal operations, when thought reaches the highest level of symbolism and is no longer constrained even by the boundaries of concrete reality (see Chapter 8). In summary, the general developmental progression is from context-bound to context-free forms of mental representation.

Piagetians go even farther in their characterization of fully symbolic forms of mental representation, for not only is the mature mental model of reality presumed to be context free, it is *content free* as well. It does not matter what specific kind of cognitive phenomenon is represented; the fundamental nature of the underlying mental representation should be the same. It is irrelevant whether the particular problem is one involving number relations, geometric relations, or taxonomic relations. Whenever a cognitive prob-

lem, of whatever content, is posed, the child's performance will be constrained in the same way by the status of the cognitive structure. Performance should be even: The child should not appear cognitively mature when performing in one domain (e.g., number) and simultaneously immature when performing in another (e.g., classification).

If mental structures are domain general, context free, and content free, then models of those structures have to be abstract, general, and broadly applicable. Indeed, Piaget's logicoalgebraic models of thought are precisely that. Extrapolating and adapting mathematical concepts, Piaget identified a mental rule system he envisioned as permitting appreciation of the logical relations uniting elements in the world. This common, unified rule system was supposed to transcend particulars of content. Thus, it should be possible to reduce spatial problem solving, numerical problem solving, and categorization to the same rule-governed, representational code.

One such rule system, **concrete operations**, includes the set of transformations mentally applicable to elements, classes, sets, and relations. These transformations characterize cognition in middle childhood. According to theory, concrete-operational stage children have internalized a system of quasi-mathematical rules, and they make logical inferences about the workings of the world in accord with those rules. Preoperational-stage children have yet to accomplish this mental feat, hence the prefix *pre*. As a consequence, their thought is characterized as less logical, less internally consistent, less rule governed, and more contextually and perceptually bound than the thought of fully operational children.

Piaget's logicomathematical proposals have been the focus of controversy on both mathematical grounds—do they work logically?—and empirical grounds—do they fit the data? One empirical difficulty is that Piaget's quasi-mathematical models predict within-subject consistency in performance across tasks and problem types; but, in actuality, we observe considerable within-subject variability. **Horizontal decalage** describes within-subject variability across tasks from different cognitive domains. In view of the observed incidence of decalage, Piaget's domain-general, context- and content-free model is criticized for not fitting the data. However, Piaget sought to describe the *modal* operation of mind—how it *can* function. Performance reflects functioning filtered through task detail. The detail could produce the appearance of conceptual instability even though the underlying capacity was, in fact, stable. Those sympathetic to the Piagetian approach explain decalage as a function of performance and dismiss such evidence as no particular challenge to the theoretical model. Others, of course, disagree. We take this debate up again in Chapter 8.

Despite continuing controversy about the feasibility of building a domain-general stage model for cognitive development, the Piagetian system is the major representation of this theoretical tack. In it, the young child (up to about age 6 or 7) is envisioned as preconceptual; the older child (from about 7 up to age 12) is, in contrast, conceptual and logical within most realistic situations. The transition between stages is a qualitative one, and profound, age-related change in children's ability to classify, categorize, and scale is predicted.

**Piaget's Theory and
the Development of Categorization**

There is more than one possible system for slicing up the world. Alternative systems for categorizing phenomena are based on different kinds of concept rules people could use to sort objects into categories. Piaget assumed that categorical decisions followed classical definitions (Markman, 1989). Classical definitions of categories specify the set of attributes

or features objects belonging to a class must have.

The *intention* of a category is the set of attributes or features that defines it. If "red triangle" constitutes a category, then the color, red, and the shape, triangle, are the defining attributes. The *extension* of the category is the set of objects qualifying as category members, those in possession of the necessary attributes. Thus, with the "red triangle" example, if a child with knowledge of the defining rule were given a group of objects varying in shape and color, then the child would sort those objects with reference to the relevant attributes. The defining rule (intention) permits correct identification of the exemplars (extension) forming a category group.

In a classical view, any category is similarly definable in terms of criterial features. It makes little difference whether the category is an arbitrarily defined one like "red triangle" or a naturally occurring one like "bird." The cognitive process for determining the intention and extension of the category is parallel. Categories differ in complexity depending on the list of essential features that must be checked to determine category inclusion; "birds" have more features than "red triangles" do. But deciding whether an object is a bird, or not a bird, or is a triangle, or not a triangle, should depend on the same cognitive scheme. Some decalage is anticipated. Children's performance on classification tasks is facilitated by perceptually salient attributes such as color, shape, and size. Children are also expected to organize objects differing on only one dimension earlier than they will be able to organize objects differing on multiple dimensions. However, this performance decalage does not signal major differences in the nature of the cognitive process underlying performance.

Definitions of concepts in a classical view are arbitrary. There are no attributes that on a priori grounds are more important than others for category definitions. Similarly, there are no a priori restrictions on the "naturalness" of combinations of multiple attributes. *Red + triangle* is no more natural a combination than *small + triangle* or *red + small*. *Little + bird* and *big + bird* are equally viable combinations. *Birds + airplanes* combine as "objects that fly" just as readily and no less naturally than *birds + bats*. There need be no assumptions about natural joints at which we have an inherent propensity to break things apart.

The combination of features is also independent. Values on one dimension, for example, size, can be combined with values on an independent second dimension, color, so any resultant combination is equally probable. *Little, red triangle* is as probable as *big, blue triangle* given that the two attributes are independent. This would not be the case if the attributes were correlated. An association would restrict the possible combinations of attribute values such that the multiplicative products would not be equally probable. For example, if size and color were correlated, then small triangles might only be red and large triangles only blue.

In a Piagetian analysis, mature categorization depends on at least three components of knowledge. First, successful classifiers know the intention and extension of the class. Second, they know that membership in one class precludes simultaneous membership in a mutually exclusive class; for example, an object cannot be both a triangle and a square nor both blue and red. Third, mature classifiers know that groups can be arranged into class hierarchies. "Little birds" and "big birds" are subordinate groups of the class "birds." "Birds" and "bats" are subordinate classes of "animals," which is part of the superordinate group "living things."

Knowledge of the hierarchical structure of classes permits certain deductions. For example, (1) an object is simultaneously a member of a subordinate and a superordinate class

within a taxonomic hierarchy; (2) what is true for members of a superordinate class is true for members of the subordinate class, although the reverse relationship need not necessarily hold; (3) since a superordinate class is achieved by combining subordinate classes, it follows that a subordinate class cannot have more members than the superordinate class. Or, more concretely, (1) an animal can be both an Arabian and a horse; (2) since horses run and eat hay, so do Arabian horses, but Arabian horses have distinctively shaped faces; (3) there are more horses than Arabian horses.

Children's abilities to classify objects and infer an object's properties from categorical knowledge are, according to a Piagetian analysis, a developmental phenomenon. Dramatic, qualitative shifts in competence correspond to the transition from the preoperational to the concrete-operational period. The younger children, because they lack the prerequisite mental representation, cannot systematically classify a series of objects into logical groups. Nor do they understand the nature of the relations among constituted groups. Objects are compared with each other in terms of the context, in terms of perceptual characteristics, and in terms of what other objects they are "next to." Young children have not yet acquired a conceptual structure to impose on stimuli. Their older counterparts, on the other hand, have constructed the supporting cognitive schemata.

Performance tasks. Categorization ability is one performance indicator of underlying conceptual knowledge. **Free classification** is the partitioning of a set of exemplars into *n* mutually exclusive groups. The rule for the grouping decision is supplied by the subjects following instructions to place similar items together. The number of groups can either be left free to vary at the subject's discretion or set by the experimenter. The subject is supposed to impose a cognitive categorical structure, which cannot be directly observed, onto a classification act, which can be. And the "structure in the head" is inferred from observation of the "partitioning on the table."

In classic studies, the stimuli vary in value on one or more dimensions predetermined by the experimenter. So, the objects have a finite set of attributes and are partitionable on the basis of a specifiable rule that makes reference to the criterial attribute(s). The boundaries between classes are concrete and clear; there are no ambiguous exemplars. If shape were the relevant dimension, and three values were represented in the exemplars (e.g., square, circle, triangle), then a subject operating with the same decision rule as the experimenter should produce three groups and appropriately place all exemplars. The performance would reveal that the subject understands the intention of the category (the decision rule) and the extension of the category (correct identification of the exemplars).

Sometimes children are given extra exemplars that they must selectively place into the category structure they created. Then they must extend their categories to encompass novel exemplars. A mature categorization performance is consistent with the predetermined decision rule. Of course, the task can be complicated by the addition of irrelevant attributes that play no part in the decision rule. Then, the irrelevant features must be ignored while the relevant features are preferentially attended to. Alternatively, relevant attributes can also be added, complicating the decision rule.

Categories form a **nominal scale** of equivalence relations. Recall from methodology classes that nominal scaling yields n classes, each of which is treated as equal in value to any other class. If the decision rule for classification is adequate, then every entity fits into one and only one of the n categories; no entities are left over. Ordering is also possible for asymmetric relations, as when objects are organized along a continuum of increasing value. The abstract rule system descriptive of operational thought enables the organization of asymmetrical relations (ordinal scaling) as well as equivalence relations (nominal scaling). Again, with reference to measurement methodology, ordinal scales provide organization for "greater than" relations among entities.

Knowledge of asymmetrical relations is assessed through **seriation**. As with free classification, subjects are given a set of objects, but these vary in value along some continuous dimension, for example, height, weight, or size. Following instructions to "put things in order," knowledgeable children form an ordinal scale with the objects, arranging them from the one having least of the quantity to one having the most of the quantity. Essentially, a mental concept of order is imposed on a group of objects creating a series where $A < B < C < D, \ldots < n$. Children who can order can also insert new objects into the constructed array and engage in **transitive reasoning** based on their representation of the ordinal scale. So, for example, the successful child will know that $D > B$ because D occurs later in the series; a direct perceptual comparison of D and B is unnecessary if children understand the logic of asymmetrical relations (Piaget & Inhelder, 1941). And again, as with categorization, seriation tasks can be complicated by adding additional attributes necessitating simultaneous ordering on multiple dimensions, for example, ordering objects that vary in both size and weight.

Several features of these tasks are important to the interpretation of developmental findings:

1. As noted, categorization and seriation tasks assess *scaling;* a system of classes constitutes a nominal scale while a seriated array describes an ordinal scale.

2. The tasks are *projective* since the subject supplies the rule when constructing the scale.

3. The dimensions of variation and the relevant attributes of exemplars to be scaled are specified a priori by the experimenter; thus, a single correct solution is predetermined. In accord with the existence of one correct, logically based solution, there are no ambiguous exemplars or unclassifiable, unorderable objects.

4. The dimensions or attributes within a problem are *independent* if more than one dimension or attribute is given.

5. Scaling behavior is used to infer underlying knowledge about the logic of classes and relations.

Failure on the child's part to impose organization and to reason about objects vis-à-vis that organization is interpreted as a corresponding failure to mentally represent concepts of order, classes, and relations.

Class inclusion is another kind of performance task (Dean, Chabaud, & Bridges, 1981; Inhelder & Piaget, 1964). Problems of this sort elicit the child's reasoning about taxonomic relations among classes. Typically, a child is presented with two sets of objects, for example, daisies and roses. Both sets have a feature in common; in this case, all are flowers. In effect, then, each of the two sets is a subset of a larger set to which both subsets belong. One of the subsets clearly contains more objects than the other; there may be more daisies than roses. The child is asked whether there are more daisies or more flowers. Since daisies (A_1) and roses (A_2) are both subsets of flowers (A), there have to be more flowers; $A_1 + A_2 = A$. The problem *context* presents the child with the easily perceived fact that $A_1 > A_2$, but the problem *question* asks for a comparison of A_1 with A. Correct solution depends on understanding the nested, class-inclusion relations existing within a hierarchy of classes. Subsets

A_1 and A_2 are mutually exclusive, but A_1 and A_2 are nested within A.

Original findings. Piagetian theory predicts that preoperational and concrete-operational children will perform quite differently on these tasks. Children in the younger group, bound as they are by perception, will rely on the way things look as the basis for organizing stimuli. When sorting objects into classes, for example, they may be swayed by which objects are located next to each other. So, if a red triangle and a red square are close together, "redness" associates them. If a blue square is next to a red square, "squareness" associates them. In the course of sorting a set of colored blocks, the perceptually bound child will alter the sorting rule as the perceptual features of object pairs shift in salience. Several transient, perceptual grouping rules take precedence over a single stable, logical grouping rule in guiding performance.

Younger children also favor *thematic associations,* in which objects go together because they are in close proximity (a saddle on a horse) or because they are in a story together (the cow jumping over the moon). The immediate context—perceptual or proximal—is the dominant influence for the preoperational child. Piagetian data were consistent with his predictions for age-related categorization phenomena (Piaget & Inhelder, 1964). Russian psychologist Vygotsky formulated a theory of conceptual development overlapping Piaget's in some respects. Vygotsky (1962) similarly found that young children produced such *chain concepts* as a consequence of the perceptual nature of their thinking.

Seriation and transitive reasoning can pose difficulties for the preoperational child because access to perceptual information is precluded by the manner in which the task is presented. For example, when two objects differing slightly in length are placed next to each other, the difference in length is perceptible.

Even young children can identify the longer object in this context. Ordering multiple objects, however, requires that a series of these pairwise comparisons be coordinated, only one of which is perceptible at any given moment. Prior comparisons must be stored in some mental representation of an ordinal scale to which subsequent comparisons can be assimilated.

Preoperational children should make individual pairwise comparisons successfully since perceptual support is available. They are more likely to encounter difficulty, however, coordinating multiple comparisons, as when constructing a whole seriated array. They will similarly be hampered in recalling the appearance of a multiobject seriated array, in extending a seriated array to include additional objects, and in inferring transitive relations among ordinally scaled items. Those latter capabilities depend on the mental representation of the concept of order rather than on the perceptual appearances of orderable objects. Again, the original Piagetian experiments and replications of them support this contention (Elkind, 1964; Inhelder & Piaget, 1964).

In class-inclusion problems, the perceptual information seduces the preoperational child into comparing A_1 with A_2 rather than A_1 with A. As a consequence, the child will respond that A_1 is indeed the larger set; the logic of classes is less salient than is the immediate context. Empirical studies conducted in the Piagetian manner attest to the reliability of this developmental phenomenon (Dean, Chabaud, & Bridges, 1981).

As Piagetian theory contends and Genevan-style experiments confirm, the performances of preoperational children and concrete-operational children are quite different. The former are bound by perception and context; the latter rely on knowledge of classes and relations. The older children who understand the logic of classes and relations solve all the described tasks as an adult would. The extent of their representational knowledge is further exemplified by their ability to generate explicit, verbal explanations for their scaling, which references the logical rules of organization. The younger children perform in a remarkably different fashion, notable for its deficiencies, idiosyncracies, and the absence of explicit formulations.

OTHER EMPIRICAL EVIDENCE

A central point in Piaget's theory of cognitive development is that developmental change is qualitative change. There is global, stagelike transition in the form of the mental representations underlying conceptual behavior. Other traditional views of concept acquisition, such as Vygotsky's (1962), Werner's (1948), and Bruner's (1964), are similar to Piaget's in this respect. Sometimes the young child's reasoning about classes and relations is characterized as perceptually bound (Piaget), as instance bound (Vygotsky), as iconic (Bruner), or as undifferentiated (Werner). The common contention is that the cognitive basis for concept formation changes in dramatic fashion sometime during childhood. Older children and adults share the same form of mental representation; younger children do not.

In traditional accounts, the incompetence of young children is profound. In many ways, this is a counterintuitive proposition. Young children can look quite competent; for example, their facility with language is remarkable (see Chapter 9). Toddlers and preschoolers use words and labels and acquire new words and new labels at an incredibly rapid rate. If labels and words are interconnected with classes and categories, it does not make obvious sense to propose that children would be accomplished in one domain (language) and naive in another (concepts), especially if cognitive development is domain-general knowledge acquisition. This picture of young children is precisely what has fueled empirical study. Investigators seek to determine whether or not preoperational children perform as incompetently as hypothesized. And, if they do, could there be an alternative explanation for their apparent deficiencies? Failure on tasks tapping knowledge of classes and relations might be due to something other than the pervasive inability to organize entities and relations. Many studies are conducted to find out what that "something" might be.

Nominal Scaling

The existence of a qualitative change in children's understanding of classes and relations depends on the interpretation of young children's failure. While it is true that young children can classify poorly (Denney, 1972; Inhelder & Piaget, 1964; Kofsy, 1966; Vygotsky, 1962), it is not always clear why they do so. Classification tasks tend to be relatively unstructured, so young children may simply sort in a manner they find interesting. Thematic collections, idiosyncratic object conglomerations, and chain concepts may interest and appeal to them, so they produce them. Other kinds of conceptual organizations may be accessible to them, too. In fact, there is evidence that subjects, including young children, who produce thematic groupings can also explain the categorical relations among objects when probed (Cole & Scribner, 1974; Smiley & Brown, 1979). Again, there is a potential decoupling between performance and underlying cognitive process.[2] That *performance* is deficient does not necessarily imply that cognitive competence is similarly deficient.

Prototypic sorting tasks often feature arbitrary concepts defined by the conjunct of two or more attributes. The experimenter defines the rule and child subjects discover it. Objects to be sorted are combinations of attributes or, similarly, possess a set of values on two or more dimensions. Thus, for example, when a set of blocks varies in size, color, and shape, any one object has a size value, a color value, and a shape value. When comparing two objects, mature categorizers usually make the comparison on a feature-by-feature basis. A big, red square and a little, blue square are identical on the form dimension, but different on the size and color dimensions. Feature-by-feature comparisons, however, require the categorizer to separate the dimensions and selectively attend to the value an object has on each.

Some evidence suggests that young children cannot isolate dimensions sufficiently well to use them this way, while older children can (Kemler & Smith, 1978; Kemler, 1983; Smith, 1981; Smith & Kemler, 1977; Shepp, 1978). Instead, young children may resort to a *holistic* sorting strategy, comparing objects as whole, inseparable units for overall similarity. The interpretation is that there is an age-related developmental shift in the basis for classification. The evidence is ambiguous, however. Even adults use the immature, holistic-comparison strategy under difficult task conditions (Smith & Kemler-Nelson, 1984), and young children are sometimes sensitive to comparative features other than overall similarity (Smith, 1985).

To clarify the ambiguity, consider what children and adults actually do when sorting multidimensional objects on free-classification tasks. Suppose objects differ on two dimensions, X and Y, both of which represent continua. On X, dimensional values can vary between the end points on the continuum and a quantity assigned accordingly ($x_1, x_2, x_3, \ldots x_n$); the same quantification of value is possible on the Y continuum ($y_1, y_2, y_3, \ldots y_n$). Any set of objects—$A$, B, C—having x and y values can be scaled in a two-dimensional space. This is depicted in Figure 4-2. Experimentally, one could vary the x and y values of objects and observe how subjects actually do scale the objects and judge degree of similarity. Scaling would reflect whether both of the separable dimensions were represented, how the dimensions were weighted ($w_1, w_2, w_3, \ldots w_n$), and how the weighted dimensions were combined.

FIGURE 4-2   Any set of objects (*A, B, C*) that differs in value on two dimensions simultaneously (*X, Y*) can be scaled in a two-dimensional space. In this depiction, objects *A* and *B* are identical on *X* but differ on *Y; B* differs from both *A* and *C* on both *X* and *Y* but is generally more similar overall to object *C*.

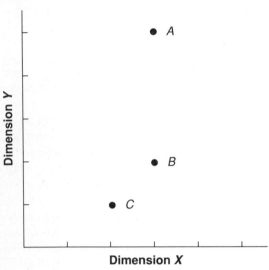

Dimension X

From "A Model of Perceptual Classification in Children and Adults" by L. B. Smith, 1989, *Psychological Review, 96*, p. 126. Copyright 1989 by the American Psychological Association. Reprinted by permission.

Conceivably, then, any object represents the computation of a value combining the dimension values with their assigned weights, or $(w_i x_i) + (w_j y_j) = A_{ij}$. Developmental change would occur in classification and judgments of similarity among objects if any of the following turned out to be age related: (1) the dimensions individuals are able to represent

(i.e., *X* or *Y*), (2) the values assigned to dimensional attributes (x_i, y_j), (3) the weights given dimensional values (w_i, w_j), and (4) the computational rule or the equation for combining weighted dimensional values.

Linda Smith (1989) conducted a series of classification studies with 2- to 8-year-old subjects and with adults. She varied the dimensional weightings of stimuli, examined the sortings of children and adults, inferred the computational rule subjects must have consulted to make the sorting decisions, and compared the empirical outcomes with predictions generated from a mathematical model. Some of these data are summarized in Figure 4-3. While there were developmental differences in classification, there were continuities as well. For instance, young children represent the same perceptual features (*X* and *Y*) as adults do, but the equations used for weighting and combining those features when judging similarity change developmentally. Those effects were predictable from Smith's mathematical model. A reasonable explanation for the observed developmental phenomenon is an apparent increase in **selective attention** to dimensional attributes associated with age and to the special status given to identity values in computation.

Two particular conclusions generated from Smith's research are that (1) even very young children can represent the attributes of objects and make similarity decisions with reference to those attributes, and (2) developmental differences in the proficiency of classification are sufficiently modeled as quantitative change. In short, the proficiency and accuracy with which children make classification com-

FIGURE 4-3   The top part of the figure depicts the values of to-be-classified objects as scaled in two- ▶ dimensional space. The bottom part depicts the outcome, the rules subjects used to sort test and control sets and the proportion using those rules.

From "A Model of Perceptual Classification in Children and Adults" by L. B. Smith, 1989, *Psychological Review, 96*, p. 137, 138. Copyright 1989 by the American Psychological Association. Reprinted by permission.

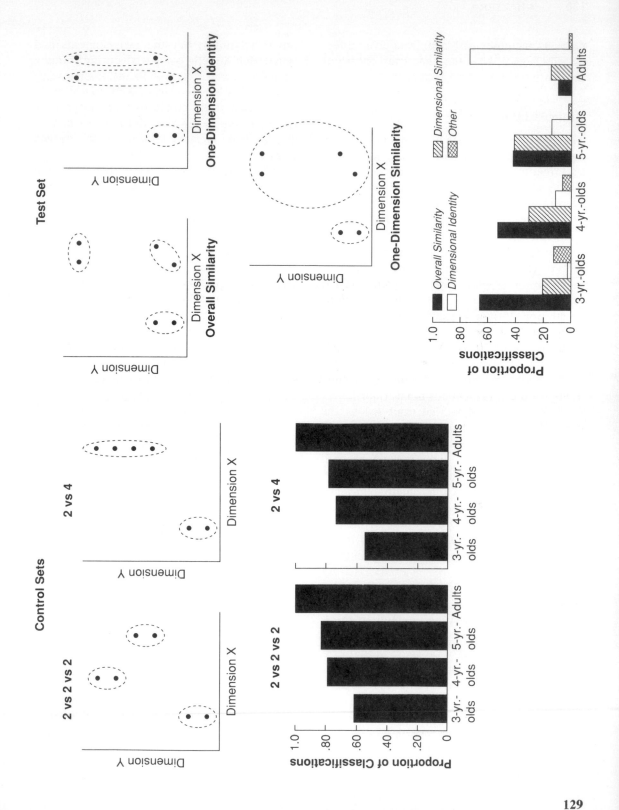

parisons increases with age. Data do not necessarily suggest that the underlying nature of the comparison process itself changes.

Ordinal Scaling

The empirical literature also provides us with evidence that young children do not always look incompetent when engaging in ordinal-scaling tasks. It is true that youngsters cannot be counted on to organize objects into an ordinal scale spontaneously. In addition, the language used in asymmetrical comparisons (e.g., bigger, smaller, more than) poses problems of clarity for them. However, children as young as 3 years of age can form ordinal scales, compare scales, and answer questions about appropriate placement within a scale when the language demands of the tasks are reduced, the task context is made more familiar, or the number of items is reduced (Siegel, 1972; Swarner, 1988). The ordinal-scaling ability of the young child is not as robust, generalized, or explicit as that exhibited by the older child, but rudiments of the skill are still detectable.

Other studies also show that young children engage in transitive reasoning. A prerequisite to success is that children must be able to represent and recall the initial premises on which a transitive inference is predicated. Children cannot be expected to infer that $A > C$ without remembering first that $A > B$ and $B > C$.

In a series of experiments, Bryant and Trabasso (1971) trained children to remember the pairwise relations between elements in an ordered series. Subjects only saw the elements two at a time and never observed the fully ordered set. Following training, children were first given a memory test. Could they remember the outcome of the individual comparisons observed during training, for example, A with B, B with C, C with D, and D with E?

Then, children were given an inference test; they had to predict which of two elements

would be longer, but the two elements had never been directly compared during training (A and C, B and D, and so forth). Even 4-year-olds could solve the transitive inference problems under these conditions at better than chance levels. When they did fail, it was predictable from memory failures for the trained comparisons necessary for the inference. In short, if a child failed to infer that $B > D$, it was attributed to a failure to recall the prerequisite relationship between B and C or between C and D. The specific experimental procedures were varied in a number of ways, but the outcome was fairly robust (Trabasso, 1975, 1977). Subsequent work reiterates the observation that preschoolers can indeed sometimes engage in transitive reasoning (Breslow, 1981; Halford, 1982).

Questions remain, however, as to whether or not the quality of the young child's performance on ordinal scaling tasks is the same as that of the older child. For instance, the probability of scaling success is increased when the number of objects is reduced; with few enough objects, the child can directly perceive quantitative differences. Then, ordinal reasoning has perceptual support. Classic tasks are, in contrast, perceptually deceiving. Even on the Bryant and Trabasso task variation, young children could form a perceptionlike image of ordered elements from the experience in training, then use the image to mediate transitive reasoning. Again, this might be interpreted as a kind of perceptual support. Whether or not this sort of cognitive ability entails the same degree of symbolic knowledge Piaget sought to elicit with classical tasks has been questioned (Chapman & Lindenberger, 1988).[3]

It is possible to train seriation skills in very young children (Bingham-Newman & Hooper, 1974). Brief observation of a model appropriately ordering an object series and verbally mediating an ordering rule is generally sufficient even for 3-year-olds (Henderson, Swanson, & Zimmerman, 1975; Swanson, Henderson, & Williams, 1979). Efficacious observational learning suggests that training clarifies task demands and elicits a competent performance from children who might have the relevant knowledge but who cannot readily access and apply it. Training demonstrates how to apply the knowledge in a proscribed task circumstance, although the generalization of the trained skill across circumstances is usually restricted (Rosser & Brody, 1981).

In an example of a training study, Rosser and Horan (1982) designed a task tapping knowledge of multidimensional scaling. In each version of the task, two dimensions were represented. For classification, objects varied in color and shape; for seriation, width and height varied. The apparatus for the tasks was a matrix into which objects (9 or 16) could be fit; these are depicted in Figure 4-4. Children were directed to organize the target objects (colored shapes on sticks varying in tallness and fatness) in the matrix. On a pretest, the preoperational children performed pretty dismally. Then, in training, children observed a model correctly filling in a 9 item matrix while describing the scaling rule. Some children observed a correct multiple-classification

performance; others observed multiple seriation.

Then, subjects were assessed again. However, they not only had to duplicate what they had observed, they had to generalize the knowledge to a more complex problem (a 16-item matrix) and to the untrained task (either classification or seriation). Training worked, but the effect was strongest for classification. Generalization was observed, but generalization effects were weaker than training effects. Horizontal decalage was evident too. Single-dimensional scaling was prerequisite to multiple-dimensional scaling; classification was easier than seriation.

In a strong interpretation of the Piagetian position, seriation and classification performance is limited in young children by the immature state of their cognitive structures and by developmental limitations on mental representation. Therefore, positive training effects should not be so readily achieved and task effects should not explain performance. The fact that preoperational children do reveal knowledge of ordinal scaling and ordinal reasoning when task demands are altered or when training is provided is theoretically problem-

FIGURE 4-4 *The Sorts of Stimuli Used by Rosser and Horan (1982) to Assess Young Children's Ability to Classify and Seriate on a Multi-Dimensional Task.*

Classification

Shape

△	○	□	
Red △	Red ○	Red □	Red
Yellow △	Yellow ○	Yellow □	Yellow **Color**
?	?	?	Blue

Seriation

Height

1"	2"	3"	
1" × 1" cube	1" × 2" rectangle	?	1" wide
?	?	?	2" wide **Width**
1" × 3" rectangle	?	3" × 3" cube	3" wide

atic. So, the empirical evidence is not entirely consistent with the traditional theoretical explanation.

Class Inclusion

Traditionalists interpret young children's failure on class-inclusion problems as proof that these youngsters do not understand the hierarchical organization of classes. The task elicits a judgment about the comparative numerosity of a subset of objects with that of its supraset. Presented with a group of five *cats* and three *rabbits,* the subsets, the child is asked to compare the numerosity of *cats* versus *animals,* the supraset. There is some inherent ambiguity here, however. The group of cats is a group of animals, the group of rabbits is also a group of animals, and, of course, the group of cats and rabbits together is a group of animals. It is not at all obvious from the task format which specific groups of animals are to be compared. Were the child to treat the rabbit-animal class as the comparison referent for the cat-animal class, then the judgment favoring the greater numerosity of the cat-animal class is quite appropriate. In short, the type of nouns used in the problem, rather than the hierarchical organization of the classes those nouns represent, may confuse young children.

The child is asked to make a part-whole comparison and to determine that the whole is more than a part of it; but the particular terms referring to the part and the whole may not clearly specify the referents. Terms such as *animal* are **class nouns;** the defining properties of a class are the properties of the individuals that make it up (Markman, 1973). Any set of two individuals, three individuals, or five individuals can be referred to by the class noun if the individuals possess the appropriate attributes. Nouns like *animals, people, flowers,* and the like, the nouns used to refer to the supraset in the class-inclusion problem, are

class nouns. The class noun *animals* in the previous example appropriately refers to the cat class (the individual cats possess the criterial attributes of animals), the rabbit class (for the same reason), and the class resulting from the union of cats and rabbits.

There are also **collective nouns** whose defining properties are those of the *set* not the individuals comprising it. So, the collective noun *family* refers to a set of objects possessing a particular organization. Breaking the set into individual family members destroys the organization. One cannot refer to individuals in a family by the collective noun; one can refer to the individuals in a class by the class noun. The referent for a collective noun, the supraset, is less ambiguous than the referent for the class noun; the latter could legitimately refer to any set, supra- or sub-, within the class-inclusion task context. Children as young as 4 years do understand the referential properties of class and collective nouns, and they understand that a class noun can refer to individual subsets within a larger set. Moreover, children make more interpretive errors with class nouns, exhibiting confusion about the exact referent of the noun on noninclusion as well as on class-inclusion tasks (Smith & Rizzo, 1982).

In several studies, Markman (1973, 1979; Markman & Siebert, 1976) changed the class-inclusion task somewhat to examine the effect of collective versus class nouns. In these studies, children were more likely to produce a correct judgment when asked, "When would you have more, when you had the children or the *family?*" They were less likely to answer correctly when asked, "When would you have more, when you had the children or the *people?*" Apparently, the type of noun used in the query, rather than the hierarchical organization of parts and whole, influenced performance. Markman argued that collections (e.g., family, forest, garden, town, and zoo) have greater psychological cohesiveness than classes. Others (Smith & Rizzo, 1982) have demonstrated that task changes that clarify the noun referents for the children facilitate performance even when class nouns are used.

Finally, Smith and Rizzo (1982, Experiment 3) have shown us the effectiveness of training class inclusion in 5-year-old children. However, the experimenters did *not* train children in class inclusion and class hierarchies per se. Children did not have the opportunity to learn to simultaneously represent a set and an included subset; they learned about the referents of set words. If young children fail class-inclusion tasks because they cannot represent hierarchical class relations, then this kind of reference-clarification training should not affect subsequent performance on class-inclusion problems. But that is not what happened.

Experimental-group children who received the training significantly improved their class-inclusion performance between pre- and posttesting when class nouns were used in the criterion task, and they outperformed a control group of children who did not receive training. When collective nouns were used, however, exposure to the pretest alone triggered significant gains for both experimental and control children. The pretest provided sufficient practice to facilitate mature performance on the collective noun form of the class-inclusion problem. These results are presented in Figure 4-5.

Making Sense of the Evidence

The data from empirical studies are confusing and ambiguous as to whether or not preoperational children are conceptually incapable as traditional theory predicts. Clearly under some circumstances, particularly on classical versions of scaling tasks, young children do not perform well. Under other circumstances—when language is simplified, when instructions are clarified, and when memory factors are controlled—young children exhibit rudimentary comprehension of nominal and ordinal scales. These data argue for early competence. Moreover, aspects of scaling are easily trained, and performance is apparently not impeded by age-defined developmental status.

The ability to comprehend the language used in a task, to understand and follow instructions, and the capacity to remember a problem's givens, however, are aspects of **procedural knowledge**. Procedures are not specific to the class and order concepts being elicited, but they are general requirements common across many assessment contexts.

FIGURE 4-5 *The Mean Proportion of Correct Answers on Pretest and Posttest on Class-Inclusion Problems as a Function of Noun Type (Class Nouns vs. Collective Nouns) and of Training Condition (Experimental versus Control).*

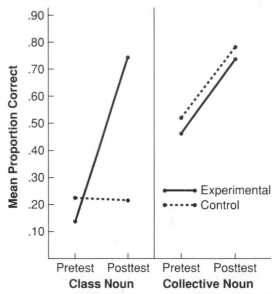

From "Children's Understanding of the Referential Properties of Collective and Class Nouns" by L. B. Smith and T. A. Rizzo, 1982, *Child Development, 53,* p. 254. Reprinted by permission.

What we hope to determine when we give children scaling tasks is the status of their **conceptual knowledge,** how much they know about order and classes. But, when a young subject fails a complex task, we do not know why. Failure will occur when the subject lacks conceptual knowledge, but failure is also certain when subjects have difficulty with the procedures necessary to display conceptual knowledge. Conceivably, a child may know something about classes and orders but not know how to demonstrate the knowledge on the particular task the experimenter gives her. When children fail at some conceptual tasks but not others, it appears that a lack of procedural knowledge is the culprit.

Even positive training can be attributed to changes in procedural knowledge. Although not the orthodox interpretation (most training studies are generated from an empiricist's perspective), training could function only to clarify task demands, to show the child what she is supposed to do. Then, she subsequently is able to display the conceptual knowledge she knew all along. So, training does not teach the child about the concepts of class and order; it merely facilitates the expression of such knowledge (see Chapter 1). Early competence is again implicated.

In short, young children have rudimentary notions of classes, concepts, and order. But it is just as true that, when traditionally assessed, children do poorly on classification tasks, seriation tasks, and on class-inclusion problems. The data are contradictory. Perhaps we should look at the phenomenon some other way.

CONCLUSION

Classification, categorization, and seriation are ubiquitous psychological phenomena. They function to make experience manageable and meaningful. They simultaneously permit the simplification of myriad encounters with reality and enrich those encounters by supporting induction. Classification, the ability to scale and group things, is the external ramification of conceptual knowledge, the mental representation of the essences of those things. And mental representations are the abstract structures that bring order to reality.

To Piaget, children's concepts were fundamentally different from those of adults. Lacking the ability to compare and contrast the features of things in an objective way, young children look instead at subjective associations—perceptual appearances, thematic relations, proximal relations, and episodic relations. Were these youngsters able to mentally represent the stable, logical relations uniting the association among elements, the unstable, transient relations would prove less seductive. The Piagetian account, like other traditionalist accounts, predicts dramatic shifts in children's performance on conceptual tasks as a reflection of qualitative shifts in the nature of the underlying conceptual organization. As Keil (1989) pointed out, despite the specifics of particular traditionalist views, all of them are a variation on a single theme: "Young children's representations are instance bound, whereas older children are able to free themselves more from particular instances to form more 'logical', abstract concepts" (p. 5).

On traditionalist-inspired tasks of nominal and ordinal scaling, young children reliably perform in an immature fashion. The groupings they create among objects are not generated from representation of classical concept definitions, taxonomic relations, or asymmetrical relations. The theoretical interpretation of that performance is controversial, for we have also seen that young children can be induced to perform in a mature manner when tasks are modified, brief training is provided, or when the extent of their knowledge is probed more thoroughly. The observation of early competence in conceptual behavior, while decidedly task specific, creates a formidable challenge to traditional theoretical explanations of conceptual development. That in itself, however, is skimpy evidence on which to mount a theoretical alternative, especially to a competence-modeling perspective.[4]

Fodor's (1972) influential critique of Vygotsky's view of conceptual development is aptly applicable to any of the traditional views, including Piaget's (Fodor, 1975, 1981). Among Fodor's criticisms, two are particularly apt. First, Fodor argues that the classical view of concept definitions embraced by Vygotsky (and also Piaget and Inhelder) is inappropriate. If we reject the classical definition as lacking psychological validity, that means people might actually use some other kind of scheme for the demarcation of categories, classes, and concepts. It follows, then, that tasks designed to tap whether or not a child possesses knowledge of classical definitions, as a means of judging the maturity of the child, are inappropriate tasks if adults do not represent concepts in classical terms either. It amounts to comparing children with a standard of "maturity" that does not even exist in the "mature."

As part of the ongoing philosophical discourse on the nature of concepts, alternatives to the classical definition scheme have regularly appeared in the contemporary literature (Rosch & Mervis, 1975; Smith & Medin, 1981). It seems that real-world concepts (e.g., animal) are not definable in the same way as the arbitrary ones (e.g., red triangle) chosen by traditional development psychologists as the focus of their tasks. However, changes in the way we understand concepts now postdate Piaget and Vygotsky's work. And, thus, there is another literature based on these newer formulations to consider.

Fodor also argued that, in general, the idea of a qualitative shift in the nature of mental representation between childhood and adulthood simply cannot work. Fodor interpreted a developmental-stage shift as a transformation from one form of mental representation to another. Essentially, since the child has one "language of thought" and the adult another, each thinks and speaks in a different language (see Keil, 1986a). How, then, could they possibly communicate without misunderstanding one another? According to traditional explanations, young children still "speak" immature "conceptualese." It is also not clear how a child could ever change "conceptualeses." How could children possibly learn a mature version of a concept if it is expressed in a "foreign" language of thought? Fodor thinks it is more likely that individuals of all ages share roughly the same representational systems. Fodor's points, however, are sufficiently profound that we will reconsider them in Chapter 11.

Still another problem, this time more specific to the development of concepts and categories, is how initial *perceptual* frameworks for grouping entities could ever give rise to *conceptual* frameworks; perception does not inform about enduring conceptual characteristics (see Spelke, 1991). Although Piaget did not make perception the basis for mature concepts, his account of conceptual development does not adequately circumvent this problem (Piatelli-Palmarini, 1980).

The Piagetian-inspired investigations with children only tell part of the story of conceptual development. To complete the account, we need to start with a different set of arguments about what concepts are and how they function in the evolution of cognition. And that is where alternative explanations begin.

ENDNOTES

1. If you ask children why two perceptually similar objects are alike, they will most likely say they *look* alike. This is not an explanation of the process that creates "likeness," but simply a restatement of the perceptual judgment. We do not have to know, explicitly, how the perceptual system operates to give us "likeness"; it is more similar to a reflex.

2. Decoupling is one translation of *decalage*.

3. A possible Piagetian-style interpretation is that perception like images are aspects of what Piaget at times called *figural thought*. Conceivably, such devices could be used to support reasoning in some circumstances. However, such reasoning devices are neither context nor content free as *operational*

thought is supposed to be. Therefore, generalized ordinal reasoning is not enabled by such cognitive mediators.

4. The data relate only to performance, not the underlying nature of cognition reflected, although not perfectly, in performance.

CHAPTER 5

SEMANTIC AND ONTOLOGICAL KNOWLEDGE: ALTERNATIVE VIEWS OF CONCEPTUAL DEVELOPMENT

INTRODUCTION

All the things that make up the world have numerous features, characteristic attributes that we use somehow to figure out what a thing is. Determining what a thing is amounts to assigning it to a category. Evaluation of the thing's features is implicated in category assignment, but modeling how features enter into the psychological decision-making process turns out to be a murky business.

In classical definitions of concepts, those that sustain traditional theories of conceptual development, certain specific features—defining attributes—determine category membership, and the decision process appears to be straightforward. Simply identify the presence or absence of those attributes and the decision should be clear. The real world, however, turns out to be a bit too complicated to nicely fit a classical model. Some kinds of things— people, pets, toys, and animals—are very familiar entities even to children. Yet these same things can be conceptually confusing to

the psychologist attempting to explain the categorization process. A person may definitely know what a familiar thing is and simultaneously not know explicitly the specific defining attributes that make it so.

The following dialogs depict sample conversations with children pressed to justify their decisions about what things are. Features are referred to, although perhaps not as an adult would reference them. Some features turn out to be more important, more definitional, than others, although this is age related too. And, then again, there is a hint about "essences," something basic to "whatness" that goes beyond features. These dialogs exemplify concretely the limitations of the traditional view as a comprehensive system for categorizing and classifying naturally occurring phenomena. In addition, the dialogs suggest how truly difficult it can be to try and figure what really makes two entities similar or different.

Dialog 1

A 3-year-old boy has just spotted a female, U.S. Army troop dressed in fatigues.

Child: Look! A G.I. Joe! (pause) No! (pause) It's a girl!
Adult: Girls can be G.I. Joes, too.
Child: No way!
Adult: But she looks like a G.I. Joe . . . she's dressed right . . . and she's driving a Jeep.
Child: No (emphatically)! G.I. Joes are *boys* . . . in true life.

Dialog 2

This conversation is between an adult and a 4-year-old who were looking at the *A* page in an alphabet book with "animal" as the *A* word.

Adult: Do you know what an animal is?
Child: Yes. A dog is an animal.
Adult: How do you know?
Child: Because . . . it has legs. Animals have legs.
Adult: Is a snake an animal?
Child: Yes.
Adult: But a snake doesn't have legs. How can a snake be an animal if it doesn't have legs?
Child: It's a *kind* of an animal.
Adult: Since snakes and dogs are both animals, how are they alike?
Child: (shrugs shoulders)
Adult: Does a dog have a brain?
Child: Yes.
Adult: Does a snake have a brain?
Child: Oh, no! (quite emphatically)
Adult: If a dog is an animal and it has a brain, and a snake is an animal too, why doesn't a snake have a brain?
Child: Because . . . a snake's head is too little . . . it would burst it!

Dialog 3

The final conversation is with a 6-year-old child.

Adult: How is Bubby (pet dog) like a person?
Child: Uh, uh . . . he's not like a person.

Adult: Does he have feelings?
Child: Yes, he has feelings.
Adult: Well, you have feelings. So, if Bubby has feelings he's like a person.
Child: It's *not* the same thing. He's *not* like a person.
Adult: How come?
Child: Well, I'll tell ya . . . he has hair, he barks, and he can't talk.
Adult: If I shave Bubby's hair and teach him to talk, will he be a person then?
Child: Not really.
Adult: Why not?
Child: Because . . . because . . . I don't know.

The child in Dialog 1 used an irrelevant feature to decide the exemplar's status as a noninstance of the category and disregarded the defining attributes. The child in Dialog 2 could correctly identify both exemplars as members of the class, but explicit knowledge of the defining features, which we presume influenced the decision, proved elusive. The child in Dialog 3 made a conceptual distinction in spite of overlapping attributes. In all three cases, the deciding feature(s) that make a thing what it is remains elusive. The boundaries between categories are clear and definite with classical definitions (either an exemplar possesses or does not possess the defining attributes); they may be less so for real-world exemplars. Recall the ambiguity in the distinction between dogs and coyotes (see Chapter 4). Thus, while the classical view of concepts seems intuitive, elegant, logical, and applicable to all concepts, it does not always work very well. Some "messier" system could turn out to be a better fit with how people actually think about these matters.

In this chapter, some "messier" alternatives to the traditional view are described and evaluated. Alternatives begin with definitions of concepts that go beyond the classic type. These definitions take their impetus from real-world entities and from the assumption that mental representation will somehow reflect those entities. Hypotheses offered to supplant the traditional view also differ in many ways. Some simply provide better and more realistic definitions with few elaborations about the acquisition of conceptual knowledge. Others are laden with theoretical implications about the nature of cognitive development. And still others propose a conceptual scaffolding that could even function as the foundation for virtually all cognitive activity. Those will be described last. We will begin with a rich notion of what concepts, classes, and categories must be.

ALTERNATIVES TO CLASSICAL DEFINITIONS

We begin by presuming that the world of things has a structure, the structure is not arbitrary or random, and certain elements go together in the structure more naturally than others. Varieties of animals, for example, share important properties that distinguish them from plants, from inanimate objects, from events, and so forth. Elements in the world cannot be combined into groups haphazardly or idiosyncratically; there are "natural joints" at which to do the cutting. So, rocks go with streams more naturally than with cars; mice join with chipmunks more easily than with moths. The mental representation of the world is psychological, not material, but it has a structure, too.

There must be some **isomorphism** between the two structures for effective species adaptation and survival. (This argument was presented before in Chapter 3 for the isomorphism of psychological and physical space.) Therefore, the developmental process of building a psychological structure to match the structure of the world must be a constrained process because the class of possible structures is restricted. Mental structures are not free to vary, if, when development is complete, they must represent the one real world in a way that is common across species members.

In the natural world, the attributes of elements do not combine in all possible ways. For example, if you encounter a creature with feathers, there is a very high probability that it also has a beak, lays eggs, and flies. Rarely, if ever, would you encounter a nonmythological feathered creature that had paws. Exceptions are possible (ostriches and penguins do not fly), which means that the association among features is less than perfect. But if you were to predict that the creature belongs to the bird class on the basis of only one feature (feathers), and then if you predicted the remaining associated features (beak, eggs, and flying), chances of accuracy are high. In short, the attributes of these phenomena are **correlated.** So, there are no talking dogs, thinking snakes, or feathered mice . . . in true life. In the classical view of concepts, attributes are treated as **independent.** Operating with a classical definition, we must check off all the defining features of an exemplar to determine its possible inclusion in a class. With correlated features, that would be both unnecessary and cognitively inefficient.

If the mental representation of classes and categories has evolved to fit with the natural world, it seems unlikely that the psychological phenomenon would operate by rules (i.e., classical definitions) not typically characteristic of the natural world. It is more likely for intuitive knowledge of concepts and classes to have a close correspondence with real-world structure. If, additionally, the classifier were especially "tuned into" the rules that organize natural phenomena into groups, then deciphering the structure of the world should proceed quickly.

The speed of knowledge acquisition comes from the limit on the number of hypotheses about the structure that need be entertained. Thus, an organism "tuned into" naturally existing rules and categories is more likely to exhibit early conceptual competence than one who is not. In effect, conceptual development may be a much easier task for children than

Piaget and others envisioned it to be if conceptual definitions are realistic and people are inherently sensitive to the divisions among things.

The classical definition has appeal because it seems reasonable to envision categories as bundles of simpler mental entities: *features, attributes,* or *properties.* We combine the features and the junction is a category. The properties are sensible, the combinations are sensible, and so there is a clear correspondence between the mental representation of a category, specified in accord with the feature-combination rule, and the actual feature structures of the objects we encounter. And, in the real world, certain sensible features tend to recur together, to cluster, or to be correlated.

One modification of the classic approach is to define concepts in terms of **clusters** of features. This has the advantage of retaining reference to the presence of category features as indicative of class membership, but the definitional variation is less rigid than the classic version. First, in the real world, features are correlated and associated, co-occurring in actual exemplars. Second, while some exemplars may exhibit many class features characteristic of the class (the child's "dog" in Dialog 2), others may exhibit fewer characteristic features (the "snake"). Some examples of a category may be "better" than others. This way of defining concepts, classes, and procedures for identifying class members lacks the "neatness" of the traditional view, but it provides a closer fit with the experienced world.

Family Resemblance and Prototypes

One cluster-concept system is the **family-resemblance** approach to defining categories; it is proposed as an alternative to the classical view (Rosch & Mervis, 1975). Family-resemblance categories are *fuzzy* categories; all the category members are generally similar to each other, but there is no one set of defining attributes that all category members must share (Mervis & Rosch, 1981; Rosch & Mervis, 1975; Smith & Medin, 1981). It may not be possible to specify the necessary and sufficient features that mark an individual as an instance of the category, but, as with members of a family, the similarity is still there. In effect there is a *pool* of features defining a given category/family.

To be a member of the category/family, the individual must have "enough" of those features. Some individuals will exemplify more of the pool; some pairs of individuals may overlap more, sharing more common features from the pool than other pairs do. Conceivably, one could scale category members as to the amount of common attributes, the degree of overlapping characteristics, or their "distance" in terms of shared features, just as one could scale degree of similarity among members of an extended family.

Investigators have looked at whether family resemblance can serve as a model for how people structure and define categories. One way to test this hypothesis is to provide subjects with a group of object names; the objects would typically be judged as sharing common category membership. For example, an investigator might give each subject the animal exemplars "bird," "dog," "lizard," "fish," and "crab." Subjects are then asked to list the attributes describing the various exemplars, and the investigator checks the lists for overlap. Based on family-resemblance notions, there should be common attributes listed across exemplars, but no one attribute need show up on all lists. "Legs" is a probable descriptor for "birds," "dogs," "lizards," and perhaps "crabs," but not "fish." Baseball, chess, bridge, and polo all belong to the category of "games." Most adults would correctly identify each exemplar as properly included in the game category and would correctly differentiate each from nongame activities. If asked to list the attributes of each, there would be overlap in characteristics between some pairs (both polo and baseball are done with a small, round thing) but little if any overlap between others (chess and polo?). This is precisely the outcome in attribute-listing studies.

These experimental procedures have some problems, however (Murphy & Medin, 1985; Tversky & Hemenway, 1984), and so interpretation of the findings is ambiguous. Because a subject fails to list an attribute for a particular exemplar does not conclusively mean he failed to consider the attribute when making categorical decisions. For example, in the previous list of animal exemplars, "self-produced locomotion" and "ability to procreate" might not make the attribute lists for a variety of reasons other than lack of relevance to the classification decision. People tend not to list attributes exhaustively, and they tend not to list attributes that characterize the superordinate class to which an exemplar belongs (Armstrong, Gleitman, & Gleitman, 1983). So, while "feathers" is a highly probable feature on lists describing birds, "skin" is not; many animals besides birds have skin.

Subjects may also have a greater tendency to list features that distinguish one exemplar from another ("lizards" are cold-blooded, a feature not shared with "dogs") rather than features in common (both "dogs" and "lizards" have four legs and a tail). Nonoverlapping attribute lists may constitute a misrepresentation of whatever underlying mental entity is presumably responsible for the observable lists.

A second procedure for testing the validity of the family-resemblance model for categorical structures is to ask subjects to judge the "goodness" with which a particular exemplar typifies a category (Rips, Shoben, & Smith, 1973; Rosch, 1973; Tversky, 1977). Apparently, people find this task to be a natural and sensible thing to do. In assessing "typicalness," the judgments should scale in an ordinal fashion. (In contrast, classical definitions yield nominal scales.) An ordinal scale permits a range of typicality judgments from most to least typical. **Prototypical instances** are highly

representative of a category and quite dissimilar from instances drawn from other categories. "Robin," for example, is a prototypic bird and shares few features with "trout" or "rabbit." **Peripheral instances** can just barely be included in the category because they also have features defining other categories as well. "Ostrich" is a peripheral instance of the "bird" category. If you conceptualize the range of exemplar typicalness spatially, for example, in a circle, then the prototypical exemplars are located at the center of the circle. Peripheral exemplars are located closer to the edge of the circle, at the boundaries, and those at the latter location might have features in common with peripheral exemplars from other categories. As illustrated in Figure 5-1, "bat" and "duck-billed platypus" are at the boundary of the "mammal" category.

When subjects are given sets of exemplars differing in "typicalness," as judged on the basis of investigator intuition or empirical pilot studies, and asked to rate them on an ordinal scale, the predicted outcome—a range of values—is observed. And there is considerable across-individual consistency in those ratings. Indeed, there are birdier birds, fishier fish, and mammalier mammals.

Subjects can also be given **verification tasks,** where they judge the truthfulness of a statement: "*A* is a member of the *B* category." *A* is the exemplar name and *B* is the category name. Obviously, subjects usually make the correct verification judgment, but they do so more quickly when *A* is a prototypic instance ("A robin is a bird") than when *A* is a peripheral instance ("An ostrich is a bird"). Verification times also form an ordinal scale from relatively short to relatively long as a function of the typicality of exemplars. This empirical finding is robust, and it is the primary kind of evidence supportive of a prototype model for categorical structures. These data challenge the adequacy of the classical definition scheme as the appropriate model for human categorical thinking.

FIGURE 5-1 When categories are conceptualized as circular spaces, prototypical exemplars are located centrally in the spaces (e.g., rabbit, robin); peripheral exemplars (e.g., bat, duck-billed platypus) are located toward the boundaries of the spaces.

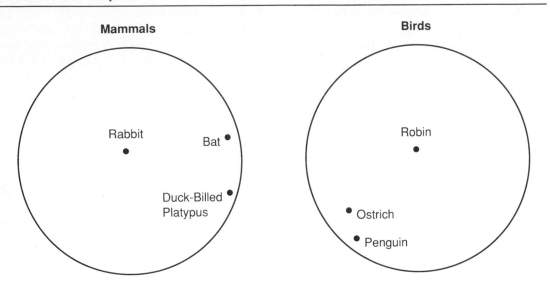

Developmental implications. Apparently, children learn typical exemplars before the atypical ones (Anglin, 1977). Perhaps instances that better exemplify a category are easier to learn than peripheral instances. For example, children may learn to identify robins and sparrows as bird instances before identifying ostriches and penguins as such. Moreover, children might acquire a category more effectively when exposed to prototypical instances rather than peripheral ones. The reasoning behind the predictions is that good exemplars should provide the most accurate basis for generalization to new instances because the prototypic ones are *maximally similar* to members of their own category and *minimally similar* to members of other categories. Robins share many more features with sparrows, hawks, canaries, and owls than they do with trout, rabbits, and crabs.

Using artificially contrived categories with a family-resemblance structure, Mervis and Pani (1980) taught child subjects labels for object categories. Some children were exposed only to good exemplars, other children only to poor exemplars. Then, children demonstrated their categorical expertise by differentiating a new set of objects, some of which were category members and some of which were not. The children exposed to the good exemplars did better. In extensions of the paradigm, children even learned better when exposed only to good exemplars as compared with exposure to the whole range of exemplars. And when exposed to the whole range, they learned the good exemplars more readily than the poor ones.

There is also evidence that children learn about *basic-level categories* before they learn about other levels of concepts within class hierarchies (Markman & Callanan, 1984). The reasoning is similar. At the basic level, exemplars of a category are maximally similar to each other and minimally similar to exemplars in other basic-level categories. So, for example, instances of the basic-level category "chair" are all much alike and clearly differ from "beds."

At the superordinate level within that specific hierarchy, however, there is less overlap among exemplars. "Chair" is an instance of "furniture," and so are "footstool" and "bureau"; the instances are not maximally similar. Extending to the subordinate level, the across-category similarities could be too great, the differences too subtle. So "armchairs," "recliners," and "rocking chairs" might not be maximally different enough. It may be that children, particularly young ones, employ an exemplar-based structure for categories (Kossan, 1981; Markman, 1989). Perhaps they represent concepts as lists of exemplars to which they compare new instances for overlap, rather than representing the concept as a list of criterial attributes.

Problems with prototypes. The situation, however, gets muddier. Armstrong, Gleitman, and Gleitman (1983), in a series of studies, replicated Rosch's (1973, 1975) procedure of having subjects rate exemplars for typicalness. Following Rosch, these investigators selected exemplars representing eight categories. Four of the categories, "fruit," "sport," "vegetable," and "vehicle," were prototype categories, but the other four were well-defined categories: "even number," "odd number," "plane geometry figure," and "female." These latter concepts are referred to as **nominal kinds** (Keil, 1989; Schwartz, 1979). A single criterion defines them, and an exemplar is either a member or a nonmember of the category on the basis of that criterion. Nominal kinds can be classically defined, and the scaling of exemplars yields a two-category nominal scale. So, for example, an integer is odd if it cannot be divided by 2 without a remainder; a figure is either a triangle or not a triangle. There is no reason to predict that some odd numbers would prove to be prototypic exemplars, capturing oddness well, while others would qualify as peripheral exemplars sharing some similarity with nonodd numbers. Subjects' judgments for exemplars drawn from classes identified as nominal kinds, and well defined at that, should not form an ordinal scale.

The findings of the studies by Armstrong et al. raise questions about the meaning of the sort of empirical data that have served to validate prototype structures for real-world classes. Armstrong et al. were able to replicate the Rosch findings; in fact, typicality ratings for exemplars in the fruit, vehicle, vegetable, and sport categories were very close to those obtained in the original investigations. "Orange" indeed is a fruitier fruit than "fig"; "baseball" is a sportier sport than "archery."

Confusingly, however, the nominal-kind exemplars also scaled in a graded fashion. The number 7 proved odder than 13; "aunt" was more female than "widow." Moreover, as it takes subjects longer to verify statements of category membership for nonprototypic exemplars (i.e., verification time for "a fig is a fruit" is longer than verification time for "an orange is a fruit"), the same holds true for statements related to well-defined category exemplars (e.g., "13 is an odd number"). In short, the empirical outcome is the same no matter what type of category selected, family resemblance categories or otherwise. How do we interpret such an outcome?

The data make sense if we contend that all categories, well defined or otherwise, are mentally represented as family-resemblance structures. Then, the ordinal scaling of exemplars from any category is a reasonable outcome. If we reject that notion, then the prototype-scaling methodologies do not distinguish empirically from concepts that may be mentally represented as family-resemblance structures from those that are unlikely to be so structured. Then, the scaling of exemplar-rating responses regardless of concept type looks like an **epiphenomenon,** an artifact of the manner in which the task is presented to and interpreted by subjects. In that case, the data tell us little about the underlying structure of the mental representation of classes and categories.

Still another interpretation is to postulate a dual nature for concepts (Osherson & Smith, 1981; Smith & Medin, 1981). There might be one mental structure associated with an *identification function* for things and events in the real world (Armstrong et al., 1983). The mentally stored identification aspect of a concept could conceivably have a prototype structure organized around "exemplariness." A second mental structure, a conceptual core or sense of the concept (Miller, 1977), encompassing a systematic categorical description functions to determine class membership. The core may not be organized in the same fashion, or even make reference to the same features, as does the structure serving the identification function.

For example, suppose a specific animal belongs to the "raccoon" category. To judge the exemplariness of the individual raccoon, we would check its size, its markings, the "mask" on its face, its handling of objects, and so forth, the observable features associated with raccoonness. However, suppose we were to dye the raccoon's fur black and paint a white stripe down its back in the manner of a skunk. We would not think the raccoon had become a skunk. The individual would not change class membership, nor would we think it had, just because of a change in appearance, in perceptual features. It might take us longer to identify the skunk-looking raccoon as a class member of the raccoon group, but the skunk-looking raccoon would still have retained its raccoon "essence." Characteristic features, as captured in a prototype conceptualization, may be associated with how we use concepts and how we normally and rapidly identify instances of concepts but not necessarily with what those concepts mean to us (Keil, 1986b).

The raccoon/skunk example raises another knotty problem: the role of features as defining attributes in conceptual representations.

Both the classical view and the family-resemblance alternative make reference to an exemplar's features as criteria for determining class membership. And yet, we can strip away those features, as with the raccoon, and still make a membership judgment.

The family-resemblance approach to concepts avoids some of the problems of the classical view and provides a methodology that has revealed interesting and robust empirical findings. However, prototype structures do not solve all of the epistemological problems. We still are not at all certain how best to define what concepts are or how they are structured. As Armstrong, Gleitman, and Gleitman (1983) concluded:

> A host of thinkers have shown us that there is enormous difficulty in explicating even so simple and concrete a concept as bird. They've shown that the difficulty becomes greater by orders of magnitude when confronted with an abstract functional concept like game. Perhaps psychologists are more than a little overexhuberant in supposing it will be easier to explicate the concept concept. (p. 305)

Natural Kinds

The family-resemblance approach to concepts has clear psychological advantages over the classical one. First, the prototype view seems to fit better with real-world divisions among entities. Second, prototype notions avoid sticky definition problems, since prototypes do not need either necessary or sufficient specifying features. Many terms that apply to naturally occurring classes of things do not have clear, feature-based definitions (Kripke, 1972; Putnam, 1975). Third, prototype views capitalize on the fact that features of real-world phenomena are both complex and occur in correlated clusters. However, mental conceptual structures cannot just be representations that tally the frequency of occurrence of correlated features in the world. Some features are more critical to the "essence" of an entity than others. So, for example, both bananas and boomerangs share the feature of being curved, but a straight boomerang is judged more anomalous than a straight banana (Medin & Shoben, 1988). Apparently, being curved is more central to the essence of a boomerang than it is to a banana.

By itself, the prototype theory of concepts does not account for why people would differentially weight some features over others in definitional importance other than by frequency of occurrence. Actual empirical frequency, however, does not always predict differential weighting (Keil, 1991). The meaning of a feature must somehow be taken into account; feature meaningfulness in turn implicates some semantic framework that gives sense to individual concepts (Murphy & Medin, 1985).

Prototype explanations also fall short of accounting for the fact that some concepts have especially rich conglomerations of correlated features. Natural-kind categories, the classes of objects found in nature (Kripke, 1971, 1972; Schwartz, 1977, 1979), are a case in point; these kinds have very complex correlated-feature structures. Not all the features are equally relevant to defining a natural kind, even though they may be ubiquitous to most exemplars; and not all the features are equally detectable either. Indeed, there may be little correlation between a feature's importance in defining a natural kind and that feature's obviousness. Yet natural kinds are fundamental classes of things in the real world about which people have elaborate knowledge and considerable familiarity.

"Dogs," "cats," and "rabbits" are all exemplars of the natural kind, "mammals." There are obvious similar feature bundles here. All have fur, legs, ears, eyes, and so forth. But if we were to continue to explore and probe the similarity of features across the three exemplars, we would discover more and more shared features—in their biological functioning, in adaptations to the environment, and so forth. In fact, the more we looked, the more we would find; and, indeed, there may be no end to the discoveries to be made. Some of the shared features can be identified with casual inspection. These are perceptually obvious, like size, texture, color, and behavior. Others are not so perceptual and are not so obvious, like the structure and operation of the circulatory and reproductive systems.

With natural kinds, we believe that unobservable properties are common across members (Markman, 1989). We expect them to share features we cannot see and may not have even thought about. It is these "deep" properties, these hidden structural properties, that account for the "surface" ones, the more superficial (and less essential) properties we readily perceive (Putnam, 1977). So, for example, we do not expect that the common physical features jointly shared by thoroughbred and Arabian horses *cause* a corresponding similarity in the internal biological structures of the two. We do expect the reverse causal relationship to be true.

With natural kinds, there is an unlimited richness to the categories. We expect to discover new facts about them if we continue to look (Gelman & Markman, 1986). The correlated structure is so rich, so connected, and so much of it is nonobvious that specialized disciplines exist for mapping the natural domains. Adults do not generalize expectations about the richness of natural-kind categories to other real-world but nonnatural-kind categories like artifacts (e.g., "furniture," "vehicles," and "tools"). There is a good possibility we would quickly discover all there is to know about "screwdrivers" and "coffee pots"; we may never find out all there is to know about "eagles" and "whales."

One advantage of categories is the role they play in supporting **induction** (Gelman, 1988). Induction is the process of drawing inferences that extend beyond available evidence (Holland, Holyoak, Nisbett, & Thagard, 1986). Thus, if two entities share category membership, it is often possible to generalize what we know about the first entity to the second. If we know something about the category "fish" and we encounter an unfamiliar individual that also happens to be a fish, then we can accurately surmise how the new individual eats, breathes, reproduces, and so forth.

Obviously, the scientifically tutored should make such inferences, but can the naive person do so? Can the child, for instance, make reasonable inferences about the shared properties of members of the same natural kind? If children can engage in induction, especially about the nonobvious, non-perceptually based attributes of natural kinds, then their immature categorical structures, which support the induction process, must overlap in important ways with mature structures (Wellman & Gelman, 1988).

Gelman and Markman (1986, 1987) pursued this line of inquiry in a series of interesting studies. Essentially, their paradigm is as follows:

1. They show children pictures of two individuals that are not members of the same natural kind, for example, a tropical fish and a dolphin.
2. The children are then taught a new fact about the individuals: that fish, for example, breathe under water but dolphins pop out of the water to breathe.
3. Then, the children are shown a third individual (shark) and informed of its category membership (fish).
4. Then they are asked if the third individual shares the same attribute as its fellow category member.

The catch is that the shark looks most like the individual with whom it does not share category membership (the dolphin) and not like the individual with whom it does share category membership (the tropical fish).

If, as Piaget and others argued, young children's categories are perceptually bound, then the greater salience of the perceptually obvious similarity between the categorically non-similar individuals should seduce children into making an incorrect inference (Flavell, 1985). We might, in short, expect them to infer that the shark pops out of the water to breathe. However, children typically do not make the error. Even 4-year-olds are more apt to generalize on the basis of nonobvious shared category membership than on the basis of perceptually obvious shared appearance. That is, most children will infer that the shark, like the fish, breathes under water. An example of the kind of stimuli Gelman and Markman used is depicted in Figure 5-2. Interestingly enough, children are able to draw inferences appropriately even when the same-category instances are referred to with nonidentical labels (e.g., "rabbit" and "bunny") and even when no labels are used (Gelman, 1988).

The fact that young children are as proficient as they are at drawing inferences about natural kinds and in generalizing properties to novel instances raises a different sort of problem. Not all properties are generalizable; to some extent, generalization of properties across objects must be constrained to only properties that are shared. Without constraints, unwarranted generalizations are possible (Goodman, 1955; Sternberg, 1982). Even within natural-kind categories, some properties are idiosyncratic to an individual. So, for example, that one rabbit is old, tired, or has a hurt foot cannot be extended to other rabbits.

With artifact categories, generalization is even more restricted. That two individuals are both chairs cannot serve as the basis for inferring that both are made of the same material (one could be wood, the other metal), in the way one could infer that two bunnies have the same organic makeup. In short, whether an inference is reasonable or not depends on the category and on the property reasoned about (Nisbett, Krantz, Jepson, & Kunda, 1983). It is possible that children may *overgeneralize,* es-

FIGURE 5-2   *The Bird, Bat, Bird Triad Used in Gelman and Markmam's Study of
Category-Supported Inference*
The lower bird resembles the bat in perceptual appearance, but the two are not members of the same *natural
kind.*

From "Categories and Induction in Young Children" by S. A. Gelman and E. M. Markman, 1986, *Cognition, 23,* pp. 183–
208. Reprinted by permission.

pecially if they are biased to expect categories of real-world phenomena to have a natural-kind structure.

To test this hypothesis, Gelman (1988) examined the extent of preschoolers' and second-graders' inferences across category and property type. The categories were natural kinds (e.g., rabbit, apple, gold) and artifacts (e.g., hammer, coat, clock). Children were taught a new property about an instance of the target category and asked if the property could be generalized to another category member. Some of the properties could only be legitimately extended to other members in natural-kind categories, for instance, what the individual had inside. Other properties could be legitimately generalized across members of an artifact category, for example, what the function of an object was. And still others were nongeneralizable by reason of idiosyncrasy (the individual being "dirty"), historical accident (e.g., "fell on the floor"), or temporal feature (e.g., "a year old").

Reiterating earlier work, the findings indicated that young children make sensible, reasoned, and principled inferences; the data are presented in Table 5-1. Even among the youngest subject group, generalization was not just based on the perceptual and surface similarity of the instances. Children expected to find deep similarities among category members, regardless of category, and their inferences revealed that. But children did not expect transient and idiosyncratic properties, the nongeneralizable ones, to extend to other members.

The major developmental difference was the age-associated distinctions children made among categories. In particular, the 4-year-olds exhibited an unstable *inferential* distinction between natural kinds and artifacts even though they understood the *literal* distinction between the categories (i.e., artifacts are human made, natural kinds are not). In contrast, the second-graders expected to find a much richer set of similarities among natural kinds

TABLE 5-1 *The Percentage of Sensible Response Patterns Produced by Children Asked to Generalize Properties across Individuals in Various Categories. A Chance Level Is .19, as Would Occur If Children Were to Make Random Judgements.*

	Preschool	Grade 2
Equally generalizable		
Natural kinds	.77	.90
Artifacts	.69	.87
Generalizable for natural kinds		
Natural kinds	.53	.87
Artifacts	.58	.74
Generalizable for artifacts		
Natural kinds	.60	.75
Artifacts	.62	.82
Nongeneralizable		
Natural kinds	.09	.30
Artifacts	.09	.26

Note: From "The Development of Induction with Natural Kind and Artifact Categories" by S. A. Gelman, 1988, *Cognitive Psychology, 20,* p. 77. Reprinted by permission.

than among artifacts, and they differentially inferred across instances as a function of category type. The younger children's inferences were not sufficiently constrained.

The studies of children's understanding of concepts in which natural-kind categories are the focus reveal some provocative outcomes. First, there is evidence of early competence; even the performances of very young children suggest conceptual sophistication. Second, in contrast to predictions of traditional theories, the young are not bound by perceptual obviousness when making conceptual inferences. Third, there are important continuities between the conceptual thinking of the young and that of their older counterparts. These outcomes are supportive of a nativistic explanation of development, because they indicate age-invariant universals of cognitive functioning. Indeed, the developmental story that emerges from the natural-kind concept studies contrasts markedly with the traditional account.

Summary

There are all kinds of categorization studies with children and alternative ways of defining what concepts and categories are. In much of the research reviewed in Chapter 4, studies spurred by traditional theories, classical definitions are preferred. These *nominal kinds* denote a concept's necessary and sufficient features. Then, again, we find *prototype* definitions, where clusters of correlated features converge in specifying what a concept is. And finally, there are *natural kinds* with their particularly rich correlated feature structures and a hint of "essentialism" that goes beyond "featureness."

Conceptual rules, like elements to be classified, could form a scale. Or, put another way, concepts themselves could scale ordinally along some dimension of complexity. One proposal (Keil, 1989) places pure nominal kinds as an anchor at one end of this dimension and pure natural kinds as the anchor at the other. The bases of differentiation are the degree of "well-definedness" and the extent of richness in conceptual structure. So, for example, at one end, the nominal kind—odd number—is well defined in accord with a single criterion, and the association among instances of the kind is limited. Instances share no other similarities, obvious or otherwise. At the other end of the scale, the natural kind—lion—is not definable with even a long list of criteria. Here, instances share a wealth of common features and similarities, and, in the end, some nonobvious "essenceness" may prove to be the ultimate grouping criteria. This proposed scale for concept types is presented in Figure 5-3.

The empirical literature, then, actually addresses diverse phenomena. The observation that young children do not usually fare well on classification tasks where nominal-kind exemplars are sorted and that they do much better on conceptual tasks based on the understanding of natural kind is not irreconcilable if the literature is actually multifaceted. Each study

FIGURE 5-3 *A Continuum that Scales Concepts on the Basis of "Well-Definedness."*
At one end, anchored by *nominal-kind* concepts, categories are defined with a single criterion. At the other end, anchored by *natural-kind* concepts, categories have rich, perhaps unlimited, conceptual structures.

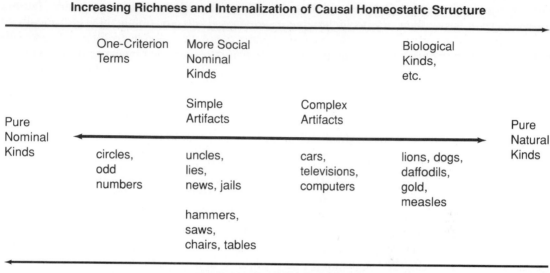

From *Concepts, Kinds, and Cognitive Development* by F. C. Keil, 1989, Cambridge, MA: MIT Press. Copyright 1989 by MIT Press. Reprinted by permission.

only tells us about a small section of the larger continuum. Viewed in this way, the developmental facts are not incompatible. Thus, it should be possible to integrate those facts. To summarize:

1. Young children often appear conceptually immature and differ from older individuals when organizing entities in accord with classical definitions and nominal kinds (see Chapter 4).
2. Children, like adults, can reference prototypelike structures when evaluating the exemplariness of entities.
3. Children seem to acquire categories in a manner consistent with feature structures.
4. With natural-kind categories, even the very young look conceptually mature.

Integrating pieces of a picture requires a frame into which the pieces fit. Just as individual concepts take their sense from some larger body of knowledge, individual developmental facts need some larger unit, too. Concepts are organized into knowledge structures, into systems that provide the "glue" and give meaning to individual concepts. Describing that structure could similarly provide a glue in which diverse empirical data make the most sense. That is where we turn next.

ONTOLOGICAL KNOWLEDGE

Cognitive development entails acquiring the ability to order experience and to construct mental models that represent the ordered product. The raw materials for model building are what result from encounters with real-world phenomena: sensation and perception, motor exploration, and self-produced activity. In Chapter 3, we saw how the raw material of encounters with physical space becomes encapsulated in mental representations of spatial relations. These represented relations are in turn integrated into a formal system, or geometry, that mediates spatial performance. Cognitive psychologists then try to determine which particular geometry depicts the mental model most adequately. Developmentalists extend the inquiry to include questions about the origins of that geometry. Whatever story is proposed, it must account for the empirical phenomenon, what we know about spatial behavior. But since data alone are seldom sufficient to disambiguate theoretical controversy, more than one formalism is possible.

Objects, elements, and events can be thought about in a similar fashion. Entities are encountered in experience with the reality of things, and those encounters must be ordered, too. The products are classes, categories, and scales—conceptual relations. Extending the parallel between space and objects, there needs to be a formalism, a "geometry," for describing how conceptual relations are ordered. What is the best geometry for categorical cognition?

Piaget answered that question. He proposed a system of domain-general operations that structures categorical cognition in the same manner as any other form of cognition. His formal model was the **groupment structures** of concrete operations. But the Piagetian proposal cannot account for the whole story. It does explain young children's unsophisticated scaling attempts when categorizing in accord with nominal concept rules and when ordering elements in accord with ordinal concept rules. It does predict the young child's failure on class-inclusion problems when class nouns are the referent for the superordinate category. The child yet to achieve concrete operational status, yet to depend on logic as the basis for reasoning, should be seduced by the perceptual, by the transient, by the obvious situational aspects of any scaling task, and many times young children are.

Other bits and pieces are *not* consistent with the Piagetian model, however. *Early competence* is obtainable on scaling problems under some task-demand conditions, so the display of competence is task specific. *Positive training effects* are obtainable, too; ideally, it should not be possible to alter a conceptual structure constrained by maturation and time. Then, finally, there are the data about young children's reasoning with natural kinds. Children's category-supported inferences with natural kinds are not dominated by the perceptual, the transient, or the obvious. Some other model could explain more of the data more sufficiently.

Constraints on Ontology

Frank Keil (1979, 1981) presented a formal system for the organization of classes and categories and concepts and meanings as an alternative to Piaget's. This "geometry of classes" is an ontological knowledge structure. **Ontology** is the branch of metaphysics concerned with the ultimate nature of things, the nature of being, what exists in the world. **Ontological knowledge,** then, is knowledge about what exists in the world or what can *be*. An **ontological knowledge structure** is the organization people bring to things, objects, elements, and events experienced in the world, a classification system that takes into account similarity in the true nature of things. For Keil, ontology provided a conceptual structure for modeling how we cut the world at its joints, for people's "naive metaphysics."

If, indeed, there is something natural, basic, real, and truly nonarbitrary about the way the world structures into like kinds, then that naturalness should be reflected in mental models describing that structure (the isomorphism issue again). And, from a developmental perspective, the structures of adults and children should not differ in important ways if the two structures are both constrained in the same way: by the way the world is organized. If it can be shown that the naive metaphysics of adults reveals a coherent and invariant structure across individuals that derives from the true nature of things, then it should also be possible to show that the metaphysics of children is very similar. It is less reasonable to argue that children's mature, natural ontological knowledge structures evolve from prior, immature, nonnatural ones. The developmental mechanism necessary to change a nonnatural system into a natural one is essentially inconceivable. In the **constraints approach** to conceptual development, Keil (1981) proposed that the ontological knowledge structures of both children and adults are importantly constrained in the same way, and so, for both, categories and classes are organized in an invariant fashion.

How can an investigator possibly assess the structure of people's ontological knowledge? These naive knowledge systems are intuitive and tacit. They influence cognitive performance but are not available to conscious introspection. It is difficult to elicit intuitive knowledge in adults and especially difficult in children. Recall, however, that conceptual knowledge is semantic and, therefore, it surfaces in language as the labels children acquire and use to stand for things (Markman, 1989). Ontological knowledge is reflected in language, too.

Consider the following line of reasoning: Specific nouns (e.g., dog) represent entities—things, events, beings, and so forth. Class nouns (e.g., animals) represent kinds of things. Predicates represent the actions and states that entities can assume, do, or be. Ontology entails what things can be, what states entities can assume, and the true nature of things constrains what they can be, what states they can assume. Ontological knowledge, therefore, could be revealed in the combinations of nouns and predicates allowable and not allowable in a language. Perhaps by looking at what combinations children and adults accept as permissible, on a semantic not a syntactic basis, we can learn something about people's intuitive ontology. Compare the two sentences, "The rabbit is hungry" and "The rabbit is an hour long." Both are grammatical and, therefore, syntactically allowable. But we automatically reject the latter sentence as a nonallowable combination. "Rabbit" represents an entity that can assume only certain states, that can only "be" certain ways, and "being an hour long" is not one of them. The possible states that go with "rabbit" are limited by the true nature of the critter.

Philosopher Fred Sommers (1959, 1963, 1965, 1971) drew a link between **predicability,** what terms can be combined with what others in language, and ontology, the natural classes inherent in the world. Both are constrained in the same way. We observe this in the sensibility of statements, that is, which terms can be logically combined with which predicates. A sensible combination is represented in the statement, "The child was delighted." This statement is allowable, imaginable, and makes sense, and its truth value can be ascertained (that is, either the child is or is not delighted).

In contrast, the statement, "The child happened yesterday," is not allowable, not imaginable, and its truth value cannot be ascertained; it is literally not possible for the child to have happened yesterday, today, or any other time. The ontological properties of the term and the predicate render the second combination conceptually impossible and intuitively inappropriate. Sommers proposed a formal constraint on ontology that dictates the structure of natural language by limiting which combinations of predicates and terms are logically permitted and which are not. Sommers (1971) referred to the constraint as the M-configuration; Keil (1979) called it the **M-constraint.**

The constraint becomes meaningful if we think about the structure of conceptual knowledge the individual creates to represent the world. Both Sommers and Keil depicted that structure as having a hierarchical form, sort of like an upside-down tree. Each point where the tree branches is a *node;* a single node is at the top of the tree, other nodes proliferate as one moves down the tree.

In a **predicability tree,** shown in Figure 5-4, the nodes represent predicates (*P*) such as "is hungry," "happened yesterday," and "is an hour long." The node at the top of the tree represents the most general class of predi-

cates, those that could be combined with virtually any term (*X*) and a sensible, allowable statement would result. Thus, if *X* "is interesting," *X* could be virtually anything; the particular predicate can be combined with any term since, ontologically, everything is either interesting or not interesting. As we move down the tree, the predicates become less general, combinable with some terms but not oth-

FIGURE 5-4 *A Predicability Tree.*
The nonterminal nodes represent classes of predicates applicable to appropriate classes of terms.

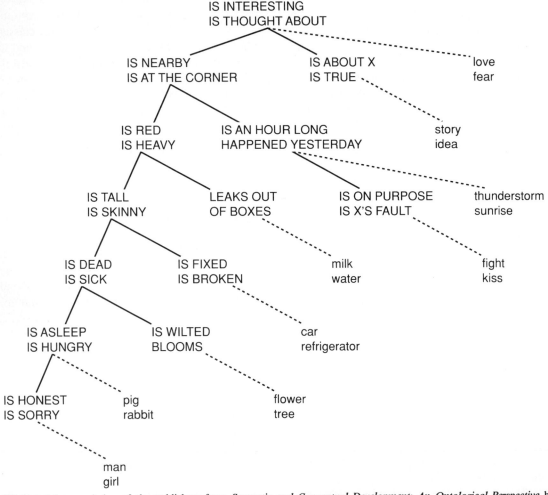

ers. The predicate "is dead," for example, could be combined only with terms used to denote living things capable of dying, not artifact terms, event terms, and so forth, which are not.

In a predicability tree, predicates occupy the nodes, but representative terms to which those predicates apply are also included to clarify how the tree works. In interpreting a tree, the rule is that a predicate (*P*) *spans* (can be combined with) all those terms (*X*) that every predicate below it spans. But the reverse is not true. So, for example, a flower (*X*) can be wilted, dead, tall, heavy, nearby, and interesting, but it cannot be sorry. The predicates and terms depicted in the tree are not meant to be exhaustive but to represent classes of predicates and terms.

Predicability trees have analogous **ontological trees** (Figure 5-5). Here the nodes are

FIGURE 5-5 *An Ontological Tree Showing the Hierarchial, Treelike Structure among Categories of Entities.*

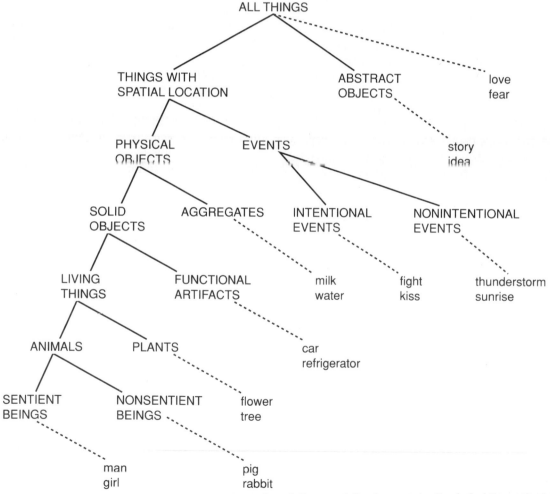

classes of things, categories, or concepts to which predicates in the previous tree can apply. Therefore, the predicate "is sorry" applies to and only to entities in the class "sentient beings"; "is sorry" cannot be applied to more general classes of things such as "animals," "physical objects," "events," and so forth. There are no "sorry trees," "sorry rocks," or "sorry parties" except in a metaphorical sense. (For more on metaphor, however, see Chapter 8.) In the ontological tree, the uppermost node is the most generalized class of entities (i.e., "all things"). As we move down the tree, through the branches, the nodes represent more restricted groupings of things. Terminal nodes (those at the ends of branches) represent the least inclusive groups. Thus, for example, the node "plants" represents a small subset of all possible "things with spatial location."

In the two trees, we find *points* or nodes and *lines* or connections that represent possible relations between points or nodes. Where there is no line, a relationship is not possible. The *M* in the M-constraint refers to the configurations or connections that are not allowable. Filling in these nonallowable connections would form an *M* or *W* pattern. According to Keil and Sommers, we do not allow combinations that would yield such a configuration. When we do, it is because of ambiguity, for example, when a single term actually has alternative meanings that permit it to refer to entities in different classes, or when a specific predicate can refer to alternative states of nature. Thus, in the following instance,

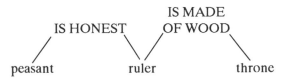

ruler is a term with two conceptually different referents (there are actually two "kinds" of rulers), and an *M* is formed on the tree. Or, in the following example,

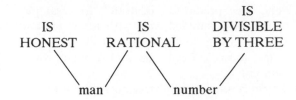

"is rational" refers to two different states of nature ambiguously referred to with the same tag, and a *W* is formed. These kinds of *M*s and *W*s are an artifact of the ambiguity of words, resolvable through context, not reflections of ontologically allowable ideas, an ambiguity at the conceptual level.

Phrased more formally, the M-constraint is a conceptual restriction that operates on these knowledge structures. The M-constraint allows no downwardly convergent nodes that create *M* or *W* patterns on the predicability tree. Thus, predicates may not have terms in common and, at the same time, terms unique to each. As Keil (1979) stated, "of all the possible ways in which predicates and terms can be organized, only those organizations that obey the M-constraint are psychologically natural" (p. 15).

The proposed ontological knowledge structure and the M-constraint that operates on it have important implications for the development of conceptual knowledge. For one, the tree could represent a very basic and intuitive skeleton for how categories are organized, which categories are judged as more similar to each other, and for what sorts of cross-categorical inductions are allowable. For example, if a child represented the following section of the tree,

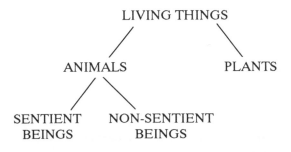

then, based on the connections allowed by the M-constraint, the child should avoid certain kinds of conceptual errors. The child should *not* confuse the properties of plants and humans, join together the category "rabbit" with the category "flower," or infer that if fish have gills, trees do, too. The child may judge that "dogs" and "people" are more similar than "dogs" and "bushes" because the first two groups are closer on the tree than the latter two groups. In short, the tree and the M-constraint predict that some conceptual errors are highly unlikely (e.g., confusing the properties of "rabbits" and "screwdrivers") while others are more likely (e.g., confusing the properties of "rabbits" and "humans"). Similarly, the tree and the M-constraint lead to the prediction that the sentence, "The idea is red," is more likely to be rejected as anomalous and unnatural than the sentence, "The pig is sorry." The structure presents a hypothesis or set of hypotheses about the nature of conceptual knowledge. Since hypotheses are predictions about observable phenomena, the viability of the proposition can be tested by comparing it with empirical data.

Studies of Ontological Knowledge

A first test of a model like Keil's is whether it can function as a representation for mature conceptual knowledge. Are the conceptual judgments of adults predictable from a formal model of ontological knowledge governed by the M-constraint? Those conceptual judgments are assessible by examining predicability, the allowable relationships between predicates and terms in language.

According to Keil (1979), several psychological phenomena reveal predicability: people's judgments about (1) anomalous sentences, (2) natural classes, (3) similar classes, and (4) natural copredications. The first kind of judgment directly taps people's intuitions about the allowability of sentences combining terms and predicates. Adults should be able

to identify and reject ontologically unallowable combinations such as, "The moon is disappointed," while accepting untruthful but allowable combinations like, "The moon is purple."

In the second kind of judgment, tasks are designed to examine which groupings of categories subjects find most natural; ontologically, the combinations of humans, animals, and plants is more natural than plants, solids, and events. Third, but along the same line of reasoning, classes should be judged as more similar the closer they are located on the ontological tree. And, finally, with copredication, adults should judge some predicate combinations as more natural and sensible than others. Thus, the combination "is honest" + "is loyal" is sensible; "is honest" + "is a week long" is awkward and not very sensible. Keil has examined all of these conceptual phenomena with adults as part of a systematic evaluation of his theoretical model. A model must survive such an assessment before it becomes useful developmentally.

The methodology used in the anomalous sentence studies exemplifies the empirical procedures. A simplified predicability tree, depicted in Figure 5-6, was constructed as the criterion, or standard. Then, a series of sentences combining predicates and terms from the tree was created; some sentences were sensible and some were anomalous. Subjects were presented with this series and were asked to determine whether each sentence was sensible or not. Data were then used to construct trees for each subject on the basis of the sentence judgments. The subjects' trees could be compared with the experimental tree and the number of M-constraint violations tabulated.

Similarly, with the other tasks, subjects' judgments about class orderings, class similarities, and the naturalness of copredications were used to construct subject trees. The outcome—the actual number of tree matches and M-constraint violations observed—can then be quantified and contrasted with the number

FIGURE 5-6 *Simplified Predicability Tree Used in the Anomaly Study with Adults.*

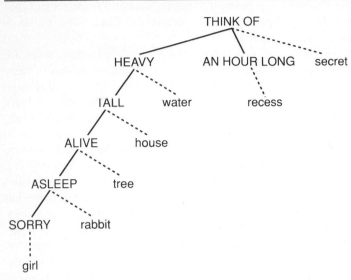

expected on the basis of chance (as would occur if ontological knowledge were not constrained).

Indeed, Keil's results were quite remarkable. The subject trees, although not always duplicates of the experimental tree, were very similar. Moreover, M-constraint violations turned out to be extremely rare. When they were observed, ambiguity in word meanings could explain their appearance. Thus, Keil concluded that the ontological knowledge structures of adults are constrained, the specific constraint appears to be the M-constraint, and the constraint is universal. The latter point is particularly important. By implication, a universal constraint should operate the same way across everybody. In short, a universal constraint should yield a knowledge structure that is constant across individuals irrespective of idiosyncratic history, experience, or, most important developmentally, of age.

The second test in the validation process was an evaluation of the developmental fit of the model; thus, Keil continued with a series of child studies. The purpose was to (1) describe the ontological knowledge structure of children, (2) test whether it, too, is governed by the M-constraint, and (3) determine the nature of age-associated changes in ontological knowledge. The methodologies pioneered in the adult studies were extended and adapted for use with children. Obviously, asking children whether a sentence is anomalous or not is tricky; child subjects will experience problems distinguishing sentences that are anomalous from ones that are not true but ontologically possible.

Keil used a procedure of asking the child whether sentences were "silly" or "okay" followed by a series of questions designed to investigate more precisely the reason for the child's judgment. So, should a child respond that the sentence, "The house is an hour long," is silly, questioning should reveal why the child judged it so. This pursuant questioning was necessary to probe deeper and to distinguish silly judgments predicated on untruthfulness—that is, "The recess was an hour long," when it might only have been 15 minutes—from silly judgments predicated on true anomaly.

The questioning procedure is exemplified in an anecdote drawn from a replication study by another investigator (Chandler, 1989). A child was being asked about the ontological properties of a "tench," a small fish. Specifically, the child had to judge whether a tench can be tall to see if he understood that physical properties are assignable to this category of entities. The child denied that the tench could be tall, a judgment that appears to be an ontological error. However, the investigator had to determine whether the error was specific to "tallness" or general to spatial proper-

ties. Therefore, the child was asked whether or not a tench could be tall if stood up on its tail. The child did accept the plausibility of a tall tench under those circumstances. Therefore, the child had not made an ontological error (denying spatial properties to a physical entity) but was confused by the specific predicate; fish, which normally swim through the water horizontally, are more apt to be thought about as "long" rather than "tall." Both are spatial predicates.

One of the target predicability trees Keil used with children is illustrated in Figure 5-7. From this, the test sentences were generated, which in turn were used to collect silly-okay judgments. Subject predicability trees were extracted from the judgment data. As was the case for adults, violations of the M-constraint were exceptionally rare for children. In fact, Keil observed that even kindergarten children scrupulously honored the constraint. Still, predicability trees constructed from children's

FIGURE 5-7 *Predicability Tree Used in the Anomaly Study with Children.*

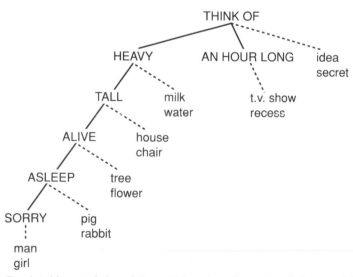

intuitions were not like the target tree or the adult trees. The trees were simpler; collapsed versions of mature trees. The trees of kindergarten children, for instance, collapsed all ontological categories into two basic ones: living and nonliving. Trees created from second-graders' protocols showed greater differentiation. Intuitions of fourth-graders represented

FIGURE 5-8 *Prototypic Trees Extracted from the Performances of Children at Different Age Levels.* The trees reveal children's intuitions and demonstrate increasing, age-associated differentiation.

Predicability Tree Showing a 5-Year-Old's Intuitions

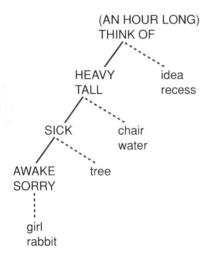

Predicability Tree Showing a 7-Year-Old's Intuitions

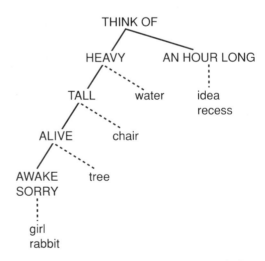

Predicability Tree Showing a 9-Year-Old's Intuitions

the same distinctions adults would make, except the youngsters failed to differentiate between humans and other animals and between abstract objects and events. Prototypic trees extracted from performances of children at different age levels are illustrated in Figure 5-8.

Keil has replicated this work with other term-predicate combinations and extended it to both younger subjects and to non-English-speaking subjects. Similar outcomes were obtained. Keil concluded that the ontological knowledge structures of children, even young ones, is constrained in the same manner as those of adults. Moreover, a rigid developmental pattern emerges in the acquisition of ontological knowledge. The trees grow in predictable, nonvariable ways, with increasing differentiation and elaboration of distinctions in a downward direction. Branches at the bottom of the upside-down tree, that is, lower placed distinctions, occur later developmentally than branches at the top of the tree. The pattern is hierarchical and stable across specific instances and particular modes of expression.

If ontological trees represent the set of fundamental categories people use to structure reality, then the age-related changes detected in these trees have implications for the nature of development. The trees do change, but by means of the proliferation of nodes. Older children do not make entirely different cuts than young children (both distinguish between living and nonliving things). Older children make more cuts, finer distinctions, within those fundamental categories common to all. This is quantitative change in contrast to the qualitative variety favored by traditionalists.

Keil's theoretical analysis of conceptual development is not free of controversy. Ontological knowledge is presumed to be deep, basic, and essential to an intuitive understanding of the world around us. Those intuitions are *reflected* in language, but it is not presumed that the intuitions are identical to the language forms used to access them. However, in most tasks used to tap ontological knowledge, the deeper, conceptual level of understanding is confounded with the more superficial, surface level of those specific language forms.

The sample sentences in a study provide a context for eliciting conceptual knowledge, but the knowledge structures extracted from people's responses to those sentences are supposed to be general and to transcend context. However, it can and has been argued that Keil's conclusions are context specific (Gerard & Mandler, 1983). Perhaps the rareness of M-constraint violations that Keil observed was a function of his particular sentence pool, his particular choice of terms and predicates. Another pool might conceivably yield a much higher proportion of M-constraint violations. Keil has countered with additional studies, extensions of the original, that varied the term-predicate pool and still led to the same conclusions (see Keil, 1989; Keil & Kelly, 1986).

A logical problem arises whenever one makes claims to the universality of a phenomenon; it only takes one *true* exception to rule out the hypothesis of universality. Thus, identifying legitimate counterexamples, either allowable statements that unambiguously violate the M-constraint or nonallowable statements that are not violations (e.g., "the man is pregnant"), presents potential troubling counterinstances.

Carey (1983, 1985) provided plausible counterexamples to challenge Keil's position. Carey did not necessarily dispute the point that ontological knowledge serves as the skeleton for conceptual knowledge, nor did she dispute the proposition that ontological knowledge changes developmentally and is reflected in age-associated changes in children's conceptual behavior. What she did dispute is that the M-constraint is the key shaper of ontological knowledge. She rejected the specific constraint proposed, not the notion that ontological knowledge is constrained. Indeed, even according to Keil, the ontological trees of young children are very simple, with few categorical distinctions.

Carey argued that the M-constraint, applied to these very simple trees, underspecifies the categorical distinctions young children are capable of drawing and the category-supported inductions they do make (Carey, 1985). Recall Markman and Gelman's work with inductions supported by natural-kind categories. Young children, those with presumably very simple ontological trees, drew stable categorical distinctions *between* classes *within* an ontological category. The M-constraint does not predict that.

In defense of the M-constraint, however, Keil has shown that young children can be led to believe that an animal can be transformed into another kind of animal through the manipulation of appearances (see Keil, 1989). Young children will accept that the transformed and painted raccoon indeed became a skunk. Those same children would not accept the transformation of an animal into an artifact. The first kind of transformation, the permitted one, is a transformation *within* categories on an immature ontological tree; the second transformation, the nonpermitted one, is a transformation *between* categories on a tree at the same level of differentiation.

According to Keil, the M-constraint operates on the hypothesis space in children's acquisition of word meaning (Keil, 1982, 1983). Apparently, children's ability to acquire meanings of unknown words from context is influenced by ontological knowledge. In tests of this hypothesis, children were asked to draw inferences about the ontological properties of words unknown to them on the basis of the contexts in which the words appeared. Even children who reported no knowledge of a word's meaning could still answer questions about the ontological properties of the word. The extent to which they could do this was consistent with their developmental level. That is, whatever the age-related distinctions

children typically incorporated in their ontological trees were the same sort of distinctions they were able to make about the ontological properties of the unknown words.

Chandler, Rosser, and Nicholson (1992) replicated this result with first-, third-, and fifth-graders. Using passages containing unknown, esoteric words reflective of Keil's ontological categories, the investigators assessed whether or not (1) children could acquire the meanings of the words from context, a marker of verbal intelligence; (2) children's intuitions about the ontological properties of the unknown words were governed by the M-constraint; and (3) there was any association between children's ontological intuitions and intelligence.

Intelligence is conceptualized as a variable, so we expect it to differ across individuals (Sternberg & Salter, 1984). The acquisition of word meaning from context is also a variable, which correlates with intelligence (Sternberg & Powell, 1983). Ontological knowledge, however, is conceptualized as a universal, a constant, and thus *not* a variable. It is an aspect of cognition that differs theoretically from intelligence (Keil, 1982) and should not correlate with measures of intelligence.

The data revealed that children did vary in their ability to acquire the meaning of esoteric words (*fop, ghee, dosser, tench,* etc.) from context, an accomplishment that, as expected, correlated with intelligence. Children understood the ontological properties of those words, however, in accord with their developmental level, whether or not they could successfully define the words. And, the extent of the children's ontological knowledge did not correlate with intelligence. The number of categorical distinctions children were able to make (that is, the amount of branching in their ontological trees) was associated with developmental level but independent of verbal intelligence.

Thus, ontological knowledge is best envisioned as a constant—the same for all individuals within a developmental period—while intelligence is a variable, differing across individuals. Ontological trees, extracted from children's responses to questions about the conceptual properties of the target words (e.g., whether the sentence, "The fop is an hour long," was silly or okay), were consistent with Keil's contentions. M-constraint violations were, again, statistical rarities. And while children did exhibit confusion about some categorical distinctions (particularly "event" and "abstract object" categories), their ontological knowledge structures seem to be constrained in precisely the expected manner.

Summary

The theoretical ramifications of Frank Keil's work go beyond the topic of classification abilities. Some of those ramifications were introduced in Chapter 1; others will come in subsequent chapters. Keil's thinking and research have done much to change the way psychologists approach development. As for conceptual development, Keil offers a coherent framework for making sense of a diverse literature: sundry studies of classification, categorization, concept acquisition, semantic knowledge, and natural kind. His proposed ontological knowledge trees represent mental models of the deepest level at which we all carve up the universe. Each branch is a basic division of kind based on the true nature of things. In sum, what is captured is an intuitive ontology, a naive metaphysics, that clarifies many observations of children's conceptual behavior.

Of particular relevance to an understanding of cognitive development generally and conceptual development specifically are three conclusions to which Keil's work points:

1. Children and adults have much in common in the way they represent a shared world. It does *not* seem likely that children are mental caterpillars to the adult's butterfly. Rather,

adult mental representations of reality are elaborate, and children's are merely less so. Where those representations overlap, children and adults share a common conceptualese and communicate easily. Where the adult's representational system is ahead of the child's and overlap is not yet attained, communication is impeded. Try, for example, convincing 4-year-olds that the earth on which they stand is a round ball floating in space.

2. Developmental change in world knowledge does occur, primarily as a differentiation process. Children, as they mature and acquire knowledge, make more and more ontological distinctions. In addition, the criteria for establishing a category of entities also changes; young children are more apt to distinguish an entity by its characteristic attributes ("uncle" as a friendly, male adult) rather than by its defining attributes (parent's brother, who could be a child). However, characteristic-to-defining shifts are a function of knowledge effects and occur at different times for different concepts (Keil, 1989). So, developmental change is reasonably envisioned as quantitative change, and even what might be construed as qualitative changes are not pervasive. This is not what traditionalists proposed as a qualitative metamorphosis in conceptual structure.

3. Ontological knowledge hierarchies, which provide the glue for concepts, also model representations of reality as divisible into separate knowledge domains. The branching indicates that there are domains for physical things, for animals, for people, and so forth. Each domain could reasonably be organized in content- or domain-specific ways. Therefore, rather than trying to model knowledge and its development in all domains with a single system—a decidedly ambitious enterprise—it may turn out that we need domain-specific systems instead. Domain specificity, in contrast to the domain generality of Piagetian-like views, allows for true decalage in development as the rule not the exception. The domain-specificity

alternative directs investigators to look at particular kinds of knowledge systems, observe how they develop and elaborate, and identify the narrower rule systems that govern these unique divisions of knowledge.

CONCLUSION

The theoretical task in studying cognition is always much the same: to figure out what kind of viable model best holds the bits and pieces of observable cognitive behavior together. The task is not easy because the bits and pieces are incomplete and sometimes contradictory. The system linking them is seldom, if ever, self-evident. The developmental extension of the task entails adding the bits and pieces from child study. The developmentalist not only wants to know what the system is like, but how it originates, changes, and grows.

The bits and pieces are aspects of performance; what we hope to explain are the cognitions underlying performance, the cognitive competence performance reflects. Competence and performance are not identical, and the discrepancy is particularly noteworthy with children. The cognitive performances of children tend to be task-specific, and so, depending on the clarity of the problems presented them, children are more or less successful. The younger the children, the greater the influence of conceptually irrelevant contextual factors. Even infants exhibit impressive if rudimentary abilities when studied with habituation procedures, stripped as they are of task-irrelevant ambiguity. Young children can look competent too.

In this chapter, for example, we have seen how capable children can be when reasoning about natural kinds. But we have also seen that competence is fragile. Children's failures are real, not artifactual, but so are their successes. Explanatory models proposed to account only for the former lead to much too conservative estimates of young children's overall conceptual ability and thus fail to account for the latter. Traditional theories, like Piaget's and Vygotsky's, do not provide the viable models for which we are looking. Early competence is neglected, and contemporary research points to precisely that.

Early competence has implications for both the timing and nature of cognition. The "early" part connotes that age of onset, the emergence of skill, predates the time predicted by empiricist- and constructivist-derived theories. Constructivist and learning theories implicitly posit the necessity of a sufficient period of time for knowledge to derive from experience. Early onset time is more consistent with a nativist-derived account, although not conclusively contraindicative of alternative stories. The "competence" part connotes an adultlike, mature expression of knowledge. Although identity is not assumed, there is important similarity between adult and child cognitive forms. It becomes logically awkward to explain how young children would derive world knowledge so like that of adults in such a short time unless knowledge acquisition is constrained. A constraint limits the form that knowledge can take; it acts somewhat like a preexisting mold that can be filled in by the raw material of experience, but that restricts from the start the options that need to be entertained. For Keil, ontological knowledge is molded in such a manner.

Constrained knowledge structures are theories about how the world works. Indeed, concepts, classes, and categories have much more meaning and cohesiveness when embedded in naive theories about that world (Gelman, 1988; Murphy & Medin, 1985). However, perhaps what individuals know about the world is constrained and systematized in multiple ways, at multiple levels. So, for example, ontology is theory of the most basic sort encompassing knowledge about how the world slices up in rudimentary divisions or domains. As such, ontology forms the backbone of our conceptual system (Carey, 1985).

Each branch on the ontology tree represents a cohesive bundle of related phenomena. The separate bundles might also be constrained such that one develops naive theories of knowledge specific to the bundle of concepts at a particular node in the overall structure. Perhaps we have domain-specific naive biologies, naive physics, or naive psychologies that constrain some clumps of conceptual knowledge and the mental representations that describe them. The relationship between ontology and specific naive theories, so characterized, might be analogous to that between philosophy and the sciences. Philosophy forms the basic, logical core on which elaboration—scientific theories—can be built.

There need not be a single constraint on conceptual knowledge, but *levels of constraints,* where a few basic constraints apply across bundles of concepts. Other constraints are more particular, restricting conceptualization only to the kind of content to which they apply. Ontology, then, forms the skeleton for conceptual knowledge; naive theory is the elaboration of that skeleton—the topic pursued in the next chapters.

CHAPTER 6

DEVELOPING IMPLICIT KNOWLEDGE OF MECHANICS AND NUMBER

INTRODUCTION

The "child as scientist" metaphor has proven a popular one for cognitive development. Language reflecting the analogy pops up everywhere in the literature. It is common, for instance, to encounter descriptors of children's behavior that link it with the realm of scientific enterprise. References to children *discovering* the workings of the world, *testing hypotheses* about that operation, *limiting the hypothesis space,* and *formulating principles* of explanation make the connection, because discovery, validation, and the establishment of natural law are the business of science.

The appeal of the Genevan perspective is partially attributable to Piaget's acceptance of the metaphor. He depicted the "infant as experimenter" deciphering the physical laws governing the behavior of objects. He envisioned, as an important achievement of the adolescent, the ability to test hypotheses in a systematic and exhaustive manner. And for all children, the hallmark of mature thinking is the representation of the rules governing natural phenomena as general abstractions—what essentially constitute scientific principles. In the Piagetian view, development entails progressive movement toward a greater and greater *objective* understanding of the workings of the universe—a scientific account. In contrast, immature thought is characterized as intuitive and *subjective,* not abstract or scientific.

There is another sense, however, in which the scientist metaphor is accepted and that is the "child as theorist." In this analogy, the child is portrayed as an *intuitive scientist* operating on the basis of naive theories about the working of the universe. The form these naive theories take is not usually explicit, but naive theories are equated with scientific theories in some respects. The assumption of a parallel between scientific and naive theory has profound implications for cognitive development.

Theories are not mere collections of facts or summaries of empirical observations. The growth of knowledge into a domain-specific theory is more than gaining expertise. With expertise, observations are accumulated and integrated into increasingly complex representations of information that support inference and reasoning vis-à-vis the domain (Chi & Glaser, 1980; Chi, Hutchinson, & Robin, 1989). But the body of knowledge remains an empirical one: organized fact. The expert possesses more empirical facts, which leads to an expanding repertoire of concepts dealing with those facts.

Theoretical knowledge, on the other hand, is presumed to go beyond empirical observation to supposition about the underlying nature of things. So, rather than being collections of facts, summaries of empirical observations, or even direct abstractions from the observed, theories are complex mental structures functioning as **explanatory systems** (Carey, 1985, 1991), complete with inferred theoretical **constructs** (Wellman & Gelman, 1988). Explanation presumes hypotheses about causal mechanisms; to hold a naive theory of some domain is to have a rudimentary explanation of how the phenomenon works.

In a naive theory of biology, for example, there must be some scheme for what causes living things to function, what makes them "alive." One 3-year-old boy's "theory" about this was revealed in a series of discussions about bodies, life, and death. Apparently, he thought that live bodies were filled up with air. So rather than containing bones and blood, (which he put in there by age 4), air was inside. This was not an isolated principle, however. It went along with his observation that the bodies of humans and animals were not "squishy," since they resisted pressure like an inner tube or balloon would. So, it was air that expanded the body's parts, giving them form, structure, and rigidity. He once observed that a rather obese individual had "too much air inside."

The principle was also consistent with needing to breathe air in order to keep filled up. Events that threatened to "let your air out"—cuts, falls, and bumps—were dangerous.

But most revealing, death occurred when one "lost one's air." Unfortunately, the discovery that life could not be returned simply by "pumping back up" caused him some distress. The construct of life as a balloon turned out not to work so well; it was consistent with some empirical observations but not with others. The lack of consistency between theory and evidence eventually became sufficient enough that he abandoned the former.

This anecdote shows how the child's explanations of life phenomena consist of a set of propositions and their ramifications, not just a hodgepodge of misfacts. For the 3-year-old, these propositions were not identical to empirical observation (he did not actually observe air inside arms), but were consistent with some of them. (He did observe and experience breathing, and he knew that deceased animals failed to do so.) And the propositions—what's inside, what threatens the body's integrity, how you die—were internally consistent.

The notion of treating child knowledge structures as if they were theoretical systems rather than some other kind of conceptual structure is interesting, novel, and quite controversial (see Carey, 1991; Keil, 1991; Kuhn, 1989). There may be many ways in which the metaphor does not work. The analogy is, nonetheless, a rich one. It allows us to draw on what we know about the workings of science, the development of the sciences, and the thinking of scientists in deciphering potentially analogous phenomena taking place in a child's mind.

In science, there is a dichotomy between **empirical knowledge,** which is tied to experience and observation in the real world, and **theoretical knowledge,** which goes beyond observation to the basic nature of things that cannot be directly observed (Yates et al., 1988). The trained scientist can separate data from theory and consider the reciprocal relationship between the two (Kuhn, 1989): that is, data inform theory, serving as the raw material for it, but, conversely, theory prioritizes data and directs data acquisition. Theories act as a set of biases affecting subsequent knowledge acquisition—which facts are deemed relevant. Could indigenous theories function this way for the intuitive scientist? For the developing child? If, indeed, these naive theories do work this way, then some kinds of learning in the very young might be especially efficient. Initial assumptions about how things work would function as a guide in the young child's search for relevant data (Gelman, 1990b).

Whatever the eventual disposition of equating scientist and child, the metaphor is proving useful in cognitive development, and the utility of metaphors validates them. This particular metaphor encourages us to look at child knowledge in a special way—to focus on its cohesiveness, its internal consistency, its explanatory value for the child, and how it functions as a glue for conceptual knowledge (Murphy & Medin, 1985). From the perspective of the theory metaphor, children's attempts to structure and systematize world knowledge, however inaccurate those attempts are judged to be, are still legitimate intellectual efforts to make sense of reality.

In the next two chapters, we explore the theory view of cognitive development, because the metaphor has yielded an intriguing picture of children's intellectual ontogenesis. The research evidence about children's knowledge acquisition in a number of conceptual domains—notably, mechanics, number, biology, and mind—has informed our thinking about conceptual development in important ways. Moreover, the empirical endeavors and the interpretations that have been spurred by this perspective have coalesced into a formidable alternative to Piagetian theory (see Carey & Gelman, 1991).

Why the division into two chapters and four domains? While it is clear that naive theories are proving to be fruitful frameworks for organizing information about phenomena, it is not clear just what the theoretical divisions should be. Some contend (see Carey, 1985)

that children start out with only one or two innate theories out of which all the others will originate. Keil (1991) referred to this as the *primal theory* view. The alternative, the *pluralistic theories* view, argues for a more diverse theory base even from the beginnings of development.

However, if we accept the proposition that all conceptual knowledge is first constrained by ontology, then the ontological knowledge structure provides a sort of reconciliation for the two discrepant positions. The initial division on the ontological knowledge tree (see Chapter 5) specifies two domains (thus, two chapters), but subsequent divisions permit an elaboration of branches. So, the elaboration of domain-specific theories following the initial division is one plausible means for organizing conceptual knowledge.

THE THEORY METAPHOR AND COGNITIVE DEVELOPMENT

According to Deanna Kuhn (1989):

The scientist (a) is able to consciously articulate a theory that he or she accepts, (b) knows what evidence does and could support it and what evidence does or would contradict it, and (c) is able to justify why the coordination of available theories and evidence has led him or her to accept that theory and reject others purporting to account for the same phenomena. . . . These skills in coordinating theories and evidence arguably are the most central, essential, and general skills that define scientific thinking. (p. 674)

Surely a child will not meet Kuhn's criteria for being scientific. But children may still be like scientists in some interesting ways.

To evaluate the utility of the "child as scientist" metaphor, we must distinguish two aspects of scientific thinking. First, scientists adopt a certain perspective toward data. To be objective (and, therefore, scientifically worthy), experimental observations must be reliable, replicable, objective, and unconfounded. Generalization of principles from observations of phenomena are only judged to be as sound and supportable as the care with which scientific procedure is followed. Method and the rules of reasoning associated with that method are the *hows* of science. The "how" of science is *domain general;* it is the style of engaging in scientific investigation that is not content specific. The rules for behaving scientifically are explicit, tutored, and conscious. Scientific reasoning in this domain-general sense is precisely what Piaget demonstrated children could not do (Kuhn, 1989).

The outcome of scientific endeavors, the *what* of science, is a second aspect of the enterprise. From observations conducted in accord with the "how rules," models that explain those observations are constructed. This is where theory comes in. Intuitive scientists, child or adult, are not as proficient as trained scientists at procuring good observations or at discriminating good ones from poor ones. Nonetheless, the intuitive scientist observes and systematizes those observations and constructs an observation-consistent explanatory theory. Formal theories serve the function of summarizing, explaining, predicting empirical outcomes, and directing subsequent inquiry; naive theories do that, too. Unlike "how rules," theories are *domain specific*. There are biological theories, physical theories, and psychological theories. The concepts contained within them are limited in scope to the particular realm of reality they are intended to explain.

Theories are composed of a set of **general propositions** about some observable phenomenon. A *proposition* is a statement about what is true. To be general, a statement must not be situation specific, in which case it would only duplicate observation (Yates et al., 1988). A statement describing living things as needing air is a proposition about what defines the concept "alive." It is general if it applies to any living thing in any situation and not just specifically to the family cat. Of course, the proposition may be derived from

observation of the family cat and other like entities, but once formulated, the proposition is at a higher level of abstraction and is broadly applicable.

The statement that the last number used when counting a set provides the cardinal value of that set is a principle about numerosity (the **cardinal principle**). It is a general principle if it applies to counting any and all sets, not just to sets of blocks or fingers and toes. Again, the cardinal principle will apply to fingers and toes and may have been constructed while counting fingers and toes. It is elevated to the status of theoretical principle only when generally extended beyond those appendages. Psychology students are familiar with the principle of *operant conditioning:* The contingent presentation of a reinforcing stimulus following a behavior increases the strength of that behavior. The principle is supposed to apply broadly across behaviors, stimuli, and organisms. Generality, however, is relative. Most statements will not apply in every situation, and hence, conditions are appended as to when it will apply. The cardinal value of a set cannot be determined if the size of the set is greater than the available number tags, for example. Some behaviors of some organisms cannot be operantly conditioned, for another.

Propositions within a theory must be internally consistent, otherwise contradiction would occur. Thus, the statements (1) living things need air and (2) living things breathe are internally consistent. The statements (1) living things breathe, (2) plants are living things, and (3) plants do not breathe are inconsistent. What distinguishes theory from some other system for listing propositions is the criterion of internal consistency.

Theories are explanatory systems that inform us about cause and effect and that tell us why and how an observed empirical event occurred. Entities are alive *because* they breathe and get air inside; loss of air *causes* death. Response strength increases *because* of reinforcement; contingent events *cause* behavior changes. Explanation permits prediction of yet to be observed empirical events as well. In this way, theories link observations in meaningful ways and permit an interpretation of what is observed. Interpretation is facilitated by explanatory devices called **constructs,** which are hypothetical entities that are themselves unobservable but that clarify observable connections between events, for example, the Piagetian "scheme" that explains (and allows us to anticipate) a child's cognitive performance.

In formal scientific theory, propositions and constructs are explicit. A theory's validity is tested when the propositions yield clearly stated hypotheses subject to empirical evaluation through means of the experiment. The scientist stands between her theory and her experiment, knowing which is which and how each influences the other, just as Kuhn (1989) described. But what happens when theory is implicit? To qualify as theory rather than as some other form of conceptual structure, knowledge systems should:

1. Contain internally consistent, general propositions.
2. Embody theoretical constructs.
3. Explain empirical phenomena.
4. Mediate the acquisition and interpretation of evidence.

Explicitness is not a fundamental requirement. If the criterion of explicitness is suspended, then the theory metaphor can help us understand children's emergent, domain-specific knowledge systems.

Conceptualizing Theory Change

Empirical and theoretical knowledge have an important relationship with one another. The former is the sum of the observations, facts, and data acquired through experimentation and experience. The latter explains empirical knowledge, augments it where the facts are scarce, and provides a cohesive, interpretive structure within which the facts make sense. With increased experimentation and experience, data proliferate and empirical knowledge accumulates. At times when the theory is working—when it is compatible with the facts—there is synchrony between empirical and theoretical knowledge. In one account of the history of science (Kuhn, 1962), these are the periods of **normal science.** During such a period, a single theory or **paradigm** predominates in spite of occasional discrepancies between theoretical interpretations and available evidence.

Sometimes, however, incoming facts are seriously at odds with the theoretical account, and considerable disharmony between the two knowledge systems results. One thing differentiating scientific theory from some other sort of formal belief system is the expectation of consistency between explanatory concepts and objective facts. Thus, there is a need to maintain an equilibrium between data and interpretation. As contradictory data accumulate, there comes pressure to reorganize, restructure, and reevaluate the theory in relation to the changing data base. Again, in the history of science, theoretical reformulations that serve to bring theory into alignment with observation are referred to as **paradigm shifts.** Scientific development can be envisioned as a succession of dominant paradigms, each prevailing for a time until empirical pressure mounts, a new replacement system evolves, and equilibrium is returned to the balance between fact and the framework for fact.

The extension of the scientific theory metaphor to the growth of knowledge in children has implications for the nature of change in naive theories. Is knowledge change during the child's development equivalent to a paradigm shift in science? Carey (1985, 1986) distinguished between two kinds of reorganizations within knowledge systems that result from the accumulation of knowledge. Both kinds of restructuring involve conceptual change.

The first is **weak restructuring.** As new facts are acquired, concepts are added and the relations among concepts and propositions become enriched. The conceptual structure accounting for observations and facts increases in complexity, supporting new inferences, elaborations, and previously unrecognized insights. But the individual concepts comprising the original structure are not incommensurate with those evolved in the course of elaborative changes. The second kind of knowledge reorganization involves **strong restructuring,** alteration at the level of the core concepts when new concepts arise that cannot be defined in terms of prior concepts (Carey, 1988, 1991). It is in this sense that naive theory change is the equivalent of a paradigm shift.

Strong restructuring requires a paradigm shift because core concepts have special meaning and a special place only within a theory. To reformulate a theory, old concepts must be altered or even discarded rather than absorbed into a new framework. In psychology, for example, the concept of reinforcement is a core concept in behaviorism that explains increases in response strength as a function of response consequences. The concept is meaningful as part of a theoretical system built on positivist notions about cause and effect, temporal associations, and so forth. Without the theoretical superstructure, the concept loses much of its importance and much of its explanatory power. Indeed, without behaviorist premises, reinforcement is an empirical phenomenon to be explained (empirical knowledge) rather than an explanatory concept itself (theoretical knowledge). Thus, with a shift to a different theoretical perspective, to a perspective built on alternative assumptions about reality, the old theory's concepts will not directly translate into the new theory's lexicon. By implication, the strong restructuring of a naive theory could create a "local incommensurability" (Carey, 1991) between a child's concepts—physical, biological,

or psychological—and those of his adult counterpart.

There are a few areas within cognitive development where children's knowledge systems have been studied and described as if they were implicit theories of natural phenomena. This research, predicated on the "child as theorist" metaphor, is relatively recent and has yet to come to full fruition. It is generally acknowledged, however, that theories, by definition, must be *domain specific.* If the propositions encompassed by a theory can be reduced to only domain-general principles of thinking or to specific reflections of domain-general knowledge, then the theory metaphor loses its utility. Naive theories may also evolve over the course of development, displaying a history much as scientific theories have had. What developmental psychologists must do is identify intuitive domains, evaluate whether a knowledge system so identified really does constitute a theory, and determine whether conceptual changes in theory during the course of development exemplify weak or strong restructuring.

Conceptualizing Theory Domains

Naive theories function to structure and constrain conceptual knowledge about identifiable segments of empirical observations (Murphy & Medin, 1985). But, ontological knowledge must constrain the initial division of observations into segments to theorize about (see Chapter 5), since ontology represents cutting the world at its natural joints. In short, the ontological knowledge structure serves as the identifier of the fundamental domains of knowledge, and for those so identified, domain-specific theories organize and explain the phenomena and facts included in the domain.

The ontological knowledge structures of adults are elaborate hierarchies. It follows that if the ontological tree is the backbone for theoretical elaboration, then adults possess several naive theories about all the information they have acquired and the events they have observed. Indeed, we know there are a multitude of formal scientific theories, associated with identifiable disciplines, that roughly correspond to the departments in a university catalogue (Carey, 1985).

Children's ontological trees are less elaborate than those of adults. The immature have accumulated less information and fewer observations that require ordering, and the distinctions drawn among those observations tend to be cruder. Thus, for example, children do not always differentiate ontologically between humans and animals. They sometimes collapse the categories of abstract entities and events (Keil, 1979), and they do not initially appreciate that plants are living things (Carey, 1985). If children possess naive theories consistent with their ontological divisions, then the scope of the phenomena to which a given immature theory applies could well differ from the mature counterpart. Children's theories tend to be cruder, less accurate, and less discriminating in the types of entities, events, and observations lumped together to constitute a single domain.

Developmental change in these rudimentary, naive theories can proceed in two ways. First, theories must change to account for new data, as when a child discovers that plants are alive. Second, as the underlying ontological tree differentiates, theories should become increasingly targeted at narrower domains, those associated with the separable nodes on that tree. What the developmentalist needs to determine is whether the concepts and constructs contained in these initial theories are the rudimentary kernels of more sophisticated theoretical systems, or "misconcepts" which, with increasing maturation, will fall by the wayside.

As Keil (1979, 1983) and others (Bullock, 1985; Carey, 1985; Gelman, 1990a; Massey & Gelman, 1988) have observed, even the youngest children can distinguish between animate and inanimate entities. This ontological division shows up on the tree structures of preschoolers and kindergarten children as well as on those of their older peers (see Chapter 5). The division constitutes a crude distinction between living, organic objects and nonliving, physical ones, although the rule governing the distinction may not be the one adults use. If ontological divisions underlie theory, then initial naive theories should reveal similar differentiations. That is, children's first theories may include (1) an intuitive physics or mechanics, which explains the actions, events, and cause-and-effect sequences applicable to all physical entities encompassed in the domain of nonliving things and (2) an intuitive biology, which explains the functioning of alive things (Carey, 1985).

But what is the basis of children's initial distinction between the animate and the inanimate? Some suggest it is movement (Carey, 1985; Laurendeau & Pinard, 1962; Piaget, 1979). Inanimate objects do not move themselves in the absence of external force, but animate objects do. Piaget (1979) contended that young children cannot distinguish between self-generated and externally caused movement and thus assume any object placed in motion is animate. In short, children overgeneralize "aliveness" on the basis of any motion. Thus, the sun and moon, which move through the sky, are alive. If this were true, then the child's initial distinction of things into separate categories on the basis of motion, without a corresponding distinction as to source of motion, would not result in nonliving, living thing differentiations that had much in common with the adult version. And the basis for the differentiation would be contrary to evidence about the ontological divisions made by young children.

Recent research challenges the Piagetian premise. There is evidence of early sensitivities to violations of the rule that inanimate objects must have an external cause of movement (Bullock, 1985; Leslie, 1984b; Richards & Siegler, 1986). Massey and Gelman (1988) pursued this line of investigation by asking young children (3- and 4-year-olds) to predict whether photographed objects would be able to move uphill and downhill by themselves. Uphill movement requires self-generated motion, something only living things should be able to do. Downhill movement, however, is possible by any nonfixed object whose mechanical form (e.g., wheels) supports it, since, once pushed, gravity sustains the motion.

The photographs were of objects unfamiliar to children drawn from different ontological categories. Two sets were of animate objects—mammals (e.g., sloth) and nonmammals (e.g., tarantula)—and three sets were inanimate—statues (e.g., of a Chow puppy), wheeled objects (e.g., an antique carriage), and rigid objects (e.g., a rowing machine). Children would be inaccurate in their predictions if they based their judgments on the presence or absence of perceptible parts associated with movements, like wheels and legs (the statues had legs), rather than on the on-

FIGURE 6-1 *Data from Massey and Gelman's Study of Young Children's Understanding of Animacy and Motion.*
The graph depicts the number of children in each age group who were judged correct in answering whether or not novel objects could go up and down hills by themselves. The children's answers depended on an ability to make the animate-inanimate distinction appropriately.

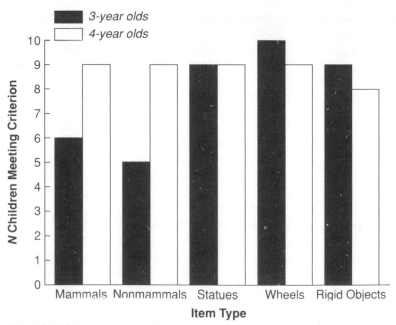

From "Preschoolers' Ability to Decide Whether a Photographed Unfamiliar Object Can Move Itself" by C. M. Massey and R. Gelman, 1988, *Developmental Psychology, 24,* pp. 307—317. Copyright 1988 by the American Psychological Association. Reprinted by permission.

tological categories to which the exemplars belonged.

It turns out that most of the children used a decision rule based on an animate-inanimate distinction. Over 70% of these children were virtually always correct and the remainder were mostly correct. Children who made errors never predicted that an inanimate object could move itself. Rather, they sometimes denied that an animate object could go uphill and downhill by itself. These data are summarized in Figure 6-1. The subjects also spontaneously justified their predictions; reference to category membership (animate-inanimate) was the most frequent explanation offered. Moreover, labels for objects, although incorrect given the novelty of the objects, tended to be drawn from the same ontological category as the target.

A distinction between animate and inanimate objects made with an implicit reference to the source of animacy appears to be a deep and fundamental distinction in the world (Gelman, 1990a). The ability to make this distinction is detectable in the behavior of young children and even infants; some propose that it is "hard-wired" (Premack, 1990). The basis for the distinction seems rooted in an early tacit understanding of causation: different causal mechanisms explain movement observed in the two classes of entities. Animate, living things are self-propelled; nonliving things are not. Hence, it is not movement per se that implies the distinction (à la Piaget), but appreciation of what source gives rise to the movement. A causal analysis of movement hinges on the nature of the moving entity but not in terms of its perceptible features. Self-propelled entities differ *inside* from those other entities not so enabled (Gelman, 1990a; Massey, 1988; Massey & Gelman, 1988).

Contemporary empirical evidence on the animate-inanimate distinction supports a basic division of the world by young children into living and nonliving objects. Initial theories, then, those implicit explanatory systems about the nature of things, should follow a similar differentiation into at least two "naive" sciences. One branch, which encompasses physical, nonliving objects, is the basis for an intuitive mechanics or physics, and it is the theory examined next.

INTUITIVE THEORIES OF PHYSICAL PHENOMENA

At the most fundamental level, what are the rules that govern the workings of the physical world in which we live? Physical objects are solid, contained entities that move when force is applied to them, stop when barriers intercept them, and fall when supports are removed from them. Moving objects proceed on paths and follow trajectories predictable from information about the forces applied to them that enable motion and those applied against them that impede motion. Laws about the nature and permanence of objects and laws about the motion and action of objects give order to physical phenomena and render the outcome of empirical events predictable.

Object-event sequences are organized in accord with the dimensions of time and space. They are rule governed in a lawful universe, and those rules apply across context and objects. Thus, the action of a ball rolling down a hill, a rock thrown off a cliff, or a projectile shot from a cannon can all be explained with reference to the same set of natural laws. To the tutored, these physical phenomena are encompassed by Newtonian physics—a formal, explicit theory. But what about the untutored? Do those who lack formal instruction in physics depend on an indigenous physics that both (1) contains rules generally applicable to these physical events and (2) functions in turn to explain those events? Do untrained people, particularly children, generate a naive physics consistent with their empirical observations?

The developmental literature addressing these questions is recent and takes its impetus from both Piagetian theory and research in object perception (Spelke, 1987, 1988b, 1990). Mechanical and physical events occur in space, over time, and are organizable as cause-and-effect sequences. Children's comprehension of the dimensions of space and time and their understanding of causality in physical systems were of considerable interest to Piaget (Piaget, 1970b). And, not unexpectedly, he viewed them as beyond the cognitive capacity of the young child. The logical basis of thought necessary to support causal reasoning and inferences about object movement and physical events in time and space, for Piaget, presupposed operational status. But some contemporary studies of children's understanding of physical phenomena and of the mechanisms of causality in physical systems challenge that view (Leslie, 1984b; Spelke 1988a, 1991).

Understanding the Actions of Material Bodies

Fundamental to an understanding of the physical world is knowledge of how objects behave in space and over time. As previously reviewed in Chapters 2 and 3, even young infants have impressive, rudimentary object knowledge (see Spelke, 1988b). Without doubt, infants' behavior toward objects attests to a very early understanding of the invariance of an object's form, the stability of an object's location (Baillargeon & Graber, 1987), and of a permanence that extends beyond immediate perception (Kellman & Spelke, 1983; Spelke, 1988b, 1990). By 7 months of age, infants are able to represent additional, more sophisticated physical properties of objects. As revealed by habituation data, these older infants seem capable of representing the physical properties of hidden objects such as size and rigidity (Baillargeon, in press). In sum, the literature tells us that from infancy on, children have knowledge of the independent existence of objects as physical entities.

However, understanding the physical principles applicable to objects is more than knowing *that* the entities exist; it involves

knowing about regularities of what they *do,* how they *move,* and how they *come to rest.* Physical knowledge involves an **intuitive mechanics.** Spelke (1989) pointed out that there are constraints on object movement that adults understand. Such knowledge permits anticipation of what will happen to an object as it moves through space. For example, an adult will infer that an unseen object to which a force is applied will move on a connected path until it encounters a barrier. Inferences like this are supported by knowledge of four constraints on object motion (see Spelke, 1989):

1. A *continuity* constraint—objects can only move through space on connected paths.
2. A *solidity* constraint—objects only move through space not occupied by other objects.
3. An *inertia* constraint—objects do not change their motion spontaneously and abruptly.
4. A *gravity* constraint—an unsupported object is subject to downward motion.

Adults understand these constraints and can mentally model them with quantitative precision. But, can children?

To determine whether infants have some understanding of these constraints, Spelke and her colleagues conducted a series of investigations (as reported in Spelke, 1989, 1991). Looking time to physical events was examined within the *habituation paradigm,* a technique described in Chapter 2. She followed this general procedure: The infant is habituated to a visual event—an object moving through space. Then, the habituation event is followed by a test event. One of these events is perceptually like the habituation event but violates one of the four constraints governing object movement. A second event is perceptually unlike the habituation event but is consistent with the physical constraint on motion. If infants dishabituate to the first test event and not to the second, then they must have detected the constraint violation. Longer looking time denotes surprise as would ensue with a violation of expectations. Thus, the crucial test event, despite its apparent similarity to the habituation event, should be at odds with infants' expectations about principles governing physical reality.

To test whether infants' expectations of object motion are consistent with the continuity and solidity constraints, Spelke and her associates habituated subjects to appropriately moving objects. In one experimental variation, depicted in Figure 6-2, a ball was lowered down a lighted stage. No barrier was present to block a full, unimpeded descent from top to bottom. Infants observed the initiation of the descent, a screen was dropped (thereby requiring the subjects to *infer* the object's path through space), and then the screen was raised

FIGURE 6-2 *The Displays Spelke (1991) Used to Evaluate Whether Infant's Honor the Solidity and Continuity Constraints on Object Movement.*
In the habituation event (left), a ball transverses the path from the top to the bottom of the frame. Infants dishabituated to the test event inconsistent with the constraints (right).

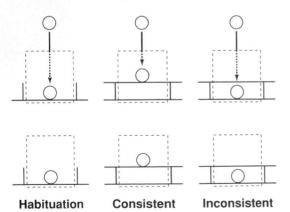

Habituation   Consistent   Inconsistent

From " Physical Knowledge in Infancy: Reflections on Piaget's Theory" by E. S. Spelke, in S. Carey and R. Gelman (Eds.), 1991, *The Epigenesis of Mind: Essays on Biology and Cognition,* Hillsdale, NJ: Erlbaum.

revealing the object at rest at the bottom of the stage.

In the test events, a barrier was interjected between the top and bottom of the stage. Again, infants watched as the ball began its descent, the screen was lowered, then the screen was raised showing the object's resting place. In the *constraint-consistent* test event, the object was at rest atop the interjected barrier, *not* in the same final location as it had been in the habituation event. In the *constraint-inconsistent* test event the object's final location was, as in the habituation event, at the bottom of the stage, which would, of course, have necessitated the object's impossibly passing through the barrier.

According to Spelke (1989), 4-month-old infants dishabituated to the constraint-inconsistent event as did 2½-month-old subjects in a second variation of the experiment. She concluded that infants are sensitive to the continuity and solidity constraints on object motion and expect objects to behave accordingly.

Infants of the same age, however, are not sensitive to the inertia and gravity constraints. They do not expect a falling object to continue to do so until it reaches an impeding surface, nor do they expect a rolling object to accelerate as it moves down an inclined plane. Other null results observed within the context of these habituation experiments indicate that infants do not infer that a rapidly moving object will continue its motion in the absence of obstacles, that it will move in a straight line, or that it will move at a constant speed. Expectations about these object-motion phenomena require a greater sophistication in physical knowledge than is available to the infant in the first year of life. Sensitivity to the solidity and continuity constraints apparently emerges first, quite early in life. Sensitivity to the other two, inertia and gravity, must develop later.

Perhaps there is something importantly different about the physical principles to which babies do and do *not* exhibit sensitivity. The solidity and continuity constraints concern the integrity of material bodies and of the spaces they take up. The principle that an object cannot pass through or skip over a barrier, for instance, is a **qualitative principle** governing physical reality. Based on such knowledge, the infant develops the expectation that an object will come to rest against a barrier. But the envisionable states of nature—at rest or in motion—according to the rule are dichotomous, hence the qualitative characteristic. So, either the object comes to rest or it does not, and the latter state elicits surprise.

The inertia and gravity constraints, on the other hand, are **quantitative principles,** expressions about the nature of velocity, speed, and the direction of motion. These expressions are about forces applied to material bodies. Predictions about the trajectory of a moving object are made by decomposing the independent vertical (gravity) and horizontal (momentum) forces acting on the object. The identity of the object is less relevant to this analysis than is an appreciation of how those forces act. Infants may have an inherent tendency to organize the physical world into material bodies (Spelke, 1991). This intuition does not automatically enable the computation of the outcome of forces applied to those material bodies.

In related research, Baillargeon (1987a & 1987c; Baillargeon, Spelke, & Wasserman, 1985) examined whether infants would dishabituate when a moving screen appeared to pass through a solid object (see Chapter 3). Babies as young as 5 months of age looked longer when the solidity constraint was violated. Older babies even dishabituated when the movement of the screen only partially (but substantially) "passed through" the object. Again, however, a rule sufficient to preclude the physical possibility of this crucial test event depends on understanding objects as material bodies, not on an understanding of sophisticated mechanics.

The literature about infants' perception and conception of objects reveals a very early appreciation of some aspects of an intuitive mechanics. Babies expect solid objects to behave in principled ways, to move on connected pathways, to maintain material identity, and to take up space. Infants' knowledge is limited and does not extend to a full understanding of all the rules governing object motion, however. What the young do understand about mechanics is probably fueled by an innate expectation that the world is made up of *things* (see Gelman, 1990b; Spelke, 1990, 1991). Knowledge of "thingness" is essential to an appreciation of mechanics, and it is a fundamental concept that perceptual sensitivities can augment (e.g., detection of form rigidity, location). But "thingness" alone underdetermines the full extent of mechanical "truths" and sometimes may even prove misleading, as we shall see.

Intuitive Understanding of Mechanics

Intuitive ideas about motion inconsistent with the fundamental principles of physics are not just characteristic of children's thinking. Many adults have misconceptions reflecting an indigenous theory of motion that differs from classic Newtonian theory. In a series of studies, McCloskey and his colleagues (Caramazza, McCloskey, & Green, 1981; McCloskey, 1983a, 1983b; McCloskey, Caramazza, & Green, 1980) examined adults' explanations and descriptions of the behavior of moving objects. The investigators wanted to find out what people believe to be true about principles of motion developed on the basis of everyday experience. McCloskey (1983a, 1983b) concluded from his data that adults' knowledge is principled, well articulated, and theoretical, but that it is *inconsistent* with fundamental physical principles. In short, many adults hold intuitive theories of motion that are wrong!

These conclusions were reached by asking subjects to solve a variety of motion problems. Many of the problems consisted of diagrams and explanations of the phenomena depicted in the diagrams. Subjects were asked to make predictions about the motion of objects depicted in the diagrams. Data were collected on both predictions and the explanations subjects gave for those predictions. Some of these problems, along with possible solutions, are depicted in Figure 6-3.

In one, the spiral-tube problem, subjects were shown a picture of a curved, metal tube and were told that a ball was to be put into one end of the tube and shot out of the other end. They were to indicate the trajectory of the exiting ball. In another problem, the diagram depicted a metal ball attached to a string twirling at high speed in a circle. The string breaks where it is attached to the ball, and subjects must predict the path of the ball after the break. In both cases, the problems are framed in such a way as to minimize the effects of friction and gravity. The correct prediction of the ball's trajectories is a straight line. However, a surprisingly high proportion of subjects (51% for the spiral-tube problem; 30% for the sling problem) provided incorrect predictions of curved, rather than straight paths.[1]

Adults do not fare much better dealing with the constraints of gravity and inertia as they affect the motion of objects. In the airplane problem, a metal ball is dropped from a plane flying at a constant speed parallel to the ground. Subjects must predict the trajectory of the ball and the position, vis-à-vis the plane, where the ball will hit the ground. In the cliff problem, a metal ball is propelled off a frictionless cliff at 50 miles per hour. Subjects again must anticipate the ball's trajectory.

In both cases, the total velocity of the ball is decomposable into independent horizontal and vertical components. The horizontal velocity is equal to that of the plane in the first problem and 50 miles per hour in the second problem. The vertical velocity is zero until the ball is dropped from the plane (Problem 1) or leaves the cliff edge (Problem 2). After the release/drop, the ball undergoes a constant vertical acceleration due to gravity (increasing vertical velocity) while still maintaining a constant horizontal velocity. Thus, both balls will fall in a parabolic arc, and, in the plane problem, the plane will be directly above the ball at the point where the latter hits the ground.

Approximately 30% of the subjects on each problem were incorrect. For the plane problem, 36% thought the ball would fall straight down; for the cliff problem, 22% drew trajectories that were not parabolic. Moreover, in behavioral tests where adults interacted with objects, they still made similar errors. For example, they misjudged where to drop a ball to hit a target on the floor when they themselves were in motion.

These findings are counterintuitive for a number of reasons. First, the extent of incorrectness is surprising, as is the observation that errors were made even by those who had been exposed to some formal instruction in physics. Second, the incorrect predictions are inconsistent with experience. If principled knowledge is generated from cumulative experience, then how could such a discrepancy result? Third, McCloskey reported consistency in judgments both within and across subjects and for both predictions and explanations. (Yates et al., 1988, however did not and disputes this point.) The interpretation is as follows: Such consistency of errors is inconceivable unless subjects have a coherent, naive theory of motion that provides a causal explanation, as theories must, for the behavior of moving objects. Subjects then try to interpret the test problems by relating them to this explanatory system. As a consequence, their predictions are not guesses but extrapolations from systematic knowledge.

According to McCloskey, this indigenous theory is not Newtonian, but it does bear resemblance to the historically earlier **impetus theory** popular during the fourteenth to sixteenth centuries. As McCloskey (1983b) stated:

FIGURE 6-3 *The Types of Problems McCloskey Used to Test Individuals' Understanding of Principles Governing Motion.*

In each case, the person is presented with a situation (left) and asked to anticipate the trajectory of an object in motion. Correct responses are at A; common misconceptions are at B. (Adapted from McCloskey, 1983b.)

A   B

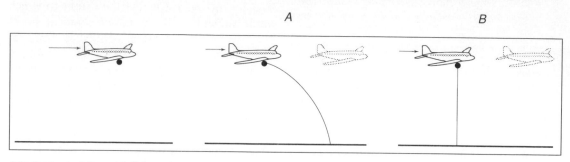

Airplane problem: Ball is to be dropped from a moving plane

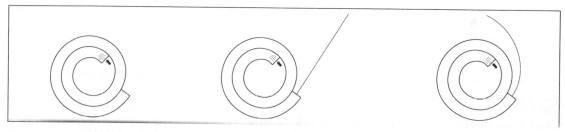

Spiral tube problem: Ball is to be shot out of the tube

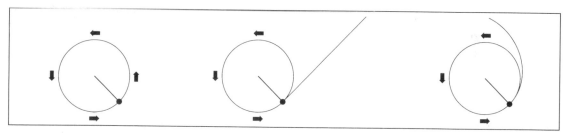

Ball and string problem: String is to break on a ball

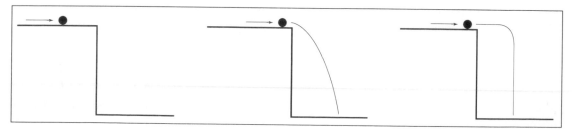

Cliff problem: A moving ball traveling at a constant speed is about to go over the edge

Many people believe that the act of setting an object in motion impresses in the object an internal force or impetus. This impetus is assumed to keep the object in motion after it is no longer in contact with the original mover. According to this view, moving objects eventually slow down and stop because their impetus gradually dissipates. This naive theory is . . . strikingly similar to the medieval theory of impetus . . . for most subjects a naive impetus theory played a prominent role in attempts to solve problems. (p. 321)

Rather than explaining motion through reference to external forces, subjects accept an explanation of motion based on the presence of internal force, a view that qualitatively distinguishes objects at rest (absence of impetus) from objects in motion (presence of impetus).[2] The ball dropped from the plane falls in a straight line to the ground because the ball presumably lacks impetus and, thus, gravity is the only influence. The ball leaving the cliff moves horizontally until its impetus dissipates, then gravity takes over. In an impetus view of mechanics, motion becomes a characteristic of the material body undergoing the motion rather than an outcome of the application and change in force.

For many motion phenomena, impetus theory is consistent with empirical observation. For example, a pushed ball will roll across the floor, gradually decelerate, and come to a stop. So, theory-based predictions about motion based on impetus principles are not totally at odds with experiences that come from living in a world with friction (White, 1983). However, impetus theory is not as broadly applicable nor as powerful as the Newtonian replacement, since the former theory does not account for changing frames of reference—the ball traveling in the moving plane is at rest in reference to the plane but in horizontal motion in reference to the ground—or acknowledge the independence of forces acting on objects. A view of motion as an object characteristic will lead to predictions about trajectory, frame of reference, and out-come of the application of force that differ from those generated from the rules of classical mechanics.

Subsequent research suggests that perhaps McCloskey overestimated the extent to which adult subjects will err on mechanical problems. When the problem context is more familiar, error rates decrease (Kaiser, Jonides, & Alexander, 1986), and when ongoing events are simulated, subjects are less error prone (Kaiser, Proffitt, & Anderson, 1985; Kaiser, Proffitt, & McKloskey, 1985). So, adults may be able to overcome their misconceptions about mechanical phenomena with effort and formal tutelage. However, McCloskey's studies have implications for how these phenomena are *initially* understood. That is where developmental study can make a contribution.

In one developmental study, Kaiser, McCloskey, and Profitt (1986) presented the spiral tube problem to children between the ages of 4 and 12 and to college students. This time the investigators compared the spiral-tube problem used in the earlier studies with a C-tube problem in which the depicted apparatus had much less curvature than the spiral contraption. Some of the findings reiterated previous studies: just 60% of the college students were correct in their prediction of the ball's path exiting the spiral tube. Generally, most subjects, regardless of age, were more likely to predict a straight-line trajectory for balls shot from the C-tube than from the spiral tube. Like the college students, the youngest subjects (preschool and kindergarten children) exhibited a 61% correct hit rate. But the older children, those in middle childhood, were correct much less often—only about 25% of the time. The investigators obtained a *U*-shaped developmental function as depicted in Figure 6-4. Here the lowest performance level is associated with the *middle* age range of subjects, rather than with the lower end, as one might expect.

It is unlikely that the youngest children organize their system of mechanical knowledge

FIGURE 6-4   Children (Preschoolers, kindergarten children, third-, fourth-, fifth-, and sixth-graders) and adults were asked to predict the trajectories of a ball exiting either a spiral tube or a *C*-shaped tube. The graph depicts the proportion of correct predictions as a function of age; the data revealed a *U*-shaped developmental function.

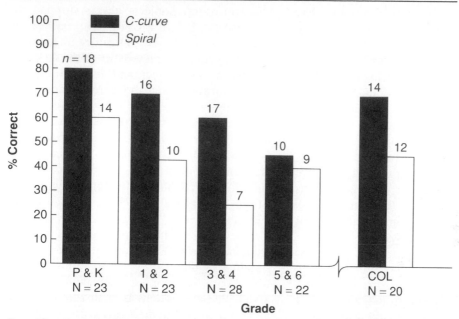

From "Development of Intuitive Theories of Motion: Curvilinear Motion in the Absence of External Forces" by M. K. Kaiser, M. McCloskey, and D. R. Proffitt, 1986, *Developmental Psychology, 22*, pp. 67–71. Copyright 1986 by the American Psychological Association. Reprinted by permission.

according to a Newtonian theory of mechanics to which they subsequently lose access. More likely, the cognitive competence responsible for the success of the young children and the college students is different; thus, the appearance of equivalence is an epiphenomenon. Perhaps young children are correct because they deal with the problems on a concrete, empirical level. Their concrete experience with trajectories, for example, with their balls, is with straight paths. So, they predict straight-line paths for the spiral-tube problem on the basis of past, everyday observation. They have not yet tried to systematize their empirical knowledge and concoct theoretical principles capable of accounting for a broad range of motion phenomena.

The college students who are correct are so because they do have access to those appropriate theoretical principles. The older children, however, are systematizing empirical knowledge into theoretical knowledge, so they no longer operate at a concrete level as their younger cohorts do. But, the children's emerging naive theory, like the theory held by the considerable proportion of adults who incorrectly anticipate curved trajectories, is not Newtonian. In sum, young children are correct because they operate atheoretically; older children are incorrect because their intuitive theory misleads them. And their intuitive knowledge may mislead them because of a strong inherent bias toward organizing the mechanical world on the basis of things and the characteristics of things (e.g., solidity) rather than on the basis of forces on things (see Spelke, 1991).

The contention that novices understand mechanics in terms of misconceptions has been made by others in addition to McCloskey (see Clement, 1983; de Sessa, 1983; White, 1983). Hegarty, Just, and Morrison (1988) characterized the rules of mechanics used by less able, less knowledgeable individuals as qualitative (e.g., about state, characteristics). In contrast, more able individuals, those who score high on psychometric tests of mechanical ability, are more likely to solve problems by referring to quantitative rules. Quantitative rules, unlike qualitative ones, express relations among continuous variables (e.g., force, speed, etc.) and permit precise computations about actions possible in physical systems.

Although Hegarty, Just, and Morrison (1988) investigated performance in adult subjects, their findings have developmental implications, too. First, younger individuals, like the mechanically less able and less experienced, might also depend on qualitative rules to represent and model causal relations in mechanical systems. Second, in the sequence of knowledge acquisition, including the developmental sequence, qualitative models could precede quantitative ones (Forbus & Gentner, 1986; White & Fredericksen, 1986).

The overriding importance of the solidity constraint on the mechanical reasoning of both children and adults was demonstrated in a series of studies by Rosser and Chandler (1991, 1992). The investigators adapted the Baillargeon apparatus, originally used with infants in a habituation context (see Chapter 3), for use with older individuals. Subjects observed a moving drawbridge occlude a solid object; the motion of the drawbridge insured a collision between it and the object sometime before the drawbridge could complete a 180 degree oscillation. The task for subjects was to anticipate where the collision would occur and to stop the screen at the point of contact.

All of the subjects, child and adult, were wrong in precisely the same way. They scrupulously honored the solidity constraint and adopted a strategy that insured adherence to that constraint. Subjects always stopped the screen short, before it could have reached the object. Because it was obligatory to focus on the "thingness" characteristics of the task—the solidity of the object and its location and salient locations on the screen—individuals uniformly misjudged the relevant mechanical characteristics of the problem. Most importantly, children and adults erred in exactly the same way: The performance of the latter was independent of formal, tutored knowledge, and all subjects honored a fundamental constraint on material bodies to which even infants adhere.

The research literature leads us to conclude that novice adults organize their understanding of physical events in terms of intuitive theory. As a consequence, their reasoning about physical systems is both rule governed and consistent, but it is less correct and less quantitative than that of experts. What is most intriguing is whether reliable misconceptions about the physical world are tied to initial biases about the way infants organize that world. An initial bias toward "thingness" insures early and efficient acquisition of knowledge about object characteristics. We have seen here and in Chapters 2 and 3 that object knowledge is an early-emerging, basic, cognitive capacity. A propensity to "thingness," however, can skew thinking in such a way that force, movement, trajectory, and like concepts are misconstrued. Motion is not a characteristic objects *have* but a consequence of the interaction of forces *applied to* them.

Summary

Children, even infants, have principled knowledge about the motion of objects. As a result, children expect object trajectories to be constrained, rule governed, and predictable. The knowledge of the naive, however, is not consistent with the rules of classic physics. In particular, the untutored do not appreciate the action of independent external forces impinging on object movement and determining momentum, velocity, speed, and outcome of force on an object's path. It is important to keep in mind, however, that a completely accurate formulation describing the movement of a real object in an environment where both gravity and friction do operate is a complex expression—a relationship among several continuous variables.

And if we interpret "intuitive" as somehow consistent with and derived from everyday experience, then the correct expression is probably not readily intuitive even though it explains the phenomenon. Untutored individuals simply may not be able to spontaneously generate such a rule. It is not surprising, therefore, that subjects who have not been taught these principles explicitly err when they depend on indigenous knowledge. The formal principles that underlie physical events are often complex and quantitative and require simultaneous consideration of multiple variables (Proffitt, Kaiser, & Whelan, 1990). The naive, children, and the nonmechanically inclined do not exhibit knowledge of the phenomenon's complexity nor its actual quantitative nature.

However, knowledge that is not "true" need not be atheoretical. Children, and the untutored generally, may have access to indigenous theories comprised of relatively workable rules. Those rules yield sufficiently "close" solutions for most everyday physical events. Then, with increasing experience, experience that must be assimilated into existing mental models, there may come a press to change the less general qualitative physical theory into a more quantitative, broadly applicable one. McCloskey's (1983a, 1983b) research suggests the developmental change is from no theory, to impetus theory, to a fac

simile of classic physics. But how might such a change come about?

In history, the change to a Newtonian mechanics represents a true paradigm shift, the sort of strong restructuring of principled knowledge to which Carey (1985) referred. Newton's laws cannot be reduced to mere refinements or elaborations of earlier physical laws because of fundamental differences about the state of nature as envisioned in the two (for, e.g., totally different laws about the difference between objects at rest and those in motion). The developmental question is whether or not the evolution from the unsophisticated, earlier physical theory in children and the naive to the more mature theory represents a paradigm shift in the individual's theoretical knowledge.

Carey (1991) interpreted her data as indicating that is, indeed, what happens. Based on children's evolving notions about matter, weight, density, and the like—all quantitative variables—Carey (1991; Smith, Carey, & Wiser, 1985) contended that the child's initial conceptualization of physical phenomena is incommensurate with the adults. Children, for instance, hold notions of weight and density that are undifferentiated and, therefore, incompatible with the mature versions of these concepts. To enable a knowledge transition, a basic reconceptualization of these concepts is necessary, beginning with the drawing of different ontological distinctions (for example, how a material/immaterial distinction is made, as with air, gas).

Spelke's (1991) position seems to differ. Knowledge of objects and their behavior enriches and elaborates with experience and maturation, but initial fundamental principles about the nature of objects are not abandoned and replaced. It follows that physical notions held by children and adults should be very much the same. To the extent those notions are misconceptions, we will observe erroneous beliefs in *both* children and adults. Any transition to a Newtonian conception of things is not a change per se, but the addition of another knowledge layer to an existing understanding of the world; perhaps a gloss of Newtonian icing envelops an indigenous cake. Spelke (1991) told us that the acquisition of the sophisticated layer takes much effort and tutelage and is aided by mathematical representation. McCloskey's work (1983a, 1983b) reminds us that knowledge evolution is not universal.

THEORETICAL KNOWLEDGE OF NUMBER

The uppermost node on the ontological tree is ALL THINGS. The supposition organizing this chapter is that a node represents an organized bundle of principled knowledge. However, a system of principles applicable to ALL THINGS would need to be very general indeed. Principles of motion are very general, but even they differentiate along the animate-inanimate distinction and apply to physical objects. This distinction creates a tree with at least two nodes. Principles that do apply to virtually all phenomena are **principles of numerosity.**

Anything can be enumerated: living things (horses in a herd), inanimate things (blocks in a box), abstract things (ideas in a passage), events (play periods in a day), and so forth. If we can identify an object as a thing, we can count it. Potentially, then, an intuitive theory of number is a likely candidate for a basic system of knowledge available even to those with access to only the crudest ontological knowledge structure, those who can organize the world around them into distinct things. This ability appears to be universal and available very early in development (Gallistel & Gelman, 1990; Gelman, 1990a).

Even animals display actions consistent with access to some rudimentary representation of number in much the same way animal behavior suggests an underlying knowledge of space (Gallistel, 1989; see Chapter 3, this volume). For instance, animal behavior implicates cognitions about **numerosity** (Capaldi & Miller, 1988a; Pepperberg, 1987) and about the ability to compute rate and determine sums, both of which are numerical *operations* (Boysen & Berntson, 1989; Gallistel, 1989, 1990). These observations in themselves are fascinating, but add to them concurrent findings indicative of precocious number knowledge in infants and very young children (Cooper, 1984; Gelman & Gallistel, 1978; Starkey & Cooper, 1980; Starkey, Spelke, & Gelman, 1983; Strauss & Curtis, 1981) and the empirical picture becomes even more intriguing.

This growing evidence—early competence for concepts of numerosity in humans coupled with access to concepts of numerosity in animals—lends credence to the proposition that some form of number representation must be preverbal, intuitive, universal, and innate (Gelman, 1990b, 1991; Starkey, Spelke, & Gelman, 1990; Wynn, in press b). The proposition remains a controversial claim, however. The data from which animal knowledge is inferred is ambiguous (Davis & Pérusse, 1988), as data from infants and young children can be (Sophian, 1987, 1988; Wynn, in press a). Similarly, the nature of these initial representations is not clear either (Meck & Church, 1983; Gallistel, 1990; Wynne a, in press b). Still, a nativist account for the acquisition of number knowledge has emerged as the strong theoretical contender.

Number represents a complex system of knowledge with a long history and about which philosophers, logicians, and mathematicians have reflected for years (Brainerd, 1979). Now, developmental and comparative psychologists have jumped into the fray because the domain is a natural focus for those investigating the innate bases of knowledge acquisition. Concepts of numerosity are found in virtually every culture studied (Saxe & Posner, 1983) and surface early in development, too (Saxe, Guberman, & Gearhart, 1988; Starkey, Spelke, & Gelman, 1990). So, the ubiquity of occurrence points to an implicit awareness of natural number preceding formal tutelage and independent of direct instruction. This is just the sort of knowledge system the cognitive developmentalist seeks to explain. In this part of the chapter, we review the evidence for infants' and children's initial understanding of number, and we explore the implications of that evidence. There is currently considerable support for principled knowledge of number as a fundamental, domain specific, cognitive capacity (Gelman, 1990a), which is applicable to the most basic branch of the ontological tree.

Knowing about Number

Just what does it mean to have knowledge of number? For example, knowing the meaning of the number eight includes knowing that (1) eight represents a set of objects with a definite numerosity. (2) It is the eighth number in an ordered set of whole integers. (3) It can be partitioned into two sets of four. (4) It is the sum of 7 + 1, 6 + 2, and 3 + 5. (5) It is the square root of 64, and so forth. Which part of that knowledge of "eightness" signifies understanding? And, to be said to "understand number" more generally, must an individual have extensive knowledge of the numerical characteristics of only some or of all possible numbers?

Numbers signify several things. First, a number represents the absolute value of the amount of entities included in a set; this is the **cardinal value** of the set. The number word is a name for an amount. Thus, the number eight represents a collection of that many things. Second, numbers are arranged in an ordered sequence—first, second, third, and so on—and so have an **ordinal value** as well. In this case, the number eight refers to the eighth position in an ordered series, a *relational* reference, rather than an indicator of numerousness.

Ordinal values inform as to place in a sequence, whereas cardinal values inform as to

the mapping between *n* objects and a specific number tag. The mature knower who understands numbers can coordinate the two kinds of values, realizing that 8 > 7 and 8 < 10, that it occurs in the eighth sequenced position (later than 7 but earlier than 10), and that it signifies a collection of eight entities. It is conceivable that the less mature knower might consistently associate the tag "eight" with eight things but be unaware of eight's position in an ordered series of integers and thus not logically conclude that 8 > 7. Similarly, a number novice might correctly organize the number word chain in sequence without knowing how many items any specific number denotes.

Historically, mathematicians have offered alternative propositions as to whether the ordinal or cardinal characteristic of number is the most rudimentary feature, serving as the foundation on which the companion features are built (Brainerd, 1973a, 1973b, 1979). For Piaget, however, the number concept was the integration and coordination of both the ordinal and cardinal characteristics (Flavell, 1963; Piaget, 1952a). And the emergence of a knowledge of number, as conceptualized this way, reflected the global, qualitative stage shift he proposed for all cognitive phenomenon predicated on the underlying groupment structures (see Chapter 4). So, a conceptual understanding of number should emerge in the period of concrete operations and not before.

Knowledge about principles of numerosity are demonstrated behaviorally in various ways. Correctly performing arithmetic operations (+, −, ×, ÷) on integers is one index of competence. Most traditional tasks that assess number knowledge involve the manipulation of numerical symbols, and children of elementary-school age can usually produce correct solutions to these problems, thereby displaying some understanding of number and of arithmetic principles. But younger children and, quite obviously, animals cannot demonstrate any knowledge they might possess when the medium of expression is symbolic in this way. These individuals may very well have some implicit set of preverbal number principles (Gelman & Greeno, 1989), but it cannot be elicited by traditional means. There is a need for alternative methods for tapping knowledge of number when the target is the extent of understanding in the very young.

For Piaget, the prerequisite for an understanding of number is **conservation**. In prototypic number-conservation tasks, subjects are shown two rows of items containing the same amount of items. The rows are arranged spatially so that the items are lined up in *one-to-one correspondence* as depicted in Figure 6-5. The subject is asked about the numerical equivalency of the rows, and their sameness is established. Then, one of the rows is transformed so that the perceptual characteristics of the row are changed, but the change is independent of number. For example, the row of items can be stretched out to render it longer than previously and longer than its nontransformed counterpart. Or, the row of items can be squished together, making it more dense than the comparison row. The transformation occurs in full view of the subject, and no items are added or taken away. The subject is again asked about the comparative numerosity of the two rows and queried as to the reasoning behind his judgment.

Piaget observed that young children, those under 5 or 6 and not yet established in the period of concrete operations, were much more likely to contend erroneously that the transformed row contained more items. Their reasoning related increased numerosity to increased length ("The longer row has more") or to increased density in cases when a squished row is identified as "more." A synopsis of the Piagetian interpretation of this counterintuitive observation is as follows: Young children fail to understand the independence of numerosity from irrelevant perceptual features (i.e., length, density of spacing) and fail

FIGURE 6-5 *Depictions of the Displays that Might Be Used to Assess Conservation of Number.*
In the top display, two rows of items are lined up in one-to-one orrespondence. A transformation occurs where the spacing in one of the rows is altered, typically by spreading the items out (bottom). If children judge the longer row (B) to have more items, the Piagetian evaluation is that they do not have a mature concept of number.

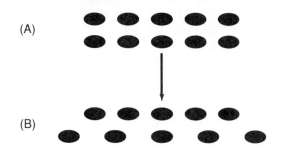

to understand the one-to-one correspondence between the items in the two rows. Despite the fact that children might actually count the number of items in each row (and still fail the conservation question), failure to conserve signaled failure to understand the *concept* of number.

The reliable observation and the accompanying explanation of the conservation phenomenon has generated so much controversy that subsequent experimental investigation of the topic has proliferated. There are a number of reviews and reanalyses of this research (see Halford, 1982; Klahr & Wallace, 1976). In its classic form, the task is complex and potentially ambiguous. The child is confronted with a perceptually misleading stimulus (as is the case in many Piagetian-inspired tasks) and asked numerosity questions framed in words (*more, same, less*) that are notorious for presenting semantic difficulties for the young (Donaldson & Balfour, 1968; Fuson & Hall, 1983; Holland & Palermo, 1975; Palermo, 1973, 1974). Therefore, a young child may fail to conserve for a variety of reasons (e.g., linguistic ambiguity). Many of these failures are attributable to task-related, rather than content-related, difficulties.

From the perspective of the 1990s, it is clear that successful conservation can be elicited from young children under a variety of simplified task-demand conditions (Bryant, 1972; Gelman, 1972; Siegel, 1978) and through training (Brainerd, 1978b). Thus, many developmental psychologists are not disposed to accept the Genevan story about the origins of number knowledge in children. But, is there an alternative theoretical view as to the origins and evolution of number knowledge in children?

Counting is another familiar aspect of numerical knowledge. It is a procedure for determining the absolute value of a set of items (Stevens, 1951). A sequence of ordered number tags is coordinated with a collection of objects or events, and those objects or events are enumerated. The last tag applied to the last item in the set reveals how many objects are included, the cardinal value associated with the set (Gelman & Gallistel, 1978). By the time children enter school, they have learned a chain of number words quite well, and they apply that chain to things. They count. The first-grader who ticks off a row of blocks, voices the accepted sequence of number words, and indicates how many blocks there are exhibits understanding of the enumeration process.

Many investigators examine counting as one index of number knowledge (Fuson, 1988; Sophian, 1988). However, counting in its socialized form with use of the accepted sequence of number tags is still beyond the capabilities of the very young child and the animal subject. But those subjects could still somehow enumerate sets without the use of the formal number chain. So counting, operationalized in some fashion, is a potential indicator of number knowledge even in these subjects.

Counting as an index of true enumeration is sometimes distinguished from three other processes: **protocounting, subitizing,** and **discriminating numerousness** (Davis & Pérusse, 1988). *Protocounting,* usually attributed to animals, refers to behavior that might be interpreted as enumeration, but the situations in which the behavior is observed are not well controlled (Braaten, 1988).

Subitizing is a problematic process and a controversial notion (Blevins-Knabe, Cooper, Starkey, Mace, & Leitner, 1987; Boysen, 1988; Gallistel, 1988). Some propose that the numerosity of small sets (set sizes of 1, 2, 3, . . . 6) is grasped directly as a consequence of perceptual processes (Siegler, 1986a). A subject looks at a set of three things and immediately perceives "threeness" in a gestaltlike fashion without the need to tick off individual entities in the set. An interpretation sometimes made is that subitizing represents a "lower" level of cognitive processing than true enumeration and is only applicable to small set sizes. A "higher" level counting process, cognitively distinguishable from subitizing, is presumably the mechanism for enumerating larger sets. The data are not clear as to the status of subitizing as distinct from counting (Burns, 1988; Gallistel, 1988; Gallistel & Gelman, 1990), but it is an issue commonly raised in discussions of numerical knowledge observed in infants, animals, and young children.

Discriminating numerousness is differential responding to sets on the basis of more qualitativelike judgments of amount. That is, a subject may note generally that a set of $n + 3$ items contains more than a set of n items but not know the absolute value of either set or the precise numerical magnitude of the difference between them.

In terms of knowledge sophistication, perhaps discriminating numerousness is less sophisticated than subitizing, both of which fall short of the knowledge signaled by true counting. The literature is not always clear as to exactly what level of sophistication is displayed when a subject emits a number-related response. Nor is it clear that the levels are even legitimately distinguishable; subitizing could represent rapid, "automated" enumeration, for example. So it can be difficult to know the extent of knowledge implicated by performance and to evaluate the nature of the subject's implicit theory of number. With those potential hurdles to interpretation in mind, we turn to a review of critical research findings. Just how much do animals, infants, and young children know about number?

The Empirical Evidence

Contrary to Piaget's predictions, considerable evidence in favor of young children's understanding of number has accumulated (Brainerd, 1979; Bryant, 1974; Gelman, 1982). Particularly important findings were reported by Rochel Gelman and her associates (e.g., Gelman & Gallistel, 1978). These investigators observed positive evidence of number knowledge and counting behavior in children, even those as young as 2½ years of age.

For example, in an innovative variation of the number conservation problem, the "magic task" (Gelman, 1972), children were presented with two plates of items, small toys typically arranged in sets of two and three. One plate from the pair was identified as the "winner" and the other as the "loser." The plates were covered, shuffled in a manner reminiscent of a shell game, and the children were asked to pick out the winner (or loser) following this shifting about. Several trials like this were conducted prior to a crucial test trial. Surreptitiously on the test trial, toys on the plate were transformed spatially (e.g., the toys were spread out) or numerically (e.g., an item was removed). The subjects exhibited surprise when the number of items changed. The children associated "winner" status with numerosity, though no mention of number had been made. They reacted when number changed impossibly, but they did not treat the spatial transformations in the same way. Ap-

parently, the subjects attended to number, and, quite spontaneously, many of them counted. Some even remarked about the number change on test trials and searched for missing items. One interpretation of these data is that young children are naturally attuned to the numerosity of stimuli, represent the cardinal value of sets, and have access to an intuitive knowledge of counting.

It is easy to overlook enumeration skills in children and to underestimate their competence, because they are often inaccurate when counting. However, failure to count well by adult standards is not the same as lacking a concept of counting. Gelman and Gallistel (1978) identified the essential features of counting and differentiated those from less essential, though generally practiced, features. For example, to keep track of how many items are in a set, the counter needs a series of tags for enumerating the items. While the counter must have *some* list of tags *(numerons),* it need not be *the* list of tags commonly used *(numerlogs).* In fact, the tags do not even have to be words at all. Gelman and Gallistel eased the criteria for what constitutes counting. And, since these investigators did not apply adult standards to child behavior, they were open to detecting early evidence of enumeration in their young subjects.

Gelman and Gallistel identified five *counting principles* or rules that govern the process of abstracting number from stimulus arrays. Those principles are:

1. *The one-to-one principle.* To enumerate a set, the counter must label each member of the set with one and only one distinctive tag. Calling the first item "one," the second "two," the third "three," and so forth until the counting is complete is an example. The counter cannot skip an item, omit or repeat a tag, or tag an item more than once. This kind of coordination between the tag sequence and countables is difficult for young children. Al-

though 2- and 3-year-old children may grasp the process implicitly (Gelman, 1982), they cannot always execute it properly. It is commonplace to observe young children attempting to count, using pointing as a strategy to monitor one-to-one correspondence, but losing the coordination between verbal labeling and motor behavior. Children do understand, despite coordination errors, that the greater the number of items to be counted, the more tags required to enumerate them. This observation is depicted in Figure 6-6 with data from Gelman and Gallistel's research.

2. *The stable-order principle.* Whatever list of number tags the counter uses, the members in the list must always appear in an invariant se-

quence. Children can use idiosyncratic strings of tags. The author's son, for example, always omitted the number seven in his initial string. Whatever the sequence, the order must be constant. Much of the time, young children honor this principle even when using some naming device other than the accepted number-name sequence.

3. *The cardinal principle.* The final count word used in the counting sequence signifies the cardinal value of the set; it tells how many things there are. Thus, in the set "one, two, three" there are *three* items. Gelman and Gallistel contended that youngsters understand this principle implicitly and can demonstrate their understanding with small set sizes espe-

FIGURE 6-6 *The Extent to Which Children Honor the One-to-One Principle When Counting.*
The graphs depict the percentage of children who achieved perfect or nearly perfect correspondence between set size and the number of tags used as a function of set size. The upper graph shows those who used exactly *N* tags for a set of *N* items; the lower graph also includes those who used N + or − tags.

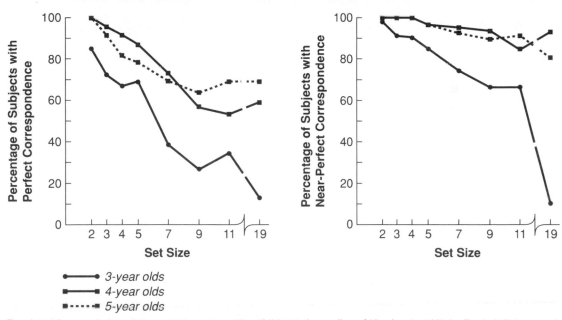

● 3-year olds
■ 4-year olds
■·····■ 5-year olds

FIGURE 6-7 *The Extent to which Children Honor the Cardinal Principle when Counting.*
The graph shows the percentage of children employing the principle, at the conclusion of an enumeration, as a function of set size.

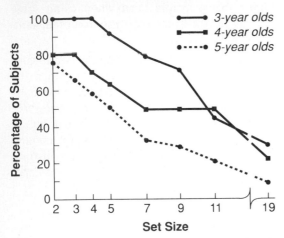

Reprinted by permission of the publishers from *The Child's Understanding of Number* (p. 124) by Rochel Gelman and C. R. Gallistel, Cambridge, MA: Harvard University Press, Copyright © 1978 by the President and Fellows of Harvard College.

cially. Data from the 1978 studies of the cardinal principle are depicted in Figure 6-7. Results like these have been reiterated and extended in subsequent studies (Fuson, Pergament, Lyons, & Hall, 1985; Gelman, Meck, & Merkin, 1986).

Whether or not children do fully understand the cardinal principle by age 2, an age when they do demonstrate counting, is a debated point. It is not unusual to observe a young child count a set, and, when asked how many items are in the set, to count again. So, it is hard to know if very young children really comprehend the special status of the last count word. In her studies, Wynn (1990) found that only older children were able to consistently provide the correct cardinal number word after counting a set. Moreover, when asked to give a specific number of things to a puppet, children differentiated into "grabbers" and "counters." Only the latter used counting as a number-determination strategy, and these, again, were the older children. Wynn concludes that children learn the cardinal principle at about age 3½.

4. The *abstraction principle* and 5. the *order-irrelevant* principle refer to what to count rather than how to count. Anything can be counted, and countables can be enumerated in any order, provided the number list is stable. These principles give a very special status to the generality of number words. A *number* label can be connected with any countable item (any member of the class of ALL THINGS); a *naming* label can only be applied to members within the more restricted class to which the label refers ("dog" only connects with CANINES). It is noteworthy as well that young children accept multiple *number tags* applied to a single countable while, at the same time, they reject multiple *labels* for a single item, (Gelman, 1982; Gelman & Gallistel, 1978; Gelman & Meck, 1986).

Young children are most accurate abstracting the numerosity of sets when set size is small, typically less than five (Siegler, 1986a; Siegler & Robinson, 1982). However, children seem to grasp the ascending order of the number sequence and the association of that with increasing magnitude (Gelman & Gallistel, 1978). Children tend to use words that appear later in the number chain when referring to sets of greater magnitude (Gelman & Tucker, 1975). They do so even when the name-number connection is wrong. A set of 19 countables, for example, might be connected with the number label "100." The cardinal value is incorrect, but an ascending order rule (the bigger the set, the higher the number word) could still have been honored in the estimate of set size.

Clearly, children make errors when they count, and they make errors when asked to reason about numbers, as on conservation tasks. What do these errors indicate? A conservative interpretation of young subjects' error-prone performance is that children lack a conceptual understanding of number in either the ordinal or cardinal sense (or both). However, conceptual competence could, in fact, be there in some rudimentary form. So, an alternative interpretation is to accept the data implicating the existence of children's conceptual knowledge and attribute errors to nonnumber-related competencies that interfere with the demonstration of that knowledge.

Gelman and her associates (Greeno, Riley, & Gelman, 1984) identified two such error-producing culprits: (1) **procedural competence** and (2) **utilization competence.** Both skills are influenced by task conditions that are not specific to number concepts. Depending on how number problems are presented to children, they may not execute a *procedure* enabling overt demonstration of whatever conceptual knowledge they do have. For example, a child who successfully counts items arranged in straight, linear rows may be unable to count the same number of items arranged randomly. The child could very well lack a tactic for monitoring and *partitioning* already counted from yet to be counted items in nonlinear arrangements. The author recalls observing a preschooler "overcounting" a circular arrangement of items because he had failed to mark the initial object counted, the item labeled "one."

Children may not understand what specific bit of conceptual knowledge is requested in a task either. The child may, for example, interpret the probe, "How many are there," asked following a successful count, as a request to recount rather than as a request for the set's cardinal value. Similarly, the probe, "Show me the 4 blocks," could refer to the set of four blocks, or the block labeled "four" in the counting sequence. Such ambiguity in task demands interferes with performance in young children. Failure to indicate a set's cardinal value is a likely result when the child does not understand what is asked and does not fully *utilize* available conceptual knowledge. Tasks useful in eliciting knowledge in the very young must be sensitive to possible barriers that will impede an exemplary performance.

The strong nativist case that Gelman and others make (Gallistel & Gelman, 1990; Gelman, 1982; Gelman & Cohen, 1988) for children's precocious knowledge of number is substantiated by corroborating data from studies with infants and animals (Antell & Keating, 1983; Gallistel, 1989; Strauss & Curtis, 1984). The significance of the infant data resides in the immaturity of the subjects. If very young infants display a sensitivity to number and a capacity to discriminate the numerosity of sets, then two implications readily follow. First, the knowledge capacities of preschoolers are less surprising and less controversial when babies show sensitivity to numerosity, too. Second, some rudimentary numerical abilities look to be innate when very young infants display them (Gelman, 1982; Starkey, Spelke, & Gelman, 1983). Similarly, a biological basis for number, rather than strictly a cultural one, is supported when animals display numberlike cognitions. It is awkward to argue for number knowledge as a consequence of socialization and schooling when animals, some of whom are quite removed from humans phylogenetically, display similar talents (Davis & Pérusse, 1988; Gallistel, 1989, 1990).

Number knowledge in babies is typically assessed within the habituation paradigm. Subjects are habituated to a stimulus display containing n objects; test displays contain $> n$ or $< n$ objects. Dishabituation denotes detection of the numerical change in the set and the capacity to discriminate numerosity. Of course, number change can be confounded with corresponding changes in numerically irrelevant characteristics such as overall pattern, amount of contrast in the display, spacing, type of object, and so forth. The studies must be carefully controlled to disentangle potentially confounding influences. With well-controlled habituation procedures, investigators have shown that babies are sensitive to numerosity, dishabituating to changes in the cardinal values of sets (Starkey & Cooper, 1980; Starkey, Spelke, & Gelman, 1983; Strauss & Curtis, 1981, 1984).

In a series of studies, Starkey, Spelke, and Gelman (1990) examined precocious responsivity to numerosity in infants between 6 and 9 months of age. Subjects were habituated to visual displays of either two or three heterogeneous items (e.g., wooden bowl, lemon, blue sponge). On test trials, the babies were presented with either numerically familiar (the same number of new objects) or numerically novel displays (a different number of new objects). The babies dishabituated to the latter; apparently, the change in number was detected and was salient enough to be perceived over and above change in other object-display characteristics. These data are presented in Table 6-1.

TABLE 6-1 *Median Duration of Looking (Seconds) in the Test Phase of Experiment 1*
Infants were habituated to either two- or three-item object displays. Test trials contained novel objects and either a familiar or novel numerosity. Infants looked longer at displays with the novel numerosity.

Habituation Displays	Test Displays	
	2 objects	*3 objects*
2 objects	6.55	7.94
3 objects	5.00	3.88

From "Numerical Abstraction by Human Infants" by P. Starkey, E. Spelke, and R. Gelman, 1983, *Cognition, 36,* pp. 97–127.

Then the investigators examined whether the detection of numerosity might be intermodal (an attempt to circumvent the subitizing criticism). This time, subjects heard a sequence of sounds, two or three drumbeats, emanating from midpoint between two visual displays, one containing two objects, the other containing three. Subjects looked longer at the visual display matching the numerosity of the auditory stimulus. In replication studies, the findings were reiterated; babies looked longer at displays where the number of items corresponded to the number of sounds. The conclusion is that infants detect distinct entities in a sequence of sounds and can relate numerical correspondences intermodally.

Evidence for animal number cognition is extensive, too (Davis & Pérusse, 1988; Gallistel, 1989, 1990). That animals discriminate numerousness is probably beyond dispute; the contention that they might count is even supportable (Boysen & Berntson, 1989; Capaldi & Miller, 1988a, 1988b). For instance, rats trained to enter a specific "burrow" in a series (for e.g., burrow 5) continued to enter that burrow even when the spacing between the burrows in the series was altered and changed (Davis & Bradford, 1986). The possibility that the rats were using a place strategy for locating the target burrow is less likely than the use of a countinglike strategy under these experimental manipulations.

What appears to be sensitivity to the absolute numerical value of sets is also reported. Apparently, when species survival favors it, animals react differentially on the basis of litter size or the number of eggs in a clutch, for example. Small litters will be abandoned if the mother has the potential of producing a second, larger litter. She, thus, saves time and energy while maximizing the number of offspring produced. Some birds will lay additional eggs if some are taken and stop laying eggs when a given number of them are present, even reabsorbing already-formed but not yet laid eggs.

The differential behavior seems to hinge on the absolute number of offspring or eggs present (Seibt, 1988). The neurological mechanism mediating number cognition in animals is being explored (see Gallistel, 1988, 1989, 1990). That animals have access to a capacity to deal with numbers seems indisputable.

Debate continues, however, about the generality of this observed number capacity in the young and in the nonhuman. With these individuals, success at abstracting and representing numerical information is often limited to small set sizes. For example, while babies can discriminate between set sizes of two and three items, they cannot do so with set sizes of four, five, and six items (Starkey & Cooper, 1980). Toddlers count fairly well with set sizes of one, two, and three items, but are much less facile as set size increases (Gelman & Gallistel, 1978). There remains the possibility that whatever knowledge is present is constrained to small numbers (Blevins-Knabe et al, 1987). Consequently, some propose that it is *subitizing,* not counting, that is the relevant abstraction process (Cooper, 1984; Davis & Pérusse, 1988; von Glasersfeld, 1982). But this is an arguable point.

First, it is not clear just what subitizing is. Is it a process distinct from other forms of enumeration? It may simply reflect very fast execution of counting in the practiced, those familiar and adept at counting. If so, since young children do not qualify as adept counters, subitizing is an unlikely strategy for them to use when abstracting numerosity (Gelman & Gallistel, 1978).

Second, the time taken to estimate the numerosity of sets increases with set size (Chi & Klahr, 1975; Mandler & Shebo, 1982). This holds true even for small sets (see Gallistel, 1988). It also takes longer to count larger sets. So counting time and reaction time for estimating set sizes show correspondence. For small set sizes, however, differences in reaction time as a function of set size are very small. The empirical fact remains: Most of the time displayed number knowledge in the young is restricted to small numerosities.

Evaluation and Summary

A *theory* is a system of principled knowledge applicable to a range of phenomena. But, it is important to distinguish *knowledge* of principles from *skill* in applying those principles. According to Gelman and colleagues, young children display knowledge of the counting principles first, and the knowledge is present prior to children's accessing the skills to apply that knowledge (Gelman & Cohen, 1988; Gelman & Greeno, 1989; Gelman & Meck, 1983; Gelman, Meck, & Merkin, 1986; Greeno, Riley, & Gelman, 1984). Lack of skill, not lack of knowledge, restricts a more generalized demonstration of innate number-specific principles of knowledge. The acquisition of skill enables an increasingly proficient display of that knowledge as children obtain the opportunity to practice the counting routine (Gelman, 1991). Envisioned in this manner, number knowledge is a domain-specific knowledge faculty (Gallistel & Gelman, 1990), a "natural domain" of competence, much like language (Gelman, 1982) and spatial ability. The number faculty is not merely reducible to some domain-general aspect of cognition (as Piaget would have it) or to an outcome of generalized learning mechanism (but see Siegler & Shipley, 1987). In a strong nativist view of number, a skeletal but principled knowledge of number is an implicit, innate faculty of the species.

So, what develops? Minimally, access to number knowledge changes with age; we observe an age-related increase in the display of numerical proficiency as children become more accurate at counting sets with greater numerosities or apply counting principles in reasoning contexts (Carpenter, Moser, & Romberd, 1982; Fuson, 1982; Miller & Gelman, 1983; Miller & Stigler, 1987; Siegler & Robinson, 1982; Siegler & Shrager, 1984). With practice and opportunity, children get better handling counting, numbers generally, and numerical reasoning as initial knowledge elaborates and expands.

There is a question of whether children's initial representation of number, which underlies early competence, is the same sort of representation they construct later. About this point there is more ambiguity (see Wynn, in press a, in press b). Gelman and Greeno (1989) assumed an innate set of preverbal *counting* principles. This existing knowledge enables children to detect quite easily the correspondence between what is implicitly known and the formal, socialized counting principles. So, children do not learn to count from scratch; they only need to re-represent existing counting principles in a new format, that is, with language. On the other hand, initial knowledge of number might not be isomorphic to socialized counting (Wynn, 1990). If not, then acquisition of counting skill might be prolonged because much more than re-representation is involved.

In formal counting, the ordinal position of the number word in the count list is the key to what the number represents. For example, 4 comes two positions after 2 in the number list, and 4 is more than 2; it is two more than 2, and so on. It is not clear if ordinality is a characteristic of early number knowledge. (Recall that babies react to varying the *cardinal* value of sets.) Perhaps a correspondence between the two systems—the linguistically representing counting system and preverbal knowledge of numerosity—is not so obvious after all. The empirical evidence is not yet sufficient to clarify this issue.

Gelman (1991) proposed a model for the initial representation of number where the numbers are like blurry blobs on a number line. Their "blobness" rather than "pointness" makes for a potential confusion between ad-

joining numerosities (e.g., mistaking "sevenness" for "eightness"), but the individual "blobs" still signify *discrete* values. This sort of representation is conducive to thinking about numbers as entities, as falling in sequence, as coming one after the other, and so on. These characteristics hold for natural number. With natural numbers, it makes sense to refer to *the* number that comes *after* 2; it is conceivable to "count on" to determine a sum. Because of a match between the notion of numbers as discrete spots in sequence—initially as innate principles and as natural numbers—some operations should be easy to learn, for example, addition and subtraction of whole numbers. Other concepts and operations are not consistent with this sort of representation; operations conducted on fractions are an example. It makes little sense to ask for the number that comes *after* 1¼. Initial knowledge should not enable knowledge constructions and the acquisition of numerical principles applicable to rational numbers (fractions) in the same way that knowledge facilitates reasoning about natural numbers (integers). Intuition should interfere with the former. And indeed, fraction concepts are difficult for most children to master (Gelman, 1991; Gelman & Meck, in press).

It is particularly noteworthy that initial knowledge of number encompasses the concept in terms of its discrete "entityness" rather than as a continuous dimension. Is this reflective, again, of a tendency to organize the world into things? It is more than curious that evidence continues to accumulate for children's predisposition to interact with (including to count) discrete, physical entities in the world (Shipley & Shepperson, 1990).

Whatever the eventual outcome of these contemporary theoretical controversies, some conclusions about children's understanding of numerosity are accepted by virtually all investigators. Implicit knowledge of number is present very, very early in life (Gallistel & Gelman, 1990). The knowledge is elaborated, extended, and made more explicit as children mature (Miller & Gelman, 1983). The fundamental enumeration principles are enriched and elaborated upon as children come to appreciate the full meaning of count words and the full implications of numerical concepts (Fuson, 1988). And all those conclusions are consistent with the contention that knowledge of number constitutes a tacit theory, even in the young, that must have roots in innate mechanisms.

CONCLUSION

The most skeletal ontological tree includes a node that encompasses ALL THINGS. From a single node, an initial branch forms: the animate-inanimate distinction. Conceivably, then, there are three primitive categories into which the world divides and to which states of existence apply. Those categories contain the entities around which principled systems of knowledge, or naive theories, form. In this initial grouping of things, distinctions between solids, liquids, events, abstractions, and so forth have yet to be made. What would seem to unite the early distinguished entities is their "objectness," a quality to which even the youngest infants are attuned (Spelke, 1988, 1989). Numerosity is a salient property of objects to which even infants respond. It is not unreasonable to surmise, therefore, that two primitive theories about the workings of the world should turn out to be an *intuitive theory of number,* primitive principles applicable to ALL THINGS, and an *intuitive mechanics,* rules about the behavior of INANIMATE OBJECTS.

The research with infants, toddlers, and preschoolers reviewed in this chapter generally confirms the proposition that youngsters have tacit conceptual knowledge about number, objects, and motion. But, that knowledge varies from the mature adult variety in several

ways. First, it is *implicit* in contrast to explicit. Youngsters cannot verbalize counting principles, explain the rule governing an object's trajectory, or formalize their rationale for reacting with surprise to an impossible physical event. They do behave in ways that appear principle governed, however. Second, children's early knowledge is *less general* than it will be later. Number knowledge, for instance, is restricted to small set sizes, to simple numerical operations, and to natural numbers. Third, youngsters may be more proficient at abstracting and representing *qualitative rules* about phenomena ("Bigger sets have higher number names," "Objects cannot pass through barriers") and less able to represent quantitative rules (e.g., the formulations of exact amount, rational numbers, velocity, and acceleration). Quantitative rules are more precise than qualitative ones and include the representation of continuous variables, not discrete entities.

The discrepancies between indigenous knowledge systems and the expert forms suggest the nature of any subsequent developmental change. With development, for instance, principles become explicitly understood; older children can explain their reasoning about number and mechanics. Piaget's evaluations of the sophistication of children's reasoning was partly based on his ability to elicit verbal justifications, or verbal rule statements, only from children aged 7 and 8 or older.

As children learn procedures and algorithms for applying knowledge and for expressing it symbolically, they increase proficiency, generalizing rudimentary concepts. Thus, they can succeed on more problems and are less likely to be tripped up by task ambiguity. Practice counting and acquisition of a longer string of number names, for example, allows elementary-school children to perform tasks involving large numerosities and to use counting as a device for adding and subtracting. Development should also improve children's ability to represent rules in the more precise quantitative form. Increasing explicitness, generality, applicability, and precision, however, are all envisionable as changes in the *degree* of knowledge, not in its original nature. But does the increase in knowledge sophistication—of physics or of number—change the original core?

The literature review in this chapter favors the view that young children have access to indigenous, rudimentary theories: an *intuitive mechanics* and a *principled understanding of number.* In the course of development, as the ontological knowledge tree differentiates, those bundles of knowledge initially lumped together in the crude structure will become differentiated, too. New theories will form.

Will the change from crude theory to differentiated theory amount to a paradigm shift? We take that issue up again in the next chapter.

ENDNOTES

1. "It is a fundamental principle of Newtonian mechanics that an object moves in a straight line unless it is acted on by an external force" (McCloskey, 1983a, p. 122).

2. In impetus theory, a fundamental distinction must be made between a state of rest (objects at rest cannot have impetus) and a state of motion (moving objects have impetus). In contrast, Newton's first law of motion holds that just as no force is required to keep an object at rest, so no force is required to keep an object moving at a constant velocity (see McCloskey, 1983a).

CHAPTER 7

NAIVE THEORIES OF BIOLOGY AND PSYCHOLOGY

INTRODUCTION

Objects are contained entities. They move and they can be counted. Concepts of motion and number are supported by highly sensible, informational characteristics of the environment, and, as we have seen, even neonates perceive motion and discriminate number. Therefore, it is reasonable that children's early theories about the workings of the world should contain principles about its perceptible features. An intuitive mechanics and an implicit understanding of number is principled knowledge about perceptually available physical phenomena. Not all that children encounter and try to figure out will be so perceptible, however. Some features of some entities, even features that mark essential properties of entities, are not easily perceived. What obvious feature, for example, defines "aliveness," "animalness," or "plantness"? What external, perceptible clue is there for an intention, a wish, or a thought?

Examine the following conversation between a mother and a 4-year-old. The context is a toy store where the child can choose only one of several possible goodies.

Mother: Which one do you want?
Child: That one. (points)
Mother: Okay. (reaches)
Child: No! Wait! I've changed my mind!
Mother: You changed your mind! Do you know what a "mind" is?
Child: (Pauses, looks at his mother, and points at his forehead placing his finger quite distinctly right in the middle) It's here.
Mother: Can you see your mind?
Child: No! I can't see my own head.
Mother: Can I see your mind?
Child: No! It's inside of me.
Mother: If you can't see your mind and I can't see your mind, how do you know its there?
Child: Because ... I can think with it.

What goes on inside bodies and heads is neither inspectible, perceptible, or obvious. Yet, children do try to decipher those phenomena. Children reason about the operation of biological and psychological systems and, possibly even construct naive theories of biology (Carey, 1985) and of mind (Astington, Harris,

& Olson, 1988). But it is not clear what data they have access to or what empirical evidence of life and thought fuels the knowledge-acquisition process.

As described in Chapter 6, the earliest differentiation on the ontological tree is between animate and inanimate entities. The inanimate branch was the subject of the last chapter. The animate branch is the subject of this one. The animate branch, a rudimentary class of living things, is differentiated into categories of plants, animals, birds, humans, and so forth in the course of development and knowledge accumulation. But does the construction of category-based theories elaborate concurrently with this development? It surely might if the thesis that ontology constrains knowledge acquisition (see Chapter 5) is indeed a legitimate premise. We next explore evidence for that connection—between naive theory, ontology, and children's cognitive development—as it applies to animate, living entities.

THEORY AND THE ANIMATE BRANCH

The sequence of ontological differentiation is from a basic, somewhat crude category of LIVING THINGS to a separation of those entities into kind. As Gelman (1990a) and others (see Chapter 6) have demonstrated, even very young children have successfully differentiated living entities into a separate category on the basis of self-propelled animacy and an **innards principle** by which the insides of animate objects are deemed causally relevant to the source of that animacy. But the knowledge is rudimentary in the young.

In Keil's (1979) research, 5-year-olds' intuitions indicated their failure to distinguish among PLANTS, NONSENTIENT BEINGS, and SENTIENT BEINGS. Seven-year-olds separated PLANT from the other two categories, but even 9-year-olds still did not make a distinction between mammals and humans. A failure to differentiate means **collapsing**

categories: having only one category where a mature individual would have two or more. Members within a category are treated the same, and a predicate appended to one is extendable to all other category members. So, from an adult perspective, in collapsed category structures, predicates will appear to span too many terms, to be overgeneralized. A 5-year-old child will accept the contention that "the rabbit is sorry"; an older person probably would not.

Changes in the branches on an ontological tree occur as categories of entities are distinguished and "moved down" to a new location. Thus, for example, objects identified as fitting criteria of "aliveness" become separated from other entities and are shifted downward on the tree. A new node is created, clearly differentiated from the NONLIVING THING node. Some classes of entities, however, will fit the judgment criteria for "aliveness" better (and developmentally earlier) than others. To children, for example, mammals might seem more alive than other forms of life. Therefore, as a new lower node is forming, some groups of things are shifted down before others, and a child's tree will differ from an adult tree in structure. At one point in development, a child's LIVING THING node might properly include mammals, birds, and insects, those classes of things having made the downward journey. Others, those adults would include in their living-thing category, such as plants, coral, and bacteria, are left behind. The resulting impression is that children's and adults' ontological knowledge are quite different, perhaps even qualitatively so.

But the child's tree is in transition. Plants, coral, and bacteria will, in time, eventually follow their living cohorts. Out of the context of developmental time, the child's tree will look different from the adult's tree, but over time, the immature tree is moving on a direct course toward the adult version. The child's is a skeletal version of the adult's.

Children's theories could differ from adult theories just as the ontological structures, the **metastructures** for those theories, also differ. Extrapolating from what we know about ontological development and generalizing it to theory development, the following seem like reasonable propositions:

1. Children's initial theories about biological systems will tend to be cruder than that of their older counterparts.
2. The examples of what constitutes biological systems will be more restricted.
3. But, some rudimentary version of a biological theory should be available as soon as the ANIMATE THINGS branch is detectable.
4. Children probably have a naive theory of mind, too, but again it is apt to be cruder and less inclusive of mental function than adult versions.
5. Whatever the form initial theories of biology and psychology take, and how ever early they emerge in rudimentary form, there will be conceptual change and developmental elaboration, which incorporates expanding experience.

The development of theory begins with facts that need figuring out; the individual has to observe something. So, if a child were to construct a theory of biology or a naive psychology, that child must have access to pertinent observations about biological and psychological systems. Part of those observations will involve who and what constitute prototypic exemplars of a biological or a psychological system. Whatever those initial prototypes are—the family dog, the bird in the window, the mouse in the cellar, or the child's own thoughts—they function as the body of *empirical* knowledge begging *theoretical* explanation.

However, the child's exemplars will not be exactly the same as those of an adult, just as children's tacit definition of "animate" is somewhat different. The mature category LIVING THING includes many, many life forms. The child's does not. The child has encountered few exemplars and has yet to pick up on all the subtle criteria that define "aliveness" in the adult sense. Evidence favors the premise, however, that even the young child has such a category (Gelman, 1990a, 1990b; Keil, 1989; but see Carey, 1985). And, very early, children have a concept of person. Most likely, therefore, the biological and psychological facts that fuel theory construction constitute a limited subset of those encompassed by a mature structure.

The observations that are important to explanations of biological and psychological phenomena require attention to nonobvious features and characteristics of entities (Wellman & Gelman, 1988). What constitutes a biological or psychological process may not be perceptible to the untrained eye (e.g., breathing, dreaming). Outward similarities in appearances may have nothing to do with theory-relevant underlying differences (e.g., dolls and children, stuffed animals and live ones). So, the would-be theory builder must not only observe the evidence but must avoid being deluded by irrelevant data as well.

Contemporary investigations favor the view that children do have access to naive theories of biology and of mind (Keil, 1991; Wellman, 1990). Their systems are not the same as those held by the tutored, but naive systems are not idiosyncratic either. They are constrained in ways quite similar to adult versions (Keil, 1989). If children build theories, they have facts; if their theories overlap with mature ones, youngsters and adults must observe similar facts. And if children's theories are fact sensitive, they must change and evolve in the face of incoming facts. At any point in time, children's theories must be consistent with the current status of empirical knowledge; as the latter changes, so must the former.

Another interchange between child and adult exemplifies the point. The child—a 5-year-old—has just observed her pet rabbit give birth. The adult and child *see* the same facts: two parents; eight little, furless, blind bunnies; and the placenta and other tissue. The interpretations of the facts are somewhat different.

Adult: Where did those baby bunnies come from?
Child: The mommy's tummy; they grew in her tummy.
Adult: How did they get there?
Child: Well, it all started with goo (referring to the placenta in the cage). The goo was in the mommy . . . and it formed into those babies . . . and the babies came out . . . and that's all there is to it!
Adult: What about the daddy?
Child: Oh . . . he's just for protection.

NAIVE THEORIES OF BIOLOGY

There are two important components of the subject matter of biology about which we acquire information. First, we must learn to identify the set of individuals who constitute a group of biological objects, a type. This **taxonomic** component of biology is about the classes of organisms, the *species,* and about the interrelationships among those classes or species. Mapping the taxonomic relations of species is a *descriptive* enterprise within biological science. Species membership is formally defined through reference to common chromosomal structure, the DNA, shared by organisms within the same classification. The genetic structure determines the other shared features of biological functioning that are more immediately perceptible than DNA, features such as physical structure, digestive and reproductive processes, and species-typical behavior.

A second component of biological science is the study of the **biological processes:** how organisms grouped together operate and func-

tion. Functions are causal processes taking place within biological systems, an appreciation of which requires reasoning about cause and effect and about mechanisms of operation. Taxonomy and function are, of course, related (since DNA ultimately determines both), but cognitions about the two may not develop in quite the same manner.

To construct knowledge of biology, children must come to understand which groups of organisms share characteristics of appearance and operation. They must decipher which of those characteristics are most relevant to decisions about organism similarity. They must figure out how organisms work. To take that knowledge a step further and organize it into a theory, children must systematize the domain-specific biological information they have acquired. And, subsequently, that system can be elaborated with increased empirical experience, evolving and restructuring as new organisms are encountered, new causal processes are discovered, and as new learning enriches existing knowledge. But how can the developmental psychologist obtain a glimpse of this evolving theoretical knowledge?

If we propose that children do have access to a naive theory of biological knowledge, it is not at all clear how to study the nature of that knowledge. It would be convenient if we could simply sit down with a child, discuss the subject of biology, and have him explain important features of his theory. Obviously, that is an unrealistic approach. Asking children for verbal explanations of biological concepts and processes may be a traditional method for attempting to extract evidence of knowledge, but it is a controversial one. Explicit scientific theories are products of formal tutelage; they are rationalized verbal reports of scientific thinking. Children, however, rarely can describe in words what they know (Karmiloff-Smith, 1988).

Still, ascribing a biological theory to an individual is presuming the individual can access a set of biological principles about what constitutes permissible and nonpermissible biological events. Adults know, for example, that birds do not hatch puppies, that all animals require food to survive, and that artifacts do not breathe, eat, and reproduce like animals do. If children's biological knowledge is principle governed, those rules should show in how children behave toward biological phenomena, even when they cannot state those principles explicitly. So investigators must be innovative. Their challenge is to design creative tasks that elicit an implicit understanding of biological principles children may not be able to explain.

A number of procedures are reported in the empirical literature. One was described previously in the discussion of children's grasp of natural-kind categories (see Chapter 5): assessing children's *inductions,* the lawfulness of inferences they draw among entities. In examining induction, the investigator assumes that children will generalize a fact about one individual only to other individuals in the same category. So, if a child learns that a rabbit gives birth to live young, and subsequently the child concedes that mice, rats, and cats also do, but that birds and turtles probably do not, then the child is treating rabbits, mice, rats, and cats as the same sort of thing and is differentiating them from birds and reptiles. Children's judgments about the generalizability of biological facts permit the investigator to infer how they might organize the biological realm of individuals according to shared biological functions. The generalization and differentiation of biological facts must be rule governed if biological knowledge is organized and theoretical. Examining how children's biological inferences are rule governed allows a peek at the status of that knowledge.

A second technique is assessing the sorts of biological transformations children accept as plausible. Can, for example, a cat be transformed into a dog (a species change) simply by donning a costume or through plastic surgery? Can a tiger's cub grow up to be a lion if

supplied with special vitamins? Acceptance of these kind-altering transformations implicates a different rule for defining a biological kind than does rejection of the transformations.

Still a third technique is to elicit directly children's reasoning about causal processes in biological systems, such as respiration, growth, and reproduction, and to infer the rules behind the reasoning. All three procedures still depend more or less on verbal protocols that carry with them problems of ambiguity and interpretation. But, the literature is intriguing, and it is telling us a great deal about the nature of children's naive biology (Keil, 1992).

A Conservative View

Conservative predictions about the status of children's biological knowledge begin with the premise that children, especially young ones, cannot possibly know much in any formal sense. The conclusion is intuitively reasonable: Children have been taught little explicitly about the biological processes that sustain life, and they are largely ignorant of the internal structures found inside bodies (Carey, 1988; Crider, 1983; Gellert, 1962). How could they be otherwise since youngsters' experience with life forms is so clearly limited?

The animal kinds with which children have their most extensive experience are themselves and the other humans with whom they interact. Throw in a few pets of limited species, some house plants, trees, and flowers, an occasional spider, bug, and bird, and you have it—the young child's typical exposure to living things. It is a rare preschooler who has much inkling of what is inside any of these creatures, and young children have yet to encounter the didactic scale models of bodies and organs found in biology books. The exception, no doubt, is the ubiquitous "ear" model many will have observed during trips to the pediatrician to treat equally ubiquitous ear infections.

If children learn biological facts in a primarily inductive fashion, then preschoolers have not had exposure to sufficient data to induce much of anything. Therefore, young children should have limited knowledge of biological principles. Moreover, from a conservative perspective, the proposal that a naive theory structures whatever biological knowledge they do have might seem implausible. Or, put another way, young children simply do not know the facts, and it takes facts to sustain a theory.

Recall, however, that children do make some distinctions between animate and inanimate entities (see Chapter 6), and their intuitions reveal such a branch in their ontological knowledge structure (Keil, 1979). A category of animate things could serve as a primitive classification of biological kind. Children use words that denote **biological kinds,** such as dog, animal, and bird; **biological states,** such as alive, dead, and sick; and **biological processes,** such as breathe and eat. Words reference concepts. But are preschoolers' biological concepts fundamentally different from those of adults even though the overt vocabulary is similar?

Conservative predictions of limited biological knowledge are consistent with the Piagetian perspective (Piaget, 1929). In this view, preschoolers are supposed to be perceptually dominated and thus predisposed to make all categorical distinctions on the basis of perceptually obvious characteristics. The important characteristics that unite different individuals into a single biological kind (guppy and shark, stinkbug and worm) are often neither obvious nor perceptual. Distinct biological kinds can share a common label—dolphin fish versus dolphin mammal—and even look similar—ants, which are insects, resemble spiders, which are not. Piagetians would predict that young children should not be able to employ nonobvious characteristics in judging similarities and differences in kind, biological or otherwise. Contemporary evidence, however, suggests that children often can (Well-

man & Gelman, 1988), at least for natural kinds.

Piaget also contended that preschool-age children are pervasively **precausal.** Thus, they are unable to reason mechanistically about cause-and-effect processes and to distinguish **mechanical causation** from **intentional causation** in any domain of knowledge. In reasoning about physical causation, a young child is likely to ascribe intentions to inanimate objects, for example, inferring that the refrigerator is cold because it wants to protect the milk. By implication, the mechanistic causal processes involved in biological systems, such as digestion, locomotion, and reproduction, should be beyond the precausal child's grasp, too. A young child might very well reason that his rabbit had babies because she was lonely and wanted someone to play with.

Notions about young children's precausal status have been challenged (Bullock, Gelman, & Baillargeon, 1982). First, young children can differentiate predictable outcomes from random outcomes (Kuzmak & Gelman, 1986) which implicates a grasp of cause-and-effect sequences. Second, there is evidence for children's early appreciation of mechanical causation (Shultz, 1982). If children do demonstrate an ignorance of biology and a lack of systematic understanding of biological principles, it is not obvious that their incompetence is ascribable to generalized inadequacies of reasoning and categorization.

Piaget proposed preoperational reasoning as guided by the principle of childhood **animism,** a tendency by the young to overattribute "aliveness" to inanimate objects. In questioning children about the concept of "alive," Piaget observed that understanding appeared to emerge in an ordered sequence of stages between no concept (Stage 0) and the mature concept (Stage 4). In the intermediate stages (1, 2, and 3), *activity* and *movement,* rather than biological processes, define life. In Stage 1, things that are active in any way are alive; in Stage 2, only things that move are alive; and in Stage 3, things that move by themselves are alive (Carey, 1985).

Laurendeau and Pinard (1962) replicated the original Piagetian studies. They found that most 4-year-olds were classifiable at Stage 0, the majority of 7-year-olds at Stages 1 and 2, and over 50% of the 10-year-olds fell into Stage 3. Carey's (1985) findings were similar when comparing the extent to which children judged inanimate objects in an animistic fashion. She also concluded that the phenomenon was robust and stable. The complied results from these studies are presented in Table 7-1.

Carey's investigations, however, went further than the others. She continued to probe children's concept of "alive," contrasting it with "dead," for example, and pursuing children's understanding of related concepts like animate, inanimate, animal, and plant. While agreeing with others that the animistic attribution of life to nonliving entities is indeed a re-

liable characteristic of children's thinking, Carey did not explain the observation as a function of children's inadequate causal reasoning or of their failure to distinguish intentional and mechanical causation. She placed her explanation in a different context, in a domain-specific rather than in a domain-general one. For Carey, apparent childhood animism results from impoverished biological knowledge. The concept of "alive" is biologically complex. Until children develop sufficient biological knowledge, which they have not accomplished as preschoolers, the distinction between living and nonliving entities is an ambiguous one. Animism declines with age as children acquire biological knowledge.

Carey (1985, 1988) remained conservative, however, because she attributed little biological knowledge to young children. They lack a *biological* concept of "alive" and "dead" as biological states. So, the distinctions youngsters draw regarding those terms are remarkably different from those of adults. And they are

TABLE 7-1 *Evidence of Animism in Children: Replications of the Original Piagetian Observations and Analysis*

		Percentage of Children at Each Stage		
Piaget's Stages		*4-year-olds*	*7-year-olds*	*10-year-olds*
Stage 0: No Concept	L & P*	73	8	0
	C**	60	0	0
Stage 1: Activity				
	L & P	23	43	22
	C	10	10	20
Stage 2: Movement				
Stage 3: Autonomous	L & P	4	10	24
movement	C	10	40	30
Stage 4: Adult Concept	L & P	0	39	54
	C	20	50	50

Adapted from *Conceptual Change in Childhood* by S. Carey, 1985, Cambridge, MA: The MIT Press. Copyright 1985 by The MIT Press. Reprinted by permission.

* Laurendeau & Pinard's (1962) replication
** Carey's (1985) replication

nonbiological distinctions. To the preschooler, "alive" things are active, real, existent, and present; death is confused with inanimate, imaginary, nonexistent, and representational. Death is avoidable, reversible, and sleeplike, not an inevitable cessation of biological functioning (Carey, 1988). Preschoolers lack the notion of the bodily machine. Knowledge of the mechanics of how the machine operates is still beyond them, so how could they possibly conceptualize life and death in bodily mechanical terms? Again, they simply do not have the facts.

More salient than the biological mechanics of bodies and animals is the *behavior* of active organisms. People and animals act and their activity is internally generated. Behavior is also readily observable and perceptible; it is also familiar since behaving is something people do. Carey contended that activity and behavior are central to the preschooler's concept of "alive." Moreover, human action is the prototype, the major example of "aliveness," for a concept of life predicated on activity. Early biological knowledge, therefore, does not involve a naive biology but an *intuitive psychology* (Carey, 1985) or, at best, a *vitalistic biology* (Carey, 1988).

Actions, behaviors, and intentions are what define "animal" for young children. Since humans, dogs, cats, and fish exhibit a lot more of those defining attributes, they are going to look a lot more alive than plants, bacteria, and coral. Carey found that for the young, the person plays the role of standard. For instance, children infer whether a specific individual (e.g., bird, mammal, bug) has an animal property (e.g., eats, sleeps, has bones) by comparing the individual to people. The more peoplelike an entity (e.g., dog versus worm), the higher the probability young children will generalize a new property to it.

Similarly, when learning a new biological fact (e.g., that an individual has a spleen), young children are more inclined to attribute the fact to another animal if the new fact was taught using people as the exemplar rather than some other animal form. This effect—differential and asymmetrical attribution—decreases with age. These data are summarized in Figure 7-1. As older children acquire more facts about the workings of more and more creatures, the similarity of any one individual to a human plays a less influential role in the induction of shared properties.

According to Carey, from 4 to 10 years of age, children's knowledge of animals, humans, and living things is elaborated, differentiated, and conceptually restructured. Children come to view animals as biological beings as well as behaving ones and to view humans as one kind of animal among many. Acquiring facts about biological processes, functions, and structures allows older children to reconceptualize a

FIGURE 7-1 *The Extent to Which Subjects Projected that Aardvarks Have Spleens (4–6) or Omenta (10–adult).*

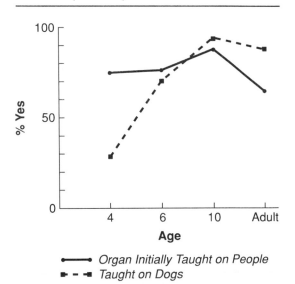

From *Conceptual Change in Childhood* by S. Carey, 1985, Cambridge, MA: The MIT Press. Copyright 1985 by The MIT Press. Reprinted by permission.

body as a machine that supports life. They also come to realize that each living thing is a solution to universal biological problems (reproduction, obtaining food). Different species share some characteristics in their solutions, but each individual meets the challenge uniquely as well. Older children's biological reasoning is supported by this rich accumulation of facts. It is this organized system of biological knowledge, this intuitive biology, that guides induction and inference for older children and adults and differentiates their thinking from that of the preschooler.

Both Piaget and Carey see young children as naive and limited in their ability to reason about biological systems. The Piagetian viewpoint posits generalized limitations in causal reasoning and pervasive childhood animism as the culprit. So, domain-general cognitive deficits constrain biological conceptualization just as they do any other type of conceptualization. In short, sophisticated biological reasoning is precluded in preoperational children because they have not yet constructed the "general-purpose" cognitive equipment. Qualitative changes in children's understanding of biological phenomena will ensue when the more sophisticated reasoning equipment comes into play.

For Carey, the limitation in reasoning is domain specific: Children lack biological information. With development, they gain expertise, which results in the enrichment of a *local* belief system. An intuitive biology emerges out of an intuitive psychology—another sort of qualitative change. Core concepts like "alive," "animal," "death," "plant," and the like are reformulated in middle childhood, forged into an explanatory conceptual system incommensurable with the earlier version. With an emerging theory, biological knowledge undergoes a developmentally driven *paradigm shift* (see Chapter 6), which occurs between the ages of 4 and 10. Only after the transition do we see, for example, evi-

dence of the concept "living thing," a superordinate category in which plant and animal have been coalesced on the basis of the mechanics of causation in biological systems.

An Alternative View

There is another possibility for how children conceptualize biology. This alternative is less conservative in attributing local knowledge to young children. While lacking explicit and specific knowledge about biological systems, children may still have access to implicit biases about how they envision the functioning of biological entities. Armed with some fundamental notions of how biological systems operate, children reason about biology in a rudimentary fashion. Moreover, tacit knowledge of the constraints on biology facilitates the acquisition of further biological information and, thus, the elaboration of a skeletal theory. As described in Chapter 1 and subsequently reiterated, constrained knowledge acquisition is rapid because constraints limit the set of hypotheses children will entertain about how some phenomenon works. Those individuals who begin the knowledge-acquisition process with rudimentary notions about how biological systems *can* work should figure out much more quickly how they *do* work.

What predictions about the emergence of a naive theory of biology in children follow given this less conservative perspective? First, young children should exhibit some knowledge of biology and an ability to reason based on that knowledge; an immature theory of biology is not simply reducible to an intuitive psychology. Second, children acquire theory-consistent biological knowledge aided by their initial intuitive biology. And, third, the development of biological knowledge does not entail theory *replacement,* as in a shift from an intuitive psychology to the intuitive biology. Theory *elaboration* and *differentiation* are alternatives to replacement. Thus, the developmental elaboration of biological knowledge need not involve qualitative change, and biological thought is not reducible to a naive psychology (Keil, 1992).

We have seen that children's explicit biological knowledge is limited. To assess implicit biological knowledge, we must tap a competence not likely to surface in spontaneous verbal accounts. Keil (see the studies reported in Keil, 1989) chose to explore children's early biological competence by examining their reactions to *transformations*. In a transformation study, a child is presented with a description of how one entity is changed into another entity, for example, a horse into a zebra, a bridge into a table, or a lizard into a stick. The following is a prototypic description, the transformation of a horse into a zebra:

> *A scientist took this horse and did an operation on it. He put black and white stripes all over its body. He cut off its mane and braided its tail like this. He taught it to run away from people. No one could ride it anymore. He taught it to eat grass instead of oats and hay. He also taught it to live out in the wild part of Africa instead of in a stable. (Keil, 1989, p. 200)*

Following this description, accompanied by supporting materials (i.e., pictures, explanations of terms like *operation*), the child is questioned about what she thinks the entity really is (e.g., "Did he change it into a zebra, or is it still a horse?") and why. Analysis of the protocols allowed Keil and his associates to determine whether children resist these transformations as true kind-altering changes. The objective is to discover what basis the child uses to establish the identity of biological entities.

There are a number of ways the basic experiment can be modified to explore children's reasoning. For instance, a transformation could change one natural kind into a closely related natural kind, as changing the horse into the zebra represents. But, it is also possible to describe much more dramatic transfor-

mations, those crossing ontological categories, as with the change of a machine into an animal, or an animal into a plant. There are also variations in the manner in which the transformations are done: quickly versus gradually, changing appearance versus changing something inside, or changing temporarily (as with a costume) versus changing permanently. The method allows for the inspection of children's ability to make judgments and to reason about biological phenomena. The ability may reveal implicit knowledge that is rule governed and theoretical, even when the youngsters cannot express the rules referenced.

In a series of studies, Keil (1989) presented these transformation stories to children in kindergarten, second grade, and fourth grade. The transformation paragraphs were of various types. Some described natural kinds where the transformation was a change within ontological category but across species—an animal into an animal, a plant into another plant. Others described the change of an artifact into some other artifact (e.g., a table into a bookcase). And the remainder described natural kinds transformed across ontological categories—an animal into an inanimate, an animal into a plant, a machine into an animal. The extent to which children resisted the transformations as truly kind altering are presented in Figure 7-2.

All children were quite willing to accept transformations of artifacts into other artifacts. Kindergartners and second-graders were somewhat willing to accept species changes, as with the horse/zebra example. But, most remarkably, even kindergarten children strongly resisted across-category changes—a lizard into a stick, a porcupine into a cactus, a toy bird into a real one. In these transformations, the perceptual, surface alterations from start to finish are not changed much but are kept relatively constant; lizards can look like sticks and toy and real birds can look alike. Still, youngsters resisted such changes, even when they could not indicate the reasons for their aver-

FIGURE 7-2 *Extent to Which Children Resisted Transformations of Kind: Across Natural Kind Types (NK/Within), and Transformations of Artifacts.*
One indicates acceptance of the transformation as kind altering, 2 indicates indecision, and 3 indicates a refection of the transformation as kind altering.

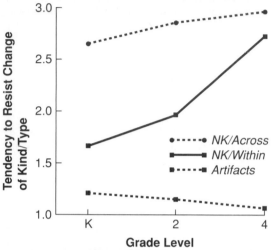

From Concepts, Kinds, and Cognitive Development by F. C. Keil, 1989, Cambridge MA: The MIT Press. Copyright 1989 by The MIT Press. Adapted by permission.

sion. An excerpt from the protocols illustrates the point:

A kindergarten child (C) rejecting a transformation of porcupine into a cactus:

C: I think he's still really a porcupine

E: And why do you say that?

C Because he started out like a porcupine.

E: Oh, OK. And even though he looks like a cactus plant you think he's really a porcupine?

C: Um hmm.

E: OK. Can you think of any other reasons why he's still a porcupine? Something you know about him?

C: (Shakes head)

E: OK. Are you sure he's a porcupine?

C: Uh huh.

E OK. (Keil, l989 p. 206)

Simultaneously, however, children who were not seduced into accepting a transformation across categories, despite the perceptual similarity that was preserved, did allow within-category transformations, and they made reference to perceptual features in doing so.

The same kindergarten child accepting the transformation of a sheep into a goat:

C: I think he changed it into a real goat. Because a sheep doesn't have horns or a beard.

E: OK. So you think even though it used to be a sheep and it came from a sheep, it's now really a goat?

C: Um hmm.

E: OK. Do you think a scientist could change a sheep into a goat? He can do that?

C: Um hmm.

E: OK. (Keil, 1989, p. 206)

From this and similar replication studies, Keil concluded that children are not necessarily bound by perceptually salient characteristics in judging the feasibility of transformations. It is clear that children resist changes at ontological boundaries. Thus, young children, but not older ones, may be quite willing to let a lion become a tiger or a mouse become a tarantula. They are unwilling to let a mouse become moss or attribute life to a toy bird. Intuitively, children have a sense that animals have special properties that distinguish them from other entities and relate to their way of biological functioning, as the protocol of a second grader exemplifies:

1. A toy bird into a real bird

   C: It's still a toy.

   E: Why?

   C: *Because you can't turn a machine into a real live thing.*

   E: So you think this is a toy bird?

   C: Well, it looks like a real bird.

   E: Yes, but you think that it is . . .

   C: A toy bird.

2. A fish into a rock

> *C:* Hmm ... I think ... well ... that it lays eggs, and it's just the outside that got crusty. So I think the inside, if they cut it open, they would see ... It would still be the insides of a fish.
>
> *E:* So you think that even though (repeats transformation), it's still a fish?
>
> *C:* Yeah. (Keil, 1989, p. 215, emphasis added)

Keil (1989) found that kindergarten children and even preschoolers will sometimes rely on surface appearances when judging the identity of individuals; thus, they are willing to tolerate changes across species boundaries. At the same time, children's biological intuitions prevent them from relying only on surface detail in all cases. They will not tolerate changes across ontological boundaries despite a correlation of features between the start and finish of a transformation. Also emerging early in development is evidence for a concept of "animalness" that goes beyond just the animacy and the observable behavior an individual displays.

If children have notions of "animalness" that are rooted in intuitive biological conceptions, rather than derived from the detection of correlated features, then they may not react to all kinds of transformations in the same way. Perhaps young subjects can be seduced into accepting some transformations as kind altering when they are biologically meaningful. The contention is that theory underlies the judgment process. If so, children should be able to differentiate biologically more plausible transformations from others that are less so. To examine this thesis, Keil (1989) manipulated the biological relevance of the transformation. The least biological transformation involved donning a costume, that is, dressing a zebra as a horse. A less superficial transformation involved repainting a horse with zebra stripes. Finally, a biologically relevant transformation involved intervening early in the animal's development to change its adult appearance. The horse/zebra transformation exemplifies a description of this type:

> *An animal doctor who was taking care of some baby horses accidentally gave a baby horse the wrong injection when it was born. So when the baby horse grew up, it had black stripes all over its body. It looked like this (a picture of a zebra). Do you think it's a horse or a zebra? (Keil, 1989, p. 222)*

Keil presented these stories to children and adults. The data are summarized in Figure 7-3. Young children rejected the biologically superficial transformation almost as often as older children and adults did. However, kindergarten subjects, and to a lesser extent second- and fourth-graders, were seduced into accepting the most biologically meaningful transformations. These latter changes imply a potential mechanism that might be responsible for the animal's surface characteristics. It is noteworthy, therefore, that children rejected transformations that operated only at the surface level (painted stripes and costumes) while accepting transformations that altered the surface as a consequence of a changed internal mechanism.

Keil concluded that children have beliefs about what sorts of mechanisms underlie animals' appearance and behavior, and children distinguish which mechanisms are related to membership in a biological kind and which are not. In short, young children, perhaps even preschoolers, do not look just at surface manifestations of kind, that is, appearances, when making biological judgments. Subjects seem to be reasoning causally, evaluating the surface changes within a biological context (see also, Gelman 1990a).

What is particularly relevant about this line of investigation is that the pattern of developmental results is not to be expected unless children's judgments—even those of young children—are theory driven. That subjects continue to alter their judgments as they mature,

FIGURE 7-3 *Extent to Which Subjects Resisted Transformations of Kind as a Function of the Biological Relevance of the Transformation.* Transformation * is the most biologically relevant, ** is the least biologically relevant. A 1 indicates acceptance of the transformation as kind altering, 2 indicates indecision, and 3 indicates a rejection.

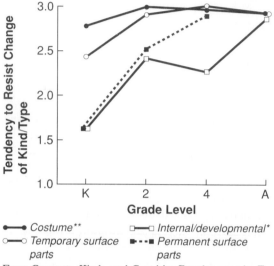

From Concepts, Kinds, and Cognitive Development by F. C. Keil, 1989, Cambridge MA: The MIT Press. Copyright 1989 by The MIT Press. Adapted by permission.

gradually accepting fewer and fewer and, finally, no transformations as kind altering, argues for a continued developmental elaboration of that theory. A perceptual to conceptual rule shift (as with Piaget) does not completely explain the experimental outcomes; children tend to use perceptual features only as a fall back rule when they lack other information on which to base their judgments. An intuitive psychology to intuitive biology shift (as with Carey) does not explain the data either, because behavioral features do not seem to have special or preeminent status for young children. Only a specifically biological theory explains these data effectively. Granted this theory is neither explicitly formed nor identical to an adult version. But, children do make reference to organisms' internal features and to

matters of lineage (i.e., what kinds of babies an organism will have) as particularly relevant facts for category decisions. Those are peculiarly biological facts.

A biological theory of some sort, a kind of **intuitive taxonomy** for structuring the biological realm, is evident in children's judgments of identity. The underlying rules responsible for the taxonomy, however, govern the operation of biological processes, such as growth, reproduction, digestion, and inheritance. Children may have intuitions about the mechanisms of operation allowable within a biological system. Thus, they may be biased to accept some mechanisms as more plausible than others (Keil, 1990; Springer & Keil, 1991), just as they are predisposed to accept certain identity transformations more readily than others. It is unlikely that such predispositions or biases will surface in children's spontaneous verbalizations; children do not know the facts of growth, reproduction, or inheritance, as Carey's work (1985) demonstrated. But experimental techniques that would allow them to differentiate plausible from implausible mechanisms might also reveal intuitive constraints on what sorts of facts they are willing to entertain.

Springer and Keil (1991) have pursued this line of inquiry. The specific causal mechanism they explored was color transmission from parent to offspring in plants and animals. To avoid the problem young children invariably face when asked to generate verbal explanations, the experimenters described possible mechanisms for color transmission to the subjects. Children were asked to choose among the options by sequentially eliminating the "silly" one, the "most wrong" one, until only their best choice remained. In this way, the biological plausibility of potential mechanisms could be manipulated.

Some of those manipulations included the presentation of nonbiological accounts. For example, there was a magical account ("The baby flower turned pink because a little man came along with a paintbrush, opened the seed carefully, and painted it pink") that might be plausible to a precausal preschooler who is predisposed to magical thinking (Piaget, 1930). There were also intentional accounts ("The baby flower turned blue because its mom wanted it to look like her when it came out") that might appeal to a child operating from an intuitive psychology. Across the several experiments, these and other accounts—animistic accounts, human agent accounts, and humuncular accounts—were pitted against the natural, biological accounts.

Children's judgments should have revealed any theoretical intuitions they had about the plausibility of biological mechanisms, and since the subjects were between ages 4 and 7, such findings should argue against conservative developmental explanations. In fact, children did prefer natural, biological accounts, rejecting the others including the psychological, magical, and animistic ones. Children's choices were not always correct by adult standards (they did not always select the genetic account), but preferred options were nonetheless descriptions of biological mechanisms. That children were also able to differentiate plausible mechanisms for what causes baby flowers to be pink and baby dogs to be brown from mechanisms that turn "baby" artifacts green further argues for the domain specificity of children's theoretical knowledge (see also Springer & Keil, 1989).

Although biological thinking changes during childhood, there is a continuity reaching back to the preschool years at least (Keil, 1992). In fact, biological matters may be uniquely construed from the start. For example, preschoolers seek different sorts of explanations for biological kinds, asking what an entity's properties are *for,* what they *do,* and what *purpose* they serve. There seems to be a presumption, perhaps a universal one, that the structure of an organism is a *design solution* to a challenge or problem posed by the environment. So, the owl's superb vision is *for* hunting at night, the scorpion's stinger is *for* protec-

tion, and the coyote's yap serves the *purpose* of announcing a kill. This **design stance** (Keil, 1992; Vera & Keil, 1991) and the search for biologically distinct functional explanations may work especially well with living things. And, when coupled with *essentialism* (an entity has an essence that defines its kind), this may be unique to the construal of biological phenomena.

Summary

The bulk of the contemporary empirical evidence supports a view of children as displaying an early competence for biological reasoning. Children are not precausal in any pervasive sense, not when it comes to causal reasoning about biological mechanisms. In judging biological identity, resisting impossible biological transformations, and rejecting implausible explanations for biological events, young children exhibit tacit understanding. It is important to keep in mind, however, that they are also frequently incorrect by adult standards. They will permit an individual to change species identity (e.g., tiger/lion, Keil, 1989). They confuse and overlap social and biological phenomena (for e.g., the parent-offspring relationship, Carey, 1985), and their preferred mechanisms for inheritance are not always genetic (Springer & Keil, 1991) or Darwinian (Keil, 1989; Springer & Keil, 1989). While children probably do have naive biological theories, their theories are, in many respects, wrong.

That a theory is incorrect does not make it any less a theory, but it does invite speculation as to what the initial, early theory is like. In Chapter 6, we saw that young children's early theories of mechanics and number are not mere simplified versions of the correct, adult variety. Early number theory seems best suited for representing integers but not rational numbers, and naive mechanics bears a resemblance to Medieval impetus theory. Children learn formal principles of mechanics and general arithmetic during the course of schooling.

Similarly, they are exposed to the principles of Mendel, the basics of DNA, and the legacy of Darwin. What might the course of the development of theoretical knowledge be like if that were not so?

As of yet, we can only speculate as to precisely what children's intuitive theories of biology are like. We know more about what they are not. In one intriguing observation, Springer and Keil (1991) noted that children tended to prefer mechanisms for inheritance that the authors described as **homeopathic,** that is, they believe that causal agents or substrates physically resemble their effects. Thus, children might reason that baby flowers are pink and baby dogs are brown because the mothers contributed pink or brown bits during the formation of their offspring. In a modern theory of genetics, genes are blueprints that are not materially identical to what is produced. But homeopathy is a historically earlier belief, predating Mendel's theory, that was widespread in folklore and mythology (Frazer, 1911; Mayr, 1982). Springer and Keil (1991) speculated that modern genetic theory may be overlaid on a homeopathic theory through the course of education. The rudiments of those homeopathic beliefs about inheritance are present in early childhood. Other evidence (Springer & Keil, 1989) suggests that young children may also be "naive Lamarkians," accepting the inheritance of acquired, biologically functional characteristics. Lamarkism, like homeopathy and impetus theory, is a historically older theoretical belief system, supplanted by its modern counterpart. The latter ones are formally taught in school, but their theoretical forerunners may precede them developmentally.

INTUITIVE THEORIES OF MIND

As adults, we know that our thoughts, ideas, intentions, wishes, fantasies, beliefs, desires, and the like are not the same sort of entities as physical things. Contents of the mind do not take up space; they do not have physical characteristics, except in a metaphorical sense. Rather, these private mental phenomena are distinct from the physical and material world of objects and things. The capacity to differentiate mental and physical entities is an ontological distinction emerging early in development, although not quite as early as the basic division between animate and inanimate objects (Keil, 1979). By age 7, children intuitively know that the statements (1) "The idea is heavy" and (2) "The thought is green" are silly since ideas and thoughts occur in the mind and cannot possess the physical properties of weight and color. Younger children, however, will sometimes permit a predicate appropriate for physical things ("is light," "is heavy") to span abstract things like ideas and thoughts (Keil, 1979).

Children's ontological intuitions are clues to their knowledge organization. Whether or not they separate mental and physical entities is important conceptually. The differentiation of the mental from the physical suggests that some "bundle" of information and facts about mental things exists within the child's knowledge organization. If the bundle is rule governed and coherent, even though implicit, then it follows that young children may have access to theoretical knowledge about mental things (Wellman, 1990). Common-sense theories of mental phenomena are *theories of mind* (Astington, Harris, & Olson, 1988; Premack & Woodruff, 1978), and an implicit theory of mind is a naive psychology (Heider, 1958). A theory of mind functions as an explanatory framework for behavior that is common in the folk psychology of adults (Forguson & Gopnik, 1988).

Possibly children have a naive theory of psychology as well as a naive theory of biology. Carey (1985) thought so. She proposed that a naive psychology preceded the emergence of a naive biology, although her version of the former suggests a theory of *behavior* rather than a mentalistic psychology. Others (Wellman, 1990) also saw evidence of this phenomenon relatively early in development and proposed that an intuitive theory of mind is indeed a documentable capacity of preschoolers. Piaget (1929) thought not. What children know about mental entities is of both conceptual and empirical interest. Recently, the question has spurred considerable research investigation and theoretical speculation (Gopnik, 1990; Leslie, 1987; Wellman, 1990).

Many cognitive and even social competencies presuppose some knowledge of the role of mental events in behavior. Predicting the actions of another individual is an example. People act with *intentions* based on their *desires,* their *goals,* and their *beliefs.* In fact, behavioral acts do not make much sense unless we consider the causes behind those acts, which most of us presume are internal, mental events or states. If a child's mother states she is hungry, and he subsequently predicts she will walk to the refrigerator and retrieve some item, then the child's prediction must be based on intuitive reasoning that his mother *desires* food and that she *intends* to satisfy her hunger with some item she *believes* to be in that location. Her behavior is most meaningful and predictable within a mentalistic context that provides the impetus for it.

As adults, we reason about and interpret our own and others' behavior in this fashion. Our language proliferates with terms that refer to mental entities (*plans, ideas, thought,* and *images,* for example) and to mental events (*remembering, dreaming, imagining,* and *reflecting*). Young children also make reference to mental phenomena, to psychological causation, and to intentions (Hood & Bloom, 1979). They begin employing terms to refer to mental state by about age 2 (Bretherton & Beeghly, 1982) and increase doing so in the following year (Johnson & Wellman, 1980; Wellman, 1985, 1988). They also become quite proficient at pretending (Leslie, 1982, 1988). So, children seem to know something of wishes, desires, and purposes, and they do talk about them. However, although children *appear* to explain their own and others' behavior through reference to mental terms, they may not be using those terms in the same manner as an adult would, nor does such usage definitively implicate an adult theory of mind.

Can children conceptually distinguish between an intention to do and the doing? A thought of a toy and a real toy itself? A negative wish and a negative deed? A bad dream and a traumatic experience? Can they truly distinguish the real and the material from the unreal and imaginistic? And, finally, can they reason about the mental and reflect on the function of cognition?

Ontological Adualism

Piaget (1929) would have supplied a very conservative answer to these questions: The child knows nothing about the nature of thought because of a fundamental inability to differentiate the realm of the mental from the realm of the physical. The cognitively mature are **dualists** for whom there is a clear distinction between mind and matter. Young children are not. Since they fail to make this distinction, they have no basis for separating a real thing from its mental image or even from its name. Thus, Piaget was willing to attribute a very strong sort of confusion to young children—a confusion of the real and the unreal. Wellman (1990) referred to this as **ontological adualism.**

A categorical blending of, what would be for the adult, ontologically separate entities produces profound effects. The first is a tendency to "physicalize" psychological phenomena (Flavell, 1963), a kind of **ontological realism** (Wellman, 1990). This is the belief that mental phenomena are real physical phenomena, for example, that dreams are external events or pictures that take place outside the self in the room and are observable by others. In this reality, thinking is equated with talking, a physically observable behavior; the mind is confused with the external head, a physically observable appendage (Broughton, 1978). Piaget called this physicalization of the mental **childhood realism.** It is a cognitive limitation that results in "a confusion between the sign and the thing signified, the thought and the thing thought of" (Piaget, 1929, p. 55). Childhood realism ignores an essential dualist distinction: There is a difference between an idea about an entity and the independently existing entity itself.

In this Piagetian reality, a child would be living in a very exotic universe. For instance, in the world of the adualist there is no difference between objective and subjective experience. Mental events are not special and private. If I think of something and that thought has physical properties and exists outside of me, then it is not private and subjective but objective, inspectible by others, and known by outside observers. Indeed, *subjective* is a nonsensicle term in an adualistic universe. A child so oriented might be convinced that others know what she is thinking, feeling, dreaming, and wishing, so there is not much need to explain the contents of her mind.

Similarly, the adualistic child should not be able to reflect on the content of her thoughts since she is unaware that she even has them. If one is unaware of one's own thoughts, then one ought to be unaware of the thoughts of others, too. And finally, it would seem quite impossible to differentiate between one's own thoughts and others' thoughts—to acknowledge different, simultaneous cognitions by different individuals about the same object—when one has yet to differentiate thought from the object of thought. Therefore, the ontological realist must by necessity be *egocentric* (Piaget, 1932).

Young children often do have difficulty adopting the perspective of another viewer either perceptually (Flavell, 1978) or cognitively (Shantz, 1983). This has been documented in the developmental literature. And, given cognitive egocentrism, the young child's *social* abilities, particularly the ability to reason

about social and psychological phenomena, should be limited, too. Children cannot be expected to contemplate the causal role of intentions and thoughts in motivating the social behavior of others if they cannot, first, comprehend intentions, and second, recognize alternative intentions. Differentiating between the mental and physical worlds is prerequisite to understanding intention, motivation, and the psychological causes of behavior (Miller & Aloise, 1989).

A second ramification of ontological adualism is a child's tendency to focus on appearances, termed **phenomenism** (Flavell, 1963). The perception of how things look and how they must really be are inseparable. Indeed, they must be. Distinguishing how things appear from how they truly are depends on analyzing the role perception plays in obtaining information about the outside world. Perception is a subjective, mental process. Without the realization that such processes exist, individuals can hardly consider what role they play. Things are as they appear. An **intellectual realism** (Flavell, 1985; Pillow & Flavell, 1985) leads the child to make errors where reality and appearance are confused, to be seduced by illusion (Flavell, Flavell, & Green, 1983), and to assume that what something looks like is the most salient aspect of what it really is (Flavell, 1977).

Third, Piaget claimed that the young child is an **epistemological realist** (Wellman, 1990). This has to do with the relationship between the thoughts an individual experiences and things out there in the real world. In this view, the young child assumes a direct connection between objects and thoughts of objects. The thought originates from the thing in the world, and it is the qualities of the object that cause the thought. Thus, for example, "a child frightened by the sight of fire, endows the fire with malicious designs" (Piaget, 1929, p. 35). Such a contention is logical if young children were to have a "copy theory" of knowledge where the mind is characterized as basically passive (Chandler & Boyes, 1982), a receiver of input rather than a constructor of representations. Interestingly enough, a passive mind copying reality is consistent with the assumptions behind empiricism (see Chapter 2), a philosophical position of which Piaget himself had a very dim view (Gruber & Voneche, 1977). Piaget attributed to young children a kind of epistemology for which he had considerable disdain.

The consequence of epistemological realism is a lack of awareness of one's own constructive mental activity which creates and originates the contents of mind. **Epistemological constructivism** (Wellman, 1990) is a more mature stance in which the constructive nature of cognition is recognized and the function of cognitive processes in achieving thoughts and ideas can be contemplated. The young child does not know the mind actively interprets, distorts, and enriches the perception of an object (Pillow, 1988) and the cognitive representation of reality. Perhaps, for Piaget, cognitive development entailed a paradigm shift from empiricism to constructivism.

Still a fourth consequence of ontological adualism is a concept we encountered in the context of naive biology in children: *animism*. This is the sort of thinking that again confuses the physical and psychological by attributing what might seem to be psychological attributes to physical phenomena. So, the young child envisions physical events, such as a river flowing or the sun rising, as signifying "on-purpose" behavior. It was Piaget's (1930) claim that young children attributed intentionlike causal processes to physical events.

The notion of an event occurring "on purpose," however, is not the same as mature psychological reasoning; it should not be confused with explaining behavior through reference to internal, mental states. Rather, it reflects **animistic causation** (Wellman, 1990), a result of the same confusion between mind and matter. There is, therefore, a general con-

fusion about the whole concept of intentionality. Intentions are overextended in some cases (i.e., to physical events), underextended in others (i.e., explaining behavior), and ignored in still others (i.e., evaluating moral acts and social behavior). When the psychological and physical worlds are not sharply differentiated, physical reality is permeated with intentions and thought is permeated with physical characteristics.

In sum, the world of young children is quite exceptional from an adult perspective and is most definitely alien and strange. As Woolley and Wellman (1990) depicted the Piagetian perspective, "the classic description of young children is that they do not differentiate reality from appearance, reality from mentality or reality from fiction until they are 7 or 8 years of age" (p. 946). Under such circumstances, it is hard to envision how adults and children could ever communicate about events, entities, wishes, experiences, or a host of other phenomena.

Evidence from the Literature

The world is not always as it seems. The sun looks to us like it revolves around the earth, not vice versa; people lie and dissimulate; paper flowers, toy animals, and movie characters may seem quite real. . . . Finding realities amidst their many guises is one of our most important cognitive tasks. This is also an everyday task facing young children, who must learn to eat real not plastic food, be cautious of real not toy animals, and distinguish events on television shows from events in the real world. (Woolley & Wellman, 1990, p. 946)

Do young children have access to a rudimentary, common-sense theory of mind that enables them to distinguish the objective and subjective, the real and the imaginary? To answer this question, we look to what contemporary investigation reveals about children's thinking about mental events, the relation of mental events to nonmental events, and the role mental events play in psychological explanation. The research reviewed in this section is diverse. The studies are not particularly similar, but generally they all yield data counter to the Piagetian conservative contention that young children—being ontological adualists and epistemological realists—are confused about appearance and reality. They are confused about the physical and the mental, unaware of the mind's role in representing reality, and, thus, oblivious to intentions, perspectives, motivations, desires, beliefs, illusions, and the subjective in general. But does the empirical literature substantiate these contentions?

Evidence is equivocal as to whether childhood animism and egocentrism are pervasive characteristics of immature thinking. Animistic causation does not seem to be typical of young children's causal reasoning (Shultz, 1982). And, as we saw in Chapter 3, egocentrism is not always a characteristic either. Even very young children, for example, can anticipate that another person will experience a different perspective from theirs if that other occupies a different viewing circumstance (Flavell, Everett, Croft, & Flavell, 1981; Lempers, Flavell, & Flavell, 1977; Masangkay, McCluskey, Sims-Knight, Vaugh, & Flavell, 1974; Salatas & Flavell, 1987).

The identification of alternative views of the same scene is evidence of a rudimentary awareness of the process of perception in determining how things look (also see Liben, 1978). Granted, young children are often incorrect in their anticipations. They sometimes make what might even be construed as egocentric errors, and the circumstances under which they appear competent are limited (Rosser, Lane, & Chandler, in press). However, that there are any circumstances under which their sensitivity to the role of perception can be elicited is counterindicative of any pervasive inability to appreciate alternative, subjective experiences. In some studies, such sensitivity is detectable in children as young as 2½ and, in many others, by age 3 (Borke, 1975;

Rosser, 1983; Rosser, Ensing, Mazzeo, & Horan, 1986). Young children sometimes can even behave nonegocentrically when asked to predict the emotional and cognitive states of another individual (Borke, 1971; Shantz, 1975).

So, it appears that very young children do display some awareness of nonanimistic causation and nonegocentric perspective. Rarely, however, can they explain the appropriate causal mechanism for a physical event (see Chapter 6), nor can they compute precisely how another individual does experience a scene or event (see Chapter 3). Limitations in computational and explanatory ability are not convincing evidence for a profound confusion of the mental and the physical, however, nor does such evidence strongly argue for a failure to differentiate between the objective and the subjective. True, young children are not as proficient as their older counterparts at figuring out and reflecting upon the perceptions and cognitions of others or at figuring out how things work. On the other hand, even the young are not oblivious to the fact things *do work* and that others *do have* perceptions and cognitions.

The appearance-reality distinction. Another issue is whether or not children are confused about appearance and reality. To overcome such a confusion, a child would have to realize that things can look different from how they really are which, again, presumes an appreciation of the role of perception and its fallibility in informing us about reality. Flavell has done a number of studies examining this issue (Flavell, 1986; Flavell, Flavell, & Green, 1987; Flavell, Green & Flavell, 1986b), as have others (for e.g., Woolley & Wellman, 1990).

Basically, in many of these investigations, subjects are confronted with objects that present an illusion in which looks and reality conflict. An example is an imitation rock resembling a piece of granite but made out of a soft spongelike material. The object *looks like* a rock and it should be hard and resistant to a squeeze, but *it is* a nonresistant, squishy sponge. Children are asked to answer two questions about objects of this sort, questions about looks and questions about reality: "When you look at this with your eyes right now, does it *look* like a sponge or does it look like a rock? . . . What is this *really and truly?* Is this really and truly a rock or really and truly a sponge?"

Three-year-olds have trouble with this kind of distinction. Either they answer with the appearances answer to both questions or the reality answer to both. Apparently, they cannot acknowledge that the object can *look* one way and *be* another. The interpretation is that young children are not aware of the role of subjectivity and their own mental representations when inspecting the object. They do not understand that the object can have two states of representation simultaneously, a subjective state and an objective state. This type of research study shows us that while 3-year-olds have difficulty with this particular distinction, the ability to handle illusion improves significantly between the ages of 3 and 5 (Flavell, 1986), although still remaining fragile into middle childhood.

The illusion distinction, however, is a special case of the more general class of appearance-reality distinctions. And although illusion seems to deceive the young, we should be cautious in overgeneralizing the finding to other sorts of distinctions. Pretense, for example, is a kind of unreality, and yet children engage in pretend play very early, even in infancy (Fein, 1981; Piaget, 1962). They do not confuse reality and pretense; they clearly know when they are pretending.

For example, a 2½-year-old boy staged elaborate dinner parties, complete with make-believe plates, food, and stuffed-animal guests. Although he did tend to opt for this form of entertainment when dinner was a bit late and he truly was hungry, he knew pretend steak did not satisfy like the real thing. Pretend is a case

of acting "as if" when the actor is clearly aware of the true situation, and it emerges toward the end of the infancy period (McCune-Nicholich, 1981; McCune-Nicholich & Fenson, 1984).

Leslie (1987) proposed that developmentally early pretense might reveal a capacity for **metarepresentation.** In order to pretend temporarily that one object is another, for example to pretend that a block is a piece of pie, the pretender must have two simultaneous mental representations of the same object and conceptually distinguish between them. One representation is the real, the objective. The other is the imaginary, the subjective, the "as if" state. The two representations are of a different quality. The objective one is real, permanent, stable, and more "true," while the subjective is unreal, temporary, transitory, and less "true." There is a single entity (the block) and two symbols for it—"toy" and "pie"—which, when the child is playing, coexist. But the child will not become confused; he will not attempt to ingest the block. When the game is over, the real, objective symbol will remain, and the imaginary, subjective one will have passed on, perhaps to be attached to some other entity in the future.

Even very young children engage in fantasy play, and they do not become confused. Such activity is an early manifestation of the ability to understand mental states, to understand in some fashion the role of representation, and thus, by implication, to appreciate the difference between what things *are* and what we can whimsically and arbitrarily signify them to be.

Indeed, there may be many types of reality-nonreality contrasts, or reality-appearance distinctions. There are contrasts between real and pretend, real and imagined, real and counterfeit, real and imitation, and so forth. We do not know how children react to all of these distinctions. Flavell's analysis addressed only one distinction, Leslie's another.

Woolley and Wellman (1990) presented evidence for roughly three levels of distinctions. The first level contrasts reality with nonreality in the broadest sense, that is, the natural with the artificial, the original with a copy, a real perceptual experience with a dream. *Real* then refers to a variety of genuine, complete, truthful qualities of objects and event.

The second level contrasts a narrower distinction between reality and appearance. There is a difference between a toy fire engine and a real one, between a child dressed as a pirate and a real pirate, between a pencil and a picture of a pencil. In the second case, the real and the not real share an important physical resemblance, but even though they look somewhat alike, they are not identical objects.

The third level involves the genuinely deceptive where "trueness" is quite difficult to determine without very close inspection. The paper flower and the sponge rock, for example, may look real and might even trick an adult. It is this narrow distinction level that encompasses illusion, where an entity is truly deceptive and its actual state cannot easily be detected. With three possible levels to consider—reality versus nonreality, reality versus appearance broadly construed, and reality versus appearance narrowly construed—the cognitive ability to distinguish the real and the not real might not emerge all at once in development.

To address this question, the investigators first examined whether young children actually produced the word *real* in their spontaneous language, since use of a word is, possibly, a comment on the state of nature. They found that young children did use the term, some at age 2 and most by age 3. Usually, the context of use was to mark the genuine aspects of objects. Second, in a series of experiments, the investigators presented sets of contrasts derived from the hypothesized levels. The contrasts were constructed with the real and the pretend, the real and the toy, the real and the picture, and finally the real and the illusion. Young children were quite good at distin-

guishing all of the contrasts except the illusion versus real one. Sometimes, they even commented explicitly on the reality and the appearance of the items.

The authors concluded that by age 3, children are not phenomenists. They can correctly conclude that a thing is not always what it appears. So, children are not *uniformly* seduced by perceptual appearance, although, as Flavell had noted, they continue to be deceived by illusion and confused by the truly tricky. Woolley and Wellman's (1990) data are supported by prior results from other work (Wellman & Estes, 1986) in which children distinguished between entities and mental representations of those entities (e.g., a real dog and a thought-about a dog). Virtually all of this research argues *for* some rudimentary understanding of mental phenomena early in development, and it argues *against* a fundamental and pervasive ontological adualism. In short, young children reveal an understanding of multiple, simultaneous perceptions when they behave nonegocentrically; multiple, simultaneous representations when they pretend; and multiple, simultaneous states of being when they resist seduction by the counterfeit, the look-alike, and the illusory.

There is a difference, however, between appreciating that the *mind has* contents separate and distinct from the entities outside of itself and understanding, in a fuller sense, just what the *mind does*. Wellman (1990), for example, differentiated between knowing about mental *contents* and knowing about mental *processes*. Young children know that something unique goes on in the head; first attempts at mental reference begin to appear in children's speech by age 2½ (Shatz, Wellman, & Silber, 1983).

But children know much less about what those unique mental activities are like, and they do not know how to differentiate among them, for example, to separate attending from comprehending from remembering from inferring (Fabricius, Schwanenflugel, Kyllonen,

Barclay, & Denton 1989). Therefore, although children display some evidence of knowledge of mental representation by about age 3, there is counterevidence, too. They do not exhibit a sophisticated understanding of the representational nature of mind and the constructive processes involved in cognitive activity even by age 10. An awareness of what psychological processes—perception, attention, memory, and inference—can do to information might have a long developmental history (Flavell, Green, & Flavell, 1986).

Desires, beliefs, and false beliefs. One of the hallmarks of a folk psychology is the ability to interpret human action, to engage in causal reasoning about intentional behavior. Interpretation and reasoning make reference to mental states, particularly an actor's beliefs—knowledge, convictions, suppositions, ideas, and opinions—and an actor's desires—wants, wishes, goals, hopes, and aspirations (Wellman & Bartsch, 1988). As adults, we take for granted that desire for an object motivates action, and beliefs about that object direct the action. So, when we *want* some ice cream and *believe* the ice cream to be in the freezer, we go to the freezer.

Both beliefs and desires are **propositional attitudes** because they are about something: There is a mental state, an object to which the mental state pertains, and a relationship between the two. Beliefs are particularly interesting, however, because they are *mental* states about *world* states and are, thus, reality directed (Wellman, 1990). The mental (thoughts), the physical (actual states of affairs), and the processes that inform the mental about the physical (perception) form a triad. The outward manifestation of the triad is intentional action toward objects. In order to reason mentally about an action, we must understand both the role of the belief-representation and the role of reality in informing the representation.

Beliefs are particularly noteworthy constructs for those who debate the legitimacy of a naive psychology and a theory of mind (Churchland, 1981, 1984; Clark, 1987; Gopnik, 1990; Stich, 1983), partly because of this special hybrid quality, a synthesis of the mental and the nonmental. That attribute makes beliefs particularly well suited for providing mental explanations for actions in the world. In a intuitive theory of mind, beliefs constitute mental causes for behaviors (Wellman, 1990). But, beliefs can be wrong; the processes that inform beliefs are fallible. And inferences about the beliefs of others can also be wrong. Reasoning about beliefs, therefore, could be construed as a tricky task potentially quite challenging for the unsophisticated.

False beliefs are a particularly knotty problem. False beliefs perform the same function as true beliefs in motivating action, but the former have been misinformed. If the car keys are on the kitchen counter, but the individual searches in his jacket, then we infer the searcher is acting on the basis of a false belief. If we discover that the individual believes the keys to be in his jacket, and we know they are on the counter, we will still correctly predict that the searcher will look in the jacket. Our correct prediction originates in a reflection on the status and function of the mental representations that demands beliefs about beliefs (Fodor, 1985).

True belief and false belief are two simultaneous, conflicting representations of the same reality. In order to reason about them, we must comprehend the cognitive processes that formed each and recognize that both perform the same function in directing behavior. This insight requires consideration of what the mind is *doing* when it receives information from outside, interprets the information to represent the outside, and directs behavior in accord with the representation. Investigators have questioned whether children have sufficient understanding of the mind's activities to do this. So, for many, the ability to reason about false belief has become the "litmus" test—proof of access to a theory of mind (Chandler, Fritz, & Hala, 1989; Wellman, 1985).

In the prototypic paradigm for studying false belief, a subject is told a brief story. One of the characters in the story is provided with incorrect information about the location of an object. The subject, of course, is privy to the correct information. The subject must predict where the misinformed character will search for the object, and, of course, to be correct the subject must ignore her own belief and judge on the basis of the false belief. Following is the story of Maxi and the chocolate, which exemplifies the nature and complexity of the narrative (from Wimmer & Perner, 1983).

[Boy doll present, representing Maxi waiting for his mother]

Mother returns from her shopping trip. She bought chocolate for a cake. Maxi may help her put away the things. He asks her: "Where should I put the chocolate?" "In the blue cupboard," says the mother.

"Wait, I'll lift you up there, because you are too small."

Mother lifts him up. Maxi puts the chocolate into the blue cupboard. [A toy chocolate is put into the blue matchbox.] Maxi remembers exactly where he put the chocolate so that he could come back and get some later. He loves chocolate. Then he leaves for the playground. [The boy doll is removed.] Mother starts to prepare the cake and takes the chocolate out of the blue cupboard. She grates a bit into the dough and then she does not put it back into the blue but into the green cupboard. [Toy chocolate is thereby transferred from the blue to the green matchbox.] Now she realizes that she forgot to buy eggs. So she goes to her neighbor for some eggs. There

comes Maxi back from the playground, hungry, and he wants to get some chocolate. [Boy doll reappears.] He still remembers where he had put the chocolate.

["BELIEF" question] "Where will Maxi look for the chocolate?"

Children younger than 4 years of age predict that Maxi will look into the green cupboard (Wimmer & Perner, 1983; see also Perner, Leekham, & Wimmer, 1987). Apparently, they are unable to separate what they know from what Maxi believes to be true. There are two simultaneous representations about reality, one of which is counterfactual, and young children seem unable to separate them. This deficit in reasoning about false belief is interpreted as a more general limitation in understanding intention, on which grasp of a folk psychology hinges.

Others (Wellman & Bartsch, 1988, 1989; Wellman & Woolley, in press) have argued that a failure on the false-belief task should not be overinterpreted as a general indictment of young children's limitations in belief-desire reasoning (but see Perner, 1989). The false-belief paradigm is a special case that requires recursive reasoning about conflicting beliefs. Wellman and Bartsch (1988) pointed out that 3-year-olds do construe human action in terms of belief, where belief is the internal mental state functioning to cause behavior—just as it is for adults. In many contexts, when causal explanations of behavior are required, young children make reference to belief.

For example, Sam wants to find his puppy, and the puppy might be under the porch or in the garage, but Sam thinks the puppy is under the porch. Three-year-olds correctly predict where Sam will look. In a series of scenarios of this nature, where the actor's belief was manipulated and subjects were asked to predict the actor's behavior in accord with the belief state, Wellman and Bartsch found young children to be generally successful.

So, why do children fail the false-belief stories when they can be quite successful in predicting belief-based action in other contexts? Wellman and Bartsch argued that youngsters have problems predicting Maxi's search behavior because *belief* is pitted against *desire;* Maxi wants the chocolate very much. Desire is a more salient action motivator for young children than belief. When desire is pitted against belief, 3-year-olds opt for desire reasoning. This explanation was extended in research by Wellman and Woolley (in press). The investigators demonstrated that even 2-year-olds can predict actions and reactions related to simple desire reasoning; they cannot simultaneously succeed on belief-reasoning tasks accessible to 3-year-olds.

Wellman (1990) concluded that a simple desire psychology is a legitimate form of naive psychology. Desire psychology constitutes an understanding of human behavior, because the role of mental states in directing action is still important, just as it is in a belief psychology. In his view, however, the desire psychology is a developmentally earlier accomplishment, a precursor to belief psychology. Children can reason about desires by age 2 and about beliefs by age 3. However, the desire-belief conflict problem, in which desire and belief are pitted against each other and desire is particularly salient, elicits the earlier, more primitive form of behavioral reasoning.

Chandler, Fritz, and Hala (1989) interpreted young chilren's failure on the prototypic false-belief task somewhat differently. These investigators argued that Maxi-type stories are complex narratives in which children must keep track of the actual location of the chocolate *and* of Maxi's movements. There is, in addition, an elaborate narrative structure to the story. This may simply prove too much for young children, whether or not they understand the role of belief in action. These procedurally excessive task demands could possibly lead to an underappreciation of children's initial theories of mind.

A similar question was raised about Piagetian-inspired empathy research with children more than a decade ago (Borke, 1978; Rosser, 1981). In empathy research, children were asked to reason about how story characters felt and thought, but the narratives were complex and the emotions projected into them conflicted among the characters and with those of the subject (see, for e.g., Urberg & Docherty, 1976), much like the conflicting beliefs in the Maxi-style stories. Young children did not fare well in this assessment context; they did much better when task demands were reduced (Borke, 1971, 1978).

One way to examine false-belief-style reasoning in a procedurally less demanding assessment context is to look at the incidence of *deception* in children's behavior (Anderson, 1986; Mitchell & Thompson, 1986), a technique that has worked well for studying epistemic states in nonhuman primates (Premack & Woodruff, 1978). Deliberate deception is an interesting behavioral choice. First, it allows the inspection of overt behavior, what a child does, as an alternative to examining just the child's verbal reasoning in response to verbal stimuli. (Again, when investigators looked at empathetic *behavior* rather than empathic reasoning [Yarrow, Scott, & Waxler, 1973], young children looked like empathizers.) Young children often experience difficulty with verbal reasoning tasks, particularly those about "as-if" situations presented in narrative form. Second, deception is directly relevant to intentional reasoning. Deception occurs when an individual deliberately distorts or fabricates information in ways *intended* to mislead others. To deceive, an individual must recognize that reality informs belief and that alternative beliefs about reality are possible given the manipulation of information. Thus, false belief can be attained. Intentions, beliefs, and false beliefs are the criterial features of a theory of mind.

Within the context of a hide-and-seek game, Chandler, Fritz, and Hala (1989) observed children's spontaneous use of deceptive strategies that could serve to delude a compatriot into searching for an object in a wrong location. The deceptive behaviors (for e.g., moving a cover from its initial location to suggest something had been hidden under it) would not occur unless the subject (1) recognized the role of perceptual information in establishing belief, (2) knew that the compatriot would rely on the information, (3) inferred that false belief could be created by manipulating that information, and (4) concluded that they could effect an action predicated on the false belief—an unsuccessful search. The investigators claimed that children as young as 2½ are quite capable of employing deceptive strategies.

Summary

The emerging picture of children's mentalistic abilities is not nearly as conservative as the one Piaget drew. Children do show some understanding of mental states very early in development. They distinguish the realm of the mental and the realm of the physical, and they do not appear to physicalize the mental either. By age 2½, toddlers make reference to mental events in their linguistic forms. They understand desire and the role desire plays in motivating behavior; they may be capable of deceit, and they can definitely partake in pretense.

Very early in infancy, children distinguish people from objects, suggesting that the domain of human behavior is unique for them, a necessary foundation for a folk psychology (Gopnik, 1990). By age 3, they begin to distinguish appearance from reality, and they are not universally seduced by the former. At the same time, these preschoolers display reasoning about belief and intention and the differentiation of their own perceptions and cognitions from those of other people. Thus, it is very unlikely that children can be properly characterized as ontological adualists or realists.

Most contemporary analysts reject the conservative Piagetian view, but argue whether some knowledge about mental life is equivalent to holding a *theory* of mind. That is not as clear. A consensus on criteria for what constitutes a naive theory is itself debatable (see Wellman, 1990; Springer, 1990). Those investigators who hold to a set of stringent criteria, referred to by Chandler et al. (1989) as "scoffers" (Flavell, Green & Flavell, 1986; Gopnik & Astington, 1988; Perner, Leekam & Wimmer, 1987; Wimmer & Perner, 1983), are not persuaded by empirical evidence for an early onset of mentalism. They doubt that the data demonstrate the level of representation and metarepresentation—the ability to reason about those representations—that would clearly signify theoretical knowledge of mind.

"Boosters" (Chandler et al. 1989), on the other hand, are convinced by the early-onset literature. Wellman (1990) has summarized interpretational differences among investigators examining theory-of-mind data. These differences in perspective on the implications of the empirical literature are depicted in Figure 7-4. It is clear from Wellman's summary that almost everyone agrees that knowledge of mind emerges between the ages of 3 to 5. Most also agree that 5-year-olds, like adults, believe our knowledge of reality is mediated by mental representations (Gopnik, 1990). In further understanding that these representations can vary among individuals, children reveal an appreciation of the constructive function of cognition in forming those representations. Although elaboration and refinement of this ability continues throughout childhood, the roots of the rudimentary, to be elaborated structure are accessible very early.

A final point at issue, however, is where this rudimentary structure comes from. What are its origins? Is knowledge of mind innate? Is it derived from exposure to the culture? Or is it constructed during the course of development? (See Clark, 1987; Gopnik, 1990.) These are questions that cannot be answered

FIGURE 7-4 *Differences Among Investigators as to When a Theory of Mind Develops.*

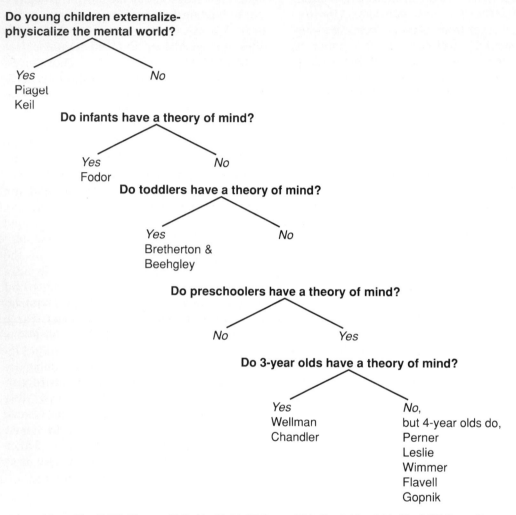

Do young children externalize-physicalize the mental world?

Yes
Piaget
Keil

No

Do infants have a theory of mind?

Yes
Fodor

No

Do toddlers have a theory of mind?

Yes
Bretherton &
Beehgley

No

Do preschoolers have a theory of mind?

No

Yes

Do 3-year olds have a theory of mind?

Yes
Wellman
Chandler

No,
but 4-year olds do,
Perner
Leslie
Wimmer
Flavell
Gopnik

Adapted from *The Child's Theory of Mind* by H. M. Wellman, 1990, Cambridge, MA: The MIT Press. Copyright 1990 by The MIT Press. Adapted by permission.

just by examining the empirical literature. We have pushed back the observable age of onset about as far as possible, given our current methodologies. No infant competence is detectable with those techniques, since even the most cognitively unelaborated of them still depend on a verbal-assessment context. So, we must reason by logic and implication.

The innateness hypothesis—human beings have an inherent understanding of mind specified a priori (Fodor, 1980)—is not particularly popular among developmentalists (see Gopnik, 1990; Wellman, 1990). Essentially, the argument for an innate origin is this: It is *compulsory* to reason about human beings in terms of intentions and beliefs, and doing so has survival value for the species (Clark, 1987). Just as evolutionary pressures act to insure an innate appreciation of the physical environment—otherwise an individual could not exist in it—so, too, do those same pressures insure a sensitivity to the social environment. The logic is appealing. Related empirical evidence, like that associated with infants' very early sensitivities to human faces (see Chapter 2) and their similarly early differentiation of humans from other objects, is consistent with the interpretation. The possible universality of a naive psychology, the tenacity with which people adhere to it, and the uniformity of subsequent developmental milestones all point to reasoning about intentions as a *bedrock* form of reasoning (Clark, 1987), a fundamental capacity of the human cognitive system.

Others argue differently. They make the point that the uniformity in the display of knowledge about intentions and beliefs could be explained in other ways. First, what exists in the world constrains how we can reason about it and restricts the degrees of freedom we have in our cognitive speculations. Second, there is a relationship between what one believes and what exists in the world (the hybrid nature of beliefs noted earlier). Unless we choose to ignore that relationship, experience should affect representation of that world and, thus, belief (Gopnik, 1990). The theory of mind available to the individual will change as experience is expanded and the outcome of experience is logically incorporated into the knowledge structures. In short, knowledge of mind is acquired; the logical structure of the knowledge may necessitate that it be acquired in a nonvariable, fixed order.

Many developmentalists argue that a theory of mind must be constructed. They debate the exact age of onset but not its constructive nature. Wellman (1990), for example, con-

tended that reasoning about mental states is present in the simple desire psychology of the 2-year-old, but early mentalistic knowledge is not representational. A representational theory of mind is characteristic of the 3-year-old, who has evolved a belief psychology out of the earlier form.

In summary, therefore, Piaget is judged to have truly underestimated children's capacity to reason about intentional systems, to differentiate intentional systems from physical ones, and to reflect on mental phenomena. Young children do not appear to inhabit a foreign universe after all. Instead they share a view of the world that has much in common with that of their older counterparts.

CONCLUSION

The literature reviewed in this chapter shows us that children have a conceptual knowledge of biology and psychology. The knowledge enables them to interpret the myriad and diverse events encountered in the course of growing up. Children can reason about biological mechanisms and psychological events by consulting those conceptual structures, and they can do so quite early in development. Investigators may argue as to precisely *when* certain reasoning competencies are reliably detectable, but there is less argument *that* such structures guide children's thinking.

Another conclusion that enjoys a high degree of consensus is that this conceptual knowledge is organized into *local* systems. It is *domain-specific* knowledge. So, the knowledge principles and rules that guide reasoning in one domain are not simple permutations of rules generalized from another. There is no *single* set of primitive principles that governs all reasoning and to which specific local principles can be reduced. Distinct biological, psychological, and physical conceptual structures are characterized by unique rule systems. The conceptual structures are uniquely constrained as well. Children expect biological systems to operate in a definite manner unlike other systems; they also expect intentional systems to follow their own restrictions. And given domain specificity, children do not confuse the two types of systems. They should not apply psychological principles when explaining biological phenomena or vice versa. That is what domain specificity implies, and it contrasts clearly with the domain-general explanations.

At issue, however, is whether those conceptual structures are most properly conceived of as theories or some other kind of representational entity (Springer, 1990). Obviously, naive theories, particularly when actualized in children, differ in important ways from the formal theories in the sciences. The former are not rationalized accounts; they are not explicit, and they may not possess the same level of internal consistency we demand of the latter. Keil (1992) pointed out that those uncomfortable with the *theory* term for these implicit-knowledge packages can substitute **explanatory belief system** without much damage to the interpretation. While the issue of the theoretical adequacy of naive systems is yet to be resolved, anything less (e.g., associative nets) does an inadequate job of explaining the coherence of exhibited knowledge in both children and adults (Murphy & Medin, 1985; Springer, 1990). Thus, the "theory theory" is garnering support.

A final speculative note concerns the explanatory adequacy of naive theories as compared with formal ones. We might question whether the indigenous biologies and psychologies, with their homeopathic underpinnings and dependence on constructs such as intention, adequately explain ordinary experience. Biologists abandoned similar notions long ago, and modern cognitive psychologists are materialists. It might seem a paradox to posit naive theories that do not work (particularly if we contend that such theories are innate and universal). Contemporary scientific theories do work better than the indigenous variety in explaining and predicting a broader range of phenomena, but the fallible, naive versions might work well enough for everyday events, for dealing with ordinary life. The next question concerns what happens to those scientifically less adequate systems when formal tutelage provides a new way to view the world? The evolution to formal theory might involve a paradigm shift; Carey seems to think so. But, then again, a formal frosting could simply come to overlay an indigenous, homeopathic biology and a naive, nonmaterialist psychology.

CHAPTER 8

THE DEVELOPMENT OF REASONING AND PROBLEM SOLVING

INTRODUCTION

Following is a conversation between a 6-year-old boy and an adult:

Adult: Do you know about dinosaurs?

Child: Oh yes, lots. I know about Tyrannosaurus Rex, Brontosaurus, Three-horn . . .

Adult: Were they big?

Child: Real big . . . bigger than this room!

Adult: They must have had to eat a lot if they were so big?

Child: Yes! Tyrannosaurus Rex was always killing everything . . .

Adult: What about the others, the plant eaters?

Child: They ate all the time . . . all day long . . . all they did was eat.

Adult: Did they have time to play?

Child: No, just eat.

Adult: You know, as the food started to disappear, do you think it took them more time or less time to find enough to eat?

Child: More time.

Adult: How do you know?

Child: . . . I'm *thinking* . . . you know . . . a nasternoid hit 'em!

Thinking is the everyday word we use for intentional mental activity. Several cognitive processes are referred to with that general term, and among them are reasoning and problem solving. These are cognitive operations that let us gain insight into the world around us, draw reasonable inferences about the complex phenomenon that confront us, and achieve our ends and goals despite the barriers that impede us. It is this ability to engage in reasoning and problem solving that permits intellectual adaptation to the environment, which is our primary mechanism of survival. In fact, these abilities were of such major importance to Piaget that for him the end product of cognitive development is the mature problem solver who, having constructed an internally consistent, abstract system of logic, can bring powerful, broadly applicable, *domain-general* cognitive equipment to bear on any particular challenge the universe dishes up and even some that it has not.

There is intentionality and deliberateness to this kind of mental activity. Deliberateness is a characteristic that contrasts thinking and reasoning with other sorts of mental activity. A ramification of this characteristic is that intentional cognition may be open to reflective examination. If so, we can study the nature of explicit thinking with procedures not applicable to nonintentional mental life. We could, for example, ask individuals directly about their logic and awareness of their own thought processes. Self-reflection provides another glimpse into the mind—a glimpse that could potentially reveal a very different picture of mental life. Piaget thought such glimpses were particularly informative, so much so that his favored methodology, the *clinical method,* was designed as a technique for eliciting self-reflective information about cognitive activity. He asked children about their own thought processes, and he asked them to explain how they solved cognitive problems. You cannot do that with implicit cognitive processes, intuitive cognitions, or with reflexlike reasoning.

Piaget was not the only one who placed great importance on this aspect of human cognition. The same interest has fueled the psychometric tradition in psychology; it has motivated those who want to measure and quantify individual differences in intelligence (Sternberg, 1985; Gardner, 1983). And interest in the domain-general aspects of cognitive ability motivates many investigators operating from an information-processing perspective—those who would model the modal workings of the mind (Anderson, 1983, 1990). What these approaches have in common is the conviction that much of what is important in human cognition depends on deliberate higher order cognitive processes (Greeno, 1989). Deliberate thinking reflects the activities of some type of **general problem solver** (Newell & Simon, 1972), a powerful device whose routines and programs are applicable in any context to serve the individual's intellectual goals.

So, what is this apparatus like? How does it develop? Those are the inquiries addressed in this chapter. First, the conceptual orientations behind this body of research will be described, along with implications for development. Then, experimental studies of reasoning and intentional thinking, as well as explanations of those data, will be reviewed. And, finally, those data will be placed in theoretical context. How do these data mesh with the developmental story emerging over the previous chapters?

A UNITARY MIND

A domain-general view of mind and cognition is quite different from what has been presented in the last few chapters. First, all variations on a "general problem solver" theme posit a *unitary* mental system (Anderson, 1990). Therefore, much of what looks like different aspects of cognition are presumably a reflection of the operation of the same mental apparatus. Contrast such a view with the *domain-specific* view emphasized in Chapters 5, 6, and 7. Domain specificity is the hypothesis that there are particular aspects of knowledge (space, number, ontology, biology, mind, and language) governed by unique principles that are not reducible to each other or directly transferable across domains. Reasoning and problem solving *within* a domain (see examples in Chapter 6) and restricted to that domain contrast with reasoning and problem solving of a more generic form. The latter is envisioned as *content independent,* with cognitive processes equally applicable *across* domains.

Second, most domain-general views acknowledge the possible existence of some unique mental faculties, but the focus is placed on the higher level cognitive functions. Those functions are explained by only *one* set of principles. By implication, these principles are central to cognition, and an understanding of them is essential to the explanation of cognition. The domain-specific view is associated with just the opposite position: There are some domain-general aspects of cognition, but a lot of important activity that goes on in the mind is modular.

Conceptions of a Central Chamber

An architectural metaphor highlights points of contrast between these two alternative perspectives on the nature of mental activity. Imagine a central chamber off of which exit several independent hallways. The hallways, each with a door that closes it off from the central chamber, run between the outside world and the central chamber itself, deep in the mind. It is in this structure that cognitive work must get done. The hallways are the conduits of information from outside to inside; the chamber serves to organize the incoming information and direct output to the problem solver in whom the structure is housed.

There are at least two ways in which the information-organization activities could get done. In one, much of the mental work is accomplished in the individual hallways; each of them is highly specialized to handle a particular type of raw data and to transform those data into a form palatable to the general-purpose central chamber. Metaphorically, these hallways are large elaborate structures, since so much work must be done in them. In contrast, the central chamber need only be a small room with sufficient space for finishing up the details of cognitive work. In the alternative floor plan, the hallways play a minimal role in compressing and translating data. The central chamber plays the maximal role. The hallways do not have to be particularly specialized for information input because the majority of the work is done in the central chamber. In this structure, the hallways are small, while the central chamber is a large, multipurpose space.

Applying the metaphor to thinking, what goes on in the central chamber is intentional, deliberate cognition. It is explicit, and the individual can reflect on and direct the mental activity that takes place there. What goes on in the hallways is implicit, reflexive, and obligatory. And because the doors are closed between the hallways and the chamber, reflection on "hallway processes" may be impossible. We are, for example, not consciously aware of the automatic processes involved in seeing or hearing. We are more likely to report conscious awareness of the deliberate mental state experienced when solving a math problem, plotting a sequence of chess moves, or designing an experiment.

Depending on which variation of the architectural analogy one prefers, there are different theoretical implications. The "big hallway" variation enables a view of cognition as made up of information-input systems (Fodor, 1983) that shape the basic nature of thought. An examination of domain-specific mental activities and their development is the experimental path to follow (see Chapters 5, 6, 7, and 9). The theories that will emerge along the way are most apt to explain the acquisition and display of particular kinds of knowledge, their degree of independence from other types of knowledge, and their role in intellectual adaptation. The "big chamber" variation suggests a different route. The goal is to come up with the very best general computational architecture for depicting the operation of that essential chamber. A quote from Anderson (1983) sums it up:

> The unitary position is not incompatible with the fact that there are distinct systems for vision, audition, walking, and so on. My claim is only that higher-level cognition involves a unitary system. Of course, the exact boundaries of higher-level cognition are a little uncertain, but its contents are not trivial; language, mathematics, reasoning, memory, and problem solving should certainly be included. . . . I claim that a single set of principles underlies all of cognition and that there are no principled differences or separation of faculties. It is in this sense that the theory is unitary. (p. 5)

In a "unitary-mind" conceptualization of thought, the exact nature of the information coming into the central chamber matters less than what manipulations and elaborations of that information will be done once it gets there. The procedures applied to information in the service of thinking should be relatively independent of the *content* of that information. Thinking rules are, in short, relatively content free and very general. What is important is the nature of these thinking rules; to what they are applied is less so.

Investigators adopting this perspective are most apt to describe these cognitive activities in terms of *strategies, heuristics, algorithms,* or *logical structures,* all of which are abstract solution devices or programs applicable across a wide variety of situations. Indeed, if this were not the case, if cognitive activities were bound instead by content and the specifics of a problem, then the unitary-mind approach would gain little over the modularity alternative. Strategies, algorithms, and structures *must* be general in order to qualify as optimally useful and powerful intellectual tools.

Since these higher order cognitive functions are envisioned as goal oriented, deliberate, and relatively slow (as contrasted with obligatory, automatic, and relatively fast), the individual employing them must have some degree of self-awareness of their use. Awareness permits reporting of mental activity. Hence, performance data sometimes take the form of verbal protocols as well as measures of the outcomes of problem solving.

In a verbal protocol, the individual describes the details of the solution process. We get a peek into what the central chamber looks like, a "section view" in architectural terms. Although self-report is not a totally reliable source of information and it requires buttressing from other sources, verbal protocols offer insight into the reasoning process (Newell & Simon, 1972). Then, the viability of that hypothesized reasoning process, constructed from the protocols, can be tested in a variety of ways.

One way, logical modeling, was favored by Piaget. Computer modeling (see e.g., Kintsch & Greeno, 1985) is another. Computer modeling entails writing a program that describes all the steps the problem solver must go through to achieve a solution. If the program runs, then the description must bc adcquate. If the output closely resembles that produced by a human problem solver, then the description is cognitively feasible as well. In short, the performance of an actual person engaging in rational thought is *simulated.*

Some varieties of problems are good contexts in which to study this aspect of cognition. Logical reasoning (Johnson-Laird, 1983), problems from intelligence tests (Pellegrino & Glaser, 1982), arithmetic problem solving (Cummins, Kintsch, Reusser, & Weimer, 1988; Kintsch & Greeno, 1985; Riley, Greeno, & Heller, 1983), scientific reasoning (Chi, Feltovich, & Glaser, 1981), and generating solutions to puzzles (Anzai & Simon, 1979) are examples of appropriate task contexts. The premises of the problem are specified; their form can be manipulated, and the correct solution is known. So, investigators can watch how the premises are used in the service of problem solution.

An example of this kind of approach is represented by studies with the Tower of Hanoi problem (see Anderson, 1990; Simon, 1975). A simplified version of the problem is depicted in Figure 8-1. In it there are three pegs and three disks with holes so that they can be stacked on the pegs; the disks differ in size. The disks start out all stacked on the first pole and must end up all stacked on the third pole in the same configuration. The disks are movable, but there are constraints on the process: (1) Only one disk at a time can be moved, and (2) a bigger disk cannot be stacked on top of a smaller disk. The investigator determines the sequence of moves necessary to achieve the

FIGURE 8-1 *Schematic Depiction of a Three-Disk Version of the Tower of Hanoi Problem.*

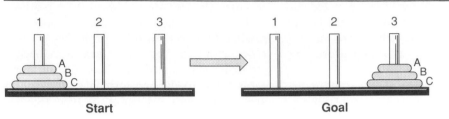

Start   Goal

From *Cognitive Psychology and Its Implications* by J. R. Anderson. Copyright © 1990 by W. II. Freeman and Company. Reprinted with permission.

problem goal in the minimum number of moves. The criterion is then a base of comparison for an individual in an empirical study, or a program routine in a computer simulation.

When abstract, problem-solving algorithms are intentionally called upon to aid reasoning and problem solving, it is the *form* of the cognitive activity that is usually primary. No one really cares about an ability to solve the Tower of Hanoi problem in particular; rather, they care about the nature of the ability that enables someone to generally solve any problem like it. The desire is to identify how the problem is mentally represented, what rules are used in solving the problem, the order and sequence in which the rules are applied, and how problem-relevant information affects the representation and the rule application. Then, the hope is to test if that cognitive analysis would hold when applied in a different but similar situation. When generality of a cognitive routine is emphasized, form takes precedent over content because it is precisely content that must be generalized across.

Developmental Implications of the Central-Chamber Metaphor

The unitary, domain-general conception of cognition has several developmental implications. First, there should be correspondence across different kinds of cognitive activities. If several separate activities are wholly or partially dependent on processing that takes place in the central chamber, then those activities must be related in some way. Relatedness shows up as a *correlation* between what might otherwise appear to be different activities. The correlation is a consequence of different activities sharing cognitive procedures. To the extent such dependence exists, both strengths and limitations in cognitive capacity will surface as overlapping adequacies (or inadequacies) in an individual's performance across tasks.

Children should demonstrate relative uniformity in performance across different kinds of problems. For, if children have acquired a particular technique that facilitates reasoning for them, we expect to see positive evidence of the application of the technique across situations similar in demand characteristics. If those children have yet to acquire a central technique, then task failure should be equally pervasive.

For example, if a child has acquired the strategy of "counting on" as a mechanism for determining the sum of combined sets (e.g., How many is 3 + 1?), then the child may draw on that strategy when faced with a variety of distinct addition problems (Siegler & Shrager, 1984). Moreover, she may be more likely to draw on the strategy for solving addition problems when she cannot easily depend on an alternative strategy: direct recall of the correct sum. Prior associative learning would facilitate recall, but when faced with less familiar problems, the child with access to the counting-on strategy has a backup procedure (Siegler, 1988).

If the strategy were to reflect some more general principle of cognitive functioning, then several things should follow:

1. The child should access the strategy under a predictable set of circumstances; in this case, access would be particularly apt under increasingly difficult task demands.
2. Use of the strategy should be a reliable and stable marker of an individual's performance style, differentiating those who have acquired the procedure from those who have not.
3. Use of the strategy should generalize across different but related tasks.

Robert Siegler and associates (Siegler, 1986b, 1988, 1989; Siegler & Shrader, 1984) identified just such a strategy. They observed individual differences in its use and its application across different but related tasks. An example of the latter is the use of the parallel, "counting down" procedure for solving subtraction problems. The investigators tested the feasibility of their contentions with computer modeling.

Stronger evidence for correspondence occurs when a *similar* backup strategy (e.g., sounding out an unknown word) is used by the same individuals who are faced with tasks drawn from a *different* domain (i.e., word identification). The task demand characteristics are similar when the problem is sufficiently difficult to preclude retrieval of an answer acquired through direct associative learning (i.e., knowing the word by sight). From repetitive prior learning, virtually every 5-year-old can recall the sum of 2 + 2, and most 5-year-old boys will recognize what N-i-n-j-a T-u-r-t-l-e spells; there is no need for any backup strat-

egy. The children are less likely to directly access the sum of 7 + 3 without counting on or to correctly identify the word e-l-e-p-h-a-n-t without sounding it out. It is reasonable to predict that, on difficult problems of both types, children who have access to backup strategies will indeed use them. The outcome turns out to be performance consistency across problems dissimilar in type (Siegler, 1988).

Across-task correlations.   The unitary model of mind leads to the following claim: Seemingly different intellectual performances will show an association to the extent those performances depend on the general cognitive apparatus. A developmental ramification of that contention is that if the status of the general apparatus changes with maturation, then the efficiency of cognitive functioning will be age related, too. Performances of all kinds, dependent on what the general apparatus does, should all be affected by the developmental status of the central chamber.

For example, some have proposed that the absolute quantity of processing resources increases with age (Hale, 1990), and so the efficiency with which children can engage in problem solving is also age related. Older children should yield faster reaction times (a marker for efficiency of processing) on tasks tapping intellectual processes than younger ones (Kail, 1986, 1988). Moreover, changes in efficiency should occur across tasks, because the limitation is a consequence of general available resources, not domain-specific ones. Hale (1990) presented evidence that changes in processing efficiency yield a linear function when assessed across age; she demonstrated the claim with children between 10 and 19 and with four different kinds of tasks. In short, children become *faster* at thinking and reasoning as they get older.

A strong interpretation of the "older is generally faster" contention predicts similar growth curves for different cognitive abilities related by dependence on central processing. Recall from Chapter 1 that a representation of a growth curve is achieved by indexing cognitive achievement on the Y axis, developmental time on the X axis, and plotting the course of change in achievement as a function of time. Similar growth curves share common characteristics such as intercept, slope, and shape, the linear function being the most straightforward.

The rationale behind predictions of growth-curve similarity is founded on notions about how central mechanisms figure in thinking. If the proficiency of central processing develops, then at some time prior to optimal operation, central processing will be a limiting factor on cognitive operations. If successful performance on related tasks depends on a central mechanism, and if that mechanism is functioning below peak values, then performance on those tasks should be limited in the same way (see Kail, 1987).

Recall however, that growth curves are generally ambiguous and subject to multiple interpretations. Growth data by themselves seldom produce definitive solutions to problems about the nature of cognitive development. Alternative explanations that are less dependent on uniform central-processing limitations can also sometimes account for similarities in slopes and intercepts across curves (Stigler, Nusbaum, & Chalip, 1988). The point, nonetheless, is that convergence in cog-nitive abilities—both in level of competence at a given point in time and in the nature of a change in competence over time—are consistent with virtually all unitary-mind approaches to the development of cognition.

Acquisition of rules. One way to approach problem solving and reasoning is to think about a problem as a representation of a relationship among variables. So, for example, the area of a rectangle is a relationship between the height variable and the width variable. Determining the area—solving the problem—depends on constructing a formula for computation from those variables. Thus, problem solution comes from knowing how variables function in a problem. The problem solver needs access to a *rule* and a *strategy,* a computational strategy, to achieve a successful performance (Siegler & Jenkins, 1989).

Robert Siegler (1978, 1981, 1983, 1984) developed the **rule-assessment procedure** as a methodology for analyzing what rules children access and use to solve a variety of problems and how those rules change in character with development. Often beginning with tasks adapted from the Piagetian literature, for example, the balance scale problem illustrated in Figure 8-2, Siegler employed a technique called **task analysis** to determine all the ways a child might solve a given problem.

In the balance-scale exemplar, the problem is to predict what will happen (balance versus

FIGURE 8-2 *The Balance Scale Used in Siegler's Research.*
Weights were placed on the pegs; the number and distance from the fulcrum varied. Children had to predict whether the scale would balance or tip as a function of weight placement.

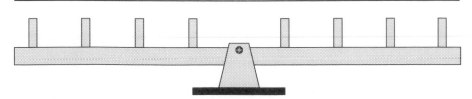

go down) as different configurations of weights are placed on the scale pegs. The relevant variables are the amount of weight (*W*) on the pegs and the distance (*D*) of the weights from the fulcrum. The correct solution that will always work is to calculate torques (i.e., combining weight and distance according to a mathematical formula). Incomplete rules, taking into account only the amount of weight or only distance, will not yield the same level of correctness across differing values of *W* and *D*.

Siegler compared models of performance, based on ideal patterns of rule use, with children's actual performances. He found that younger children (5-year-olds) used a "weight-only" rule; in fact, not until ages 13 and 17 did children consistently use the formal rule relating *W* and *D*. He attributed the failure of the young children to *encode* the relevant variables (Siegler, 1984).

The rule-assessment methodology, along with similar approaches, has been applied to a variety of cognitive problems (see Klahr & Robinson, 1981; Siegler, 1978, 1981, 1983). What is typical of these techniques is an analysis of problems in terms of *problem representations* and *solution strategies*. Solution rules identify the *components* of processing—attending, encoding, transforming, computing, and so forth—in a domain-general way. Developmental change is conceptualized as differential, age-related efficacy with which these components can be brought to bear (see also, Klahr, 1984; Sternberg, 1984).

In order for a reasoning or problem-solving strategy to be applicable across tasks, it must be generalizable. To be generalizable it must not be bound to the context in which it was initially acquired or first applied. Achieving generality requires extracting the rule from the context in which it was acquired and translating it into a more widely applicable form. The greater the applicability of a rule or algorithm, the more abstract it needs to be. As an example, compare an addition statement expressed concretely—3 + 2 = 5—and the algebraic statement expressed abstractly—*a* + *b* = *c*. The latter represents the sums of all integer combinations rather than being limited to only one. The operation of the central chamber is going to increase in efficiency as the rules, algorithms, and strategies available there become more abstract.

Children, however, acquire strategies for solving problems in particular situations, and the rules are often quite concrete. Gradually, the rules transfer across contexts as the child learns to use them more broadly, but transfer may be constrained by time, experience, and opportunity.

An example can be drawn from studies of children's ability to solve conservation problems (Brainerd, 1978a). Conservation problems come in many forms—conservation of number, of mass, of weight, and so forth. During middle childhood, youngsters come to solve most forms of the problem successfully. The different types of problems are not all solved at the same time, an asynchrony referred to as **horizontal decalage** (Piaget, 1952b).

Presumably, children eventually solve all forms of the conservation problem after acquiring a general rule about the invariance of quantity, a rule that will apply equally well to all conservation problems. However, when children are first mastering the concept, they come up with less generalizable rules; for example, they could solve a conservation of number problem by counting. A counting strategy, however, will not help them solve a conservation of mass, weight, or volume problem. Counting is content specific because it only works for number. Formation of the more powerful, general rule occurs developmentally later than the formation of the restricted rule.

The technique of approaching problem solving and reasoning as the acquisition and extension of rules and strategies places the emphasis of analysis on general cognitive activities taking place in the central chamber. More generally applicable rules and strategies are associated with increases in age; efficacy of execution is also correlated with increases in age. So, as children get older, they should get better and faster, regardless of the domain from which a problem is drawn.

Predictions about developmental onset. Deliberate, conscious, broadly applicable thinking routines, especially those on which the individual can reflect, are not likely to surface early in development. There are three reasons for that. First, such an accomplishment requires appreciating what the mind does, and while the initial seeds of a concept of mind are displayed by preschoolers, an understanding of mental operations, of mental actions, does not emerge until later (see Chapter 7). Second, deliberate use of mental operations presumes not only awareness but explicit control of those operations. Again, this is an unlikely achievement for young children. Indeed, young children, for whatever reason, can rarely explain their problem solutions even for successful performances, as the anecdote at the beginning of the chapter exemplifies. Third, the ability to apply a strategy or rule across contexts must somehow be related to experiences in application, and the amount of experience possible is developmentally constrained.

In short, intentional reasoning on which the individual can reflect is not something for which we expect evidence of early competence. Competence is more likely to arise relatively late in development, emerging initially in limited task situations and subsequently generalizing across multiple-task situations. The first prediction, therefore, is for a *discontinuity* between the problem-solving capacities of the mature and the immature. And, predicated on a unitary model of mind, a second prediction is for *correspondence* among intellectual performances similarly rule governed. So, we expect younger children's competence to be restricted and tied to the concrete in a uniform manner across tasks, while older children, armed with powerful, abstract algorithms, rules, and strategies, will experience equally broad successes.

DEVELOPMENT OF DEDUCTIVE REASONING

Reasoning is a deliberate process of thought that allows the derivation of new information from old. A distinguishing feature of reasoning is that it is based on systematic principles that establish specific relations between premises, the old information, and conclusions, the new. Depending on the nature of the premises, the conclusion that follows is either necessary, probable, or possible. We know this formal set of principles relating premises to conclusions as **logic**.

Logic is a subdiscipline of philosophy that specifies what it means for an argument to be correct. The purpose of logical principles is to guarantee the validity of the arguments that follow the rules. Thus, logic is a kind of symbolic formalism, not unlike mathematics, for relating evidence and arguments in a rule-governed way. Adherence to this formalism as a strategy for deriving solutions to problems encountered—either real or hypothetical—is examined in the study of human reasoning. Much of the research on reasoning has been designed to compare human performance with the prescriptions of logic (Anderson, 1990). Logic, then, provides a *form* for problem solving and a *theory* of thinking.

Following is an example of logical reasoning: If a person accepts the truth of the premise, "All dogs are black," then he knows that any dog he encounters must also be black. The conclusion follows from the premise by *necessity;* if the premise is true, then the conclusion *has* to be true. On the other hand, if the person has encountered mostly black dogs, again he might conclude that the next dog he meets will also be black, but that conclusion is only *probably* true. It does not necessarily follow since the next dog could just *possibly* be brown; there is no premise that precludes "brownness" in the next encounter.

These conclusions are *inferences* about the nature of future information from known or past information, but they are different kinds of inferences. Inferences, or arguments, can be classified as *inductive* or *deductive* depending on whether the construction of the argument calls for a conclusion that is merely probable or one that is necessary and certain. The first example, therefore, describes a deductive inference, and the second, an inductive one. For an argument to be inductively valid, the conclusion must be probable if the premises are true; for deductive validity, the conclusion is necessarily true if the premises are true.

However, the necessary truth of the deductive inference does not depend on its plausibility in the real world, only on the nature of the premise. If the premise had been, "All dogs are green," the conclusion that the next dog would be green is still logically valid even though it is empirically implausible. In deductive reasoning, the conclusion *must* be true if the premise is true.

The only secure form of inference, then, is deduction (Johnson-Laird, 1990) because it is strictly logical and does not require *empirical* validation with real-world data. The logical principles alone guarantee validity. Indeed, if the conclusion does not follow logically from the premises, then the deduction is fallacious even though it may be highly plausible and may lead to a conclusion that is correct in the world. For instance, if a child infers, given (1) all dogs are black, that (2) the next dog he encounters may be black, brown, or white, he has drawn a fallacious conclusion even though, in the real world, he may be correct. It is the form of the argument, not what the argument is about, that functions as the criterion for determining the validity of those arguments.

The rules of reasoning and inference are of interest to psychologists because the ability to think in a rule-governed manner is an intriguing human competence entailing thought independent of context. The study of this thought could reveal something about the "syntax" of reasoning, and that syntax just might qualify as the abstract formalism central to a unitary model of mind. The study of deductive reasoning in particular should serve this purpose, since the ability to reason deductively entails a grasp of the concept of necessity attributed to conclusions on the basis of the argument form alone (Black & Overton, 1990).

One route to explaining reasoning in people is to describe a **mental logic** containing the rules that direct the inferential process. The assumption is that the problem solver has access to a formal system, and the system underlies the deductive capacity of the reasoner. The theoretician's job is to model the system and describe how the system influences real people in problem-solving situations. The second assumption is that, somehow, in the course of development, children must gain access to this system of mental logic. If we accept the contentions that (1) a mental logic is at the root of problem solving, and (2) the efficacy of mental logic is age related, then we must explain the ontogenesis.

The Piagetian Explanation

According to Black and Overton (1990), Piaget's theory is recognized as the standard contemporary treatment of the development of deductive reasoning. This makes sense given what we know about Piaget. Recall from earlier chapters that form and flexibility of thought and the individual's ability to generalize cognitive routines across contexts, content, and situations are what most interested Piaget. He saw cognitive structures as highly abstract, symbolic formalisms—the antithesis of situation-bound reasoning strategies. For Piaget, development entailed the sequential evolution of thought from very situation-bound forms, sensorimotor thought, to the most symbolic forms, those of formal operations. His models of deductive competence are the **class logic** of the concrete period (see Chapter 4) and the **propositional logic** of the formal period.

At each stage of development, the child's thinking becomes increasingly symbolic. The achievement of object permanence, the first major developmental hallmark, is the initial evidence for symbolic representation. In the preoperational period, we see expanding representational activity in the form of language acquisition and *iconic* thought (i.e., the ability to symbolize in mental pictures). With the attainment of operational thought, representation becomes truly coordinated and systematic (Inhelder & Piaget, 1958). It is then that thinking can be formally modeled.

Piaget (1957) uses the concept of **mental operations**—actions that have become internalized, reversible, and coordinated into an integrated whole—to capture the nature of logical thought. Mental operations permit the transformation and organization of data about the real world so that they can be used sensibly in the service of problem solving (Gray, 1990; Parson, 1958).

There are two levels of operational thought, however. They are differentiated on the basis of how closely mental life is constrained by physical reality. Concrete-operational thought is tied to the concrete, the real, the physical "facts" of experience. It is quite possible to reason logically about those "facts," as evidenced by the considerable success youngsters in middle childhood display with classification, seriation, and enumeration problems. Presented with a problem about the workings of the physical world, children at the concrete level of development appear logical and reasonable, and their behavior is most definitely rule governed (see Chapters 4 and 6 for examples). In fact, concrete operations are mature, adultlike intellectual adaptations to what is empirically real (Gray, 1990).

The limitation of concrete-operational thought is just that, a tight connection to the empirically real. The same level of intellectual prowess does not extend to either the hypothetical or to premises contrary to empirical fact, the nonreal. The concrete operational child cannot deduce whether the next dog she meets will be green, given that all dogs are green, because she rejects the premise on empirical grounds, that is, dogs are not really green. She cannot reason about the logical validity of the form of the argument independent of the empirical validity of the premise's content. The form of the argument is its *syntax;* what the argument refers to is its *semantic* content, or its meaningful connection to the real world. For a child denying the existence of green dogs, semantics take precedence over syntax.

So, while both concrete and formal operational stage individuals can reason and problem solve, only those in the latter group have evolved a truly formal, abstract system of mental operations applicable to any and all conceivable content (Inhelder & DeCaprona, 1990). The more abstract representation, if *p,* then *q,* replaces the concrete representation, if all things are black, then this thing is black, when the formal level is achieved. A point of contrast between concrete and formal thinking is the difference between reasoning about what is possible in *all* possible worlds and reasoning about what is possible in the actual world—only one of those possible. Formal thought begins to become available around 10 to 12 years of age (Piaget, 1986, 1987a, 1987b). Similarly, formal deductive reasoning seems to emerge at about the same time (Byrnes & Overton, 1988; Overton, Ward, Noveck, Black, & O'Brien, 1987).

Essentially, Piaget argued that development involves a succession of increasingly powerful logical systems (Fodor, 1980). *Powerful* is a synonym for generality of application, and this logical system is applicable to any problem, no matter how abstract. For example, school-age children can reason about numerosity quite effectively with the rules of arithmetic since numbers quantify real things. It is only in adolescence, however, that the more abstract algebraic system becomes manageable. A comparison of the logical structures available at each Piagetian stage of development is depicted in Figure 8-3. Logical problem solving and reasoning are carried out by individuals of both concrete and formal operational status, but only the latter have access to the abstract variety (Overton, 1990).

In sum, Piaget's developmental system describes a sequential mental metamorphosis in which increasingly efficient cognitive systems incorporate and replace their less efficient forerunners. The concrete-operational system is less efficient than its formal counterpart because it is fact bound. As we gain experience in the real world, facts about that world accumulate. At some point, the sheer number of facts adding to the pile become overwhelming. It is then that a fact-bound reasoning system must prove nonefficacious, and it is then that an abstract formulation would simplify things and increase cognitive efficiency by accounting for "lumps" of facts with fewer principles.

For example, recall the rule that $2 + 3 = 5$, therefore, $5 - 2 = 3$. A rule of that sort is applicable to all two-term addition problems for

FIGURE 8-3 *Relationship between Piaget's Stages of Development and the Forms of Logical Reasoning Available to the Problem Solver.*

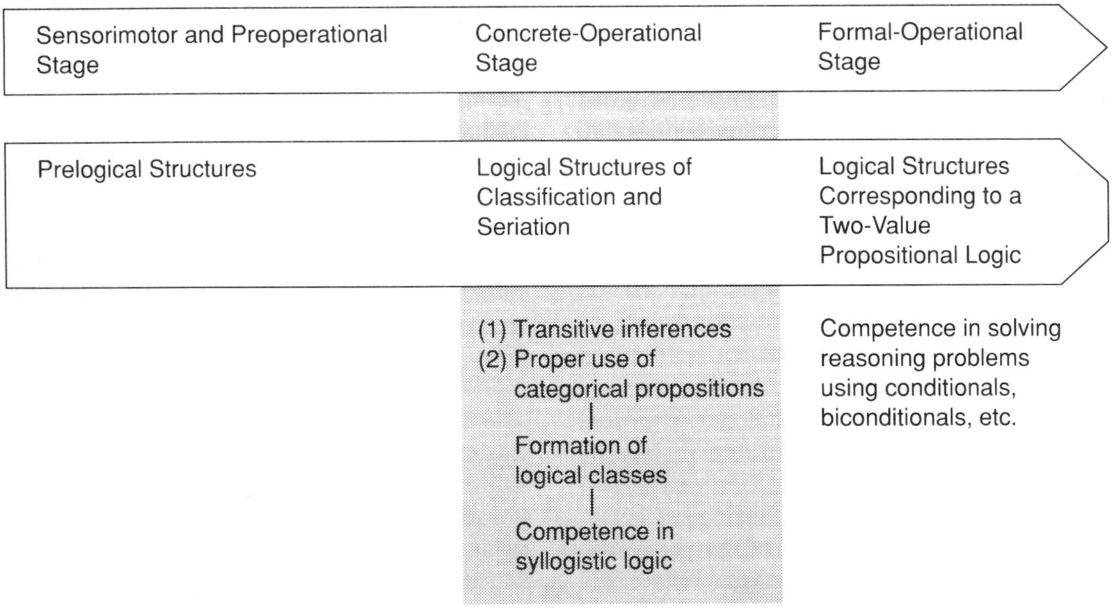

Sensorimotor and Preoperational Stage	Concrete-Operational Stage	Formal-Operational Stage
Prelogical Structures	Logical Structures of Classification and Seriation	Logical Structures Corresponding to a Two-Value Propositional Logic
	(1) Transitive inferences (2) Proper use of categorical propositions | Formation of logical classes | Competence in syllogistic logic	Competence in solving reasoning problems using conditionals, biconditionals, etc.

From "Reasoning, Logic, and Thought Disorders: Deductive Reasoning and Developmental Psychopathology" by J. S. Black and W. F. Overton, in *Reasoning, Necessity, and Logic* by W. F. Overton (Ed.), 1990, Hillsdale, NJ: Erlbaum. Copyright 1990 by Lawrence J. Erlbaum, Inc. Reprinted by permission.

integers. In a nonefficient, fact-bound system of arithmetic reasoning, there would need to be a separate rule statement of that type for every single combination, every arithmetic fact. On the other hand, in an abstract algebraic system, a single expression, such as $a + b = c; c - b = a$, will suffice for all combinations. In this way, the second system is more efficient than the first in accounting for "lumps" of addition facts.

For a second example, recall your own introduction to probability (which you may have encountered when you took statistics). You learned initially to compute the expected probabilities of two-outcome events (e.g., coin tosses) by listing all the possible combination of outcomes and their relative frequencies across n trials. That's the empirical method and it works pretty well when n is small. But as n increases, the empirical strategy becomes increasingly cumbersome and even approaches "undoability." That is when the more efficient expression $(p + q)^n$ is preferable; the abstract expression for the expansion of the binomial greatly simplifies the computation of combinations and probabilities.

When individuals attain a formal level of mental operations, their mental logic is fully abstract, efficient, and disembedded from specific content. As a consequence, they are able to conceive of possibilities, to engage in hypothetical-deductive thought and combinatorial and proportional reasoning, and to speculate about propositions that are contrary to fact (Gray, 1990). They can do so by consulting the **propositional calculus** that Piaget proposed as a design for the evolved, mature, cognitive structure (Overton, 1990).

Revisions, Extensions, and Alternatives

Many evaluations of Piagetian theory focus on whether real people perform the way the theory predicts, questioning whether the theory is *psychologically valid*. In evaluating the shift from preoperational to concrete-operational thinking, for example, critics contend that young children are not as incompetent as expected. Early competence is often interpreted as counterindicative of theoretical validity. In evaluating the shift from concrete to formal operational thought, however, another question is added to the argument: Do older subjects evidence the *extent* of competence the theory predicts? Do those in the appropriate age range actually perform in as competent a manner as expected? For the theory to have validity at this developmental level, most adolescents and adults should reason according to formal principles. Ironically, a lack of competence, as well as the detection of early competence, is taken as counterindicative evidence.

Studies of deductive reasoning, which is dependent on formal thinking, are a case in point. Controversy exists as to whether adults, those clearly past the age of predicted onset of formal operations, do in fact demonstrate the capacity to reason successfully on complex deductive reasoning tasks. Some evidence supports the existence of these abilities in adults (Bady, 1979; Bucci, 1978; Byrnes & Overton, 1986; 1988; Clement & Falmagne, 1986; Moshman, 1979; Moshman & Franks, 1986; O'Brien & Overton, 1980, 1982), but other findings tend to dispute the claim (Johnson-Laird, 1990; Wason & Johnson-Laird, 1972).

The more troublesome of the deductive logic problems is not conditional reasoning of the form "if p, then q; p exists therefore q exists"—what is called **modus ponens.** It is the **modus tollens** form "if p then q; not q therefore not p, which is the most troublesome (Anderson, 1990; Rips & Marcus, 1977; Taplin, 1971; Taplin & Staudenmayer, 1973; Staudenmayer, 1975). When problems are presented in the latter form, even educated adults can be induced to draw invalid conclusions.

The failure of many adults on the modus tollens argument was demonstrated in experiments by Wason (Wason & Johnson-Laird, 1972). In one of these experiments, subjects were presented with four cards such as:

E K 4 7

The task was to judge the validity of the following argument: If a card has a vowel on one side, then it has an even number on the other. Subjects were to turn over *only* those cards necessary to make the correctness judgment. Just 10% of the subjects choose the correct combination: $E(p)$ and $7(q)$.[1] Only those cards could lead to the discovery of potential counterexamples and disconfirmation (Evans, 1982; Johnson-Laird, Legrenzi, & Sonino-Legrenzi, 1972). The ability to evaluate a proposition by seeking falsifying counterexamples demands formal operational reasoning (Beth & Piaget, 1966). Nonetheless, the difficulty adults experience on this reasoning task has been replicated many times (see, for e.g., Cheng, Holyoak, Nisbett, & Oliver, 1986).

The observed shortcomings of adults to reason deductively is important for two major reasons. First, if failures are reliable and pervasive, then how could that be, given the reality of formal operational thought? Or, put another way, if formal operations (p), then deductive reasoning (q); not q. People who have not been formally exposed to principles of logic make logical mistakes. Indeed, even those exposed can experience difficulty (Cheng, Holyoak, Nisbett & Oliver, 1986). Second, the factors that tend to affect failure rates are often related to the specific situational, content-related, and pragmatic factors in the problem. These factors are part of the semantics, or meaning, of the problem vis-à-vis the real world, not the syntax of argument form. Adults, for example, perform much better when tasks are formally equivalent to the Wason card task, but with familiar content

(Cox & Griggs, 1982) and when the rule is pragmatically sensible (Cheng & Holyoak, 1985).

Johnson-Laird (1983; 1990) argued that people should not make mistakes, semantic and pragmatic content should not influence task solutions, if formal operations correctly describe the adult mental structure. Taken together, the fact that adults err and the fact that errors are often accounted for by problems of context (Cheng & Holyoak, 1985, 1989) calls into question the very existence of a content-independent, domain-general form of reasoning in anyone, child or adult.

Another type of inference problem involves **syllogistic reasoning**. Again, the individual must draw a valid conclusion from given assertions, but the assertions are statements containing quantifiers. For example:

1. All *a* are *b*
   All *b* are *c*

   .˙. all *a* are *c*

2. None of the *a* are *b*
   All of the *c* are *b*

   .˙. None of the *a* are *c*

3. Some of the *a* are *b*
   All of the *b* are *c*

   .˙. ?

Adults do not always draw valid conclusions from these pairs of premises, depending on the specific terms embedded in the premises and on whether they understand the statements (semantics again). On some problems (for e.g., #1) success rates are very high, but less so for others. Johnson-Laird contended that individuals build mental models of who's who as presented in the premises. For instance, given the statements

All the artists (*a*) are beekeepers (*b*)
All the beekeepers (*b*) are chemists (*c*)

The subject can construct a scenario where actors play roles, joint or otherwise. According to the first premise,

$a = b$
$a = b$
$a = b$

add the second

$b = c$
$b = c$

putting them together

$a = b = c$
$a = b = c$
$a = b = c$
$\quad\;\; b = c$
$\quad\;\; b = c$

and so it follows

$a = c$

However, the complexity of the mental modeling required can increase as the premises change, the quantifiers change, and as competing models/outcomes need to be represented. The claim is that, as the modeling increases in complexity, the probability of drawing valid conclusions decreases. The prediction fits the data for both adult and child subjects (see Johnson-Laird, 1983). Even adults will not always appear logical and reasonable; children as young as 9 will succeed with some of the less cumbersome syllogisms (Johnson-Laird). However, performance is not a function of age per se; it is a function of the semantics of the problem. And that is another aspect of context.

Context effects produce unevenness and inconsistency in performance, rather than intertask consistency and correlation. The situation is made more confusing, however, by the observation that even context effects are capricious (Griggs, 1983; Wason, 1983). So, the questions remain: (1) Is the tactic of employing any logical formalism as a theory of thought reasonable? (2) If so, is Piaget's version a viable formalism?

Competence over performance. One way to attempt answering these questions is to distinguish competence, what the human mind is capable of doing, from performance, what people tend to do in actual situations. Those two aspects of human cognition need not be the same nor need they be accounted for with the same set of explanatory principles. As adults, we all know the principles of addition and subtraction, but we still make accounting errors in our checkbooks. We all know how to form grammatically correct sentences, but we utter ungrammatical phrases in oral discourse. If we were to describe the state of what we know just from our arithmetic errors and our poorly formed conversational scraps, the picture might be quite unflattering.

Overton (1990) dichotomized theoretical efforts to account for reasoning into competence and procedure theories. The former describe idealized accounts representing operations of the mind. The resultant model abstraction, or structure, is supposed to be relatively enduring, universal, and applicable to a broad range of phenomena. It is what must underly and be responsible for successful logical reasoning when we do see it. Procedure or process theories describe and explain the problem representations and reasoning algorithms people actually utilize in real time with local problems. In short, competence theories model the syntax and procedure theories model the semantics of thinking. From one perspective, what has been called the rationalist perspective, it is the *potential* for employing abstract reasoning strategies—however imperfectly—that is the relevant aspect of logical thinking on which to focus (Evans, 1982). And that is competence.

Piagetian theory is a competence theory for hypothetico-deductive thought (Inhelder &

Piaget, 1958). Formal operational structures are idealized abstractions that describe the optimal performance of the fully adapted intellect. Like any other cognitive structure in a constructivist scheme, formal operational structures are acquired through the equilibration process (Piaget, 1986). In the course of adjusting to the press of environmental events, the individual creates a mental representation of the environment; the mental construction is the best adapted to and coordinated with the totality of what is experienced. Once created, however, the representation does not merely reduce to the sum of those experienced units; it is more because it must be both in synchrony with experience *and* be an internally consistent, balanced system. Self-regulatory processes (of a biological nature) insure that the structure that fulfills such a criterion will be universal for the species.

One reason the display of formal thinking may be more elusive than the concrete version is because of the intensity of the environmental press spurring cognitive metamorphosis. Gray (1990) pointed out that concretelike stages of development are forced upon every normal human being by the structure of the physical world and the circumstances of human existence. Without a representation of real space, for instance, an individual could not get around; without an understanding of causation in physical, biological, and social systems, people would never know what was going to happen next. Failure to navigate the physical environs and to anticipate real events would prove a threat to survival. Formal thinking, on the other hand, is not a necessary condition of survival (Neimark, 1975). We will not die from failing a conditional reasoning problem presented as *ps, qs, Es* and 7s. Thus, for many individuals, the full fruition of formal thinking need not ever be actualized. The failure to display such competence, however, does not result because the mind *cannot* function as proposed, but because it *does not*

have to at all times to serve the needs of the organism.

The facts remain: (1) People *do not* always and spontaneously employ formal logical rules to test the validity of implications, especially when the relationship between *p* and *q* is an arbitrary one (as in the Wason card task). (2) People *can* reason in accord with logical rules at least by adolescence, and probably earlier (Johnson-Laird, 1990), when premises and assertions are meaningful and familiar. Reasoning probably cannot be fully disassociated from the individual's knowledge of the topic reasoned about (Pieraut-Le Bonniec, 1990). That would help account for the simultaneous observation of failure and success as a function of context. However, the interpretation of the two seemingly paradoxical observations remains challenging.

That people make deductive errors and reason with varying efficiency as a function of content is not in itself sufficient grounds for rejecting the formal approach (Falmange, 1990). People also make grammatical errors in language, yet the utility of formalizing a grammar, a language syntax, is rarely disputed. So, it is not unreasonable to propose that people could, in fact, possess a syntax of logic but have difficulty gaining access to it. Performance failure occurs not because of an absence of competence but because of impediments to access. Those impediments, content-related **moderator variables,** could interpose between the reasoning task and the performance outcome and produce inconsistencies in performance across problems varying in content.

Consistency in reasoning performance across tasks varying in content is age related. Young adolescents and children are more apt to display task-specific success; consistency of success across tasks is more characteristic of older adolescents and adults (Overton, 1990; see also, Murray, 1990). These findings make sense if we initially accept the legitimacy of describing a formalism and then explaining variation in performance as a function of access to that formalism. Experience, learning, and the acquisition of world knowledge, all of which are also age related, would affect accessibility.

Logical statements are abstractions, but the statements people are faced with are real sentences. Each sentence has a particular form, a particular content, and it is uttered in a particular context (Scholnick, 1990). Many times, the sentence begins with an "if" clause: If *A,* then *B.* For example: (1) If it is raining, then Tommy plays inside; (2) If Dean cleans his room, then he can earn a dollar; (3) If Mommy is not in the house, then she is in the barn.

There is also the language of quantifiers— *all, some, none*—as in syllogistic problems. There is an obvious parallel between the *language* of the sentence and the *form* of the logic. Many have called attention to this parallel (Braine, 1990; Falmange, 1980, 1990). Perhaps language development and logical competence are interrelated such that the acquisition of the ability to comprehend certain forms (like "if" clauses) facilitates deductive reasoning. Children who understand the meaning of "if", ones considerably younger than formal operations, can reason with conditionals (such as in the sample sentences) when the scripts are familiar (French & Nelson, 1985). Johnson-Laird reported that 9-year-olds can draw valid conclusions when they have a reasonable grasp of quantifiers (Johnson-Laird, 1983), and for 11-year-olds, grasp of the quantifiers and the ability to make syllogistic inferences are positively correlated (Johnson-Laird, 1990).

Braine (Braine, 1990; Braine, Reiser, & Rumain, 1984; Braine & Rumain, 1983) assumed that one important function of deduction is to understand discourse, what people imply in the sentences they speak. In Braine's view, reasoning is a tool for doing this, but he

differentiates ordinary, natural, or **primary logic** from **secondary logic.** The latter is the product of formal education and is much more erudite than the former, which he proposed is a universal and probably automatic reasoning skill.

Primary logical skills are envisioned as **inference schemes** with which an individual can match the form of an incoming sentence and draw reasonable conclusions. For example, the sentence presented previously, "If Mommy is not in the house, she is in the barn," is of the *modus ponens* form, which is on Braine's list of primary inference schemes. Even a young child, one capable of matching the sentence with the scheme, when asked, "Mommy is not in the house. Where is she?", will deduce correctly that she must be in the barn. The *modus tollens* form of the conditional is not on Braine's primary list, however. And he would attribute success with that form to reasoning based on secondary skills achieved with formal education and familiarity with legalistic arguments.

Inference schemes can vary in length and in the number of logical connections that must be made. But with primary schemes, those that do not overly tax the capacities of the individual for processing oral discourse, success can be elicited even early in childhood. Some chains are longer and would overtax the processing capacity of the younger child (Case, 1985a). The longest and most complex would tax any individual who does not have access to the logical chain in the form of written discourse. Braine's system, then, is one way to explain the paradoxical facts.

Performance over competence. Sentences have form and meaning. Explanations of logic that focus on the common features of syntax between logic and language still stress the importance of form. Those who think that meaning is primary offer alternative views. Meaning is contained in the content or subject of the sentence. Reasoning about content is based on an individual's knowledge of the world, belief systems, and so forth. The child who determines that Mommy must be in the barn may not do so because of an appreciation of premises and conclusions, but rather, because he knows of his mother's fondness for her horses. Reasoning from a semantic basis does not emphasize form over content.

Johnson-Laird (1983, 1990) challenged the formal approach because, in his view, it simply does not accurately represent how people think about problem situations. He characterized explanatory systems that focus on the symbolic manipulations in accord with formal rules, as *mental logic* approaches, and he concluded that there is little unambiguous empirical evidence to support them. His alternative is the aforementioned **mental model** approach, in which implicit semantic representations of arguments and premises enable reasoning based on content. The reasoning people use in everyday life takes this mental model form and it is not accessible to introspection. He cited as support for his position the following observations:

1. The content of premises can have a decisive effect on the conclusions people draw (Wason & Johnson-Laird, 1972).
2. In reality, people are quite concerned with matters of truth and falsity, not validity and invalidity.
3. Most people's bias is towards verifying (as opposed to falsifying) hypotheses.
4. People are influenced by their beliefs and their prejudices both in the conclusions they draw (Oakhill & Johnson-Laird, 1985) and in the evaluation of conclusions already drawn (Evans, Barston, & Pollard, 1983).

According to Johnson-Laird, none of these observations is predicted from a theory of reasoning that proposes as a basic operation the quasisyntactic manipulation of formal, uninterpreted symbols (Johnson-Laird, 1983).

Johnson-Laird (1990) assumed that deductive inferences are made on the basis of three main steps:

> The reasoner imagines how the world would be if the premises were true, taking into account any general knowledge that is triggered by their interpretation. This representation is remote from the linguistic form of the premises and consists of a mental model of the relevant state of affairs, i.e., a model that is close in form to the perception of the relevant events, with a mental token for each relevant individual, property and relation.
>
> The reasoner formulates a novel conclusion that is true in the model, i.e., a conclusion establishing something that was not explicitly presented in the premises. If there is no such conclusion, then the reasoner considers that there is nothing that follows from the premises.
>
> The reasoner attempts to construct an alternative model of the premises that refutes the conclusion drawn in the previous step. If there is no such model, then the conclusion is valid. If there is such a model, then the reasoner returns to the previous step, and attempts to formulate an informative conclusion that is true in all the models so far constructed. If the reasoner is uncertain about the existence of such a model, then the conclusion is drawn on a tentative basis. (p. 96)

What the individual must do, essentially, is construct a mental model of what is proposed in an argument, and then mentally manipulate the model to see if it can be made consistent with the conclusion drawn from the argument. If the model cannot be so transformed, then the argument is invalid. The elements in the model are what the argument is about.

The development of an ability to do this will depend, first, on the child's ability to understand the meaning of the words presented in the argument, particularly the meanings of quantifiers (*all, some,* etc.), connectives (*and, or, if,* etc.), and relational terms. Second, the child must have sufficient capacity in working memory to hold on to models and countermodels in order to make comparisons. And finally, the child must have the ability to search for counterexamples.

Johnson-Laird assumed that both the development of language and development of working memory are innately programmed and maturationally constrained. Therefore, success on reasoning tasks will also be age related. His argument, however, was that the apparent reasoning limitations of children are not best explained by limitations in syntactic representations, but semantic ones. His model for how reasoning ability might develop in children is depicted in Figure 8-4.

The mental model proposal is not the definitive solution to the development of deductive reasoning, however. First, its reasonableness depends on conclusions about language development—which we will evaluate in Chapter 9, and memory development, the subject of Chapter 10. His assumptions about the ontogenesis of these two capacities would compromise his analysis if they prove to be untenable. We shall see. Second, what is the ability to search for counterexample? Might that not be the sort of logical thinking skill that others propose? There is the possibility that Johnson-Laird's model builds in logical capacity implicitly, in which case its development still begs explanation (see Scholnick, 1990).

Whether you put much stock in the vagaries of performance as a function of task content (e.g., context effects) is not an empirical issue but an evaluative one. If you think

FIGURE 8-4 *Johnson-Laird's Representation of Important Landmarks in the Development of Deductive Reasoning.*

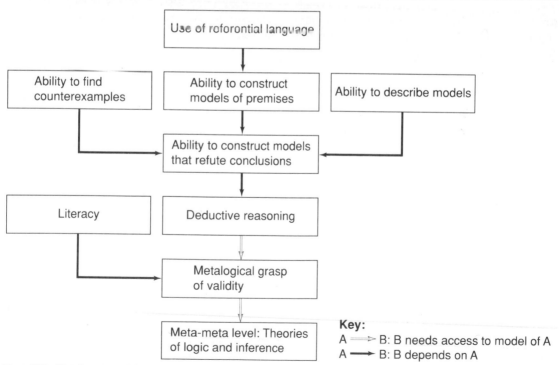

the task of the developmental psychologist is to describe an ideal *model* for asymptotic mental functioning and the origins of such, then you might relegate context effects to the status of nuisance variable. The argument is that context effects result from experimental details unrelated to the important conceptual issues and interfere with theory construction. On the other hand, if *modal* functioning and its evolution are your concerns, context effects are centrally important. Pursuit of the model mind might even be conceived as a somewhat silly enterprise if real people do not operate that way.

Either perspective alone is a little unsatisfying. A full account of developmental phenomena must allow for the explanation of both the optimal sequence for the evolution of deductive reasoning and the variations in experience, maturation, semantic content, and so forth that influence the display of optimal functioning. The only qualification—which would make the two tasks antagonistic enterprises—is if explanations generated from the study of one type of development should turn out to be incompatible with the explanations of the other.

A Metalogic Alternative

Before we try to make sense out of the literature on deductive reasoning and its development, read the following excerpts from real conversations between an adult and a 6-year-old child:

Excerpt 1
Adult: Listen to me a moment. . . . All sheep are green. Tommy has a sheep. What color is Tommy's sheep?
Child: Green.
Adult: How did you know that Tommy's sheep had to be green?
Child: Because . . . it rolled in the grass so much.

Excerpt 2
Adult: The ball in my hand is either red or green. It is not red. What color is it?
Child: Green.
Adult: How do you know it's green without looking?
Child: Because you said . . . it's not red.

Excerpt 3
Adult: The ball in my hand is either red or green or yellow. It is not red. What color is it?
Child: Green.
Adult: How do you know it isn't yellow?
Child: Because . . . I'm smart!

In two out of the three excerpts, the child makes the correct deduction. However, there is a difference between the child's reasoning and an adult version; indeed, that is what makes the conversations humorous. Perhaps the difference also suggests something relevant about the development of deductive reasoning.

There is a difference between making correct deductions by *implicitly* following logiclike rules and describing the rule system consulted *explicitly*. There is also a difference between drawing conclusions about how things usually are in the world and drawing logical conclusions counter to how things are. To do the latter, a person must understand that, when reasoning, the rule system takes precedence over reality. And again, to do so requires explicit knowledge of the rule system and how it works. The child in the examples is fairly competent at drawing correct inferences, and he attempts a statement of one of the simpler rules, but he does not fully understand the notion of necessity. Moreover, his inference ability is not independent of his empirical knowledge. When he draws the appropriate deduction in Excerpt 1, he concocts an empirical explanation (not a logical one) to account for it; he knows that sheep are really white.

Research on deductive reasoning has provided three sorts of evidence generally viewed as challenging a Piagetian theoretical formulation. The first is evidence of content or *knowledge effects:* People are more apt to reason logically about premises and conclusions connected to their world knowledge. So, access to rules of deductive logic is apparently not context independent (as abstract algorithms are supposed to be in a domain-general model). The second is evidence of *early competence:* Even preschool children perform well on simple inference tasks, behaving much as adults would (Braine & Rumain, 1983; Thayer & Collyer, 1978). This argues against *any* developmental story for logic since it is evidence of cognitive continuity across children and adults. And the third is evidence of *late incompetence:* the pervasive illogicality of adults on many reasoning tasks, which presents a challenge to the psychological validity of any formal system. Of course, the tasks are different across research with children and adults, and task nonequivalence contributes to the confusion. Still, there may be some sensible explanation that can help salvage a semblance of a developmental story for deductive reasoning from this messy mass of experimental data.

Moshman (1990) distinguished between *logic* and *metalogic.* The use of basic logic calls for competence of an implicit sort. (Moshman calls it "unconscious".) And it is a cognitive capacity established and accessible by about age 5 or 6. This capacity is comparable to Braine's (1990) *primary inference schemes,* logical skills necessary for human survival and for the comprehension of discourse, and, therefore, expected to emerge early and be universal. Metalogic consists of two components:

1. *Metalogical strategies* are rules for reasoning that invoke the explicit distinction between premises and conclusions and the purposeful use of this knowledge in the service of thinking. Examples would include generating multiple possibilities consistent with premises (Markovits, 1984), seeking counterexamples to conclusions (Johnson-Laird, 1983), and coordinating the construction of a line of argument (Johnson-Laird, 1975).

2. *Metalogical understanding* is an explicit conception of the nature of logic itself, such as grasping the concept that a conclusion must be consistent with all possible states of affairs permitted by the premises. Metalogic, this explicit, conscious component of reasoning, is sophisticated and relatively late developing; it consists of an awareness of how a formal thought system works, above and beyond the ability to use it.

This conceptualization of reasoning leads to a four-stage developmental sequence modeling progression toward greater and greater rationality in thinking, enabled by the development of metalogic. Stage 1 individuals (preschool children) use inference implicitly, not by deliberately thinking about premises and conclusions but about facts (permitting the success achieved in Excerpt 2).

In Stage 2 (elementary school years), children grasp and extend the concept of necessity, distinguish the necessary from the merely plausible, and recognize the possibility of gaining knowledge through inference. So, the Stage 2 child possesses rudiments of metalogic not available to the Stage 1 child. (The Stage 2 child would succeed on Excerpt 3).

By Stage 3 (beginning around age 11), people separate empirical truth from logical validity (and would reason logically on Excerpt 1); they achieve an explicit grasp of logical form. The Stage 3, adolescent deduces there must be more molecules in the world than there are grains of sand on all the beaches, even though she has not counted the grains and collected the empirical proof. And in Stage 4 (only achieved by some adults),

TABLE 8-1 *Moshman's Model for the Development of Metalogical Understanding*

Stage	Explicit Object of Understanding	Knowledge Implicit in Reasoning (Subject)
Stage 1 Explicit Content Implicit Inference	*Content*	*Inference:* Conclusion deduced and, thus, distinct from premises
Stage 2 Explicit Inference Implicit Logic	*Inference:* Conclusion deduced from and, thus, related to premises	*Logic:* Form of argument distinct from empirical truth of premises and conclusions (necessity)
Stage 3 Explicit Logic Implicit Metalogic	*Logic:* Relation of argument form and empirical truth of premises and conclusions (validity)	*Metalogic:* Formal logical system distinct from natural language
Stage 4 Explicit Metalogic	*Metalogic:* Interrelations of logical systems and natural languages	

From "The Development of Metalogical Understanding" by J. S. Black and D. Moshman, in *Reasoning, Necessity, and Logic* by W. F. Overton (Ed.), 1990, Hillsdale, NJ: Erlbaum. Copyright 1990 by Lawrence J. Erlbaum, Inc. Reprinted by permission.

metalogical development has progressed sufficiently to enable reasoning about logical systems themselves. These stages are summarized in Table 8-1.

Moshman's (1990) metalogic analysis fits the data better than the original Piagetian version does. Implicit logic is available early in development. Explicit logic is displayed later, and illogicality can extend into adulthood (presumably on tasks requiring Stage 4 attainments). But, where does explicit reasoning, or metalogic, come from? What are its origins? How does it arise? What are the developmental mechanisms that enable access to it? The Piagetian account applied to the development of deductive logic is conceptually weak because these questions are answered only through reference to vaguely described developmental processes. Any other account—even one that provides a more complete, descriptive reformulation of performance on logical tasks—will suffer a similar weakness unless those questions are adequately addressed.

Currently, Moshman's system provides a useful framework for thinking about the development of deductive reasoning. But, for now, the development of explicit, generalized reasoning skills remains somewhat of a mystery. We know deductive reasoning is age related, task related, content related, and knowledge related. Whether, if at all, a domain-general cognitive function is implicated still remains unclear.

DEVELOPMENT OF ANALOGICAL REASONING

Deductive reasoning and inductive reasoning are two of the "thinking" strategies that have attracted the attention of developmentalists. At least part of the interest in studying these skills is due to their potential for revealing something about domain-general aspects of cognition. Reasoning appears to be a content-independent cognitive capacity. A second impetus for study comes about from the Piagetian formulation of these skills as late developing. Thus, adults presumably have significant domain-general reasoning abilities, important intellectual skills, that are not available to young children.

In a strong interpretation of the structuralist perspective, these abilities are not available until adolescence. The developmental implications of a maturational constraint on young children's reasoning are somewhat surprising; it is counterintuitive to envision children as this intellectually deficient. Such implications invariably attract attention. Another of these skills, **analogical reasoning ability,** occupies a similar place in the domain-general, unitary-mind view of things. And these skills have undergone similar interpretation, reinterpretation, and investigative histories.

Analogical reasoning is reasoning about similarity relations among elements. Successful analogical reasoning occurs when an individual infers one relation—from a pair of terms, a story, a system, or a problem description—and constructs the same relation with another pair of terms, story, system, or description. Therefore, the task is to *abstract* the first relation and transfer or *generalize* that abstraction to another relation. The second step represents the ability to reason about a **higher order relation,** a relation between relations. Because generalizing the relation across content implicates the need to abstract or disembed the relation from the specific elements that expressed it, the skill reasonably appears to be a domain-general capacity.

The most familiar form of this reasoning task is the verbal analogy problem encountered on psychometric measures of intelligence and ability. These problems are of the form *a: b:: c: d.* For examples, *bird: feather:: dog: fur; bicycle: handlebars:: car: steering wheel;* or a numerical version, *3: 1:: 9: 7:: 4:?* The individual must determine the relation

between the first pair of terms and extend it to the second pair of terms, typically by supplying the fourth term. So, in the problem *hot: cold:: soft: ?,* the first task is to recognize that the relation expressed between *a* and *b* is antonymous. The second task is to recognize the need to express the identical relation between *c* and *d.* And the third task is to supply the element that constructs the target relation. Problem solving is disembedded from content when the relation is extended, or generalized, to the second pair. These are the classical versions of analogical reasoning tasks (Goswami, 1991), but there are other versions as well.

Metaphors presume analogical thinking since they express the relation that *x* is like *y.* For examples, a cloud is like a sponge and a plant stem is like a drinking straw (Gentner, 1988). Systems can also share a relational correspondence, for example, the analogous structures of the solar system and an atom (Gentner, 1983). Stories can share structural similarities (Gentner & Toupin, 1986) such that the actions of characters and sequence of events in one story can be mapped onto similar elements in a second story. (Anyone who watches much series television can attest to that.) And problems can be analogously solved.

An example of this last analogy is taken from an actual experiment (Holyoak, Junn, & Billman, 1984). Children were presented with a tricky problem to solve: They had to transfer small rubber balls from one bowl to another, but the second bowl was beyond their reach. Implements that could be used to solve the problem were provided: a cane (for bringing the target bowl closer), a hollow tube (for rolling the balls through), a sheet of paper (for rolling into a tube), and so forth. In order to see if they could transfer a solution across problems, children were first read a story about an analogous problem. The base story was about a genie who wanted to transfer jewels from one bottle to another. Solutions in the story varied: The genie used his "magic staff" to pull the second bottle closer versus rolling his "magic carpet" into a tube to roll the jewels between bottles. The structure of the story problem (called the *base*) and the structure of the real problem facing the children (called the *target*) are obviously similar. Also, the genie's solutions were applicable to the children's task.

The form of the analogy, then, is: $Problem_B : Solution_B :: Problem_T : Solution_T$ (Holyoak, 1984). Successful analogical reasoning is demonstrated when the subjects apply the solution strategy that they heard about in the prior story to the problem facing them. Again, reasoning suggests disembedding the solution from the story content and generalizing it to a different content.

Analogical reasoning can prove difficult for the young child. As an example, consider the following set of relations among terms—*car: steering wheel:: bicycle: handlebars:: boat: rudder:: horse: reins*. Across the pairs, the relation is a functional one (e.g., a steering function). The child must understand the relation expressed in the base pair. Then, the child must be able to disembed the steering function from the specific means of travel (cars) and generalize it to other means of travel (bicycles, boats, and horses). A prerequisite, however, to providing a correct *d* term in any of the four-term combinations is knowledge of the precise mechanism for steering appropriate in the other context.

Some contexts are predictably more familiar (cars, bicycles) and some perhaps less so (boats, horses). Failure is likely if the child (1) cannot understand the initial relation *a:b;* (2) cannot disentangle the relation from the initial context, fixating on *a*s; or (3) cannot supply a specific *d* term. Only the second possibility potentially involves a domain-general ability. The first and third could be explained as a limitation in knowledge—as a domain-specific limitation. When the author gave this series to her son, he correctly supplied the d term for bicycles and horses, and he described

the function depicted; but he could not supply the *d* term for boats. He hasn't had much experience with boats and doesn't know how they steer.

When children cannot supply the correct *d* term that preserves the analogy, they may give something else—a term invoking an associative relation (*boat: sail*), a taxonomic relation (*boat: water*)—or they may inappropriately overgeneralize a previously mentioned *d* term (*boat: steering wheel*). In their failure to supply the target *d* term, it may look like they are reasoning in a different manner than adults or older children. But this cannot be determined unless the precise source of the failure is identifiable.

Domain-General Explanations

Domain-general accounts of analogical reasoning focus on the *process* of reasoning, on the abstraction and construction of similarity relations among terms. The particular terms themselves are of less direct relevance, except that, as a consequence of varying them, it becomes possible to assess the generality of reasoning (so important to domain-general cognitive processes). Therefore, investigators typically vary the specific relation between *a* and *b* (e.g., associative, functional, causal, etc.) and examine whether the individual can still equate the relation with the *c, d* pair. This is where higher order reasoning about an abstraction comes in: the construction of a *relation between relations*.

In a Piagetian view, reflection upon and reasoning about the contents of thought, that is, thinking about thought, is a sophisticated, late-developing achievement. Essentially the mind consciously operates on its own products, representations at least one processing loop removed from concrete reality. It follows, then, that analogical reasoning, like its deductive counterpart, should prove beyond the cognitive capacities of children until the achievement of formal operations when operating on symbolic abstractions becomes possible. That is, in fact, the prediction (see Goswami, 1991).

Piaget studied analogical reasoning with a picture version of the classic *a: b:: c: d* analogy task (Piaget, Montangero, & Billeter, 1977). Children sorted pictures into pairs (*a:b* and *c:d* relations) and then generated the analogies by sorting the pairs into sets of four. Through successive probes, the children's extent of knowledge was more deeply examined. The criteria for success were generation of the original relations, construction of the analogy, and rejection of false countersuggestions. A false countersuggestion was an experimenter-supplied substitution for the d element which, while still forming a sensible relation with c, destroyed the equivalence relation across pairs.

A fully competent reasoner should be able to generate the initial sets, explain the relation—requiring explicit knowledge of analogy—and resist countersuggestion. The data, as interpreted, were consistent with theoretical prediction: only formal-operational-stage children could consistently reason analogically and grasp the quasimathematical nature (i.e., =) of the similarity relation. Preoperational children were only able, at best, to build the initial pairwise associations; concrete-operational children could sporadically coordinate the pairs into an analogy, but they could not reliably resist the countersuggestions.

Developmental effects similar to those detected in the Piagetian-inspired investigations also have been found by others (Gallagher & Wright, 1979; Levinson & Carpenter, 1974; Lunzer, 1965). Again, success on analogical reasoning tasks was age related, with age 12 being the approximate point where shifts in performance were most likely to be observed. However, even in these studies (as in the Piagetian original), occasional analogical reasoning was observed in younger children, although the items associated with precocious success were limited (e.g., to concrete versus abstract associations). The investigators generally tended to discount these sporadic successes, noting that the higher order reasoning, so important in the theoretical analysis of these cognitive problems, was still not demonstrated by young subjects.

Goswami (1991) contended, however, that the causes behind the failures of young children in these studies is not clear. Alternative interpretations are plausible. One alternative is the possibility that failures and successes are a function of specific knowledge effects. For example, in the numerical analogy 5:125, 4:64, 2:8:,: 3:?, failure would be insured by insufficient mathematical knowledge (not knowing the concept of raising a number by the power of 3) even if considerable reasoning skill were accessible. Young children have less specific knowledge than older children; extent of knowledge is confounded with developmental status. In many studies, extent of knowledge is neither controlled nor independently evaluated.

Other investigators, those not Piagetian in theoretical allegiance, have still observed developmental, age-related changes in children's ability to solve analogy problems. Sternberg and his associates (Sternberg & Nigro, 1980; Sternberg & Rifkin, 1979), for example, approached intelligence as a set of combined component cognitive skills that is called into service when the individual performs a cognitive task (e.g., the items included on intelligence tests). These investigators, operating from an **information-processing perspective,** identified the set of component skills underlying performance on specific reasoning problems. Classical analogy problems are one of the kinds often studied (Alderton, Goldman, & Pellegrino, 1985; Sternberg, 1977).

By identifying the components and designing tasks that allow independent assessment of each component, it is possible to precisely evaluate how individuals compare in their ability to execute cognitive operations.

Note that the operations are envisioned as domain general, although the exact combination varies across task content. This research agenda has yielded greater understanding of the nature of intelligence and the source of individual differences in intelligence than that provided by the theoretically impoverished psychometric approach. In developmental extensions of componential theory, children varying in age are compared as to whether and how efficiently they execute the identified components.

Some of the components involved in analogical reasoning and relevant to developmental inquiry are (1) *encoding* the meanings of the terms given in the analogy, (2) *inferring* the relation between *a* and *b*, (3) *mapping* the relation between the *a* and *c* terms, and (4) *applying* an analogous relation to the *b* term to generate the solution. Sternberg and Rifkin (1979) found that children became faster at executing components with age (reaction time is typically assessed in these studies), but children below age 8 seldom evidenced any use of mapping. The authors concluded that it is the mapping component that requires the recognition of the higher order relation. Even though younger children recognize the lower order relation (*a* to *b*), they do not appreciate the higher order similarity relation.

In subsequent research (Sternberg & Nigro, 1980), the age effect was again observed. The authors concluded that younger children depend heavily on *association* (*apple* goes with *tree*, *water* goes with *boat*, etc.) as a substitute for full analogical reasoning. Even when younger children are distracted by an incorrect *d* term, it tends to be one that is an associate of *c* that does not fulfill the analogy (Goldman, Pellegrino, Parseghian, & Sallis, 1982). Although the impetus for the work is not Piagetian, the conclusions turn out to be consistent with structuralist predictions.

In sum, the robustness of a developmental effect is attested to not only by Piagetian-inspired research but by results of other research as well—and on a variety of analogical tasks (see also Gentner, 1988; 1989). Even the timing of the predicted age shift (about 12 years) turns out to be similar. If we were to stop evaluating the literature at this point, we would probably conclude that (1) analogical reasoning reflects a domain-general cognitive function and (2) it develops. But precisely *why* would a child produce what is described as an "associative" response? Is there an alternative explanation not fully consistent with these conclusions?

Evidence of Early Competence

In the general view of things, it is not clear what an associative response is, really. All possible nonidiosyncratic *d* terms are associates of some kind or another. For example, *sail, rudder, water, wind, float,* and *seagull* are all legitimate associates of *boat,* but each association is predicated on a different kind of relation. In an experiment, the correct *d* term is the one identified as preserving the same relation as in *a:b.* Any other *d* that has some connection with *d* qualifies as an "associate."[2] Therefore, to describe a young child's response as associative is somewhat vague. It is quite possible that an associative response is a "default" response; that is, the child provides *some* associate of *c* when she hasn't quite figured out *the* associate being asked for.

There are two important ramifications of this interpretation. First, in supplying any associate of *c,* the child demonstrates some implicit knowledge about analogical reasoning; she knows *one* of the rules underlying the task at hand: *a* and *b* are related, so make *c* and *d* relate, too. Thus, associative responding is evidence of continuity in development because the rule is one prerequisite to the identification of the correct *d* term as well as its incorrect associates. Second, if the child supplies a–d, but not the –d, what has prevented her from discriminating among possible d options? Insufficient domain-general knowledge seems an incomplete explanation when she apparently does understand some domain-general requirements of the task.

In one test of the associate claim (reported in Goswami, 1991), investigators narrowed down the "associate" group to *thematic* associations (e.g., *dog* and *bone*). Recall from Chapter 4 that young children often prefer thematic grouping over other forms, including categorical grouping. In the analogy study, an experimental condition was devised in which a thematic associate was pitted against an analogy associate in a multiple-choice, picture version of the task. For example, in the *bird: nest:: dog: doghouse* relation, *bone* was one of the distractors. Other distractors were appearance matches—another *dog*—and category matches—a *cat*. The child, then, had four d options to choose among. There was also a control condition: The c term was presented with the four d options without the initial establishment of the analogy (the *a:b* pair was omitted). Choices in the control condition, therefore, reflect the associates children spontaneously prefer.

If children can reason analogously, however, their choices in the experimental condition (*a:b* relation presented) should differ from their choices in the control condition (*a:b* not presented). In fact, preference for the analogous d was significantly higher in the experimental condition, even in children as young as 4! Provided young children *understood* the meaning of the *a:b* relation, they could demonstrate analogical reasoning and were not especially seduced by thematic associates. Insufficient knowledge, however, could constrain correct responding, facilitating a thematic choice as a fallback strategy.

There is more evidence of early competence in children's analogical reasoning (Alexander, Willson, White, & Fuqua, 1987;

Goswami, (1989). Goswami and Brown (1989) used causal relations as the basis of their analogies; knowledge of causal processes in physical systems emerges early among children's conceptual competencies (see Chapter 6). In the analogy study, the a and b terms expressed a relation of before and after a causal event, for example, *car: wet car, playdough: cut playdough*. The c term offered another before state, that is, *apple*, and d options included a correct after state, *cut apple*. Four- and 6-year-olds were very successful; 3-year-olds were partly successful. Most illuminating, however, was the finding that the extent of analogical reasoning was predictable from prior knowledge of the causal relations expressed in *a:b*.

Indeed, as long as the relational basis for an initial analogy in a reasoning task remains within the boundaries of what we expect to be children's prior knowledge, then early competence shows up across a variety of task types (Brown, 1989; Brown & Kane, 1988; Brown, Kane, & Echols, 1986). With classic analogics, the initial relation must be understood; with problem analogies, task similarity between base and target must be recognized (Brown, Kane, & Long, 1989; Crisafi & Brown, 1986). And younger children may need more "hints" than older ones to facilitate generalization (Holyoak, Junn, & Billman, 1984). So, the claim that analogical reasoning is beyond the reach of young children is seriously compromised by an abundance of evidence for early competence.

The detection of early competence is enabled by a knowledge effect. When knowledge is present, successful performance on analogical reasoning tasks follows. However, knowledge effects may very well be idiosyncratic, explaining individual differences in success as a function of expertise related to task content. An expertise-related knowledge effect would not be developmentally interesting (although, any unexplained task effect challenges a domain-general view of cognition). But what we are seeing is a *reliable* age-associated knowledge effect, one that is specifically developmental. The ability to reason through analogy seems to be related to conceptual knowledge (Brown, 1989; Vosniadou, 1989), and conceptual knowledge elaborates and differentiates in predictable ways with development (Keil, 1981; 1989). One of the developmentally earliest ontological distinctions is between animate and inanimate entities (Keil, 1979). Conceptual knowledge of the workings of the inanimate is grasped early (Gelman, 1990a; also see Chapter 6), and analogical reasoning shows up early with these contents.

A child may ably transfer a relation across terms (i.e., generalize between *a* and *c*) when the ontological distinctions between the terms is well established. Metaphor is a form of analogy and comprehending a metaphor could conceivably reflect domain-general analogical reasoning. On the other hand, appreciating a metaphor could also be constrained by domain-specific knowledge. Some metaphors will be grasped earlier than others as a function of elaboration in ontological knowledge.

As an example, here are three metaphors: (a) "The battery is dead," (b) "The ocean roared," and (c) "The lies flowed out of her mouth." Literally, these sentences represent unacceptable combinations of terms and predicates (see Chapter 5). In (a) and (b) a living-thing predicate is paired with a nonliving-thing term; in (c) a liquid-thing predicate is combined with an abstract-thing term. To understand the metaphor, a child must (1) understand the ontological distinction underlying other terms, (2) know which predicates cannot literally be combined with terms from those ontological categories, and (3) recognize the implication of the analogy in an otherwise (4) inappropriate pairing. Numbers (3) and (4) cannot occur in the absence of (1) and (2); and (1) and (2) are age-related achievements. Specifically, the liquid- versus abstract-object distinction occurs later than the living- versus nonliving-thing distinction.

The following snippets are taken from a metaphor experiment (Chandler, Rosser, & Narter, 1993) and demonstrate possible developmental influences on the comprehension of metaphor:

Metaphor 1: "The battery is dead"; the subject is 9 years old.

Experimenter: What are batteries?
Child: Batteries are things that have energy in them and you can put them in mechanical things and the batteries will make them run. (*She understands the term.*)
Experimenter: What does "dead" mean?
Child: If a person or an animal is dead then its not alive anymore. (*She understands the predicate.*)
Experimenter: What does it mean when I say, "The battery is dead"?
Child: The batteries can't work anymore. They aren't energized anymore. (*She understands the relation.*)
Experimenter: When I say, "The battery is dead," does it mean the same thing as, "The person is dead"?
Child: No. A person is really alive and it breathes. The battery isn't alive. It doesn't breathe. (*She understands the use of analogy in metaphor.*)

The same analogy with a 6-year-old.

Experimenter: What are batteries?
Child: You put them in cars. It starts the car.
Experimenter: What does "dead" mean?
Child: . . . like an animal is dead . . . but that's not a very nice thing to say.
Experimenter: What does it mean when I say, "The battery is dead"?
Child: The car won't go. The battery doesn't work anymore.
Experimenter: When I say, "The battery is dead," does it mean the same as, "The animal is dead"?
Child: No. A battery is electricity. An animal is alive.

Metaphor 2: "The ocean roared."

Nine-year-old's response to the final metaphor question: The ocean can't roar like a lion. A lion makes sound and so does the ocean, but the ocean isn't alive and breathing.

Six-year-old's response: Lions and tigers and bears roar. . . . Oceans make waves and they crash (*nontranscribable depictions of sound*) like that.

Metaphor 3: "The lies flowed out of her mouth."

Nine-year-old's response to the metaphor question: That means she lied a lot, but the lies aren't made out of water. It's just a figure of speech.

Six-year-old (who had much trouble with the predicate): I don't know what you're talking about. . . . Leave me alone!

Summary

There are many types of analogical reasoning tasks, classic *a: b:: c: d* analogies, problem analogies, and metaphors among them. Many have been administered to children in an attempt to discover the factors—developmental and otherwise—that influence the efficiency of reasoning. As a whole, the findings are confusing, just as we saw for studies of deductive reasoning. Some research, especially Piagetian-inspired and information-processing work, supports an interpretation of reasoning as late developing, where there is discontinuity between the performances of younger and older children. And these studies point to a developmental shift around age 12. Other research leads to the attribution of competence to much younger children, children as young as 3 in some cases. These data argue conversely for developmental continuity. So what is to be concluded?

Age does account for part of the variance in analogical reasoning tasks; older children do better. They are able to exhibit reasoning across more tasks than younger children. Per-

formance of the mature is more robust, and only older subjects have access to explicit knowledge of their reasoning strategies. Knowledge effects also account for some of the variance. When prior knowledge is controlled, assessed independently, or experimentally manipulated (as in a training condition), the age effect is mitigated and reasoning performance is predictable from extent of prior knowledge. In most studies, developmental status and extent of prior knowledge are confounded and inseparable. It is clear, however, that younger children do their best when reasoning tasks are consistent with their conceptual and ontological knowledge. Young children rarely explain their analogical reasoning strategies, and they may not use them spontaneously. Because their reasoning is most appropriately describable as implicit, they may need hints as to how and when to generalize relations.

Analogical reasoning in older children, particularly adolescents, is generalized. It, therefore, does appear to qualify as a domain-general cognitive process—accessible, deliberate, explainable, and broadly applicable. Analogical reasoning in the young is constrained by conceptual knowledge; it appears to be a domain-specific cognitive process—implicit, not explainable, and narrowly applicable. Perhaps a distinction that separates out metalogic aspects of reasoning, like Moshman (1990) has proposed for deductive reasoning, will lead to a fuller accounting of the data (Goswami, 1991). But that is not certain. It is clear that separating domain-general from domain-specific cognitive functioning in developmental inquiry is not an easy endeavor. We have not yet achieved a clear separation for analogical reasoning.

CONCLUSION

The theoretical purpose, consistent with a unitary model of mind, is to describe, or model, a set of principles that governs rational thought.

Whether the set is a group of component intellectual processes, a sequence of computer programs, or a holistic operational structure, the modeling enterprise is a similar one. All such models constitute a formalism, an abstract rule system. The conceptual implication is that the syntax of thought best captures the properties of mind. The developmental ramifications of unitary models were previously described:

1. Across-task correlations are expected since central processing is implicated in all cognitive operations.
2. It is general rules that are acquired, and general rules transcend the specifics of content.
3. Generalized cognitive skills of this sort are expected to have a relatively late developmental onset.

So, do the data support these developmental predictions? Yes . . . but. Explicitly expressed, deliberately accessed, explainable cognitive strategies are not reliably observed until late childhood or early adolescence, *but* implicitly usable ones are implicated even in the performances of young children. Explicitly available strategies are generalizable across tasks, *but,* specific content will sometimes impede their application. Task context can make the mature look illogical, incompetent, and immature. Conversely, in other contexts, the immature will look logical, competent, and mature. There are across-task correlations and age associations in reasoning performance, *but,* a substantial portion of the variance is not accounted for by those associations.

How can these conclusions be interpreted? One route is to separate *competence* from *performance.* The "buts" all have to do with performance variation as a function of task, context, experimental detail, and so on. Competence models, which are predictive of developmental phenomena, are extractable from the morass. Then, of course, performance—the

data—is, in fact, not well explained; some would find that an unsatisfactory state of affairs. An alternative route is to differentiate the ability to use *logic* and reasoning, which is apparently a capability of both the mature and the immature depending on the circumstances, from *metalogic.* The latter is the deliberate use of reasoning and an understanding of its formal, syntactic properties. Metalogic is a late-onset competence, and the status of its developmental state predicts age-related performance pretty well. The remaining difficulty is to identify the impetus for its emergence and ontogenesis. Where does metalogic, metareasoning capacity, come from? That remains a mystery.

The problem is that we can never really separate the *syntax* of reasoning from the *semantics* of reasoning.[3] Semantics is the meaning of referents reasoned about. Meaning implicates knowledge about how the world works. That, too, is a developmental phenomenon, but world knowledge does not seem to emerge in the same way thought "syntax" is theoretically supposed to. Knowledge effects turn out to be a challenge to a domain-general, unitary view of mind. And knowledge effects reliably occur. It is going to take a more comprehensive developmental story to account for all the empirical information we have collected about reasoning and problem solving from research with children. We explore that developmental story in Chapter 11.

ENDNOTES

1. One educated adult, on whom the author tried this task, said *all* the cards must be turned over to determine the "truth" of the premise. That is what an individual would do to establish the *empirical* validity, rather than the *logical* validity, of the premise.

2. The best definition of an associate is empirically determined. Subjects are given lists of terms and they supply connected terms. The response terms with high frequencies are then defined as associates. This is seldom independently assessed in developmental studies.

3. In the psychometric literature on the assessment of intelligence and ability, this confounding is an item effect. And it continues to be a problem. The issue of *test bias* is a problem of semantics that results in observed group differences in performance. Attempts to produce bias-free (semantic-free?) tests have not fared much better than attempts to independently measure the syntax of reasoning.

CHAPTER 9

CHILDREN'S LANGUAGE ACQUISITION

INTRODUCTION
THE TASK OF ACQUIRING LANGUAGE
THE FACTS OF LANGUAGE DEVELOPMENT
EXPLANATIONS OF THE ACQUISITION PHENOMENON
CONCLUSION

INTRODUCTION

The acquisition of language is one of the growing child's most marvelous of feats. Virtually every child in every society accomplishes it in seemingly effortless fashion, yet it is a rare parent who attempts to teach it deliberately. In a period of about three years, an otherwise fairly naive individual will come to master the basics of an extraordinarily complex representational system. And there will be no exceptions. Some children will exhibit mastery of chess, and some will not; some will achieve skill with computers or creativity in music, and others will not. All will acquire the language of their social community unless extreme deprivation or organic insult severely interrupts the normal flow of human experience. Explaining the incredible ubiquity of language acquisition, when the thing to be acquired is itself so immensely complicated, is a challenge to cognitive and developmental psychologists, linguists, and biologists, indeed to all cognitive scientists.

Once children begin talking and displaying their accumulated language knowledge, most of what they say is appropriate and well formed, but not every utterance is exactly correct. The following scenarios exemplify some of the uniqueness of child language, the mistakes, simplifications, and distortions which just might reveal to us something about the nature and course of this impressive developmental accomplishment:

Scenario 1

A 3-year-old asks his mother what she is doing: "What doing Mommy?" Mother replies that she is watching television, the program—"Miami Vice." Subsequently, Father asks the child where Mother is. The child's reply is, "Watching *'Her Ami Vice.'*"

Scenario 2

A 14-month-old is about to utter a simplified but meaningful version of a sentence in context. He picks up a block, smashes a small cricket that has entered his play space, and issues the summary statement, "Bug go!"

Scenario 3

A 2-year-old is intermittently watching a video playing for others on television; she observes the Starship Enterprise advance to warp speed. Her comment: "Airplane go bye-bye."

Scenario 4

An 11-month-old has used the word *stick* to refer to a piece of wood lying on the ground that can be picked up and thrown for the family dog. The baby has yet to acquire a word for *tree*. But he fills the gap anyway by creating a suitable alternative that communicates much of the essence of the concept—"heavy stick"—when pointing to a tree.

Scenario 5

A 4-year-old spent the weekend with a family member other than her parents. When asked about the adequacy of care, her critical reply is "Very not so good."

Scenario 6

A 6-year-old has decided to give up on backpacking. After one overnight hike, he decided he truly didn't care for the case of "attitude sickness" brought on from overexertion in the high mountains.

These scenarios suggest various features of child language that will be more thoroughly examined in this chapter: its rule-governed nature, its relationship to the meaning of events, and its seeming simplicity as compared with the mature form. However, common across the scenarios is their originality. Child language is a creative endeavor consisting of novel utterances generated by young speakers. These utterances are not merely inaccurate approximations or impoverished imitations of what adults say. What children themselves say is meaningful and usually contextually appropriate, and even when not in a form identical to the adult version, it communicates. Adults

hearing such scenarios—and all parents have their own set of language anecdotes—find them understandable, remarkable, and often humorous. And parents typically delight in their child's speech, rarely correcting it even when it is ungrammatical. Perhaps more so than any other behavioral content, language provides us with a window on the mind, and child language allows a glimpse of the developing mind. It is not surprising, then, that language acquisition is one of the most important topics in cognitive science (Pinker, 1989).

Adult language is a sophisticated domain of knowledge. It is a complex system with a structure and set of specifiable rules that permit the speaker to generate an infinite number of utterances. Infants produce no such utterances, while 4-year-olds are highly articulate. How do young children efficiently internalize the rules governing language so that their speech blossoms in a relatively short time? Moreover, the feat is not only the norm, it is universal. All languages are complex and all children acquire language during early childhood as a function of being human.

Any theory of mind must account for language acquisition—its ubiquity, universality, and human uniqueness. And in the attempts to do so, some familiar theoretical themes emerge. One is the issue of domain specificity: Does language constitute a special domain of knowledge whose principles of organization are not shared with other cognitive domains (Chomsky, 1975, 1986; Fodor, 1983)? If it does, then language acquisition must depend on the acquisition of a special rule system enabled through the operation of a distinct mental organ specially adapted to deciphering language. The explanation of language development must be specific to linguistic content if modularity represents the state of affairs. If accessing the rules governing language production constitutes problem solving of a more generic, domain-general sort that primarily taps the cognitive operations of powerful central processing (Anderson, 1983), then explanations need not refer to a language module specialized for the processing of linguistic input. Some general inductive process will suffice.

Another related theme is the extent to which the ability to acquire language is an innate, biologically determined human capacity. Any theoretical perspective must allow for some sort of innate species-specific capacity in language acquisition; language is, after all, a *human* achievement. The issue is about how complex innate knowledge needs to be to get the job of language learning done. This is where theories differ: the importance placed on innate mechanisms and on the necessary complexity of those mechanisms. For example, perhaps human beings are only equipped with a bias to attend to linguistic stimuli, or perhaps they have a tendency to detect patterns and regularities. The task, then, is to describe how basic biological mechanisms process language "input" in order to arrive at a grammar and a lexicon, but the emphasis is placed on input.

As an alternative, there may be complex innate mechanisms that essentially dictate the form of the behavioral product. Again, biological givens and environmental input interact to yield language development, but without a full description of the innate mechanisms and how they function specific to language, the product becomes unpredictable. So, the task is changed and the emphasis of explanation is on the nature and intricacy of innate mechanisms. Empiricists and nativists do spirited battle, sometimes quite zealously, over the extent of innate language knowledge and over how such knowledge functions as the impetus for language development.

One major catalyst for the contemporary study of language acquisition was Chomsky's, nativist, critical review (1959) of B. F. Skinner's, the supreme empiricist, book *Verbal Behavior* (1957). Skinner explained language acquisition simply as the learning of another behavior elicited, maintained, and shaped by parental application of the principles of operant conditioning to children's verbal responses. Language, in Skinner's view, was not modular, was not domain specific, did not constitute behavior of a special sort, did not require a unique learning mechanism, and was definitely not dependent on the existence of elaborate, language-specific, innate knowledge.

Generally, empiricists deny the necessity of postulating complex, domain-specific capacities to explain behavior. Chomsky took issue with the Skinnerian orientation on language behavior, pointing out, among other things, how theoretically vacuous it was. Using language and its acquisition as an example, Chomsky challenged the utility of general learning principles (e.g., reinforcement), as well as the philosophical framework that gives them prominence, for adequately explaining cognitive phenomena. His arguments so impressed the psychological community at the time that it changed the course of study in language development and, for that matter, cognition in general. So, the philosophical battle lines were drawn and remain drawn, though not to quite the degree seen during the 1950s. And although empiricist ideas persist in modified form, it would be difficult to find a purely operant account of language development in the contemporary literature.

Language acquisition is a highly technical and complicated subject, most of which is beyond the scope of this text. On the other hand, the emergence and elaboration of a child's language is intricately connected with the rest of cognition. We often examine cognitive ability via the vehicle of language; we even use language facility as a reliable marker for general intelligence. In short, cognition and language are sufficiently intertwined that the development of the latter cannot be slighted. Therefore, in this chapter the important conceptual issues in language development, available evidence from empirical study of the phenomenon, and current attempts to account for this most important of human achievements are explored.

The first topic is an analysis of the acquisition task facing the child: What is language and what must the language learner achieve to become a proficient speaker of a language? The second topic is an examination of the objective evidence: What is the course of language development actually like in real children? And the final topic is an inspection and evaluation of the theoretical stories: Which mechanisms can account for what we know about language and about how children become proficient language users?

THE TASK OF ACQUIRING LANGUAGE

If you have ever been in a room surrounded by people speaking a foreign language unknown to you, perhaps you have some taste of the enormity of the task facing the young would-be language learner. The stream of sounds is rapid and unintelligible; it is not obvious where the stream breaks into meaningful units. You would not automatically be able to seize upon the properties of the speech stream that are relevant to this particular variety of linguistic expression—something you do effortlessly and automatically with your own language. With a strange language, you would be challenged to pick out a word, a phrase, or a sentence, or to connect the sounds with the events and objects to which they refer. Only where the sound units, phrases, and such are similar to your native tongue would you demonstrate much expertise.

But the youngster acquiring a first language has no native tongue. The language learner's task is to somehow pair the indefinite number of sounds to the indefinite number of meanings (Gleitman, Gleitman, Landau, & Wanner, 1988), given a rich, complicated acoustic milieu and the many possible

things there are in the world to talk about. However, the number of tenable hypotheses possible for linking speech sound to meaningful referents is infinite.

Language is describable as a complex set of rule systems for pairing sound with meaning such that communication between speakers becomes possible. First, there is a rule system governing which specific sounds should qualify as speech sounds, since the human vocal apparatus is capable of producing many. This rule system is **phonology,** and the **phonemes** are the units of sound included in a language. Every language uses a finite set of phonemes as the building blocks of speech, and the sets vary across different languages. *R* and *L,* for example, are differentiated phonemes in English, but these sounds are not distinguished in Japanese. Other phoneme contrasts irrelevant in English are important distinctions in other languages, so not all sounds are language phonemes. The child must identify the set that will be relevant to the language of her social community. And some of the distinctions come slowly.

Second, there is a rule system for putting sounds together into meaningful units. This is **morphology,** the rules governing the formation of **morphemes**—words and additions to words that carry meaning. *Dog* is a morpheme; *dog/s* is two morphemes because the added *s* denotes multiple individuals. *Travel* is one morpheme; *travel/ed* is two—the *ed* indicating a past action. Some morphemes are *free* morphemes that can stand alone as meaningful units; *dog* and *travel* qualify. Others are *bound* morphemes, like the *-s* and *-ed,* which have meaning only when connected to other units. As children develop, the length of their utterances increases, and the number of morphemes per expression grows. Those who study language development quantify this growth with an index called **mean length utterance** (MLU). The index is a measure of the average number of morphemes in a child's speech sample at a given point in development.

An interesting feature of words underscores an important characteristic of language: The connection between the word and its referent is totally arbitrary. In English, *dog* identifies a particular mammal, but some other combination of sounds—*glub* or *wap*—could do just as well. There is no inherent similarity between the signified and the signifier. Language is an arbitrary symbolic system, unlike some others. For example, in spatial representation, the symbol (i.e., map) has a real correspondence, a true similarity, to the thing represented (i.e., spatial region). Only a very few language symbols (e.g., words like *buzz* or *swish*) demonstrate a correspondence in sound to the referent. Most connections between word and referent are not of this nature. Once the connection is made, however, it cannot be arbitrarily changed; we cannot use the word *dog* to signify a feline, a party, a thunderstorm, or some other noncaninelike entity.

Morphemes are connected in linearly ordered strings to form sentences and phrases: "The cat chased the mouse." "It is raining." "Who did John hit?" The rule system governing the generation of phrases and sentences is **syntax** or grammar. Based on a grammar, all sentences in a language, but no nonsentences, can be generated (Pinker, 1979). So, syntax is the set of rules for the organization of words into well-formed, understandable sentences. The arrangement and sequencing of words specifies the relationship of the words to one another, and it is what makes a sentence more than the sum of the meanings of the words in it. In short, syntax is about sentence structure, and structure both implicates meaning and affects comprehensibility.

Although sentences are formed in accord with syntactical rules, those sentences are about things, states, and events in the world. There is a connection between utterances and happenings; sentences have meanings. **Seman-tics** links language to its referents. Words refer to entities out there in the world; sentences describe happenings, occurrences, and states in that world. The words in a sentence fill semantic categories such as AGENT, PATIENT, GOAL. In English, the subject of the verb is frequently the AGENT, the doer of an action, as in "Dean broke the bike." The object—the receiver of the action, in this case "bike"—is often the PATIENT. Sometimes the PATIENT can also function as a subject, as in "The bike broke." In this way, the sentence tells us what happened to an entity as a consequence of the action of another entity. These semantic relations, the themes words play in sentences, also constrain the sensibility of utterances.

And, finally, language is used in a social context: Individuals communicate with other indviduals. The social conventions, the rule system governing how language is used, are referred to as **pragmatics.** Turn taking in conversation is an example, as is the use of greetings and saying "thank you" and "please" in accord with cultural expectation. It is disconcerting when people do not adhere to social convention in their use of language. Indeed, some rule breaking, for example, interrupting a speaker, elicits negative social sanctions.

To summarize, language encompasses the structuring of sounds (or signs) into organized units logically patterned to describe events in the world and to be used in a social context. Aspects of all these rule systems—phonology, morphology, syntax, semantics, pragmatics—can either be constant or can vary across the different natural languages people in the world speak. Within a given linguistic community, possessing expertise in language means exhibiting mastery of all the rules sufficiently well to communicate—to produce meaningful utterances and to comprehend what is said in return. *Knowing* a language corresponds to knowing the set of rules for producing and recognizing sentences in the language; *learning* language corresponds to inducing that set of rules. But does the learner start the induction process from scratch?

The Impossibility of Learning Language

If we propose that the child learns language from scratch, then we must first determine if the task can be accomplished by any learner. The essence of this judgment is whether we can conceive of any learning device or program sufficiently powerful to induce the rules governing language from the input data—the finite set of utterances a child hears during her first few years of life. The child's input is simultaneously enormous—she will hear thousands of utterances—and limited. She will not be exposed to all varieties of possible language constructions, nor will she be exposed to language in written text. What she will hear is oral language produced by a limited number of speakers talking about a limited number of subjects in a limited variety of contexts. To address the feasibility of language acquisition, we would have to determine whether our hypothetical learning device is able to induce the four major rule systems governing language from this data set.

Rules are not the same as sentences. The former are abstract, general, and subtle and govern the formation of large classes of sentences. In order to produce sentences, the learner must acquire the abstractions and disembed them from the context of the specific utterances heard, which exemplify the rules. Across utterances, the words and the context are variables. To acquire the rule, the learner must detect the constants, the regularity, across the variation. Drawing a parallel to visual perception (recall Chapter 2), the learner must extract the invariants when faced with stimuli in a state of flux.

Language is *constrained*. A constraint is a negative statement about a language (Fodor & Crain, 1987). That means there are restrictions on the class of utterances qualifying as correct and acceptable sentences. The class would be larger if there were no constraints operating. So, constraints limit what can be said and still be understood. For example, the utterance, "Jenny can ride a two-wheel bicycle," is meaningful, appropriate, and correctly formed. But the utterance, "Jenny ride bicycle can two-wheel a," is meaningless, inappropriate, and incorrectly formed. "Cheese pizza" and "pizza cheese" have different meanings as a function of word order. Order is constrained in the production of meaningful sentences in English. The competent speaker must have access to implicit knowledge of the constraints to generate correctly formed sentences and to accurately distinguish those instances from meaningless, garbled, noninstances.

The grammar of the language encapsulates the constraints and functions as a set of specifications enabling the production of any and all possible acceptable sentences in a language. The task for the language learner, then, is to extract this set of specifications from a finite set of instances. It turns out that this is actually quite impossible. There is an infinite set of grammars that can "explain" a finite set of utterances. According to Pinker (1979), it is "impossible for *any* learner to observe a finite sample of sentences of a language and always produce a correct grammar for the language" (p. 225). In sum, for any finite data set, the group of possible rule systems that could potentially be induced from the sample sentences is simply too large (see Pinker, 1989).

Suppose the language-learning scenario went something like this: In the process of extracting rules governing language from environmental input (e.g., sample sentences), the learner hypothesizes a plausible rule from the data. Since the learner has yet to identify the constraints on language constructions, the exact set of correct rules (and hence the set of all correct constructions) is unknown. As a consequence, the learner's plausible language will include constructions outside the restricted set of the target language. The state of affairs can be conceptualized as circles, as depicted in Figure 9-1. One alternative representation is of partially overlapping circles and another, concentric circles.

Envisioning this state of affairs as concentric circles, the inside smaller circle represents the target language, while the outside larger circle is the learner's plausible language. To solve the language induction problem, those language constructions falling outside the smaller circle (or beyond the Circle A in the partially overlapping model) must be abandoned. So, our learner, with hypothetical rule in hand, generates a test sentence. If we provide our learner with a "language informant" of some sort, the learner can try out the test sentence on the informant and obtain infor-

FIGURE 9-1 *Relationships among the Set of Plausible Languages (B) and the Target Language (A) a Learner Must Acquire.*
To be competent in a language, the learner must abandon the usages that lie outside Circle A.

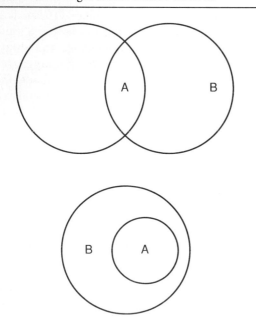

mation about the validity of the rule. So, for example, the learner, who has been exposed to lots of input about how to form the past tense by adding *-ed*—as in fish*ed,* stopp*ed,* travel*ed,* walk*ed,* and so forth—creates the plausible test sentence, "I goed to the park".

This scenario points to one role for the environment in language learning. An effective means for restricting the group of candidate constructions on an a posteriori basis is if the environment affords feedback about the formation of utterances. Sentences generated in accord with *the* correct rules are reinforced while others are rejected. The negative evidence is particularly important because it applies to those constructions falling outside the circle formed by the target language. In short, negative feedback provided for inappropriate sentence instances serves as a unique source of linguistic information. Then, gradually, the language learner can differentiate instances of rule-governed language from those that are not and can pare down the circle of possible constructions to the limits of the target circle.

But is this scenario realistic? There are serious reservations as to whether the environment supplies this sort of feedback. Apparently, there is little negative data available to the learner, that is, little information about what is *not* in a language (Baker, 1979; Wexler & Culicover, 1980).

First, most of what people say is appropriate; there are relatively few mistakes. So noninstances are really statistical rarities providing little if any opportunity for a learner to observe what *not* to do. When you consider the sheer number of violations possible in a constrained system as compared to the relatively few forms allowable, many more errors should be observed. Even children do not violate syntactic rules to the degree expected under the hypothesis of trial-and-error learning.

Second, negative feedback is seldom provided when sentences are grammatically wrong, especially in the case of young children beginning to speak. In a classic study, Brown and Hanlon (1970) found that parents did not provide feedback to young speakers contingent on grammar. Instead, parents were more apt to respond on the basis of the potential truthfulness of an utterance than on the basis of its well-formedness. Although appropriately stated, "The cow is blue" invites parental correction since cows seldom come in that hue. "Look, cow brown" lacks grammatical touches but would be accepted as a legitimate observation. Others (Demetras & Post, 1985; Hirsch-Pasek, Treiman, & Schneiderman, 1984) have reiterated the observation of a lack of parental input and correction.

It does not appear that young language learners get much if any systematic negative feedback for their syntax, and what feedback they do get underdetermines the correctness of their productions. So, the environment does not provide the learner with a reliable "language informant," which raises an important question: What would dispose a child who used inappropriate sentences—for example, "Look what I builded." "I deaded the cockroach." "Why the baby crying?"—to abandon the usage in the absence of corrective feedback?

If constraints are negative statements about language, that is, what *cannot* be said, and if there exists no negative data available from which to acquire information about the constraints, then how can the constraints be learned? This is a paradox of language learning. To create correct sentences, an individual has to have some sort of knowledge of the constraints, but little if any information is available to permit this knowledge acquisition. Learning of language from scratch is, in short, highly implausible. This paradox leads many to conclude that constraints must be unlearned; they must operate a priori (Chomsky & Lasnik, 1977).

Still another problem for language learners is deciphering the connection between words and their referents in the real world. As was pointed out in Chapter 4, the context in which a child first hears a word is extremely complex. Why would the child necessarily conclude that a label for an object, for instance, *rabbit,* refers to the whole animal rather than to some feature of the rabbit, some uniqueness of the context in which the rabbit is found, some idiosyncratic behavior the rabbit is exhibiting, and so forth. Again, the potential hypotheses for connecting words with referents are simply too numerous to enable efficient learning. Indeed, the possible connections could be infinite.

Given that (1) the possible connections between sounds and meanings are infinite; (2) the possible rules inferable from a set of sample sentences are infinite; and (3) the possible connections between words and referents are also infinite, the induction problem in language learning is simply outrageous. Our hypothetical learner cannot learn language from scratch; we are going to have to provide some help. Help comes in the form of built-in biases that function to restrict the set of potential hypotheses about language constructions the learner ever entertains in the first place.

Recall from Chapter 1 that the concept of constraints is important in developmental theory because knowledge of the constraints governing a cognitive domain limits the hypothesis space about what can be true in the domain. A priori knowledge of the constraints on language would function just this way. Some possible but incorrect hypotheses about linguistic constructions would simply never be considered, and hence negative data about the validity of the constructions would not be needed. Then, the nature of the theoretical problem changes. While the young child is going to acquire a language during early childhood, he has the capacity to learn *any* language in that time. If we attribute too little or too unelaborate a priori knowledge of language to the child, we cannot explain the reality of universal acquisition. If we attribute too much, too specific, or too elaborate a priori knowledge, we risk being unable to explain the flexibility of the language forms children do acquire. The problem is to identify the particular constraints that will do the job.

Some Facts about the Formal Nature of Language

An important notion in cognitive development is the distinction often made between competence and performance. Competence is the status of an individual's underlying knowledge displayed in, but not identical to, performance. Performance is subject to the vagaries of situational and utilization factors that mediate the production of what is known. So, performance cannot always be used to evaluate unambiguously what an individual knows. We usually assume that the degree of competence is greater than what is revealed in observed performance. This is a reasonable assumption. How could a person accomplish a cognitive or linguistic act (performance) for which an underlying knowledge base (competence) did not exist?

In language development, competence denotes tacit knowledge of the rules forming the foundation for the generation of sentences, knowledge that is essential to rule-governed language production. Performance is the less than perfect reflection of tacit knowledge. In speaking, we exhibit false starts, use incomplete sentences, misuse or incorrectly choose words, and make grammatical errors on occasion, but not necessarily because of inadequate language competence. Rather, the context may distract us, competing thoughts and activities may interfere, or another speaker may interrupt us, and so forth.

When explaining the language capabilities of young children, competence is the focus. However, performance data comprise the language sample. But, it is not always easy to link the two such that performance is diagnostic of competence. This is particularly true because children's sentences are normally short. Short

sentences simply cannot allow for the demonstration of intricate language knowledge even if the child possessed it (Bloom, 1990a). With language, the relationship between production and knowledge is particularly complicated. Competency itself is decomposable into multiple levels of knowledge.

Chomsky (1957, 1965), who sought to produce a competence theory of language, distinguished between the surface structure of a language and its deep structure. **Deep structure** is the underlying organization of an utterance as expressed in an abstract code or representation, a sort of "mathematics of language." **Surface structure,** on the other hand, is the external version of the sentence, as in the string of words actually produced in a spoken message. This surface structure is language specific, because the details of how something is said vary somewhat across different language families. So, language competency includes knowledge of surface structure and sentence formation and knowledge of that underlying, deeper structure.

An elaborate system of rules is required to arrive at the deep structure from the surface form and to translate deep structure into the surface version. For Chomsky, a **transformational grammar** describes how translations are possible across levels. **Phrase-structure rules** generate a sentence's deep structure; **transformational rules** generate the surface structure. When comprehending language, the incoming surface structure string is translated, in accord with these rule systems, into its deep-structure message. When producing language, the order of the processing is reversed.

Phrase-structure grammar enables the decomposition of a complete sentence into its subcomponents or *constituents* and specifies the relationship between those constituents. For example, consider the sentence (*S*): "The boy kicked a football." This sentence can be decomposed into two major components: (1) a noun phrase (*NP*)—"the boy"—and, (2) a verb phrase (*VP*)—"kicked the football." A short-hand for the outcome of the decomposition is $S \rightarrow NP + VP$. Then each phrase can be further decomposed. The *NP* is analyzed into a determiner (*D*) and the noun (*N*), or $NP \rightarrow D + N$; the *VP* is reexpressed as a verb (*V*) and a noun phrase, or $VP \rightarrow V + NP$, and the last *NP* becomes $NP \rightarrow D + N$. The result of the component analysis is described via a tree diagram that schematizes the abstract structure underlying this particular sample utterance. An example with this sentence appears in Figure 9-2.

This deep structure is manipulated in a variety of ways (through transformation rules) to generate other related surface structures, such as a passive sentence—"A football was kicked by the boy."—or a question—"Did the boy kick a football?" These transformation rules encapsulate the generational nature of language; a multitude of surface forms can be produced from a finite syntactic core.

If language is envisioned as multileveled, then constraints can operate at each level. There are language-specific constraints that limit the acceptable sentence formations for a particular language. This is the sense of grammar most of us are familiar with—the rules for constructing declaratives, questions, and the like in our own language. At a more basic, foundational level, however, there are constraints applying to all languages. The family of natural languages is restricted; not all possible languages are represented in the sample people in the world actually speak.

Again, if existing languages and all possible languages are represented as concentric circles, then the natural languages constitute the smaller, interior of the two circles, and constraints are implicated. Since there are constraints that apply to all languages as a set, then there must be language **universals,** principles of grammar governing the acceptability of utterances generatable in any language system. Indeed, it turns out that languages do not vary without limit, and there is a large number of universal properties shared by all languages (Comrie, 1981; Greenberg, 1978; Shopen, 1985). A **universal grammar** is a set of specifications for the shape of permissible kinds of languages (Chomsky, 1965, 1975, 1980).

Language systems vary, but the variation exhibited is bounded. Linguists attempt to characterize those bounds (Goodluck, 1986) in part by comparing and analyzing the sorts of sentence strings represented in languages. By focusing on exemplar sentences in languages and contrasting them with unacceptable and anomalous strings, the linguist can describe the formal characteristics of the "finished product," that is, sentences producible by a fully competent speaker of a language. This analysis yields the end state of language acquisition, and the end state sets limits on the developmental story. Because of this fact, linguistics becomes one source of hypotheses for the developmental psychologist examining child language, and formal theories of language sometimes serve as conceptual models for language acquisition.

Languages are organized. Some, including English, impose relatively rigid word orders

FIGURE 9-2 *A Tree Diagram Depicting the Analysis of the Sentence, "The boy kicked the football," Broken into its Constituents.*

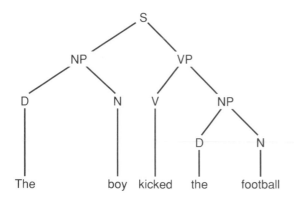

on sentences; others do not. Three frequent word orders characteristically found in human languages are:

1. Subject-Verb-Object (SVO).
2. Subject-Object-Verb (SOV).
3. Verb-Subject-Object (VSO).

With order rules, phrases and sentences can be embedded within one another yielding a hierarchical structure. For example, the sentence "The boys played ball" can be embedded in the larger string, "She is thinking about the boys who played ball," or even "He knows she is thinking about the boys playing ball."

Essentially, phrases function as modifiers for other phrases. Depending on the preferred basic word-order type, the embedded phrases will be placed in different locations in the string. Placement, in turn, influences the outcome of how a transformation affects the string, as in transforming a declarative into a question or substituting a pronoun to reference a noun. Since languages are structured and cohesive, a single decision, for example, whether SVO or SOV is the preferred order in a language, has cascading effects throughout the language on what else can be said (Goodluck, 1986).

The rules in a language system are not independent. Given one rule, only certain others will be compatible with it, and remaining rules are not free to vary. If subsequent rules in a particular language are not free to vary and instead follow from some very basic prior rules, then each sentence the learner hears actually could carry a great deal of information about allowable constructions in the target language.

Linguistic analysis suggests that learning language could proceed plausibly if the learner had access to tacit knowledge of the limits on possible language systems. The knowledge would place some constraints on the kinds of errors the learner would make, acting as a sort of mandate against hypothesizing "wild" grammars. Since a universal grammar func-

tions as a set of blueprints for possible languages to be learned, access to such knowledge would simplify the task of linguistic knowledge acquisition by babies and young children.

THE FACTS OF LANGUAGE DEVELOPMENT

Explaining language acquisition begins with describing what language children produce as they develop the ability to communicate. This descriptive record is the data, and just like formal linguistic analysis, it, too, places limits on the plausibility of a theoretical story. Any such story must account for and predict these data. From the record, it is possible to chart the *sequence* with which certain language forms arise, to estimate the *timing* of the linguistic landmarks (e.g., first words, first multiword combinations), and to identify acquisition *universals,* landmarks that show up in virtually all children's language records.

Information about sequence, timing, and developmental universals reveals whether or not young children display any systematic bias in what language they learn and when they learn it. Bias reflects a tendency to follow one particular developmental route toward the final product—competent use of language—rather than some other route. That is essentially what happens when the set of potential final products is restricted from the onset. In this way, bias will result from the action of constraints in the language-acquisition process. So by looking at the input—what others say to babies and young children—and at the output—what babies and young children produce in their own language samples—we attempt to decipher how the learning process gets started and the nature of the course it takes.

But how do we get that record? There are basically two methods. A common and widely used technique is simply to collect naturalistic accounts of what children say both within and across different languages. The data base is a dairy of sorts, recording the spontaneous utterances of subjects and the circumstances surrounding those utterances. The records, of course, require intensive collection and usually can only involve a small number of children (see Brown, 1973). However, the records from different investigators are compiled and shared thereby increasing the total sample. Developmental psycholinguists collect their sample of sentences to analyze just as other linguists do; the difference is the source of those sentences—actual child speech. Subsequently, wider samples are collected as a test of whether a particular conclusion, inferred from the data of a few, is generalizable to the many (deVilliers & deVilliers, 1973, 1978) and generalizable across languages.

A second method, also widely used, is the controlled experiment. In language experiments, the investigator elicits a particular language sample from children in a setting in which the context is carefully controlled. For instance, a child may hear a series of utterances: "Big Bird patted Ernie," "Ernie patted Big Bird," "Ernie was patted by Big Bird." Then the child may be asked to act out the sentence with puppets or perhaps to select a picture of the action described. Then, the investigator can evaluate whether the child understood the action signified by the words, structure, and syntax of the utterance. In the example, a child who is not yet able to deal with a passive construction might be misled, possibly by the order of the words, into thinking it was Ernie doing the patting in the third sample utterance.

Sometimes, made-up words are used as stimuli in experimental studies. These artificial stimuli function to test the child's understanding of abstract language rules. For instance, a child might be shown a picture of an entity and told: "This is a zat." Then the child is shown a picture of two such entities and

asked to complete the phrase: "Now there are two _____." A child who can utilize the rule for forming regular plurals in English should supply *zats* for the phrase ending. Experiments like this (see for e.g., Berko, 1958) are very useful in attempts to gauge the extent to which children comprehend and use the rules governing the formation of utterances, even though their rule knowledge may only be tacit. Then again, the child may be taught the *zat*-object connection and asked which of a set of like objects also qualify as *zats*. The child's choices reveal the basis on which he is willing to generalize a noun to other entities (see for e.g., Jones, Smith, & Landau, 1991).

The intense and careful study of a few children allows for the compilation of information about the natural course of language development in ecologically valid environments—those in which children are engaged in communicating about things of concern to them. Then, the extension of the same sort of descriptive methodology to a larger group of children enables a test of the generality of language phenomena originally observed with just a few. Since the aim of the research is often to identify common, if not universal, features of language development, the generality of specific acquisitions is a fundamental concern. Finally, those descriptive accounts serve as the basis for the formulation of specific hypotheses about how language development proceeds. The experiment provides a context for testing and evaluating those hypotheses.

In language development, meaning is paired with sound or sign; the sounds (signs) are acoustical (gestural) information provided as environmental input to the learner. So, it follows that to fully understand the acquisition process, we must evaluate that input and determine what role it plays, what contribution it makes to learning. What do babies hear (see)? It might seem intuitive that the baby's linguistic milieu will be extremely complex and varied, but that is a judgment made from an adult perspective. The nature and extent of the complexity and variability in the input from the infant's perspective could differ.

Input to Language Acquisition

Recall from Chapter 2, research has shown us that even very young infants are sensitive to the acoustical characteristics that differentiate phonetic units in language (Kuhl, 1987). For example, babies under 4 months of age can already discriminate many, if not all, of the phonetic distinctions made in English (Eilers, 1980; Eimas & Tartter, 1979; Kuhl, 1979; Morse, 1978), and the capacity does not seem to be a function of the specific linguistic environment in which infants are reared. Such responsivity to language sounds is an impressive feat; it is all the more remarkable because babies demonstrate this precocious responsivity before they systematically produce the sounds themselves and before they have had sufficient time for extensive exposure to the input.

The capacity is not limited to an ability to discriminate sounds presented in isolation, for even in larger contexts, as when phonetic units are embedded in multisyllabic strings, discrimination is still observed (Jusczyk, Copan, & Thompson, 1978; Goodsitt, Morse, Ver Hoeve, & Cowan, 1984). As expected, discriminability is made more difficult as the context of the input becomes more complex. There are data, however, showing how infants recognize similarity among syllables if those units share initial consonants or share other phonetic features (Hillenbrand, 1983, 1984; Kuhl, 1980). In short, young infants come equipped with an initial set of capabilities particularly well suited for processing the raw material necessary for language learning.

Responsivity to the sounds of a language is a start, but babies must detect how the sound is segmented. Conversation forms a stream of sound. Essential to comprehension is the ability to pick out the pieces from the flow onto which meaning will be mapped. The language sounds babies hear directed to them is streamlike, not disconnected instances of individual sounds. Breaking up the stream at the correct points can be a difficult task. This is attested to by the observation that even older children make mistakes (recall the "My Ami Vice" example at the beginning of the chapter). Segmentation errors underscore the difficulties inherent in organizing the sound flow into the correct chunks. But errors aside, for the most part, children talk in whole words, not halves of words or words-and-a-half (Gleitman, Gleitman, Landau, & Wanner, 1988).

The environment may provide the baby with some assistance in what is called child-directed (CD) speech or **motherese** (Snow & Ferguson, 1977). Although adult speech to babies and children is connected, just as adult speech to other adults is, there are some important differences. Child-directed speech is simpler in syntactic form and semantic content. An exaggerated intonation and a slower tempo make CD speech acoustically different in prosodic character (Fernald & Simon, 1984). Some of these prosodic modifications include higher pitch, more distinctive pitch contours, slower tempo, longer pauses, and increased emphatic stress, all of which give "motherese" a distinct "song" (Garnica, 1977; Newport, Gleitman & Gleitman, 1977; Papousek, Papousek, & Bourstein, 1985).

There are other differences between CD and adult-directed speech as well. The former is characterized by fewer words per utterance, more repetition, better articulation, and decreased structural complexity. Because of the character of CD speech, the adjusted input directed at babies is different in important ways from what adults hear most of the time. That difference may exploit the acoustical sensitivities with which babies come equipped.

Mothers use this special speech with babies not only in English-speaking communities but in other language communities, too (Cooper & Aslin, 1990; Fernald & Simon, 1977; Grieser & Kuhl, 1988). And babies, even newborns and 1-month-olds, prefer CD speech to the adult-directed variety (Cooper & Aslin, 1990). Apparently, the enhanced acoustical features of CD speech elicit and maintain infant attention (Fernald, 1985; Werker & McLeod, 1989). In this way, the attention function of CD speech could facilitate the infant's detection and discrimination of segmental contrasts (Kemler-Nelson, Hirsch-Pasek, Jusczyk, & Wright-Cassidy, 1989).

So, because of the way adults automatically and nondeliberately talk to babies, the babies' task in segmenting the speech stream may be made easier than it at first seems. The sound streams babies hear, differentially attend to, and prefer are special. Gleitman and associates (1988) referred to this as a **natural coadaptation** where mothers are inclined to provide a particular sort of input to which babies are particularly inclined to attend.

As their child grows and language develops, parents adjust their CD speech in accord with the child's needs. Parents increase the complexity of what they say in accord with the child's progress and simplify utterances when the child seems not to understand (Bohannon & Warren-Leubecker, 1988). Two techniques, **recasts** and **expansions,** occur when a parent restates what a child says, thereby reformulating and/or extending the child's production into a more mature, sometimes more correct form (Bohannon & Stanowitz, 1988). A parent hearing a child say "Dog go!" may elaborate the sentence making it, "Yes, its time for the dog to go outside." "Daddy work" may become "Daddy is going to work now." "Mommy horse" expands into "Mommy is riding her horse." Then, of course, parents are always restating and paraphrasing their children's early sentences in order to translate for other listeners. Usually, it takes a well-trained ear to decipher the essence of a message delivered in a phonetically truncated, and often bungled, early utterance.

Parents do not use child-directed speech deliberately in an attempt to teach language to their children. More likely, parents employ it unconsciously because it works both to get youngsters attention and to get them to obey. Nor does CD appear to be a necessary precondition for language acquisition. Investigators have generally failed to discover a strong relationship between the extent of maternal speech adjustments and infants' level of language development (Gleitman, Newport, & Gleitman 1984; Murray, Johnson, & Peters, 1990; Scarborough & Wyckoff, 1986). And while "motherese" is a pervasive phenomenon, its role in syntactic development remains particularly unclear (Bohannon & Hirsch-Pasek, 1984; Furrow & Nelson, 1986).

"Motherese" does not qualify as *the* mechanism responsible for language acquisition. The stress patterns, however, that typify "motherese" may facilitate the task for the child already prepared by nature to seize upon linguistically relevant features of the sound stream. Stress makes thing acoustically salient. The sound stream is bracketed by stress into words and bracketed by intonation into the phrases marking clauses (Gleitman & Wanner, 1984; 1988). In "motherese," these stress patterns are exaggerated, potentially making the breaks associated with segmentation even more highly salient. It is, therefore, noteworthy that it is the stressed items that show up earlier in development than nonstressed items (Gleitman & Wanner, 1988). Perhaps sensitivity to the sound characteristics of "motherese" serves as a kind of *bootstrap* that enables the young learner to extract linguistically functional units from what would otherwise be too unmarked and too continuous a sound stream.

Researchers in the social learning tradition (Bandura, 1986) have emphasized the role of **imitation** in children's acquisition of conceptual rules, including language rules (Rosenthal

& Zimmerman, 1978; Whitehurst & Vasta, 1975; Whitehurst & DeBaryshe, 1989). This is not imitation in the sense of mimickry but of a more general kind. The contention is that the sentences produced by speakers in the child's environment are patterned, rule-governed utterances that differ mainly in content and specifics. Children abstract the rules underlying classes of utterances from exposure to these modeled exemplars. Subsequently, the child uses the abstracted code to guide generation of new utterances—unique in particular words, but rule governed nonetheless. Imitation, then, is of the sentence *form* and does not yield a sentence *match* (Snow, 1983; Whitehurst & Novak, 1973).

Since CD speech is limited in the range of linguistic forms modeled (i.e., sentences tend to be shorter and less structurally complex), the number of syntactic rules that actually vary across sample utterances may be limited, too. So, there might actually be only a few regularities or patterns that describe the multitude of specific exemplars. In that case, the few regularities would be more salient which, from a social learning perspective, should facilitate rule acquisition. Then again, remember that rules within a language are interconnected and not free to vary. So, the acquisition of a single rule limits the potential variability in the rules yet to be acquired. Rule learning from models could be *progressive:* With each rule acquired, the range of plausible patterns extractible from subsequent utterances is smaller than it otherwise would have been. There have been many experimental demonstrations of the feasibility of the acquisition of rules through imitative learning. Also, children are proficient at regularity detection (Maratsos, 1982) and do notice consistent linguistic patterns.

The implications of the outcomes of modeling studies, however, are ambiguous. Regularity detection and the extraction of rules from modeled input are possible strategies for acquiring language from input. It is not clear what conceptual basis gives rise to those strategies, or why the right regularities are the ones attended to. The issue is whether observational learning of general rules constitutes an *explanation* for language development or a phenomenon in language development to be explained. We do not know which mechanism enables the child to pick up the correct patterns from varied input.

"Motherese," expansions, recasts, clarification questions, and modeled rule-governed exemplars are all instances of *positive evidence;* they provide information about what *to* say. A big concern in language acquisition, however, is *negative evidence*—input about what *not* to say. As noted earlier, descriptive data reveal an absence of negative input to children. So, it is not clear why children would abandon an incorrect form—constructions like "I deaded the bug," I ated the cookie," "The movie was very not so funny," "Give it to me the milk," and "Button me my blouse"—in the absence of correction. The utterances communicate and parents are not apt to react negatively unless the statements are untrue.

Little if any overt input is available to explain the subsequent substitution of grammatically correct replacements for earlier versions. What then would be the impetus for a switch? At various points during the course of language development, children do make regular mistakes. They later abandon those forms for correct versions. Why? The "no negative evidence" problem remains a real challenge for any theory of language acquisition.

The Output:
Child Language

The empirical literature shows us that babies are by nature sensitive to input relevant to language. They seem biologically prepared to develop language as a function of species membership. And the environment provides them with an abundance of data to fuel acquisition. Still, infants under 1 year of age do not use language. They do not utter words or sentences or engage in conversation. They do lots of other languagelike things, however, that are precursors to the monumental accomplishments to come.

The preverbal period. From birth, babies make noises. The initial noises are physiological in nature—sounds associated with respiration, eating, signaling discomfort (crying), and so forth (Kaplan & Kaplan, 1971). Gurgling is an apt description of these initial noises, and they are distinctively not language. By around 2 months of age, *gooing* emerges when babies begin producing single-syllable vowel sounds ("ah," "oo") and consonant-vowel sounds ("goo," "ba," "da"). These more languagelike *babbles* are frequently accompanied by signs of positive emotion, such as smiling and laughing (Blount, 1982). By 6 months, babies engage in *reduplicative babbling* (Ferguson, 1983), stringing together identical sounds in chains, as in "bababababa" or "dadadada." For the most part, the repeated sounds are consonant-vowel combinations. Then, by the end of the first year, babbling loses its reduplicative nature and becomes even more speechlike. Babies start to combine different sounds (*goo + ba + um*) and the stress and intonation patterns make this "speech" appear conversationlike without intelligible words (Clumech, 1980). It is in this late phase of babbling that infants produce many of the sounds they will produce in their first true words (Ferguson & Macken, 1983; Vihman & Miller, 1988).

Preverbal development is probably a maturationally driven phenomenon (deVilliers & deVilliers, 1978; Sachs, 1985). In terms of maturational sequence, these preverbal sound patterns are not random; they follow a predictable course (Oller, 1986; Roug, Lundberg & Lundberg, 1989; Stark, 1986). Generally, that course is from limited babbling—only a few sounds represented—to a broad range of sounds, to the speechlike babbles of the 12-month-old. Also, children from different language backgrounds are very similar in bab-

bling development despite those differences (Anderson & Smith, 1987; Oller & Eilers, 1982) and produce a similar repertoire of early sounds.

Like hearing babies, deaf babies and babies of deaf parents babble even though they receive different sorts of acoustical input (Lenneberg, Rebelsky, & Nichols, 1965; Stoel-Gammon & Otomo, 1986), but for infants with hearing disabilities, there appears to be a delay in the onset of reduplicated babbling and a reduced number of well-formed syllables. Some investigators question whether complex forms of verbal babbling occur at all in these babies (Oller & Eilers, 1988). Recently, however, Pettito and Marenette (1991) observed that deaf babies "babble" with sign gestures at exactly the same age babies exposed to English do. Given how similar the phonetic development of babbling is across infants of quite different language groups, biological processes simply must play a role in this behavioral accomplishment if the regularity is to be explained.

Toward the end of the first year, while still maintaining speechlike babbles, babies produce their first true words with clear meaning. The origins of the first word invite speculation. Perhaps word use gradually emerges from early languagelike forms. Origination could result from a **babbling drift** (Brown, 1958) where babbles become increasingly wordlike as a consequence of feedback from the environment. Were this the case, then babbling should initially contain many sounds, only some of which are like the phonemes in the child's target language. With feedback, that range should narrow until the class of target phonemes is what remains.

Although there is some evidence in favor of a babbling drift (Kuhl & Meltzoff, 1988), preverbal development does not generally follow this course. Babbling begins with a narrow set of sounds, then conversely, the sound range expands by the end of the first year when word use begins. Arguments for and against the origins of language in babbles and the relevance of babbling to true language production depend on the perspective we assume on the continuity between babbling and true speech. In accepting babbling drift, we are assuming a continuity view. However, verbalizations change when babies begin using words, a change that signals evidence of discontinuity as well.

The shift from babbling to word use is a gradual one (Bates, O'Connell, & Shore, 1967). Late in the first year, babies begin uttering certain sounds and sound combinations more frequently. For the author's son, one of these was "bubba". Then, the frequent combinations are attached to particular objects, situations, or people (for "bubba" it was the family pets, bugs, horses and so forth), so the sounds are wordlike in use. But, since these terms do not always correspond or sometimes even resemble an adult form, word use is not necessarily identified.

Before long, however, forms become clearly recognizable—"dada" in the father's presence, "baa" when playing with a round thing, or "caa" as the family feline jumps onto the bed. Typically, parents notice clear first words when babies are 11 to 12 months of age; the range is from 8 to 18 months (Whitehurst, 1982). Babbling continues, along with gesturing and other attempts at communication (Dobrich & Scarborough, 1984; Vihman & Miller, 1988). **Jargon stretches,** babbled sequences with real words embedded in them (Mcnyuk, Menn, & Silber, 1986), also occur.

Early lexical development.   While production of the first word, a developmental landmark for the beginning of language, occurs toward the end of the baby's first year, the addition of more words comes quickly. By 18 months, the average child has a **lexicon,** a vocabulary, of about 50 spoken words (Benedict, 1979). This is when many investigators report observing a **naming explosion,** a phenomenon wherein babies start connecting labels to virtually everything. Apparently, about this time babies realize words are symbols that can be attached to things (Goldfield & Reznick, 1990; Gopnik & Meltzoff, 1987b). By age 6, the lexicon has grown to about 14,000 words (Templin, 1957), so between 18 months and 6 years, children add about nine new words per day to their vocabulary (Clark, 1983). Through a process of **fast mapping,** children are able to connect a new word to its referent after only a brief encounter (Carey, 1978).

There are regularities in these early vocabularies. First words generally refer to manipulable or moving objects (*ball, doggie, truck*) and events that have salient properties of change (*bye-bye, open, up, more*). Rarely do early words refer to objects that just sit there, do not move, or things that are not played with (*chair, window*). Most words in beginning vocabularies are the names of objects and things, that is, nouns. Nouns are understood earlier, spoken earlier and more frequently, and pronounced better than are other classes of words (Caramata & Leonard, 1986; Gentner, 1982; Maratsos, 1988). Children also acquire words for actions (Clark, 1983) and the majority of these are verbs (*go, give, eat*). By at least age 3 and probably much earlier, they can distinguish words for objects and words for actions (Brown, 1957). Children rarely use words for absent objects, disappearing objects (*all gone*), or the outcome of events on objects (*broke*) until they have attained the conceptual knowledge usually associated with Piaget's Sensorimotor Stage 6 (Gopnik & Meltzoff, 1986, 1987a).

In order to enlarge the vocabulary during this early phase of language acquisition, infants must discover the connection between words and their referents in the world. But this is not such an easy feat. Presumably, the connection is facilitated by the provision of **ostensive** definitions, labels in conjunction with pointing. Labeling increases babies' attention to objects even over and above pointing alone (Baldwin & Markman, 1989). With ostensive definitions, however, the precise connection between the thing and its name is still ambiguous.

To make any connection, the language learner has to already have some expectation that a spoken label is related in some way to things in the world; otherwise, the information conveyed in the definition is going to be irrelevant. Then, for any finite amount of information about a new word meaning, there will still be numerous hypotheses that will suffice as a possible connection (Pierce, 1957; Quine, 1960). How is a baby to know that the word *man* refers to a category of individuals rather than to a particular man, what the man is wearing, the fact that the man is smiling or has brown hair, what the man is doing, and so forth? If a baby had to entertain and systematically eliminate all but the first hypothesis, the task would take an inordinate amount of exposure. Perhaps it would not be accomplishable at all. The problem is much like the one alluded to previously—inducing grammatical rules from a finite set of utterances. Word learning is also a problem of induction. And, again, from a finite set of encounters connecting a label and its potential referents, an infinite number of generalizations are possible (Goodman, 1983).

In reality, babies acquire the connections between words and their referents very rapidly during the early expansion of the lexicon. Youngsters must access some set of reasonable beliefs about possible word meanings that enables them to narrow the possibilities. Some construals of word meaning seem to be more "natural" than others. In short, there must be constraints on the process of mapping word and referent.

That, indeed, seems to be the case. First, infants have a word learning bias for nouns. Nouns are the preponderant terms in children's early vocabularies, and nouns are names for things. Some of children's early words are pronouns and proper nouns (*Mommy, Bubba*) which are names for specific things. Remember, one of the first principles babies utilize to organize the perceptual and physical world is the concept of objectness (see Chapters 2, 3, and 6). They conceive of a reality of things as bounded, solid individuals (Spelke, 1991). "Thingness" places a constraint on how babies partition stimuli, and "thing connections" apparently constrain word acquisition as well, a reminder that lexical and conceptual development are mutually intertwined (Waxman, Shipley, & Shepperson, 1991).

Second, children do not treat labels just as names for specific things but as names for categories of things (Markman & Hutchinson, 1984; Waxman & Gelman, 1986; Waxman & Kosowski, 1990). They interpret a new word as an object-category label (Au, 1985; 1990; Baldwin, 1989; Taylor & Gelman, 1988), and if they already have a word for a particular category (e.g., *dog*), then they assume a new word (*coyote*) must refer to another category of things or to a subset of the original category (Taylor & Gelman, 1988, 1989).

In order to explain some of these word-learning biases, investigators have attempted to describe the sorts of word learning constraints that seem to operate during the expansion of the lexicon. Markman (1990) identified two: (1) the *whole-object constraint,* a novel label is likely to refer to a whole object, not its parts, substance, or other properties, and (2) a *taxonomic constraint,* labels refer to objects of the same kind. So, for example, a child learning the word *cat* is biased in assuming that the word references a whole animal and a class of like whole animals at that.

Consistent with these biases is the observation that children do not treat new words as synonyms for old ones and resist accepting two labels for the same object (Hutchinson, 1986; Macnamara, 1982; Markman & Wachtel, 1988). The author's son emphatically denied that the thorny tree in the backyard could be both an "owie bush" and a mesquite, or that "Bubba" was simultaneously a dog and a

Golden Retriever. For little ones, two words denote two categories of things, and those categories are apt to be mutually exclusive (Markman, 1989; Markman & Wachtel, 1988). The operating bias for young children is that objects can only have one name. In **lexical contrast theory,** Clark (1983; 1987) proposes the operating principle of *contrast* for how children acquire word-referent mappings. Children assume that the meaning of each new word is unique and differs in meaning from the words they already know. So upon hearing a new label, they figure out its particular connection to things in the world by contrasting it with old words and old connections.

Categories carve the world up into kinds of things, labels name the cuts, and categories form hierarchies. Children acquire knowledge about this hierarchical organization of things during the toddler and preschool years when they are also acquiring language. As their knowledge of taxonomies elaborates, so should the kinds of word-category connections they are willing to accept. At age 2, a child is less inclined to accept anything but a basic-level label for an item, for example, "horse" for the creature who lives in the barn. Soon, however, two names will be acceptable if they represent different levels of classification, as in *horse* and *animal* (Au & Glusman, 1990). And it does not take long for the child to acknowledge that horse has a proper name (e.g., "Cassie) and a series of descriptive labels—*horse, mammal, vegetarian, animal,* and so on— as its particular place in the hierarchy of things in the world becomes more clearly understood.

That children have inherent tendencies to treat new words in particular ways (Waxman, 1990; Woodward & Markman, 1991) is the proposition that word learning is constrained. Those constraints function to simplify the task by eliminating from the very start the possible connections between word and referent that are ever entertained.

Although there are similarities between them, children do not have the same taxon-

omies as adults do; children's are, for one, less elaborate. Also, youngsters do not know as many names for things. So, in order to reference all the things there are to talk about and all the cuts made among those things, children connect their labels to referents in some unadultlike ways. They make mistakes as they extend their limited language resources to the utmost (Clark, 1978).

One form of error is **overextension,** applying a name to a wider set of entities than is appropriate, for example, using the word *truck* for any vehicle; *cat* for cats, bunnies, raccoons, and skunks; or *ball* for balls, apples, donuts, and other round things. Such errors reveal limitations in conceptual understanding, less elaborate hierarchies, and limitations in vocabulary (Behrend, 1988; Hoek, Ingram, & Gibson, 1986). Children do not make overextensions randomly but apply the label to similar referents. As vocabularies grow, finer distinctions between entities are made, and then overextended words are applied to an appropriately narrower range of referents (Rescorla, 1980).

Underextensions also occur when children do not apply the label to a sufficiently broad class of exemplars. Failing to recognize that *dog* refers to a larger class of exemplars than just to the family pet or denying that a penguin is indeed a bird are instances of this error. **Coining** is the creation of new words to fill in gaps for yet to be acquired words (Clark, 1982, 1983). "Heavy stick" in the scenario at the beginning of the chapter, "owie-bush," "lawn-lady" for gardener, and "Bubba-dogs" for golden retrievers are all examples.

As children acquire more words and expand the lexicon, these problems of generalization become less obvious. Then, children abandon the extension errors and the created words that have temporarily sufficed to fill in the gaps of language knowledge. Given the principles of **mutual exclusivity** (Markman & Wachtel, 1988) and/or **lexical contrast** (Clark, 1987), abandonment of old usages as new word are acquired is expected. Youngsters do not accept multiple words to denote the same classes of things, so they have to give up the old one or the new one. A second principle of Clark's lexical contrast theory (Clark, 1983, 1987, 1988, 1990) is that when a choice between names must be made, children replace current ones with those they decide are more conventional or accepted.

Explaining precisely how children project word meanings from original entities to similar entities could reveal something about the underlying basis of semantic distinctions. Landau, Smith, and Jones (1988) reported a **shape bias** in extensions among 2- and 3-year-old children. When presented with novel objects varying in size, shape, and texture, subjects extended a new noun applied to one object to other same-shaped objects across large and salient variations in size and texture. The investigators contended that the "same name only if same shape" rule characterized children's judgments. In a subsequent study (Jones, Smith, & Landau, 1991), half the objects provided had eyes—a property strongly associated with certain material kinds. This time children extended the name of "eyeless objects" to other objects on the basis of shape and of "eyed objects" on the basis of shape and texture. The implication of both findings is that projection of noun names is based on perceptual properties.

Soja, Carey, and Spelke (1991) took issue with Landau et al.'s (1988) contention. They used a wider range of entities—objects (e.g., a cup) and nonsolid substances (e.g., play-dough)—with novel, made-up names. The findings for noun projection turned out to be more complicated this time; shape was only relevant for object-connected nouns. The investigators concluded that the following rules better characterized the 2-year-old's judgments: If solid object, conclude word refers to shape; if nonsolid substance, conclude word refers to texture. The distinction between objects and nonsolid substances is an important one because it is an *ontological distinction* (see Chapter 5) made by adults and older children.

These young toddlers apparently made that distinction in their projection rules. Thus, by implication, ontology constrains the course of word learning from the very beginning, and provides more evidence for the intertwined character of conceptual and lexical development.

The word-learning constraints identified here work pretty well for explaining the acquisition of *nouns,* and particular nouns at that: **count nouns**—(dog, cup) nouns referring to individuals that can be enumerated, and to some extent **mass nouns,** which refer to substances (milk, dirt). But not all the words young children acquire are nouns of this sort. They also learn nouns for events (nap, bath), nouns referring to time and place (week, beach), and nonnouns, too. The object constraints do not explain the acquisition of these other words as well, if at all. It may be that young word learners also know something about the grammatical categories into which words fall (noun, verb) and word learning constraints could be category specific (Bloom, in press; Gleitman, 1990). The acquisition of words and the acquisition of syntax may, in fact, not be independent processes.

The development of grammar. Between 1 and 2 years of age, children produce mostly one-word utterances. This early, one-word speech is not confined to the labeling of things, however. It is used in communication almost like one-word sentences or **holophrases** (Dore, 1975, 1985). "Up" may communicate the intent, "Pick me up, Mommy." "Milk" could suffice for, "Give me more milk, please." Then, by around the end of the second year, children start to combine words into two-word phrases or **duos.**

Examples such as "allgone milk," "bye-bye Mommy," "horsey go," "Dean truck" are skeletal in nature and have an MLU of 2.0. The sentences lack little, unstressed words, like articles and prepositions, and word endings, like plurals, possessive markers, and verb endings, that would increase the MLU

(Brown, 1973). In fact, this skeletal speech has been described as *telegraphic* because, like a telegraph, it has sufficient words to get the message across without wasting resources on the nonessential niceties of expression. While there is apparently no consistent word-order combination, or common syntax, that typifies these early duos across children (Maratsos, 1982) a variety of semantic relations are expressed in these sentences. Some of the relations are summarized in Table 9-1.

Between 2 and 3 years of age, MLU moves toward 3.0 and beyond as children combine multiple words and form simple sentences. Children acquiring English tend to respect adult word order in these early utterances (Pinker, 1989), such as in the SVO sequence, "Dean play truck," "Mommy sit chair," and "Doggie run ball." This early speech is simplified with sentence length varying from three to eight words (Pinker, 1989), but it is rule governed and contains a range of syntactic categories. Valian (1986), for example, collected speech samples from children aged 2 to 2½ years who produced sentences of MLU 2.93 to 4.14. She found evidence of six syntactic categories in these utterances—determiner, adjective, noun, noun phrase, preposition, and prepositional phrase—and concluded that even

these young children have to be credited with possessing considerable syntactic knowledge.

During this developmental period, youngsters also acquire the grammatical morphemes: word endings, articles, auxiliaries, and the little bound morphemes that flush out sentences and lead to an overall increase in MLU. Now phrases like "Mommy's horse," "Bubba chase cat*s*," and "kitty sleep*ing*" appear in children's repertoires. Brown (1973) documented the order in which these grammatical morphemes appear in the speech of English-speaking children between 1½ and 3½ years of age. The sequence of acquisition like what he observed and like what has subsequently been replicated by others (deVilliers & deVilliers, 1973; Kuczaj, 1977), is summarized in Table 9-2. It turns out that the order of attainment is very regular, but it is not related to adult's frequency of morpheme use in the children's environments (Pinker, 1981). Brown (1973) contended that a morpheme's structural and semantic complexity predicted fairly well its timing of acquisition in the sequence. For instance, it is less complex to add an *s* marking plurality than it is to use an auxiliary verb (e.g., to be), which requires adding a word and changing the ending of a verb, too, as in "I *am* go*ing*."

Children make some telling errors while they are flushing out their speech with grammatical touches. A particularly interesting error is **overregularization**. One example is **morphological generalization** in which constructions such as *mouses, foots, goed,* or *builded* appear in children's speech. Apparently, as children begin to acquire the inflections that mark plurality or tense, they apply those patterns in the irregular case.

Irregular verbs like *break, bring,* and *go* are treated as if they belonged to the regular paradigm of *walk, open,* and *jump* (Berko, 1958; Cazden, 1968; Kuczaj, 1977) even by children who had previously used the correct irregular form first. Verbs that mark change of

TABLE 9-1 *Semantic Relationships Typically Expressed by Children during the Two-word Phase of Sentence Production*

Relation	Example
Agent-action	"Bubby bark"
Action-object	"Give juice"
Agent-object	"Daddy block"
Action-location	"Go store"
Entity-location	"Horsey barn"
Possessor-possession	"My kitty"
Entity-attribute	"heavy stick"
Demonstrative-entity	"that ball"

TABLE 9-2 *Order of Acquisition for 14 English Morphemes*

Morpheme	Example
1. Present progressive	"I go*ing*"
2–3. in, on	"*on* horsey"; "*in* truck"
4. plural	"two bunn*ies*"
5. Past irregular	"Bubby *ran*"
6. Possessive	"Mommy*'s* briefcase"
7. Uncontractible copula	"There it *is*"
8. Articles	"there *the* stick"; "that *a* car"
9. Past regular	"he walk*ed*"
10. Third-person regular	"She ride*s* one"
11. Third-person irregular	"he *has* on"
12. Uncontractible auxiliary	"this *is* going"
13. Contractible copula	"he*'s* nice"
14. Contractible auxiliary	"they*'re* runn*ing*"

state (e.g., break, drop) tend to be inflected for past tense first, followed by those denoting activity (e.g., run) (Bloom, Lifter, & Hafitz, 1980), and even later, those that already sound like regular past-tense forms are regularized. *Hit* may become *hitted, ride* becomes *rided,* and *stop* becomes *stop(t)ed* (Bybee & Slobin, 1982). There are also incidences of **lexicosyntactic overgeneralization,** for example, "Who deaded my kitty cat" (Bowerman, 1974), in which the wrong verb is extended into an otherwise appropriate construction, and **syntactic overgeneralization,** for example, "How he can be doctor?" or "I turned off it" (Fodor & Crain, 1987), in which regular word order is inappropriately overextended.

Overregularization has important implications for any explanation of language development. It exposes language learners as pattern makers developing language rules from input rather than mimicking just what they hear. Children do not hear adults say *breaked, goed, bringed,* or *deaded,* yet youngsters gener-

ate such forms. However, if children are conceptualized as a rampant pattern makers, what mechanisms would limit their overgeneralization? There are many more overgeneralizations possible than are actually exhibited in children's speech, so instances of the error are not the norm in language acquisition (Fodor & Crain, 1987). Also, children do eventually achieve the correct rules rather than overly generalized rules. What can account for the change? What would account for the grammatical shift in the absence of direct negative feedback (which we have learned does not exist)?

There are a number of potential hypotheses, but none of them are totally satisfactory. In a *competition model* (MacWhinney, 1987), the child's incorrect rules compete with correct forms modeled by others. Alternate ways of expressing the same thing vie for one syntactic "niche." Hence, one way must eventually be eliminated. In extending the logic of *contrast theory* (Clark, 1987), perhaps multiple constructions are no more acceptable to children than multiple tags or synonyms are. So, when there are two possible constructions, for example, *broke* and *breaked,* one must go. The conventional one, the one adult's use, is the winner and the other is dropped. While such explanations are consistent with the data, it is not at all clear why rules cannot happily coexist (they often do for a time, see Kuczaj, 1977). It is not clear either how a child identifies a particular modeled sentence as a competitor for a preferred usage; the overgeneralized exemplar and the correct exemplar do not occur in exactly the same context where the child could choose between them. And it is not clear why the correct form is always favored.

While children have made great strides in language acquisition by the age of 3½, there is still more to come. They must master the complexity of forming negatives (Tager-Flusberg, 1989). Early forms are often in error, for example, "Daddy no work today," where the auxiliary is omitted. Children also must master the transformations required in the construction of questions. Early questions are typically marked by rising intonation (Bowerman, 1973), for example, "Daddy work?", "Where Daddy go?", "What you doing?", rather than a change in the ordering of words and the addition of auxiliaries. The appropriate constructions come later. **Conjunctions** connecting sentences and verb phrases ("Mommy got home *and* we played"; "I got dressed *and* brushed my teeth") appear later, as do **embeddings** ("I think he's my best friend") and **passive sentences** ("Susan was hit by John").

Having started to use words at about 12 months, by the time children go off to kindergarten at about 5 years of age, they are truly articulate. Although there is still more to come and much vocabulary to be learned, children can express most of what they wish to say in appropriately formed constructions by the beginning of the elementary school years. This transformation—from gurgling babbler to proficient language user in a little over 3 years—is what all the fuss is about.

EXPLANATIONS OF THE ACQUISITION PHENOMENON

A theory of language acquisition must also explain language development, and a fully satisfactory account of the developmental story does not yet exist. However, some contenders are more plausible than others. It is possible to identify limitations (constraints again) that restrict the set of reasonable theoretical explanations. The developmental data are one constraint on potential accounts. The logical feasibility of any proposed acquisition mechanism is another. But there are others.

The human being learning language is a biological system and biological operation places a constraint on what the organism can do and when in the course of physical maturation it can do it. The language learner is also an information-processing system with finite limitations on processing capacity—another constraint. To sort out the contenders, we must evaluate the theoretical accounts with all of these constraints in mind.

The Biology of Language

Undeniably, language is fundamentally biological in nature. First, the human vocal apparatus is uniquely adapted for speech; this structural adaptation has been accomplished at considerable sacrifice to the efficiency of other activities such as breathing, chewing, and swallowing (Lieberman, 1984). Second, the neural circuitry in the left hemisphere of the brain appears specific to language processing (Pinker, 1989); damage or injury to that circuitry can selectively affect language capacity (Pinker, 1989; Pinker & Bloom, 1990), either leaving it intact while other cognitive function is impaired or vice versa. And third, language capacity is a species-specific phenomenon, a fact that implicates human biology and selective evolutionary processes in its origination (Pinker & Bloom, 1990). But all theoretical explanations of language acquisition, not just nativist accounts, in some way recognize the contributions of biology to development.

A stronger nativist case rests on whether language development is maturationally determined (Gleitman, 1981; Lenneburg, 1967). The contention is that the growth of language demonstrates a *maturational function* (see Chapter 1) in which age and biological maturity provide the best predictor of timing, extent, and sequencing of linguistic accomplishment. An important ramification of a maturational function, almost a "smoking gun" for a nativist view, is the detection of a *critical period* for language learning. A developmental accomplishment is said to exhibit a critical period when there is an age-associated change in the ability to learn—a peak in learning at some maturationally definable period with a subsequent decline in the ability to acquire facility at a later time (Newport, 1991). By implication, given the same extent of environmental input, acquisition should be better during the peak period and significantly worse after that period.

Recall from Chapters 1 and 2 that critical periods are associated with peak periods of *synaptogenesis* in which the organism is neurologically primed to profit from the expected experiences (like language input) provided by the environment because of an abundance of synapses ready for pruning. Synaptic density peaks at about age 2 in humans (Pinker, 1989). It is subsequent to that time when we observe a true flourishing in early language capacity.

However, determining whether or not the critical period phenomenon holds for language development is not easy. The evidence for the function is all indirect. The experimental procedures necessary to really address the question are simply not applicable in the study of language. With other hypothesized critical-period phenomena such as the development of vision, animals can serve as subjects. The onset of input or deliberate deprivation of input vis-à-vis maturational status is manipulated, and the effects are observed. The connection between maturational priming and accomplishment is investigated directly. Since humans are the only organisms who exhibit language naturally, the results of deprivation experiments on animals do not apply, and the extension of the animal paradigm to human subjects is ethically ruled out.

Virtually all human beings are exposed to linguistic input during early childhood unless the natural course of development is grossly interrupted. Investigators do sometimes turn to "natural" experiments, however, and identify individuals for whom the range of experience with linguistic input is outside the norm, perhaps even vastly so. The hope is that examination of individuals with exceptional learning histories will clarify the role of experience and biology in language acquisition.

One body of data relevant to the maturational case is the study of individuals deprived of exposure to language by horrendous life circumstances. One such person, Genie (Curtiss, 1977), was isolated by an abusive parent from age 1 until after puberty when she was discovered, removed from the home, and immersed in English. Another, Chelsea (Curtiss, 1988), was isolated until age 32. The critical-period hypothesis predicts a decline in the ability to acquire language after puberty when the brain has achieved a mature state. In fact, the findings with Genie and Chelsea are consistent with that thesis. For both women, acquisition of English syntax was strikingly abnormal with limited, if any, features of syntax or morphology successfully mastered (Newport, 1991). However, since the experiences of these persons were so outside the norm and involved deprivation in such a broad sense, any generalization to the normal course of language acquisition is problematic.

Also relevant is the study of children with impairments that restrict their access to the usual form of linguistic input. For example, deaf children do not hear spoken sentences, blind children are denied a visual context in which to connect label and referent, and Down syndrome children may have impaired learning capacity. Interestingly enough, Gleitman (1981) observed that such children still acquire language in much the same way as unimpaired children despite differences in their accessibility to input. Similarities in sequence and timing of language achievements point to (albeit, very indirectly) a biological impetus for language acquisition. The logic is that if the sequence of language development is consistent across individuals (i.e., a constant), but experience is a variable, then the variability cannot explain the consistency.

Some of the most interesting data come from studies of deaf children acquiring American Sign Language (ASL) (Newport, 1991). ASL is a true natural language with the same grammatical complexity, structural properties, and developmental patterns revealed in other natural languages (Klima & Bellugi, 1979; Newport & Meier, 1985). But, unlike the language exposure of hearing infants, deaf children's exposure to ASL varies in timing. Some children are exposed from birth by signing parents, so these babies' experiences mirror hearing children's exposure to spoken language. Other deaf children are not exposed to signing until later. Thus, this is a natural experiment in which the timing and extent of exposure to input are ex post facto variables.

Elissa Newport and her colleagues (Newport, 1981, 1988, 1991; Newport & Meier, 1985; Newport & Supalla, 1990) have studied subjects living this natural experiment whose exposure to ASL varied from birth to postpuberty. The investigators separated subjects, on the basis of time of exposure, into native (from birth), early (ages 4–6), and late (after age 12) learners of ASL. They assessed mastery of basic word order and aspects of morphology acquisition. Acquiring words and the rules for basic word order were not affected by age at first exposure, but the acquisition of aspects of morphology was. Those exposed to ASL late demonstrated a lack of control over all but the simplest aspects of grammar quite unlike that of native signers. Like Genie and Chelsea, timing of exposure was associated with selective impairment in skills: the impairment of facility with syntax. These results support a critical-period interpretation for at least one aspect of language acquisition.

In this literature and in related studies (see Newport, 1991), the particular aspect of language acquisition most impaired by the late onset of exposure to linguistic input turns out to be syntax, not vocabulary, not the development of a lexicon, and not even the basic ordering of words in skeletal sentences. Syntax and morphology are aspects of knowledge that are peculiar to language as a form of representation. So, syntax, perhaps more than any other aspect of language, appears to be domain specific. That we also observe selective effects of input deprivation on the mastery of syntax adds strength to the domain-specificity contention.

The Learning Mechanism

Given an organism primed to acquire language by biological nature, we still require a mechanism for constructing language rules from input. To reiterate points made earlier, language is rule governed, and learning language means inducing those rules from available data. The data are sample utterances presented to the learner. These utterances demonstrate regularities in construction and form. The rules explain and predict the regularities. What the learner must do is arrive at the rules from observation of those regularities. We have seen that the child acquiring language is a rule maker; overregularization (*breaked, mouses*) clearly attests to that. The experimental demonstration of modeling effects on language rules is an empirical validation of the point. But what is the rule-making mechanism?

One proposal builds on the co-occurrence of regularities in sentences and on the notion that, in principle, co-occurrences can be quantified and frequencies can be detected. Regularities are statistical; the learner might be equipped to detect statistical regularities reflecting the operation of language rules and to arrive at the rules as a consequence. Perhaps the learner sets up a giant correlation matrix in his mind, noticing which words appear in which positions (e.g., nouns usually come first), which words appear next to which other words (e.g., articles appear before nouns), which words take which suffixes (e.g., many words inflected with -s refer to plural entities), and so forth. Syntactic categories and rules arise as the learner discovers how certain properties are correlated across large sets of exemplars (Pinker, 1989). The statistical regularities are there; all we need to hypothesize is a learner capable of finding them.

There are two reasons why this account of the learning mechanism fails to become the winning contender. First, if our learner were open to any kind of co-occurrence, and to posit otherwise is to build in constraints, the hypothetical correlation matrix would have to be extremely large to provide slots for all possible combinations. Most of these slots would never have any entries. Since natural languages themselves are constrained, actual co-occurrences constitute a much smaller set than all possible co-occurrences. So, the hypothesis predicts an information-processing system of greater complexity and power than needed to detect the statistical regularities actually represented in natural languages. Mother Nature is usually much more economical.

Second, the rules governing the formation of appropriate sentences are often subtle, convoluted, not readily accessible, and subject to a multitude of exceptions (for e.g., irregular verbs, the formation of questions). A regularity detector is very apt to pick up on a co-occurrence from sample sentences and inappropriately generalize it to another example. Borrowing from Pinker (1989), examine the following sample sets:

1. a. John saw Mary with her best friend's husband.
    b. Who did John see Mary with?
    c. John saw Mary and her best friend's husband.
    *d. Who did John see Mary and?

2. a. The baby seems to be asleep.
    b. The baby seems asleep.
    c. The baby seems to be sleeping.
    *d. The baby seems sleeping.

3. a. Irv drove the car into the garage.
    b. Irv drove the car.
    c. Irv put the car in the garage.
    *d. Irv put the car.

(The * denotes a logical generalization of an apparent rule that yields an unacceptable sentence.) In each case, a regularity can be extracted from the transformation of (a) into (b); but when the regularity is applied to (c), an erroneous construction, (d), is the outcome. Errors like these should occur frequently if rule makers are at work; children should end up with overly general grammars. But they don't. Errors, especially syntactic ones, are rare and overgeneralization is not rampant, which is a good thing given the negative evidence problem. So, this mechanism *overpredicts* erroneous constructions.

A final problem for the correlational approach is how the truly naive learner, which is what the young child is, enters the system and gets the process started in the first place. For example, to detect how auxiliaries and subjects co-occur in sentences ("He has the flu." "She is sleeping." "How have you been?"), the child would need to know something already about what those categories of words are. To posit prior knowledge, either of word categories to get the child started or of limits on co-occurrence combinations to simplify the matrix, is to hypothesize constraints. The statistical-extraction approach is an attempt to avoid elaborate constraints on the learner and to explain learning instead as a function of input in interaction with a general-purpose regularity detector. Given the questionable feasibility of correct rule identification from finite input, the probable limitations on processing capacity in the young child, and the actual infrequency of erroneous overgeneralization of detectable regularities, this account is rather implausible.

An alternative to distributional analysis, rule extraction from statistical frequencies, is **parameter setting** (Chomsky, 1981, 1986), Chomsky's more recent alternative to the transformational theory presented earlier in the chapter. This learning mechanism takes into account that language rules exhibited in actual natural languages are not free to vary but represent a small subset of all possible rule forms. A learner who is designed to exploit the fact that there are limits on all possible language forms has an advantage: she need not consider all the nonfilled, nonrepresented cells in the correlation matrix.

Natural languages are built on the same general plan with some variations possible on that plan. The variations are conceptualized as *parameters,* values within the rule equation that can vary within limits. So, one language may set the parameter at one value and another at a different value; in both cases, the equation in which the parameter is contained is the same. For example, a verb can occur in a variety of locations (different values) within the structure of a sentence (equation), but it cannot occur anywhere within the sentence. In English, the verb precedes the object; in German, it follows the object. A learner would need to determine which position (parameter setting) is appropriate in the target language. However, the learner need only consider a limited set of possibilities (e.g., before, after) to make the choice. Indeed, one sample utterance could set the parameter if only two options are available to choose among and if the learner has prior knowledge of the option range.

Instead of a massive correlation matrix, we can envision a group of switches; each switch can take a limited range of positions. To begin, a switch is set in the "default" position, a sort of "rule to use in the absence of additional information" option. But incoming sentences can reset the switch to the appropriate value for that target language. The parameters correspond to language universals and the values in settings correspond to the variations possible in natural languages. Recall that rules within any one language are interrelated; one parameter setting restricts even further the extent of variation in other parameter settings. So, a single sentence ends up conveying a lot of information about which settings are appropriate in the target language.

Parameter setting is a viable and efficient mechanism for figuring out the rules governing language, and it fits the learning mechanism to the particular learning problem: language acquisition. The mechanism also predicts learnability from *positive evidence* because of the cascading implications of information conveyed in a well-formed utterance. Given sentence samples that set one parameter, the child may deduce what else must be true of her language in this interconnected system. If anything, parameter setting could *underpredict* actual errors made by children rather than overpredicting them. The child never even entertains all the possible constructions that could be made but, in fact, do not appear in the languages people speak. The parameter-setting mechanism works to restrict the hypothesis space; a restricted space is consistent with universal and rapid language acquisition.

A parameter-setting mechanism is not without explanatory problems, however. One is determining "default values." Another is identifying the universal rules. We are still left with questions about the nature of a child's initial language representation. And, how does the child get started either extracting regularities or determining parametric values in the first place?

Getting Started: Semantic Bootstrapping

Children learning language have to figure out what a string of words says about the world. For example, in the sample utterance, "The big dog runs down the road," the words and the order among them convey information about an incident. At least two aspects of that sentence are obvious. First, it is made up of words and each word refers to something out there, physical and real: *dog* and *road* reference entities, *runs* describes an action, and *down* makes a spatial reference. So, the words have semantic implications. Second, the words play syntactic roles in the sentence. *Dog* is a noun acting as the subject, *runs* is a verb, and *down* is a preposition. However, the syntactic categories to which words belong and their semantic characteristics arc not independent. Nouns tend to be things and verbs tend to denote actions. Not all nouns are things—*idea bedtime,* and *wish* are not things in the usual sense—but all things are nouns. Not all verbs are actions—*exist* and *have* are not—but all actions are verbs.

Perhaps the young language learner can exploit the less than perfect relationship between the semantic and syntactic characteristics of sentences to get things started. This is the **semantic bootstrapping hypothesis** (Grimshaw, 1981; Macnamara, 1982; Pinker, 1984), and it conveys the notion that children use semantic information to figure out what utterances say and to determine the linguistic categories into which words fit. The basic idea is that children somehow "pull themselves up by the bootstraps" and use meaning to access the representational system (Pinker, 1989).

Semantic bootstrapping is intuitively appealing, fits well with what we know about children's early cognitive abilities, and also fits with the facts of early language development. For instance, we know infants are tuned into "thingness" as a specifier of objects; they also demonstrate appreciation of object-action sequences. In this sense, infants know about the simple causal relations among entities in an incident. Then, again, the whole-object bias in word learning is documented for the acquisition of count nouns; the frequency of nouns referencing things in children's early vocabularies attests to a "thing" bias as well. If children know the meaning of key words in a sentence, they also know quite a bit about what that sentence says. "Dog run" conveys a partially overlapping meaning for the full sample sentence. Consistent, too, is the respect young learners pay to word order; perhaps they are honoring the conceptual order in which things can happen. Lexical development, then, might help young learners figure out what longer streams mean, giving them that much needed "leg up."

Other aspects of the language spoken to children increase the plausibility of the semantic bootstrapping hypothesis. One is stress and prosody; in the speech children hear, the words central to meaning and gist are apt to be the ones stressed, not the little connecting words and the inflections (e.g., *the* and the *-s* on *runs* in the sample sentence).

Then there is processing capacity; young children simply cannot encode and hold as much information as adults can. Thus, a long sentence that an adult could easily store, with all its linguistic intricacies, could prove a bit much for the child. A simplified version, a shorter truncated facsimile, would match the child's capacities better. Shorter sentences contain *less* linguistic information for the child to deal with, and consequently there are *fewer* rules to induce. Perhaps children effectively process "The big dog runs down the road" as "Big dog run," and lose or ignore the rest of it. Young children produce shorter sentences than do their older counterparts, and processing limitations are a viable reason for that observation, too (Bloom, 1990a). Attending to part of an utterance, the stressed part, because of limited processing abilities could help young children get started and prevent their being overwhelmed with complexity and unmanageable information.

The semantic bootstrapping hypothesis makes good sense as a possible account for how early language acquisition proceeds. The account builds on cognitive capacities that babies and very young children are known to have. These capacities are not totally specific to language as a form of representation, however. Perceptual knowledge, object knowledge, ontological knowledge, a primitive understanding of mechanics and number, and a rudimentary grasp of causal processes are faculties that arise early and are well in place when children start producing first sentences of the telegraphic variety. Armed with nonlinguistic but still domain-specific skills, children acquiring language are not starting from scratch; they may be exploiting what they already know about the world in deciphering how language maps onto that world. An implication of this account is that children derive *syntactic* categories and rules from their knowledge of *conceptual* categories and rules and the correspondence between the two systems.

But what adults and children know about language cannot simply be reduced to conceptual knowledge. Even the speech of the youngest subjects reveals knowledge of the syntactic categories of words (Valian, 1986), as well as of the conceptual categories they represent. And children tend not to produce sentences that would be permissible conceptually but that would violate syntactic rules. Why not? It seems that children must also know a great deal about language that is linguistically specific.

To explore this possibility, we can look at how young children order words in phrases because word-order rules, at least as they apply in English, are not governed only by conceptual constraints. Bloom (1990b) examined the ordering of adjective-noun combinations in language samples taken from 1- and 2-year-old children. In English, adjectives can precede nouns, but they cannot precede proper nouns or pronouns. That means the combination "big dog" is allowable but "big he" or "big Fred" is not. *Dog, Fred,* and *he* may refer to the same entity in a given incident—if the dog is male and is named Fred—but *big* cannot modify *Fred* or *he*. Bloom (1990b) found that young children do not violate this constraint in their early language. Apparently, they discriminate between the syntactic category, noun—a general category, like "dog," to which innumerable individual dogs belong—and a noun phrase (NP), like "the dog," which refers to a particular individual. Pronouns and proper names are treated as NPs, referring as they do to a particular individual. And, just as "big the dog" is unallowable, so is "big he" or "big Fred." The fact that young children

learning English make these distinctions attests to their appreciation of the language-specific syntactic rules governing utterances.

But how do children come to honor what would seem to be purely syntactic constraints on language constructions? That is not clear. Perhaps this sort of knowledge, knowledge about the purely formal aspects of language, is innate, too. Or, semantic knowledge could assist children in determining linguistic categories of words and phrases (Bloom, 1990b, in press). It is clear that knowledge about the syntactic characteristics of language shows up very early in children's speech. They seem to know something of the syntactic categories to which words belong and they honor constraints on the ordering of syntactic categories in their first multiword sentences. Children are quite good at acquiring purely grammatical distinctions without apparent semantic support, for example, gender markings as an abstract grammatical feature (Karmiloff-Smith, 1979; Pinker, 1989). How do they do this? That remains largely a mystery. But to extrapolate from Pinker (1987, 1989), children probably use all the information available—a combination of semantic, correlational, and prosodic cues—to arrive at a grammatical analysis that works best for all that input taken together.

CONCLUSION

Language has many aspects—phonology, morphology, semantics, and syntax. Learning language entails learning a lot of things. A complex achievement such as this may draw on more than a single intellectual faculty. Some of the faculties may be specific to language learning, but all of them need not be. We know the task is accomplished by all normal human beings in similar fashion within a specific time frame, and the process is relatively impervious to all but the most extreme variations in environmental and experiential differences. What we need to determine is the particular intellectual tools that allow for the acquisition of language within the known parameters of the developmental story and that are still consistent with the constraints of logic, learnability, biology, and the cognitive status of the young child.

To begin the process of deciphering linguistic input so as to map meaning and structure to sound, infants must be sensitive to the acoustical features of the input. It turns out that, indeed, they are amazingly sensitive to those acoustical features most relevant to phonological distinctions that are critical to the basic building blocks of language. Interestingly enough, this capacity is not necessarily unique to language learning; it is not even unique to humans. Other animals make similar distinctions, yet a language is not within their natural capacity. It is as if human languages exploit the acoustical capacities and sensitivities with which the future language user comes equipped. So, at least one of the perceptual/cognitive components that plays a role in language acquisition is not domain specific to language per se; it may not even be specific to the species.

The first definitive evidence of language use is the child's production of words at around the end of the first year of life. Word use is a developmental landmark because, at the very least, it reveals a grasp of the mapping between representational units and their referents in the world. Children tend to produce words that reference the things they know about: individual objects, the actions of objects and themselves, and the events in their daily routine. There is a connection between cognitive achievements—perceptual knowledge, object knowledge, ontological knowledge, rudimentary causal knowledge—and word acquisition, the generalization of words to other entities, and the use of words in commenting on reality.

Despite considerable overlap between the general cognitive achievements and the language achievements of babies, however, the-

acquisitions cannot be reduced to the same thing. Even these youngsters reveal some grasp of the syntactic categories to which their early words belong, and syntax *is* domain specific for language. Thus, while conceptual development and language development are intertwined, they are still separable threads.

When young children start using sentences, which are short and unadorned consistent with the processing capacities of the immature, their language has a semantic look to it. The rudimentary combinations link object words, action words, and agent words in skeletal descriptions of incidents and happenings in a child's world. But even in these early utterances, young speakers honor syntactic constraints, restrictions that go beyond any semantic requirements on constructions. So again, the interconnectedness of semantic and syntactic development is clear, but given children's sensitivity to the purely structural aspects of language, syntax is not simply an epiphenomenon of grasping semantics.

The connection between semantics and syntax and the hypothesis that syntactical knowledge may be derivable from semantic knowledge suggests how language learning may build on domain-specific knowledge that is not specific to language. Of particular focus is what babies know about objects. Recalling Chapters 2, 3, and 6, we have seen that one of the baby's earliest capabilities is in organizing the physical landscape into things, into individual entities. Early emerging also is the ability to enumerate things as individuals. Words map to things, and children even seem sensitive to the difference between generic things (marked by nouns) and individuated things (marked by pronouns and proper nouns) (Bloom, 1990b). Potentially, knowledge of things and ontological knowledge about the distinctions among things and what they can be and do (see Chapter 5) have profound ramifications for the development of the lexicon (Bloom, in press) and other aspects of language acquisition as well.

Once the production of sentences is underway, the addition of syntactic rule markers in children's language elaborates. We see a flourishing of syntactic knowledge, and, again, syntactic knowledge is domain-specific to language. It is this capacity for grammar that clearly marks a human achievement, unique to a linguistic representational system, and that most looks like a biologically driven, critical-period phenomenon.

To fully explain this fascinating developmental accomplishment, we must determine the intellectual components, the a priori knowledge, with which learners must begin in order to get the job done. It is clear that babies *must have* some such initial tools, otherwise language acquisition is highly unlikely, but it is less clear what specifically the tools *must be*. They have to be sufficient so that through some mechanism, such as parameter setting, positive evidence enables the determination of how thing are said in the target language.

However, we must remember how flexible children are, capable of learning any language with equivalent ease (or difficulty). So, the set of tools cannot be overly general or overly specific. Semantic constraints may hold across languages, but syntactic constraints vary, albeit within limits. Because language rules are interrelated and because one rule decision has cascading effects on others, the set of initial constraints necessary to get the process started need not be lengthy. But what are these first principles like? Are they semantic? Syntactic? A combination of both? And what of those default values? Trying to answer these questions ought to keep cognitive scientists, linguists, and developmental psychologists busy for a long while yet.

CHAPTER 10

THE DEVELOPMENTAL BASIS
OF MEMORY

INTRODUCTION

A first-grader prepares to leave his house to catch the school bus, but he must collect his odds and ends before departing—homework, soccer ball, lunch money, library books. He goes through his mental list, retrieving each item from where he *remembered* leaving it the night before. His search complete, the items stored in his backpack, he's off for another day. He can anticipate what will happen this day as he *recalls* the sequence of usual events: announcements, spelling test, reading group, math center, and so forth. He *recognizes* the faces of his friends as he gets off the school bus, and he *remembers* to give that note from his mother to the teacher. The Pledge of Allegiance he *recites verbatim.*

Before long, it is time for the spelling test; he must *recall* the 10 words he learned during the past week. Then, it is math time and he must *retrieve* the sums he has *memorized* and the procedure for subtracting integers. In reading, he has to tackle new words, *remembering* all the sound-letter associations as he

goes. Just before lunch, it is time for library, but—whoops! He *forgot* to bring back that second library book he checked out last week. He starts to *reminisce* about yesterday evening: Where did he put that book after reading it with Dad just before bedtime? He can't remember that, but he can *remember the gist* of what the story was about. In fact, he certainly has remembered a lot of details, rules, facts, procedures, sequences, and meanings necessary to get him successfully through this complex day.

The act of remembering is familiar, pervasive, and ubiquitous in our mental lives. Virtually every cognitive task draws on memory in some manner, and, indeed, *cognition* and *memory* can seem even synonymous. There is an everyday need for memory in real settings, so, intuitively, no one doubts the psychological reality and importance of this cognitive process. We have personally experienced recognition of the familiar, recall of prior learning, reconstruction of a past event, reminiscence of a previous encounter, and forgetting—often at crucial times—of a fact, rule, principle, procedure, or item.

The interconnectedness of memory to other cognitive functions seems unquestionable, too. For instance, it might seem obvious that there is a connection between memory and reasoning, memory and inference, memory and problem solving, and memory and thinking (Weinert & Perlmutter, 1988). The intuitive premise is that we could not possibly mentally manipulate, transform, and reconstruct represented information in the service of some cognitive performance unless we had encoded and stored the information in the first place and then retrieved it as needed from "file cabinets" in the mind. Information storage is, in many ways, the common-sense notion of what memory is all about.

Another equally common-sense notion about memory is the idea that it gets better with development up to some optimal point. We often take for granted that older children and adults remember things better than younger children and that elderly people show a diminishing proficiency. Both contentions reflect a presumption that the capacity is age related. And, interestingly enough, ample experimental data show how older is often better when it comes to memory performances (Kail, 1990). Then again, we are apt to think about memory as some generic capacity, some basic operation of the mind we can access and apply as needed, with varying degrees of proficiency, in any context, and to any content. In fact, many of these common-sense notions about memory and its development seem so self-evident we might not think to question them. However, in exploring the processes of cognition, things seldom turn out to be quite as self-evident as they might at first appear.

The sort of memory performances exhibited by the first-grader in the anecdote are familiar instances of the cognitive operation. First, they depend on explicit, human capacities: the child is aware of a deliberate and conscious effort to recall information of various sorts. Second, the contents retrieved are symbolic representations—sums, words, passages, semantic interpretations—many of them verbal in nature. This is the sense of memory we tend to associate with the process.

But there are other senses. For example, sometimes memory is implicit (Schacter, 1987) without awareness, deliberateness, or consciousness as to its operation. Infants exhibit performances dependent on memory, too (indeed, habituation presumes it; see Chapters 2, 3, & 6). Yet we do not typically attribute memory in the usual sense to infants, and few of us are able to recall events from our own infancy, a phenomenon called **infantile amnesia** (Campbell & Spear, 1972). Animals routinely exhibit memory, too, for example, spatial memory (see Chapter 3). So memory is not just a human capacity after all. In short, memory can be both explicit and implicit, conscious and unconscious, deliberate and nondeliberate, a human and a nonhuman capacity, and so forth. Clearly, this is no simple cognitive operation of obvious character.

The study of memory has a long empirical history. In fact, for decades memory has been pivotal in cognitive investigations. The literature reveals historical biases that have carried over into the study of memory development. Notions about what memory is like, about its nature, and about how it must function influence research decisions. Prototypic paradigms of investigation are evident in the memory literature. (Recall from Chapter 1 that paradigms are like frames that determine the view we get of a cognitive phenomena.) The study of memory development has primarily been an extension of adult studies to child subjects (Kail, 1990), so those paradigms frame our view of the phenomenon in children, too. To evaluate the literature on child memory and to appreciate the implications of memory data for theory in cognitive development, we must be aware of the initial biases that direct empirical efforts.

First, memory is usually approached as a domain-general cognitive function (see Anderson, 1990). Think back to the architectural metaphor of the mind introduced in Chapter 8. Memory is one of the operations that go on in the central chamber; a domain-general view of the process is the "big-chamber" view. Memory is envisioned as a generic operation of the mind brought to bear on a variety of contents and representations.

The aim of memory study is to characterize the system, describe how it works, and identify factors that influence proficiency. Because the inclination is toward domain generality, the particular content to be remembered becomes less crucial than the process of remembering. There is no logical need to posit different memories for different content. In fact, the exact nature of the information to be recalled can become quite irrelevant. So, many investigators have historically opted to study memory for arbitrary lists of items, nonsense material, made-up syllables (e.g., DAX), digit strings, and so forth. The rationale is that memory for arbitrary, experimenter-created material not rich in meaning is preferable, because it equalizes the effects of prior learning across subjects. Any observed experimental effect is a memory effect, not an information effect or a learning effect.

Distinctions in memory performances are sometimes made on the basis of broad differences in content, for example, between implicit and explicit memory, between declarative and procedural memory (Anderson, 1990), and between semantic and episodic memory (Tulving, 1984). *Declarative memory* is memory for facts, events, lists, rules, principles, and so forth, while *procedural memory* is memory for how to do things such as ride a bike, type, or execute a tennis serve. *Semantic memory* refers to information we have about the world in general, whereas *episodic memory* is for specific events that occurred at a particular time and place, stored with an autobiographical reference (Tulving, 1972). Disasso-

ciations between those components are sometimes observed (Kolb & Wishaw, 1985), but the primary focus of traditional memory research has been on the description of a single, unitary system. And most of the research has targeted semantic and declarative memory (see Tulving & Donaldson, 1972).

A second major bias is an associationist one. Much current thinking about memory is rooted in the empiricist philosophical tradition (see Chapters 1 and 2), and the prevailing experimental methods are rooted in this view as well (Perlmutter, 1988). One particular ramification of this state of affairs is the idea that cognition can be simplified or reduced to a set of more elementary cognitive processes, capacities, or components which is then variously combined in the service of intellectual activity. Memory, the retention of veridical (accurate) representations of encoded information, is one of the most important of these elementary processes (Brainerd & Reyna, in press; Perlmutter, 1988).

The notion that complex intellectual performances are reducible to a series of less complex cognitive acts is consistent with the associationist view of the world. So, too, is the notion that memory somehow involves a stamping in of an impression or perception on a receiving medium that preserves a trace for subsequent recall. The task is to uncover the influences affecting the durability of the traces, the stimuli and conditions that activate the traces, and the extent of trace strengthening or decay over time. Again, there is no inherent necessity to posit an effect for the nature or the complexity of the impression so preserved. Laws of behavior sufficient to explain memory for simple events are assumed to generalize to complex events and across the content of those events.

Finally, much contemporary research in memory is framed within the information-processing perspective, which builds on a computer metaphor of the human cognitive system (Anderson, 1983; Perlmutter, 1988). Computers transfer, store, and manipulate information; within this metaphor, memory is the storage and retention of information for subsequent retrieval. The image is of a series of "receptacles" and memory is the process through which information is transferred from input through the various storage receptacles until retrieval becomes necessary, and a recall performance becomes the output. In fact, one of the early information-processing models was much like this in character (see Atkinson & Shiffrin, 1968), and contemporary revisions retain much of the flavor of the originals (Anderson, 1990).

The "language" of memory reflects the computer metaphor, too; the terms *encoding, activation, duration, interference,* and *retrieval* all suggest data storage over time. The metaphor points to researchable hypotheses about storage capacity, information loss, information accessibility, and so forth. Paradigms appropriate for addressing such hypotheses also follow the metaphor. Procedures are designed to uncover how information, of whatever variety, moves through the cognitive system and how the mind's file cabinets organize the information and function to hold onto it for subsequent access in real time.

All these biases find their way into the child memory literature. Memory-performance effects documented on adults are examined in children and similar procedures are extended. More often than not, performance turns out to be age related, with children performing less well than adults. The results lead to the common wisdom that memory develops (Brown & DeLoache, 1978; Kail, 1990; Weinert & Perlmutter, 1988). But what develops? Capacity? Organization? Accessibility? And how is memory development connected with the rest of cognitive development? These are the questions addressed in this chapter.

But, first, mechanisms of development are always constrained by at least two things in addition to what we know of the mature end state. The two things are (1) the biological substrate in which the cognitive mechanism is instantiated and (2) the initial state of the organism, the starting point for development. So, we begin by examining the biology of memory. Then we proceed to an examination of infant memory. Third, with those two constraining factors in mind, we evaluate the empirical literature on memory change in children and the implications of that literature for cognitive development more generally.

THE BIOLOGY OF MEMORY

It is an essential fact that an animal modifies its nervous system in response to events during its lifetime. The brain's architecture is plastic and can be changed by experience (Greenough 1984; Rosenzweig & Bennett, 1978). The result is an observed change in behavior. This adaptive capacity—to change as a function of experience—is the ability to learn and remember. Learning is the process of acquiring new information; memory is the persistence of learning revealed at a later time. So, memory is the expected consequence of learning (Squire, 1987). There can be no memory, however, without altering the behavior of the nervous system (Teyler, 1986). The capacity for memory is a special case of a more general phenomenon—**neuronal plasticity:** functional and structural changes at the level of the neuron that have a lasting effect on patterns of neuronal connections. To be useful to the organism in affecting subsequent behavior, the neural alterations, both structural and functional, must be relatively enduring.

Mechanisms of Neural Alteration

Since mature neurons have lost the capacity to divide after the period of neurogenesis in early, primarily prenatal, development, there are no new neurons generated to account for plasticity across the life span. Instead of multiplying, the existing neurons must grow. The synapse is the critical site of cell change and of plasticity (Hebb, 1949; Eccles, 1953; Kandel, 1977); thus, synaptic change is the basic component of memory at the biological level. Recall from earlier discussions in Chapters 1 and 2 that neurons interact and communicate at synaptic sites and form complex systems of interconnections, or circuits. Therefore, the more synaptic material—and there are approximately 10^3 to 10^4 synapses per neuron (Squire, 1987)—the greater the patterns of interconnectivity possible. A specific pattern of connections is unique to a response, serving as the biological foundation for that response. As patterns elaborate and change, a greater variety of responses becomes possible. A memory can be conceptualized as a pattern of neuronal interactions that has been previously sculpted by the animal's experience. There can be no memory, however, unless those interconnections are accessible in the future.

The exact cellular mechanism through which synaptic connections change is beyond the scope of this text, but the effect of the mechanism is variation in the efficacy with which specific connections can be made. Activated connections, those that have occurred in response to experience, become easier to make than inactivated ones. Frequently activated connections become strengthened and increasingly efficacious in communication. Experience triggers a pattern of connections and repeated experience functions to solidify the pattern.

Kolb and Wishaw (1985) used the analogy of water running down a hill. If water is poured onto the top of a hill, it will cut a channel in the soil as it travels toward the base of the hill. The top of the hill is the input or activation of a neuronal connection; the bottom of the hill is the response—the animal's reaction to the activation. Additional water poured on the hill will tend to take the same route as the first, deepening the existing channels and enabling the animal to make the same reaction again. One way to think about memory is as the route furrowed down the hill and left behind when the water has past; sensory experience is the water flowing through the routes of the brain. A *trace* of that flow is left behind, like the furrows in the soil. That is the memory. So, memory is the process and aftermath of neuronal connectivity.

Greenough, Black, and Wallace (1984, 1987) proposed two basic processes through which experience modifies neural circuitry. The first, *experience-expectant* synaptic change was described in Chapters 1 and 2. The mechanism here is excess *synapse elimination* as a function of experience following *synapse overproliferation* early in life. Selective synapse pruning efficiently sculpts the neural substrate for those capabilities essential to the survival of the organism when the target experience is ubiquitous for the species. Much experience, however, is idiosyncratic and individual. Since experience-expectant synaptic change makes the animal susceptible to the effects of deprivation, it cannot logically be the mechanism to account for the incorporation of idiosyncratic experience. Too many animals would be rendered defective if it were, which would not be good for species survivability.

Experience-dependent synaptic change is a more likely neural mechanism to account for learning and memory other than critical period phenomena. In experience-dependent processes, new synapses are created and strengthened in response to experience. In fact, rats reared in enriched environments, which presumably offer more opportunity for experience and learning, show an increase in gross cortical weight and thickness, in size of the neuron cell bodies, in the number and length of dendritic branches (on which synapses form), and in synapse diameter (Squire, 1986). With more dendrite and more synapses, more neuronal interconnectivity results.

These synaptic change processes provide a "how" for memory. Experience is the impetus for learning, strengthening some connections and weakening others; the connections so activated lay the foundation for remembering. But it is a dynamic process of continual sculpting as new experiences, new learning, and new memories are formed. It follows that the content of memory should change as interfering information is acquired (competing connections), as rehearsal occurs (strengthening connections), with overlearning (more strengthening), and as subsequent learning episodes affect preexisting memory.

Expanding the hill metaphor, depending on the initial amount of water, the furrows in the soil will differ in depth, extent of side channeling, and how far down the hill the route proceeds. More water and continued surges of water will deepen established channels, create new channels, and bypass previously formed but small side channels. If we think of the channel network as analogous to a mental representation, then as time passes after initial learning (the first surge of flow), representations of events should lose detail (the bypassed small channels) while remaining elements of the same representations become more marked and strongly connected (established larger channels) (see Squire, Cohen, & Nadel, 1984). Some of what is stored in memory is forgotten; some is made stronger and more easily accessible.

Memory is distinct from sensing and perceiving information; all the information present during learning is not present during remembering. The pattern of connectivity associated with remembering a representation must be triggered in a different way than is first perceiving information. This analysis raises questions about what structures in the brain operate in establishing memory traces and in reactivating them. Those structures could be distinct from or overlapping with the ones involved in perceiving, acquiring, and responding to information in the first place.

The Anatomy of Memory

The collection of neural changes representing a memory is the **engram** (Squire, 1986), and the objective of much contemporary research in neuroscience is to locate engrams in the brain. In short, the concern is with *where* memories are. Two methods are useful in pursuing this search.

One method uses animal models that make it possible to associate localized damage to specific neural structures and the subsequent effect on behavior or to correlate localized brain activity with performance on memory tasks. As an example, recall from Chapter 3 that Adele Diamond's studies showed how monkeys who had sustained damage to the prefrontal cortex were unable to demonstrate location memory on an A-not-B-like search task. Also as described in Chapter 3, rats who had sustained damage to the hippocampus revealed deficits in spatial memory in the water-maze task. Animal models provide some basis for associating structure and function in memory studies, but many memory performances of interest to psychologists are not within the response repertoire of animal subjects, for example, recall of verbal material. Something else is needed.

Another useful strategy is to study human memory pathology (Kolb & Wishaw, 1985; Squire, 1986, 1987) in which, because of brain injury or disease, individuals exhibit memory impairment in the absence of other cognitive deficits. This is the condition of **amnesia,** the partial or total loss of memory. The study of patients suffering such disorders enables neuroscientists to decipher the associations between specific locations of brain damage and specific expressions of memory impairment. The study of animal models of brain functioning, amnesia, and human memory pathology (Mishkin & Appenzeller, 1987; Squire, 1986, 1987) has yielded considerable insight into the mystery of memory.

Although the picture is far from clear and the search is far from over, it seems that no single brain structure or region is solely responsible for memory storage and retrieval (Berman, 1986). The structures currently proposed as most involved in memory trace formation are the *cerebellum, hippocampus, amygdala,* and *cerebral cortex* (Thompson, 1986).

The cortical areas are implicated since those are the neural systems that ordinarily participate in perception, analysis, and processing of information to be learned, and memories most often originate in sensory impressions. Information storage is tied to the specific processing areas engaged during information acquisition, for example, visual processing and visual cortex (Squire, 1986).

Many neural systems participate in the representation of a complex event, but particular brain systems have a unique role to play in the representation process. The cerebellum is implicated in the performance of skilled movements, motor learning, and classical conditioning in mammals (Thompson, 1986). It is the amygdala and the hippocampus, however, two structures in the limbic system located on the inner surface of the temporal lobes in both hemispheres, whose removal or damage has a profound effect on a range of memory performances (Mishkin & Appenzeller, 1987). These structures have become the focus of much current investigation (Kesner, 1986; Squire, 1986, 1987).

The hippocampus, described in Chapter 3 in relation to spatial mapping, is particularly interesting because of its location, its unique geometric features, and its complex patterns of connectivity both internal to the structure and in projections to other brain regions. It clearly appears as a structure only in the

mammalian brain, in organisms viewed as having an adaptive advantage in the capacity to change their behavior in response to environmental press. Lesions to the hippocampus affect working memory, temporal memory, and spatial memory (O'Keefe & Nadel, 1978; Olton, 1983; Rawlins, 1985). Combined lesions to the hippocampus and amygdala affect global memory (Mishkin, Spiegler, Saunders, & Malamut, 1982), creating an amnesialike condition in animals.

A number of individuals reviewing the neuroscience literature make claims for multiple memory systems, not all of which depend equally on hippocampal involvement (Cohen & Squire, 1980; Hirsch, 1974; O'Keefe & Nadel, 1978). Sutherland and Rudy (1989) differentiated processes enabling memory for what they refer to as *simple associations* and those enabling memory for *configural associations.* The former are the sorts of traces on which memories established during conditioning would depend. The latter are more complex forms of connections as in learning and memory for relations, patterns, and cognitive maps. It is these forms that much of the research literature points to as hippocampal dependent.

From a developmental perspective, the role of the hippocampus formation in memory is particularly intriguing because the formation is late developing. In most of the brain, neurogenesis is a prenatal process. However, the generation of certain neurons (*granule cells*) in the hippocampus (and, incidentally, the cerebellum) occurs postnatally (Bayer & Altman, 1987; Eckenhoff & Rakic, 1988; Mangan, 1992). Thus, the generation of neurons in this structure differs from what is seen in neocortical development.

In fact, recent evidence with humans indicates that up to 20% of the granule cells of a substructure of the hippocampus formation called the *dentate gyrus* are formed postnatally. Proliferation continues up to 6 months of age, and immature cells (as evidenced by incomplete dendritic development) have been observed in brains of 15-month-old children (Seress, 1991). Extrapolations from these and other data (Nadel & Zola-Morgan, 1984) date the likely time when the human hippocampus should be approximating adult levels of functioning at 24 months. Behavioral data from spatial memory tasks are consistent with that projection (Mangan, 1992).

Tentative identification of the structures involved in memory and the concurrent study of individuals with memory disorders has led Squire (1986) to distinguish several varieties of memories on the basis of the neurological literature. First, the amnesia data provide evidence for distinguishing short-term, limited-capacity, immediate memory from long-term memory; the former is not impaired in amnesia patients.

Second, within the domain of long-term memory, there is a distinction between *declarative memory,* which is explicit, conscious, and inclusive of facts, episodes, lists, and routes, and *procedural memory,* retention of motor skills and operations and implicit knowledge. Squire subsumed the processes of habituation and simple conditioning under the procedural category. Again, these memory functions are not usually affected in amnesia patients. Squire further contended that procedural learning, knowledge, and memory are phylogenetically old and not restricted to mammals. The capacity for declarative knowledge, on the other hand, is phylogenetically recent, "reaching its greatest development in mammals with the full elaboration of medial temporal structures, especially the hippocampal formation and associated cortical areas" (Squire, 1986, p. 1615).

Implicit memory is also not usually affected in amnesiacs (Warrington & Weiskranz, 1982). As noted previously, implicit memory is memory without conscious awareness, without a deliberate attempt to recall specific information. Implicit memory is experimentally induced with a technique called **priming** (Graf & Schacter, 1985).

In priming, subjects are exposed to stimuli, such as a study list comprised of pairs of words (e.g., *mold-bread; jail-strange*). Then they are subsequently tested for recall of the stimuli. However, subjects can be tested in the usual explicit memory form—cued recall—in which one member of a word pair is presented and its associate recalled. Or, subjects can be tested in a priming condition. Then a word fragment is provided, such as *mold-bre___* or *bre___* and the subject completes the word. Amnesia patients fare worse than normals on the explicit memory tests, but they do just as well on the primed memory task. Therefore, information presented at an earlier time affects performance at a later time—which is, after all, what memory is. Possibly, amnesia patients are able to learn and form associations (Graf & Schacter, 1986; Kihlstrom, Schacter, Cork, Hurt, & Behr, 1990) but cannot access them in explicit form.

Priming effects may result from the operation of a distinct memory system—*a perceptual representation system*—disassociated from declarative memory (Tulving & Schacter, 1990) and accessed only through modality-specific cues, for example, picture fragments for visual information or word fragments for verbal information. Declarative memory, the memory system in which the role of the hippocampus is implicated, is not modality specific.

Summary

Much debate remains as to how best to conceptualize the nature of memory systems. And although there is controversy and differences in proposed models, much of the neurological evidence supports a view of memory as multiple structures organized around different information-storage systems. That explains why memory performances are differentially affected by pathologies—lesions or disease—and the type of performance probe used experimentally. The neuroscience literature generally supports distinctions and disassociations between immediate and long-term memory, implicit and explicit memory, and procedural and declarative memory. A structural feature of the brain associated with most theories positing distinctive memory systems is the role of the hippocampal formation. The precise involvement of this brain structure is not yet clear, but it is particularly implicated in explicit, declarative forms of memory. Squire's (1986) taxonomy of memory is represented in Figure 10-1.

The neurological record does not yield the definitive story of memory development. First, the data are too tenuous and constantly emerging. Second, the neurological level is substantially removed from the level of behavioral analysis. What the record provides is a backdrop against which to evaluate the developmental literature. It serves as a constraint on the plausibility of theoretical accounts of what develops and how development proceeds for those cognitive performances we associate with memory. Memories have neural substrates; remembering has analogous neural processes.

What we conclude about how memory operates and emerges at the cognitive level cannot be incompatible with the evidence reviewed here—the structure and function of those processes in the brain. Following are some points to keep in mind as we delve into behavioral literature:

1. The close association between the acquisition of knowledge (learning) and remembering it (memory) as revealed in overlapping circuitry.
2. The disassociability of distinct memory systems in the brain that are supported by brain anatomy.
3. The possible differential rates of maturation in the brain structures presumed to underlie memory performance.

FIGURE 10-1 *A Tentative Taxonomy of Memory Derived from the Neurological Record.*

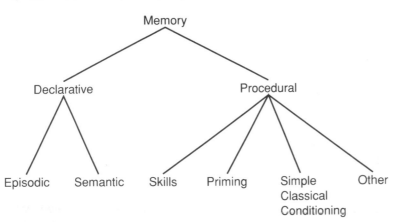

From "Mechanisms of Memory" by L. R. Squire, 1986, *Science, 232,* pp. 1612—1919. Adapted by permission of the American Association for the Advancement of Science. Copyright 1986 by the AAAS.

We may find that these three points have particularly profound developmental ramifications.

INFANT MEMORY

A multiple-systems view of memory, in which one system is instantiated in different brain structures with different maturational time tables than another, leads to predictions about memory in infancy that contrast with a single-system view. First, infants should not exhibit memory components (e.g., declarative aspects of memory) presumably mediated by late-developing structures. At the same time, infants should express memory abilities mediated by early-developing structures. Extrapolating along these lines, infant memory performances might have much in common with those of amnesiacs, particularly variable success on memory tasks as a function of the type of task (see Schacter, Moscovitch, Tulving, McLachlan, & Freedman, 1986), because the same structures—the hippocampus and amygdala—are below optimal levels of functioning in pathology and in immaturity.

Second, changes in memory capabilities should correlate with development. As the underlying structures mature, subsequent improvement in memory systems dependent on those structures will follow. These points follow from a proposition of *discontinuity* between memory as it exists in infants and memory in older individuals, and the source of discontinuity is the maturational status of neural structures supporting memory processes in younger and older individuals.

The hypothesis of an age-related discontinuity in memory should be empirically testable through the examination of infant memory. That seems like an appropriate testing ground for evaluating the multiple-systems model. The proposal postulating important memory differences in infants as compared to older individuals is the cornerstone of a number of neurologically based models of human memory development (Bachevalier & Mish-kin, 1984; Nadel & Zola-Morgan, 1984; Schacter & Moscovitch, 1984; Squire, 1986).

As in many other areas of cognitive development, infant research should clarify appropriate models. Unfortunately, disambiguating points of theoretical controversy is not a straightforward process. Assessing infant memory is methodologically difficult; equating infant tasks with standard memory tasks is virtually impossible. So, the data elicited from infants remain open to alternative interpretation.

A presumption in many classical developmental theories is that early experience is somehow especially salient and critical for developmental progress. Indeed, the presumption has become incorporated into lay thinking. We tend to take for granted the substantial importance of infancy and infant experience for later development; it seems self-evident. At the same time, people cannot recall those early experiences. Memory for events prior to about 3 or 4 years of age is almost universally absent (Kail, 1990). So, a mystery arises: How can early experience exert such a powerful effect on later behavior if no memory of that experience exists?

There have been many attempts to account for this infantile amnesia, ranging from the Freudian account with its emphasis on *repression,* to those that posit retrieval difficulties as the culprit. Most accounts accept the fact of infant memory, otherwise early experience could not carry over to later development. But infant memory has to be accessed in a different way. The proposition is that infant memory must take a nonlinguistic form since the infant is not yet a language user. Thus, the older individual, who is a language user, may have lost the ability to retrieve these early nonlinguistically coded memories.

The experiential and environmental context in which infant memories are established is so different from later developmental contexts that the individual has no cues for getting at and activating memories that may have been established. Then again, if different brain structures mediate early and late memories, perhaps access is structure specific. The reliability of infantile amnesia as a cognitive phenomenon is an undeniable given. The phenomenon reiterates the point that there are differences between memory as an infant might experience and express it and the counterpart function in more mature individuals. We are not quite certain why that should be so.

Returning to the water-hill metaphor of memory, a response revealing a memory trace is made when the water reaches the bottom of the hill. Then, recall of a previous encounter, recognition of a familiar perceptual event or reconstruction of a prior response becomes evidence that furrowing accomplished by the water's travel has been sustained. It is not clear, however, what the infant's response signaling the presence of preexisting furrowing should look like. What can an infant do to reveal the influence of prior learning?

Some behaviors in an infant's response repertoire indicative of the operations of memory are clear from studies in other areas of infant cognition. Preference for novelty is an example (Friedman, Nagy, & Carpenter, 1970; Slater, Morison, & Rose, 1982, 1983, 1984; Werner & Siqueland, 1978). Presumably, to look longer at a novel stimulus as compared to a previously presented, familiar one, the infant must be able to store some semblance of the previous stimulus across trials. The necessary time of storage may only be a few seconds, but it must be of sufficient duration to permit some rudimentary comparison process between the novel stimulus and a "representation" of the old stimulus. Similarly, habituation must capitalize on some form of memory. The baby cannot dishabituate to a change in stimulation without recognition of the change. And since the "old" stimulation is removed before the "new" stimulation is presented, rudimentary memory is again implicated.

You know already from Chapters 2, 3, and 6 that even very young infants display preferences for new stimuli, respond to novelty, and exhibit habituation-dishabituation very early in life. Obviously, this notion of "memory" is not a duplicate of the cognitive operation present in adults, but some sort of storage capacity is implicated. Even neonates can remember high-contrast visual stimuli for at least 3 minutes (Gotlieb & Sloane, 1989). Duration of storage may be brief, but a storage function certainly appears to play a role.

Rudimentary search behavior leads to the same conclusion. Visual search for an absent object, as Diamond's and Baillargeon's data have shown (see Chapter 3), is an expressed capability well before the first birthday. It is illogical to expect search for an object without presuming some memory of that object. Similarly, dishabituation to surprising, constraint-violating, physical events (see Chapter 6) could not occur if the constraint-consistent event were not represented.

These infant performances, however, are very different from the kinds of memory performances typically expected from older individuals. An adult may be asked to recall a familiar stimulus by producing it, for example, supplying a previously encountered word or completing a word fragment. Or an adult may be asked to recognize which words on a list were seen before on a prior learning trial. An animal may have to find a hidden object, locate a familiar spot in a maze, or retrace an old route. But the prelinguistic, nonmotoric infant has neither the verbal capacities to perform human adult memory tasks nor sufficiently mature motor skills to do what rats and monkeys do. So, how do we know if the water got to the bottom of the hill?

Evidence from Conditioning Studies

It is a fact that babies can be **operantly conditioned** (Rovee-Collier & Gekoski, 1979). In conditioning, the subject learns an association between a stimulus and a response, for example, that a specific action (R) will produce a reinforcing consequence (S^+). During the training phase of conditioning, the person acquires the *S-R* contingency and the response rate increases as a function of the reinforcement.

When the conditioning is occurring, discriminitive stimuli (S^D) are also present; these stimuli signal the onset of the contingency, that it is in operation. On a later occasion, introduction of those S^Ds (discriminative stimuli) can reinstate posttraining levels of responding. If the conditioning has affected behavior in a lasting way, then that is reflected in the response rate; responding will approximate postacquisition levels when cued. If the conditioning is only transitory, the response rate should return to preacquisition, baseline levels despite the presence of signaling S^Ds.

Since babies can be successfully conditioned, they must have acquired the contingency (learning). And, if, on a subsequent occasion, the target response rate increases in the presence of the original S^Ds, then the association between the S^Ds, the response, and the reinforcement also has been acquired (more learning). Most critically, if there is a separation in time between initial learning and those subsequent postraining trials, then the associations have to have been remembered. Therefore, memory is implicated in the conditionability of infants.

The operant conditioning paradigm holds promise as a mechanism for studying memory in infant subjects for a number of reasons. First, conditionability is broadly applicable to a variety of responses, some of which, like simple motor ones, such as kicking and head turning, are within the response repertoires of even young babies.

Second, the responses selected for reinforcement are usually what we think of as "voluntary" and *emitted* as compared to the reflexive, *elicited* ones associated with classical conditioning. The classical conditioning paradigm is used quite productively in the study of memory in invertebrates (see Davis, 1986), but operantly conditioned responses intuitively

seem to have more in common with the deliberate sort of behaviors typically associated with recall in humans.

Third, by assessing the durability of conditioning over time, it is possible to evaluate extinction, which in memory terms is *forgetting.* Finally, there are the phenomena of generalization and discrimination—the extent to which the reinforced response can be reinstantiated later with similar but not duplicate S^Ds. From a memory perspective, if the subject responds at posttraining levels to exactly the same S^Ds as used in training but not to changed S^Ds, then they must remember the particular features of those original S^Ds.

Carolyn Rovee-Collier and her associates (Rovee-Collier, 1984, 1990; Rovee-Collier & Fagen, 1981; Rovee-Collier, Sullivan, Enright, Lucas, & Fagen, 1980) have cleverly exploited the operant conditioning paradigm in order to study memory in human infants. Essentially, in these studies an infant's kicking behavior is operantly conditioned. While the baby lies in a crib or playpen, his ankle is connected by a ribbon to a mobile over the crib. A kick (R) activates the mobile and makes it move (S^+). The sight of the motion is reinforcing to babies, so the rate of kicking, the operant response, increases as conditioning ensues. Subject babies undergo brief training sessions to establish the connection between the sight of the mobile (S^D), the kicking (R), and the reinforcing motion.

Kicking rate can be quantified and expressed as a measure of operant kicking strength when compared with the baseline—the spontaneous kicking rate. After establishing the operant learning, the investigators can check its durability by reintroducing the unattached mobile and observing possible changes in kicking strength as a consequence. By varying time between initial learning and reassessment, the investigators quantify how long the conditioning memory lasts. By reactivating the conditioning in intervening sessions, they assess whether memory can be strengthened and forgetting delayed. By varying features of the S^Ds on testing trials, they can examine whether babies seem to remember the specific features associated with the training stimuli.

The basic idea is that the subject is trained to perform a distinctive response in a particular setting. The subject is subsequently returned to that setting after a delay, and the experimenter "asks" the subject to remember the contingency. The question to be evaluated is: Does the subject emit the response in the presence of the original information? For Rovee-Collier, the paradigm has much in common with the *cued-recall paradigm* used in the study of memory in children and adults (Spear, 1978).

Rovee-Collier used two variations of the operant conditioning paradigm (Rovee-Collier, 1990). In the **simple forgetting paradigm**, infants are initially conditioned on consecutive days and assessed for recall after a determined interval, which can range from 1 to 42 days after training. With this technique, the investigators evaluate the durability of conditioning, which is in effect memory, and they observe the *forgetting function*—the rapidity of memory loss plotted against time.

In the **reactivation paradigm**, conditioning is established just as in the other paradigm. But, after a sufficient interval has passed to insure forgetting (determined from data generated under conditions in the first paradigm), a very brief reminder of conditioning is presented. Then retention is measured. In either paradigm, details of the conditioning context can be manipulated, too: the features of the mobile itself, the features of the crib bumper present during conditioning, and so forth.

As for simple forgetting, retention is very high when the interval is a single day, and memory gradually decreases over a period of several days. Two-month-old babies forget faster and retain less than 3-month-old babies do (Greco, Rovee-Collier, Hayne, Griesler & Earley, 1986); 6-month-old babies exhibit bet-

ter memories and more durable memories than their younger cohorts (Hill, Borovsky & Rovee-Collier, 1988). These data are presented in Figure 10-2. Forgetting is generally complete about 6 to 8 days after training (Hayne, 1988; Sullivan, Rovee-Collier, & Tynes, 1979) but increasing the duration of training sessions or the number of them significantly prolongs retention (Enright, Rovee-Collier, Fagen, & Caniglia, 1983; Ohr, Fagen, Rovee-Collier, Hayne, & Vander Linde, 1989; Vander Linde, Morrongiello, & Rovee-Collier, 1985).

Clearly, infants are capable of remembering a contingency over long periods of time and can demonstrate their memories by emitting the operant response when subsequently presented with an appropriate S^D. These data, then, support long-term memory as a capacity of infants.

FIGURE 10-2 *Forgetting Functions for 2-, 3-, and 6-Month-Old Infants Operantly Conditioned to Kick in the Presence of a Mobile.*
Recall of the conditioned effect was assessed subsequent to the initial learning to evaluate memory.

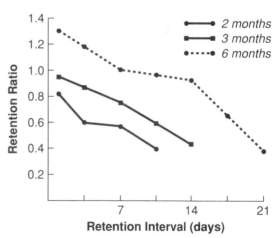

From "Continuities in Infant Memory Development" by W. L. Hill, D. Borovsky, and C. Rovee-Collier, 1988, *Developmental Psychobiology, 21,* pp. 43—62. Copyright 1988 by the American Psychological Association. Reprinted by permission.

There is, however, great specificity to these memories. At assessment one day after training, when absolute retrieval is greatest, babies do not respond above baseline when cued with a novel mobile (changed S^D). Apparently, their memory is highly specific, allowing them to differentiate the features of the training mobile from the changed features of the novel mobile. They do not respond in the presence of the novel stimulus because they "know" it is not the correct S^D. They could not "know" that without somehow having preserved a detailed representation of the correct S^D. Similarly, if the context is different at assessment (e.g., the crib liner) and memory is assessed one day after training, babies do not respond above baseline either. So, again, their memory must include the particular features of the distinctive entities involved in the learning environment, and the contingency is not retrieved by entities with only generally similar features.

Somewhat paradoxically, if the interval between training and assessment is increased, memory performance with the changed S^Ds is actually better; retrieval of the response does generalize to similar but not the exact context and stimulus. In sum, at short intervals, memory is better and specific; at longer intervals, it is weaker but more general (Rovee-Collier & Sullivan, 1980). The investigators attribute this outcome to the specificity of what is remembered and to differential decay of what is remembered over time. Memory for the details of the training context are forgotten more rapidly than those for its general features (Borovsky, 1987).

Extending the water-hill metaphor, it is as if the training "water" leaves a distinct, sharp channel down the hill. But with time, the edges of the channel erode and become less distinct. Recall assessed soon after training reveals the sharpness of the trace, showing up as recall only to a particular cue. But, later, recall is fuzzier. Because it is fuzzier, a variety of cues only somewhat similar to the original now reactivate the trace.

Memories are made more durable with reactivation. Reactivation is not retraining; it simply involves the reintroduction, after forgetting should have occurred, of only the original training S^Ds, not the contingency. Infants who receive such a reminder exhibit near perfect retention upon long-term retention assessment whereas nonreminded infants have forgotten the contingency (Hayne, Rovee-Collier, & Perris, 1987; Hill, Borovsky, Rovee-Collier, 1988). It is as if the reminder "water" significantly deepens the original furrowing, thereby strengthening the memory.

The specificity of the reactivation intervention is intriguing and complex. Apparently, babies remember the general features associated with the training event better than the specific features. In all these results, however, the efficacy of memory is extremely context specific. Whether to reactivate those traces or to elicit evidence of recall, the setting needs to be almost a duplicate of the training setting. What seem like minor changes (e.g., the print on the crib bumper) alter the effect. These are not flexible memories variously accessed through multiple cues. Instead, they are narrowly accessible traces of past events tapped only with an remarkably narrow range of cues.

Continuity versus Discontinuity in Infant Memory

There is little doubt that infants are capable of learning and memory. When short-term, immediate memory is tapped, babies differentiate novel and familiar stimuli, preferring the former and habituating to the latter. On visual paired comparison tasks, delayed nonmatching to sample tasks, habituation tasks, and object search tasks (Diamond, 1990a, 1990b, 1990c, 1991), babies exhibit performances consistent with the operations of memory. Most times, delays between initial processing of information and assessment of storage must be brief (tens of seconds), and as delays increase in length, evidence for memory decreases. This, however, is characterized as a quantitative cognitive change.

When long-term memory is assessed, as with the operant conditioning paradigm, results are also positive. Infants can remember an established contingency for days, which is evidence for long-term memory. In short, infants remember, and they remember some information for relatively long periods of time.

The issue is not so much that infants remember, but what the implications of this positive evidence are for the nature of memory development. There are two alternative stances. In one, a case is made for the *continuity* in functioning between infant, child, and adult since all individuals exhibit commonalities in their abilities to remember. Diamond (1991), for example, argued that young children do remember the location of a hidden object when delays are brief. She attributed any limitations in the demonstration of memory to problems of motor control over search actions (Diamond, 1990a, 1990b). Those problems originate in the immaturity of the frontal cortex. Lack of memory is not the culprit in failure to search—a conclusion supported by others as well (Baillargeon & Graber, 1988).

Rovee-Collier (1990) and colleagues (Hill et al., 1988) also made arguments for continuity in memory across age. The evidence is the capacity of babies 2 to 6 months of age to recall contingencies. The argument is that babies do get better at remembering with age (Rovee-Collier, 1990), but it is not parsimonious to posit that they remember differently. These baby data, in addition to monkey data about the effects of lesioning the frontal cortex, seem to point to developmental continuity in memory. Age-related differences in memory performances are attributed to nonmemory functions (motor control) or context effects that restrict retrieval (specificity of recall).

Others (Moscovitch, 1985; Schacter & Moscovitch, 1984) argue for *discontinuity* and time the point of change at around 8 months

of age when the A-not-B error is overcome (see Schacter, Moscovitch, Tulving, McLachlan, & Freedman, 1986). Acceptance of this rationale presumes one also accepts the A-not-B error prior to 8 months as a real memory failure rather than an artifactual one (but see Diamond, 1991). The majority of the evidence leading to this conclusion comes from the study of amnesia patients who make what appear to be some of the sorts of errors babies would make. In these cases, however, it is the hippocampus formation that is implicated (Mishkin & Appenzeller, 1987). A less than optimally functioning hippocampus, whether because of lesion, disease or immaturity, is interpreted as a *memory* deficit not a *performance* deficit (à la Diamond). In a discontinuity interpretation, infants' capacity for memory is not denied; rather, the argument is made that infant memory performances reflect a distinct, early maturing memory system, not mediated by the hippocampus formation.

It is not at all clear how to resolve this argument. The data for the role of the hippocampus in declarative memory is very compelling. The evidence for the memory capacity of infants is also. There are problems with both, however. Equating performances of amnesiacs and infants is fraught with difficulty. Amnesiacs are adults who, virtually by definition, do not have other impaired cognitive functioning. Therefore, they can learn, solve problems, and access strategies to retain information over short-term intervals.

Memory functions are intertwined with other cognitive functions in complex ways. Infants are *generally* cognitively immature. With infant performance deficits, it is not easy to determine whether a memory deficit or some other cognitive deficit underlies performance failure. Keeping in mind the possible nonequivalency of tasks, both babies and amnesiacs demonstrate the capacity for memories associated with what Moscovitch refers to as the early-developing system: implicit memories, motor memories, immediate memory.

Amnesiacs with hippocampal-amygdala damage fail declarative memory tasks. We cannot really determine whether infants would fail declarative memory tasks because we have no way to evaluate that. Recalling contingencies for motor behaviors and recalling object locations within a visual search paradigm might not qualify as the appropriate tasks to assess the infant equivalent of declarative memory.

The incredible specificity of infant recall in the conditioning paradigm raises some interesting questions, too. Perhaps that lack of flexibility in recallability is much like what is associated with priming. Priming works to elicit memory in amnesiacs when the recall cue is modality specific to initial information input; otherwise, it does not. The hippocampus formation is not implicated in implicit memory as tapped by a priming task.

Contingency recall by babies is highly specific to the retrieval cue employed, too. It, like a priming cue, cannot vary from the context of input. One can make a good case that the phenomenon of recalling contingencies by babies has more in common with priming of implicit memory than with the cued-recall tasks for tapping declarative memory in older individuals.

While resolution is not achieved, there is no evidence as of yet that counterindicates a multiple-memory-system view. Habituation, visual preference, and recall of operant contingencies could all reflect operation of an early-developing system distinct from the late-developing one. Different brain structures are implicated in each, and they are structures that do not share the same developmental time table.

The emerging picture of memory development has continuities and discontinuities. The continuity is that both infants and older individuals display the capacity for memory. However, there is a possible discontinuity between infancy and later age periods. But by 24 months of age, supporting brain structures should be functioning in a mostly mature manner. Therefore, there is no compelling neurological reason to suspect that subsequent changes in memory functioning should reflect additional discontinuities. Growing children have much to learn, lots of connections to form, many channels to carve, strengthen, and elaborate. We should be able to account for those subsequent changes by continuous growth processes.

DEVELOPMENTAL CHANGES IN MEMORY PERFORMANCE

It is an empirical truism that on any given memory task, an older child will assuredly remember more items than a younger child will. Although we know that memory proficiency increases with age, why that should be so is less clear. We already know that younger children typically perform less well than older children do on a range of cognitive tasks, but the reasons behind performance differences are seldom obvious. The same is true of memory-performance differences.

Moreover, memory and the remaining operations of cognition are intertwined, enmeshed processes. Teasing apart the unique contributions of memory to cognitive functioning is not easy; identifying specifically what it is about memory that develops is not easy either. Older children have spent much time learning, elaborating their learning, practicing what they have learned, and reactivating and strengthening memories; they also have experienced demands to remember. Younger children are less exposed to all of this. So the question is, Are there developmental differences constrained to the memory component of cognition that account for these age differences in performance?

Generally, investigators have identified three possible ways in which memory might change with development. The first is in *capacity*. Possibly, the hardware underlying memory changes with age such that the older child actually has more memory "machinery." The second is *control* over memory processes. Older children may have access to strategies that help them do something to remember, such as organizing, elaborating, and rehearsing incoming information for later retrieval. And third, there is *content*, the substantive nature of the material to be recalled. This is sometimes referred to as a *knowledge effect* because meaningful items held in memory are part of what the individual knows about the world, and those items are intertwined with prior knowledge.

The influence of the domain-general perspective on cognition and particularly the information-processing-derived computer metaphor influences how memory development is conceptualized and how memory change is studied. First, there is a distinction between the "hardware" and the "software" supporting memory operations just as we differentiate the computer-as-machine from how it functions to manipulate data. The hardware is analogous to the neural circuitry of the brain while software references the programs—the algorithms, data-processing procedures, and data representations the machine accesses and uses when acting on incoming information. These metaphoric computers have capacities, space limitations, processing limitations, differences in available programs, and so forth; the extension to child-as-computer follows.

Second, by implication, we should be able to identify and characterize these processing systems in some generic way, just as we might characterize the general characteristics of computing systems. If any capacity limitations are identified and described, they constitute *system limitations*, not particular task limitations. This is an important distinction. If memory is to be a primary focus of developmental investigation, then it is that process, that system, that we must be able to characterize. If, on the other hand, memory effects turn out to be an epiphenomenon of other cognitive operations—reasoning, language

acquisition, conceptual knowledge, and so forth—then outlining the characteristics of memory operations generically might be the wrong focus.

In the next section, we review and evaluate the literature on developmental changes in those aspects of memory that seem to change with development. Most of the research has been conducted from an information-processing perspective (see Kail, 1990). With the neurological evidence in mind, we will consider what the empirical picture means in the larger theoretical picture, what contribution it makes.

There is an interesting note to keep in mind, however. Piaget is one cognitive developmentalist who did not place much stock in the contribution of memory per se to intellectual functioning (Piaget & Inhelder, 1973). In his view, memory reflected everything else going on in the ontogenetic evolution of the cognitive structures. Older children remember better because their cognitive structure is operational, organized, and accessible to reflection. Younger children are cognitively immature and that shows up as a pervasive performance decrement—conceptually, spatially, numerically, and also in terms of memory ability.

Changes in Capacity

Questions about capacity changes concern the hardware of memory: how the structure of the system might evolve in age-related ways that permit increasingly greater amounts of information to be held in storage. In a common-sense explication, we might think of memory as composed of a finite number of slots into which incoming information can be put and held for varying durations. Quite possibly, the number of slots increases with development. If so, then there would be structural constraints on how much information an immature individual could hold.

Extrapolating along these common-sense lines, suppose there were 3 available slots at age 4, 9 at age 7, 15 at age 12, and so forth (The numbers are arbitrarily chosen for illustration purposes). The 4-year-old should appear deficient at any recall task necessitating more than three slots. As an example, consider remembering a number sequence with more than three integers or repeating verbatim a sentence with more than three words. Seven-year-olds could remember everything a 4-year-old could and also could succeed on memory tasks requiring even more slots, for example, repeating a phone number or remembering their home addresses. Thus, as the number of slots increase in the structural architecture, capacity to hold items in memory increases, and the result is changes in memory performance proficiency.

Most research about age-related changes in proficiency focus on *short-term* or what is often called **working memory.** There has been little reason to postulate any capacity changes in either sensory memory or long-term memory. At least from age 5 through adulthood, people demonstrate roughly the same capacity for a sensory store (Morrison, Holmes, & Haith, 1974). Children may take longer to encode information when they are younger (Hoving, Spencer, Robb & Schulte, 1978), but generally, the structural features of sensory memory are developmentally invariant after infancy. Similarly, there is no reason to suspect developmental changes in long-term memory capacity either (Siegler, 1991). Long-term capacity seems to be limitless. There is little risk of overcrowding, of pushing old information out as new data come in. If there is a capacity bottleneck in memory, it has to be located in short-term store.

Working memory is conceptualized as the "file cabinet" where information is held while cognitive work is being done with it. Work examples include (1) a set of integers to be added, (2) a series of words in a sentence to be comprehended, or (3) the premises from which an inference is to be drawn. Recall from earlier chapters (4, 8, and 9, particularly), that young children exhibit limitations in transitive reasoning, their produced sentences tend to be short, and they experience difficulties on deductive reasoning tasks. All these observed empirical facts have been attributed at one time or another to limitations in holding adequate material in short-term memory long enough to get the cognitive job done. The intuition behind this rationale is that failures in reasoning will occur if the child does not possess the cognitive equipment to apply a reasoning process to premises *or* if a child does not have access to the premises because limited memory capacity constrains access to the premises.

The problem with hypotheses about the potential limited capacity of working memory is creating a way of evaluating memory relatively independent of content. Memory is supposed to be a domain-general operation. The goal is to identify characteristics of the operation, including capacity, that cut across particulars of item content. Older children and adults know more content than younger children do and conceivably have relevant representations in long-term memory on which they can draw. Therefore, on a memory task, prior knowledge, as well as current working memory capacity, are bound to affect performance adequacy.

But the two influences are confounded. The young child who performs poorly on a memory task supposedly tapping short-term memory but including meaningful material with potential connections to items in long-term memory may do so because of capacity limitations, prior knowledge limitations, or both. True, young children have less knowledge, fewer stored representations than older ones, but that is not strictly a capacity issue.

To avoid the confounding problem, the capacity of short-term storage is typically assessed with *non*meaningful material. The favorite stimuli are strings of items, digits, letters, or the like. A series of digits, for example, 7, 10, 5, 3, 8, is presented to the person who then reproduces them in the sequence given. The number of digits recalled is an index of memory span or memory capacity (Knopf, Körkel, Schneider, & Weinert, 1988). Memory span increases with age: 2-year-olds generally reproduce about two items, 5-year-olds about four, and adults about seven.

In Dempster's (1981) summary of several studies of memory span, this age-related increase in performance was reliable whether the items to be recalled were digits, letters, or words. A summary of the data is presented in Figure 10-3. Traditional verbal memory span as measured on standardized intelligence tests goes from about two items at age 2½ to about five items at age 7 (Woodworth & Schlosberg, 1954). If recalling items from a nine-item list, 2½-year-olds remember about 20%, 4-year-

olds about 40% (Perlmutter & Myers, 1979). In short, the empirical finding is fairly stable.

While the finding is reliable, the interpretation is more elusive. The empirical data could be explained by a developmental change in capacity, but there are alternative explanations as well. Information is kept active in short-term memory by using a number of rehearsal strategies, such as repeating the items, chunking the items, or making up an image of the items. It has long been recognized that older children are more likely to rehearse than younger children (Flavell, Beach, & Chinsky, 1966; Kail, 1990; Ornstein, Baker-Ward, & Naus, 1988). So, performance differences could be attributed not to capacity, but to rehearsal.

Then again, older children have a lot more familiarity with the stimuli—numbers, letters, and words. School-age children know about

FIGURE 10-3 *Memory Span for Digits as a Function of Age.*

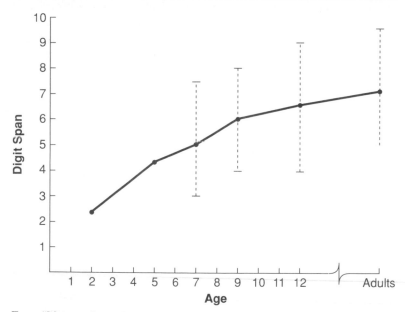

these things and have past experiences with these things in ways that younger children have not. As a consequence, performance effects could be a ramification of knowledge effects (Carey, 1990). In fact, there is no compelling reason, on the basis of these empirical data, to conclude that age-related changes in memory capacity underlie age-observed performance changes on digit-span-type tasks.

Pascual-Leone (1970) pursued the hypothesis of short-term memory capacity limitations in short-term memory. He proposed that the available computing space, what he called the **M-space,** increased in size during development. There are two components in M-space—e and k. E is the amount of space for general information about how to solve a task; k is the space available for information specific to the task at hand including relevant items and procedures to apply (analogous to the "slots" in an earlier example). E does not change in capacity with development, but k does. According to Pascual-Leone (1970), k increases by one unit every other year between age 3 (where $k = 1$) and age 16 (where $k = 7$) (see Kail, 1990).

A number of tests of the M-space hypothesis have been conducted (Case, 1972; Case & Serlin, 1978; Pascual-Leone, 1970; Scardamalia, 1977). Using digit stimuli, for example, children were presented with n ordered digits (e.g., 3, 8, 12) and a final digit (e.g., 10) to be appropriately placed in the sequence (between 8 and 12). The number of digits was equal to or greater than the hypothesized available M-space (for 6-year-olds, $e + 2$).

It was predicted that children would correctly solve the problem when $n = k$ and the digits are remembered; when $n > k$, proficiency would decrease (Case, 1972). The data were consistent with the predictions but the meaning of that outcome is ambiguous. To make the predictions, assumptions had to be made about the operations of memory; some of those assumptions may be incorrect, for ex-

ample, how individual items are dropped when $n > k$. Many investigators remain unconvinced by the experiments (Trabasso, 1978; Trabasso & Foellinger, 1978). Then there are those stimuli again; older children know a lot more about numbers than younger ones do, especially how they sequence in an ordinal chain (see Chapter 6).

Case (1985a) addressed possible capacity limitations in memory as a constraint on children's cognitive functioning. But unlike Pascual-Leone, Case did not contend that the overall space available in short-term memory increases with development. Instead, he divided the total resource space into *operating space* and *short-term storage space*. The total space is developmentally fixed, but the available space can be split between the two components.

To solve a given problem, the individual needs space to carry out the operation, for example, performing addition on a set of integers, and space to hold the items to be operated on (like k). Overall proficiency in problem solving, like the ability to add longer and longer strings of integers, will increase if, as Pascual-Leone proposed, k-space increases with age. Overall proficiency will also increase if operating space demands decrease with development, freeing up more resources for storage. That is Case's argument. Operating space needs decrease as cognitive operations become more automated through practice and become less resource demanding as a consequence. Thus, capacity overall does not change; allocation of resources changes and mimics capacity change. Although it is an inferential leap from behavioral data to neuropsychological evidence, there is probably good reason to suspect that practice, which increases with age, makes memories more efficient. (It is that water again.) There is much less reason to suspect that the actual capacity to lay down memories is age related; the hill is there for the furrowing.

Performance changes with development. Does capacity change or does it not? Unfortunately, the experimental data do not allow us to differentiate definitively whether it does or does not. Much of the data is consistent with an overall capacity change; much of it is equally consistent with an allocation change. We cannot disconfirm one or the other hypothesis. Since the data are indeterminate, the issue is unresolved, and we might conclude that this line of study has led to an investigative dead end. Most developmentalists do not yet see compelling evidence for capacity changes in memory sufficient to explain the reliably observed age-related changes in memory performance (Kail, 1990; Siegler, 1991). The explanation would seem to lie somewhere else.

Changes in Control Processes

Content in short-term memory—a list of words, a series of numbers, a spoken sentence—decays rapidly. In early models of the memory system, short-term memory was viewed as an information bottleneck between sensory memory, which is modality specific, short lasting but roomy, and long-term memory, which is amodal, long lasting, and even roomier. But to get from sensory input to the long-term store, intuitive wisdom had it that information must get through this bottleneck or be lost indefinitely. Information in short-term store had to be kept active long enough to solve an immediate problem, or it had to be transformed into a representation storable in the long-term system. These ideas persist in contemporary perspectives in which short-term memory is envisioned as having limited capacity with a finite number of slots.

Common sense informs most adults that new, incoming information does have a high probability of loss. We will not recall the grocery list or the series of errands that need doing without some effort. Therefore, we typically engage in behaviors to help this process happen. When we look up a new phone number, we repeat it until we can either write it down (a permanent store) or dial the phone. To remember a list of words—*elephant, bicycle, hat*—we create an image of the three items interacting—an elephant wearing a hat and riding a bicycle—to make those individual items more memorable. Then again, to remember a long list of words, we can organize them into conceptual categories—fruits, animals, artifacts, and so forth.

When faced with the demand of remembering information for later retrieval from long-term store, most of us will engage in some type of activity to increase the probability of recall. Some children make up stories with their vocabulary words in an attempt to insure recall.

When the author was in college, she was faced with a task demanding verbatim recall of several pages from a interview manual. Each page was comprised of a list of statements. In order to insure memorability, the author came up with an elaborate code for each page that embedded the first letter of the sentences in a list, for example *L-P-H-I-T,* for a five-item list. Then, each sentence was learned and associated with its letter, the letter codes were learned and associated with each page. Upon the demand to recall, with page numbers as the retrieval cues, the code was produced and used as a cue to replicate the verbatim sentences in sequence. This may seem like a rather silly way to test for remembered knowledge (as it certainly seemed at the time), but the techniques were effective in facilitating recall.

Devices applied to information to be recalled are **mnemonic skills** (Ornstein, Baker-Ward, & Naus, 1988). They are deliberate, intentional, goal-directed techniques, *strategies,* or plans for the storage and retrieval of items from memory. Psychologists have amassed a rich data base regarding age-related changes in the use and accessibility of memory strategies (Chi, 1983; Kail, 1990; Kail & Hagen, 1977; Ornstein, 1978). Three of the most often studied of these mnemonics are:

1. *Rehearsal,* repetition of items to be recalled as in repeating them over and over.
2. *Organization,* the structuring of items into categories or sets on some conceptual basis.
3. *Elaboration,* embedding the items in some meaningful unit like an image or story.

Numerous studies reveal that older children are more likely than younger children to generate and utilize strategic plans to aid remembering (Bjorklund, 1990; Bjorklund & Muir, 1988; Kail, 1990; Schneider & Pressley, 1989). Prior to age 7, it seems, children typically are not strategic; but around that time, they begin to use the simplest rehearsal strategy—overt or covert repetition of items to be remembered. Flavell, Beach, and Chinsky (1966) observed that when asked to recall pictorial stimuli following brief delays, only 10% of 5-year-olds rehearsed to help remember the stimuli while 60% of 7-year-olds and 85% of 10-year-olds did. Older children are typically more proficient in the use of repetition strategies, rehearsing more items from a list to be recalled, as compared to younger children (Cuvo, 1975; Ornstein, Naus, & Liberty, 1975; Ornstein, Naus, & Stone, 1977).

Organization is the next strategy that emerges developmentally. When 5- to 11-year-olds were given a task to remember a group of pictures, the 10- and 11-year-olds first organized the pictures into groups based on category membership. Younger children rarely did (Moely, Olson, Halwes, & Flavell, 1969).

Elaboration appears to be the last of the three to develop (Pressley, 1982). Although older children spontaneously display strategic behavior, younger children can be trained in mnemonic skills (Harnishfeger & Borklund, 1990; Ornstein, Naus, & Stone, 1977; Pressley & Levin, 1978; Shriberg, Levin, McCormick, & Pressley, 1982), although they do not always generalize their newly acquired skills across situations (Brown, Bransford, Ferrara, & Campione, 1983).

As opposed to just closing one's eyes and furrowing one's brow in a passive attempt to remember, deliberate, active attempts at remembering presume some level of conscious awareness of what memory is, what it does, and what its limitations are. This cognitive skill is termed **metamemory** (Flavell & Wellman, 1977; Flavell, 1979). Then it makes sense to come up with plans for getting around those limitations. Older children usually predict more accurately what they will be able to remember (Schneider & Pressley, 1989).

Knowing about and then compensating for anticipated shortcomings in a mental process depends on knowing something about the operation of the mental domain. In Chapter 7, evidence was presented about children's understanding of mind. And indeed, it is around middle childhood that children begin revealing an adultlike understanding of mental processes (Fabricius et al., 1989). However, children are aware of mindful things considerably before that time (Wellman, 1990). Perhaps the case from the empirical literature of the young child as a passive, nonstrategic, and, hence, without a very good memory, leaves some key evidence out.

If we assume that knowledge of memory as an operation is prerequisite to engaging in any activity to affect that process, then is there any evidence that young children possess the prerequisites? Wellman (1988) contended that there is such evidence. Preschoolers, even 2½-year-olds, demonstrate understanding of mental verbs, such as *remember, think, know, pretend* (Johnson & Wellman, 1980; Macnamara, Baker, & Olson, 1976; Shatz, Wellman, & Silber, 1983; Wellman & Estes, 1987; Wellman & Johnson, 1979). Three-, 4-, and 5-year-old children know about memory specifically

(Wellman, 1977; Yussen & Bird, 1979) and can make predictive judgments about their certainty in knowing and probable accuracy in remembering (Cultice, Sommerville, & Wellman, 1983; DeLoach & Brown, 1984), a phenomenon referred to as **feeling-of-knowing** (Hart, 1965).

The deployment of a strategy to remember also presumes an *intention* to remember. Do young children demonstrate such an intention in their mnemonic attempts? Again, Wellman's (1988) conclusion is yes. In trying to remember, in trying to attend to items to be remembered, and in differentially engaging in these behaviors as a function of instructional set (i.e., under memory demands), these youngsters reveal an intention to remember (Somerville, Wellman, & Cultice, 1983). They also reveal a conviction that such deliberate effort will pay off (Miller & Zalenski, 1982; Wellman, Collins, & Glieberman, 1981).

It would seem, then, that young children have the necessary foundation for engaging in strategic remembering. But do they? Again, Wellman (1988) contends that they do, but not necessarily in the narrow way that investigators have traditionally defined the term *strategy*.

Three-year-olds will look at and touch a hiding place when instructed to remember where an object is located (Wellman, Ritter, & Flavell, 1975) more often than if just told to wait for the object. Similarly, in studies where children as young as 2½ knew they would have to remember where a doll was hidden after a delay, they would do all sorts of strategic things in the interim, such as pointing to the location; saying the doll's name aloud, sometimes with its location; maintaining attention to the location; and so forth (DeLoach & Brown, 1979; DeLoach, Caseate, & Brown, 1985). The behaviors do not fit the usual category of deliberate strategies, which are typically verbal and conceptual (e.g., verbal repetition, conceptual clustering), but they qualify

as deliberate, intentional, and goal-directed attempts to effect the memory process. That does qualify as a sort of strategy.

Unfortunately, young children's strategies are often *faulty;* they just don't work very well (see for e.g., Baker-Ward, Ornstein, & Holden, 1984). So, very young children may not be the best strategy users and certainly are not as adept as their older counterparts. But that is not the same as being nonstrategic.

Whether or not young children use memory strategies raises questions about the nature or memory development after infancy. If, indeed, young children can be characterized as nonstrategic with a shift to a strategic pose around middle childhood, then a developmental discontinuity is proposed. However, that does not seem to be the case. Wellman's (1988) arguments are convincing. He maintained that young children, toddlers included, are strategic in a broad sense, but they get better at enlisting a wider range and a more efficient set of strategies as they grow and acquire more knowledge about memory specifically and strategic behavior generally. Such a proposition is consistent with memory changes as reflective of a continuous developmental process.

So far, age-related performance differences in memory tasks have been variously attributed to capacity effects and to strategic effects. We have seen that the latter could explain the former. Perhaps knowledge effects can explain most all of it. That is where we turn next.

Changes in Knowledge

Most of the time in real life, remembering is not about nonmeaningful stimuli, pages of verbatim sentences, and arbitrary strings of digits. There are times when we must recall such material, but most acts of remembering are for meaningful material: the general idea of a paragraph, the plot of a novel, the definition of a word, or the sum of two integers.

This is *semantic* memory, the storage of substantive material. In common-sense terms, it is acquired knowledge, what Piaget called "memory in the wider sense" (Piaget & Inhelder, 1973).

Piaget and Inhelder distinguished this sense of memory from memory in the strict sense, defined as memory for particular attributes of stimuli experiences in a particular setting. When information is retrieved from semantic store, it is rarely going to be in the form it was originally encountered. That is, we do not usually recall specific sentences we read without some deliberate attempt to do so. Memory is for gist, for meaning, for message, for sense. And it is often **reconstructive** (Bartlett, 1932). The implication of reconstruction is that new incoming information is incorporated and interpreted in accord with existing prior knowledge, and what is recalled is a new entity rather than a trace of what came before. Over time original memories change but not only through loss, decay, or forgetting. It is possible that original memories can become more—more elaborate, more enriched, more meaningful, and even better—as new information and old information become enmeshed in a long-term store (see Liben, 1975; Paris & Lindauer, 1977).

This fits with the neurological evidence, too. Neural connections constituting memories are not static but change as new connections, new inputs, and new experiences are incorporated into the neural substrate.

We have all had the experience of finding it easier to recall information about which we already had prior knowledge. For example, it is easier to remember a location of a specific building when you already know the general area, and it is easier to remember the name of a specific dinosaur when you know something about the varieties dinosaurs come in. Knowledge is organized into networks or structures of interrelated facts, concepts, and associations. The greater the knowledge, the richer those connections and associations among facts and concepts are going to be. The more elaborate the structure, the greater the possibility for access to a particular fact and the more material retrievable from a single cue.

Generally, older children know more about the world and more about individual topic areas than younger children. The former have prior knowledge, networks of facts within which to organize new information. And since the new and the old get intertwined in semantic store, prior knowledge will affect recall of the new. But younger does not always mean less knowledgeable.

Chi (1978) conducted a definitive study with children (10-year-olds) and adults in which subjects had to recall two kinds of stimuli. The first were the usual digit stimuli so often used in memory-span studies, and not surprisingly, the adults outperformed the children in predictable ways. The second kind of stimuli were arrangements of playing pieces on a chess board. This time the children were the superior performers. Why? Because they were chess experts with extensive prior knowledge as compared with novice adults. The children's prior chess knowledge enabled them to organized the stimuli into meaningful and familiar configurations. Thus, they had a *knowledge* advantage and displayed a *memory* advantage as a consequence. These data are depicted in Figure 10-4.

Chi was able to render age and expertise independent, and when she did, it was expertise not age that predicted the empirical outcomes. This is not an isolated finding. Children can equal or outperform their older counterparts when the content is something they are familiar with and know well, for example, soccer rules (Schneider, Korkel, & Weinert, 1987). Indeed, the role of knowledge in memory performance functions prominently in contemporary information-processing accounts of memory (Bjorklund 1987; Chi & Ceci, 1987).

Chi subsequently carried this line of investigation further. Chi and Koeske (1983) ex-

FIGURE 10-4 *The Number of Digits Recalled Compared with the Number of Chess Piece Arrays Recalled by Children and Adults.*

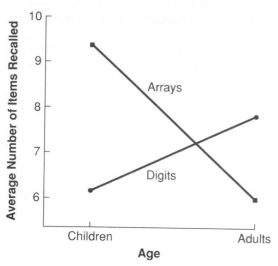

From "Knowledge Structures and Memory Development" by M. T. H. Chi, in R. Siegler (ed.), 1978, *Children's Thinking: What Develops?*, Hillsdale, NJ: Erlbaum.

amined a 5-year-old boy with an unusually extensive knowledge of dinosaurs. From analysis of the boy's responses to dinosaur queries and of his dinosaur books, the investigators developed a diagnostic model of that knowledge, a semantic network model. The model enabled the investigators to predict what the boy would remember about specific dinosaurs, for example, whether a particular exemplar was a meat eater or not, on the basis of how the knowledge domain was thought to be organized.

This, and research like it, shows clearly that memory is a function of expertise; experts remember more and better than novices when the material to be remembered is related to the area of prior knowledge. In demonstration cases, children can be the experts. But most of the time, older children are more knowledgeable than younger children and adults are more knowledgeable than children about a

great many topics. If expertise supports memory, then the older the better for memory performance.

The implication of these findings is that knowledge effects alone could explain age-related differences in memory performance (Carey, 1990). Moreover, in the process of acquiring domain-specific information, an individual also probably acquires strategic ways for organizing that information (Wellman, 1988), just as the young dinosaur expert's performances revealed. Since it is virtually impossible to derive stimulus materials for memory experiments that are not in some way related to materials in the real world, then it is impossible to behaviorally evaluate the processes of memory independent of content. Knowledge and memory are confounded.

Summary

What are we to conclude about what develops in memory? Capacity is not a particularly viable contender for developmental change. Apparent changes in capacity can be explained by greater efficiency of processing, by greater familiarity with the items typically used to assess memory span (see Chi, 1976), and by greater automaticity of memory operations with practice. Strategic behavior has been the favored developmental focus for some time. Indeed, the proposition that use of memory strategies increases with development has been the preferred view (see Kail, 1990; and chapters in Weinert & Perlmutter, 1988). Increased use of strategies can even explain apparent capacity effects.

But the wisdom of attributing performance differences to strategy development is called into question, too (Wellman, 1988). Virtually all memory performance effects can be attributed to knowledge effects, and while knowledge and age often increase together, exceptions are possible. Those exceptions raise the real questions about whether, after infancy, memory develops at all. Perhaps, the appearance of memory development is an epiphenomenon of other developments.

Carey (1990) took the perspective that the domain-general level is not the correct locus to describe developmental change. Developmental change is occurring at the domain-specific level: in conceptual knowledge, in number knowledge, in theoretical knowledge, and so on. The ramification is that age-related increases in domain-specific knowledge and expertise-specific knowledge only masquerade as developmental changes in general memory function.

CONCLUSION

Despite our common intuitions about it, memory, its nature, and how it evolves with maturation turn out to be complex phenomena. It has been one of the most researched cognitive functions in psychology's history, and yet, at the conclusion of this chapter, it is still not possible to present *the* developmental story for memory. But the study of memory and the empirical findings yielded from that study remind us of by now familiar themes.

Memory is a psychological function actualized in a biological system and supported by a biological substrate. Neuroscientists and behavioral scientists have tried to elucidate the function. However, the research traditions are separate if not independent. The neuroscientists tell us about how the brain works when we remember, about what happens at the level of the neuron and the cortical structures. In recent years, this research has revealed much about the workings of the brain in memory. We know something of the structures implicated and of the maturational timetables for those structures. That evidence points to a de-

velopmental discontinuity between infant memory and later memory of a certain kind— declarative memory—and continuity for other memory types—procedural memory, habituation, and the memories associated with conditioning

The empirical record for the nature of memory development after infancy is not integrated with the neurological record. This is behavioral research, primarily influenced by an information-processing perspective and predicated on a computer analogy, not a biological metaphor. So, memory research after infancy shifts its emphasis to domain-general procedures for managing data in the mind. This course of study has not always led to productive outcomes. Research into the development of memory capacity has proved indefinitive. Investigations of whether memory mnemonics and strategies develop is now in question. And all too often, serious reservations surface about whether we have even been studying the right thing (Perlmutter, 1988). The one clear and uncompromised fact is that children usually perform better on memory tasks as they get older. However, memory changes across childhood are most likely to be best characterized as changes in efficacy and proficiency—evidence for a continuous developmental process.

The most supportable interpretation so far is that memory effects may reduce to knowledge effects. Knowledge effects are implicated when the cognitive structures elaborate with experience and learning. So learning, knowledge acquisition, and memory remain interconnected, confounded, cognitive functions. And since age is correlated with amount learned, knowledge acquisition, and memory, it is not all that clear what actually develops to yield those ubiquitous performance effects.

CHAPTER 11

THE FUNDAMENTAL ISSUES REVISITED

INTRODUCTION
THE NATURE-NURTURE ISSUE
THE CONTINUITY-DISCONTINUITY ISSUE
THE DOMAIN-GENERAL VERSUS DOMAIN-SPECIFIC ISSUE
A SOMEWHAT SPECULATIVE DEVELOPMENTAL STORY
A FINAL NOTE

INTRODUCTION

While this book was in preparation, the author watched her son grow from babyhood to first grade. Through enormous changes, he has transformed from a dependent infant who could not sit up to an independent young boy who rents his own videos. We have passed innumerable, memorable landmarks—first words ("up"), first sentences ("bug go"; "hammaburg, cheesaburg, fies"), first Lego structures, and many first discoveries. We have had major philosophical discussions about death, about why dinosaurs became extinct, about why the earth does not fall out of space, and about whether a trillion is really more than infinity. The extent of change in such a relatively short period of time is remarkable and salient. Sometimes the changes stand out in recollection, overshadowing the concurrent fact that this lanky 6-year-old—now mostly arms and legs—is the very same person as the fat baby—then all head and tummy—for whom thoughts of infinity were far from foremost on his mind. That often tends to be the case with development: The age-related changes in behavior and capability that accompany physical growth are obvious and easy to see. There are, however, vital continuities, too—those subtle consistencies of style, character, disposition, and mental functioning that link the individual with himself across time.

In Chapter 1, fundamental issues about human cognition and its development were introduced, issues that challenge any theoretical effort to explain these complex phenomena. In Chapters 2 through 10, the empirical literature in proscribed areas of development was evaluated. Now, it is time to return to the broader perspective, to try and piece together a picture that makes the most psychological sense given what we know about children's behavior, to tell the story of cognitive development as best we can. Variants of those fundamental themes, reformulated here in more sophisticated fashion, will guide the construction of our story.

THE NATURE-NURTURE ISSUE

Questions about whether biology or environment propel development tend to be intractable and simplistic. Definitive answers are naive. Neither extreme empiricism nor extreme nativism can fully account for the rich, complex interplay between biology and experience. We have seen repeatedly how both play a role, both contribute to growth and the acquisition of cognitive skills. However, the scales need not be balanced. Were we to stack up the empirical data, the facts we have observed about cognitive development, the bulk of the evidence could tip the scales toward one of the alternatives. At the very least, some potential explanations will be eliminated; they will not fit the data and will not remain as contenders when the scales are measured.

And which way will those scales tip? Probably toward nativism. There are two major reasons: First, there is the proliferation of evidence in recent years attesting to the amazing cognitive capacities of the infant and even of the newborn. And second, there is evidence for the phenomenon of *privileged learning* (see Marler, 1991). Right from the beginning, organisms seem to come equipped with initial biases toward particular kinds of environmental input. Such attuneness can be quite specific, as a young sparrow's differential attention to the song patterns of same-species individuals demonstrates. These initial *modes of construal* imply that the organism is not equally receptive to all perceptible stimuli. In short, the young individual takes *innate stances* in her orientation toward the world.

Empiricists and Piagetians postulate a naive infant because both perspectives reject a priori knowledge. It is illogical and inconsistent to propose either experientially driven or constructively driven mechanisms for development and, at the same time, to propose an initial state for the immature individual that includes some knowledge of the world she will develop in. Empiricists and constructivists would have to posit one set of principles to explain initial knowledge and a second to explain subsequent knowledge. It is more logical, parsimonious, and internally consistent with the philosophical assumptions of both positions to begin with a naive infant.

In these views, biology provides the neonate with an initial repertoire of physical behaviors and reflexes and perceptual systems with which to start the chain of events—the interactions with the environment. But biology does not provide preexisting mental representation. Any initial "attuneness" would have to be at the level of peripheral processing—sensation, perception, reflexlike responses—not at the level of *belief.* Therefore, evidence that suggests very early knowledge and competence at the level of belief argues against the hypothesized naive, unbiased, initial state of the individual.

If we have learned one truism in the last 20 years of developmental study, it is that babies are smart. With the introduction of the habituation paradigm, investigators have been able to assess just how smart they are. Babies detect *meaningful* units of physical stimuli—phonemes, objects, numerosities, geometric features, faces, and so forth. And babies discriminate meaningful units from other meaningful units. They exhibit a semblance of memory. They react when experimental events violate natural law. One initial stance of human neonates may be to organize the world into individual entities and to *believe* the world is comprised of these lawfully related individuals. A bias toward "individuating" sets development on a particular, constrained course. Indeed, the "individuating" baby stands in sharp contrast to the Piagetian "solipsistic" one.

It could be argued that from birth, sophisticated sensory systems enable the newborn infant to extract environmental information very efficiently and thus gain *perceptual* capability and expertise early in life. Such capacity does not imply the *concept* of an individual. In this way, object percepts, spatial percepts, and perhaps even number percepts are responsible for habituation performances. Percepts need not connote a mental content or mental representation, that is, initial belief.

Spelke (1988a; 1991), however, argued convincingly that this interpretation cannot explain all the evidence; the organization of a perceptual display into constraint-governed, meaningful units must be guided by *conceptual* knowledge. Otherwise, the organization of stimulation into surfaces consistent with existent physical laws would be underdetermined by the stimulus layout. Since light and sound stimulation are actually continua (i.e., *dimensions* not *discrete entities*), why would the baby necessarily pick out things (objects and phonemes) in them? Object beliefs are at the root of habituation performances in babies, not object percepts according to Spelke. The case for initial modes of construal permeated by beliefs—conceptual knowledge of objects, motion, and rudimentary principles of mechanics—is a convincing one.

Many of the cognitive accomplishments we attribute to babies are shared by other animals too (e.g., space and number, see Gallistel, 1990). That connection also strengthens the nativist case. Individual species have, through evolutionary pressures, successfully adapted to this physical universe. It makes logical sense that some features of that universe, the detection of which is crucial to survival, should somehow become ingrained in those animals' nervous systems. When we detect competencies in species phylogenetically related to us (e.g., nonhuman primates, other mammals), it suggests that we, too, may possess some biologically derived, cognitive capacities.

There is also a problem with the developmental mechanism empiricist, nurture-driven views must posit for knowledge acquisition—

some version of regularity detection. The notion there is that statistical regularities, *or correlations,* among stimuli exist in the universe. The regularities constitute a pattern and a pattern is a structure. The organism, therefore, needs only to be a *regularity detector* and the pattern will be discovered and extracted from sense data. There are some problems with this contention.

First, since there are no assumptions about specific stimuli within the physically sensible range having greater attraction than others, a general-purpose regularity detector would have to be sensitive to any and all regularity. Yet, animals are not (see, Gallistel et al., 1991). The salience of stimuli varies across species. Some birds, for instance, are very sensitive to the arrangement of stars in the night sky, presumably to acquire navigation abilities, and human babies are particularly sensitive to the acoustics of speech. A general-purpose regularity detector would have to have *greater* extraction capabilities than the animal needs to insure survival; that is inefficient programming.

Second, it is not clear how universally shared, complex mental representations could be derived from correlational data. For a statistical analogy, that is what exploratory factor analysis does with correlational matrices. But, unless the analytic procedures are constrained by a priori restrictions on data manipulations, more than one mathematical solution results. Which one would represent the world as it is? As soon as parameters within the hypothetical matrix are held constant, set, or specified a priori, then innate biases are introduced and "nature" rears her head again. In short, we cannot get there from here, where *there* is cognitive maturity and *here* is a belief-free, blank slate.

Then again, consider what we have learned about brain development. Much of the hardware in human babies—the brain structures, cell layers, even connecting pathways—is laid down prenatally. Granted, brain development continues after birth, but the initial foundation already established before birth will place limits on what can happen later. And, indeed, even what happens later may be endogenously controlled. The biological evidence is inconsistent with a "blank slate" view of the neonate, although it does allow for potential developmental flexibility in response to the environment. What is intriguing is the close association between when brain regions and connections come on line in a mature sense and when certain cognitive competencies are detectable. Diamond (1990a, 1991) has demonstrated this connection for object knowledge, particularly the $A\bar{B}$ error (see Chapter 3). The prototypic $A\bar{B}$ error is detected prior to the maturation of the dorsolateral prefrontal cortex but not after (also see Chapters 9 and 10).

None of these bits of evidence by themselves definitively establishes a nativist-oriented conceptual explanation of cognitive development—the nature view—as *the* correct position. Brain growth allows for postnatal plasticity, and the cognitive capacities of the human newborn are not the same as knowledge exhibited later. Those facts allow for potentially profound experiential influences on development.

However, none of the facts are compatible with a naive infant. It is more reasonable to envision an attuned infant, equipped with initial modes of construal, rudimentary beliefs, and impressive information-processing equipment, ready to bring structure to the raw data of experience. This truly is interactionism, but those innate biases will skew the course of growth. Not all developmental achievements are equally probable because of the *individual's* capacities. This is what tips the scales toward nativism. The argument is summarized in Table 11-1.

THE CONTINUITY-DISCONTINUITY ISSUE

In general form, questions about whether development is continuous or discontinuous, representing quantitative change or qualita-

TABLE 11-1 *Summary of the Nature-Nurture Issue*

Question		Resolution		Evidence
In the balance of nature and nurture, does the evidence tip the scales?	→	Yes, tentatively toward nativism and away from a "blank slate."	→	1. Early conceptual competencies of the infant and neonate.
				+
				2. Evidence for "priveleged learning" in animals and humans.
				+
				3. Detected cognitive capacities of other animals.
				+
				4. The extent of prenatal brain development.
				+
				5. The implausibility of structure building through associationism.

tive change, are as intractable and unanswerable as are nonspecific questions that pit nature versus nurture. There are both continuities and discontinuities in development. To examine the issue sensibly, we must first refine the questions. Three, issue-related questions that are answerable follow:

1. Are there consistencies in cognitive ability and cognitive processing that transcend age and unite the infant, child, and adult?
2. Are there also verifiable and important differences between the functioning of the mature and the immature that reveal reliable associations with age?
3. Is there evidence of major, pervasive, age-related shifts in cognitive functioning and mental representation?

The detection of similarities in cognition across individuals and across the immature and the mature is a more recent thrust in developmental studies than is the detection of differences. Finding the latter is easier, partly because of the scientific methodologies we use. Much empirical research relies on statistical techniques that allow us to compute associations among variables. When we observe an association between a behavioral variable and some other potentially influential variable—an empirical effect—those techniques permit mathematical quantification of the strength of the effect. That strength index denotes the degree of robustness of our observation (i.e., its potential replicability). Use of such procedures is the norm in psychological inquiry. Piaget may have used anecdotes and descriptive accounts in support of his theoretical hypotheses, but the contemporary psychological community demands some mathematical buttressing of a researcher's observations.

More often than not, mathematical support is in the form of correlations or similar numerical quantities. Whatever the exact statistic, computation depends on the presence of systematic variability connecting some measure of cognitive function and some experimental or subject characteristic. Frequently, in developmental research, the subject characteristic is age. While age is not an independent variable in the experimental sense, it is a rough, available, and observable index of less observable maturational processes—cumulative experience, acquired knowledge, neurological growth, and so forth. Developmentally associated cognitive change surfaces as a statistically significant relation between the age variable and performance variables. These associations are almost ubiquitous across decades of developmental inquiry. They tell us how infants, children, and adults perform differently on cognitive tasks, and knowledge of age permits better than chance prediction of cognitive performance.

The demonstration of continuity, on the other hand, is the detection of *no* association between age and performance, a finding of *no* statistical effect. In short, a continuity hypothesis is the null hypothesis that (recall from earlier chapters) is usually ambiguous. So, the statistical techniques that have served psychologists so well do not serve as well in the pursuit of answering continuity questions. Continuities are constants, while statistical methods exploit variability.

Research designed to uncover consistencies of cognitive functioning across development must be less methodologically orthodox than the traditional variety. Keil's (1979) research (see chapter 5) with the M-constraint is an example. Violations of the M-constraint are supposed to be rare (ideally, nonexistent) and *nonvariable* regardless of age. Thus, the correlation between frequency of violation and age must be essentially zero[1]—a null effect. But that is not a statistically pleasing outcome.

One way around the dilemma is to come up with a mathematical model of the phenomenon in question—a rather sophisticated enterprise—or, if possible, to compute the actual probability of an observation. For example, a researcher could determine the probability of obtaining by chance alone identical ontological trees from subjects who differ in age. A chance probability represents a condition where no M-constraint is operating. The actual probability so computed turns out to be infinitesimal (Chandler, Rosser, & Nicholson, 1992).

The interpretation is that if the outcome is highly unlikely without the operation of the M-constraint, the validity of the M-constraint is supported. Of course, the interpretation can be challenged (see, Carey, 1985). The legitimate contrast may not be between observations predicted under the M-constraint versus observations predicted by chance (no M-constraint). Rather, the contrast should be between observations predicted under the M-constraint versus observations predicted with some other constraint. The statistical answer only evaluates the former contrast. Perhaps the contrast is a "straw man." Any statistical argument for demonstrating continuity, however, is an indirect one. The reasoning is certainly less direct than in the discontinuity case.[2]

Another challenge confronting those who would search for continuities in cognitive performance is what task to use. It is easy to create cognitive tasks that differentiate younger and older subjects; demands on procedural and utilization competence will invariably produce bias against the former. If continuities exist, they are most likely the result of similarities in conceptual competence. Therefore, continuity-sensitive tasks must be ones in which procedural demands are either greatly reduced or separated from conceptual demands in order to isolate the source of bias. Such tasks *can* be successfully designed. The studies of Rochel Gelman, Susan Gelman, Frank Keil, Ellen Markman, Elizabeth Spelke, Henry Wellman, and many others who work with preschoolers and infants attest to it.

What is remarkable, given the methodological difficulties, is how many developmental continuities we do observe when we look. Perceptually, infants, children, and adults are attuned to similar arrangements of the physical layout: moving surfaces indicating edges, vectors indicating the direction of motion, dot swarms suggesting biological movement, and visual flux revealing geometric form. Similar conceptual sensitivities to number, space, natural kinds, ontological distinctions, laws of mechanics, and so on, are detectible in young children, older children, adults, and even infants. Both children and adults consult theorylike knowledge structures to support causal reasoning about physical things, biological things, and mental things (see Chapters 6 and 7). Despite a methodological tradition rooted in the analysis of individual variation and developmental variation, a fact is now quite clear: Cognitive continuities universally cut across that individual and developmental variation.

Consistencies in cognitive functioning between immature and mature individuals coexist with marked and reliable differences. No doubt about it, there is age-related developmental change that is salient, important, and distinguishes the cognitive status of infant, toddler, child, and adult. Infants may conceptualize something about objects, but initially, only common movement defines "objectness." A more complex conceptualization comes later (Chapter 2).

Similarly, infants appreciate some constraints on object motion—solidity and continuity constraints—but not others—inertia and gravity constraints (Chapter 6). Young infants do not produce language (Chapter 9), although they babble with languagelike intonation patterns and discriminate phonemic contrasts. Babies are sensitive to numerosity, to cardinal and ordinal values, but their representation of number may differ from that of the older person (Chapter 6). Indeed, infants are not the same kind of cognitive creatures as are their older counterparts.

During the infancy period, bursts of change in behavioral functioning coincide with the maturation and involvement of implicated brain regions (e.g., the frontal cortex, visual cortex, and hippocampus). There are clear and reliable differences, for example, between the visual sensitivities of infants at 4 weeks and those at 8 weeks (maturation of the visual system implicated). Spatial location is responded to differently by babies under 8 months of age and those older (prefrontal cortex implicated), and with the onset of self-propelled locomotion, the organization of space changes yet again (hippocampus, among other structures, implicated). Most of these behavioral changes have been connected empirically with neurological changes, at least with animals, and these age-related behavioral effects serve to separate infant and toddler.

Still other differences emerge as the individual moves into and through childhood. Language acquisition flourishes (Chapter 9). Implicit, if crude, reasoning about mechanical (Chapter 6), biological, and psychological systems (Chapter 7) first surfaces and then elaborates in sophistication. Geometric representations guiding spatial behavior look increasingly Euclidean as the child moves from toddlerhood, to preschool age, to school age. By the time the child enters first grade, she looks cognitively much more like the adult she will become than the infant she once was.

The behavioral changes that occur between 3 and about 10 years of age do not seem as dramatic and profound in quality as those earlier changes. The cognitive performances of the young are more fragile, more task specific, and less generalized than those of their older counterparts. Increase the set size and, in young children, counting skill deteriorates; increase the number of objects in a spatial array, and children's geometric judgments look "egocentric"; increase the number of items to

be remembered, and recall falters; increase the complexity of logical and relational rules necessary to solve a problem, and the young look illogical.

So, when tasks are complicated, younger children do not display the same degree of expertise as older ones do. But, when the tasks are kept simple and unambiguous, the younger and older child look cognitively similar. Task complexity, sometimes even conceptually irrelevant complexity, is more apt to impede performance in the less mature.

So, performance is a function of age. However, these effects represent differences in the *degree* of proficiency, not in the *kind* of proficiency. One variety of developmental change, then, is in the *generality* of cognitive ability, in the *applicability* of that ability across situations, and in the *robustness* of the display of knowledge across variability of context. All increase with age.

A second kind of change occurs when children's knowledge elaborates with their growing maturity. We see this in studies of children's semantic development (Chapters 4 and 5). Ontological trees are increasingly differentiated from the two- to three-branched structures of the young child to the four-plus-branched structures of the older child. Conceptual categories are expanded to include more, and less prototypic, exemplars; the defining characteristics of classes and categories become less feature bound. Conceptual knowledge structures become more organized, more hierarchical, and more interconnected. The younger child might surmise that a rabbit can be sorry while the older child will reject the premise; the difference is attributable to an increased differentiation in ontological knowledge that accompanies development. Similarly, the more elaborate knowledge structures of the older child will support inferences that clearly seem beyond the young one's grasp. In short, older children have access to richer knowledge structures, but *richer* need not imply *different*. All of these behavioral changes can be explained with quantitative elaborations of the growing child's cognitive structures.

There are ways, however, in which *different* does appear to be an applicable characterization for developmental change. For instance, a young child will allow a transformation of kind (e.g., a horse into a zebra) that an older child will reject. And although neither child will accept a change across ontological boundaries (e.g., a lizard into a stick), it does seem that children of different ages are defining a kind in alternative ways (Keil, 1989). While still open to conflicting interpretation, a shift in the way in which an individual identifies a kind, a characteristic- to defining-feature shift (Keil & Batterman, 1984), could be construed as a qualitative change. Similarly, the knowledge systems that organize biological and psychological phenomenon may undergo qualitative alteration. Although the evidence is far from definitive, a vitalistic biology may be replaced by a truer biological version; desire-psychology is transformed into belief-psychology.

Carey argued that these sorts of theoretical reorganizations reflect *strong restructurings,* paradigm shifts in knowledge systems equivalent to those that have occurred in the evolution of science (see Carey, 1991). Paradigm shifts are not reducible to successive elaborative changes but to changes in kind. On the other hand, recent evidence (see Keil, 1992; Springer & Keil, 1991) also tells us that even preschoolers exhibit nonvitalistic biological reasoning and reject nonbiological explanations for biological phenomenon. And the ways infants, children, and naive adults understand physical phenomena are more alike than different (Spelke, 1991). So, it is not clear. There *may be* developmentally related qualitative changes in knowledge and cognition as the naive theories of the child evolve, but these changes, too, may still turn out to be reducible to the elaborative kind.

There is yet another change that suggests alteration in kind: The emergence of *explicitness* in cognition. Young children's conceptual knowledge is primarily *implicit*. We see this when we attempt to extract explanations from young children about what they know; they simply cannot provide us with any even when what they know makes sense. Implicit knowledge seems to defy conscious access, to defy reflection and deliberate manipulation. When knowledge is explicit, on the other hand, it is itself a content to be mentally operated on, thought about, and formalized. Does that process, consciously thinking about what one knows in a deliberate fashion, significantly change what it is one knows? If so, such a change might be characterized as qualitative. That was one of Piaget's contentions. Where the capacity to exhibit explicit knowledge comes from, and how that capacity subsequently affects the state of existing implicit knowledge when it does come, are questions yet to be answered.

In response to the first two questions at the beginning of this section, it is clear that there are *both* continuity and discontinuity, across-age similarities and age-related differences, in cognitive development. Whether consistency or change is most frequently observed, however, is not independent of cognitive content. For instance, continuity stands out for knowledge and thinking about "natural" domains—language, space, number, concepts, untutored knowledge of mechanics and biology. These are also the domains of knowledge referenced most often in arguments supporting the nativist case. Developmental differences are most pronounced in other cognitive areas—explicit reasoning, aspects of procedural knowledge, strategy use, problem solving with arbitrary and school-based tasks, formal and tutored knowledge. These domains have been referenced in the building of the empiricist and the constructivist cases.

One response to the continuity-discontinuity issue, particularly the third question, is more definitive: There is little support for the kind of pervasive, profound, qualitative shifts in cognition predicted from Piagetian and neo-Piagetian perspectives. This does not mean that some aspects of thinking (e.g., some forms of explicit reasoning, perhaps naive theoretical knowledge systems) do not change dramatically, but the concept of stage, implying as it does a broad metamorphosis in thinking, is not a viable, explanatory construct. Behavioral effects that turn out to be both reliable and the rule in empirical study—context effects, knowledge effects, early competence, developmental continuities, and so forth—have to be treated as exceptions to the rule in stage theory. When exceptions begin to outnumber theory-derived, rule-consistent observations (which, albeit, do exist), then the integrity of the rule itself is called into question. Arguments against pervasive, qualitative, developmental change can be constructed on logical, empirical, and neurological grounds.

The logical argument against pervasive cognitive shifts is based on two major premises (see Fodor, 1972). First, a form of cognitive structure constitutes a "language" for thought. If there are two forms (one version for the earlier, less mature state, and a second version for the later, more mature state), then there are two "languages." If the languages show a one-to-one mapping, a correspondence, such as languages derived from the same language family would show (e.g., Spanish and French), then translation from one language to the other would not pose an insurmountable barrier. Understanding and communication between individuals thinking different "languages" of this sort would not be impossible because there are common formalisms.

However, qualitative differences in the languages of thought imply no such mapping or formal correspondence. Then, there would be a translation problem. Without common points of reference, how could thinkers of two qualitatively different languages communicate? On the other hand, if there are common points of reference, then, by definition the languages must not be qualitatively different.

Children, even infants, do share meanings with adults, although those meanings are not always identical. The very fact that children and adults make similar conceptual distinctions (as with ontological distinctions and with natural kinds), that they understand and use similar tokens for phenomena (as with labels), and that adults can describe what children know raises serious questions about the feasibility of dramatically different, alternative modes of thinking. Obviously, simple use of the same words does not constitute definitive evidence of shared meanings, but the burden of proof is on those who would make claims about significantly different meanings.

A second premise concerns a mechanism for change. How can one system really evolve onto another without there being common elements between the first and the second system? The reasoning goes something like this: (1) A developmentally advanced concept is expressed in Language 2. (2) The developmentally immature learner only understands the world in Language 1. (3) There is no overlap between Languages 1 and 2. Then, it is not conceivable how a Language 1 thinker could learn anything represented in Language 2 terms. This line of logic, carried to its extreme, leads to the proclamation that nothing is learnable and development is, in fact, impossible. The only alternative position is that overlap between 1 and 2 must exist initially. (Or, more strongly, 1 and 2 must be identical.)

This is not an easy criticism to rebut from a stage perspective. If the mental models associated with each sequential stage of development are qualitatively different, then we are faced with at least three languages of thought in Piagetian theory.[3] There must be mechanisms for metamorphosis that transcend the translation problem.

However, the theoretical mechanisms of transition in Piagetian theory, that is, adaptation and equilibration, are conceptually vague. It is not clear how transitions across stages are supposed to occur, how they would operate, logically, or what they would look like, behaviorally. The definition of qualitative difference and qualitative change, on which the particular criticism hinges, is a stringent one, and the argument reflects one extreme view. Even if one is not sympathetic to that extreme view, the solid conclusion is still clear: Pervasive, qualitative, developmental change is logically implausible. (For a plausible explanation of qualitative change in local domains, however, see Carey, 1991.)

On empirical grounds, experimental findings do not support qualitative shifts of the Piagetian variety either. First, evidence attesting to early competence and to cognitive continuity across age suggests a striking likeness between individuals in different stages. Second, there are context effects on reasoning and thinking. This means that the display of knowledge is very often a function of the particular circumstances under which a subject must perform. Context, then, will explain the performances observed more parsimoniously than will age, and, in fact, the young can look cognitively mature or the old cognitively immature depending on the circumstances.

Traditionally, Piagetian theory has not dealt with context effects as a central issue, treating them instead as a sort of nuisance variable or explaining them away with the concept of horizontal decalage.[4] This tact may be changing in neo-Piagetian thinking (see Chapters 8 and 10). However, it is not clear whether the qualitative-shift notion can survive with theoretical integrity and, simultaneously, have context effects fully taken into account.

The potential elegance of a stage construct based on sequential qualitative metamorphoses in cognition is this: Knowledge of developmental stage should permit accurate prediction of cognitive performance across tasks. To use a statistical analogy, this predic-

tion is conceptualized as a within-subject consistency, a subject effect (or, for a developmentally constituted group of subjects, an age effect). Contextual influences create within-subject variability, and a task factor explains the variance. Given there is a finite amount of variance in performance to be explained, to the extent it is attributable to a "task" effect, it is not attributable to a "stage" effect. And then, the utility of the stage concept is lost.

A counterargument is that the concept of stage is meant to describe the evolution of an underlying *competence*, not the vagaries of surface *performance* (see Chapter 8). Performance can be unstable while, simultaneously, competence remains stable and truly diagnostic of cognition. The resolution of this argument depends on the importance one puts on performance variation, on the relevance of context effects. And that is not strictly an empirical issue.

One could conceivably dismiss context effects as experimental artifact. Then, evidence of task specificity is not potentially damaging to the conceptual integrity of qualitative shifts or to stage notions. But a third body of evidence remains a threat: evidence of knowledge effects. Knowledge effects are more predictable and consistent than context effects; and they are prevalent in the literature, too (Ceci, 1989). Many studies demonstrate how knowledge about a topic facilitates cognitive functioning at a mature level, but the accelerated level of reasoning is confined to a local domain. So, for example, a young child who happens to know a lot about horses could tell you all sorts of "horse facts," describe "horse behavior," discriminate subtle "horse categories," and make inferences about "horse characteristics," while remaining relatively naive, perhaps, about number concepts, mechanical concepts, or kinship concepts. What we have, again, is unevenness in performance.

Prior, local knowledge influences memory (Chapter 10), induction and inference (Chapter 5), the comprehension of metaphor (Chapter 5, Chapter 9), deductive reasoning (Chapter 8), and a host of other cognitive operations. Apparently, in areas where a child has acquired knowledge and expertise, the knowledge enables what appears to be a mature level of cognitive functioning. However, the effect is not pervasive. Immature reasoning in other domains occurs simultaneously. This *developmental dyssynchrony* does threaten the stage concept, because stage connotes *generality* and knowledge effects show, again, specificity in thinking capacity.

Then there is the neurological case. It follows that pervasive changes in behavioral functioning reflecting a similarly profound restructuring of cognitive organization should have correlates in brain development. It is not clear what brain events would qualify as supportive evidence, but we can speculate. Certainly, major periods of synaptogenesis and neurogenesis are likely contenders. There is evidence of postnatal neurogenesis in some brain regions and postnatal episodes of synaptogenesis concurrently across many brain regions. Delayed involvement of certain brain structures could also signal qualitative changes in functioning. Important, late-maturing structures such as the frontal cortex and the hippocampus are relevant to this line of reasoning. The hippocampus in particular is implicated in memory and in spatial cognition (see Chapters 3 and 10), and there are important maturational changes in how the formation connects with other brain regions, changes that also occur postnatally.

The evolution of the interconnectedness of brain regions, growth spurts in the complexity of synaptic networks, and alterations in the degree of involvement of particular brain structures could all affect cognitive functioning in a manner that could be described as developmentally qualitative. Other brain changes look more developmentally quantitative, however: gradual synapse deletion, experience-dependent synapse elaboration, myelination, lateralization, and so forth. The question pertaining to the continuity-discontinuity issue is this: Do what appear to be neurological qualitative changes correlate in timing with hypothesized behavioral qualitative changes?

Most of the dramatic, maturationally related brain events summarized in previous chapters, events that might logically precipitate qualitative changes in cognition, occur during the first 24 months of life. Many changes do take place after that time, after the infancy period, but later changes lack the abrupt quality of those earlier ones. Recall from Chapter 1 that abruptness in the episodes of growth defines discontinuity in development, and discontinuity is one observable feature of a qualitative shift. Postinfancy brain development does not particularly support an argument for postinfancy qualitative change (although a case can be made for the qualitative nature of brain maturation changes during infancy). A lack of evidence for distinct developmental stages at the *neurological* level does not preclude the plausibility of such stageness at the *representational* level—the level addressed by traditional theory. Still, a lack of evidence is cause for caution as another reason to be skeptical about propositions of pervasive, age-related metamorphoses in thinking.

If age-associated behavioral differences are accounted for by context effects, knowledge effects, and knowledge-driven elaborations of cognitive functioning, none of which are solely developmental, then is the concept of development really a useful one? In defense of development, there are some clear "facts" about children's growth that cannot be fully explained by continuities, context effects, knowledge effects, and the like. First, infants, although smart, are very unlike their older counterparts in a variety of cognitively important ways.

Second, even beyond infancy, children who differ in age do, in fact, look different, act different, and exhibit different preferences and propensities. Age demarcations within the childhood period, which have social legitimacy, probably have some nonarbitrary, intuitive wisdom behind them as well. It is not just convention that sets 3 as the appropriate age for preschool, 5 as the age for real school, or eighth or ninth grade as the time to introduce algebra. There is some sense to it—a reflection of how maturation will mitigate socialization and learning.

Third, development seems to set limits on cognitive acceleration achieved through the provision of knowledge. It is very difficult, probably impossible, to get a 6-year-old to reason about number or physics or biology in the same way an adolescent would.

Piaget astutely observed that there *are* time-associated constraints on how growing children reason and think. These time-related constraints on cognition are not the whole story, but they reflect one type of developmental principle. We may be experiencing some confusion now as to what these developmental principles should look like or from where they originate.[5] But the "facts" of child behavior continue to attest to development as a reality. The questions, arguments, and evidence are compressed in Table 11-2.

THE DOMAIN-GENERAL VERSUS DOMAIN-SPECIFIC ISSUE

Throughout preceding chapters, there has been tension between domain-specific and domain-general views of development, between the growth of local structures and the growth of global ones. Whether cognitive development arises from domain-general or domain-specific principles of knowledge acquisition is another of those vigorously debated conceptual issues (see e.g., Behrend, 1990; Ceci, 1989; Nelson, 1990; Sternberg, 1989). The question is as intractable as the nature versus nurture and the continuity versus discontinuity queries—unresolvable when framed in global form. Perhaps a semblance of a qualified response can be attempted, however.

First, the precise meaning of the terms must be considered, and second, an account of how each figures into our elaborating must be fashioned.

Domain-general knowledge structures are the kind associated with, though not limited to, Piagetian-style conceptualizations of development (see, particularly, Chapters 4, 8, and 10). The primary characteristic is of a single, generic, cognitive system that can operate on any problem the environment (or a perverse experimental psychologist) dishes up. So, the system is independent of content and context, is broadly applicable to all phenomena, and is reducible to a common set of cognitive rules. We roughly equate the operations of the system with cognitive activities to which we ascribe mental terms: *encoding, memory, inductive reasoning, deductive reasoning, comprehending, problem solving,* and so on. The content of a cognitive task is in the form of a problem representation; task solution takes place when the operation is applied to the representation.[6]

These operations are the same sorts of intellectual capacities traditionally tapped by standardized psychometric measures. The primary assumption behind such testing is that the capacity is separable from the particular content—the items—used to assess it, and thus, the capacity is independently measurable. Developmental theories describe the evolution of these capacities and age-related changes in efficacy; psychometric approaches explain individual variations in efficacy. However, there are similar underlying assumptions common to all domain-general accounts of cognition:

1. The most parsimonious model of cognition consists, primarily, of a single, prominent system.
2. It should be possible to outline a single set of rules by which the system operates.
3. Those rules are applicable across a broad range of content and within a multitude of intellectual contexts.

TABLE 11-2 *Summary of the Continuity-Discontinuity Issue*

Question	Resolution	Evidence
Are there age-transcending cognitive continuities in development?	→ Yes →	1. Perceptual sensitivities of infant, child, adult similar. + 2. Conceptual continuities in number, space, ontology, natural kind, laws of mechanics, etc. + 3. Theorylike knowledge structures consulted by child and adult +
Are there age-related developmental differences in cognition?	→ Yes →	1. Conceptual differences detected between competencies of infants and children. + 2. Increases in extent of cognitive proficiency with age. + 3. Knowledge elaboration and differentiation with age. + 4. Naive theoretical systems evolve and change. + 5. Knowledge becomes explicit with increases in age.
Are there sequential, pervasive, qualitative shifts in cognition organization with development?	→ No →	1. Such shifts are logically implausible. + 2. Cognitive continuities across hypothesized stages/levels. + 3. Context effects on thinking and reasoning → within-stage performance unevenness. + 4. Knowledge effects facilitate reasoning confined to local domains → developmental dyssynchrony. + 5. Brain events do not support qualitative change after infancy.

Domain specificity has at least two meanings (Ceci, 1989). However, all views hypothesizing domain-specific, local knowledge structures share a common feature: rejection of the independence of cognitive activity and the context acted upon. How well the individual is able to function cognitively depends on the degree of local knowledge called into service. Therefore, we cannot explain intellectual performance without accounting for the unique combination of local knowledge (the "facts" one knows) and what an individual can do with that knowledge.

For example, a 4- or 5-year-old who is very familiar with the Teenage Mutant Ninja Turtle stories and characters will show sophisticated, turtle-relevant reasoning: *encoding* subtle differences among the four turtles (which has something to do with headgear and weapons), *remembering* details of turtle history (a convoluted story), *explaining* the action of mutagens in the turtles' transformation, and *inferring* how each turtle would extricate himself from a nasty jam with the Shredder as a function of the turtle's personality, beliefs, desires, and prototypic behaviors.

There is a distinction, however, in the type of local knowledge addressed in various definitions of domain specificity. The Ninja Turtle instance exemplifies local knowledge of essentially any kind, any body of information about which an individual gains expertise. A person can gain expertise in playing chess or bridge, in differentiating wildflowers or horse feeds, in the history of ancient artifacts, in the organization of stars into constellations, in the intricacies of psychological research, and so on. Another label for knowledge of this sort is **expertise-specific knowledge** (Keil, 1982).

Knowledge acquisition of the expertise variety is apt to be idiosyncratic—a function of an individual's peculiar experiences, interests, and history of exposure to things. Expertise does affect cognitive processing; the person will demonstrate greater degrees of cognitive proficiency in domains where she has accumulated the greatest amount of information. However, a second sort of domain-specific knowledge acquisition references local structures with a special status. These are domains of knowledge to which all individuals are specially attuned, and expertise is given as a function of the stances each takes because one is human. Expertise-specific knowledge exhibits individual differences and variation; domain-specific knowledge should not.

This second type of local knowledge structure is most important to the tension between theoretical conceptualizations of development. And the assumptions underlying this version of domain specificity contrast sharply and significantly with those outlined for domain generality. They are:

1. The most plausible model for cognition consists of multiple systems, faculties, or modules.
2. Each system is uniquely constrained and operates by a special set of rules that are not reducible to a common list.
3. Each rule system is applied to a single kind of content.

The number of domains is limited, most probably to space, number, ontology, language, and possibly to mechanics, biology, and mind. The way we think about phenomena within the domains is *obligatory* and reflexive. In sum, these are "natural" domains of knowledge for which it makes sense to posit a species-level attuneness with an evolutionary origin. This is *tacit, intuitive* knowledge, *implicit* knowledge, *universal* knowledge. In contrast, domain-general knowledge is most reasonably characterized as *explicit* and *universal;* the expertise-specific variety is characterized as sometimes *implicit,* sometimes *explicit, tutored,* and *idiosyncratic.*[7]

Which kind of knowledge acquisition is implicated in development? All of them—domain-general, expertise-specific, and domain-specific knowledge—are implicated. The three are invariably intertwined in complex ways in the course of development, too. And how might this three-routed cognitive growth process take place? That is the topic of next and final section.

A SOMEWHAT SPECULATIVE DEVELOPMENTAL STORY

The neonate faces a visually rich, elaborately noisy, variously simulating, wondrously complicated universe. It is a universe that must be coped with and made sense out of quickly, however, because in less than 9 months the baby will be crawling around the world under her own power—maneuvering through it, banging on it, sucking it, stacking and throwing bits of it, experimenting with elements in it. In 24 months she will be ably running about, climbing, swinging, exploring, hiding, and finding things. She will be out the door into the expanded world of the play group, preschool, or day-care center. And in 5 years or so, she'll be off to school where, with 25 or more other little ones, she'll begin an even more circuitous journey toward adulthood. Of course, she'll need help figuring things out along the way—help from parents, grandparents, teachers, playmates, pets, and numerous others. But she is not without resources. Sometime between conception and that first day of school, she gained access to some pretty powerful cognitive equipment—equipment that will serve her well—so that even on her own she can capably extract vital information and build a structure of knowledge from those myriad events to come.

Several different sorts of encounters, experiences, and challenges face our little traveler. Some of them have faced every human being universally, such as the task of organizing space so she can find her way through it; the problem of figuring out how things move, go, fall, stop and how many there are so she doesn't fall, bump things, or get run into; and the mystery of communicating with others and anticipating what those around her will do, so she doesn't get into too much trouble. Evolution and biology may have prepared our traveler for these events with "special-needs" cognitive equipment. Other encounters will be culturally unique but common to our traveler's cohorts such as learning to read and spell and to do mathematics and geography and figuring out how fax machines and PCs work. Evolution could not have specifically prepared our traveler for these events, but some "general-purpose" cognitive apparatus and the "special-needs" equipment can be

called into service. Then, again, there also will be personally unique experiences, such as learning about her family history, learning the rules of Nintendo, Monopoly, soccer, and baseball, learning to ride horses and to read horse stories, and so much more. Our traveler may need all her cognitive equipment (and lots of help from others) to benefit maximally from these experiences. So what will a developmental account of the journey look like?

Cognitive development is the evolution of three separate strands of intellectual capacity. There is a strand for domain-specific knowledge acquisition, one for expertise-specific knowledge acquisition, and another representing domain-general cognitive operations. Each strand differs in developmental pathway and onset time. Each is more or less involved in cognitive performance as a function of the nature of the task or problem confronting the individual. As maturation and growth proceed, the strands become increasing intertwined and dependent; probably, as well, all three become changed through the network of interconnections that forms. In fact, teasing apart the strands in the mature person may be next to impossible, the "intertwinedness" having become so complicated. With hypothesized different onset times, however, separating the strands in the immature person is potentially more likely.

Domain-specific knowledge, comprised of a set of finite modules, is in operation first. The rudimentary format of these modules is innately specified, and these are what constitute the often documented cognitive abilities of infants. These primitive, fundamental, knowledge systems prepare the individual for survival in the world and enable preliminary adaptation to the developmental environment. Early exploratory behaviors, actions, and discoveries serve to enrich these knowledge systems which form the *core* of cognition. With time (time during which both maturational and experiential processes can operate), the core elaborates, affecting more and more observable behaviors. By the time the child is a toddler or preschooler, considerable evidence of cognitive sophistication is apparent, provided the tasks used to elicit reasoning are domain-relevant ones. Domain-specific knowledge underlies cognitive continuity between the young child, the older child, and even the adult.

Expertise-specific knowledge acquisition gets underway once the child is sufficiently able to derive benefit from unique encounters. While time of onset is not specifiable, it must follow domain-specific knowledge acquisition because of the interconnected relationship between the two; late infancy or toddlerhood is a reasonable guess. Domain-specific processes pave the way and provide the limits for what can be thought about and mentally represented. So, while this second strand of knowledge acquisition is not especially developmental, it is interconnected with domain-specific knowledge acquisition such that the latter limits what sorts of expertise are acquirable.

For example, extensive, idiosyncratic experience with blocks, Legos, and manipulables may enable a preschooler to become a proficient expert, but acquired Lego knowledge will not violate the rules of domain-specific spatial knowledge. Expertise-specific knowledge functions to enable the enrichment and elaboration of the core. Therefore, in expertise domains, as well as in "natural" domains, the child is going to look cognitively sophisticated. But the sophistication—the inferences, inductions, insights, and mental transformation—will evaporate when children must move beyond those natural domains.

Again, with time, experience, and increased expertise, the cognitive core elaborates, differentiates, restructures, reorganizes, forms new connections, and enables richer inferences. The basic rules of the core (i.e., domain-specific constraints) are never violated during the enrichment process, and all this mental activity remains primarily implicit. These youngsters cannot explicate for us how those infer-

ences, inductions, and transformations take place; they cannot externalize the workings of their minds for us and themselves to inspect. But at some point, sometime in middle childhood, that changes. Explanations emerge in cognitive behavior, and children begin to explicitly tell us what they think and how they reason.

Explanations and externalizations of mental processes come with the third, and perhaps most elusive of the strands: domain-general knowledge. It constitutes knowledge of facts, strategies, procedures, operations, algorithms, and reasoning schemes deliberately brought to bear in intellectual activity. It is neither as content- nor context-bound as domain-specific and expertise-specific thinking. But, where does this cognitive strand originate? That is not clear. What are its limits? That is not clear either, but it is what Piaget sought to explain. Explicit, domain-general cognition may arise from the elaboration of other strands when some cross-domain principle or relationship becomes apparent to the organizer. Or, explicit reasoning may emerge when the language faculty enables the expression of previously implicit rules. Domain-general knowledge could even constitute an innate cognitive capacity of its own, perhaps with a maturationally late onset time.

Karmiloff-Smith (1991) suggested that, at some point in development, we become capable of *representational redescription* of mental contents. Essentially, aspects of knowledge, known at first only implicitly and encapsulated in specific domains, become reexpressed by the mind. And when they do, the explicit reformulation is accessible to other parts of the mind. When and how such a process should come about is not yet clear.

Whatever their nature, domain-general (or domain-neutral) aspects of cognition are for now ethereal and elusive and perhaps will prove the most difficult strand on which to get a grasp theoretically. One reason for the elusiveness is that we cannot observe domain-general cognition without a real context (and either domain-specific, expertise-specific, or a combination of both provides that) except with artificial tasks. Those can prove notoriously difficult even for adults, and context effects extend to adults as well. Thus, domain-general development is probably what we are most unsure of. However, once explicit reasoning is a capacity available to the individual, its operation may even further alter the elaboration of the cognitive core. While each strand may begin independently, by the time a mature mind emerges, the interweaving of the strands is remarkable.

A FINAL NOTE

I often ask my son to give me his ideas about some of the matters I am trying to explain. So, I have asked him for one last contribution:

Author: Dean, do you know how babies get to kids?

Child: I don't know.

Author: Well, what do you think? How is a baby different from you?

Child: It must be the brain.

Author: (*Demanding an explicit-explanation*) What do you mean? What happens to the brain?

Child: Ummm . . . it gets bigger, and bigger, and bigger. . . . *I don't know!*

Author: (*Checking to see if a constraint will be violated*) Well, babies can become kids . . . can kids become babies?

Child: (*Denying the violation*) No way!

Author: Why not?

Child: Because kids are older than babies.

And that is one indisputable final truism about development.

ENDNOTES

1. Recall from your statistics course that the magnitude of correlations is affected by the range in the variables. When the range in one of the variables is restricted, so is the possible size of the correlation. When the range is a single point value—no variation—then the correlation has to be zero.

2. Actually, this problem always occurs when one directs inquiry to the *confirmation* of a hypothesis rather than to its *disconfirmation.* Scientific procedure is predicated on the logic that only disconfirmation is, in fact, truly possible. One need only observe a single black swan to reject the hypothesis that all swans are white. On the other hand, the observation of thousands of white swans does not rule out the possibility of someday discovering that disconfirmatory, single black one.

3. The three are *sensorimotor thought,* spanning the infancy and preoperational period; *concrete-operational thought,* described by the groupment structures; and *formal-operational thought,* the groups and lattices of the final stage.

4. While the concept of *horizontal decalage* appears to explain context effects, it really doesn't. Instead, the term is a descriptive one, an acknowledgment that performance variability across tasks is an empirical reality. We are not given why this should be the case theoretically.

5. The counterargument is, of course, that time constraints on competence only reflect the time it takes anyone to acquire sufficient knowledge, thus reducing, again, development to a knowledge effect. The controversy is probably unresolvable since knowledge-acquisition time and developmental time are perfectly confounded in the natural course of things.

6. Note, that both the *operation* of the general system and the *formation* of problem representations could be conceptualized as developmental phenomena. Piaget at one time roughly distinguished the two as *operational* and *figural* thought, although it was the former that was theoretically central.

7. Here, *universal* means present in all normal individuals whereas *idiosyncratic* implies significant individual differences. Consistent, age-related effects are possible for both.

REFERENCES

Aadlard, J., Beatty, W. W., & Maki, R. H. (1985). Spatial memory of children and adults assessed in the radial maze. *Developmental Psychobiology, 18,* 163–172.

Abramov, I., Gordon, J., Hendrickson, A., Hainline, L., Dobson, V., & LaBossiere, E. (1982). The retina of the newborn human infant. *Science, 217,* 265–267.

Acredolo, L. P. (1977). Developmental changes in the ability to coordinate perspectives of a large scale space. *Developmental Psychology, 13,* 1–11.

Acredolo, L. P. (1978). Development of spatial orientation in infancy. *Developmental Psychology, 14,* 224–234.

Acredolo, L. P. (1979). Laboratory versus home: The effect of environment on the 9-month-old infant's choice of spatial reference system. *Developmental Psychology, 15,* 666–667.

Acredolo, L. P. (1985). Coordinating perspectives on infant spatial orientation. In R. Cohen (Ed.), *The development of spatial cognition.* Hillsdale, NJ: Erlbaum.

Acredolo, L. P. (1988a). From signal to "symbol": The development of landmark knowledge from 9 to 13 months. *British Journal of Developmental Psychology, 6,* 369–372.

Acredolo, L. P. (1988b). Infant mobility and spatial development. In J. Stiles-Davis, M. Kritchevsky, & U. Bellugi (Eds.), *Spatial cognition: Brain bases and development* (pp. 157–166). Hillsdale, NJ: Erlbaum.

Acredolo, L. P., & Evans, D. (1980). Developmental changes in the effects of landmarks on infant spatial behavior. *Developmental Psychology, 16,* 312–318.

Alberts, J. R. (1984). Sensory-perceptual development in the Norway rat: A view toward comparative studies. In R. Kail & N. E. Spear (Eds.), *Comparative perspectives on the development of memory* (pp. 65–102). Hillsdale, NJ: Erlbaum.

Alderton, D. L., Goldman, S. R., & Pellegrino, J. W. (1985). Individual differences in process outcomes for verbal analogy and classification solution. *Intelligence, 9,* 69–85.

Alexander, P. A., Willson, V. L., White, C. S., & Fuqua, J. D. (1987). Analogical reasoning in young children. *Journal of Educational Psychology, 79,* 401–408.

Altman, J., & Das, G. D. (1965). Autoradiography and histological evidence of postnatal neurogenesis in rats. *Journal of Comparative Neurology, 124,* 319–336.

Anderson, J. R. (1983). *The architecture of cognition.* Cambridge, Mass: Harvard University Press.

Anderson, J. R. (1990). *Cognitive psychology and its implications.* New York: Freeman.

Anderson, J. R., & Rosenfeld, E. (Eds.). (1988). *Neurocomputing: Foundations of research.* Cambridge, MA: The MIT Press.

Anderson, M. (1986). Cultural concatenation of deceit and secrecy. In R. W. Mitchell & N. S. Thompson (Eds.), *Deception: Perspectives on human and nonhuman deceit.* Albany, NY: State University of New York Press.

Anderson, R., & Smith, B. L. (1987). Phonological development of two-year-old monolingual Puerto Rican Spanish-speaking children. *Journal of Child Language, 14,* 57–78.

Anglin, J. M. (1977). *Word, object, and conceptual development.* New York: W. W. Norton.

Anooshian, L. J., & Siegel, A. W. (1985). From cognitive to procedural mapping. In C. J. Brainerd & M. Pressley (Eds.), *Basic processes in memory development: Processes of memory development.* New York: Springer-Verlag.

Antell, S. E., & Keating, D. P. (1983). Perception of numerical invariance in neonates. *Child Development, 54,* 695–701.

Anzai, Y., & Simon, H. A. (1979). The theory of learning by doing. *Psychological Review, 86,* 124–140.

Appelbaum, M. I., & McCall, R. B. (1983). Design and analysis in developmental psychology. In P. H. Mussen (Series Ed.) & W. Kessen (Vol. Ed.). *Handbook of Child Psychology,* (Vol. 1, pp. 416–476). New York: Wiley.

Armitage, S. E., Baldwin, B. A., & Vince, M. A. (1980). The fetal sound environment of sheep. *Science, 208,* 1173–1174.

Armstrong, S. L., Gleitman, L. R., & Gleitman, H. G. (1983). On what some concepts might not be. *Cognition, 13,* 263–308.

Arterberry, M. E., & Yonas, A. (1988). Infants' sensitivity to kinetic information for three-dimensional object shape. *Perception and Psychophysics, 44*(1), 1–6.

Ashmead, D. H., Clifton, R. K., & Perris, E. E. (1987). Precision of auditory localization in human infants. *Developmental Psychology, 23*(5), 641–647.

Aslin, R. N. (1981a). Development of smooth pursuit in human infants. In D. F. Fisher, R. A. Monty, & J. W. Senders (Eds.), *Eye movements: Cognition and visual perception* (pp. 31–51). Hillsdale, NJ: Erlbaum.

Aslin, R. N. (1981b). Experiential influences & sensitive periods in perceptual development: A unified model. In R. N. Aslin, J. R. Alberts, & M. R. Peterson (Eds.), *Development of perception: Psychobiological perspectives: Vol 2. The Visual System.* New York: Academic Press.

Aslin, R. N. (1987). Visual and auditory development in infancy. In J. D. Osofsky (Ed.), *Handbook of infant development* (pp. 5–97). New York: Wiley.

Aslin, R. N. (1988). Anatomical constraints on oculomotor development: Implications for infant perception. In A. Yonas (Ed.), *Perceptual development in infancy: The Minnesota symposia on child psychology* (Vol. 20, pp. 67–104). Hillsdale, NJ: Erlbaum.

Aslin, R. N., Pisoni, D. B., & Jusczyk, P. W. (1983). Auditory development and speech perception in infancy. In M. M. Haith & J. J. Campos (Eds.), *Handbook of child psychology: Infancy and developmental psychobiology,* (Vol. 2, pp. 573–687). New York: Wiley.

Aslin, R. N., & Salapatek, P. (1975). Saccadic localization of visual targets by the very young human infant. *Perception and Psychophysics, 17,* 293–302.

Aslin, R. N., & Smith, L. B. (1988). Perceptual Development. In M. R. Rosenzweig & L. W. Porter (Eds.), *Annual Review of Psychology,* (Vol. 39, pp. 435–474). Palo Alto, CA: Annual Reviews, Inc.

Astington, J. W., Harris, P., & Olson, D. (1988). *Developing theories of mind.* New York: Cambridge University Press.

Atkinson, J. (1984). Human visual development over the first 6 months of life. A review and a hypothesis. *Human Neurobiology, 3,* 61–74.

Atkinson, R. L., & Shiffrin, R. M. (1968). Human memory: A proposed system and its control processes. In K. W. Spence & J. T. Spence (Eds.), *The Psychology of motivation and learning* (Vol. 2). New York: Academic Press.

Au, T. K. (1985). Children's word-learning strategies. *Papers and Reports on Child Language Development, 24,* 22–29.

Au, T. K., & Glusman, M. (1990). The principle of mutual exclusivity in word learning: To honor or not to honor? *Child Development, 61,* 1474–1490.

Bachevalier, J., & Mishkin, M. (1984). An early and late developing system for learning and retention in infant monkeys. *Behavioral Neuroscience, 98,* 770–778.

Bady, R. J. (1979). Students' understanding of hypothesis testing. *Journal of Research in Science Teaching, 16,* 61–65.

Baillargeon, R. (1987a). Object permanence in 3.5- and 4.5-month-old infants. *Developmental Psychology, 23,* 655–664.

Baillargeon, R. (1987b). *Reasoning about the height and location of a hidden object in 4.5- and 6.5-month-old infants.* Paper presented at the meeting of the Society for Research in Child Development, Baltimore, MD.

Baillargeon, R. (1987c). Young infants' reasoning about the physical and spatial properties of a hidden object. *Cognitive Development, 2,* 179–200.

Baillargeon, R. (in press). The object concept revisited: New directions. In H. W. Reese (Ed.), *Advances in child development & behavior* (Vol. 23). New York: Academic Press.

Baillargeon, R., & Graber, M. (1988). Evidence of location memory in 8-month-old infants in a nonsearch AB task. *Developmental Psychology, 24,* 502–511.

Baillargeon, R., Spelke, E. S., & Wasserman, S. (1985). Object permanence in five-month-old infants. *Cognition, 20,* 191–208.

Baker, C. L. (1979). Syntactic theory and the projection problem. *Linguistic Inquiry, 10,* 533–582.

Baker-Ward, L., Ornstein, P. A., & Holden, D. J. (1984). The expression of memorization in early childhood. *Journal of Experimental Child Psychology, 37,* 555–575.

Baldwin, D. (1989). Priorities in children's expectations about object label reference: Form over color. *Child Development, 60,* 1291–1306.

Baldwin, D. A., & Markman, E. M. (1989). Mapping out word-object relations: A first step. *Child Development, 60,* 381–398.

Bandura, A. (1986). *Social foundations for thought and action: A social cognitive theory.* Englewood Cliffs, NJ: Prentice Hall.

Banks, M. S. (1988). Visual recalibration and the development of contrast and optical flow perception. In A. Yonas (Ed.), *Perceptual development in infancy: The Minnesota symposium on child psychology* (Vol. 20, pp. 145–196). Hillsdale, NJ: Erlbaum.

Banks, M. S., & Ginsburg, A. P. (1985). Early visual preferences: A review and a new theoretical treatment. In H. W. Reese (Ed.), *Advances in child development & behavior* (pp. 207–246). New York: Academic.

Banks, M. S., & Salapatek, P. (1981). Infant pattern vision: A new approach based on the contrast sensitivity function. *Journal of Experimental Child Psychology, 31,* 1–45.

Banks, M. S., & Salapatek, P. (1983). Infant visual perception. In M. M. Haith, & J. J. Campos (Eds.), *Handbook of child psychology: Infancy and developmental psychobiology* (pp. 435–572). New York: Wiley.

Banks, M. S., Stephens, B. R., & Hartmann, E. E. (1985). The development of basic mechanisms of pattern vision: Spatial frequency channels. *Journal of Experimental Child Psychology, 40,* 501–527.

Barrera, M. E., & Maurer D. (1981). The perception of facial expressions by the three-month-old. *Child Development, 52,* 203–206.

Bartlett, F. C. (1932). *Remembering*. Cambridge, England: Cambridge University Press.

Bates, E., O'Connell, B., & Shore, C. (1967). Language and communication in infancy. In J. D. Osofsky (Ed.), *Handbook of infant development* (2nd ed.). New York: Wiley.

Bateson, P. P. G. (1979). How do sensitive periods arise and what are they for? *Animal Behavior, 27,* 470–486.

Bayer, S. A., & Altman, J. (1987). Directions in neurogenic gradients and patterns of anatomical connections in the telencephalon. *Progress in Neurobiology, 29,* 57–106.

Behrend, D. A. (1990). Constraints and development: A reply to Nelson (1988). *Cognitive Development, 5,* 313–330.

Behrend, D. A. (1988). Overextensions in early language comprehension: Evidence from a signal detection approach. *Journal of Child Language, 15,* 63–75.

Beilin, H. (1984). Cognitive theory and mathematical cognition: Geometry and space. In B. Gholson & T. L. Rosenthal (Eds.), *Applications of cognitive-developmental theory* (pp. 49–93). New York: Academic Press.

Benedict, H. (1979). Early lexical development: Comprehension and production. *Journal of Child Language, 6,* 183–200.

Berg, C. A., & Sternberg, R. J. (1985). Response to novelty: Continuity versus discontinuity in the course of development. In H. W. Reese (Ed.), *Advances in child development and behavior,* (Vol. 19, pp. 2–48). Orlando, FL: Academic Press.

Berg, W. K., & Berg, K. M. (1979). Psychophysiological development in infancy: State, sensory function, and attention. In J. D. Osofsky (Ed.), *Handbook of infant development*. New York: Wiley.

Berko, J. (1958). The child's learning of English morphology. *Word, 14,* 150–177.

Berman, R. F. (1986). Studies of memory processes using electrical brain stimulation. In J. L. Martinez & R. P. Kesner (Eds.), *Learning and memory: A biological view*. New York: Academic.

Bertenthal, B. I., & Campos, J. J. (1984). A reexamination of fear and its determinants on the visual cliff. *Psychophysiology, 21,* 413–417.

Bertenthal, B. I., & Campos, J. J. (1987). New directions in the study of early experience. *Child Development, 58,* 560–567.

Bertenthal, B. I., Campos, J. J., & Barrett, K. (1984). Self-produced locomotion: An organizer of emotional, cognitive, and social development in infancy. In R. Emde & R. Harmon (Eds.), *Continuities and discontinuities in development* (pp. 175–210). New York: Plenum.

Bertenthal, B. I., Campos, J. J., & Haith, M. M. (1980). Development of visual organization: The perception of subjective contours. *Child Development, 51,* 1072–1080.

Bertenthal, B. I., Dunn, S., & Bai, D. (1986). Infants' sensitivity to optical flow for specifying self-motion. *Infant Behavior and Development, 9,* 35.

Bertenthal, B. I., Proffitt, D. R., Cutting, J. E. (1984). Infant sensitivity to figural coherence in biomechanical motions. *Journal of Experimental Child Psychology, 37,* 213–230.

Bertenthal, B. I., Proffitt, D. R., Kramer, S. J., & Spetner, N. B. (1987). Infants' encoding of kinetic displays varying in relative coherence. *Developmental Psychology, 23,* 171–178.

Bertenthal, B. I., Proffitt, D. R., Spetner, N. B., & Thomas, M. A. (1985). The development of infant sensitivity to biomechanical motions. *Child Development, 56,* 531–543.

Beth, E. W., & Piaget, J. (1966). *Mathematical epistemology and psychology*. Dordrecht: Reidel.

Bialystok, E. (1989). Children's mental rotations of abstract displays. *Journal of Experimental Child Psychology, 47,* 47−71.

Bialystok, E., & Vallance, D. (1989). *Calculation of perspective change.* Paper presented at the biennial meeting of the Society for Research in Child Development, Kansas City, Missouri.

Bijou, S. W., & Baer, D. M. (1961). *Child Development: Vol. I. A systematic and empirical theory.* New York: Appleton-Century-Crofts.

Bijou, S. W., & Baer, D. M. (1978). *Child development: A behavior analysis approach.* Englewood Cliffs, NJ: Prentice Hall.

Bingham-Newman, A. M., & Hooper, F. H. (1974). Classification and seriation instruction and logical task performance in the preschool. *American Education Research Journal, 11,* 379−393.

Bjork, E. L., & Cummings, E. M. (1984). Infant search errors: Stage of concept development or stage of memory development? *Memory & Cognition, 12,* 1−19.

Bjorklund, D. F. (1987). How age changes in knowledge base contribute to the development of children's memory: An interpretive review. *Developmental Review, 7,* 93−130.

Bjorklund, D. F. (1990). *Children's strategies: Contemporary views of cognitive development.* Hillsdale, NJ: Erlbaum.

Bjorklund, D. F., & Muir, J. E. (1988). Children's development of free recall memory: Remembering on their own. In R. Vasta (Ed.), *Annals of Child development* (Vol. 5). Greenwich, CT: JAI.

Black, J. E., & Greenough, W. T. (1986). Induction of pattern in neural structure by experience: Implications for cognitive development. In M. E. Lamb, A. L. Brown, & B. Rogoff (Eds.), *Advances in developmental psychology* (Vol 4, pp. 1−50). Hillsdale, NJ: Erlbaum.

Black, J. S., & Overton, W. F. (1990). Reasoning, logic, and thought disorder: Deductive reasoning and developmental psychopathology. In W. F. Overton (Ed.), *Reasoning, logic, and necessity* (pp. 255−298). Hillsdale, NJ: Erlbaum.

Blass, E. M., Ganchrow, J. R., & Steiner, J. E. (1984). Classical conditioning in newborn humans 2−48 hours of age. *Infant Behavior & Development, 7,* 223−235.

Blevins-Knabe, B., Cooper, R. G., Starkey, P., Mace, P. G., & Leitner, E. (1987). Preschoolers sometimes know less than we think: The use of quantifiers to solve addition and subtraction tasks. *Bulletin of the Psychonomic Society, 25,* 31−34.

Bloom, L., Lifter, K., & Hafitz, J. (1980). The semantics of verbs and the development of verb inflection in child language. *Language, 56,* 386−412.

Bloom, P. (1990a). Subjectless sentences in child language. *Linguistic Inquiry, 21,* 491−504.

Bloom, P. (1990b). Syntactic distinctions in child language. *Journal of Child Language, 17,* 343−355.

Bloom, P. (in press). Possible names: The role of syntax-semantic mappings in the acquisition of nominals. *Lingua.*

Blount, B. G. (1982). The ontogeny of emotions and their vocal expression in infants. In S. A. Kuczaj (Ed.), *Language development* (Vol. 2). Hillsdale, NJ: Erlbaum.

Boden, M. A. (1979). *Jean Piaget.* New York: Viking.

Bohannon, J. N., & Hirsch-Pasek, K. (1984). Do children say as they're told? A new perspective on motherese. In L. Feagons, C. Garvey, & R. Golinkoff (Eds.), *The origins and growth of communication.* Norwood, NJ: Ablex.

Bohannon, J. N., & Stanowitz, L. (1988). The issue of negative evidence: Adult responses to children's language errors. *Developmental Psychology, 23,* 684−689.

Bohannon, J. N., III, & Warren-Leubecker, A. (1988). Recent developments in child-directed speech: We've come a long way, baby-talk. *Language Sciences, 16,* 89−110.

Bomba, P., & Siqueland, T. (1983). The nature and structure of infant form categories. *Journal of Experimental Child Psychology, 35,* 294−328.

Borke, H. (1971). Interpersonal perception of young children: Egocentrism or empathy? *Developmental Psychology, 5,* 263−269.

Borke, H. (1975). Piaget's mountains revisited: Changes in the egocentric landscape. *Developmental Psychology, 11,* 240−243.

Borke, H. (1978). Piaget's view of social interaction and the theoretical construct of empathy. In L. S. Siegel & C. J. Brainerd (Eds.), *Alternatives to Piaget: Critical essays on the theory.* New York: Academic.

Bornstein, M. H. (1978). Visual behavior of the young human infant: Relationships between chromatic and spatial perception and the activity of underlying brain mechanisms. *Journal of Experimental Child Psychology, 26,* 174−192.

Bornstein, M. H. (1984). A descriptive taxonomy of psychological categories used by infants. In C. Sophian (Ed.), *Origins of cognitive skills.* Hillsdale, NJ: Erlbaum.

Bornstein, M. H. (1985). Habituation of attention as a measure of visual information processing in human infants: Summary, systematization, & synthesis. In G. Gottlieb & N. A. Kransnegor (Eds.), *Measurement of audition and vision in the first year of postnatal life: A methodological overview* (pp. 253–300). Norwood, NJ: Ablex.

Bornstein, M. H. (1988). Perceptual development across the life cycle. In M. H. Bornstein & M. E. Lamb (Eds.), *Developmental psychology: An advanced textbook* (2nd ed., pp. 151–204). Hillsdale, NJ: Erlbaum.

Bornstein, M. H., Ferdinandsen, K., & Gross, C. G. (1981). Perception of symmetry in infancy. *Developmental Psychology, 17,* 82–86.

Borovsky, D. B. (1987). *Determinants of retention in 6-month-old infants.* Unpublished master's thesis, Rutgers University, New Brunswick, NJ.

Bower, T. G. R. (1967). The development of object-permanence: Some studies of existence constancy. *Perception and Psychophysics, 2,* 411–418.

Bower, T. G. R. (1974). *Development in infancy.* San Francisco, CA: Freeman.

Bower, T. G. R. (1977a). *A primer of infant development.* San Francisco, CA: Freeman.

Bower, T. G. R. (1977b). Comment on Yonas et al., "The development of sensitivity to information for impending collision." *Perception & Psychophysics, 21,* 281–282.

Bower, T. G. R., Broughton, J. M., & Moore, M. K. (1971). Development of the object concept as manifested in the tracking behavior of infants between 7 and 20 weeks of age. *Journal of Experimental Child Psychology, 11,* 182–193.

Bower, T. G. R., & Patterson, J. G. (1973). The separation of place, movement, and object in the world of the infant. *Journal of Experimental Child Psychology, 15,* 161–168.

Bower, T. G. R., & Wishart, J. G. (1972). The effects of motor skill on object permanence. *Cognition, 1,* 165–172.

Bowerman, M. (1973). *Early syntactic development.* Cambridge, England: Cambridge University Press.

Bowerman, M. (1974). Learning the structure of causative verbs: A study in the relationship of cognitive, semantic, and syntactic development. In E. Clark (Ed.), *Papers and reports in child language development* (No. 8, pp. 142–178). Stanford, CA: Stanford University Committee on Linguistics.

Bowlby, J. (1958). The nature of the child's tie to his mother. *International Journal of Psychoanalysis, 39,* 350–373.

Bowlby, J. (1969). *Attachment & Loss: Vol. 1. Attachment.* New York: Basic Books.

Boysen, S. T. (1988). Kanting processes in the chimpanzee: What (and who) really counts. *Behavioral & Brain Sciences, 11,* 580.

Boysen, S. T., & Berntson, G. G. (1989). Numerical competence in a chimpanzee. *Journal of Comparative Psychology, 103,* 23–31.

Braaten, R. F. (1988). Protocounting as a last resort. *Behavioral & Brain Sciences, 11,* 581.

Braine, M. D. S. (1990). The "natural logic" approach to reasoning. In W. F. Overton (Ed.), *Reasoning, logic, and necessity* (pp. 135–158). Hillsdale, NJ: Erlbaum.

Braine, M. D. S., & Rumain, B. (1983). Logical reasoning. In J. H. Flavell & E. M. Markman (Eds.), *Handbook of child psychology: Vol. 3. Cognitive Development* (pp. 264–340). New York: Wiley.

Braine, M. D. S., Reiser, B. J., & Rumain, B. (1984). Some empirical justification for a theory of natural propositional logic. In G. H. Bower (Ed.), *The psychology of learning and motivation: Advances in research and thinking* (Vol. 18, pp.313–371). New York: Academic.

Brainerd, C. J. (1973a). Mathematical and behavioral foundations of number. *Journal of General Psychology, 88,* 221–281.

Brainerd, C. J. (1973b). NeoPiagetian training experiments revisited: Is there any support for the cognitive-developmental stage hypothesis? *Cognition, 2,* 349–370.

Brainerd, C. J. (1973c). The origins of number concepts. *Scientific American, 228,* 101–109

Brainerd, C. J. (1978a). *Piaget's theory of intelligence.* Englewood Cliffs, NJ: Prentice Hall.

Brainerd, C. J. (1978b). Learning research and Piagetian theory. In L. S. Siegel & C. J. Brainerd, *Alternatives to Piaget: Critical essays on the theory.* New York: Academic Press.

Brainerd, C. J. (1978c). The stage question in cognitive-developmental theory. *Behavioral and Brain Sciences, 2,* 173–213.

Brainerd, C. J. (1979). *The origins of the number concept.* New York: Praeger.

Brainerd, C. J., & Reyna, V.F. (in press). Memory independence and memory interference in cognitive development. *Psychological Review.*

Bremner, J. G. (1978). Egocentric versus allocentric spatial coding in nine-month-old infants. Factors influencing the choice of code. *Developmental Psychology, 14,* 346–355.

Bremner, J. G. (1985). Object tracking and search in infancy: A review of data and a theoretical evaluation. *Developmental Review, 5,* 371–396.

Breslow, L. (1981). Reevaluation of the literature on the development of transitive inferences. *Psychological Bulletin, 89,* 325–351.

Bretherton, I., & Beeghly, M. (1982). Talking about internal states: The acquisition of an explicit theory of mind. *Developmental Psychology, 18,* 906–921.

Brody, L., Zelazo, P., & Chaika, H. (1984). Habituation-dishabituation to speech in the neonate. *Developmental Psychology, 20,* 114–119.

Bronson, G. W. (1974). The postnatal growth of visual capacity. *Child Development, 45,* 873–890.

Broughton, J. (1978). Development of concepts of self, mind, reality, and knowledge. In W. Damon (Ed.), *New directions for child development.* San Francisco: Jossey-Bass.

Brown, A. L. (1976). The construction of temporal succession by preoperational children. In A. D. Pick (Ed.), *Minnesota symposium on child psychology* (Vol. 10). Minneapolis: University of Minnesota Press.

Brown, A. L. (1989). Analogical reasoning and transfer: What develops? In S. Vosniadou & A. Ortony (Eds.), *Similarity and analogical reasoning* (pp. 369–412). Cambridge: Cambridge University Press.

Brown, A. L., & DeLoache, J. S. (1978). Skills, plans, and self-regulation. In R. S. Siegler (Ed.), *Children's thinking: What develops?* Hillsdale, NJ: Erlbaum.

Brown, A. L., & Kane, M. J. (1988). Preschool children can learn to transfer: Learning to learn and learning by example. *Cognitive Psychology, 20,* 493–523.

Brown, A. L., Kane, M. J., & Echols, C. H. (1986). Young children's mental models determine analogical transfer across problems with common goal structure. *Cognitive Development, 1,* 103–121.

Brown, A. L., Kane, M. J., & Long, C. (1989). Analogical transfer in young children: Analogies as tools for communication and exposition. *Applied Cognitive Psychology, 3,* 275–293.

Brown, A. L., Bransford, J. D., Ferrara, R. A., & Campione, J. C. (1983). Learning, remembering, and understanding. In P. H. Mussen (Ed.),

Handbook of child psychology: Vol. 3. *Cognitive development.* New York: Wiley.

Brown, R. (1957). Linguistic determinism and the part of speech. *Journal of Abnormal and Social Psychology, 55,* 1–5.

Brown, R. (1958). *Words and things.* New York: Free Press.

Brown, R. (1973). *A first language: The early stages.* Cambridge, MA: Harvard University Press.

Brown, R., & Hanlon, C. (1970). Derivational complexity and order of acquisition in child speech. In Hayes, J.R. (Ed.). *Cognition and the development of language.* New York: Wiley.

Bruner, J. S. (1964). The course of cognitive growth. *American Psychologist, 19,* 1–15.

Bruner, J. S., Goodnow, J. J., & Austin, G. A. (1956). *A study of thinking.* New York: Wiley.

Bruner, J. S., Olver, R. R., & Greenfield, P. M. et al. (1966). *Studies in cognitive growth.* New York: Wiley.

Bryant, P. E. (1972). The understanding of invariance by very young children. *Canadian Journal of Psychology, 26,* 79–96.

Bryant, P. E. (1974). *Perception and understanding in young children.* New York: Basic Books.

Bryant, P. E., & Trabasso, T. (1971). Transitive inferences and memory in young children. *Nature, 232,* 457–459.

Bucci, W. (1978). The interpretation of universal affirmation propositions. *Cognition, 6,* 55–77.

Bullock, M. (1985). Animism in childhood thinking: A new look at an old question. *Developmental Psychology, 21,* 217–225.

Bullock, M., Gelman, R., & Baillargeon, R. (1982). The development of causal reasoning. In W. F. Friedman (Ed.). *The developmental psychology of time.* New York: Academic.

Bullock, T. H. (1984). Comparative neuroscience holds promise for quiet revolutions. *Science, 225,* 473–478.

Burns, R. A. (1988). Subitizing and rhythm in serial numerical investigations with animals. *Behavioral and Brain Sciences, 11,* 581–582.

Bushnell, I. W. R. (1979). Modification of the externality effect in young infants. *Journal of Experimental Child Psychology, 28,* 211–229.

Butterworth, G., Jarrett, N., & Hicks, L. (1982). Spatiotemporal identity in infancy. Perceptual competence or conceptual deficit. *Developmental Psychology, 18,* 435–449.

Bybee, J. L., & Slobin, D. I. (1982). Rules and schemes in the development and use of the English tense. *Language, 58,* 265–289.

Byrnes, J. P., & Overton, W. F. (1987). Reasoning about certainty and uncertainty in concrete, causal, and propositional contexts. *Developmental Psychology, 22,* 793–799.

Byrnes, J. P., & Overton, W. F. (1988). Reasoning about logical connectives: A developmental analysis. *Journal of Experimental Child Psychology, 46,* 194–218.

Campbell, B. A., & Spear, N. E. (1972). Ontogeny of memory. *Psychological Review, 79,* 215–236.

Campos, J. J., Benson, J., & Rudy, L. (1986). *The role of self-produced locomotion in spatial behavior.* Paper presented at the meetings of the International Conference on Infant Studies, Beverly Hills, CA.

Campos, J. J., Hiatt, S., Ramsay, D., Henderson, C., & Svejda, M. (1978). The emergence of fear on the visual cliff. In M. Lewis & L. A. Rosenblum (Eds.), *The origins of affect.* New York: Plenum.

Capaldi, E. J., & Miller, D. J. (1988a). Counting in rats: Its functional significance and the independent cognitive processes which comprise it. *Journal of Experimental Psychology: Animal Behavior Processes, 14,* 3–17.

Capaldi, E. J., & Miller, D. J. (1988b). A different view of numerical processes in animals. *Behavioral and Brain Sciences, 11,* 582–583.

Caramata, S., & Leonard, L. B. (1986). Young children pronounce object words more accurately than action words. *Journal of Child Language, 13,* 51–65.

Caramazza, A., McCloskey, M., & Green, B. (1981). Naive beliefs in "sophisticated" subjects: Misconceptions about trajectories of objects. *Cognition, 9,* 117–123.

Carey, S. (1978). The child as word learner. In M. Halle, J. Bresnan & G. A. Miller (Eds.), *Linguistic theory and psychological reality.* Cambridge, MA: MIT Press.

Carey, S. (1983). Constraints on the meanings of natural kind terms. In B. Seiler & W. Wannenmacher (Eds.), *Concept development and the development of word meaning.* Berlin: Springer Verlag.

Carey, S. (1985). *Conceptual change in childhood.* Cambridge, MA: MIT Press.

Carey, S. (1986). Cognitive science and science education. *American Psychologist, 41,* 1123–1130.

Carey, S. (1988). Conceptual differences between children and adults. *Mind and Language, 3,* 167–181.

Carey, S. (1990). On some relations between the description and explanation of developmental change. In G. Butterworth & P. Bryant (Eds.), *Causes of development: Interdisciplinary perspectives.* Hillsdale, NJ: Erlbaum.

Carey, S. (1991). Knowledge acquisition: Enrichment or conceptual change? In R. Gelman & S. Carey (Eds.), *The epigenesis of mind: Essays on biology and cognition.* Hillsdale, NJ: Erlbaum.

Carey, S., & Gelman, R. (1991). *The epigenesis of mind: Essays on biology and cognition.* Hillsdale, NJ: Erlbaum.

Carpenter, T. P., Moser, J. M., & Romberg, T. A. (Eds.). (1982). *Addition & subtraction: A cognitive perspective.* Hillsdale, NJ: Erlbaum.

Carroll, J. J., & Gibson, E. J. (1981). *Infant's differentiation of an aperture and an obstacle.* Paper presented at the Society for Research in Child Development, Boston, MA.

Carter, P., Pazak, B., & Kail, R. (1983). Algorithms for processing spatial information. *Journal of Experimental Child Psychology, 37,* 284–304.

Case, R. (1972). Validation of a neo-Piagetian capacity construct. *Journal of Experimental Child Psychology, 14,* 287–302.

Case, R. (1985a). *Intellectual development: Birth to adulthood.* New York: Academic.

Case, R. (1985b). *Intellectual development: A systematic reinterpretation.* New York: Academic.

Case, R., & Serlin, R. (1978). A new processing model for predicting performance on Pascual-Leone's test of M-space. *Cognitive Psychology, 11,* 308–326.

Castro, C. A., Paylor, R., & Rudy, J. W. (1987). A developmental analysis of the learning and short-term-memory processes mediating performance in conditional-spatial discrimination problems. *Psychobiology, 15,* 308–316.

Cazden, C. B. (1968). The acquisition of noun and verb inflections. *Child Development, 39,* 433–448.

Ceci, S. J. (1989). On domain-specificity . . . more or less general and specific constraints on cognitive development. *Merrill-Palmer Quarterly, 35,* 131–142.

Chandler, K. (1989). *Variability in ontological knowledge and its relationship to intelligence.* Unpublished doctoral dissertation, University of Arizona, Tuscon.

Chandler, K., Rosser, R., & Narter, D. (1993). *The effects of developmental status, ontological knowledge, and verbal ability on children's understanding of metaphor.* Paper presented at the biennial meeting of the Society for Research in Child Developmental. New Orleans, LA.

Chandler, K., Rosser, R. A., & Nicholson, G. C. (1992). The relationship between ontological knowledge structure and intelligence in children. *Cognitive Development, 7,* 63–80.

Chandler, M., & Boyes, M. (1982). Social-cognitive development. In B. B. Wolman (Ed.), *Handbook of developmental psychology.* Englewood Cliffs, NJ: Prentice Hall.

Chandler, M., Fritz, A. S., & Hala, S. (1989). Small-scale deceit: Deception as a marker of two-, three-, and four-year-olds' early theories of mind. *Child Development, 60,* 1263–1277.

Chang, H. W., & Trehub, S. E. (1977). Infants' perception of temporal grouping in auditory patterns. *Child Development, 48,* 1666–1670.

Changeaux, J. P. (1980). Genetic determinism and epigenesis of the neuronal network: Is there a biological compromise between Chomsky and Piaget? In M. Piatelli-Palmarini (Ed.), *Language and Learning* (pp. 185–197). Cambridge: MA: Harvard University Press.

Chapman, M., & Lindenberger, U. (1988). Functions, operations, and decalage in the development of transitivity. *Developmental Psychology, 24,* 542–551.

Cheng, P. W., & Holyoak, K. J. (1985). Pragmatic reasoning schemas. *Cognitive Psychology, 17,* 391–416.

Cheng, P. W., & Holyoak, K. J. (1989). On the natural selection of reasoning theories. *Cognition, 33,* 285–313.

Cheng, P. W., Holyoak, K. J., Nisbett, R. E., & Oliver, L. M. (1987). Pragmatic versus syntactic approaches to training deductive reasoning. *Cognitive Psychology, 18,* 293–328.

Chi, M. T. H. (1976). Short term memory and limitations in children: Capacity or processing deficits? *Memory and Cognition, 4,* 559–572.

Chi, M. T. H. (1978). Knowledge structures and memory development. In R. S. Siegler (Ed.), *Children's thinking: What develops?* Hillsdale, NJ: Erlbaum.

Chi, M. T. H. (1983). *Trends in memory development research.* Basel, Switzerland: Karger.

Chi, M. T. H., & Ceci, S. J. (1987). Content knowledge: Its role, representation and restructuring in memory development. In H. W. Reese (Ed.), *Advances in child development and behavior* (Vol. 20). New York: Academic.

Chi, M. T. H., & Glaser, R. (1980). The measurement of expertise: Analysis of the development of knowledge and skill as a basis for assessing achievement. In E. L. Baker & E. S. Quellmalz (Eds.), *Educational testing and evaluation: Design, analysis, and policy.* Beverly Hills, CA: Sage.

Chi, M. T. H., Feltovich, P. J., & Glaser, R. (1981). Categorization and representation of physics problems by experts and novices. *Cognitive Science, 5,* 121–152.

Chi, M. T. H., Glaser, R., & Rees, E. (1982). Expertise in problem solving. In R. Sternberg (Ed.), *Advances in the psychology of human intelligence* (Vol. 1). Hillsdale, NJ: Erlbaum.

Chi, M. T. H., Hutchinson, J. E., & Robin, A. F. (1989). How inferences about novel domain-related concepts can be constrained by structured knowledge. *Merrill-Palmer Quarterly, 35,* 27–62.

Chi, M. T. H., & Klahr, D. (1975). Span and rate of apprehension in children and adults. *Journal of Experimental Child Psychology, 19,* 434–439.

Chi, M. T. H., & Koeske, R. D. (1983). Network representation of a child's dinosaur knowledge. *Developmental Psychology, 19,* 29–39.

Childs, M. K., & Polich, J. M. (1979). Developmental differences in mental rotation. *Journal of Experimental Child Psychology, 27,* 339–351.

Chomsky, N. (1957). *Syntactic structures.* The Hague: Mouton.

Chomsky, N. (1959). A review of B. F. Skinner's verbal behavior. *Language, 35,* 26–58.

Chomsky, N. (1965). *Aspects of the theory of syntax.* Cambridge, MA: MIT Press.

Chomsky, N. (1975). *Reflections on language.* New York: Random House.

Chomsky, N. (1980). *Rules and representations.* New York: Columbia University Press.

Chomsky, N. (1981). *Lectures on government and binding.* Dordrecht: Foris.

Chomsky, N. (1986). *Knowledge of language: Its nature, origin, and use.* New York: Prager.

Chomsky, N. (1988). *Language and problems of knowledge.* Cambridge, MA: MIT Press.

Chomsky, N., & Lasnik, H. (1977). Filters and control. *Linguistic Inquiry, 8,* 425–504.

Churchland, P. (1981). Eliminative materialism and propositional attitudes. *Journal of Philosophy, 78,* 67–90.

Churchland, P. (1984). *Matter and consciousness.* Cambridge, MA: Bradford Books/MIT Press.

Clark, A. (1987). From folk psychology to naive psychology. *Cognitive Science, 11,* 139–154.

Clark, E. V. (1978). Strategies for communicating. *Child Development, 49,* 977–987.

Clark, E. V. (1982). The young word-maker: A case study of innovation in the child's lexicon. In E. Wanner & L. R. Gleitman (Eds.), *Language ac-*

quisition: The state of the art. Cambridge, England: Cambridge University Press.

Clark, E. V. (1983). Meanings and concepts. In J. H. Flavell & E. M. Markman (Eds.), Handbook of child psychology: Vol. 3. Cognitive development. New York: Wiley

Clark, E. V. (1987). The principle of contrast: A constraint on language acquisition. In B. MacWhinney (Ed.), Mechanisms of language acquisition: The 20th annual Carnegie symposium on cognition. Hillsdale, NJ: Erlbaum.

Clark, E. V. (1988). On the logic of contrast. Journal of Child Language, 15, 317–335.

Clark, E. V. (1990). On the pragmatics of contrast. Journal of Child Language, 17, 417–431.

Clement, C. A., & Falmange, R. J. (1987). Logical reasoning, world knowledge, and mental imagery: Interconnections in cognitive processes. Memory & Cognition, 14, 200–307.

Clement, J. (1983). A conceptual model discussed by Galileo and used intuitively by physics students. In D. Gentner & A. L. Stevens (Eds.), Mental models. Hillsdale, NJ: Erlbaum.

Clifton, R. K., Gwiazda, J., Bauer, J. A., Clarkson, M. G., & Held, R. M. (1988). Growth in head size during infancy: Implications for sound localization. Developmental Psychology, 24(4), 477–483.

Clumech, H. V. (1980). The acquisition of tone. In G. H. Yeni-Komshian, J. Kavanaug, & C. A. Ferguson (Eds.), Child Phonology: Vol. 1. Production. New York: Academic.

Cohen, N. J., & Squire, L. R. (1980). Preserved learning and retention of pattern analyzing in amnesia: Dissociation of knowing how and knowing that. Science, 210, 207–209.

Coie, J. D., Costanzo, P. R., & Farnill, D. (1973). Specific transitions in the development of spatial perspective-taking ability. Developmental Psychology, 9, 167–177.

Cole, M., & Scribner, S. (1974). Culture and thought: A psychological introduction. New York: Wiley.

Coleman, P. D., Flood, D. G., Whitehead, M. C., & Emerson, R. C. (1981). Spatial sampling by dendritic trees in visual cortex. Brain Research, 214, 1–21.

Coleman, P. D., & Riesen, A. H. (1968). Environmental effects on cortical dendritic fields: I. Rearing in the dark. Journal of Anatomy, 102, 363–374.

Comrie, B. (1981). Language universals and linguistic typology: Syntax and morphology. Basil Blackwell.

Cooper, L. A. (1975). Mental rotation of random two-dimensional shapes. Cognitive Psychology, 7, 20–43.

Cooper, L. A. (1976). Demonstration of a mental analog of an external rotation. Perception and Psychophysics, 19, 296–302.

Cooper, L. A., & Mumaw, R. J. (1985). Spatial aptitude. In R. F. Dillon & R. R. Schmeck (Eds.), Individual differences in cognition (Vol. 2, pp. 67–94). New York: Academic.

Cooper, L. A., & Podgorny, P. (1976). Mental transformations and visual comparison processes: Effects of complexity and similarity. Journal of Experimental Psychology: Human Perception and Performance, 2, 503–514.

Cooper, L. A., & Shepard, R. N. (1973). Chronometric studies of the rotation of mental images. In W. G. Chase (Ed.), Visual information processing (pp. 75–176). New York: Academic.

Cooper, R. G. (1984). Early number development: Discovering number space with addition & subtraction. In C. Sophian (Ed.), Origins of cognitive skills. Hillsdale, NJ: Erlbaum.

Cooper, R. P., & Aslin, R. N. (1990). Preference for infant-directed speech in the first month after birth. Child Development, 61, 1584–1595.

Cornell, E. H. (1979). The effects of cue reliability on infant's manual search. Journal of Experimental Child Psychology, 28, 81–91.

Cornell, E. H., & Heth, C. D. (1979). Response versus place learning by human infants. Journal of Experimental Psychology: Human Learning and Memory, 5, 188–196.

Cotman, C., Taylor, D., & Lynch, G. (1973). Ultrastructural changes in synapses in the dentate gyrus of the rat. Brain Research, 63, 205–213.

Cowan, W. M. (1979). The development of the brain. Scientific American, 241, 112–113.

Cox, J. R., & Griggs, R. A. (1982). The effects of experience on performance in Wason's selection task. Memory & Cognition, 10, 496–502.

Cox, M. V. (1978). Order of the acquisition of perspective-taking skills. Developmental Psychology, 14, 421–422.

Cox, M. V. (1980). Visual perspective taking in children. In M. Cox (Ed.), Are young children egocentric? London: Bastford Academic.

Crabtree, J. W., & Riesen, A. H. (1979). Effects of the duration of dark rearing on visually guided behavior in the kitten. Developmental Psychobiology, 12, 291–303.

Crain, B., Cotman, C., Taylor, D., & Lynch, G. (1973). A quantitative electron microscope study of synaptogenesis in the dentate gyrus of the rat. *Brain Research, 63,* 195–204.

Crick, F. (1979). Thinking about the brain. *Scientific American, 241,* 219–282.

Crider, C. (1983). Children's conceptions of the body interior. In R. Bibace & M. Walsh (Eds.), *Children's conceptions of health, illness and bodily functions.* San Francisco: Jossey-Bass.

Crisafi, M. A., & Brown, A. L. (1986). Analogical transfer in very young children: Combining two separately learned solutions to reach a goal. *Child Development, 57,* 953–968.

Crnic, L. S. & Pennington, B. F. (1987). Developmental psychology and the neurosciences: An introduction. *Child Development, 58,* 533–538.

Cultice, J. C., Somerville, S. C., & Wellman, H. M. (1983). Preschoolers' memory monitoring: Feeling-of-knowing judgments. *Child Development, 54,* 1480–1486.

Cummins, D. D., Kintsch, W., Reusser, K., & Weimer, R. (1988). The role of understanding in solving word problems. *Cognitive Psychology, 20,* 405–438.

Curtiss, S. (1977). *Genie: A psycholinguistic study of a modern day "wild child."* New York: Academic.

Curtiss, S. (1988). *The case of Chelsea: A new test case of the critical period for language acquisition.* Unpublished manuscript, University of California, Los Angeles.

Cutting, J. E. (1981). Coding theory adapted to gait perception. *Journal of Experimental Psychology: Human Perception and Performance, 7,* 71–87.

Cutting, J. E., & Kozlowski, L. T. (1977). Recognizing friends by their walk: Gait perception without familiarity cues. *Bulletin of the Psychonomic Society, 9,* 353–356.

Cutting, J. E., Proffitt, D. R., & Kozlowski, L. T. (1978). A biomechanical invariant for gait perception. *Journal of Experimental Psychology: Human Perception and Performance, 4,* 357–372.

Cuvo, A. J. (1975). Developmental differences in rehearsal and free recall. *Journal of Experimental Child Psychology, 19,* 65–78.

Cynader, M., & Chernenko, G. (1976). Abolition of direction selectivity in the visual cortex of the cat. *Science, 193,* 504–505.

Dannemiller, J. L., & Stephens, B. R. (1988). A critical test of infant pattern preference models. *Child Development, 59,* 210–216.

Darwin, C. (1859). *On the origin of species.* London: John Murray.

Darwin, C. (1871). *Descent of man.* London: John Murray.

Davis, H., & Bradford, S. A. (1986). Counting behavior by rats in a simulated natural environment. *Ethology, 73,* 265–280.

Davis, H., & Prusse, R. (1988). Numerical competence in animals: Definitional issues, current evidence, and a new research agenda. *Behavioral and Brain Sciences, 11,* 561–615.

Davis, W. J. (1986). Memory: Invertebrate model systems. In J. L. Martinez & R. P. Kesner (Eds.), *Learning and memory: A biological view.* New York: Academic.

Dean, A. L. (1976). The structure of imagery. *Child Development, 47,* 949–958.

Dean, A. L. (1979). Patterns of change in relations between children's anticipatory imagery and operative thought. *Developmental Psychology, 15,* 153–163.

Dean, A. L., Chabaud, S., & Bridges, E. (1981). Classes, collections, and distinctive features: Alternative strategies for solving inclusion problems. *Cognitive Psychology, 13,* 84–112.

Dean, A. L., Duhe, D., & Green, D. (1983). The development of children's mental tracking strategies on a rotation task. *Journal of Experimental Child Psychology, 36,* 226–240.

Dean, A. L., & Harvey, W. O. (1979). An information-processing analysis of a Piagetian imagery task. *Developmental Psychology, 15,* 474–475.

Dean, A. L., & Scherzer, E. (1982). A comparison of reaction time and drawing measures of mental rotation. *Journal of Experimental Child Psychology, 34,* 20–37.

de Boysson-Bardies, B., Sagart, L., & Durand, C. (1984). Discernible differences in the babbling of infants according to target language. *Journal of Child Language, 11,* 1–5.

DeCasper, A. J., & Fifer, W. P. (1980). Of human bonding: Newborns prefer their mothers' voices. *Science, 208,* 1174–1176.

DeCasper, A. J., & Spence, M. J. (1986). Prenatal maternal speech influences newborns' perception of speech sounds. *Infant Behavior and Development, 9,* 113–150.

DeLoache, J. S. (1980). Naturalistic studies of memory for object location in very young children. In

M. Perlmutter (Ed.), *New directions for child development: Children's memory*. San Francisco: Jossey-Bass.

DeLoache, J. S. (1984). Oh where, oh where: Memory-based searching by very young children. In C. Sophian (Ed.), *Origins of cognitive skills*. Hillsdale, NJ: Erlbaum.

DeLoache, J. S., & Brown, A. L. (1979). Looking for Big Bird: Studies of memory in very young children. *Quarterly Newsletter of the Laboratory of Comparative Human Cognition, 1*, 53–57.

DeLoache, J. S., & Brown, A. L. (1983). Young children's memory for the location of objects in a large scale environment. *Child Development, 54*, 888–897.

DeLoache, J. S., & Brown, A. L. (1984). Intelligent searching by very young children. *Developmental Psychology, 20*, 37–44.

Demany, L. (1982). Auditory stream segregation in infancy. *Infant Behavior & Development, 5*, 215–226.

Demetras, M. J., & Post, K. N. (1985, April). *Negative feedback in mother-child dialogues*. Paper presented at the biennial meeting of the Society for Research in Child Development, Toronto.

Dempster, F. N. (1981). Memory span: Sources of individual and developmental differences. *Psychological Bulletin, 89*, 63–100.

Denney, N. W. (1972). A developmental study of free classification in children. *Child Development, 43*, 221–232.

deSessa, A. A. (1983). Phenomenology and the evolution of intuition. In D. Gentner & A. L. Stevens (Eds.), *Mental models*. Hillsdale, NJ: Erlbaum.

de Villiers, J. G., & de Villiers, P. A. (1973). A cross-sectional study of the acquisition of grammatical morphemes in child speech. *Journal of Psycholinguistic Research, 2*, 267–278.

de Villiers, J. G., & de Villiers, P. A. (1978). *Language acquisition*. Cambridge, MA: Harvard University Press.

Diamond, A. (1985). Development of the ability to use recall to guide action, as indicated by infants' performance on AB̄. *Child Development, 56*, 868–883.

Diamond, A. (1988a). Differences between adult and infant cognition: Is the crucial variable presence or absence of language? In L. Weiskrantz (Ed.), *Thought without language* (pp. 337–370). Oxford, England: Clarendon Press.

Diamond, A. (1988b). The abilities and neural mechanisms underlying AB̄ performance. *Child Development, 59*, 523–527.

Diamond, A. (1990a). The development and neural bases of memory functions, as indexed by the AB̄ and delayed response tasks, in human infants and infant monkeys. *Annals of the New York Academy of Sciences, 608*, 267–317.

Diamond, A. (1990b). Developmental time course in human infants and infant monkeys, and the neural bases of inhibitory control in reaching. *Annals of the New York Academy of Sciences, 608*, 637–676.

Diamond, A. (1990c). Rate of maturation of the hippocampus and the developmental progression of children's performance on the delayed non-matching to sample and visual paired comparison tasks. *Annals of the New York Academy of Sciences, 608*, 394–426.

Diamond, A. (1991). Neuropsychological insights into the meaning of object concept development. In S. Carey & R. Gelman (Eds.), *The epigenesis of mind: Essays on biology and cognition*. Hillsdale, NJ: Erlbaum.

Diamond, A. (in press). Frontal lobe involvement in cognitive changes during the first year of life. In K. Gibson, M. Konner, & A. Peterson (Eds.), *Brain and behavioral development*. New York: Aldine Press.

Diamond, A., & Goldman-Rakic, P. S. (1983). Comparison of performance on a Piagetian object permanence task in human infants and rhesus monkeys: Evidence for involvement of prefrontal cortex. *Society for Neuroscience Abstracts, 9*, 641.

Diamond, A., & Goldman-Rakic, P. S. (1985). Evidence that maturation of the frontal cortex underlies behavioral changes during the first year of life: 1. The AB̄ task. 2. Object retrieval. *Society for Research in Child Development Abstracts, 5*, 85.

Diamond, A., & Goldman-Rakic, P. S. (1986). Comparative development in human infants and infant rhesus monkeys of cognitive functions that depend on prefrontal cortex. *Neuroscience Abstracts, 12*, 742.

Dineen, I. T., & Meyer, W. J. (1980). Developmental changes in visual orienting behavior to featural versus structural information in the human infant. *Developmental Psychobiology, 13*, 123–130.

Dobrich, W., & Scarborough, H. S. (1984). Form and function in early communication: Language and pointing gestures. *Journal of Experimental Child Psychology, 38,* 475−490.

Dodwell, P. C. (1963). Children's understanding of spatial concepts. *Canadian Journal of Psychology, 17,* 141−161.

Dodwell, P. C., Humphrey, G. K., & Muir, D. W. (1987). Shape and pattern perception. In P. Salapatek & L. Cohen (Eds.), *Handbook of infant perception* (Vol 2, pp. 1−79). New York: Academic Press.

Donaldson, M., & Balfour, G. (1968). Less is more: A study of language comprehension in children. *British Journal of Psychology, 59,* 461−471.

Dore, J. (1975). Holophrases, speech acts, and language universals. *Journal of Child Language, 2,* 21−40.

Dore, J. (1985). Holophrases revisited: Their "logical" development during dialogue. In M. D. Barrett (Ed.), *Children's single-word speech.* New York: Wiley.

Eccles, J. C. (1953). *The neurophysiological basis of mind: The principles of neurophysiology.* Oxford: Clarendon Press.

Eckenhoff, M. F., & Rakic, P. (1988). Nature and fate of proliferative cells in the hippocampal dentate gyrus during the lifespan of the rhesus monkey. *Journal of Neuroscience, 8,* 2729−2747.

Eilers, R. E. (1980). Infant speech perception. In G. H. Yeni-Komshian, J. F. Kavanaugh & C. A. Ferguson (Eds.), *Child phonology: Vol. 2. Perception.* New York: Academic.

Eilers, R. E., Gavin, W., & Wilson, W. R. (1979). Linguistic experience and phonemic perception in infancy: A cross linguistic study. *Child Development, 50,* 14−18.

Eilers, R. E., Wilson, W. R., & Moore, J. M. (1977). Developmental changes in speech discrimination in infants. *Journal of Speech and Hearing Research, 20,* 766−780.

Eimas, P. D. (1974). Auditory and linguistic processing of cues for place of articulation by infants. *Perception and Psychophysics, 16,* 513−521.

Eimas, P. D. (1975a). Auditory and phonetic coding of the cues for speech: Discrimination of the /r-l/ distinction by young infants. *Perception and Psychophysics, 18,* 341−347.

Eimas, P. D. (1975b). Developmental studies of speech perception. In L. B. Cohen & P. Salapatek (Eds.), *Infant perception: From sensation to perception* (Vol. 7). New York: Academic.

Eimas, P. D., & Miller, J. L. (1980). Discrimination of the information for manner of articulation by young infants. *Infant Behavior and Development, 3,* 367−375.

Eimas, P. D., Siqueland, E. R., Jusczyk, P. & Vigorito, J. (1971). Speech perception in infants. *Science, 171,* 303−306.

Eimas, P. D., & Tartter, V. C. (1979). On the development of speech perception: Mechanisms and analogies. In H. W. Reese & L. P. Lippett (Eds.), *Advances in child development and behavior* (Vol 13). New York: Academic.

Elkind, D. (1964). Discrimination, seriation, and the numeration of size and dimensional differences in young children: Piaget replication of Study VI. *Journal of Genetic Psychology, 104,* 275−296.

Elliot, L. L., & Katz, D. R. (1980). Children's pure tone detection. *Journal of the Acoustical Society of America, 67,* 343−344.

Enright, M. K., Rovee-Collier, C. K., Fagen, J. W., & Caniglia, K. (1983). The effects of distributed training on retention of operant conditioning in human infants. *Journal of Experimental Child Psychology, 36,* 512−524.

Evans, J. St. B. T. (1982). *The psychology of deductive reasoning.* London: Routledge & Kegan Paul.

Evans, J. St. B. T., Barston, J., & Pollard, P. (1983). On the conflict between logic and belief in syllogistic reasoning. *Memory and Cognition, 11,* 295−306

Fabricius, W. V., Schwanenflugel, P. J., Kyllonen, P. C., Barclay, C. R., & Denton, S. M., (1989). Developing theories of the mind: Children's and adults' concepts of mental activities. *Child Development, 60,* 1278−1290.

Falmagne, R. J. (1980). The development of logical competence: A psycholinguistic perspective. In R. Kluwe & H. Spada (Eds.), *Developmental models of thinking* (pp. 171−197). New York: Academic Press.

Falmagne, R. J. (1990). Language and the acquisition of logical knowledge. In W. F. Overton (Ed.), *Reasoning, logic, and necessity* (pp. 171−197). Hillsdale, NJ: Erlbaum.

Fantz, R. L. (1958). Pattern vision in young infants. *Psychological Record, 8,* 43−47.

Fantz, R. L., Fagan, J. F., III, & Miranda, S. B. (1975). Early visual selectivity as a function of pattern variables, previous exposure, age from birth and conception, and expected cognitive deficit. In L. B. Cohen & P. Salapatek (Eds.),

Infant perception: From sensation to cognition (Vol. 1). New York: Academic.

Fantz, R. L., Ordy, J. M., & Udelf, M. S. (1962). Maturation of pattern vision in infants during the first six months. *Journal of Comparative and Physiological Psychology, 55,* 907–917.

Fantz, R. L., & Yeh, J. (1979). Configural selectivities: Critical for development of visual perception and attention. *Canadian Journal of Psychology, 33,* 277–287.

Fein, G. G. (1981). Pretend play in childhood: An integrative review. *Child Development, 52,* 1095–1118.

Fenson, L., Vella, D., & Kennedy, M. (1989). Children's knowledge of thematic and taxonomic relations at two years of age. *Child Development, 60,* 911–919.

Ferguson, C. A. (1983). Reduplication in child phonology. *Journal of Child Language, 10,* 239–243.

Ferguson, C. A., & Machen, M. A. (1983). The role of play in phonological development. In K. E. Nelson (Ed.), *Children's language* (Vol 4). Hillsdale, NJ: Erlbaum.

Fernald, A. (1985). Four-month-old infants prefer to listen to motherese. *Infant Behavior and Development, 8,* 181–195.

Fernald, A., & Simon, T. (1984). Expanded intonation contours in mothers' speech to newborns. *Developmental Psychology, 20,* 104–113.

Fifkova, E. (1968). Changes in the visual cortex of rats after unilateral deprivation. *Nature, 220,* 379–381.

Fifkova, E. (1970). The effect of unilateral deprivation on visual centers in rats. *Journal of Comparative Neurology, 140,* 431–438.

Fischer, K. W. (1980). A theory of cognitive development: The control and construction of hierarchies of skills. *Psychological Review, 87,* 477–531.

Fischer, K. W. (1983). *Levels and transitions in children's development.* San Francisco: Jossey-Bass.

Fischer, K. W. (1987). Relations between brain and cognitive development. *Child Development, 58,* 623–632.

Fischer, K. W., & Pipp, S. L. (1984). Processes of cognitive development: Optimal level and skill acquisition. In R. Sternberg (Ed.), *Mechanisms of cognitive development* (pp. 45–80). New York: Freeman.

Fishbein, H. D., Lewis, S., & Keiffer, K. (1972). Children's understanding of spatial relations:

Coordination of perspectives. *Developmental Psychology, 7,* 21–23.

Flavell, J. H. (1963). *The developmental psychology of Jean Piaget.* Princeton, NJ: Van Nostrand.

Flavell, J. H. (1971). Stage-related properties of cognitive development. *Cognitive Psychology, 2,* 421–453.

Flavell, J. H. (1977). *Cognitive development* (1st ed.). Englewood Cliffs, NJ: Prentice Hall.

Flavell, J. H. (1978). The development of knowledge about visual perception. In C. B. Keasey (Ed.), *Nebraska Symposium on Motivation, 1977.* Lincoln, NE: University of Nebraska Press.

Flavell, J. H. (1979). Metacognition and cognitive monitoring. *American Psychologist, 34,* 906–911.

Flavell, J. H. (1982). Structures, stages, and sequences. In W. A. Collins (Ed.), *The concept of development: The Minnesota symposium on child psychology,* (Vol. 15, pp. 1–28). Hillsdale, NJ: Erlbaum.

Flavell, J. H. (1985). *Cognitive development* (2nd ed.). Englewood Cliffs, NJ: Prentice Hall.

Flavell, J. H. (1986). The development of children's knowledge about the appearance-reality distinction. *American Psychologist, 41,* 418–425.

Flavell, J. H., Beach, D. H., & Chinsky, J. M. (1966). Spontaneous verbal rehearsal on a memory task as a function of age. *Child Development, 37,* 283–299.

Flavell, J. H., Botkin, P. T., Fry, C. L., Wright, J. W., & Jarvis, P. E. (1968). *The development of role-taking and communication skills in children.* New York: Wiley.

Flavell, J. H., Everett, B. A., Croft, K., & Flavell, E. R. (1981). Young children's knowledge about visual perception: Further evidence for the Level 1–Level 2 distinction. *Developmental Psychology, 17,* 99–103.

Flavell, J. H., Flavell, E. R., & Green, F. L. (1983). Development of the appearance-reality distinction. *Cognitive Psychology, 15,* 95–120.

Flavell, J. H., Green, F. L. & Flavell, E. R. (1986). Development of knowledge about the appearance-reality distinction. *Monographs of the Society for Research in Child Development, 51,* Serial No. 212.

Flavell, J. H., Flavell, E. R., & Green, F. L. (1987). Young children's knowledge about the apparent-real and pretend-real distinctions. *Developmental Psychology, 23,* 816–822.

Flavell, J. H., & Wellman, H. M. (1977). Metamemory. In R. V. Kail & J. W. Hagen (Eds.), *Perspectives on the development of memory and cognition*. Hillsdale, NJ: Erlbaum.

Flavell, J. H., & Wohlwill, J. F. (1969). Formal and functional aspects of cognitive development. In D. Elkind & J. H. Flavell (Eds.), *Studies in cognitive development: Essays in honor of Jean Piaget*. New York: Oxford University Press.

Fodor, J. A. (1972). Some reflections on L. S. Vygotsky's *Thought and Language*. *Cognition, 1*, 83–95.

Fodor, J. A. (1975). *The language of thought*. Cambridge, MA: Harvard University Press.

Fodor, J. A. (1980a). Methodological solipsism considered as a research strategy in cognitive psychology. *Behavioral and Brain Sciences, 3*, 66–109.

Fodor, J. A. (1980b). On the impossibility of acquiring "more powerful" structures. In M. Piattelli-Palmarini (Ed.), *Language & learning: The debate between Jean Piaget & Noam Chomsky* (pp. 142–162). Cambridge, MA: Harvard University Press.

Fodor, J. A. (1981). *Representations*. Cambridge, MA: MIT Press.

Fodor, J. A. (1983). *The modularity of mind*. Cambridge, MA: MIT Press.

Fodor, J. A. (1985). Fodor's guide to mental representation: The intelligent auntie's vade-mecum. *Mind, 94*, 76–100.

Fodor, J. D., & Crain, S. (1987). Simplicity and generality of rules in language acquisition. In B. MacWhinney (Ed.), *Mechanisms of language acquisition*. Hillsdale, NJ: Erlbaum.

Forbus, K. D., & Gentner, D. (1986, December). *Learning physical domains: Toward a theoretical framework* (tech. tep.). Urbana–Champaign: University of Illinois.

Ford, M. (1979). The construct validity of egocentrism. *Psychological Bulletin, 86*, 1169–1188.

Foreman, N., Arber, M., & Savage, J. (1984). Spatial memory in preschool infants. *Developmental Psychobiology, 17*, 129–137.

Forguson, L., & Gopnik, A. (1988). The ontogeny of common sense. In J. Astington, P. Harris, & D. Olson (Eds.), *Developing theories of mind*. New York: Cambridge University Press.

Fox, R., & McDaniel, C. (1982). The perception of biological motion by human infants. *Science, 218*, 486–487.

Franz, R. L., & Miranda, S. B. (1975). Newborn infant attention to form of contour. *Child Development, 46*, 224–228.

Frazer, J. G. (1911). *The golden bough: Vol. 1. The magic art and the evolution of kings*. (3rd. ed.). London: Macmillan.

Freedland, R. L., & Dannemiller, J. L. (1987). Detection of stimulus motion in 5-month-old infants. *Journal of Experimental Psychology: Human Perception and Performance, 13*, 566–576.

French, L. A., & Nelson, K. (1985). *Children's acquisition of relational terms: Some ifs, ors, and buts*. New York: Springer-Verlag.

Friedman, S., Nagy, A. N., & Carpenter, G. C. (1970). Newborn attention: Differential response decrement to visual stimuli. *Journal of Experimental Child Psychology, 10*, 44–51.

Furrow, D., & Nelson, K. (1986). A further look at the motherese hypothesis: A reply to Gleitman, Newport, & Gleitman. *Journal of Child Language, 13*, 163–176.

Fuson, K. C. (1982). An analysis of the counting–on solution procedure in addition. In T. P. Carpenter, J. M. Moser, & T. A. Romberg (Eds.), *Addition and subtraction: A cognitive perspective*. Hillsdale, NJ: Erlbaum.

Fuson, K. C. (1988). *Children's counting and concepts of number*. New York: Springer-Verlag.

Fuson, K. C., & Hall, J. W. (1983). The acquisition of early number word meanings. In H. Ginsburg (Ed.), *The development of children's mathematical thinking*. New York: Academic.

Fuson, K. C., Pergament, G. G., Lyons, B. G., & Hall, J. W. (1985). Children's conformity to the cardinality rule as a function of set size and counting accuracy. *Child Development, 56*, 1429–1439.

Fuster, J. M. (1980). *The prefrontal cortex*. New York: Raven Press.

Gallagher, J. M., & Wright, R. J. (1979). Piaget and the study of analogy: Structural analysis of items. In J. Magary (Ed.), *Piaget and the helping professions* (Vol. 8, pp. 114–119). Los Angeles: University of Southern California.

Gallistel, C. R. (1988). Counting versus subitizing versus the sense of number. *Behavioral and Brain Sciences, 11*, 585–586.

Gallistel, C. R. (1989). Animal cognition: The representation of space, time, and number. *Annual Review of Psychology, 40*, 155–189.

Gallistel, C. R. (1990). *The organization of learning*. Cambridge, MA: Bradford Books/MIT Press.

Gallistel, C. R., Brown, A. L., Carey, S., Gelman, R., & Keil, F. C. (1991). Lessons from animal learning for the study of cognitive development. In S. Carey & R. Gelman (Eds.), *The epigenesis of mind: Essays on biology and cognition*. Hillsdale, NJ: Erlbaum.

Gallistel, C. R., & Gelman, R. (1990). The what and how of counting. *Cognition, 34,* 197–199.

Garcia, R. (1980). Developmental epistemology and fundamental problems in the theory of knowledge. *Cashiers de la Foundation Archives Jean Piaget* (No 1, pp. 49–78). Geneva, Switzerland: Foundation Archives Jean Piaget.

Gardner, H. (1973). *The quest for mind: Piaget, Levi-Strauss, and the structuralist movement*. New York: Knopf.

Gardner, H. (1985). *The mind's new science*. New York: Basic Books.

Gardner, H. (1983). *Frames of mind: The theory of multiple intelligences*. New York: Basic.

Garner, W. R. (1974). *The processing of information and structure*. Hillsdale, NJ: Erlbaum.

Garnica, O. (1977). Some prosodic and paralinguistic features of speech to young children. In C. E. Snow & C. Ferguson (Eds.), *Talking to children: Language input and acquisition*. Cambridge, MA: Cambridge University Press.

Gellert, E. (1962). Children's conceptions of the content and functions of the human body. *Genetic Psychology Monographs, 65,* 291–411.

Gelman, R. (1972). Logical capacity of very young children: Number invariance rules. *Child Development, 43,* 75–90.

Gelman, R. (1982). Basic numerical abilities. In R. J. Sternberg (Ed.) *Advances in the psychology of human intelligence*, (Vol. 1, pp. 181–206). Hillsdale, NJ: Erlbaum.

Gelman, R. (1990a). First principles organize attention to and learning about relevant data: Number and the animate-inanimate distinction as examples. *Cognitive Science, 14,* 79–106.

Gelman, R. (1990b). Structural constraints on cognitive development. *Cognitive Science, 14,* 3–9.

Gelman, R. (1991). Epigenetic foundations of knowledge structures: Initial and transcendent constructions. In R. Gelman & S. Carey (Eds.), *The epigenesis of mind: Essays on biology and cognition*. Hillsdale, NJ: Erlbaum.

Gelman, R., & Baillargeon, R. (1983). A review of some Piagetian concepts. In J. H. Flavell & E. M. Markman (Eds.), *Carmichael's manual of child psychology* (Vol. 3). New York: Wiley.

Gelman, R., & Cohen, M. (1988). Qualitative differences in the way Down Syndrome and normal children solve a novel counting problem. In L. Nadel (Ed.), *The psychobiology of Down Syndrome*. Cambridge, MA: Bradford Book/MIT Press.

Gelman, R., & Gallistel, C. R. (1978). *The child's understanding of number*. Cambridge, MA: Harvard University Press.

Gelman, R., & Greeno, J. G. (1989). On the nature of competence: Principles for understanding in a domain. In L. B. Resnick (Ed.), *Knowing and learning: Issues for a cognitive science of instruction*. Hillsdale, NJ: Erlbaum.

Gelman, R., & Meck, E. (1983). Preschoolers' counting: Principles before skill. *Cognition, 13,* 343–359.

Gelman, R., & Meck, E. (1986). The notion of principle: The case of counting. In J. Hiebert (Ed.), *Conceptual and procedural knowledge: The case of mathematics*. Hillsdale, NJ: Erlbaum.

Gelman, R., & Meck, E. (in press). Early principles aid early but not later conceptions of number. In J. Bideaud & C. Meljac (Eds.), *Les chemins du nombre*. Paris: Les Presses Universitaires De Lille.

Gelman, R., Meck, E., & Merkin, S. (1986). Young children's numerical competence. *Cognitive Development, 1,* 1–29.

Gelman, R., & Tucker, M. F. (1975). Further investigations of the young child's conception of number. *Child Development, 46,* 167–175.

Gelman, S. A. (1988). The development of induction with natural kind and artifact categories. *Cognitive Psychology, 20,* 65–95.

Gelman, S. A., & Markman, E. M. (1986). Categories and induction in young children. *Cognition, 23,* 183–208.

Gelman, S. A., & Markman, E. M. (1987). Young children's inductions from natural kinds: The role of categories and appearances. *Child Development, 58,* 1532–1541.

Gentner, D. (1983). Structure-mapping: A theoretical framework for analogy. *Cognitive Science, 7,* 2.

Gentner, D. (1988). Metaphor as structure-mapping: The relational shift. *Child Development, 59,* 47–59.

Gentner, D. (1982). Why nouns are learned before verbs: Linguistic relativity versus natural partitioning. In S. A. Kuczaj (Ed.), *Language development: Vol. 2. Language, thought, and culture*. Hillsdale, NJ: Erlbaum.

Gentner, D., & Toupin, C. (1986). Systematicity and surface similarity in the development of analogy. *Cognitive Science, 10,* 277–300.

Georgopoulos, A. P., Lurito, J. T., Petrides, M., Schwartz, A. B., & Massey, J. T. (1989). Mental rotation of the neuronal population vector. *Science, 243,* 233–236.

Gerard, A. B., & Mandler, J. M. (1983). Sentence anomaly and ontological knowledge. *Journal of Verbal Learning and Verbal Behavior, 22,* 105–120.

Gesell, A. L. (1928). *Infancy and human growth.* New York: Macmillan.

Gibson, E. J. (1969). *Principles of perceptual learning and development.* New York: Appleton-Century-Crofts.

Gibson, E. J. (1982). The concept of affordances in development: The renascence of functionalism. In W. A. Collins (Ed.), *Minnesota symposia on child psychology, Vol. 15: The concept of development.* Hillsdale, NJ: Erlbaum.

Gibson, E. J. (1984). Perceptual development from the ecological approach. In M. E. Lamb, A. L. Brown, & B. Rogoff (Eds.), *Advances in developmental psychology.* Hillsdale, NJ: Erlbaum.

Gibson, E. J. (1987). Introductory essay: What does infant perception tell us about theories of perception? *Journal of Experimental Psychology: Human Perception and Performance, 13*(4), 515–523.

Gibson, E. J., Owsley, C. J., & Johnston, J. (1978). Perception of invariants by five-month-old infants: Differentiation of two types of motion. *Developmental Psychology, 14,* 405–415.

Gibson, E. J., Owsley, C. J., Walker, A., & Megaw-Nyce, J. (1979). Development of the perception of invariants: Substance and shape. *Perception, 8,* 609–619.

Gibson, E. J., & Spelke, E. S. (1983). The development of perception. In J. H. Flavell & E. M. Markman (Eds.), *Handbook of child psychology: Cognitive development* (pp. 1–76). New York: Wiley.

Gibson, E. J., & Walk, R. D. (1960). The "visual cliff." *Scientific American, 202,* 64–71.

Gibson, E. J., & Walker, A. (1984). Development of knowledge of visual and tactual affordances of substance. *Child Development, 55,* 453–460.

Gibson, J. J. (1950). *The perception of the visual world.* Boston: Houghton Mifflin.

Gibson, J. J. (1962). Observation on active touch. *Psychological Review, 69,* 477–491.

Gibson, J. J. (1966). *The senses considered as perceptual systems.* Boston: Houghton Mifflin.

Gibson, J. J. (1979). *The ecological approach to visual perception.* Boston: Houghton Mifflin.

Giffen, K. Van, & Haith, M. M. (1984). Infant visual response to Gestalt geometric forms. *Infant Behavior and Development, 7,* 335–346.

Gleitman, L. R. (1981). Maturational determinants of language growth. *Cognition, 10,* 103–114.

Gleitman, L. R. (1990). The structural sources of word meaning. *Language Acquisition, 1,* 3–55.

Gleitman, L., Gleitman, H., Landau, B., & Wanner, E. (1988). Where learning begins: Initial representations of language learning. In F. J. Newmeyer (Ed.), *Linguistics: The Cambridge survey, Vol III: Language: Psychological and biological aspects.* New York: Cambridge University Press.

Gleitman, L., Newport, E., & Gleitman, H. (1984). The current status of the motherese hypothesis. *Journal of Child Language, 11,* 43–79.

Gleitman, L. R., & Wanner, E. (1984). Richly specified input to language learning. In E. L. Rissland & M. Arbib (Eds.), *Adaptive control of ill-defined systems.* New York: Plenum.

Gleitman, L. R., & Wanner, E. (1988). Current issues in language learning. In M. H. Bornstein & M. E. Lamb (Eds.), *Developmental psychology: An advanced textbook.* Hillsdale, NJ: Erlbaum.

Goldberg, S. (1976). Visual tracking and existence constancy in 5-month-old infants. *Journal of experimental child psychology, 22,* 478–491.

Goldfield, B. A., & Reznick, J. S. (1990). Early lexical acquisition: Rate, content, and vocabulary spurt. *Journal of Child Language, 17,* 171–183.

Goldfield, E. C., & Dickerson, D. J. (1981). Keeping track of location during movement in 8-to-10-month-old infants. *Journal of Experimental Child Psychology, 32,* 48–64.

Goldman, S. R., Pellegrino, J. W., Parseghian, P. E., & Sallis, R. (1982). Developmental and individual differences in verbal analogical reasoning. *Child Development, 53,* 550–559.

Goldman-Rakic, P. S. (1974). An alternative to developmental plasticity: Heterology of CNS structures in infants and adults. In D. G. Stein, J. Rosen, & N. Butters (Eds.), *Plasticity and recovery of function in the central nervous system* (pp. 149–174). New York: Academic.

Goldman-Rakic, P. S. (1987). Development of cortical circuitry and cognitive function. *Child Development, 58,* 601–622.

Goodluck, H. (1986). Language acquisition and linguistic theory. In P. Fletcher & M. Garnon (Eds), *Language acquisition: Studies in first language development*. Cambridge, England: Cambridge University Press.

Goodman, N. (1955). *Fact, fiction, and forecast*. Cambridge, MA: Harvard University Press.

Goodman, N. (1983). *Fact, fiction, and forecast*. Cambridge, MA: Harvard University Press.

Goodnow, J. (1977). *Children drawing*. Cambridge, MA: Harvard University Press.

Goodsitt, J. V., Morse, P. A., Ver Hoeve, J. N., & Cowan, N. (1984). Infant speech recognition in multisyllabic contexts. *Child Development, 55,* 903–910.

Gopnik, A. (1990). Developing the idea of intentionality: Children's theories of mind. *Canadian Journal of Philosophy, 1,* 87–111.

Gopnik, A., & Astington, J. W. (1988). Children's understanding of representational change and its relation to the understanding of false belief and the appearance-reality distinction. *Child Development, 59,* 26–37.

Gopnik, A., & Meltzoff, A.N. (1986). Words, plans, things, and locations: Interactions between semantic and cognitive development in the one-word stage. In S.A. Kuczaj & M.D. Barrett (Eds.), *The development of word meaning: Progress in cognitive development research*. Berlin: Springer–Verlang.

Gopnik, A., & Meltzoff, A. N. (1987a). The development of categorization in the second year and its relation to other cognitive and linguistic developments. *Child Development, 58,* 1523–1531.

Gopnik, A., & Meltzoff, A. N. (1987b). Early semantic developments and their relationship to object permanence, means-ends understanding and categorization. In K. Nelson & A. VanKleek (Eds.), *Children's language* (Vol 6). Hillsdale, NJ: Erlbaum.

Goswami, U. (1989). Relational complexity and the development of analogical reasoning. *Cognitive Development, 4,* 251–268.

Goswami, U. (1991). Analogical reasoning: What Develops? A Review of research and theory. *Child Development, 62,* 1–22.

Goswami, U., & Brown, A. L. (1989). Melting chocolate and melting snowmen: Analogical reasoning and causal relations. *Cognition, 35,* 69–95.

Gotlieb, S. J., & Sloane, M. E. (1989). *Memory in human neonates*. Paper presented at the meeting of the Society for Research in Child Development, Kansas City, MO.

Gottlieb, G. (1983). The psychobiological approach to developmental issues. In M. M. Haith & J. J. Campos (Eds.), *Handbook of child psychology: Vol. 2. Infancy and developmental psychobiology* (pp. 1–26). New York: Wiley.

Gould, J. L. (1986). The locale maps of honey bees: Do insects have cognitive maps? *Science, 232,* 861–863.

Graf, P., & Schacter, D. L. (1985). Implicit and explicit memory for new associations in normal and amnesic subjects. *Journal of Experimental Psychology: Learning, Memory, and Cognition, 11,* 501–518.

Granrud, C. E. (1986). Binocular vision and spatial perception in 4- and 5-month-old infants. *Journal of Experimental Psychology: Human Perception and Performance, 12,* 36–49.

Granrud, C. E., Yonas, A., & Peterson, L. (1984). A caparison of responsiveness to monocular and binocular depth information in 5- and 7-month-old infants. *Journal of Experimental Child Psychology, 38,* 19–32.

Granrud, C. E., Yonas, A., Smith, I. M., Arterberry, M.E., Glicksman, M. L., & Sorknes, A. (1984). Infants' sensitivity to accretion and deletion of texture as information for depth at an edge. *Child Development, 55,* 1630–1636.

Grant, K. W., Ardell, L. H., Kuhl, P. K., & Sparks, D. W. (1985). The contribution of fundamental frequency, amplitude envelope, and voicing duration cues to connected discourse perception by speechreaders. *Journal of the Acoustical Society of America, 77,* 671–677.

Gratch, G. (1975). Recent studies based on Piaget's view of object concept development. In L. B. Cohen & P. Salapatek (Eds.), *Infant perception: From sensation to cognition* (Vol.2, pp. 51–99). New York: Academic.

Gratch, G. (1976). Review of Piaget infancy research: Object concept development. In W. F. Overton & J. M. Gallagher (Eds.), *Knowledge and Development: Advances in research and theory* (Vol. 1). New York: Plenum.

Gratch, G. (1982). Responses to hidden persons and things by 5-, 9-, and 16-month-old infants in a visual tracking situation. *Developmental Psychology, 18,* 232–237.

Graton, L. G., & Yonas, A. (1988). Infants' sensitivity to boundary flow information for depth at an edge. *Child Development, 59,* 1522–1529.

Gray, W. M. (1990). Formal operational thought. In W. F. Overton (Ed.), *Reasoning, logic, and necessity*. Hillsdale, NJ: Erlbaum.

Greco, C., Rovee-Collier, C., Hayne, H., Griesler, P., & Earley, L. (1986). Ontogeny of early event memory: I. Forgetting and retrieval by 2- and 3-month-olds. *Infant Behavior and Development, 9*, 441–460.

Greenberg, J. (1978). *Universals of human language: Vol. 4. Syntax*. Stanford, CA: Stanford University Press.

Greeno, J. G. (1989). A perspective on thinking. *American Psychologist, 44*, 134–141.

Greeno, J. G., Riley, M. S., & Gelman, R. (1984). Conceptual competence and children's counting. *Cognitive Psychology, 16*, 66–94.

Greenough, W. T. (1984). Structural correlates of information storage in the mammalian brain: A review and hypothesis. *Trends in Neuroscience, 7*, 229–233.

Greenough, W. T., Black, J. E., & Wallace, C. S. (1987). Experience and brain development. *Child Development, 58*, 539–559.

Grieser, D. L., & Kuhl, P. K. (1988). Maternal speech to infants in a tonal language: Support for universal prosodic features in motherese. *Developmental Psychology, 24*, 14–20.

Griggs, R. A. (1983). The role of problem content in the selection task and in the THROG problem. In J. St. B. T. Evans, (Ed.), *Thinking and reasoning: Psychological approaches* (pp. 16–47). London: Routledge & Kegan Paul.

Grimshaw, J. (1981). Form, function, and the language acquisition device. In C. L. Baker and J. McCarthy, (Eds.), *The logical problem of language acquisition*. Cambridge, MA: MIT Press.

Grossberg, S. (1982). *Studies of mind and brain: Neural principles of learning, perception, development, cognition, and motor control*. Boston: Reidel.

Gruber, H. E., & Voneche, J. J. (1977). *The essential Piaget*. New York: Basic Books.

Grusser, O. J. (1983). Multimodal structure of the extra personal space. In A. Heir & M. Jeannerod (Eds.), *Spatially oriented behavior* (pp. 327–352). New York: Springer-Verlag.

Hagan, J. J., Alpert, J. E., Morris, R. G. H., & Iverson, S. D. (1983). The effects of central catecholaminergic depletion on spatial learning in rats. *Behavioral Brain Research, 9*, 83–104.

Haith, M. M. (1966). The response of the human newborn to visual movement. *Journal of Experimental Child Psychology, 3*, 235–243.

Haith, M. M. (1980). *Rules that babies look by*. Hillsdale, NJ: Erlbaum.

Haith, M., Bergman, T., & Moore, M. (1977). Eye contact and face scanning in early infancy. *Science, 198*, 853–855.

Haith, M. M., & Campos, J. J. (1977). Human infancy. *Annual Review of Psychology, 28*, 251–293.

Haith, M. M., Hazan, C., & Goodman, G. S. (1988). Expectation and anticipation of dynamic visual events by 3.5-month-old babies. *Child Development, 59*, 467–479.

Hale, S. (1990). A global developmental trend in cognitive processing speed. *Child Development, 61*, 653–663.

Halford, G. S. (1982). *The development of thought*. Hillsdale, NJ: Erlbaum.

Hall, W. G., & Oppenheim, R. W. (1987). Developmental psychobiology: Prenatal, perinatal and early postnatal aspects of behavioral development. *Annual Review of Psychology, 38*, pp. 91–128.

Harnishfeger, K. K., & Bjorklund, D. F. (1990). Children's strategies: A brief history. In D. F. Bjorklund (Ed.), *Children's strategies: Contemporary views of cognitive development*. Hillsdale, NJ: Erlbaum.

Harris, L. J. (1978). Sex differences in spatial ability: Possible environmental, genetic, and neurological factors. In M. Kinsbourne (Ed.), *Asymmetrical function of the brain*. Cambridge: Cambridge University Press.

Harris, L. J. (1979). Sex-related differences in spatial ability: A developmental psychological view. In C. Kopp (Ed.), *Becoming female: Perspectives on development* (pp. 131–181). New York: Plenum.

Harris, P. L. (1975). Development of search and object permanence during infancy. *Psychological Bulletin, 82*, 332–344.

Harris, P. L. (1987). The development of search. In P. Salapatek & L. B. Cohen (Eds.), *Handbook of infant perception* (pp. 155–207). New York: Academic.

Hart, J. T. (1965). Memory and the feeling-of-knowing experience. *Journal of Educational Psychology, 56*, 208–216.

Hayne, H. (1988). *The effect of multiple reminders on retention by 3-month-old infants*. Unpublished doctoral dissertation, Rutgers University, New Brunswick, NJ.

Hayne, H., Rovee-Collier, C., & Perris, E. E. (1987). Categorization and memory retrieval by three-month-olds. *Child Development, 58*, 750–760.

Hays, W. L. (1988). *Statistics for psychologists* (4th. ed.). New York: Holt, Rinehart & Winston.

Hebb, D. O. (1949). *The organization of behavior.* New York: Wiley.

Hecox, K. (1975). Electrophysiological correlates of human auditory development. In L. B. Cohen & P. Salapatek (Eds.), *Infant perception: From sensation to cognition* (Vol. 2, pp. 151–191). New York: Academic.

Hegarty, M., Just, M. A., & Morrison, I. R. (1988). Mental models of mechanical systems: Individual differences in qualitative and quantitative reasoning. *Cognitive Psychology, 20,* 191–236.

Heider, F. (1958). *The psychology of interpersonal relations.* New York: Wiley.

Held, A., Hein, R., & Gower, E. C. (1970). Development and segmentation of visually controlled movement by selective exposure during rearing. *Journal of Comparative and Physiological Psychology, 73,* 181–187.

Henderson, R. W., Swanson, R., & Zimmerman, B. J. (1975). Training seriation responses in young children through televised modeling of hierarchically sequenced rule components. *American Educational Research Journal, 12,* 479–489.

Heumann, D., & Leuba, G. (1983). Neuronal death in the development and aging of the cerebral cortex of the mouse. *Neuropathology and Applied Neurobiology, 9,* 297–311.

Hickey, T. L. (1977). Postnatal development of the human lateral geniculate nucleus: Relationship to a critical period for the visual system. *Science, 198,* 836–838.

Hickey, T. L., & Peduzzi, J. D. (1987). Structure and development of the visual system. In P. Salapatek & L. Cohen (Eds.), *Handbook of Infant Perception* (Vol. 1, pp. 1–42). New York: Academic.

Hill, W. L., Borovsky, D., & Rovee-Collier, C. (1988). Continuities in infant memory development. *Developmental Psychobiology, 21,* 43–62.

Hillenbrand, J. (1983). Perceptual organization of speech sounds by infants. *Journal of speech and hearing research, 26,* 268–282.

Hillenbrand, J. (1984). Speech perception by infants: Categorization based on nasal consonant place of articulation. *Journal of Acoustical Society of America, 75,* 1613–1622.

Hirsch, H. V. B., & Spinelli, D. N. (1970). Visual experience modifies distribution of horizontally and vertically oriented receptive fields in cats. *Science, 168,* 869–871.

Hirsch, R. (1974). The hippocampus and contextual retrieval of information from memory: A theory. *Behavioral Biology, 12,* 421–444.

Hirsch-Pasek, K., Treiman, R., & Schneiderman, M. (1984). Brown and Hanlon revisited: Mother's sensitivity to ungrammatical forms. *Journal of Child Language, 11,* 81–88.

Hoek, D., Ingram, D., & Gibson, D. (1986). Some possible causes of children's early word overextensions. *Journal of Child Language, 13,* 477–494.

Holland, J. H., Holyoak, K. J., Nisbett, R. E., & Thagard, P. R. (1986). *Induction: Processes of inference, learning, and discovery.* Cambridge, MA: Bradford Books/MIT Press.

Holland, V. M., & Palermo, D. S. (1975). On learning "less": Language and cognitive development. *Child Development, 46,* 437–443.

Holyoak, K. J. (1984). Analogical thinking and human intelligence. In R. J. Sternberg (Ed.), *Advances in the psychology of human intelligence* (Vol. 2, pp. 199–230). Hillsdale, NJ: Erlbaum.

Holyoak, K. J., Junn, E. N., & Billman, D. O. (1984). Development of analogical problem-solving skill. *Child Development, 55,* 2042–2055.

Hood, L., & Bloom, L. (1979). What, when, and how about why: A longitudinal study of early expressions of causality. *Monographs of the Society for Research in Child Development* (Serial No. 181).

Horan, P. F., & Rosser, R. A. (1983). The function of response mode in the coordination of perspectives. *Contemporary Educational Psychology, 8,* 347–354.

Horton, M. S., & Markman, E. M. (1980). Developmental differences in the acquisition of basic and superordinate categories. *Child Development, 51,* 708–719.

Hoving, K. L., Spencer, T., Robb, K. Y., & Schulte, D. (1978). Developmental changes in visual information processing. In P. A. Ornstein (Ed.), *Memory development in children.* Hillsdale, NJ: Erlbaum.

Hutchinson, J. E. (1986). Children's sensitivity to the contrastive use of object category terms. *Papers and Reports on Child Language Development, 25,* 49–56.

Huttenlocher, J., & Newcombe, N. (1984). The child's representation of information about location. In C. Sophian (Ed.), *The origin of cognitive skills* (pp. 81–111). Hillsdale, NJ: Erlbaum.

Huttenlocher, J., & Presson, C. C. (1973). Mental rotation and the perspective problem. *Cognitive Psychology, 4,* 277–299.

Huttenlocher, P. R. (1979). Synaptic density in human frontal cortex——developmental changes and effects of aging. *American Journal of Mental Deficiency, 88,* 488–496.

Huttenlocher, P. R. (1979). Synapse elimination and plasticity in the developing human cerebral cortex. *American Journal of Mental Deficiency, 88*(3), 197–227.

Hyde, J. S. (1981). How large are cognitive gender differences? A meta-analysis using *w* and *d. American Psychologist, 36,* 892–901.

Inhelder, B., & de Caprona, D. (1990). The role and meaning of structures in genetic epistemology. In W. F. Overton (Ed.), *Reasoning, logic, and necessity.* Hillsdale, NJ: Erlbaum.

Inhelder, B., & Piaget, J. (1958). *The growth of logical thinking from childhood to adolescence.* New York: Wiley.

Inhelder, B., & Piaget, J. (1964). *The early growth of logic in the child.* New York: Harper & Row.

Jackendoff, R. (1989). What is a concept, that a person may grasp it? *Mind and Language, 4,* 68–102.

James, W. (1890). *Principles of psychology* (Vol. 1). New York: Holt.

Johansson, G. (1973). Visual perception of biological motion and a model for its analysis. *Perception and Psychophysics, 14,* 201–211.

Johansson, G. (1978). Visual event perception. In R. Held, H. W. Leibowitz, & H. L. Teuber (Eds.), *Handbook of sensory physiology: Vol. 8. Perception* (pp. 675–712). Berlin: Springer-Verlag.

Johnson, C. N., & Wellman, H. M. (1980). Children's developing understanding of mental verbs: "Remember," "know," and "guess". *Child Development, 51,* 1095–1102.

Johnson, M. H. (1988). Memories of mother. *New Scientist, 18,* 60–62.

Johnson, M. H. (1990). Cortical maturation and the development of visual attention in early infancy. *Journal of Cognitive Neuroscience, 2,* 81–95.

Johnson, M. H. (in press). Cortical maturation and perceptual development. In H. Bloch & B. Bertenthal (Eds.), *Sensory motor organisation and development in infancy and early childhood.* Dordrecht: Kluwer Academic Press.

Johnson-Laird, P. N. (1975). Models of deduction. In R. J. Falmagne (Ed.), *Reasoning: Representation and process in children and adults.* Hillsdale, NJ: Erlbaum.

Johnson-Laird, P. N. (1983). *Mental models.* Cambridge, MA: Harvard University Press.

Johnson-Laird, P. N. (1990). The development of reasoning ability. In G. Butterworth & P. Bryant, (Eds.). *Causes of development.* Hillsdale, NJ: Erlbaum.

Johnson-Laird, P. N., Legrenzi, P., Sonino-Legrenzi, M. (1972). Reasoning and a sense of reality. *British Journal of Psychology, 63,* 395–400.

Johnson-Laird, P. N., Oakhill, J. V., & Bull, D. (1986). Children's syllogistic reasoning. *Quarterly Journal of Experimental Psychology, 38,* 35–58.

Jones, S. S., Smith, L. B., & Landau, B. (1991). Object properties and knowledge in early lexical learning. *Child Development, 62,* 499–516.

Jusczyk, P. W. (1981). Infant speech perception: A critical appraisal. In P. D. Eimas & J. L. Miller (Eds.), *Perspectives on the study of speech* (pp. 113–164). Hillsdale, NJ: Erlbaum.

Jusczyk, P. W., Copan, H., & Thompson, E. (1978). Perception by 2-month-old infants of glide contrasts in multisyllabic utterances. *Perception and Psychophysics, 24,* 515–520.

Jusczyk, P. W., & Thompson, E. (1978). Perception of a phonetic contrast in multisyllabic utterances by 2-month-old infants. *Perception and psychophysics, 23,* 105–109.

Just, M. A., & Carpenter, P. A. (1985). Cognitive coordinate systems: Accounts of mental rotation and individual differences in spatial ability. *Psychological Review, 92,* 137–171.

Kail, R. (1985). Development of mental rotation: A speed-accuracy study. *Journal of Experimental Child Psychology, 40,* 181–192.

Kail, R. (1986). Sources of age differences in speed of processing. *Child Development, 57,* 969–987.

Kail, R. (1987). *Impact of extensive practice on speed of cognitive processes.* Paper presented at the Society for Research in Child Development meeting, Baltimore.

Kail, R. (1990). *The development of memory in children.* New York: Freeman.

Kail, R., & Hagen, H. (1977). *Perspectives on the development of memory and cognition.* Hillsdale, NJ: Erlbaum.

Kail, R., Pellegrino, J., & Carter, P. (1980). Developmental changes in mental rotation. *Journal of Experimental Child Psychology, 29,* 102–116.

Kaiser, M. K., Jonides, J., & Alexander, J. (1986). Intuitive reasoning about abstract and familiar physics problems. *Memory and Cognition, 14,* 308–312.

Kaiser, M. K., McCloskey, M., & Proffitt, D. R. (1986). Development of intuitive theories of motion: Curvilinear motion in the absence of external forces. *Developmental Psychology, 22,* 67–71.

Kaiser, M. K., & Proffitt, D. R. (1987). Human sensitivity to the dynamics of collisions. *Perception and Psychophysics, 38,* 533–539.

Kaiser, M. K., Proffitt, D. R., & Anderson, K. (1985). Judgments of natural and anomalous trajectories in the presence and absence of motion. *Journal of Experimental Psychology: Learning, Memory, and Cognition, 11,* 795–803.

Kaiser, M. K., Proffitt, D. R., & McCloskey, M. (1985). The development of beliefs about falling objects. *Perception & Psychophysics, 38,* 533–539.

Kandel, E. R. (1977). Neuronal plasticity and the modification of behavior. In J. M. Brookhart & V. B. Mountcastle, (Eds.), *Handbook of physiology. The nervous system.* Bethesda, MD: American Physiological Society.

Kant, I. (1924). *Critique of pure reason.* New York: Macmillan.

Kapadia, R. (1974). A critical examination of Piaget-Inhelder's view on topology. *Educational Studies in Mathematics, 5,* 419–424.

Kaplan, E., & Kaplan, G. (1971). The prelinguistic child. In J. Elliot (Ed.), *Human development and cognitive processes.* New York: Holt, Rinehart, and Winston.

Kaplan, G. A. (1969). Kinetic disruption of optical texture: The perception of depth at an edge. *Perception and Psychophysics, 6,* 193–198.

Karmel, B. Z., & Maisel, E. B. (1975). A neuronal activity model for infant visual attention. In L. B. Cohen & P. Salapatek (Eds.), *Infant perception: From sensation to cognition,* (Vol. 1). New York: Academic.

Karmiloff-Smith, A. (1979). *A functional approach to language acquisition.* New York: Cambridge University Press.

Karmiloff-Smith, A. (1988). The child is a theoretician, not an inductivist. *Mind and Language, 3,* 184–195.

Karmiloff-Smith, A. (1991). Beyond modularity: Innate constraints and developmental change. In R. Gelman & S. Carey (Eds.), *The epigenesis of mind: Essays on biology and cognition.* Hillsdale, NJ: Erlbaum.

Kaufman, F., Stucki, M., & Kaufman-Hayoz, R. (1985). Development of infants' sensitivity for slow and rapid motions. *Infant Behavior and Development, 8,* 89–98.

Keil, F. C. (1979). *Semantic and conceptual development: An ontological perspective.* Cambridge, MA: Harvard University Press.

Keil, F. C. (1981). Constraints on knowledge and cognitive development. *Psychological Review, 88*(3), 197–227.

Keil, F. (1982). Intelligence and the rest of cognition. *Intelligence, 6,* 1–21.

Keil, F. C. (1983). Semantic inferences and the acquisition of word meaning. In T. Seiler & W. Wannenmacher (Eds.), *Conceptual development and the development of word meaning* (pp. 103–124). Berlin: Springer Verlag.

Keil, F. C. (1984). Mechanisms in cognitive development and the structure of knowledge. In R. J. Sternberg (Ed.), *Mechanisms of cognitive development.* New York: Freeman.

Keil, F. C. (1986a). On the structure-dependent nature of cognitive development. In I. Levin (Ed.), *Stage and structure: Reopening the debate.* Norwood, NJ: Ablex.

Keil, F. C. (1986b). The acquisition of natural kind and artifact terms. In W. Demopoulous & A. Marras (Eds.), *Language learning and concept acquisition* (pp. 135–153). Norwood, NJ: Ablex.

Keil, F. C. (1989). *Concepts, kinds, and cognitive development.* Cambridge, MA: Bradford Books/MIT Press.

Keil, F. C. (1991). The emergence of theoretical beliefs as constraints on concepts. In S. Carey & R. Gelamn (Eds.), *The epigenesis of mind: Essays on biology and cognition.* Hillsdale, NJ: Erlbaum.

Keil, F. C. (1992). The origins of an autonomous biology. In M. R. Gunnar & M. Maratsos (Eds.), *Modularity and constraints in language and cognition: The Minnesota symposium on child psychology* (Vol. 25). Hillsdale, NJ: Erlbaum.

Keil, F., & Batterman, N. (1984). A characteristic-to-defining shift in the development of word meaning. *Journal of Verbal Learning and Verbal Behavior, 23,* 221–226.

Keil, F. C., & Kelly, M. H. (1986). Theories of constraints and constraints on theories. In W. Demopoulous & A. Marras (Eds.), *Language learning and concept acquisition* (pp. 173–183). Norwood, NJ: Ablex.

Kellman, P. J. (1984). Perception of three-dimensional form by human infants. *Perception and Psychophysics, 36,* 353–358.

Kellman, P. J. (1988). Theories of perception and research in perceptual development. In A. Yonas (Ed.), *Perceptual development in infancy: The Minnesota symposium on child psychology* (Vol. 20, pp. 267–282). Hillsdale, NJ: Erlbaum.

Kellman, P. J., Gleitman, H., & Spelke, E. S. (1987). Object and observer motion in the perception of objects by infants. *Journal of Experimental Psychology: Human Perception and Performance, 13,* 586–593.

Kellman, P. J., & Short, K. R. (1985). *Infant perception of partly occluded objects: The problem of rotation.* Paper presented at the Third International Conference on Event Perception and Action, Uppsala, Sweden.

Kellman, P. J., & Short, K. R. (1987). Development of three-dimensional form perception. *Journal of Experimental Psychology: Human Perception and Performance, 13,* 545–557.

Kellman, P. J., & Spelke, E. S. (1983). Perception of partly occluded objects in infancy. *Cognitive Psychology, 15,* 483–524.

Kellman, P. J., Spelke, E. S., & Short, K. (1986). Infant perception of object unity from translatory motion in depth and vertical translation. *Child Development, 57,* 72–86.

Kemler, D. G. (1982). Classification in young and retarded children: The primacy of overall similarity relations. *Child Development, 53,* 768–779.

Kemler, D. G. (1983). Holistic and analytic modes in perceptual and cognitive development. In T. J. Tighe & B. E. Shepp (Eds.), *Perception, cognition, and development: Interactional analyses.* Hillsdale, NJ: Erlbaum.

Kemler, D. G., & Smith, L. B. (1978). Is there a developmental trend from integrality to separability in perception? *Journal of Experimental Child Psychology, 26,* 498–507.

Kemler-Nelson, D. G., Hirsch-Pasek, K., Jusczyk, P. W., & Wright-Cassidy, K. (1989). How the prosodic cues in motherese might assist language learning. *Journal of Child Language, 16,* 53–68.

Kenny, S. L. (1983). Developmental discontinuities in childhood and adolescence. In K. W. Fischer (Ed.), *Levels and transitions in children's development* (pp. 81–96).San Francisco, CA: Jossey-Bass.

Kermoian, R., & Campos, J. J. (1988). Locomotor experience: A facilitator of spatial cognitive development. *Child Development, 59,* 908–917.

Kesner, R. P. (1986). Neurobiological views of memory. In J. L. Martinez & R. P. Kesner (Eds.), *Learning and memory: A biological view.* New York: Academic.

Kessen, W. (1967). Sucking and looking: Two organized congenital patterns of behavior in the human newborn. In H. W. Stevenson, E. H. Hess, & H. L. Rheingold (Eds.), *Early behavior: Comparative and developmental approaches.* New York: Wiley.

Kessen, W. (1984). The end of the age of development. In R. J. Sternberg (Ed.), *Mechanisms of cognitive development* (pp. 81–96). New York: Freeman.

Kihlstrom, J. F., Schacter, D., Cork, R., Hurt, C., & Behr, S. (1990). Implicit and explicit memory following surgical anesthesia. *Psychological Science, 1,* 303–306.

Kintsch, W., & Greeno, J. G. (1985). Understanding and solving arithmetic problems. *Psychological Review, 92, 109*–129.

Kirk, R. E. (1982). *Experimental design: Procedures for the behavioral sciences.* Belmont, CA: Brooks Cole.

Klahr, D. (1984). Transition processes in quantitative development. In R. J. Sternberg (Ed.), *Mechanisms of cognitive development* (pp. 101–140). New York: Freeman.

Klahr, D., & Robinson, M. (1981). Formal assessment of problem solving and planning processes in preschool children. *Cognitive Psychology, 13,* 113–148.

Klahr, D., & Wallace, J. G. (1976). *Cognitive development: An information processing view.* Hillsdale, NJ: Erlbaum.

Klima, E., & Bellugi, U. (1979). *The signs of language.* Cambridge, MA: Harvard University Press.

Knopf, M., Körkel, J., Schneider, W., & Weinert, F. E. (1988). Human memory as a faculty versus human memory as a set of specific abilities: Evidence from a life-span approach. In F. E. Weinert & M. Perlmutter (Eds.), *Memory development: Universal changes and individual differences.* Hillsdale, NJ: Erlbaum.

Knudsen, E. (1983). Early auditory experience aligns the auditory map of space in the optic tectum of the barn owl. *Science, 222,* 939–942.

Knudsen, E. I., & Knudsen, P. F. (1990). Sensitive and critical periods for visual calibration of sound localization by barn owls. *Journal of Neuroscience, 16,* 222–232.

Koffka, K. (1935). *Principles of Gestalt psychology.* New York: Harcourt, Brace, & World.

Kofsy, E. A. (1966). A scalogram study of classificatory development. *Child Development, 37,* 191–204.

Kolb, B., & Wishaw, I. Q. (1985). *Fundamentals of human neuropsychology.* New York: Freeman.

Kossan, N. E. (1981). Developmental differences in concept acquisition strategies. *Child Development, 52,* 290–298.

Kosslyn, S. M., Heldmeyer, K. H., & Locklear, E. P. (1977). Children's drawings as data about internal representations. *Journal of Experimental Child Psychology, 23,* 191–211.

Kramer, S. (1986). *Infants' detection of motion in random-dot kinematograms.* Paper presented at the International Conference on Infant Studies, Los Angeles, CA.

Kripke, S. (1971). Identity and necessity. In M. K. Munitz (Ed.), *Identity and individuation.* New York: University Press.

Kripke, S. (1972). Naming and necessity. In D. Davidson & Harman (Eds.), *Semantics of natural language.* Dordrecht: Reidel.

Kuchuk, A., Vibbert, M., & Bornstein, M. H. (1986). The perception of smiling and its experiential correlates in three-month-old infants. *Child Development, 57,* 1054–1061.

Kuczaj, S. A., II. (1977). The acquisition of regular and irregular past tense forms. *Journal of Verbal Learning and Verbal Behavior, 16,* 589–600.

Kuhl, P. K. (1979). The perception of speech in early infancy. In N. J. Lass (Ed.), *Speech and language: Advances in basic research and practice.* New York: Academic.

Kuhl, P. K. (1980). Perceptual constancy for speech-sound categories in early infancy. In G. H. Yeni-Komshian, J. F. Kavanaugh, & C. A. Ferguson, (Eds.), *Child phonology: Vol. 2. Perception.* New York: Academic.

Kuhl, P. K. (1987). Perception of speech and sound in early infancy. In P. Salapatek & L. Cohen (Eds.), *Handbook of infant perception* (Vol. 2, pp. 275–382). Orlando FL: Academic.

Kuhl, P. K., & Meltzoff, A. N. (1982). The bimodal perception of speech in infancy. *Science, 218,* 1138–1141.

Kuhl, P. K., & Meltzoff, A. N. (1984). The intermodal representation of speech in infants. *Infant Behavior and Development, 7,* 361–381.

Kuhl, P. K., & Meltzoff, A. N. (1988). Speech as an intermodal object of perception. In A. Yonas (Ed.), *Perceptual development in infancy: The Minnesota symposia on child psychology* (Vol. 20, pp. 235–266). Hillsdale, NJ: Erlbaum.

Kuhn, D. (1974). Inducing development experimentally: Comments on a research paradigm. *Developmental Psychology, 10,* 590–600.

Kuhn, D. (1989). Children and adults as intuitive scientists. *Psychological Review, 96,* 674–689.

Kuhn, T. (1962). *The structure of scientific revolutions.* Chicago: University of Chicago Press.

Kuzmak, S. D., & Gelman, R. (1986). Young children's understanding of random phenomena. *Child Development, 57,* 559–566.

Lakoff, G. (1987). *Women, fire, and dangerous things: What categories reveal about the mind.* Chicago: University of Chicago Press.

La Mantia, A., & Rakic, P. (1984). The number, size, myelination and regional variations in the corpus callosum and anterior commissure of the developing rhesus monkey. *Society of Neuroscience Abstracts, 10,* 1373.

Lampl, M., & Emde, R. N. (1983). Episodic growth in infancy: A preliminary report on length, head circumference and behavior. In K. W. Fischer (Ed.), *Levels and transitions in children's development* (pp. 21–36). San Francisco: Jossey-Bass.

Landau, B. (1988). The construction and use of spatial knowledge in blind and sighted children. In J. Stiles-Davis, M. Kritchevsky, & U. Bellugi (Eds.), *Spatial Cognition: Brain bases and development* (343–372). Hillsdale, NJ: Erlbaum.

Landau, B., Gleitman, H. & Spelke, E. (1981). Spatial knowledge and geometric representation in a child blind from birth. *Science, 213,* 1275–1278.

Landau, B., & Spelke, E. (1985). Spatial knowledge and its manifestations. In H. M. Wellman (Ed.), *Children's searching: The development of search skill and spatial representation.* Hillsdale, NJ: Erlbaum.

Landau, B., & Spelke, E. (1988). Geometric complexity and object search in infancy. *Developmental Psychology, 24,* 512–521.

Landau, B., Spelke, E., & Gleitman, H. (1984). Spatial knowledge in a young blind child. *Cognition, 16,* 225–260.

Landau, K. B., Smith, L. B., & Jones, S. S. (1988). The importance of shape in early lexical learning. *Cognitive Development, 3,* 299–321.

Langley, P., Simon, H. A., Bradshaw, G. L., & Zytkow, J. M. (1987). *Scientific discovery.* Cambridge, MA: MIT Press.

Laurendeau, M., & Pinard, A. (1962). *Causal thinking in the child.* New York: International Universities Press.

Laurendeau, M., & Pinard, A. (1970). *The development of the concept of space in the child*. New York: International Universities Press.

Lempers, J. D., Flavell, E. R., & Flavell, J. H. (1977). The development in very young children of tacit knowledge concerning visual perception. *Genetic Psychology Monographs, 95*, 3–53.

Lenneburg, E. (1967). *Biological foundations of language*. New York: Wiley.

Lenneberg, E. H., Rebelsky, F. G., & Nichols, I. A. (1965). The vocalizations of infants born to deaf and hearing parents. *Human Development, 8*, 23–37.

Leslie, A. M. (1982). Discursive representation in infancy. In B. de Gelder (Ed.), *Knowledge and representation*. London: Routledge & Kegan Paul.

Leslie, A. M. (1984a). Infant perception of a manual pick-up event. *British Journal of Developmental Psychology, 2*, 19–32.

Leslie, A. M. (1984b). Spatiotemporal continuity and the perception of causality in infants. *Perception, 13*, 287–305.

Leslie, A. M. (1987). Pretense and representation: The origins of "theory of mind." *Psychological Review, 94*, 412–426.

Leslie, A. M. (1988). Some implications of pretense for mechanisms underlying the child's theory of mind. In J. W. Astington, D. R. Olson, & P. L. Harris (Eds.), *Developing theories of mind*. New York: Cambridge University Press.

LeVay, S., Wiesel, T. N., & Hubel, D. H. (1980). The development of ocular dominance columns in normal and visually deprived monkeys. *Journal of Comparative Neurology, 191*, 1–51.

Levinson, P. J., & Carpenter, R. L. (1974). An analysis of analogical reasoning in children. *Child Development, 45*, 857–861.

Liben, L. S. (1975). Evidence for developmental differences in spontaneous seriation and its implications for past research on long-term memory improvement. *Developmental Psychology, 11*, 121–125.

Liben, L. S. (1978). Perspective-taking skills in young children: Seeing the world through rose-colored glasses. *Developmental Psychology, 11*, 87–92.

Liben, L. S. (1988). Conceptual issues in the development of spatial cognition. In J. Stiles-Davis, M. Kritchevsky, & U. Bellugi (Eds.), *Spatial cognition: Brain bases and development* (pp. 167–194). Hillsdale, NJ: Erlbaum.

Liben, L. S., Patterson, A. H., & Newcombe, N. (1981). *Spatial representation and behavior across the life span*. New York: Academic.

Liberman, A. M., Harris, K. S., Eimas, P., Lisker, L., & Bastian, J. (1961). An effect of learning on speech perception: The discrimination of durations of silence with and without phonemic significance. *Language and Speech, 4*, 175–195.

Liberman, A. M., Harris, K. S., Hoffman, H. S., & Griffith, B. C. (1957). The discrimination of speech sounds within and across phoneme boundaries. *Journal of Experimental Psychology, 54*, 358–368.

Liberman, A. M., Harris, K. S., Kinney, J. A., & Lane, H. (1961). The discrimination of relative onset-time of the components of certain speech and non-speech patterns. *Journal of Experimental Psychology, 61*, 379–388.

Lieberman, P. (1984). *The biology and evolution of language*. Cambridge, MA: Harvard University Press.

Linn, M. C., & Peterson, A. C. (1985). Emergence and characterization of sex-differences in spatial ability: A meta-analysis. *Child Development, 56*, 1479–1498.

Lohman, D. F. (1979). *Spatial ability: A review and reanalysis of the correlational literature*. Technical Report No. 8. Office of Naval Research and Advanced Research Projects Agency. Contract No. N00014-75-C-0882. Stanford University.

Lohman, D. F. (1988). Spatial abilities as traits, processes and knowledge. In R. Sternberg (Ed.), *Advances in the psychology of human intelligence* (Vol. 4, pp. 181–248). Hillsdale, NJ: Erlbaum.

Lunzer, E. A. (1965). Problems of formal reasoning in test situations. In P. H. Mussen (Ed.), European research in child development. *Monographs of the society for research in child development, 30*, (Serial No. 100).

Lynch, K. (1960). *The image of the city*. Cambridge, MA: MIT Press.

Maccoby, E. G., & Jacklin, C. N. (1974). *The psychology of sex differences*. Stanford, CA: Stanford University Press.

Macnamara, J. (1982). *Names for things: A study of human learning*. Cambridge, MA: MIT Press.

Macnamara, J., Baker, E., & Olson, C. L. (1976). Four-year-old's understanding of pretend, forget, and know: Evidence for propositional operations. *Child Development, 47*, 62–70.

MacWhinney, B. (1987). The competition model. In B. MacWhinney (Ed.), *Mechanisms of language acquisition*. Hillsdale, NJ: Erlbaum.

Mandler, G., & Shebo, B. J. (1982). Subitizing: An analysis of its component processes. *Journal of Experimental Psychology: General, 11*, 1–22.

Mandler, J. M. (1983). Representation. In J. H. Flavell & E. M. Markman (Eds.), *Handbook of child psychology: Cognitive development* (Vol. 3). New York: Wiley.

Mandler, J. M. (1988). The development of spatial cognition: On topological and Euclidean representation. In J. Stiles-Davis, M. Kritchevsky, & U. Bellugi (Eds.), *Spatial cognition: Brain bases and development* (pp. 423–432). Hillsdale, NJ: Erlbaum.

Mangan, P. (1992). *Spatial memory abilities and abnormal development of the hippocampal formation in Down Syndrome*. Unpublished doctoral dissertation, The University of Arizona, Tucson, AZ.

Maratsos, M. P. (1982). The child's construction of grammatical categories. In E. Wanner & L. R. Gleitman (Eds.), *Language acquisition: The state of the art*. Cambridge, England: Cambridge University Press.

Maratsos, M. P. (1988). The acquisition of formal word classes. In Y. Levy, I. M. Schlesinger, & M. D. S. Braine (Eds.), *Categories and processes in language acquisition*. Hillsdale, NJ: Erlbaum.

Marini, Z., & Case, R. (1989). Parallels in the development of preschoolers' knowledge about their physical and social worlds. *Merrill Palmer Quarterly, 35,* 63–87.

Markman, E. M. (1973). Facilitation of part-whole comparisons by use of the collective noun "family." *Child Development, 44,* 837–840.

Markman, E. M. (1979). Classes and collections: Conceptual organization and numerical abilities. *Cognitive Psychology, 11,* 395–411.

Markman, E. M. (1989). *Categories and naming in children: Problems of induction*. Cambridge, MA: MIT Press.

Markman, E. M. (1990). Constraints children place on word meanings. *Cognitive Science, 14,* 57–77.

Markman, E. M., & Callanan, M. A. (1984). An analysis of hierarchical classification. In R. J. Sternberg (Ed.), *Advances in the psychology of human intelligence* (Vol. 2). Hillsdale, NJ: Erlbaum.

Markman, E. M., & Hutchinson, J. E. (1984). Children's sensitivity to constraints on word meaning: Taxonomic vs. thematic relations. *Cognitive Psychology, 16,* 1–27.

Markman, E. M., & Siebert, J. (1976). Classes and collections: Internal organization and resulting holistic properties. *Cognitive Psychology, 8,* 561–577.

Markman, E. M., & Wachtel, G. F. (1988). Children's use of mutual exclusivity words. *Cognitive Psychology, 20,* 121–157.

Markovits, H. (1984). Awareness of the "possible" as a mediator of formal thinking in conditional reasoning problems. *British Journal of Psychology, 45,* 367–376.

Marler, P. (1991). The instinct to learn. In R. Gelman & S. Carey (Eds.), *The epigenesis of mind: Essays on biology and cognition*. Hillsdale, NJ: Erlbaum.

Marmor, G. S. (1975). Development of kinetic images: When does the child first represent movement in mental images? *Cognitive Psychology, 7,* 548–559.

Marmor, G. S. (1977). Mental rotation and number conservation: Are they related? *Developmental Psychology, 13,* 320–325.

Martin, J. L. (1976). An analysis of some of Piaget's topological tasks from a mathematical point of view. *Journal for Research in Mathematics Education, 7,* 8–24.

Masangkay, Z. S., McCluskey, K. A., McIntyre, C. W., Sims-Knight, J., Vaugh, B. E., & Flavell, J. H. (1974). The early development of inferences about the visual percepts of others. *Child Development, 45,* 357–366.

Massey, C. M. (1988). *Development of the animate-inanimate distinction in preschoolers*. Unpublished doctoral dissertation, University of Pennsylvania, Philadelphia.

Massey, C. M., & Gelman, R. (1988). Preschoolers' ability to decide whether a photographed unfamiliar object can move itself. *Developmental Psychology, 24,* 307–317.

Maurer, D. (1985). Infant's perception of facedness. In T. Fields & N. Fox (Eds.), *Social perception in infants* (pp. 73–100). Norwood, NJ: Ablex.

Maurer, D., & Barrerra, M. E. (1981). Infants, perception of natural and distorted arrangements of a schematic face. *Child Development, 52,* 196–202.

Maurer, D., & Lewis, T. L. (1979). A physiological explanation of infant's early visual development. *Canadian Journal of Psychology, 33,* 232–252.

Maurer, D., & Martello, M. (1980). The discrimination of orientation by young infants. *Vision Research, 3,* 201–204.

Maurer, D., & Salapatek, P. (1976). Developmental changes in the scanning of faces by young infants. *Child Development, 47,* 523–527.

Mayr, E. (1982). *The growth of biological thought*. Cambridge, MA: Harvard University Press.

McCall, R. B. (1979). The development of intellectual functioning in infancy and the prediction of later I.Q. In J. D. Osofsky (Ed.), *Handbook of infant development* (pp. 707–741). New York: Wiley.

McCall, R. B. (1983). Exploring developmental transitions in mental performance. In K. W. Fischer (Ed.), *Levels and transitions in children's development* (pp. 65–80). San Francisco: Josey-Bass.

McCloskey, M. (1983a). Intuitive physics. *Scientific American, 248,* 122–130.

McCloskey, M. (1983b). Naive theories of motion. In D. Gentner & A. L. Stevens (Eds.), *Mental models.* Hillsdale, NJ: Erlbaum.

McCloskey, M., Caramazza, A., & Green, B. (1980). Curvilinear motion in the absence of external forces: Naive beliefs about the motion of objects. *Science, 210,* 1139–1141.

McCune-Nicholich, L. (1981). Toward symbolic functioning: Structure of early use of early pretend games and potential parallels with language. *Child Development, 52,* 785–797.

McCune-Nicholich, L., & Fenson, L. (1984). Methodological issues in studying early pretend play. In T. D. Yawley & A. D. Pellegrini (Eds.), *Child's play: Developmental and applied.* Hillsdale, NJ: Erlbaum.

McGee, M. G. (1979). Human spatial abilities: Psychometric studies and environmental, genetic, hormonal, and neurological influences. *Psychological Bulletin, 6,* 889–918.

McGurk, H., & MacDonald, J. (1976). Hearing lips and seeing voices. *Nature, 264,* 746–748.

Meck, W. H., & Church, R. M. (1983). A mode control model of counting and timing processes. *Journal of Experimental Psychology: Animal Behavior Processes, 9,* 320–334.

Medin, D. L., & Shoben, E. J. (1988). Context and structure in conceptual combinations. *Cognitive Psychology, 20,* 158–190.

Mehler, J., Bertoncini, J., Barciere, M., & Jassik-Gerschenfeld, D. (1978). Infant recognition of mother's voice. *Perception, 7,* 491–497.

Mehler, J., Jusczyk, P. W., Lambertz, G., Amiel-Tison, C., & Bertoncini, J. (1988). A precursor of language acquisition in the four-day-old infant. *Cognition, 29,* 143–178.

Meiback, R. C., Ross, D. A., Cox, R. D., & Glick, S. D. (1981). The ontogeny of hippocampal energy metabolism. *Brain Research, 204,* 431–435.

Meicler, M., & Gratch, G. (1980). Do 5-month-olds show object conception in Piaget's sense? *Infant Behavior and Development, 3,* 265–282.

Meltzoff, A. N. (1985). The roots of social and cognitive development: Models of man's original nature. In T. M. Fields & N. Fox (Eds.), *Social perception in infants* (pp. 1–30). Norwood, NJ: Ablex.

Meltzoff, A. N. (1988). Infant imitation and memory: Nine-month-olds in immediate and deferred tests. *Child Development, 59,* 219–225.

Meltzoff, A. N., & Borton, R. W. (1979). Intermodal matching by human neonates. *Nature, 282,* 403–404.

Menyuk, P., Menn, L., & Silber, R. (1986). Early strategies for the perception and production of words and sounds. In D. Fletcher & M. Garmon (Eds.), *Language acquisition* (2nd ed.). Cambridge, England: Cambridge University Press.

Menzel, E. W. (1973). Chimpanzee spatial memory organization. *Science, 182,* 943–945.

Mervis, C., & Pani, J. R. (1980). Acquisition of basic object categories. *Cognitive Psychology, 12,* 496–522.

Mervis, C., & Rosch, E. (1981). Categorization of natural objects. In M. R. Rosenzweig & L. W. Porter (Eds.), *Annual review of psychology* (Vol. 32). Palo Alto, CA: Annual Reviews, Inc.

Miller, G. A. (1977). Practical and lexical knowledge. In P. N. Johnson-Laird & P. C. Wason (Eds.), *Thinking: Readings in cognitive science.* Cambridge, England: Cambridge University Press.

Miller, K., & Gelman, R. (1983). The child's representation of number: A multi-dimensional scaling analysis. *Child Development, 54,* 1470–1479.

Miller, K., & Stigler, J. W. (1987). Counting in Chinese: Cultural variation in a basic cognitive skill. *Cognitive Development, 2,* 279–305.

Miller, P. H., & Aloise, P. A. (1989). Young children's understanding of the psychological causes of behavior: A review. *Child Development, 60,* 257–285.

Miller, P. H., & Zalenski, R. (1982). Preschoolers' knowledge about attention. *Developmental Psychology, 18,* 871–875.

Mishkin, M., & Appenzeller, T. (1987). The anatomy of memory. *Scientific American, 256,* 80–90.

Mishkin, M., Spiegler, B. J., Saunders, R. C., & Malamut, B. J. (1982). An animal model of global amnesia. In S. Corkin, K. L. Davis, J. H. Growdon, E. J. Usdon, & R. J. Wurtman (Eds.), *Toward a treatment of Alzheimer's Disease.* New York: Raven Press.

Mitchell, R. W., & Thompson, N. S. (Eds.) (1986). *Deception: Perspectives on human and nonhu-*

man deceit. Albany: State University of New York Press.

Moely, B. E., Olson, F. A., Halwes, T. G., & Flavell, J. H. (1969). Production deficiency on young children's clustered recall. *Developmental Psychology, 1,* 26–34.

Moore, M. K., Borton, R., & Darby, B. L. (1978). Visual tracking in young infants: Evidence for object identity or object permanence? *Journal of Experimental Child Psychology, 25,* 183–198.

Moore, M. K., & Meltzoff, A. N. (1978). Imitation, object permanence and language development during infancy: Toward a neo-Piagetian perspective on communicative and cognitive development. In F. D. Minifie & L. L. Lloyd (Eds.), *Communicative and cognitive abilities––Early behavioral assessment*. Baltimore, MD: University Park Press.

Morris, R. G. M. (1981). Spatial localization does not require the presence of local cues. *Learning and Motivation, 12,* 239–260.

Morris, R. G. M. (1983). An attempt to dissociate "spatial-mapping" and "working memory" theories of hippocampal function. In W. Seifert (Ed.), *Neurobiology of the hippocampus* (pp. 405–432). New York: Academic.

Morris, R. G. M. (1984). Developments of a water-maze procedure for studying spatial learning in the rat. *Journal of Neuroscience Methods, 11,* 47–60.

Morris, R. G. M., Garrud, P., Rawlins, & O'Keefe, J. (1982). Place navigation impaired in rats with hippocampal lesions. *Nature, 297,* 681–683.

Morrison, F. J., Holmes, D. L., & Haith, M. H. (1974). A developmental study of the effect of familiarity on short-term visual memory. *Journal of Experimental Child Psychology, 18,* 412–425.

Morrongiello, B. A. (1988). Infants' localization of sounds along the horizontal axis: Estimates of minimal audible angle. *Developmental Psychology, 24,* 8–13.

Morrow, L., & Ratcliff, G. (1988). The neuropsychology of spatial cognition. In J. Stiles-Davis, M. Kritchevsky, & U. Bellugi (Eds.), *Spatial cognition: Brain bases and development* (pp. 5–32). Hillsdale, NJ: Erlbaum.

Morse, P. A. (1978). Infant speech perception: Origins, processes, & Alpha Centauri. In F. Minifie and L. L. Lloyd (Eds.), *Communicative and cognitive abilities-early behavioral assessment*. Baltimore, MD: University Park Press.

Moscovitch, M. (1985). Memory from infancy to old age: Implications for theories of normal and pathological memory. *Annals of the New York Academy of Sciences,* pp. 78–96.

Moshman, D. (1979). Development of formal hypothesis-testing ability. *Developmental Psychology, 15,* 104–112.

Moshman, D. (1990). The development of metalogical understanding. In W. F. Overton (Ed.), *Reasoning, necessity and logic: Developmental perspectives*. Hillsdale, NJ: Erlbaum.

Moshman, D., & Franks, B. A. (1986). Development of the concept of inferential validity. *Child Development, 57,* 156–165.

Mower, G. D., Christen, W. G., & Caplan, C. J. (1983). Very brief visual experience eliminates plasticity in the cat visual cortex. *Science, 221,* 178–180.

Muir, D., & Field, J. (1979). Newborn infants orient to sounds. *Child Development, 50,* 431–436.

Muller, A. A., & Aslin, R. N. (1978). Visual tracking as an index of the object concept. *Infant Behavior and development, I,* 309–319.

Murphy, G. L., & Medin, D. L. (1985). The role of theories in conceptual coherence. *Psychological Review, 92,* 289–316.

Murray, A. D., Johnson, J., & Peters, J. (1990). Fine-tuning of utterance length to preverbal infants: Effects on later language development. *Journal of Child Language, 17,* 511–525.

Murray, F. B. (1990). The conversion of truth into necessity. In W. F. Overton (Ed.), *Reasoning, logic, and necessity* (pp. 205–226). Hillsdale, NJ: Erlbaum.

Nadel, L. (1988). Landmarks: Neurobiological perspectives. *British Journal of Developmental Psychology, 6,* 383–385.

Nadel, L., & Zola-Morgan, S. (1984). Infantile amnesia: A neurobiological approach. In M. Moscovitch (Ed.), *Infant memory*. New York: Plenum.

Neimark, E. D. (1975). Intellectual development during adolescence. In F. D. Horowitz (Ed.), *Review of child development research* (Vol. 4, pp. 543–594). Chicago: University of Chicago Press.

Nelson, C. A. (1987). The recognition of facial expression in the first two years of life: Mechanisms of development. *Child Development, 58,* 889–909.

Nelson, C. A., & Horowitz, F. D. (1983). The perception of facial expressions and stimulus motion by 2- and 5-month-old infants using holographic stimuli. *Child Development, 54,* 868–877.

Nelson, C. A., & Horowitz, F. D. (1987). Visual motion perception in infancy: A review and synthesis. In P. Salapatek & L. Cohen (Eds.), *Handbook of infant perception* (Vol. 2). Orlando, FL: Academic.

Nelson, K. (1973). Structure and strategy in learning to talk. *Monographs of the Society for Research in Child Development*, p. 38149.

Nelson, K. (1979). Explorations in the development of a functional semantic system. In W. A. Collins (Ed.), *Minnesota symposia on child psychology: Vol. 12. Language and communication*. Hillsdale, NJ: Erlbaum.

Nelson, K. (1990). Comments on Behrend's "Constraints and development." *Cognitive Development, 5,* 331–339.

Nelson, T. M., & Bartley, S. H. (1961). Numerosity, number, arithmetization, and psychology. *Philosophy of Science, 28,* 178–203.

Nersessian, N. (in press). How do scientists think? Capturing the dynamics of conceptual change in science. In R. Giere (Ed.), *Minnesota studies in the philosophy of science:Vol. 15. Cognitive models of science*. Minneapolis, MN: University of Minnesota Press.

Newcombe, N. (1988). The paradox of proximity in early spatial representation. *British Journal of Developmental Psychology, 6,* 376–378.

Newell, A., & Simon, H. A. (1972). *Human problem solving*. Englewood Cliffs, NJ: Prentice Hall.

Newport, E. (1981). Constraints on structure: Evidence from American Sign Language and language learning. In W. A. Collins (Ed.), *Minnesota symposia on child psychology: Vol. 14. Aspects of the development of competence*. Hillsdale, NJ: Erlbaum.

Newport, E. (1988). Constraints on learning and their role in language acquisition: Studies of the acquisition of American Sign Language. *Language Sciences, 10,* 147–172

Newport, E. (1991). Contrasting conceptions of the critical period for language. In R. Gelman & S. Carey (Eds.), *The epigenesis of mind: Essays on biology and cognition*. Hillsdale, NJ: Erlbaum.

Newport, E. L., Gleitman, H., & Gleitman, L. R. (1977). Mother, I'd rather do it myself: Some effects and non-effects of maternal speech style. In C. A. Ferguson & C. E. Snow (Eds.), *Talking to children*. New York: Cambridge University Press.

Newport, E., & Meier, R. (1985). The acquisition of American Sign Language. In D. I. Slobin (Ed.), *The cross-linguistic study of language acquisition* (Vol. 1). Hillsdale, NJ: Erlbaum.

Newport, E., & Supalla, T. (1990). *A possible critical period effect in the acquisition of a primary language*. Unpublished manuscript, University of Rochester, New York.

Nisbett, R. E., Krantz, D. H., Jepson, C., & Kunda, Z. (1983). The use of statistical heuristics in everyday inductive reasoning. *Psychological Review, 90,* 339–363.

Oakhill, J. V., & Johnson-Laird, P. N. (1985). Rationality, memory, and the search for counterexamples. *Cognition, 20,* 79–94.

O'Brien, D., & Overton, W. F. (1980). Conditional reasoning following contradictory evidence: A developmental analysis. *Journal of Experimental Child Psychology, 30,* 44–60.

Odom, R. D. (1978). A perceptual salience account of decalage relations and developmental change. In L. S. Siegel & C. J. Brainerd (Eds.), *Alternatives to Piaget*. New York: Academic.

Ohr, P., Fagen, J. W., Rovee-Collier, C., Hayne, H., & Vander Linde, E. (1989). Amount of training and retention by infants. *Developmental Psychobiology, 22,* 69–80.

Okaichi, H. (1987). Performance and dominant strategies on place and cue tasks following hippocampal lesions in rats. *Psychobiology, 15,* 58–63.

O'Keefe, J., & Nadel, L. (1978). *The hippocampus as a cognitive map*. Oxford, England: Oxford University Press.

O'Keefe, J., Nadel, L., Keightly, S., & Kill, D. (1975). Fornix lesions selectively abolish place learning in the rat. *Experimental Neurology, 48,* 152–166.

O'Keefe, J., & Speakman, A. (1987). Single unit activity in the rat hippocampus during a spatial memory task. *Experimental Brain Research, 68,* 1–27.

Oller, D. K. (1986). Metaphonology and infant vocalizations. In B. Lindblom & R. Zetterstrom (Eds.), *Precursors of early speech*. New York: Stockton.

Oller, D. K., & Eilers, R. E. (1982). Similarity of babbling in Spanish- and English-learning babies. *Journal of Child Language, 9,* 565–577.

Oller, D. K., & Eilers, R. E. (1988). The role of audition in infant babbling. *Child Development, 59,* 441–449.

Olton, D. S. (1977). Spatial memory. *Scientific American, 236,* 82–98.

Olton, D. S. (1983). Memory functions and the hippocamus. In W. Seifert (Ed.), *Neurobiology of the hippocamus*. New York: Academic.

Ornstein, P. A. (1978). *Memory development in children*. Hillsdale, NJ: Erlbaum.

Ornstein, P. A., Baker-Ward, L., & Naus, M. J. (1988). The development of memory skill. In F. E. Weinert & M. Perlmutter (Eds.), *Memory development: Universal changes and individual differences*. Hillsdale, NJ: Erlbaum.

Ornstein, P. A., Naus, M. J., & Liberty, C. (1975). Rehearsal and organization processes in children's memory. *Child Development, 26,* 818–830.

Ornstein, P. A., Naus, M. J., & Stone, B. P. (1977). Rehearsal training and developmental differences in memory. *Developmental Psychology, 13,* 15–24.

Osherson, D. N., & Smith, E. E. (1981). On the adequacy of prototype theory as a theory of concepts. *Cognition, 9,* 35–58.

Overton, W. F. (1990). Competence and procedures: Constraints on the development of logical reasoning. In W. F. Overton (Ed.), *Reasoning, logic, and necessity* (pp. 1–32). Hillsdale, NJ: Erlbaum.

Overton, W. F., Ward, S. L., Noveck, I. A., Black, J., & O'Brien, O. P. (1987). Form and content in the development of deductive reasoning. *Developmental Psychology, 23,* 22–30.

Oviatt, S. L., (1980). The emerging ability to comprehend language: An experimental approach. *Child Development, 51,* 97–106.

Owsley, C. (1983). The role of motion in infant's perception of solid shape. *Perception, 12,* 707–717.

Paivio, A. (1971). *Imagery and verbal processes*. New York: Holt, Rinehart & Winston.

Palermo, D. S. (1973). More about less: A study of language comprehension. *Journal of Verbal Learning and Verbal Behavior, 12,* 211–221.

Palermo, D. S. (1974). Still more about the comprehension of less. *Developmental Psychology, 10,* 827–829.

Papousek, M., Papousek, H., & Bornstein, M. (1985). The naturalistic vocal environment of young infants: On the significance of homogeneity and variability in parental speech. In T. M. Field & N. A. Fox (Eds.), *Social perception in infants*. Norwood, NJ: Ablex.

Paris, S. G., & Lindaur, B. K. (1977). Constructive aspects of children's comprehension and memory. In R. V. Kail, Jr., & J W. Hagen (Eds.), *Perspectives on the development of memory and cognition*. Hillsdale, NJ: Erlbaum.

Parker, T. W., & Walley, R. E. (1988). Effect of low-intensity hippocampal stimulation on spatial versus working memory in rats. *Behavioral Neuroscience, 102,* 653–661.

Parsons, A. (1958). Translator's introduction: A guide for psychologists. In B. Inhelder & J. Piaget (Eds.), *The growth of logical thinking from childhood to adolescence* (pp. 12–24). New York: Basic.

Pascual–Leone, J. A. (1970). A mathematical model for the transition rule in Piaget's developmental stages. *Acta Psychologica, 32,* 301–345.

Pellegrino, J. W., & Glaser, R. (1982). Analyzing aptitudes for learning: Inductive reasoning. In R. Glaser (Ed.), *Advances in instructional psychology* (Vol. 2, pp. 269–345). Hillsdale, NJ: Erlbaum.

Pellegrino, J. W., & Kail, R. (1982). Process analyses of spatial aptitude. In R. J. Sternberg (Ed.), *Advances in the psychology of human intelligence*. Hillsdale, NJ: Erlbaum.

Penner, S. (1987). Parental responses to grammatical and ungrammatical child utterances. *Child Development, 58,* 376–384.

Pepperberg, I. M. (1987). Evidence for conceptual quantitative abilities in the African grey parrot: Labeling of cardinal sets. *Ethology, 75,* 37–61.

Perlmutter, M. (1988). Research on memory and its development: Past, present, and future. In F. E. Weinert & M. Perlmutter (Eds.), *Memory development: Universal changes and individual differences*. Hillsdale, NJ: Erlbaum.

Perlmutter, M., & Myers, N. A. (1979). Development of recall in 2- to 4-year-old children. *Developmental Psychology, 15,* 73–83.

Perner, J. (1989). Is "thinking" belief? Reply to Wellman and Bartsch. *Cognition, 33,* 315–319.

Perner, J., Leekham, S. R., & Wimmer, H. (1987). Three-year-olds' difficulty with false belief: The case for a conceptual deficit. *British Journal of Developmental Psychology, 5,* 125–137.

Perrett, D. I., Rolls, E. T., & Caan, W. (1982). Visual neurons responsive to faces in the monkey temporal cortex. *Experimental Brain Research, 47,* 329–342.

Peters, R. P. (1973). Cognitive maps in wolves and men. In W. F. E. Preiser (Ed.), *Environmental Design Research* (Vol. 2, pp. 247–253). Stroudsburg, PA: Dowden, Hutchinson, & Ross.

Pettito, L.A., & Marentette, P. F. (1991). Babbling in the manual mode: Evidence for the ontogeny of language. *Science, 251,* 1493–1496.

Piaget, J. (1929). *The child's conception of the world.* London: Routledge & Kegan Paul.

Piaget, J. (1930). *The child's conception of physical causality.* London: Routledge & Kegan Paul.

Piaget, J. (1932). *The moral judgement of the child.* New York: Harcourt, Brace.

Piaget, J. (1950). *The psychology of intelligence.* London: Routledge & Kegan Paul.

Piaget, J. (1952a). *The child's concept of number.* New York: W. W. Norton.

Piaget, J. (1952b). *The origins of intelligence in children.* New York: International Universities Press.

Piaget, J. (1954). *The construction of reality in the child.* New York: Basic Books.

Piaget, J. (1957). *Logic and psychology.* New York: Basic Books.

Piaget, J. (1962). *Play, dreams, and imitation in childhood.* New York: W. W. Norton.

Piaget, J. (1970a). *Structuralism.* New York: Basic Books, 1970.

Piaget, J. (1970b). *The child's conception of movement and speed.* London: Routledge & Kegan Paul.

Piaget, J. (1971). *Biology and knowledge.* Chicago: University of Chicago Press.

Piaget, J. (1979). *The child's conception of the world.* Totowa, NJ: Littlefield, Adams.

Piaget, J. (1980). The constructivist approach. *Cahiers de la Foundation Archives Jean Piaget, No. 1,* 3–10.

Piaget, J. (1986). Essay on necessity. *Human Development, 29,* 301–314.

Piaget, J. (1987a). *Possibility and necessity: Vol. 1. The role of possibility in cognitive development.* Minneapolis, MN: University of Minnesota Press.

Piaget, J. (1987b). *Possibility and necessity: Vol 2. The role of necessity in cognitive development.* Minneapolis, MN: University of Minnesota Press.

Piaget, J., & Inhelder, B. (1941). *Le dèveloppement des quantitès physiques chez l'enfant.* Neuchâtel: Delachaux et Niestlè.

Piaget, J., & Inhelder, B. (1956). *The child's conception of space.* London: Routledge & Kegan Paul.

Piaget, J., & Inhelder, B. (1971). *Mental imagery in the child.* New York: Basic Books.

Piaget, J., & Inhelder, B. (1973). *Memory and intelligence.* New York: Basic Books.

Piaget, J., Inhelder, B., & Szeminska, A. (1948). *La gèomètrique spontanèe de l'enfant.* Paris: Presses Universitaires de France.

Piaget, J., Inhelder, B., & Szeminska, A. (1960). *The child's conception of geometry.* London: Routledge & Kegan Paul.

Piaget, J., Montangero, J., & Billeter, J. (1977). Les Correlats. In J. Piaget (Ed.), *L'abstraction reflechissante* (pp. 115–129). Paris: Presses Universitaires de France.

Piatelli-Palmerini, M. (1980). *Language and learning: The debate between Jean Piaget and Noam Chomsky.* London: Routledge & Kegan Paul.

Pick, H. L. (1988). Perceptual aspects of spatial cognitive development. In J. Stiles-Davis, M. Kritchevsky, & U. Bellugi (Eds.), *Spatial cognition: Brain bases and development* (pp. 145–156). Hillsdale, NJ: Erlbaum.

Pieraut-Le Bonniec, G. (1990). The logic of meaning and meaningful implication. In W. F. Overton (Ed.), *Reasoning, logic, and necessity* (pp. 67–86). Hillsdale, NJ: Erlbaum.

Pierce, C. S. (1957). The logic of abduction. In *Essays in the philosophy of science.* New York: Liberal Arts Press.

Pillow, B. H. (1988). The development of children's beliefs about the mental world. *Merrill-Palmer Quarterly, 34,* 1–32.

Pillow, B. H., & Flavell, J. H. (1985). Intellectual realism: The role of children's interpretations of pictures and perceptual verbs. *Child Development, 56,* 664–670.

Pinker, S. (1979). Formal models of language learning. *Cognition, 1,* 217–283.

Pinker, S. (1981). On the acquisition of grammatical morphemes. *Journal of Child Language, 8,* 477–484

Pinker, S. (1984). *Language learnability and language development.* Cambridge, MA: Harvard University Press.

Pinker, S. (1987). The bootstrapping problem in language acquisition. In B. MacWhinney (Ed.), *Mechanisms of language acquisition.* Hillsdale, NJ: Erlbaum.

Pinker, S. (1989). Language acquisition. In D. N. Osherson and H. Lasnik (Eds.), *An invitation to cognitive science: Vol. 1. Language.* Cambridge, MA: MIT Press.

Pinker, S., & Bloom, P. (1990). Natural language and natural selection. *Behavioral and Brain Sciences, 13,* 713–733.

Plomin, R. (1988). The nature and nurture of cognitive abilities. In R. J. Sternberg (Ed.). *Advances in the psychology of human intelligence* (Vol. 4). Hillsdale, NJ: Erlbaum (pp. 1–34).

Plomin, R., DeFries, J. C., Loehlin, J. C. (1977). Genotype-environment interaction and correlation in the analysis of human behavior. *Psychological Bulletin, 84,* 309–322.

Pokorny, J., & Yamamoto, T. (1981). Postnatal ontogenesis of hippocampal CAI area in rats: I. Development of dendritic arborization in pyramidal neurons. II. Development of ultrastructure in Stratum lacunosum and molecular. *Brain Research Bulletin, 7,* 113–130.

Prechtl, H. F. R. (1984). Continuity and change in early neural development. In H. F. R. Prechtl (Ed.), *Continuity of neural functions from prenatal to postnatal life* (pp. 1–15). Philadelphia: Lippincott.

Premack, D. (1990). The infants' theory of self-propelled objects. *Cognition,, 36,* 1–16.

Premack, D., & Woodruff, G. (1978). Does the chimpanzee have a theory of mind? *The Behavioral and Brain Sciences, 4,* 515–526.

Pressley, M. (1982). Elaboration and memory development. *Child Development, 53,* 269–309.

Pressley, M., & Levin, J. R. (1978). Developmental constraints associated with children's use of the keyword method of foreign language vocabulary learning. *Journal of Experimental Child Psychology, 29,* 391–402.

Presson, C. C. (1980). Spatial egocentrism and the effect of an alternative frame of reference. *Journal of Experimental Child Psychology, 29,* 391–402.

Presson, C. C. (1987). The development of landmarks in spatial memory: The role of differential experience. *Journal of Experimental Child Psychology, 44,* 317–334.

Presson, C. C., & Ihrig, I. (1982). Using mother as a spatial landmark: Evidence against egocentric coding in infancy. *Developmental Psychology, 18,* 699–703.

Presson, C. C., & Montello, D. R. (1988). Points of reference in spatial cognition: Stalking the elusive landmark. *British Journal of Developmental Psychology, 6,* 378–381.

Presson, C. C., & Somerville, S. (1985). Beyond egocentrism: A new look at the beginnings of spatial representation. In H. Wellman (Ed.), *Children's searching: The development of search skill and spatial representation.* Hillsdale, NJ: Erlbaum.

Proffitt, D. R., Kaiser, M. K., & Whelan, S. M. (1990). Understanding wheel dynamics. *Cognitive Psychology, 22,* 342–373.

Putnam, H. (1975). *Mind, language, & reality: Philosophical papers* (Vol. 2). Cambridge, England: Cambridge University Press.

Putnam, H. (1977). Is semantics possible? In S. P. Schwartz (Ed.), *Naming, necessity, and natural kinds.* Ithaca, NY: Cornell University Press.

Pylyshyn, Z. W. (1979). The rate of "mental rotation" of images: A test of a holistic analogue hypothesis. *Memory and Cognition, 7,* 19–28.

Pylyshyn, Z. W. (1981). The imagery debate: Analogue media versus tacit knowledge. *Psychological Review, 88,* 16–45.

Querleu, D., & Renard, K. (1981). Les perceptions auditives du feotus humain. *Medicine et Hygiene, 39,* 2102–2110.

Quine, W. V. O. (1960). *Word and object.* Cambridge, MA: MIT Press.

Quine, W. V. O. (1961). *From a logical point of view.* Cambridge, MA: Harvard University Press.

Quine, W. V. O. (1981). Five milestones of Empiricism. In W. V. O. Quine (Ed.), *Theories and things.* Cambridge, MA: MIT Press.

Rader, N., Bausano, M., & Richards, J. E. (1980). On the nature of the visual-cliff-avoidance response in human infants. *Child Development, 51,* 61–68.

Rakic, P. (1986). Mechanisms of ocular dominance segregation in the lateral geniculate nucleus: Competitive elimination hypothesis. *Trends in Neuroscience, 9,* 11–15.

Rakic, P., Bourgeois, J. P., Zecevic, N., Eckenhoff, M. F., & Goldman-Rakic, P. S. (1986). Isochronic overproduction of synapses in diverse regions of the primate cerebral cortex. *Science, 232,* 232–235.

Reese, H. W., & Overton, W. F. (1970). Models of development and theories of development. In L. R. Goulet & P. B. Baltes (Eds.), *Life-span developmental psychology: Research and theory.* New York: Academic.

Rescorla, L. A. (1980). Overextension in early language development. *Journal of Child Language, 7,* 321–335.

Richards, D. D., & Siegler, R. S. (1986). Children's understandings of the attributes of life. *Journal of Experimental Child Psychology, 42,* 1–22.

Richards, J. E., & Rader, N. (1981). Crawling-onset age predicts visual cliff avoidance in infants. *Journal of Experimental Psychology: Human Perception and Performance, 7,* 382–387.

Richards, J. E., & Rader, N. (1983). Affective, behavioral, and avoidance responses on the visual cliff: Effect of crawling onset age, crawling experience, and testing age. *Psychophysiology, 20,* 633–642.

Riesen, A. H. (Ed.).(1975). *The developmental neuropsychology of sensory deprivation.* New York: Academic.

Rieser, J. J. (1979). Spatial orientation of 6-month-old infants. *Child Development, 50,* 1078–1087.

Riley, M. S., Greeno, J. G., & Heller, J. I. (1983). Development of children's problem-solving ability in arithmetic. In H. P. Ginsberg (Ed.), *The development of mathematical thinking.* New York: Academic.

Rips, L. J., & Marcus, S. L. (1977). Supposition and the analysis of conditional sentences. In M. A. Just & P. A. Carpenter (Eds.), *Cognitive processes in comprehension.* Hillsdale, NJ: Erlbaum.

Rips, L. J., Shoben, E. J., & Smith, E. E. (1973). Semantic distance and the verification of semantic relations. *Journal of Verbal Learning and Verbal Behavior, 12,* 1–20.

Rogers, B., & Graham, M. (1982). Similarities between motion parallax and stereopsis in human depth perception. *Vision Research, 22,* 261–270.

Rosch, E. (1973). On the internal structure of perceptual and semantic categories. In T. E. Moore (Ed.), *Cognitive development and the acquisition of language.* New York: Academic.

Rosch, E., & Mervis, C. B. (1975). Family resemblances: Studies in the internal structure of categories. *Cognitive Psychology, 7,* 573–605.

Rosch, E., Mervis, C. B., Gray, W. D., Johnson, D. M., & Boyes-Braem, P. (1976). Basic objects in natural categories. *Cognitive Psychology, 8,* 382–439.

Rose, S. A., & Ruff, H. A. (1987). Cross-modal abilities in human infants. In J. D. Osofsky (Ed.), *Handbook of infant development* (pp. 318–362). New York: Wiley.

Rosenthal, T. L., & Zimmerman, B. J. (1978). *Social learning and cognition.* New York: Academic.

Rosenzweig, M. R., & Bennett, E. L. (1978). Experiential influences on brain anatomy and brain chemistry in rodents. In G. Gottlieb (Ed.), *Studies on the developmental of the nervous system* (Vol 4). New York: Academic.

Ross, G. (1980). Categorization in 1- to 2-year-olds. *Developmental Psychology, 16,* 391–396.

Rosser, R. A. (1981). Social learning theory and the development of prosocial behavior: A system for research integration. In R. W. Henderson (Ed.), *Parent-child interaction: Theory, research, and prospects.* New York: Academic.

Rosser, R. A. (1983). The emergence of spatial perspective taking: An information-processing alternative to egocentrism. *Child Development, 54,* 660–668.

Rosser, R. A., & Brody, G. H. (1981). Acquisition of a concrete operational rule through observational learning: How abstract is the acquired abstraction? *Merrill-Palmer Quarterly, 27,* 3–13.

Rosser, R. A., & Chandler, K. (1991). *Children's understanding of constraints on motion: Developmental change in the ability to anticipate object-object contact.* Paper presented at the convention of the Society for Research in Child Development, April 18–20, Seattle, Washington.

Rosser, R. A., & Chandler, K. (1992). *The influence of first principle knowledge on the mechanical intuitions of children and adults.* Paper presented at the 22nd Annual Symposium of the Jean Piaget Society, May 28–30, Montreal, Canada.

Rosser, R. A., Chandler, K., & Lane, S. (in press). Children's computation of viewpoint from locational descriptions: Initial steps in the coordination of perspectives. *Child Study Journal.*

Rosser, R. A., Ensing, S. S., Glider, P. J., & Lane, S. (1984). An information-processing analysis of children's accuracy in predicting the appearance of rotated stimuli. *Child Development, 55,* 2204–2211.

Rosser, R. A., Ensing, S. S., & Mazzeo, J. (1985). The role of stimulus salience in young children's ability to discriminate two-dimensional rotations: Reflections on a paradigm. *Contemporary Educational Psychology, 10,* 95–103.

Rosser, R. A., Ensing, S. S., Mazzeo, J., & Horan, P. (1986). Visual perspective taking in children: Further ramifications of an information-processing model. *Journal of Genetic Psychology, 146,* 379–387.

Rosser, R. A., & Horan, P. F. (1982). Acquisition of multiple classification and seriation from the observation of models: A social learning approach to horizontal decalage. *Child Development, 53,* 1229–1232.

Rosser, R. A., Horan, P. F., Mattson, S. L., & Mazzeo, J. (1984). Comprehension of Euclidean space in young children: The early emergence of understanding and its limits. *Genetic Psychology Monographs, 110,* 21–41.

Rosser, R. A., & Lane, S. (1987). *Developmental evidence for a non-holistic solution strategy on mental rotation problems.* Paper presented at the biennial meeting of the Society for Research in Child Development, Baltimore, MD.

Rosser, R. A., Stevens, S., Glider, P., Mazzeo, J., & Lane, S. (1989). Children's solution strategies and mental rotation: Evidence for a developmental shift. *Genetic, Social, and General Psychology Monographs, 115,* 183–205.

Rothblat, L. A., & Schwartz, M. (1979). The effect of monocular deprivation on dendritic spines in visual cortex of young and adult albino rats: Evidence for a sensitive period. *Brain Research, 161,* 156–161.

Roug, L., Landberg, I., & Lundberg, L. J. (1989). Phonetic development in early infancy: A study of four Swedish children during the first eighteen months of life. *Journal of Child Language, 16,* 19–40.

Rovee-Collier, C. K. (1984). The ontogeny of learning and memory on human infancy. In R. Kail & N. E. Spear (Eds.), *Comparative perspectives on the development of memory.* Hillsdale, NJ: Erlbaum.

Rovee-Collier, C. K. (1990). The "memory system" of prelinguistic infants. In A. Diamond (Ed.), *The development and neural bases of higher cognitive functions.* New York: The New York Academy of Sciences.

Rovee-Collier, C. K., & Fagen, J. W. (1981). The retrieval of memory in early infancy. In L. P. Lipsitt (Ed.), *Advances in infancy research* (Vol. 1). Norwood, NJ: Ablex.

Rovee-Collier, C. K., & Gekoski, M. J. (1979). The economics of infancy: A review of conjugate reinforcement. In H. W. reese & L. P. Lipsitt (Eds.), *Advances in child development and behavior* (Vol 13). New York: Academic.

Rovee-Collier, C. K., & Hayne, H. (1987). Reactivation of infant memory: Implications for cognitive development. In H. W. Reese (Ed.), *Advances in child development and behavior, Vol. 20.* 185–219. New York: Academic Press.

Rovee-Collier, C. K., & Sullivan, M. W. (1980). Organization of infant memory. *Journal of Experimental Psychology: Human Learning and Memory, 6,* 798–807.

Rovee-Collier, C. K., Sullivan, M. W., Enright, M., Lucas, D., & Fagen, J. (1980). Reactivation of infant memory. *Science, 208,* 1159–1161.

Rozin, P. (1976). The evolution of intelligence and access to the cognitive unconscious. In J. M. Sprague & A. A. Epstein (Eds.), *Progress in psychology and physiological psychology.* New York: Academic.

Rudy, J. W., & Paylor, R. (1988). Reducing the temporal demands of the Morris Place Learning task fails to ameliorate place-learning impairment of preweanling rats. *Psychobiology, 16,* 152–156.

Rudy, J. W., Stadler-Morris, S., & Albert, P. (1987). Ontogeny of spatial navigation behaviors in the rat: Dissociation of "proximal" and "distal" cue-based behaviors. *Behavioral Neuroscience, 101,* 62–73.

Sachs, J. (1985). Prelinguistic development. In J. Berko Gleason (Ed.), *The development of language.* Columbus, OH: Merrill.

Salapatek, P. (1975). Pattern perception in early infancy. In L. B. Cohen & P. Salapatek (Eds.), *Infant perception: From sensation to cognition* (Vol. 1). New York: Academic.

Salapatek, P., & Cohen, L. (1987). *Handbook of perception* (Vol. 2). New York: Academic.

Salatas, H., & Flavell, J. H. (1987). Perspective-taking: The development of two components of knowledge. *Child Development, 47,* 103–109.

Saxe, G. B., Guberman, S. R., & Gearhart, M. (1988). Social processes in early development. *Monographs of the Society for Research in Child Development, 52.* (Serial No. 216).

Saxe, G. B., & Posner, J. K. (1983). The development of numerical cognition: Cross cultural perspectives. In H. P. Ginsberg (Ed.), *The development of mathematical thinking.* New York: Academic.

Scarborough, H., & Wyckoff, J. (1986). Mother, I'd still rather do it myself: Some further non-effects of "motherese." *Journal of Child Language, 13,* 431–437.

Scardamalia, M. (1977). Information processing capacity and the problem of horizontal decalage: A demonstration using combinatorial reasoning tasks. *Child Development, 48,* 28–37.

Scarr, S., & McCartney, K. (1983). How people make their own environments: A theory of genotype environment effects. *Child Development, 54,* 424–435.

Schacter, D. L. (1987). Implicit memory: History and current status. *Journal of Experimental Psychology: Learning, Memory, and Cognition, 13,* 501–518.

Schacter, D. L., & Moscovitch, M. (1983). Infants, amnesics, and dissociable memory systems. In M. Moscovitch (Ed.), *Infant memory: Its relation to normal and pathological memory in humans and other animals* (pp. 173–216). New York: Plenum.

Schacter, D. L., & Moscovitch, M. (1984). Infants, amnesics, and dissociable memory systems. In M. Moscovitch (Ed.), *Advances in the study of communication and affect: Vol. 9. Infant memory.* New York: Plenum.

Schacter, D. L., Moscovitch, M., Tulving, E., McLachlan, D. R., & Freedman, M. (1986). Mnemonic precedence in amnesic patients: An analogue of the A$\overline{B}$ error in infants? *Child Development, 57,* 816–823.

Schiff, W. (1965). Perception of impending collision: A study of visually directed avoidant behavior. *Psychological Monographs, 79* (Whole No. 604).

Schmidt, H., & Spelke, E. S. (1984). *Gestalt relations and object perception in infancy.* Paper presented at the International Conference on Infant Studies, New York.

Schneider, W., Korkel, J., & Weinert, F. E. (1987). *The knowledge base and memory performance: A comparison of academically successful and unsuccessful learners.* Paper presented at the American Educational Research Association, Washington, DC.

Schneider, W., & Pressley, M. (1989). *Memory development between 2 and 20.* New York: Springer–Verlag.

Scholnick, E. K. (1990). Three faces of if. In W. F. Overton (Ed.), *Reasoning, logic and necessity* (pp. 159–182). Hillsdale, NJ: Erlbaum.

Schwartz, M., & Day, R. H. (1979). Visual shape perception in early infancy. *Monographs of the society for research in child development, 44* (Serial No. 182).

Schwartz, S. P. (1977). Introduction. In S. P. Schwartz (Ed.), *Naming, necessity, and natural kinds.* Ithaca, NY: Cornell University Press.

Schwartz, S. P. (1979). Natural kind terms. *Cognition, 7,* 301–315, 382–439.

Seibt, U. (1988). Are animals naturally attuned to number? *Behavioral and Brain Sciences, 11,* 597–598.

Seress, L. (1991). *Granule cells in primate dentate gyrus and their development.* Paper presented at The Dentate Gyrus and Its Role in Seizures: An International Symposium, Irvine, CA.

Shantz, C. U. (1975). The development of social cognition. In E. M. Hetherington (Ed.), *Review of child development research* (Vol. 5). Chicago: University of Chicago Press.

Shantz, C. U. (1983). Social cognition. In J. H. Flavell & Markman, E. M. (Eds.), *The Handbook of Child Psychology: Vol. III. Cognitive Development.* New York: Wiley.

Shantz, C. U., & Watson, J. (1970). Assessment of spatial egocentrism through expectancy violation. *Psychonomic Science, 18,* 93–94.

Shatz, M., Wellman, H. M., & Silber, S. (1983). The acquisition of mental verbs: A systematic investigation of the first reference to mental state. *Cognition, 14,* 301–321.

Shepard, R. N. (1981). Psychophysical complementarily. In M. Kubovy & J. R. Pamerantz (Eds.), *Perceptual organization* (pp. 279–341). Hillsdale, NJ: Erlbaum.

Shepard, R. N. (1984). Ecological constraints on internal representation: Resonant kinematics of perceiving, imaging, thinking, and dreaming. *Psychological Review, 91,* 417–447.

Shepard, R. N. (1988). The role of transformations in spatial cognition. In J. Stiles-Davis, M. Kritchevsky, & U. Bellugi (Eds.), *Spatial cognition: Brain bases and development* (pp. 81–110). Hillsdale, NJ: Erlbaum.

Shepard, R. N., & Cooper, L. A. (1986). *Mental images and their transformation.* Cambridge, MA: MIT Press.

Shepard, R. N., & Metzler, J. (1971). Mental rotation of three-dimensional objects. *Science, 171,* 701–703.

Shepp, B. (1978). From perceived similarity to dimensional structure: A new hypothesis about perceptual development. In E. Rosch & E. B. Lloyds (Eds.), *On the nature and principle of formation of categories.* Hillsdale, NJ: Erlbaum.

Shipley, E. F., & Shepperson, B. (1990). Countable entities: Developmental changes. *Cognition, 34,* 109–136.

Shopen, T. (1985). *Language typology and syntactic descriptions: Vol 2. Complex constructions.* New York: Cambridge University Press.

Shriberg, L. K., Levin, J. R., McCormick, C. B., & Pressley, M. (1982). Learning about "famous" people via the keyword method. *Journal of Educational Psychology, 74,* 238–247.

Shultz, T. R. (1982). Rules of causal attribution. *Monographs of the Society for Research in Child Development* (Serial No. 194).

Siegel, L. S. (1972). The development of the concept of seriation. *Developmental Psychology, 6,* 135–137.

Siegel, L. S. (1978). The relationship of language and thought in the preoperational child: A reconsideration of nonverbal alternatives to Piagetian tasks. In L. S. Siegel & C. J. Brainerd (Eds.), *Alternatives to Piaget: Critical essays on the theory.* New York: Academic.

Siegel, L. S., & Brainerd, C. J. (1978). *Alternatives to Piaget: Critical essays on the theory*. New York: Academic.

Siegler, R. S. (1978). The origins of scientific reasoning. In R. S. Siegler (Ed.), *Children's thinking: what develops?* Hillsdale, NJ: Erlbaum.

Siegler, R. S. (1979). What young children do know. *Contemporary Psychology, 24,* 613–615.

Siegler, R. S. (1981). Developmental sequences within and between concepts. *Monographs of the Society for Research in Child Development, 46,* (Whole No. 189).

Siegler, R. S. (1983). Five generalizations about cognitive development. *American Psychologist, 38,* 263–277.

Siegler, R. S., (1984). Mechanisms of cognitive growth: Variation and selection. In R. J. Sternberg, (Ed.), *Mechanisms of cognitive development*. New York: Freeman.

Siegler, R. S. (1986a). *Children's thinking*. Englewood Cliffs, NJ: Prentice Hall.

Siegler, R. S. (1986b). Unities across domains in children's strategy choices. In M. Perlmutter (Ed.), *Minnesota symposium on child development, Vol. 19*. Hillsdale, NJ: Erlbaum.

Siegler, R. S. (1988). Individual differences in strategy choices: Good students, not-so-good students, and perfectionists. *Child Development, 59,* 833–851.

Siegler, R. S. (1989). How domain-general and domain-specific knowledge interact to produce strategy choices. *Merrill-Palmer Quarterly, 35,* 1–26.

Siegler, R. S. (1991). *Children's thinking*. Englewood Cliffs, NJ: Prentice Hall.

Siegler, R. S., & Jenkins, E. (1989). *How children discover new strategies*. Hillsdale, NJ: Erlbaum.

Siegler, R. S., & Robinson, M. (1982). The development of numerical understandings. In H. W. Reese & L. P. Lipsitt (Eds.), *Advances in child development and behavior*. New York: Academic.

Siegler, R. S., & Shipley, C. (1987). The role of learning in children's strategy choices. In L. S. Liben (Ed.), *Development and learning: Conflict or congruence?* Hillsdale, NJ: Erlbaum.

Siegler, R. S., & Shrager, J. (1984). Strategy choices in addition and subtraction: How do children know what to do? In C. Sophian (Ed.), *Origins of cognitive skills*. Hillsdale, NJ: Erlbaum.

Simon, H. A. (1975). The functional equivalence of problem-solving skills. *Cognitive Psychology, 7,* 268–288.

Skinner, B. F. (1938). *The behavior of organisms: An experimental analysis*. New York: Appleton-Century-Crofts.

Skinner, B. F. (1957). *Verbal behavior*. New York: Appleton-Century-Crofts.

Slater, A., Morison, V., & Rose, D. (1982). Visual memory at birth. *British Journal of Psychology, 73,* 519–525.

Slater, A., Morison, V., & Rose, D. (1983). Perception of shape by the newborn baby. *British Journal of Psychology, 1,* 135–142.

Slater, A., Morison, V., & Rose, D. (1984). Habituation in the newborn. *Infant Behavior and Development, 1,* 183–200.

Slater, A., & Sykes, M. (1977). Newborn infants' visual responses to square wave gratings. *Child Development, 48,* 545–554.

Smiley, S. S., & Brown, A. L. (1979). Conceptual preference for thematic or taxonomic relations: A nonmonotonic age trend from preschool to old age. *Journal of Experimental Child Psychology, 28,* 249–257.

Smith, C., Carey, S., & Wiser, M. (1985). On differentiation: A case study of the development of the concepts of size, weight, and density. *Cognition, 21,* 177–238.

Smith, E. E., & Medin, D. L. (1981). *Categories and concepts*. Cambridge, MA: Harvard University Press.

Smith, J. D., & Kemler-Nelson, D. G. (1984). Overall similarity in adult's classification: The child in all of us. *Journal of Experimental Psychology: General, 113,* 137–159.

Smith, L. B. (1979). Perceptual development and category generalization. *Child Development, 10,* 705–715.

Smith, L. B. (1981). The importance of overall similarity of objects for adults' and children's classifications. *Journal of Experimental Psychology: Human Perception and Performance, 1,* 811–824.

Smith, L. B. (1985). Young children's attention to global magnitude: Evidence from classification tasks. *Journal of Experimental Child Psychology, 39,* 472–491.

Smith, L. B. (1989). A model of perceptual classification in children and adults. *Psychological Review, 96*(1), 125–144.

Smith, L. B., & Kemler, D. G. (1977). Developmental trends in free classification: Evidence for a new conceptualization of perceptual development. *Journal of Experimental Child Psychology, 24,* 279–298.

Smith, L. B., & Rizzo, T. A. (1982). Children's understanding of the referential properties of collective and class nouns. *Child Development, 53,* 245–257.

Snow, C. E. (1983). Saying it again: The role of expanded and deferred imitations in language acquisition. In K. E. Nelson (Ed.), *Children's language* (Vol. 4). Hillsdale, NJ: Erlbaum.

Snow, C. E., & Ferguson, C. (1977). *Talking to children: Language input and acquisition.* Cambridge, England: Cambridge University Press.

Soja, N., Carey, S., & Spelke, E. S. (1991). Ontological categories guide children's inductions of word meaning: Object terms and substance terms. *Cognition, 38,* 179–211.

Somerville, S. C., & Haake, R. J. (1983). *Selective search skills of infants and young children.* Paper presented at the Society for Research in Child Development meeting, Detroit, MI.

Somerville, S. C., Wellman, H. M., & Cultice, J. C. (1983). Young children's deliberate reminding. *Journal of Genetic Psychology, 143,* 87–96.

Sommers, F. (1959). The ordinary language tree. *Mind, 68,* 160–185.

Sommers, F. (1963). Types and ontology. *Philosophical Review, 72,* 327–363.

Sommers, F. (1965). Predicability. In M. Black (Ed.), *Philosophy in America.* Ithaca, NY: Cornell University Press.

Sommers, F. (1971). Structural ontology. *Philosophia, 1,* 21–42.

Sophian, C. (1984a). *Origins of cognitive skills.* Hillsdale, NJ: Erlbaum.

Sophian, C. (1984b). Spatial transpositions and the early development of search. *Developmental Psychology, 35,* 369–390.

Sophian, C. (1987). Early developments in children's use of counting to solve quantitative problems. *Cognition and Instruction, 4,* 61–90.

Sophian, C. (1988). Limitations on preschool children's knowledge about counting: Using counting to compare two sets. *Developmental Psychology, 24,* 634–640.

Sophian, C., Larkin, J. H., & Kadane, J. B. (1985). A developmental model of search: Stochastic estimation of children's rule use. In H. M. Wellman (Ed.), *Children's searching,* (pp. 185–214). Hillsdale, NJ: Erlbaum.

Sophian, C., & Sage, S. (1983). Developments in infants' search for displaced objects. *Journal of Experimental Child Psychology, 35,* 143–160.

Spear, N. E. (1978). *The processing of memories: Forgetting and retention.* Hillsdale, NJ: Erlbaum.

Spelke, E. S. (1985). Perception of unity, persistence, and identity: Thoughts on infants' conceptions of objects. In J. Mehler & R. Fox (Eds.), *Neonate cognition* (pp. 89–113). Hillsdale, NJ: Erlbaum.

Spelke, E. S. (1987). The development of intermodal perception. In Salapatek, P. & Cohen, L. (Eds.), *Handbook of infant perception,* (Vol. 2, pp. 233–273). New York: Academic.

Spelke, E. S. (1988a). Where perceiving ends and thinking begins: The apprehension of objects in infancy. In A. Yonas (Ed.), *Perceptual development in infancy: Minnesota symposium on child development,* (Vol.20, pp. 197–234). Hillsdale, NJ: Erlbaum.

Spelke, E. S. (1988b). The origins of physical knowledge. In L. Weiskrantz (Ed.), *Thought without language.* Oxford, England: Clarendon Press.

Spelke, E. S. (1989). Early cognitive functioning. In C. von Euler (Ed.), *Neurobiology of early infant behavior.* London: Macmillan Press.

Spelke, E. S. (1990). Principles of object perception. *Cognitive Science, 14,* 29–56.

Spelke, E. S. (1991). Physical knowledge in infancy: Reflections on Piaget's theory. In S. Carey & R. Gelman (Eds.), *The epigenesis of mind: Essays on biology and cognition.* Hillsdale, NJ: Erlbaum.

Springer, K. (1990). In defense of theories. *Cognition, 35,* 293–298.

Springer, K., & Keil, F. C. (1989). On the development of biologically specific beliefs: The case of inheritance. *Child Development, 60,* 637–648.

Springer, K., & Keil, F. C. (1991). Early differentiation of causal mechanisms appropriate to biological and non-biological kind. *Child Development, 62,* 767–781.

Squire, L. R. (1986). Mechanisms of memory. *Science, 232,* 1612–1619.

Squire, L. R. (1987). *Memory and brain.* New York: Oxford University Press.

Squire, L. R., Cohen, N. J., & Nadel, L. (1984). The medial temporal region and memory consolidation. In L. Weiskranz & E. Parker (Eds.), *Memory consolidation.* Hillsdale, NJ: Erlbaum.

Stark, R. E. (1986). Prespeech segmental feature development. In P. Fletcher & M. Garman (Eds.), *Language acquisition: Studies in first language development* (2nd ed.). New York: Cambridge University Press.

Starkey, P., & Cooper, R. S. (1980). Perception of numbers by human infants. *Science, 210,* 1033–1035.

Starkey, P., Spelke, E., & Gelman, R. (1983). Detection of intermodal numerical correspondences by human infants. *Science, 222,* 179.

Starkey, P., Spelke, E., & Gelman, R. (1990). Numerical abstraction by human infants. *Cognition, 36,* 97–127.

Staudenmayer, H. (1975). Understanding conditional reasoning with meaningful propositions. In R. J. Falmagne (Ed.), *Reasoning: Representation and process* (pp. 55–79). Hillsdale, NJ: Erlbaum.

Stephens, B. R., & Banks, M. S. (1985). The development of contrast constancy. *Journal of Experimental Child Psychology, 40,* 528–547.

Stephens, B. R., & Banks, M. S. (1987). Contrast discrimination in human infants. *Journal of Experimental Psychology: Human Perception and Performance, 13*(4), 558–565.

Steri, A. S., & Pecheux, M. G. (1986). Tactual habituation and discrimination of form in infancy: A comparison with vision. *Child Development, 57,* 100–104.

Steri, A. S., & Spelke (1988). Haptic perception of objects in infancy. *Cognitive Psychology, 20*(1), 1–23.

Sternberg, R. J. (1977). Component processes in analogical reasoning. *Psychological Review, 84,* 353–378.

Sternberg, R. J. (1980). Capacity of young children. *Science, 208,* 47–48.

Sternberg, R. J. (1982). Natural, unnatural, and supernatural concepts. *Cognitive Psychology, 14,* 451–488.

Sternberg, R. J. (1984). Mechanisms of cognitive development: A componential approach. In R. J. Sternberg, (Ed.), *Mechanisms of cognitive development.* New York: Freeman.

Sternberg, R. J. (1985). What is an information-processing approach to human abilities? In R. J. Sternberg (Ed.), *Human abilities: An information-processing approach* (pp. 1–5). New York: Freeman.

Sternberg, R. J. (1989). Domain-generality versus domain-specificity: The life and impending death of a false dichotomy. *Merrill-Palmer Quarterly, 35,* 115–129.

Sternberg, R. J., & Nigro, G. (1980). Developmental patterns in the solution of verbal analogies. *Child Development, 51,* 27–38.

Sternberg, R. J., & Powell, J. S. (1983). Comprehending verbal comprehension. *American Psychologist, 38,* 878–893.

Sternberg, R. J., & Rifkin, B. (1979). The development of analogical reasoning processes. *Journal of Experimental Child Psychology, 27,* 195–232.

Sternberg, R. J., & Salter, W. (1984). Conceptions of intelligence. In R. J. Sternberg (Ed.), *Handbook of human intelligence* (pp. 3–20). New York: Cambridge University Press.

Stevens, S. S. (1951). Mathematics, measurement, and psychophysics. In S. S. Stevens (Ed.), *Handbook of experimental psychology.* New York: Wiley.

Stich, S. (1983). *From folk psychology to cognitive science.* Cambridge, MA: Bradford Books/MIT Press.

Stigler, J. W., Nusbaum, H. C., & Chalip, L. (1988). Developmental changes in speed of processing: Central limiting mechanism or skill transfer? *Child Development, 59, 1144*–1153.

Stiles-Davis, J. (1988). Developmental change in young children's spatial grouping activity. *Developmental Psychology, 24,* 522–531.

Stoel-Gammon, C., & Otomo, K. (1986). Babbling development of hearing-impaired and normally hearing subjects. *Journal of Speech and Hearing Disorders, 51,* 33–41.

Strauss, M. S., & Curtis, L. E. (1981a). *Infant perception of patterns differing in goodness of form.* Paper presented at the meeting of the Society for Research in Child Development, Boston, MA.

Strauss, M. S., & Curtis, L. E. (1981b). Infants' perception of numerosity. *Child Development, 52,* 1146–1152.

Strauss, M. S., & Curtis, L. E. (1984). Development of numerical concepts in infancy. In C. Sophian (Ed.), *Origins of cognitive skills.* Hillsdale, NJ: Erlbaum.

Sullivan, M. W., Rovee-Collier, C. K., & Tynes, D. M. (1979). A conditioning analysis of infant long–term memory. *Child Development, 50,* 152–162.

Sutherland, R. J., & Dyck, R. H. (1984). Place navigation by rats in a swimming pool. *Canadian Journal of Psychology, 38,* 322–347.

Sutherland, R. J., Kolb, B. A., & Whishaw, I. Q. (1982). Spatial mapping: Definitive disruption by hippocampal or medial frontal cortex damage in the rat. *Neuroscience Letters, 31,* 271–276.

Sutherland, R. J., & Rudy, J. W. (1989). Configural association theory: The role of the hippocampal formation in learning, memory, and amnesia. *Psychobiology, 17,* 129–177.

Sutherland, R. J., Whishaw, I. Q., & Regehr, J. C. (1982). Cholinergic receptor blockage impairs spatial localization following electrolytic, kainate-, or colchicine-induced damage to the hippocampal formation in the rat. *Behavioral Brain Research, 7,* 133–153.

Swanson, R. A., Henderson, R. W., & Williams, E. (1979). The relative influence of observation, imitative motor activity, and feedback on the induction of seriation. *Journal of Genetic Psychology, 135,* 81–91.

Swarner, J. C. (1988). *Ordinal size scaling in preschool children.* Unpublished doctoral dissertation, University of Arizona, Tuscon.

Tager-Flusberg, H. (1989). Putting words together: Morphology and syntax in the preschool years. In J. Berko Gleason (Ed.), *The development of language.* Columbus, OH: Merrill.

Taplin, J. E. (1971). Reasoning with conditional sentences. *Journal of Verbal Learning and Verbal Behavior, 10,* 218–225.

Taplin, J. E., & Staudenmayer, H. (1973). Interpretation of abstract conditional sentences in deductive reasoning. *Journal of Verbal Learning and Verbal Behavior, 12,* 530–541.

Taylor, M., & Gelman, S. (1988). Adjectives and nouns: Children's strategies for learning new words. *Child Development, 59,* 411–419.

Taylor, M., & Gelman, S. (1989). Incorporating new words in the lexicon: Preliminary evidence for language hierarchies in two-year-old children. *Child Development, 60,* 625–636.

Tees, R. C. (1979). The effects of visual deprivation on pattern recognition in the rat. *Developmental Psychobiology, 12,* 485–497.

Tees, R. C., & Cartwright, J. (1972). Sensory preconditioning in rats following early visual deprivation. *Journal of Comparative and Physiological Psychology, 81,* 12–20.

Tees, R. C., Midgely, G., & Nesbit, J. C. (1982). The effect of early visual experience on spatial maze learning in rats. *Developmental Psychobiology, 14,* 425–438.

Teller, D. Y. (1979). A forced-choice preferential looking procedure: A psychophysical technique for use with human infants. *Infant Behavior and Development, 2,* 135–153.

Templin, M. (1957). *Certain language skills in children: Their development and interrelationship.* Institute of Child Welfare Monograph 26. Minneapolis: University of Minnesota Press.

Termine, N., Hrynick, T., Kestenbaum, R., Gleitman, H., & Spelke, E. S. (1987). Perceptual completion of surfaces in infancy. *Journal of Experimental Psychology: Human Perception and Performance, 13,* 524–532.

Teyler, T. J. (1986). Memory: Electrophysiological analogs. In J. L. Martinez & R. P. Kesner (Eds.), *Learning and memory: A biological view.* New York: Academic.

Thayer, E. S., & Collyer, C. E. (1978). The development of transitive inference. *Psychological Bulletin, 85,* 1327–1343.

Thomas, D. G., Campos, J. J., Shucard, D. W., Ramsay, D. S., & Shucard, J. (1981). Semantic comprehension in infancy: A signal detection analysis. *Child Development, 52,* 798–803.

Thompson, R. F. (1986). The neurobiology of learning and memory. *Science, 233,* 941–947.

Thurstone, L. L. (1938). *Primary mental abilities.* Chicago: University of Chicago Press.

Tieman, S. B., & Hirsch, H. (1982). Exposure to lines of only one orientation modifies dendritic morphology of cells in the visual cortex of the cat. *Journal of Comparative Neurology, 211,* 353–362.

Timney, B., Mitchell, D. E., & Cynader, M. (1980). Behavioral evidence for prolonged sensitivity to effects of monocular deprivation in dark-reared cats. *Journal of Neurophysiology, 43,* 1041–1054.

Tolman, E. C. (1948). Cognitive maps in rats and men. *Psychological Review, 55,* 189–208.

Trabasso, T. (1975). Representation, memory, and reasoning: How do we make transitive inferences? In A. D. Pick (Ed.), *Minnesota symposia on child psychology* (Vol. 9). Minneapolis: University of Minnesota Press.

Trabasso, T. (1977). The role of memory as a system in making transitive inferences. In R. V. Kail & J. W. Hagen (Eds.), *Perspectives on the development of memory and cognition.* Hillsdale, NJ: Erlbaum.

Trabasso, T. (1978). On the estimation of parameters and the evaluation of a mathematical model: A reply to Pascual-Leone. *Journal of Experimental Child Psychology, 26,* 41–45.

Trabasso, T., & Foellinger, D. B. (1978). Information processing capacity in children: A test of Pascual-Leone's model. *Journal of Experimental Child Psychology, 26,* 1–17.

Trehub, S. E. (1976). The discrimination of foreign speech contrasts by infants and adults. *Child Development, 47,* 466–472.

Trehub, S. E., Bull, D., & Thorpe, L. A. (1984). Infants' perception of melodies: The role of melodic contour. *Child Development, 55,* 821–830.

Tulving, E. (1972). Episodic and semantic memory. In E. Tulving & W. Donaldson (Eds.), *Organization of memory.* New York: Academic.

Tulving, E. (1984). Relations among components and processes of memory. *Behavioral and Brain Sciences, 7,* 257–268.

Tulving, E., & Donaldson, W. (1972). *Organization of Memory.* New York: Academic.

Tulving, E., & Schacter, D. (1990). Priming and human memory systems. *Science, 247,* 301–306.

Turner, A. M., & Greenough, W. T. (1985). Differential rearing effects on rat visual cortex synapses. I. Synaptic and neuronal density and synapses per neuron. *Brain Research, 329,* 195–203.

Tversky, A. (1977). Features of similarity. *Psychological Review, 84,* 327–352.

Tversky, B., & Hemenway, K. (1984). Objects, parts, and categories. *Journal of Experimental Psychology: General, 113,* 169–193.

Urberg, K. A., & Docherty, E. M. (1976). Development of role-taking skills in young children. *Developmental Psychology, 12,* 198–204.

Uzgiris, I. C., & Hunt, J. McV. (1970). *Assessment in infancy: Ordinal scales of psychological development.* Urbana, IL: University of Illinois Press.

Valian, V. (1986). Syntactic categories in the speech of young children. *Developmental Psychology, 22,* 562–579.

Vander Linde, E., Morrongiello, B. A., & Rovee-Collier, C. (1985). Determinants of retention in 8-week-old infants. *Developmental Psychology, 21,* 601–613.

Van Giffen, K., & Haith, M. H. (1984). Infant visual response to Gestalt geometric forms. *Infant Behavior and Development, 7,* 335–346.

Vera, A., & Keil, F. C. (1988). *The development of induction about biological kinds: The nature of the conceptual base.* Paper presented at the 1988 meeting of the Psychonomics Society, Chicago, IL.

Vihman, M. M., & Miller, R. (1988). Words and babble at the threshold of language acquisition. In M. D. Smith & J. L. Locke (Eds.), *The emergent lexicon.* Orlando, FL: Academic.

Volkman, F. C., & Dobson, M. V. (1976). Infant responses to ocular fixation to moving visual stimuli. *Journal of Experimental Child Psychology, 22,* 86–99.

von Glasersfeld, E. (1982). Subitizing: The role of figural patterns in the development of numerical concepts. *Archives de Psychologie, 50,* 191–218.

Voneche, J. (1980). Introduction. *Cashiers de la Foundation Archives Jean Piaget, No. 1,* 1–2.

Vosniadou, S. (1989). Analogical reasoning as a mechanism in knowledge acquisition: A developmental perspective. In S. Vosniadou & A. Ortony (Eds.), *Similarity and analogical reasoning* (pp. 413–437). Cambridge, MA: Cambridge University Press.

Vygotsky, L. S. (1962). *Thought and language.* Cambridge, MA: MIT Press.

Vygotsky, L. S. (1986). *Thought and language.* Cambridge, MA: MIT Press.

Walk, R. D. (1966). The development of depth perception in animals and human infants. *Monographs of the Society for Research in Child Development, 31,* (5, Serial No. 107).

Walk, R. D., & Gibson, E. J. (1961). A comparative and analytical study of visual depth perception. *Psychological Monographs, 75* (15, Whole No. 519).

Walk, R. D., & Walters, C. P. (1973). Effects of visual deprivation on depth discrimination of hooded rats. *Journal of Comparative and Physiological Psychology, 85,* 559–563.

Walker, D., Grimwade, J., & Wood, C. (1971). Intrauterine noise: A component of the fetal environment. *American Journal of Obstetrics and Gynecology, 109,* 91–95.

Warrington, E., & Weiskranz, L. (1982). Amnesia: A disconnection syndrome? *Neuropsychologia, 20,* 233–248.

Wason, P. C. (1983). Realism and rationality in the selection task. In J. St. B. T. Evans (Ed.), *Thinking and reasoning: Psychological approaches* (pp. 44–75). London: Routledge & Kegan Paul.

Wason, P. C., & Johnson-Laird, P. N. (1972). *Psychology of reasoning: Structure and content.* London: B. T. Batsford.

Waxman, S. (1990). Linguistic biases and the establishment of conceptual hierarchies: Evidence from preschool children. *Cognitive Development, 5,* 123–150.

Waxman, S., & Gelman, R. (1986). Preschoolers' use of superordinate relations in classification and language. *Cognitive Development, 1,* 139–156.

Waxman, S. R., & Kosowski, T. D. (1990). Nouns mark category relations: Toddlers' and preschoolers' word-learning biases. *Child Development, 61,* 1461–1473.

Waxman, S. R., Shipley, E. F., & Shepperson, B. (1991). Establishing new subcategories: The role of categories labels and existing knowledge. *Child Development, 62,* 127–138.

Weinert, F. E., & Perlmutter, M. (Eds.). (1988). *Memory development: Universal changes and individual differences.* Hillsdale, NJ: Erlbaum.

Wellman, H. M. (1977). Preschooler's understanding of memory-relevant variables. *Child Development, 48,* 1720–1723.

Wellman, H. M. (1985a). A child's theory of mind: The development of conceptions of cognition. In S. R. Yussen (Ed.), *The growth of reflection in children.* New York: Academic.

Wellman, H. M. (Ed.) (1985b). *Children's searching: The development of search skill and spatial representation.* Hillsdale, NJ: Erlbaum.

Wellman, H. M. (1988a). First steps in the child's theorizing about the mind. In J. Astington, P. Harris, & D. Olson (Eds.), *Developing theories of mind.* New York: Cambridge University Press.

Wellman, H. M. (1988b). The early development of memory strategies. In F. Weinert & M. Perlmutter (Eds.), *Memory development: Universal changes and individual differences.* Hillsdale, NJ: Erlbaum.

Wellman, H. M. (1990). *The child's theory of mind.* Cambridge, MA: Bradford Books/MIT Press.

Wellman, H. M., & Bartsch, K. (1988). Young children's reasoning about beliefs. *Cognition, 30,* 239–277.

Wellman H. M., & Bartsch, K. (1989). Three-year-olds understand belief: A reply to Perner. *Cognition, 33,* 321–326.

Wellman, H. M., Collins, J., & Glieberman, J. (1981). Understanding the combination of memory variables: Developing conceptions of memory limitations. *Child Development, 52,* 1313–1317.

Wellman, H. M., Cross, D., & Bartsch, K. (1987). Infant search and object permanence: A meta-analysis of the A-not-B error. *Monographs of the Society for Research in Child Development, 51*(3).

Wellman, H. M., & Estes, D., (1986). Early understanding of mental entities: A reexamination of childhood realism. *Child Development, 57,* 910–923.

Wellman, H. M., & Estes, D. (1987). Children's early use of mental terms and what they mean. *Discourse Processes, 10,* 141–156.

Wellman, H. M., & Gelman, S. A. (1988). Children's understanding of the nonobvious. In R. J. Sternberg (Ed.), *Advances in the Psychology of Human Intelligence* (Vol. 4). Hillsdale, NJ: Erlbaum.

Wellman, H. M., & Johnson, C. N. (1979). Understanding mental processes: A developmental study of *remember* and *forget. Child Development, 50,* 79–88.

Wellman, H. M., Ritter, K., & Flavell, J. H. (1975). Deliberate memory behavior in the delayed reactions of very young children. *Developmental Psychology, 11,* 780–787.

Wellman, H. M., & Woolley, J. D. (in press). From simple desires to ordinary beliefs: The early development of everyday psychology. *Cognition.*

Werker, J. F., Gilbert, J. H. V., Humphrey, K., & Tees, R. C. (1981). Developmental aspects of cross-language speech perception. *Child Development, 52,* 349–355.

Werker, J. F., & McLeod, P. J. (1989). Infant preference for both male and female infant-directed talk: A developmental study of attention and affective responsiveness. *Canadian Journal of Psychology, 43,* 230–246.

Werker, J. F., & Tees, R. C. (1984). Cross-language speech perception: Evidence for perceptual reorganization during the first year of life. *Infant Behavior and Development, 7,* 49–63.

Werner, H. (1948). *Comparative psychology of mental development.* New York: International Universities Press.

Werner, H. (1957). The concept of development from a comparative and organismic point of view. In D. B. Harris (Ed.), *The concept of development.* Minneapolis: University of Minnesota Press.

Werner, J. S., & Siqueland, E. R. (1978). Visual recognition memory in the preterm infant. *Infant Behavior and Development, 1,* 79–94.

Wexler, K., & Culicover, P. W. (1980). *Formal principles of language acquisition.* Cambridge, MA: MIT Press.

White, B. Y. (1983). Sources of difficulty in understanding Newtonian dynamics. *Cognitive Science, 7,* 41-65.

White, B. Y., & Fredericksen, J. R. (1986, March). *Qualitative models and intelligent learning environments* (Tech. Rep.). BBN Laboratories.

White, S. H. (1968). The learning-maturation controversy: Hall to Hull. *Merrill-Palmer Quarterly, 14,* 187–196.

Whitehurst, G. J. (1982). Language development. In B. B. Wolman (Ed.), *Handbook of developmental psychology.* New York: Wiley.

Whitehurst, G. J., & DeBaryshe, B. D. (1989). Observational learning and language acquisition: Principles of learning, systems, and tasks. In G. E. Speidel & K. E. Nelson (Eds.), *The many faces of imitation in language learning.* New York: Springer-Verlag.

Whitehurst, G. J., & Novak, G. (1973). Modeling, imitation training, and the acquisition of sentence phrases. *Journal of Experimental Child Psychology, 16,* 332–345.

Whitehurst, G. J., & Vasta, R. (1975). Is language acquired through imitation? *Journal of Psycholinguistic Research, 4,* 37–59.

Wiesel, T. N., & Hubel, D. H. (1963). Single-cell responses in striate cortex of kittens deprived of vision in one eye. *Journal of Neurophysiology, 26,* 1003–1017.

Wimmer, H., & Perner, J. (1983). Beliefs about beliefs: Representation and constraining function of wrong beliefs in young children's understanding of deception. *Cognition, 13,* 102–128.

Winestock, S. I., & Bilaystok, E. (1989) *Reconstruction of abstract shapes.* Paper presented at the biennial meeting of the Society for Research in Child Development, Kansas City, MO.

Wishart, J. D., & Bower, T. G. R. (1982). The development of spatial understanding in infancy. *Journal of Experimental Child Psychology, 33,* 363–385.

Wohlwill, J. F. (1973). *The study of behavioral development.* New York: Academic.

Wohlwill, J. F. (1980). Cognitive development in childhood. In O. G. Brim & J. Kagan (Eds.), *Constancy and change in human development* (pp. 359–444). Cambridge, MA: Harvard University Press.

Wood, C. C. (1976). Discriminability, response bias, and phoneme categories in discrimination of voice onset time. *Journal of the Acoustical Society of America, 60,* 1381–1389.

Woodward, A. L., & Markman, E. M. (1991). Constraints on learning as default assumptions: Comments on Merriman and Bowerman's "The mutual exclusivity bias in children's word learning." *Developmental Review, 11,* 137–163.

Woodworth, R. S., & Schlosberg, H. (1954). *Experimental Psychology.* New York: Holt.

Woolley, J. D., & Wellman, H. M. (1990). Young children's understanding of realities, nonrealities, and appearances. *Child Development, 61,* 946–961.

Wynn, K. (1990). Children's understanding of counting. *Cognition, 36,* 104–143.

Wynn, K. (in press a). Children's acquisition of the number words and the counting system. *Cognitive Psychology.*

Wynn, K. (in press b). Evidence against empiricist accounts of the origins of numerical knowledge. *Mind and Language.*

Yarrow, M. R., Scott, P. M., & Waxler, C. Z. (1973). Learning concern for others. *Developmental Psychology, 8,* 240–260.

Yates, J., Bessman, M., Dunne, M., Jertson, D., Sly, K., & Wendelboe, B. (1988). Are conceptions of motion based on a naive theory or on prototypes? *Cognition, 29,* 251–275.

Yonas, A. (1981). Infants' responses to optical information for collision. In R. N. Aslin, J. R. Alberts, & M. R. Peterson (Eds.), *Development of perception: Psychobiological perspectives: Vol. 2. The visual system* (pp. 313–334). New York: Academic.

Yonas, A., Arterberry, M. E., & Granrud, C. E. (1987a). Four-month-old infant's sensitivity to binocular and kinetic information for three-dimensional object shape. *Child Development, 58,* 910–917.

Yonas, A., Arterberry, M. E., & Granrud, C. F. (1987b). Space perception in infancy. In R. Vasta (Ed.), *Annals of child development* (pp. 1–34). Greenwich, CT: JAI.

Yonas, A., & Owlsley, C. (1987). Development of visual space perception. In P. Salapatek & L. Cohen (Eds.), *Handbook of infant perception* (Vol. 2, pp. 80–122).

Yonas, A., Petersen, L., & Lockman, J. (1979). Young infants' sensitivity to optical information for collision. *Canadian Journal of Psychology, 33,* 268–276.

Yonas, A., Sorknes, A. C., & Smith, I. M. (1983). *Infant's sensitivity to variation in target distance and availability of depth cues.* Paper presented at the Society for Research in Child Development, Detroit, MI.

Yoneshinge, Y., & Elliot, L. L. (1981). Puretone sensitivity and ear canal pressure at threshold in children and adults. *Journal of the Acoustical Society of America, 70,* 1272–1276.

Young-Browne, G., Rosenfeld, H. M., & Horowitz, F. D. (1977). Infant discrimination of facial expression. *Child Development, 48*, 555–562.

Yuodelis, C., & Hendrickson, A. (1986). A qualitative and quantitative analysis of the human fovea during development. *Vision Research, 26,* 847–855.

Yussen, S. R., & Bird, J. E. (1979). The development of metacognitive awareness in memory, communication, and attention. *Journal of Experimental Child Psychology, 28,* 300–313.

Zimmerman, B. J., & Rosenthal, T. L. (1974). Observational learning of rule-governed behavior by children. *Psychological Bulletin, 81,* 29–42.

Zola-Morgan, S., & Squire, L. R. (1986). Memory impairment in monkeys following lesions limited to the hippocampus. *Behavioral Neuroscience, 100,* 155–160.

NAME INDEX

SUBJECT INDEX

Note: Page numbers followed by t, f, or n denote tables, figures, or endnotes, respectively.